The Way of the
Beloved

A Spiritual Path for Couples

Robert and Diana Van Arsdale

TRUE DIRECTIONS | iUniverse

AN AFFILIATE OF TARCHER PERIGEE

THE WAY OF THE BELOVED
A SPIRITUAL PATH FOR COUPLES

iUniverse books may be ordered through booksellers or by contacting:

iUniverse
1663 Liberty Drive
Bloomington, IN 47403
www.iuniverse.com
1-800-Authors (1-800-288-4677)

Because of the dynamic nature of the Internet, any web addresses or links contained in this book may have changed since publication and may no longer be valid. The views expressed in this work are solely those of the author and do not necessarily reflect the views of the publisher, and the publisher hereby disclaims any responsibility for them.

Any people depicted in stock imagery provided by Thinkstock are models, and such images are being used for illustrative purposes only. Certain stock imagery © Thinkstock.

ISBN: 978-1-4917-9609-2 (sc)
ISBN: 978-1-4917-9610-8 (hc)
ISBN: 978-1-4917-9611-5 (e)

Library of Congress Control Number: 2016918674

Print information available on the last page.

iUniverse rev. date: 12/08/2016

Contents

· ACKNOWLEDGEMENTS ·

The two decades long project of writing this book has left us indebted to more people than we can adequately acknowledge. First, with deep gratitude we thank our Teacher, Herman Rednick, who guided us to the Path of Love and gave us the teaching of the Way of the Beloved and who told us on three separate occasions to write this book. Without Herman we would not have become a beloved couple and we would never have known of the spiritual potential of the love between man and woman. We are also grateful to Torkom Saraydarian and Lama Karma Dorje for their direct and subtle help and for their encouragement of our work.

We could not have written this book without the editing expertise, critical comments and invaluable suggestions of the friends and students who read our manuscript in its various stages of development. We are most grateful to Robert Ricci, Jane Lipman, Anna Racicot, Alice Herter, Rachel Sayre, Janet Voorhees and Guilford Webb.

Also we could not have written this book without the dedication, the love, the many shared experiences and the financial help of the innumerable couples attending our classes over the last 27 years. We never charged a fee for our classes, but those students who wished to contribute to our work could make donations in accordance with how much they valued the teachings and how much they could afford. These donations provided the financial means to bring this project to completion. Many couples will recognize themselves in the book and although we cannot name them all, we thank each of them for their support. To those couples and individuals who have continued over a long period of time to walk the Path of the Beloved or who have encouraged and contributed to our work we offer special thanks. Among them are: Joan Eilers and Charlie Deans, Ron and Nancy Barber, Elaine Germano and Robert Ricci, Tim Harrington and Sherril Howard, Mari Bankey, Anna Urizar, Ann Frerichs, Hattie Stone, Steve and Anna Racicot, Leo and Leslie

Katz, Tim and Connie Long, Scott and Julia Butler, Ross Raderstorf and Carla McPherson, Alan and Michelle Katz, Liz Lyons and Ralph Marra, Athena Kelly, Anne Kious, Jane Lipman, Cynthia Olson, Hans Petersen and Tracee Hudson, Rachel Sayre, Bill and Helena Rose-Swift, Joan and Adriaan Vanderhor, Janet Voorhees and Lois and Richard Winar.

We also appreciate the time and effort that Charles Dillon has put in, managing the many donations to our Beloved Book Fund, as Treasurer of Earth Journey, Inc. for the past twelve years. And we thank Howard and Patsy Bach for allowing us the seclusion of their charming "madam's cottage" in Bisbee, for our writing retreats. Lastly, we are grateful to the "book cooks" who prepared numerous, healthy, gourmet meals for us so that we could focus more intensely on the writing—thanks to Joan Vanderhor, Janet Voorhees, Joan Eilers, Anna Urizar and Claire Long.

· INTRODUCTION ·

*I have thought of a little book on the path of the beloved ...
Humanity desperately needs this kind of instruction. There
are great feelings of loneliness and isolation in the world. The
path of the beloved is the path of union. Through union, man
[woman] realizes that he [she] is not alone, but a part of a great
and glorious spiritual reality.*

Herman Rednick[1]

I

The Way of the Beloved is our attempt to put into book form what we have
been teaching to small groups of couples for more than 27 years. The Beloved
classes offer an ageless teaching for the transformation of the love between
man and woman into a way for spiritual development, adapted to the needs
of contemporary relationships. In our classes we do not give lectures or
engage in philosophical or psychological discussions. The Way of the Beloved
is an integrated body of experiential exercises and meditations based on
universal spiritual principles which may be used by couples to actualize the
creative potential of their relationship through the intensification of love and
compassion.

It has taken us more than 32 years of work, as a couple, to make this book
possible. We were married in 1971 at age 36. Each of us had 3 children, former
partners, and new spouses of former partners, creating a complicated extended
family, not untypical in today's world. It did not take very long before the
subterranean volcanoes erupted into our life together and raging emotional
storms began to dominate the relationship. Our personalities were struggling
fiercely with each other, and we began to feel that we were faced with an
impossible task. It was also in 1971 that our mentor, Herman Rednick,[2]

began to reveal to his students a new teaching which he called "The Beloved Yoga." With a sense of desperation, we realized that there was no way out for us, except to make the struggle of our relationship part of our spiritual quest. We believed that to grow spiritually, we had to work through our impasse—now, with each other—or the same blocks would return to each of us at a later time. Out of necessity we blindly began to apply the principles of The Beloved Yoga teaching to our daily interactions. It seemed like a very long time before we saw any changes, but we did persist. And 5 years later we had a breakthrough into a realm of greater love. We were opened to experiences of loving communion which we had never imagined would be possible. All our hopes and invocations were exceeded. From the process of moving through the pain and mystery of our own marriage, and the guidance and spiritual wisdom flowing through our teacher, we were able to develop a series of classes for other couples seeking to intensify the love in their relationship. Our classes present a unique way for couples to transform their relationships into the arena and expression of their spiritual quest.

This is not a book *about* couples, but a book *for* couples. It is a book for intensifying the love between a man and a woman. It begins with the invoking of more love; it is concerned throughout with practical ways to become more loving; and it ends with the vision of love fulfilled. It is a book for realizing the Union of Opposites through spiritual love; thus it becomes a book for developing universal compassion. It presents a way, a path, a yoga[3] of love, and as such, it becomes comprehensible and meaningful only if one walks in this way—i.e., actually practices the various exercises presented. The Way of the Beloved is for those who want to become "walkers in the way." All the discussions of concepts, footnotes, references, observations, etc. are presented to explain, encourage, convince, and inspire the reader to actually practice the exercises. As Claude Bragdon explained: "liberation is not achieved by knowledge of a specific kind, but by *action*. This accounts for the fact that the world-saviors taught conduct and not theosophy."[4]

Just 20-30 years ago it would have been a great surprise to most couples to find out that building a loving relationship takes considerable work and risk. By and large Americans have had, until quite recently, a fairy tale vision of marriage. Indeed, many still believe that when they marry they should "live happily ever after." Against all the contemporary experience to the contrary, they continue to maintain vague expectations that this kind of fantasy relationship will actually be their destiny. However, it has now become common knowledge that a life of fulfillment and joy does not happen automatically to a man and woman just because they have fallen in love. The intimate daily interactions of two ego-oriented, multifaceted personalities, living in an increasingly tense and complex society, have thoroughly overcome the fairy-tale vision. And today, most men and women seem to experience a helpless despair when they contemplate the actual conditions of their intimate relationships. They are confronted almost on a daily basis with the critical question of whether or not it is possible to build a fulfilling life of love and spiritual growth *together*.

The process of developing a loving relationship can be compared to climbing a high and unexplored mountain.[5] We may have some idea of what the summit is like, and we really want to reach it, so we start the climb with optimism and enthusiasm. We quickly discover that there are some fine views and beautiful meadows along the path. There are also rocks, some small and some quite large, which often block the way. There are steep places to scale and many areas where there is no trail at all. We find, or more usually, we make, our own pathway to the unknown top. Some places on the mountain require taking risks if we are to climb any higher. There is the danger of exposure to intense elemental forces, of slipping, of falling down and maybe getting seriously hurt. But from time to time, we can catch glimpses— numinous oracles—of the higher peaks. And when that happens we know that, although the climb is most difficult, the rewards of fulfillment and joy are greater than we had ever hoped or imagined was possible. We call the journey of a couple who are climbing the mountain of spiritual love together, "The Way of the Beloved."

II

It is almost a universal belief today that any real *spiritual* work must be done by each individual acting in isolation. As Plotinus expressed it in the 3rd. century A.D., the spiritual journey is one of "the alone to the Alone."[6] Throughout recorded history, the recommended approach to any profound spiritual development was to withdraw from family and society and go into seclusion as a hermit or into a monastery community to meditate and pray. This ascetic path was considered the *only* path—the *necessary* way to spiritual achievement. Consequently, most traditions explicitly taught that contact with the opposite sex was one of the greatest dangers to spiritual progress.

However, today, most spiritual seekers, particularly in the West, are fully involved in a life of relationships (marriage, family, and work), and they find themselves searching, often in vain, for a path that they can follow to spiritual completeness and enlightenment.[7] There is now a path which is open to them. The cycle is shifting toward a balanced participation of men and women in the world, and women are taking their rightful place of equality in all activities, including love relationships. The path of the beloved couple has become accessible to seekers everywhere.

During this entire 2500 year historical cycle—at least since Heraclitus and the Book of Genesis—the conception of the union of opposites as a spiritual goal for a man and a woman has been known, but to only a few. In the East, the spiritual potential of the "polarities" was developed by the Hindu and Buddhist Tantrics.[8] Miranda Shaw tells us that, "The Tantric ideal of inclusivism and the utopian vision of men and women as companions in the spiritual quest were like embers that could be fanned into flame whenever a teacher or cultural setting supported their expression."[9] To our knowledge, in the West there has never been any systematic or sustained elaboration of a yoga of polarity.[10] Nevertheless, the idea that man and woman are destined to unite through love in a greater spiritual whole has been presented by the Bible, Plato, and the Neoplatonists in ancient times and the Kabbalists and Alchemists in the Medieval period. In modern times there have been a few great thinkers who have ventured into this territory of the potential spiritualization of the man/woman relation, but, so far, there has been little recognition of their vision. For example, among well-known thinkers we would mention, Jacob Boehme, Teilhard de Chardin, Paul Tillich and Martin Buber.[11]

Today psychic storms sweep unabated across our land and there is great turmoil between men and women, much more than in any previous age. Without a doubt, humanity's greatest need is to activate and intensify the love nature. We must all learn (indeed, in Western religions we are commanded) to truly love another "as our own self," whether this be husband, wife, neighbor, stranger, or even enemy. Religious and spiritual traditions, the world over, present this teaching as the only way to awaken the slumbering spiritual heart within each of us. Selfless love is humanity's next step in evolution. It is not an accident then, that we notice more and more that what is most lacking in our relationships is love. The interaction of man and woman is the fundamental encounter of the individual with *the other* and, for most of us, this is the testing ground of our personal and spiritual development as well as the promise of any future evolution of the Spirit.

It is our belief that the path of the beloved couple shall become the yoga for the coming age.[12] The Way of the Beloved is a new *type* of yoga because it is based on a co-intentional or mutual practice by a man and a woman who are united in a life and in the world by their love for each other. This is a new approach to the potential of the intensification of the love between a man and a woman. It is not a temporary strategy to advance the spiritual development of the individuals involved in the relationship. The Way of the Beloved leads to a *joint enlightenment* —an unprecedented spiritual creation!

This path of the beloved is not restricted to a chosen few. It is open to any couple willing to do the work of transformation through the intensification of love. It is not necessary to withdraw from the world. All aspects of this yoga can be practiced by sincere seekers wherever they live, whatever their worldly destiny, and regardless of what religion or tradition they may follow.

The Way of the Beloved actively affirms and sets out a program to realize that the purpose of all love between man and woman is fulfilled in the mystical union of "opposites," and that the joining of our separated beings into a new coherent creation, a spiritual at-one-ment, is the true destiny (the *telos*) of gender. Despite the fears of many, this new union does not diminish or obliterate individuality, but *fulfills* it. Each individual is elevated, moving toward her or his[13] full spiritual potential. [14] This union is not a creation of nature, but the conscious and intentional realization of a reality greater than nature by a man and woman whose intense love and devotion blends them, "as one, in the seamless cloak of immortality."[15] Moreover, we believe that this coherent united functioning is the consummation of the ancient and enigmatic separation of the sexes and the next step in the ascent of human consciousness. This may be the first time in history when a man and a woman can unite, through selfless love, the seemingly separate, self-conscious sense of individuality into a greater whole, thus fulfilling the heretofore mostly hidden, transcendent purpose of gender.

This is a pioneering effort that beloved couples make, for the "way," which has been closed and obscure until now is entering the mainstream of modern consciousness. Throughout history, even when the true purpose of the sexes was revealed, there was very little said about how to achieve it. The *Way of the Beloved* is our attempt to present a systematic and practical way to walk this path.

Today there are many indications that an awareness of the need for a spiritual approach to the man/ woman relationship is beginning to emerge in our society: e.g., books on marriage and relationships are being published at an unprecedented rate, couples' groups and workshops are becoming ubiquitous, and marriage and family therapy is practically mandatory in some social circles. In many prescient insights Teilhard de Chardin clearly expressed this need as early as 1934. For example, "It is not in isolation (whether married or unmarried), but in paired units, that the two portions, masculine and feminine, of nature are to rise upwards towards God. … Spirituality does not come down upon a 'monad' but upon the human dyad."[16]

More frequently of late we are being asked about the applicability of the Way of the Beloved to the same-sex couple. Although both gay male and lesbian couples have gained much from our classes and workshops, the ultimate realization of this path of the beloved is predicated on the spiritual union of the opposite polarities in the incarnate forms of a man and a woman. Nevertheless, developing more love for another person or persons is a universal and necessary undertaking for every human being, and there is much in our presentation of the beloved path that is useful in same-sex relationships or in any human relationship, i.e., parent-child, sister-brother, friendship, etc. No matter what type of relationship one has with another person, more love for that beloved-other benefits her or him, our self and all of humanity.[17]

III

Structurally, the Way of the Beloved is a program of progressive stages. It is a path to be consciously walked from the love that is known to the heights of universal compassion. The "mystical path," described in the world's esoteric traditions makes reference to three levels of attainment.[18] In *The Way of Beloved* we have called these three major divisions: (1) "Exercises for the Path of Love—Working Towards Harmony;" (2) "Entering the Way;" and (3) "The State of the Beloved— Spiritual Union:"

> (1) Part One introduces concepts and exercises to help each person overcome barriers in the personality which prevent the expression of love. This section of the book presents specific, structured exercises designed for couples to use individually and together. The focus is on the commonly recognized issues encountered in any relationship, such as communication, goals, commitments, and transforming negativity. The purpose of the exercises is to motivate couples to increase love in their relationship and to develop skills and techniques to achieve greater harmony. These exercises are based on fundamental spiritual practices that we have adapted for the interactive lives of couples, and they are also useful with other people in one's life, e.g., co-workers, friends, children, family members, etc.

(2) In Part Two we present a plan for the development of what might have been called in an earlier time, "the virtues." We articulate experiential techniques, but they require a less structured practice than those in Part One, i.e., they are more "meditative." Rather than skill-building, the focus is on a reorientation towards selfless loving. Although we have given the sections familiar sounding titles, (e.g., Devotion, Trust, Affirmation, Forgiveness, etc.), our approach is a "spiritualization" of the common understanding of these concepts. These become identified as processes of interaction between a man and woman, and each is offered in such a way that it can become a stepping stone for a couple to enter "The Path of Love" and thus prepare for higher spiritual aspirations. The overall purpose of this section is to provide ways for a couple to realize that stage where "the mind ... is kindled to the burning of love"[19] and where the aspiration becomes a deep desire to reach a love and union on higher, spiritual levels.

(3) Part Three is overtly spiritual and relies more on meditation techniques to cultivate the spiritual potential of the man/woman relationship. The concepts embodied and implied in The Way of the Beloved are not sectarian or dogmatic, and no specific beliefs are necessary, except perhaps that love is a spiritually transformative power available to all. We use the word "spiritual" in a most general sense and our students come from many traditions: Christian, Buddhist, Hindu, Sufi, Jewish, Esoteric, etc. The chapters in Part Three open up for a receptive couple the possibilities of attaining "higher consciousness." This section explores the mysteries of polarity, the dynamics and differences between masculine and feminine in the experience of love, the process of reestablishing the "flow" of love, the use of the theophanic imagination to see the divine aspect in the beloved, the union of opposites (the hermetic marriage), and the couple as a unit of service in the body of humanity. The presentation of the stage of Union (*unio mystica*, At-one-ment) reveals the culmination of the Way of the Beloved. Our teacher told us many times that the path of the beloved is a straight path to the spiritual heights and its potential is unlimited.

IV

To orient the reader within the subject matter, it should be said that The *Way of the Beloved* is our "root text." It is the outcome of 32 years of meditation, study, and daily experience in the lived relationship of a man and woman striving on the path of the beloved. Consequently, we have put all of our knowledge, skill, insight, aspiration, devotion to the path, and reverence for our teacher into this book. Ortega y Gasset expressed a thought which strikes a deeper and more personal note for us:

> Love is complete when it culminates in a more or less clear desire to leave, as testimony of the union, a child in whom the perfections of the beloved are perpetuated and affirmed. This third element, precipitated by love, seems to sum up its essential meaning in all its purity. The child is neither the father's nor the mother's: he[she] is the personified union of the two and is a striving for perfection modeled after flesh and soul. ... Plato was right: love is a desire to generate in perfection ... [20]

The Way of the Beloved is a concretization, neither one's nor the other's, of our love and life as a loving couple; it is a striving for perfection modeled after our mind, heart and soul—it is our child, yet not after the flesh. It was only after we had experienced the power and potential of the Way of the Beloved that we decided to share what we had learned with other couples. Indeed, it was not until much later, as the writing of this book progressed, that we began to research the historical and philosophical aspects of the man/woman relationship. Parts One and Two of the book were directly derived from our own daily practice of the Beloved Yoga. Part Three is an expression of the *glimpses* we were given during those most intense times of blending and communion, where we began to see the unlimited spiritual potential which is possible on this path. Since The *Way of the Beloved* is the culmination of our experience on The Path of Love, we have attempted to present a comprehensive unfolding of this path to spiritual growth and union. This is a *complete yoga,* i.e., through following the Way of the Beloved a man and a woman can climb the "ladder of love" and reach the heights of spiritual realization.

We wrote this book together, literally. It is a blended and unified effort to represent each of our personal perspectives. We worked on every sentence, every concept, and every exercise to create an intimate harmonization of the masculine and feminine aspects. It has been a labor of love, but a very long process, sometimes arduous in the extreme, sometimes swift and sure with inspiration, yet often written, of necessity, during painful episodes of chronic illness. A few other couples have blended their talents to produce a truly united product. Indeed, echoing the foregoing, John Stuart Mill said, about his collaboration with his wife Harriet in writing his famous essay, *On Liberty*: "there was not a sentence of it that was not several times gone through by us together, turned over in many ways, and carefully weeded of any faults, either in thought or expression, that we detected in it."[21] Throughout this process we have been sustained by the spiritual legacy of our beloved teacher and the certain direction that he set for us.

The concepts, exercises, and meditations in this book are designed to be put into active practice in your life. Some of them are to be done thoroughly once and then not repeated for perhaps 3-5 years. Most exercises, however, need to be integrated into the daily fabric of life over a period of time. In our classes two-week intervals are often not long enough for couples to really grasp the concept and begin the exercise. Indeed, the transformative promise of some exercises may take years to realize. The structured program that we present to our classes requires a full year to complete after which there are monthly meditation meetings and semi-annual retreats. Doing the work consistently over a long period of time is necessary if the habitual patterns of interaction are to be transformed. The Way of the Beloved will be truly comprehended only if it becomes a "lived" experience. Without daily practice the "Way" becomes just another intellectual episode in a busy life. Therefore, this book may best be used as a reference and a resource to assist in the practice of the exercises. All the exercises lead to greater love, so we encourage couples to use the ones that suit their preferences, and leave the others on the shelf, so to speak, for later consideration. Almost any one of the exercises practiced with intensity and devotion over a period of time could take a couple far along the path to a higher loving.

Many people believe that they need to understand something before they are willing to commit the energy and time to actually doing it. For these persons there are brief discussions of every concept and reasons and strategies for the practical implementation of each exercise. The extensive notes and references are included to expand the possibilities for further understanding, particularly for those seekers who desire to go beyond the text and to research further into the history and philosophy of the spiritual potential of the man/ woman relationship. We recommend that the reader put the endnotes aside, at first, in order to follow the flow of the text. Upon second reading, he or she may choose to explore those which are of particular interest.

We offer this book with the heartfelt desire to benefit and assist those who are seeking a spiritual path which they can walk together as a couple. If The Way of the Beloved touches anyone in such a way that more love enters his or her life, then we will have achieved our purpose.

80 03

· PART ONE ·

EXERCISES FOR THE PATH OF LOVE

In our world today it is so easy for a marriage
to become a battle of egos and misunderstandings.

We want to be right.
We want to compete.
We have forgotten to love.
What does it matter who is right?
Aren't we both moving toward the light?

Love is the key.
Love is the power.
Love is the open door.
Love is all we need and it brings to us everything that we seek.
Let the power of love be our guide.

—Herman Rednick[1]

Building a loving relationship takes work. As in any other endeavor, the benefits you receive will vary according to how much energy you put into the process. If you work with sincerity every day, you will achieve more than if you are casual.

The Chapters in Part One are written for couples who are willing to actually *practice* the exercises that are presented. Reading through these Chapters

1

may be of interest and, perhaps, even serve to increase your understanding of what it will take to be more loving, but the true meaning and, therefore, the real usefulness of the concepts and exercises can be realized only if they are tested in the daily experience of your life. It is in the attempts to practice these techniques that the details of our instructions become relevant and useful.

CHAPTER 1

• 1.1 THE INVOCATION OF LOVE •

*Love is the most universal, the most tremendous
and the most mysterious of the cosmic forces.*
—Pierre Teilhard de Chardin[1]

In its mysterious and unpredictable way, love sweeps into our life and suddenly our world is changed. We begin to glow with a magical radiance and there is an atmosphere of beauty around us. We feel a new and inexplicable sense of wholeness, a joy which transports us beyond our ordinary, everyday state of being. The very presence of our beloved one makes us happy. We are fulfilled, complete, the world is bursting with unexpected, limitless possibilities, and each of us believes the *other* person to be the source of this wondrous state.

What most of us experience as love is, no doubt, a mixture of illusion and longing, romanticized desires and wish-fulfilling fantasy. Yet, at the same time, love as we know it, is a reflection of the great spiritual truth which has been taught by every Wisdom Tradition since time without measure: i.e., Love is the cause of all creation and the sustaining power in all that lives. Indeed, *Love is the greatest power on earth.* [2]

The 20th century theologian, Paul Tillich, said, "I have given no definition of love. This is impossible, because there is no higher principle by which it could be defined."[3] But even though we may not be able to define it, love can be felt and known at some level by every one of us.

Most of us associate love with the strong feelings it evokes in us, yet love is much more than feelings and emotions.[4] Love is that most powerful, creative energy which, when it streams through our being, affects every level of our life—physical, emotional, mental and spiritual.

In our self-centered and materialistic culture, we suffer greatly from a poverty of love. For many of us, the shared values of social and cultural traditions have lost their cohesive power and, as history amply demonstrates, these secular cultural forces only appear to connect people, they are only temporary artifacts and they inevitably break down. In our world today, the atmosphere is clouded by a pervasive feeling of separation and alienation from one another. And we are constantly showered with seemingly rational explanations to excuse and justify the bitterness, violence, anger and fear that characterize our relations with one another. Where is love?

The development of love is the underlying true purpose for the blended life of a man and woman—as well as the communal life of all humanity—and love is the only *real* power that can hold us together. Indeed, love is the only power that can move us toward a more noble and lofty, spiritual destiny. We must begin now, as the Bible tells us, to "love one another."[5] If a man and a woman living together were to actively and intentionally focus on the renewal and intensification of their love for each other, their relationship could become a creative vehicle for deep fulfillment and spiritual growth. In truth, there is nothing that can stop us. Despite how we might feel, despite every apparent obstacle or problem, *in this moment, we can begin to love.*[6]

The purpose of The Way of the Beloved is to develop love in the relationship between a man and a woman. Since love on its own will not sustain itself in this relationship, we must continually and intentionally renew its presence, in our heart and in our life. Therefore we go directly to the essential core of The Way of the Beloved with an exercise that builds on the love we already know. It is a practice of remembrance and invocation which recalls, rekindles and intensifies love in a simple and direct way.

• THE EXERCISE •

- If you are alone, sit in a comfortable position in a quiet room. Close your eyes and relax. Mentally put aside the cares and problems of your day. Think of the one you love and visualize him or her in your mind's eye. When you see or feel the presence of your loved one, say the words, "I love you, … [person's name] …"(silently). Repeat the words over and over. Sustain the visualization and repetition for 2 or 3 minutes.
- If you are together, sit comfortably next to each other in a quiet room. You may hold hands or touch each other—or not, as you prefer. You

may look at each other or close your eyes. You will find it easier to focus on the exercise if you close your eyes. Put aside any conflicts, duties or problems between you. If you are looking at each other, say, "I love you, ... [person's name] ..."(silently to one another). If your eyes are closed, visualize or feel the other person in your mind's eye as you repeat the words. Keep repeating the words as you hold the image for 2 or 3 minutes.

- You may begin by recalling a time, perhaps that beginning time when you both were delightfully, surprisingly, spontaneously in love. Recall what it was like, remember what the other person was like, and feel what you were feeling at that time of new love between you. As you say, "I love you ... [name] ...,"the remembrance of your love can make it *present* to you and that love becomes your experience at this very moment.

- Afterwards, writing notes of your experience will increase your awareness.

This exercise sounds simple—it is simple—but it produces powerful effects. Through this exercise you are invoking and drawing into your awareness the love you already know. "Re-member" literally means to "form-again." Remembering love cannot fail to turn your relationship in a positive direction. Do it, and observe the effects. If there is harmony in your relationship, this practice will intensify the love between you. If there is conflict and unhappiness in your relationship, this practice will help to center you. As you recall the love you have had for each another, you actively invoke love to become your state *now*.

Many people say that they want more love in their relationship, but usually they have no idea of how to do it. Those who actually do the Invocation of Love each day, tell us that the effects are far reaching. The exercise can be done at any time, anywhere, during a 5-minute break at the office or a few silent moments at home. A particularly good time to stop everything else and focus on love is just before you leave the house in the morning or just before you go to bed at night. It does not matter whether you are alone or together, or whether the other person knows what you are doing or not. Wherever or whenever you do it, regular practice will intensify the love in your relationship and make you more aware of your love for each other for at least a few more minutes each day.

For example, one couple doing this work was building a house. Every morning one of them would go in the pickup truck to get building materials and the other would take the children to their play-school and bring lunch to the building site. When they met at the building site, the first thing that they did was to sit down on their beautiful piece of land and spend five minutes doing this Invocation of Love together. The hustle and bustle of preparations were left behind and they began their construction work in love and harmony. Another woman told us that she does the Invocation while she is stopped at red lights in city traffic. And a businessman said that the 20 minute drive to work every morning had become a time of beaming out love to his wife instead of worrying about the work day to come.

Reactions to this exercise are varied: Some people are filled with keen anticipation and others become frightened or shy. Some couples report that they remember the exercise in the middle of an argument and are suddenly unable to continue fighting. Some find the exercise difficult to do because they are feeling angry or resentful toward their partner. YOU CAN DO THIS EXERCISE REGARDLESS OF YOUR FEELINGS.

Of course, when you are feeling separated from your loved one and in a negative state, you will not want to love the person you consider to be the source of your pain. However, this is precisely the time to remember the love instead of perpetuating the separating emotions. You can choose now to love your partner, even if you feel like doing just the opposite.

For more than twenty-five years we have been starting our classes for couples with the Invocation of Love. Couples come in from their busy workday full of concerns, worries, and distracting thoughts, but 2-3 minutes of focusing on the love for each other brings a tangible softening and intensification of the atmosphere in the room. If you do this exercise regularly and with sincerity, more love will flow through you and you will feel and see a difference in your relationship. A man in one of these classes recently wrote:

> Often in the early morning my beloved and I sit in meditation … we silently repeat the love invocation. Starting the day this way not only connects me with Joan, but also creates for me a quiet, solid foundation that throughout the day gives me an ease and lightness of being that makes for an effortless and satisfying day. My heart, without prompting, will say, "Joan, I love you." I know how different it is when, for whatever reason, I rush out of the house to meet the day crashingly head on …

In the last few months, the lessons have sunk in. I now see and experience that negativity disappears when I love. Getting myself into a state of loving changes the world. Now, in the heat of the battle, or more often right after, when I am still shaking with anger and fear, I say the simple love invocation. And when I stay with it, the fear, and anger, and hurt dissipate. I see clearly that my work is to love my beloved. I trust the rest will follow.

The Invocation of Love is simple, effective and, above all, practical. It is practical because the simple act of turning your mind and heart toward your partner with love brings love into your life at this very moment. The Invocation of Love is something beautiful and *spiritual* that you can do everyday for the rest of your life.

Only so long as they loved did they live!
For only love, like life, which love is, has no Why or Wherefore,
No thing which would precede it;
Hence love alone is an absolute end in itself,
The end or perfection of all things, As well as their beginning,
To which everything else serves as a means.
It is true to say of it: They say love has no law.
Why not? Because love is itself The Supreme Law! [7]

• 1.2 VISION, GOALS AND COMMITMENTS •

We are used to thinking that everything happens to us because of past causes. This is a very incomplete thought. There are more causes and far stronger causes in the future, but we do not call them causes; we use different names. For example, goals are causes; visions are causes; promises, decisions, intentions are causes; a deeper understanding is a cause. All these causes affect our life in much deeper ways than the causes of the past because these new causes are formulated by the will operating on higher levels and in greater insight.

—Torkom Saraydarian[8]

A relationship between a man and woman without a goal or a vision is destined to flounder in the churning sea of life's events. Rising and falling on waves of emotion there is no guiding principle to steady its passage through modern life. For many the external goals of career, family, and success are not enough to provide the required energy to overcome the conflicting forces in the world that pull couples apart.

Most of us enter into a love relationship with some ideas of what we *want* from the other person and what sort of life we would like to lead, but often we are unaware of our deeper expectations and hopes. Until the middle of the twentieth century, most people's hopes and expectations of marriage and family life were consistent with the accepted social conventions and institutions of the times. But with the breakdown and realignment of the traditional social structures and the extensive intermarriage between different racial and cultural groups within our diverse society, the ideals of marriage and family have become vague and confused. How can a marriage succeed if a person's deepest hopes, expectations and ideals are not brought consciously into the relationship?

Having a goal awakens us to a sense of purpose in our relationship. It gives us something to strive for, a reason for being together. It provides us with a means to grow, to surpass what we have already accomplished and to reach for a greater achievement. If our goals are conscious, then they become a power that guides and energizes our thoughts, feelings, and actions. If two people have a common goal in life, they gather greater energy to support and give meaning to their striving. A couple brings a sense of purpose into focus when they verbalize and give form to the goals and commitments of their relationship.

The subject of commitment carries a strong emotional charge or potency. In the modern world where traditional norms have disintegrated, it is not at all clear what we are committing ourselves to, or what our responsibilities will become when we enter into a love relationship. Under such conditions of cultural uncertainty, it is not surprising that people experience fear and reluctance when faced with the issue of commitment. What can equal the power of attraction or repulsion, the joy or pain, the exaltation or despair of our love relationships? It is in this most intimate loving relationship that we must examine our natural and habitual inclinations and develop new ideas of responsibility and commitment.

We believe that the love between man and woman has an unlimited potential for spiritual growth and fulfillment. Thus as a couple develops deeper commitments to their relationship and strives for higher goals together, they can bring forth a beautiful and creative vision of the fulfillment of their combined destiny. This vision can be a great inspiration, even if it seems fantastic and totally unattainable. Such a vision becomes an image to reach toward. The image is like a magnet which radiates upon us its unseen power, as we strive to enliven it and make it a reality within our own consciousness.[9]

People usually find that there are two or three major goals for their relationship and life as a couple. When they recognize this, they discover that some of their other goals are subordinate and lose their importance as the major aspirations are fulfilled. For example, a woman told us that her primary goal was, "to love and support her husband at all times" and consequently her desire for a greater income and material comfort had become relatively unimportant. Also several men have reported that their desire for "better sex" was really a way of expressing the greater desire for more love in the relationship. They had found that sex was subordinate to more intense lovingness and it no longer was such a big issue when the love was flowing.

Aim for the highest goals you can imagine. If you set moderate goals, your inspiration and therefore your achievement will be moderate. If you aim for something 'higher', you have a greater possibility of achieving something higher. The goal itself becomes a power in your life, stimulating and inspiring you to move towards its realization.

A similar process occurs with commitments. There is a whole spectrum of levels of commitment to another person, ranging from casual dating, to an intense dedication to uniting through love in every area of life. As with goals, the deeper and more far-reaching the commitment, the greater the possibility for growth and higher achievement.

Commitments are related to goals and often they are overlapping. In most relationships we usually assume what the other person is committed to and these assumptions are never brought out into the open or verified unless a crisis occurs. In a crisis we may make the painful discovery that we had thought that the other person was committed in ways that she or he really is not, or we are completely unaware of a commitment that is expected of us. If couples clarify their commitments, bring them into focus, and make them specific, both people know where the relationship stands and what they can expect from one another.

Goals, commitments and visions are not static. They change as people and conditions change. For this reason, we recommend that couples reevaluate their goals and commitments periodically, perhaps once every 2-3 years. This exercise is designed to help you become aware of the present state of your goals and commitments, and to decide how you might wish to change them so that your relationship can grow in love.

It is possible and preferable, to develop clear goals on many levels of life. Some suggestions to help you identify and organize your goals are as follows:

PHYSICAL
money
health
social life
personal appearance
employment/career
house/property
recreation/vacations

EMOTIONAL
romance & emotional expression
communication
family life/relatives/in-laws
children
sexual relations
sharing of feelings, needs, desires, longings
hopes/aspirations

MENTAL
outlook on life
art
interests
sharing of ideas/beliefs
philosophy of life
politics
social issues

SPIRITUAL
prayer
death
religious activities
spiritual path
meditation
church
creativity

• THE EXERCISE •

PART A (To be done by each person individually: Find a quiet place where you will not be disturbed for 1/2 hour or more. It may take a few days to complete this first part.)

1. Write a list of your goals for the relationship. Remember that many goals may be unconscious, so you will probably have to "dig" for them. Put down whatever you can think of, no matter how trivial or significant.
- Do not edit at this point. There are many different kinds of goals. For example, there are goals of acquiring possessions or of having children. There are satisfactions we may want, like emotional support, harmonious companionship, good sex, etc. Also many couples hope to share ideas and intimate thoughts with each other, or things of a religious and spiritual nature.
- Identify which are the 2 or 3 most important goals for you in this relationship.

2a. Make a list of your commitments. Be specific about what you are willing or not willing to do for the sake of the relationship.
- For example, you might have statements like the following: "I am committed to sharing all our possessions, including money." "I'm willing to spend all our weekends together, but not to give up my Thursday night bridge game. "I will be sexually faithful to you."
- Write down every one that you can think of.

2b. Make a list of what you think your partner might be committed to in the relationship. This is a way to check your assumptions about your partner's commitments.

3. When you feel that your lists are adequate, close your eyes and do the Invocation of Love for a few minutes. Then, imagine your greatest dream, your most exalted vision—an imaginary scene—that embodies the highest fulfillment of the love between you and your partner. This will be an exciting and joyous thing to do—let yourself go! It is important not to inhibit your imagination. Do not say, "Oh, this is not practical" or "This could never happen in a million years." If you allow what you think is practical or feasible today to limit your tomorrows, then your future will not be any different from today. You cannot grow, if you do not hope for something better.

- It is important to write down your vision for the future of your relationship because this action will bring it more into form. When you write it as a story, a scene, a poem, a song—any way at all—you have taken the first step toward concretizing your ideal.[10]

4. Evaluation: Read over your lists of goals and commitments. If you wish, change, delete, or add new material. Try to make changes towards the highest values you can think of, or towards bringing more love into your relationship.

PART B (To be done together in private, no children, phone, or interruptions that you can prevent. This can be a special sharing and you will never do it the *first* time again.)

1. Share your lists of goals with each other. Take your time and enjoy the interchange and discovery. You'll probably find that you have several goals in common.

- Make a list of these. Choose which are the most important to both of you.
- Discuss all the goals from the point of view of bringing more love and harmony into your relationship.

2. Share and compare your commitment lists as you did with the goals. Don't be surprised if there are great differences in your commitments. This is not a final product. Your relationship is in the process of changing and it is useful for both of you to become aware of your commitments.

- Do not be disappointed if your partner does not share the same commitments that you have to the relationship. Do not think you have been betrayed if your partner does not have some of the commitments that you thought she or he did. To bring your assumptions out into the open, is the purpose of this exercise. This may be the first time that this area has been made explicit between you.
- Decide together upon those changes that will bring more love to your relationship.

3. After talking about commitments, you may reveal to each other your vision for the relationship. Do the Invocation of Love for a few minutes. Make a little ceremony out of this sharing and have a good time together.

4. The last part of this exercise is to put your creative energies together to invoke a joint vision of the highest fulfillment for your relationship. You could describe it as a movie unfolding in front of you, or as a story that you are writing together. It may express itself in other artistic forms, like poetry or prose, a joint musical composition, or a painting. Or it may be a quiet loving time of talking together about your dreams and hopes. When was the last time you did that?

଼ଠ

The following are three diverse examples of how this part of the exercise has been done by students of The Way of the Beloved:

Vows/Intentions/Aspirations

I vow to focus my Loving Awareness upon you, My Beloved, as my life's highest intention.

I vow to <u>celebrate</u> our Love, Life and Light together.

I vow to help you achieve happiness in your own way.

I vow not to be competitive.

I vow not to say "nothing" when you ask if something is the matter, and there really is.

I vow not to elevate my fear of being a fool or my fear of being wrong above my Love for you.

I vow not to aggrandize myself and blame you.

I vow to ask for help from you and others along the Way.

I vow not to switch my "position" in the midstream of an argument when I suspect that I am "losing."

I vow to be Loving instead of right.

I vow to Love you if you withdraw or leave, even when you are just thinking about it.

I vow not to judge you.

I vow to be your supportive witness and companion in times of pain and sickness.

I vow to forgive, and then to *really* forget it.

13

I vow to receive your Love as you offer it to me; not just in the ways that I want or am accustomed to.

I vow not to ever know who you are, I am, or we are as fixed identities. We are ever-changing, growing, dissolving and transforming beings walking the Beloved Path.

(together)

We vow to discover Our True Nature.

We vow to choose Love, any/way and all/ways.

℠ℚ

What do I feel is my goal with you?

It is to reach deep within and bring out the best I have for you.

It is my sincerest, most selfless, unconditional LOVE and understanding

—for I do love you, and this is what I offer, my love.

My commitment is devotion to this goal.

There shall be no secret rooms within, hidden from your knowing;

no secret, separative thoughts which make distances and coolness;

only openness and honesty, trust and caring, and

I am devoted to nourishing both.

℠ℚ

This exercise is usually a joyful activity for both people. Couples feel that this exercise brings them closer together. Some have even found their wedding vows and reread them from a new perspective. They recalled the way they felt when they first got together, and were reminded of the positive reasons that they joined with each other in life.

One young couple we know had been together about five years. They had married young, and although they cared for each other and had a relatively peaceful relationship, they felt lost about how to proceed. While working on their goals and commitments they looked at their wedding ceremony for the first time in five years. The purpose and enthusiasm of those early years was restored to them and when we saw them again they were glowing. Couples could get remarried every few years! The enactment of the wedding ceremony invokes and restores the forces that brought you together. Could not anniversary celebrations, as well, become times of renewal for your relationship?

Of course this exercise can also bring up areas of difficulty and conflict. One person may have a goal to which the other is unsympathetic or even opposed. There may be a real disagreement about what you are committed to in the relationship. This is an opportunity to make things explicit and to work them out together. If it is not possible to reach an agreement on certain issues, we suggest that you use the Invocation of Love to change the atmosphere of the conflict. This often creates a climate in which to find a resolution. Also it is certainly acceptable to leave an issue unresolved for the present. Even if this feels uncomfortable, it may be necessary—your relationship is a process of growth, not a static perfection, or imperfection.

• 1.3 GRATITUDE •

It has been many centuries, but the people of this small Chinese village still remember the story of the wise old farmer. He was about 80 at the time, yet he had a young son, to whom he was very attached. He had prayed for many years for a son, and then in his sixties, his younger wife had delivered a fine son, but she died in childbirth. In his late teens, the son was tall and handsome and cared for his father and their small farm with devotion and efficiency. The whole village considered the man lucky to have such an admirable son.

Unique among his neighbors the man owned a great black stallion, which had come to him as part of his wife's dowry. This was the only horse in the entire village, as no one could afford such a luxury, and despite his wife's death the man was considered the luckiest person in town.

One morning the man and his son discovered that the stallion had knocked down the gate during the night, and run off. The village was surrounded on three sides by heavily forested mountains, and when domestic animals strayed into the woods, they were seldom seen again. In this close-knit village neighbors cared about one another, and it was not even noontime, when several were gathered at the old man's house to console him on his bad luck. However they became perplexed when the man said to them, "Bad luck, maybe! How do I know if my horse's disappearance is good luck or bad luck? I am a simple farmer, what do I know of the ways of heaven?

Then the son jumped up and said, "Father, I will go into the forest and bring our horse back. He should be easy to track." The father consented, and the son left quickly to follow the fresh trail. The neighbors were amazed, since few had the courage to go into the dark and unknown woods, and they said to the father, "You are very lucky to have such a brave son!"

The old farmer did not reply, but when the son had not returned after two days, the neighbors were back at his house more concerned than before. They kept repeating that this was really very bad luck. But the old peasant replied as before, "How can we say 'good luck' or 'bad luck'? We do not know the laws of heaven."

The very next morning the son returned home, not only with the stallion, but also with seven wild mares that the stallion had captured. That day everyone in the village who could walk, came to their house to congratulate the man and his son on their great good luck, and of course to see the horses. But in the midst of the celebrating the old man stood, and addressing his happy neighbors said, "I am thankful to heaven to have my son back and for these beautiful horses. And my heart is glad to see my neighbors so happy, but who can say if these events are good luck or bad luck?" Thinking that the old man was losing it, and somewhat taken aback, his friends shouted, "Surely you can see that this is the best luck that anyone in our village has had in a very long time—maybe ever." The old farmer replied, "My friends, I understand how you feel, but I cannot know the consequences of these momentous happenings. So I shall not say if this is good luck or bad; only that I am thankful for whatever heaven sends."

It was about 2 months later, that the old farmer's son was badly injured while breaking the wild mares. His leg was broken in 3 places, and he might have died, but a barefoot doctor came by at just the right time. It was going to be many months before the son could walk at all, and then he probably would have a limp. Again the neighbors came to console the old man, to bring food, and to help out. It was indeed difficult for the father to take care of his son and do all that was needed for the horses and the farm, and he was grateful for his neighbors' assistance. But they kept telling him that his son's serious injury was obviously an example of bad luck. Could he not see that now?

The old man was very tired, but he replied not unkindly to his friends, "You say that one thing is 'good luck' and that another is 'bad luck', but then bad things come from the 'good luck' and good things come from the 'bad luck', how can this be? I cannot judge these things on the basis of what I want or don't want to happen. I have heard that in the ancient past there were sages who could read the future in the stars, but I am a simple man and all I can do in the face of destiny is to accept with thankfulness everything that heaven sends me."

The old farmer's neighbors were beginning to make some sense of what he had been telling them, because they had been unable to foresee the consequences of what had been happening, and they could not understand how bad could come of good, or good could come of bad. Perhaps, the ways of heaven are inscrutable to men.

This story came to its conclusion only a week later, when a petty warlord from the next province swept through the village and took all of the able-bodied young men to be slaughtered in his hopeless last battle. Only the wise old farmer's son was left, because he could not even walk at the time ...

This is probably an old Taoist story, although it does seem to be fairly well known in the West today.[11] This wisdom has been expressed in many ways and in many cultures,[12] but the basic human dilemma is timeless, universal, and of intimate concern to everyone: e.g., "What is the most enlightened way to meet the events in my life, especially the ones that I do not like, but cannot change? We all must ask ourselves, "What is the purpose of my pain and suffering, disappointments and frustrations, even happiness and joy? And what would be the wisest approach to these inevitable human experiences?"

Much of the world's literature for the past 4,000 years has been deeply concerned about humanity's apparent powerlessness in the face of the awful things that can, and do, happen to us. If we resist the experience that comes to us out of the flux of the world, we will deny it or distort it, and therefore we will miss the value and the lesson inherent in the event. If we are strongly focused on what we like and don't like, we become happy or sad, satisfied or frustrated, calm or angry depending on our emotional evaluation of each event and condition. Consequently, our life experiences become a stimulus to an unending sequence of positive and negative reactions. A life focused in the emotions is chaotic, like a wood chip tossed about in a stormy sea. In modern holistic psychology there is a clear trend toward the recognition that

> every experience, no matter how hurtful and sad it may seem at the moment, is an opportunity to learn, to grow, and to evolve toward higher levels of human awareness. In that sense, there are no *negative* experiences, no *mistakes*, no need to blame ourselves for our past choices. There is only more information to draw upon in making constructive decisions in the future.[13]

All the great spiritual traditions in the world tell us that even though we may be unable to comprehend the ultimate meaning and purpose behind life's events—the ways of heaven— if we meet the conditions of our life with a spirit of gratitude (thankfulness), we will learn from every experience and mature in wisdom and love. Thus our goal in life would be to live in a state of gratitude, meeting all events and conditions with thankfulness, remembering that in some unknown way they are helping us to grow spiritually. That is why it has been said that, "it is the mark of the lost that they cannot give thanks, just as it is a mark of the initiated that they cannot give thanks enough."[14]

In our closest relationship, gratitude is the key that opens the door to love. Therefore, gratitude is necessary, not only for the conditions that we approve of and like, but for every quality and characteristic of our partner, for every thought and action, large or small, whether it is agreeable to us or not. If our goal is to live in a state of gratitude with our loved one, then we must be grateful for every experience arising out of our interactions. To many people this sounds inside out or backwards! How can we be grateful for things we don't like and actions we don't approve of? Why *should* we be grateful for these things?

Working to become more grateful helps to create within us the ability to love another person even when he or she does not fulfill our desires or behave in the ways that we want. It is this effort to become grateful for every experience that helps us to see that there is a hidden purpose behind events, and that within each experience with this other person, there is an opportunity for us to learn and to grow in love. Through our gratitude for every quality that the other person expresses, faults and virtues alike, we grant to the other the freedom of his or her own individuality in an atmosphere of acceptance, love and forgiveness. *Gratitude is not approval, nor is it passive acceptance. It is an active, outgoing, positive energy which frees our mind and heart to bring forth a flow of love.* [15]

Most persons have been conditioned to think that they should disapprove of what they don't like, and that they should condemn and try to change those who embody or express these characteristics. This ungratefulness results in a life of constant criticism and resentment, which leads to painful alienation and separation from others. How can love live in an atmosphere of resentment? Gratitude transcends the very issue of disapproval. It means that you can love "the person," even if you may disagree with her or his actions or character.

In our teaching we have found that people seldom question the *concept* of gratitude. They say, quite sincerely, that they would like very much to be grateful all the time, but that they do not know how to work toward achieving this state of being. The following exercise has helped many to bring the spirit of gratitude into their thoughts and actions as they go through the activities of their daily lives.

೫ ೦೪

• GRATITUDE EXERCISE •

You will need a pencil and paper and some quiet and privacy to begin this exercise. Write down a short list of qualities, characteristics, habits, actions, opinions, etc., that you have observed in your partner and in the interactions between you. Include some positive, some negative, some important, or not so important items. The list need not be long—3 to 6 is a good start.

- *FOR EXAMPLE,*
- "Tom drinks much too much!"
- "Every time I tell a story, Melanie interrupts me."
- "Juan is a loving father."
- "I miss Mark terribly when he is away."
- "Ellen has always supported me in my problems at work."

In front of each item on your page, write, "I am grateful that …" and after each one write, "because …"

- *FOR EXAMPLE,*
- "I am grateful that Juan is a loving father because …"
- "I am grateful when Nathan leaves his socks under the coffee table because …"

Now finish each sentence, taking enough time to think of a good reason for being grateful for this particular characteristic or interaction. Start with the positive ones, if you find that easier.

- *FOR EXAMPLE,*
- "I am grateful Juan is a loving father, *because* it makes me happy that our children will grow up with the love and security that I never had."
- "I am grateful that Ellen has always supported me in my problems at work, *because* she continued to stand by me even when I had given up. Without her support we would have lost everything."

- "I am grateful for Carol's beautiful smile *because* it turns me on."
- "I am grateful that John/Carol spends money foolishly *because* it helps me to recognize that what I call foolish is relative and that my way may not be any better."
- "I can be grateful when Tim drinks too much *because* I need to develop the strength to confront him in a constructive way, which I could never do with my ex-husband.

Repeat the completed sentence over and over again, perhaps with eyes closed. Visualize the scene, until you begin to feel some truth in what you are saying.

The best way to use this exercise is to do it every day, for the rest of your life—can we ever become too grateful? As you practice the repetition of your sentences with a heartfelt intensity you will see a subtle change in your attitudes. The daily effort to reinterpret your experiences in the light of gratitude will turn your heart and mind toward your partner and your relationship in new and creative ways. Becoming more grateful will dissolve anger and resentment between you, and your life together will begin to look like it has a purpose for growth.

Completing the sentences in the exercise is a way for you to give new meaning to your experiences. Your understanding, and therefore your reasons for gratefulness, may change as you work from day to day. Modify your sentences when you think of "better" endings. As you work with your sentences every day, you can expand your list to include new items and more reasons to be grateful.

It may be difficult to complete some sentences. As we have discussed (see Note #19), many make the mistake of attempting to become grateful for the negative condition itself, instead of reinterpreting their experience of it.

One man said that he did not know how to even begin to be grateful for the hurt done to his wife by her family. As he put it, "these hurts have their cause outside of our relationship." He was trying to be grateful for a lifetime of hurtful acts against his beloved, and this confusion of intent was paralyzing his efforts to do the exercise. He had some comprehension that it was his angry response to these hurtful acts that he needed to work on—he had no illusions that he could change his wife's family patterns—but his anger kept him focused on the events themselves. Two months later, at our

21

next meeting, he had found a way to move out of his resentment, toward gratitude for this difficult experience. He had remembered something that the Dalai Lama had said about how our enemies were more useful to our spiritual development than the Buddha.[16] He realized that his wife's family was providing him the opportunity to learn compassion, and that his wife was being given this opportunity too—her persecutors were their teachers! Adopting this viewpoint and believing in its truth, which transcends the actual events, has made it possible for him to work toward gratitude.

Being in a state of gratitude does not mean that we passively accept a negative condition or action. Being in a state of gratitude means that we can learn from all our experiences and meet the circumstances and conditions of life directly.

The young wife of a man who had begun drinking at the age of 13, knew that she was unable to confront him about his weekend disappearances and his increasingly abusive behavior. He had always denied that he was an alcoholic, but something had to be done because he was getting worse, and she was pregnant. When she began the gratitude exercise she quickly saw how she avoided confrontation, or even conversation, with him about the drinking, because of a deep sense of weakness and a concomitant fear of his reactions. Working to be grateful for the situation despite her fear, she found that she could call-up a new strength from within herself. And over a period of time her strength increased and her anger and resentment subsided. She said that it was not unlike awakening from a 5 year nightmare of hurt and blame. She was helpless until she was able to reinterpret her experience of anger and resentment and recognize that this situation was being given to her that she might become a stronger person. Through her husband's drinking she became a whole and independent person for the first time in her life, and although she got him to go to AA for awhile, and she had gained much strength and skill through Alanon, he never became sober. Indeed, two years later she had to leave him.

We must hang on to gratitude as one hangs on to a log in the ocean after a shipwreck.

—Torkom Saraydarian[17]

If you are having trouble thinking of a reason to be grateful for something, stop trying to think of a *real* reason and make one up. Be creative; too much rationality can paralyze your efforts. For example, write down the first thing that pops into your mind, even if it sounds ridiculous and unrelated. An apparently absurd reason can be as effective as one that is *perfectly reasonable.* There is more truth to the imagination than we often realize. Another way to work through an impasse is to use the statement, "I am grateful for ..., **because** *it gives me an opportunity to be grateful."* or "I am grateful for ..., **because** *I want to live in a state of gratitude and this experience is giving me a good opportunity to learn how."* Others have been able to utilize the statement, "I am grateful for this experience **because** *I know that, in some way, it is teaching me something."* As you become more creative with your sentences, totally unexpected revelations are possible!

Undoubtedly, it will be very difficult to feel grateful for some of your experiences. In fact, it may seem impossible to find a reason to be grateful for them. These are the "hard ones" or this is where you are "blocked," and you will have to put considerably more effort into them. Don't give up; it may even take years of work to become grateful for some of these issues!

However, some very difficult and emotionally-loaded situations can be changed almost instantly when you see them in a new light: Once right in class, as the couples were thinking of reasons to be grateful, a woman in an 8 year long living-together relationship, wrote about how her partner would become self-absorbed, and how she felt shut-out and abandoned. Then, she came up with the following: "I am grateful when Andy shuts me out because my feelings of hurt and abandonment tell me how important our relationship is to me. My strong reaction means that I really do care about him, more than I ever knew." We seldom witness an *aha*! experience like this, and we saw an instant transformation take place. The fear and anger fell away from her, and were replaced by awe and delight for this discovery of love.

And in a lighter vein, a woman in her 60's, who had been married to the same man for over 40 years, came to class after 2 weeks of working on this exercise with a timely and humorous testimonial. She, and many of her women friends, had been grousing together for years about men leaving the toilet seat up. She remembered being "really bugged" that her husband seldom put the toilet seat down when he was finished, and to her this was a personal and vulgar affront. It had become a symbol of male selfishness and thoughtlessness. She had found the following reason to be grateful for this: "I am grateful that Lance leaves the toilet seat up because, at least, it constantly reminds me that there is a man in the house." And she added that most of her women friends were divorced and living alone.[18]

It is essential to spend as much time and energy on being grateful for the qualities you like and enjoy in your relationship, as you do on the difficult areas. Recalling the gratitude that you have for those things which you spontaneously appreciate, is the way you come to understand what gratitude feels like, and therefore you know what it is that you are invoking into all the areas of your life.

Gratitude for the things you like is also your protection against taking your life together for granted. How many things can you think of that used to delight you, that have now become ordinary occurrences you hardly notice anymore? A friend remembered how thrilled she was in the first months of her marriage, when her husband came home each evening and they had dinner together. She realized that she now *expected* this to happen, and it had lost its magic. Through becoming grateful, once again, that her husband came home each evening for dinner, their delight in being together was recharged, and she felt more love in their daily rituals. Gratefulness prevents the possibility of things becoming humdrum, boring, or dull. If you take things for granted the resulting boredom and resentment will snuff out the very life of your marriage, no matter how exciting your love used to be.

Do not mistake satisfaction or approval for gratitude. Just because you approve of the other person's actions does not mean that you are actively loving her or him. Satisfaction is a passive and precarious state based on constantly changing personal preferences, and so easily disrupted by events we cannot alter or causes that we do not understand. Gratitude is an active, positive, and outgoing state leading to a flow of love.

If we can remember to **DO IT**, it is a beautiful experience to be grateful for what we like in our partner. Is it not then even more wondrous and growth-promoting, to be grateful for the opportunity to give love to another when we would not spontaneously do so? When gratitude for each experience lives within us, everything that happens to us becomes a step in our spiritual growth. When we are in a state of gratitude, our heart is open to a flow of love and every problem becomes a luminous opportunity in the course of our life.

Many years ago a student, who was a Lutheran Deaconess working as a pastoral counselor in a large city hospital, was so inspired by the positive effects that the gratitude exercise had had on her that she introduced it to her co-workers. She thought, "Why should I use this exercise only with my husband? It could be so helpful to our counseling team and so useful in our work with the patients." She introduced the concept of gratitude and the exercise at the next staff meeting, and was not surprised at the immediate positive effects that this practice had on the entire staff.

Indeed, as Paul Tillich said, "there are no limits to situations in which to thank."[19] We *can* be grateful for every experience, knowing that it is helping us to mature in love. Indeed, over the 20 years that we have been teaching this exercise to couples, the overwhelming majority of both women and men have told us that gratitude has been the most direct and most useful practice for bringing more love into their life.

> *Gratitude is the song of the heart. With every grateful feeling, there arises a golden offering to the spiritual presence … Let us be continuously grateful for every person we see or think about. We are grateful for the sunlight or the healing night, for our magnetic breath, for all colors and all sounds. Thus, through this little golden key, we shall open the gate to the temple.*
>
> —Herman Rednick[20]

25

CHAPTER 2

• 2.1 COMMUNICATION AS COMMUNION •

> *Love shone through the cloud which had come between the Lover and the Beloved, and made it to be as bright and splendid as the moon by night, as the day star at dawn, as the sun at midday, and as the understanding in the will. And through that bright cloud, the Lover and the Beloved held conversation.*
>
> —Ramon Lull[1]

People are concerned about many aspects of their relationships, but of the great variety of questions asked of us, the issue most often mentioned is communication.[2] Has there ever been a time in history when people were as aware of the absence of genuine communication with one another, as they are today? Every way we turn we see conflict, misunderstanding, and intolerance. Couples have such busy, separate lives that sometimes they hardly even get to see each other, let alone talk with one another. If they can negotiate the mechanics of their typical harried and stressful days with any congeniality or positive interaction, it is considered an achievement. Many married couples find that they can no longer talk to each other in an intimate and meaningful way. And they are deeply disturbed about the sense of loneliness that they feel. It is not uncommon to be married and yet tormented by pervasive feelings of isolation. People feel alone and cut-off from one another. The very nature of our modern Western civilization seems to be to separate one person from another, men from women, all of us from the natural world and from the spirit of love.

The lack of *real* communication in one's life is almost always felt to be a serious problem. People want and need the warmth and close contact with others. And mostly, they need the companionship, sharing, and intimacy of a loving partner. If they do not have this special relationship in their life, they will seek it out with great energy and motivation. And if the relationship with their chosen partner is lacking in genuine communication and closeness, they desperately seek elsewhere for a person or group with whom they can feel a sympathetic contact.

Do we even know what it is that we are looking for?[3] Bookstores and libraries have shelves full of books about techniques and exercises to improve communication skills.[4] Couples study how to negotiate to "get what they want" or perhaps how to "get to YES".[5] And they attend workshops and seminars to learn sophisticated methods of expressing and sharing their feelings. We have met many couples who have read books on communication, participated in communication workshops and negotiation seminars, and are familiar with numerous techniques that they can use, and yet they are still unhappy, dissatisfied, and frustrated, still feeling separated from one another.

The central, yet elusive, secret of communication, is simple and close by, if we know where and how to look for it. The essence of true communication is disclosed in the connecting power of love. When we are connected through love to another person, we are in communion with him or her. Thus, true communication is *communion*. As Brother David Steindl-Rast has said, "communion is not only the fruit, but the root of communication. ... communication also presupposes communion."[6]

The secret of experiencing communion with another, is found by "opening our eyes" through love, to the underlying community that already exists between us. The experience of communion is like a window to the truth that lies at the foundation or ground of all our interpersonal encounters: at the heart of everything there is a Oneness of Being. The almost universal perception that we are separate beings has been accurately called "the great lie."[7] Experiencing ourselves as separate is, in fact, an illusion. We feel separate when we are not in communion with others. The sense of separation, this so-called "cloud of Illusion" or "Maya,"[8] is a direct result of humanity's descent from a spiritual existence into material life. Love is the only power that can bridge this gap between us and shine through the cloud. Indeed, love alone can bring the experience of communion, but communication, without love, cannot put us in communion with another. Love is the rainbow that lights that bridge over the chasm of separation. It is the creative force that will tell us how to reach another and meet the other directly in the reality of communion.

Certain results flow naturally from loving communication:

- When love is flowing through us to another person, we feel that we are in communion with him or her.
- Love makes us feel close to him or her.
- Through love, we make contact with the being, or truth, of the other person.
- Through the eyes of love, we can see deeply into another person.[9]
- Through love, we can blend with another person's uniquely different individuality.
- When love flows through our heart to another, we can read their heart, and sometimes, even their thoughts.
- Through love, we can reach out to touch the deepest core of another's being—the most intimate and sacred places.
- Through love we can 'see' what it is that another person needs: We can 'hear' their cry for acknowledgment, or appreciation, or affection; or we can recognize a need for firmness and confrontation.

> My heart has become an ocean, beloved, since You have poured Your love into it.
>
> —Hazrat Inayat Khan[10]

When we are filled with love, we are able to see into the depths of the other person, and we feel that we are expressing the truest and deepest part of our own self. With a heart full of love we have no fear. We are free to say what needs to be said, and we know when to speak out and when it is better to remain silent. We feel an inner core of strength centering us and a flow of inner power sustaining us.

Thus, it is not words that bridge the gap that separates us, but love. If communication skills which help people to understand and negotiate with one another, or techniques which help people to express their thoughts and feelings more easily, are used *without love*, they do not bring about genuine communication. Without love there is no real communication— no communion. Without love there is only loneliness, isolation, and separation.

The state of communion with another human being may be rare in our life-experience, yet we all know it when it happens. We may not be able to say what it was that happened to us, but we cannot fail to recognize the experience—it is unmistakable.[11]

Indeed, we have a sense of *real* contact with the other person:

- This may take the form of our discovering that we can *identify* with the other. Thus a feeling of deep recognition arises within us and then we may experience true empathy with the other person.
- Or we may discover, with wonder and awe, an expansive feeling of difference between our self and the other person—an affirming recognition of the other's uniqueness or individuality.
- We have the sense of being profoundly understood by the other person, and the sense of a new and deeper understanding of her or him. The feelings of merging or blending are often experienced during communion.
- We have an inner knowledge that we are expressing ourselves deeply and truly, and that the other person is doing the same; and we are both aware that this is happening.
- We have the sense of knowing the *inner being* of the other person and of simultaneously being *seen* and *known* by them. In the marriage relationship, this knowing and seeing can bring a new depth of communion which, through the intensification of love and devotion to one another, may lead to a mystical experience of transcendence.

In his inimitable prose Thomas Merton has summarized our meanings and intentions in this Section:

> True communication on the deepest level is more than a simple sharing of ideas, conceptual knowledge, or formulated truth. The kind of communication that is necessary at this level must also be "communion": beyond the level of words, a communion in authentic experience which is shared not only on a "preverbal" level but also on a "postverbal" level.
>
> And the deepest level of communication is not communication, but communion. It is wordless, it is beyond words, and it is beyond speech, and it is beyond concept. Not that we discover a new unity. We discover an older unity. My dear brothers [and sisters], we are

already one. But we imagine that we are not. And what we have to recover is our original unity. What we have to be is what we are.[12]

So, if we have recognized its many benefits, what can we do to learn to truly communicate with our partner? If we want to have a deeper communion with another, we need to learn how to **LISTEN!**

• 2.2 LISTENING •

The best way for you to serve your [partner] and help yourself is to be very still ... and listen. Listen with your mind and heart. Listen with your hands and feet. Listen with your whole being. Let your being become like a gigantic ear. And listen in awareness as your [partner] speaks. Thus without the reasoning mind, but through straight knowledge, your being from the center shall respond to the call.

—Herman Rednick[13]

How can we develop a sense of true and loving communion with our partner? The way to begin is to learn to listen with great love. When we listen with love, we listen with much more than our ears and our mind. We listen with the "heart."[14] The heart has a much greater ability to touch others than any of our senses or our mind. The heart is the true center of our being. Within the heart is the quality of compassion or unconditional love and it is through the silence of the heart that the "voice of intuition" comes to us. Thus when we listen with our heart we are more perceptive, and we become more attuned to seeing and knowing "who" the other person is and what he or she is expressing to us. The following listening exercise has helped many to practice inner silence and begin to truly hear the other person in a spirit of love.

∞ ♋

• LISTENING EXERCISE •

Decide upon an issue or a question which you want to explore or that you need to talk about. Both of you may explore the same topic, or you may each choose a different one. Spend some time— it could be as much as several days, if necessary—thinking about what you want to communicate to your partner, and write down some notes about your thoughts. Or even better, write a detailed letter to the other person. Then set a time to meet when there will be no distractions, phone calls, children, etc. During the exercise each person will have a turn to practice listening for at least 6 minutes while the other person is the "speaker". The exercise takes no more than 15 minutes to complete, but many people find that they spontaneously wish to continue for a longer period of time. It is best to be open-ended, if possible.

Observe the following guidelines:

- A kitchen timer or stop watch will help you to accurately time the sequences of the exercise.
- Begin with the Invocation of Love. This sets the tone for a flow of loving communication.
- For 3 minutes: The speaker reads aloud from the letter or notes that she or he has prepared, and/or tells the other person his or her thoughts and feelings on the chosen issue.
- The listener DOES NOT SPEAK AT ALL during these 3 minutes.
- For the next 3 minutes: Both people focus on amplifying and exploring more deeply, the speaker's thoughts & feelings. The listener may ask questions.
- These 6 minutes end the first sequence. You may switch roles, if you wish, or you may stop at this point, or you may want to dialogue, whatever seems best at the time.

• WHEN YOU ARE THE SPEAKER •

Remember to speak with the awareness that you love the other person, even if what you have to say is difficult. You may read your letter or use the notes that you have written, or just talk spontaneously. Describe what is going on inside of you in as much detail as you can. Increase your own awareness by delving more deeply to discover what thoughts, feelings, emotions, perceptions, and observations you want to express to your partner.

Use images and word pictures, such as: "I feel …"; or "I/it feels like …"; "It reminds me of …"; "It reminds me of how I felt when …" Try to describe your perceptions and observations with sentences like: "It seems to me that …"; "It makes me think that …"; "It looks to me like …"

Most of us look forward to having the opportunity to express ourselves, to be listened to, and to be heard. At the same time, it is necessary to carefully avoid using the occasion to vent negativity or to get back at the other person. Try to tell your story just as you experience it, without cloaking or distorting it with any motive other than the desire to discover, reveal and share yourself with your partner. Therefore AVOID explaining, analyzing, intellectualizing or theorizing about your experience; justifying or defending yourself; blaming or accusing the other person; *dumping garbage* (such as complaining, whining, or feeling sorry for yourself); or looking for a solution to your situation.

For the first three minutes of this exercise, the speaker reads his or her letter and/or talks freely, without interruption. **The listener remains silent.** In this way, the listener is able to practice giving the speaker her or his full attention, and the speaker knows that she or he has at least three minutes to express himself or herself without interruption. Most people find that three minutes go by very quickly, and they still have plenty to say, but occasionally someone may finish speaking before the time is up. Should this happen, the speaker may feel ill at ease, or stuck. This need not become a problem. The listener can simply acknowledge that he or she has heard the other person, and can begin to ask questions that will elicit more and expand upon the speaker's experience.

• WHEN YOU ARE THE LISTENER •

Do the Invocation of Love with your partner before you start the exercise. This will help you to remember to listen with your heart. Focused listening may not always be easy or comfortable. Focused listening involves some risk because it opens up the possibility of hearing something new and different, and maybe even something you have been avoiding.

To listen with a heart of love requires that:

- We become inwardly silent.
- We turn towards the other person with love.
- We give the other person our full, complete attention.

In order to become inwardly silent, we must first eliminate the many external sounds, noises, and demands that distract us and clamor for our attention. We must be in a quiet environment. Our daily world is noisy with the constant stimulation of radios, T.V.s, music, traffic, conversations, telephones ringing, cars driving by, sirens, and so on. We have to make a deliberate effort to find a quiet place and time to be silent.

Next we must begin to quiet down the flow of noisy thoughts and emotions that fill our inner world with constant dialogue. We are rarely free from mental responses, thoughts, formulas, random daydreams, plans, "what to say to whom," "how I should have done so and so," "when will I get to do such and such," etc., combined often with a corresponding surge of feelings — anxiety, excitement, dismay, etc.. Exterior silence can be arranged with some thought and planning. Interior silence, however, is a great achievement—it is an art, a skill, and the result of loving devotion and discipline, which must be developed and practiced with concentration and consistency, over a period of time.

Give the speaker your full attention. When there is inner silence—a quiet mind and a loving heart—we can turn towards the other person and offer her or him our full attention. We are ready to receive what he or she offers us. This maxim is well-known and can be found in the literature on mediation, meditation and spiritual development. A recent example is from Mother Meera, "In silence one can receive more because all one's activities become concentrated at one point."[15]

When your attention is focused on the other person, you can begin to listen:

- You can listen to the *content* of what is being expressed. This is the most tangible level of your exchange, and helps you to understand what your partner is presenting to you.
- You can listen for the *feeling* or *quality* of the other person. The words may be amiable, but they might carry a tone of anger or frustration. Or the words may be difficult and uncomfortable, while the tone is gracious and gentle.
- You can listen to the **whole** of what is being expressed, even if you don't like one aspect or part of it. We stop listening to the other person if we get caught or "hung up" in a phrase or a sentence that disturbs us; the whole process is interrupted and we have lost the flow of communication.
- You can listen to the **person** even if you don't like what is being said. If you remember always hat you love this person and that s/he is the most important person in your life, there will be much less distortion of what you hear and see coming towards you from the other.

During the first 3 minutes of the exercise, when you may not speak, you have the greatest opportunity to practice inner silence. This is the time to become aware of the internal activities that prevent you from listening to anything more than the most superficial levels of what is being said. At first the work will be to notice what processes keep interfering with your attempts to become silent. Once you become aware of what you are doing, you can learn to turn from the active habitual mind and focus your loving attention on your partner.

• SOME THINGS TO NOTICE AND AVOID •

Do not prepare an answer or think of what your response will be. If you are thinking about your side of the issue—indeed, if you are thinking about anything at all—you are not listening. This constant thinking and preparing is such a "natural" or habitual mental activity that almost everyone in our culture recognizes that he or she is doing it all the time. It may not be easy to stop the rambling flow and turn your attention towards your partner with love. Learning to do this is part of what we are practicing in this exercise.

If you find that you disagree, or even that you agree with what the other person is saying, you are no longer listening to the speaker. If you reject what you hear or see, or if you criticize or judge, or evaluate by any standard, you are not listening. You stop hearing the other person if you hold on to your own point of view, or if you have any opinion, positive or negative, about what is being communicated.

If you are busy formulating arguments, you stop hearing the other person. In order to listen, you must be poised with a silent mind, not yet committed to a point of view. Try to suspend these activities of the mind as you turn in love towards your partner.

Do not make suggestions, offer aid, or try to solve the problem. If your mind is occupied with trying to figure out solutions, you are not able to listen. Presenting a solution when it has not been asked for, even if offered with the best of intentions, cuts off the flow of communication and the person is no longer being heard.

During the next 3 minutes when you may speak you are still a *listener*, i.e., your focus is exclusively on the speaker. You do not respond, reply, or express your point of view. You are focused only on what the speaker is expressing. You may draw the speaker out by asking questions:

"Tell me more about …"; "Is it like …?"; "Have you felt like … before?"

Acknowledge that you have heard the person:

"I understand ..." & "I hear you ..."

Try to acknowledge the person in their language mode, rather than yours. Check to see that you have understood the other person:

"When you say ..., does it mean ...?";
"Are you saying, ... (paraphrase in your own words) ...?"

You may ask if there is any way that you can help or anything that you can do. Notice how different this is from offering suggestions or solutions to the other person, especially when she or he has not asked for them.

•USES OF THE EXERCISE •

The skill of focused listening is one of the most basic achievements of a compassionate person. It is useful in all areas of interpersonal relationships. Especially in intimate love relationships, listening with love is a fundamental activity leading to an experience of communion. The skill of listening is something that few ever master, but we can become very good at it. In order to become a better listener, we need to practice, and there are several ways to use this exercise with our partner to accomplish this goal. The first way to use the exercise is as a structured practice. How to do this is described above. As a couple, you decide to choose a topic and listen to each other within the confines of the instructions. Creating an artificially strict set of rules within which to practice a specific skill is commonly used in many sports, music and other kinds of physical and mental endeavors. Just as it works in those activities, it works equally well to develop listening skills.

The listening exercise may also be used spontaneously in your everyday life as a couple. When an issue arises, particularly one that is difficult to talk about, a good strategy for interchange is to use the technique of remaining silent and listening. Many couples have told us that this approach has made it possible for them to discuss certain issues for the first time.

Another possibility is to end the exercise after one person has spoken for 3-4 minutes with the listener being silent. Stopping at this point with no dialogue, no reciprocity, just "letting it be ..." can provide an opportunity for both people to hold an unresolved ambiguity for awhile, or perhaps to absorb a new point of view.

The technique of taking "turns" listening and speaking about the same subject can be very revealing of the different ways that you each see that same situation or event. This can help you to "understand" your partner in ways that were not accessible before. Dialoguing in this way can lead to a transformation of your communication and subsequently to more meaningful patterns of verbal interaction.[16]

Finally, the listening exercise can be used as a way to "get together," to share experiences, to commune with one another, or to engage in that almost extinct form of human activity, "intimate talking."

> About 6 years ago we worked with a couple who had been married for 35 years, but for the last 20 of those years their interactions had become progressively mechanical. There had been problems with alcohol, prescription drugs, overeating, children, money, and careers, which had over the years reduced them to cohabiting strangers. Now, in their middle 50's they had decided do something to become loving partners again, so they took our Way of the Beloved classes. When they practiced the listening exercise for the first time, they found that each exchange led to another, and that they could not stop talking. Seven hours later, at 3 AM, they realized that the 20 year cycle of disengagement and non-communication had been broken. They continued to work together and were able to reestablish a loving and fulfilling relationship after many years of separation and hurt.

ဆာ ○ ○ ಣ

To facilitate and stimulate your structured practice of the listening exercise, we have appended a list of questions which can help you and your partner explore your relationship.

• SUGGESTED TOPICS FOR THE LISTENING EXERCISE •[17]

1. What are my feelings about being married to you?
2. About what area of our life am I most able to talk with you? How do I feel about this?

3. In what area of our life together am I least able to communicate with you?
4. What are my hopes about our future together? How do I feel about this?
5. What are my fears about our future together? How do I feel about this?
6. What feeling/perception do I have that I find most difficult to share with you?
7. What feeling/perception do I have that I find most difficult to face in myself?
8. What was a specific occasion when I felt closest to you? (Describe in detail)
9. How do I feel when I want to be with you and you are somewhere else?
10. How do I feel when I want to be with you and you have something else to do?
11. How do I feel after sex?
12. How do I feel when I want to have sex and you don't?
13. How do I feel when I need to hear a response from you and you are silent?
14. What are the qualities which most attracted me to you?
15. What are the qualities which I admire most in you?
16. I feel I need your help specifically in …
17. Do I love you and accept you as you are?
18. Do I feel that you love me and accept me as I am?
19. What do I appreciate most about you?
20. How do I feel when we argue?
21. In what area of our life am I most open to listening to you?
22. In what area of our life am I least open to listening to you?
23. How do I feel when you do something I dislike?
24. How do I feel when you do something that I like?
25. How do I feel when I do something you dislike?
26. How do I feel when I do something you like?
27. What am I most grateful for in our relationship?
28. In what area of our life is it most difficult for me to feel gratitude?

• 2.3 PATTERNS OF SHARING •

We are always communicating, whether we are aware of it or not. Without intention, the tone of our being radiates in all directions and the quality of our thoughts and emotions reaches others. In addition our body language, posture, and moods, reveal to others what is happening within us. Thus we cannot not communicate.

Words are important, but they communicate only a part of who we are and are not essential to the expression of love. You do not need to talk to your partner in order to love her or him. You do not need to identify or know what your feelings are and you do not need to be an expressive, demonstrative person in order to love. People of few words tend to think of themselves as poor communicators, because the societal standard is apparently based on quantity of verbiage. This is unfortunate. Everyone may have known a person who speaks very little and seems shy and reticent, but who radiates good will and invites close contact. It is the quality of our attitudes and emotions towards others that determines the depth and character of our communication patterns. It does not matter whether one is expressive or reserved, social or private, anyone can evoke, experience, and communicate love to another person. Our motives and what is in our heart are what really count in human interactions and are the basis for communion with others.

In the spirit of self-exploration, we can examine our patterns of sharing with our partner. The patterns of our interactions are seldom explicit to us. They are underlying patterns which are tacit, i.e., silent. In his article, "On Dialogue,"[18] David Bohm explains that "'Tacit' means that which is unspoken, which cannot be described—like the tacit knowledge required to ride a bicycle. It is the *actual* knowledge, and it may be coherent or not." The Sharing Assessment is an exercise to bring into awareness these underlying communication patterns. Even though we are communicating in many ways, the Sharing Assessment focuses on the patterns of how we *speak* to one another.

ഇരു

• DESCRIPTION OF THE EXERCISE •

We will explore our verbal communication patterns in the following ways:

- First we will look at the *quality* or *tone* of our interactions.
- Then we will investigate the *quantity*, *extent* or *depth* of our verbal sharing.
- Lastly we will be able to evaluate how we speak to one another in order to set goals for improvement.

In his, now almost classic, treatise on Tantric Buddhism, Herbert Guenther tells us that "it is through our moods and judgments of feeling that we communicate with other persons and the world around us. Although communication is mostly related to words, more important is the timbre of the voice which clearly reflects my mood, and my mood may colour the whole situation."[19] Especially in a love relationship, the tone quality carried or embodied by our spoken interactions is more important than the words we exchange. What do we mean by the tone quality of the spoken word? All our verbal exchanges are influenced by our state of mind and heart. Thus, our changing states of emotion, our moods, our mental postures, or our physiological dispositions affect the color, flavor, taste, note, rhythm, or tonal qualities of what we are saying. This tone quality is independent of the words, meaning or content of what is being said. Our whole being rides on the words that we speak,[20] and it is all present for those "who have ears to hear." We are often acutely aware of the tone quality we hear in what is being spoken to us. And we may know quite a lot about how we respond to these different tone qualities, but often we do not consider how our own state of heart, mind and body affects those who listen to us.

There are innumerable variations in the tones expressed by different couples. How many couples do you know who talk in angry, critical tones to each other, as if they were locked in some eternal debate? We have known couples who talk to each other as if they were negotiators trying to work out a contract for the tenuous co-existence of two warring tribes whose conflicts go back a thousand years and can never be resolved. We have also met many couples who "share" everything, especially all of their feelings and emotions in great detail with no inhibitions, and the quality of their interaction sounds like they are participating in a business conference. Sometimes we hear an affectionate sounding couple, or a couple who speak cordially to one another, and occasionally we hear a couple whose speech carries love. In assessing your patterns of verbal sharing, you must know more about how the tone quality of your speech affects your partner. You **can** learn to express more love!

In addition to the tone quality of your speaking with each other, you must explore the quantity, extent and depth of your verbal exchanges. We are not referring to the quantity of information exchanged nor to the superficial chatter that constantly takes place between so many people, but about the degree of communion that you are able to achieve with one another. Ask yourself, "How much of my life do I talk about with my partner?" or "How much of my 'self' do I share?" or "How willing am I, to reveal the deeper, more intimate levels of my nature? The answers to these questions will tell you something important about the degree of closeness and intimacy in your relationship. Part 1 of the exercise is an exploration of these questions.

• THE EXERCISE •

PART I

Each person should work individually and privately for several days or more and complete the following:

- Write a list of all the areas of your life that you and your partner talk about easily and naturally.
- Write another list of those areas that are "mixed", sometimes it's all right to talk about them, sometimes it's not all right to talk about them; sometimes it go smoothly, sometimes there's tension, or fear, or anger, or misunderstanding.
- Write a third list of those areas that you keep private and to yourself. Include things that you talk about with others, but not with your partner, and secrets that you may never have revealed to anyone.

Do not censor yourself, this is your own list. No one else need ever see what you have written, if you do not wish it. These lists are for the purpose of self-exploration; you are trying to learn more about how you speak to your loved one. Try not to make any value judgments at this point. Look upon your lists as road maps, neither good nor bad—patterns showing you where you are. Think about and include all areas of your life as you construct these lists. For example, you may consider events of your day, conversations with other people, problems at work, thoughts, feelings, hopes, fears, dreams, fantasies, plans for the future, etc. (Consult the list of categories given in Section 1.2 Goals and Commitments for ideas.)

Next to each item on your first two lists, make notes which describe the tone quality of these expressions.

- For example, loud, angry, fearful, gentle, affectionate, cold, argumentative, negotiating, business-like, tentative, caring, uncaring, critical, accepting, shallow, intensely emotional, etc. (Use the list of emotion words in Appendix #1, for additional descriptive terms.)

Reread everything that you have written so far and mark those items which you find to be positive or satisfactory and those which you think are negative or could be improved.

Close your eyes and do the Invocation of Love for 3 minutes. Now from a quiet place of love feel the sincerity of your intention to speak with a tone of love to your partner.

- Make a commitment to be more loving and more positive in the quality of your communication.
- Visualize yourself speaking from your heart with an expression of beauty and love. This does not mean that you will be "weak" and "ineffective". Love is a power that fills a person with great inner strength.
- Feel your intention, and make an additional commitment to listen deeply and to "hear" your partner from your heart of love without judgment or criticism, meeting whatever is said to you with gratitude and compassion.
- Visualize yourself "hearing" and loving the other person as you listen.

PART II

Set aside a time when you can be together with no interruptions and do the following:

- Compare and share your lists. Share as much as you choose or as much as you are able, at your own discretion.
- Discuss and become aware of what is shared in your relationship and what isn't. Try not to be judgmental. At this point you're trying to look at **how** you've been communicating up to now. (There will be opportunity later on to evaluate.)

Make explicit the "unspoken" patterns such as:

"We talk easily about ... but we are not yet ready to talk about ... ";

"... must never be said between us!";

"I am afraid to talk about ... ";

"I notice that you never mention anything about ... "

- Some areas to discuss might be sex, in-laws, step-children, money, business, illness, politics, religion, emotional needs and desires, fantasies, the past, the future, etc.
- You may not wish to mention your private or secret areas, but you may decide to say that you do have them.

Decide how you might improve your communication and bring more love to your relationship by changing the way you speak and listen.

- Sit silently together and do the Invocation of Love.
- Then talk about your mutual commitment to speak and listen in a loving manner. Talk about how you both will do this—be specific.
- Evaluate and keep a daily record of the extent and the quality of communication in your relationship.

❧❧

• DISCUSSION OF THE EXERCISE •

The purpose of this exercise is to inspire you with the desire to fill your daily encounters with love. These explorations should help you work toward speaking from a heart of love and toward listening to your partner without judgment or criticism. The sincere commitment to speak and listen with compassion indicates that you will put your good intentions into practice and make them a reality in your life. Therefore, when you disagree with each other or begin to argue, emotions may be strong but you will make an effort to avoid nastiness or fighting. If you hurt each other, it will happen unintentionally because you have *slipped*, and not because you have meant to be hurtful.

Although both of you are participating, either one of you can change the quality of your interaction (This approach is discussed in detail in Section 3.2 "Transforming Negativity," the part titled, "Why Should I Change?"). For instance, a common problem in couples relationships is described by Suzette

Elgin in her book, *Genderspeak.* She says, "A great deal of the time, when people hear someone say something they don't immediately understand, they assume that it's false and try to imagine what could be wrong with the person saying it …"[21] This immediate impulse to make a negative assumption about another is so deeply embedded in our culture that it has become a social reflex. An effective way to overcome this reaction is to *interpret* what your partner is saying in the most *positive* way. One way this can be accomplished is by assuming that what the other person is saying is true for them, and then by trying to imagine in what way it could be true.[22] Another way, is to assume that the other person has a positive intention, and then try to imagine in what way this could be so. Here are two actual accounts that illustrate the use of this kind of reframing technique in marriage:

> About 15 years ago, we heard the following story from our friend, Sara. She was in her middle 40's at that time and was a successful artist with 3 teenage children. She and her second husband, Eric, had been married almost 5 years when the incident occurred: One Spring afternoon Sara was in the kitchen busily cutting up vegetables for dinner, when Eric passed by and without even slowing down said, "You should use the smaller knife." What a blow! She was taken by surprise and Eric was out of the room before she could react. Righteous anger welled up in her and she thought, "He puts me down like that all the time. He must think that I am just not good enough for him. How arrogant can he be?" Just as she was beginning to get really angry, much like the dinner that was boiling on the stove, she remembered the technique of "trying to give the most positive interpretation" to Eric's demeaning remark. Sara asked herself, "If there is any possible *positive* interpretation for Eric's criticism, what could it be?" The moment she asked this question the answer rose up in her as if from some new place in her psyche. She thought, "I know that Eric really wants to make things better for me. He's always telling me that he wants to fix things for me. Could it be that this is a way of showing that he cares about me and wants to help me?" In that instant, something changed for Sara. She was able, for the first time, to *detach* from her defensive reaction. Along with feeling hurt and angry, she was aware that she was loved, and she began to feel a sweet appreciation of her husband. Now that she felt Eric's intent might have been to help her, as clumsy and inept as his attempts to express it were, she could love him. And she was free

to even try the smaller knife if she chose. She didn't have to stand her ground and defend herself. But she did resolve to talk to Eric about a different way to try to make things better for her.

John worked hard and he was beginning to do quite well. He and his wife, Ann, had a good life, his construction business was booming, they owned their home outright, and their two sons were doing very well in school. John and Ann were in our couples' class because they wanted to make their "good relationship" into a more fulfilling marriage. Lately, Ann had been telling him that she missed him and wanted him to talk to her more. John told her that the long hours he worked and the stress of building a business were unavoidable and that the day would come when he could spend more time with her and the boys, but this did not seem to do any good. He really got irritated one night when he returned home late and Ann was immediately *at* him, *pumping* him about every little detail of his complicated day. John asked himself, "What does she want? Is she trying to manage and control my whole life?" He was beginning to feel that maybe Ann was dissatisfied with him, the way he was, and wanted to change him; or maybe she no longer wanted him at all. During this painful monologue, John remembered the couples' class, and thought of the idea of "trying to interpret what Ann was saying in the most positive way." For some reason he became calmer and then he remembered that Ann had often said to him, that because she cares so much for him, she wants to share everything with him. This led John to ask himself, "If she loves me, why would she badger me so much? Why doesn't she leave me alone to do what I have to do? Then wouldn't I have more time for her? How could her inquisitiveness be positive?" And then it suddenly struck him that what he called "badgering" and "attempts to control him" could be Ann's way of trying to share a life with him, to get closer, and to *be with* him during the day. "This was her way of being loving!" With this realization his mood and the direction of his thinking changed abruptly. For the first time he realized that Ann might not want to control him or get rid of him, it could be just the opposite! She really appreciated all the work he did and wanted to share in it with him. He wondered how he could have misinterpreted the situation so completely and he saw that he could now try to meet her need for more loving contact without such a negative reaction. He could now feel the care and love behind the questions which before had seemed so manipulative. Needless to say, John's realization changed his attitude toward Ann's behavior, dramatically.

These two accounts illustrate that if you make a positive assumption with loving intention, your confusions about the intent and meaning of your partner's actions may be clarified before you automatically judge her or him. In these examples both Sara and John had attributed the opposite meaning to their partner's behavior than what was revealed after applying the technique. The use of this technique alone can reduce conflict and open up options you never knew you had.

It is popular today to talk about cultivating openness and honesty in a relationship. Openness and honesty are important, but without love, they can be destructive, separating, and part of a struggle of selfish wills. As love grows, so does communion. With the intensification of love, two people become closer, and they want to reveal themselves more and share more of themselves in the relationship. Your pledge to give positive responses and listen with your heart, non-judgmentally, develops an atmosphere that allows for more sharing and a deeper revealing of the innermost areas of your being. If you desire to become united in a closer relationship you will begin to want to share all areas of life, physical, emotional, mental and spiritual. For a relationship to be the most intimate and creative that it can be the freedom to have complete sharing is the eventual goal. Furthermore sharing everything is not a matter of quantity. This kind of sharing is a matter of quality and intention and the absence of deliberately withholding anything from your partner. It would be impossible to relate and share every word, every thought, every feeling and interaction that has occurred in one's life. Indeed, if love is intense enough, a couple will feel closely connected even when they have little time to talk together.

It may not be productive to try to reveal everything immediately. As you work with making your communication and your lives more loving, confidence and trust will develop and you will be more willing to take some risks with each other. There is no timetable for this. Every couple has a different path to travel. One woman told of this breakthrough in her relationship:

> It was part of a great crisis in our relationship. We had been married five years and had had many serious struggles with each other, but

this one was *it*. We were both determined that we had to come through it together, and become closer. It was so emotional. We said that we really did love each other and that because of this we would tell all and share all, and do it in the spirit of love, not any other way. Not only would we tell all of our private thoughts and secrets, we would not exclude the other one from any part of our life. It was like a sudden jump upwards. All of a sudden we both felt that we never ever had to be alone again. We were like two innocent children. When I was away from home I couldn't wait to get back to tell Walter everything that had happened. And when a problem came up at work or with another person I would have the thought that I could tell Walt and that we'd talk about it, and he'd listen and share with me. He would say similar things too, like, "I was just waiting and waiting for you to get back. I could feel you coming and I knew you'd be here soon."

When there is an atmosphere of love and non-critical listening, it becomes possible to share the more difficult and secret areas. Some people experience the sharing of secrets as a great freedom—freedom from the burden of having to hide a shameful deed or failure. These people often report that it was harder for them to tell of it, than it was for their partner to listen without judgment. In one very close and happy marriage, the man searched his mind to see if there was anything he hadn't told his wife. He found some sexual fantasies which he had "neglected" to ever mention to her. When he told her about them, with some trepidation, her response was a mild, "Oh!"

There is a great variation in such sharing. Since each couple's situation is different, you will have to evaluate where each of you is and what can be handled at any point. Listening with your heart requires an abundance of forgiveness. You must have some confidence that you will be heard and understood without judgment and with great forgiveness before you can actually take the risk of revealing your deepest self.

If your relationship is loving, and you are actively trying to share everything with each other, begin to search for the "mushrooms" growing in the dark closets of your fearfulness. Mushrooms are thoughts or feelings that have some potency or relevance in the relationship, but we keep them to ourselves out of fear or shyness or out of a desire to hold on to them and perpetuate them. Mushrooms may be incidents that have happened to you or things you have done that you are ashamed of. They may be forbidden fantasies or feelings. When kept to oneself they tend to grow and fester, as if being fed by the withholding. Even if a relationship appears harmonious, mushrooms can separate or alienate a woman and man. Try to overcome your resistance to sharing and bring these mushrooms into the relationship. If this is done with a spirit of love, and at the right time, the atmosphere will become clearer, and both of you will notice a difference. Mushrooms cannot live in the light.

Even in the best of relationships, misunderstandings occur. In fact, they occur frequently. Actually, they are occurring all the time. Accepting this as a fact of life rather than a fault of yourself, your partner, or your relationship, can save you much grief, and hours of fighting and dealing with hurt feelings. Many people feel that they have to explain themselves down to the last, minuscule detail, before they are satisfied that they are completely understood. How much more conducive to togetherness it is to let misunderstandings disappear into the ever-flowing river of gratitude and love. Love and compassionate generosity, will bridge the gap of misunderstanding much better than explanations ever can.

No doubt it is helpful to identify misunderstandings as they happen. Otherwise they can become an obscure and overlooked problem. Try to notice when your partner says one thing and you hear it differently from the way that it was intended. Or you say or do something and your partner seems to totally *mis*interpret your meaning. Or you say something and your partner seems to hear you, but you feel that it doesn't really register or sink-in. You can tell when these things are happening by noticing the non-verbal signals at the time of the interchange or the confusing consequences that result from these misunderstandings.[23] The listening exercise is a good way to gain clarity when there are confusions of intentions and meanings. Within that format you can ask the right questions to disclose the intentions and meanings behind what the other person is saying without your emotionally loaded misperceptions coloring the results.

A sense of timing is a great art, a delicate skill, and an absolute necessity. A College Administrator we know, has displayed prominently on the wall in her office a relevant quote from The Buddha:

> *If it is hurtful and untrue, don't say it;*
> *If it is helpful and untrue, don't say it;*
> *If it is hurtful and true, don't say it;*
> *If it is helpful and true, choose the right time.*

If you are in a positive, loving state, your intuition will tell you when it is the right time to speak and when to remain silent. You will be sensitive enough to your partner to be able to see whether or not he or she is ready (i.e. receptive) to hear what you have to say. And you will be prepared to wait, if necessary, until he or she is ready.

Different personality types will need to cultivate different strategies to overcome their particular hindrances to loving communication. A person who says everything spontaneously and immediately with strong emotional affect may have to realize that sometimes it is more loving to try to control or tone down the instant expression and wait for a more opportune moment to speak. This person needs to recognize that just because he or she is ready to talk doesn't mean that the other person is. An emotional person may deliberately have to take time-out to modify her or his emotional state before saying another word (see Sec. 3.2 "Transforming Negativity"). Or the quiet person whose natural mode is to remain silent and avoid saying something or confronting an issue may have to overcome powerful resistances in finding a way to speak out and say what must be said. The reticent person who has difficulty saying anything at all and who feels exposed and anxious when speaking, can practice speaking lovingly and gradually learn to overcome his or her diffidence.

As you get closer, watch for the tendency to think that the other person knows something about you that he or she really does not, or the tendency to make decisions and plans that involve your partner without consulting her or him first. These can be forms of "taking the other person for granted", and also of taking the closeness of the relationship for granted: "Oh, I thought I told you that ... ", or, "Didn't you know that ...?" This discovery may be a sign that you are neglecting the other person or the relationship, and that you are drifting backwards into old patterns. If this occurs, catch it before it goes too far. It can become a reminder that you have to be aware, if you want a loving relationship. You have to create the love and closeness in your relationship. It will not happen on its own automatically.

The flow of communication between two people fluctuates constantly. Sometimes it may stream harmoniously for days or weeks, and then, gradually or suddenly, it will be different. It may change as our moods vary or as the necessities of life influence us and carry us away from a focus on the relationship. Close communication can be broken because of our own negativity, fear, ignorance, selfishness, distraction, absorption in something else, or just lack of awareness. Sometimes the flow is lost for unknown, seemingly inexplicable reasons. There seem to be cycles in the stream of communication and the expressions of love in a relationship, just as there are cycles in all areas of our life. Therefore, loving communication must be constantly reestablished.[24] If you are working to intensify your love, close and deep communion will be one result of your efforts.

CHAPTER 3

• 3.1 FIRST STEPS TOWARD TRANSCENDING SELFISHNESS •

Narcissus was the failure of love … He stood for a danger that has fascinated as well as repelled us for centuries: the danger that the individual will become so enamored of his mind and flesh, that society will go untended and God go unloved; or, perhaps more secretly, that each of us will go unloved. For Narcissus is never ourselves, he is always the other one who cannot see us.

—Paul Zweig[1]

Most people view their relationship with the opposite sex as a means to satisfy their own needs and desires. Each individual is trying to *get* something from the other person and from the relationship. This approach leads, sooner or later, to a conflict of personalities, and not to an experience of joy or fulfillment. What kind of a fulfillment can we find, if it is based on taking from others?[2]

"Narcissist" is a term used to describe those people who are obsessively trapped in their own egos. We also say that they are "egoists," "egocentric," "selfish," or "self-absorbed." These are people who not only satisfy their own desires regardless of others, but who also do not experience anyone else as a true *other*. Eric Fromm in his enormously popular book, *The Art of Loving*, repeated what has been known to us at least since the time of the Periclean Greeks: "the main condition for the achievement of love is the *overcoming* of one's *narcissism*. The narcissistic orientation is one in which one experiences as real only that which exists within oneself, while the phenomena in the outside world have no reality in themselves, but are experienced only from the viewpoint of their being useful or dangerous to one."[3] This is so common today that we all can probably think of an example. Here is one that is close to us:

> We have an old friend who would make decisions and commitments that involved his wife's participation without consulting her. He would invite people home for dinner or to spend the night and not inform her in advance—he would often just show-up with the unannounced guest. Also he would give away money or even personal items without talking to his wife about it. When anyone asked him about this behavior, he would reply innocently, "Well, what's wrong with that? We are one, aren't we?" He had a vague belief that in some *spiritual* sense, perhaps because they had had a church ceremony, that he and his wife must be united, and therefore his agenda should be her agenda. This distortion of a great spiritual ideal was the result of a blinding self-absorption, which prevented him from recognizing his wife as a separate and unique being—equally as real as he is.

It is not uncommon today to find marriages *based* on selfishness.[4] Indeed, even when two people believe that they love each other, an "*unhappiness* comes in, because the love which *dominates* them is not a love of each for the other **as that other really is**."[5] The extent to which a person acts out of selfish desires and motives, is the extent to which that person will not experience other people as separate individuals possessing as equal a reality as himself or herself. Seldom do egoists realize that they are experiencing others as reflections of their own inflated desire life. They are convinced that they are right and that they know what others *really* need and want—even despite what the others may say about it.[6]

We are all a mix of selfishness and genuine care for others. This mixture of opposing forces in people lies along a vast continuum, from the saint to the megalomaniac. It may be said, that today selfishness has become the primary source of unhappiness in intimate relationships between men and women![7]

> There was a young couple in our family who after living together for about 3 years, got married and had 2 children. They seemed as happy and *normal* as we could expect of any couple in their 20's. But after 4-5 years we began to notice a pattern of disengagement on the part of the husband which seemed a strange way to deal with problems and conflict in the relationship. When a crisis arose, whether it was

emotional, financial, or with the children, his immediate response was to say something like, "I need some space," "I haven't been taking care of myself lately," "I have been denying myself too much," etc. And he would take off backpacking for a week or two, or he would buy himself something that they could not afford, or he would find a new way to "have more fun." This, of course, left his wife to deal with the situation alone. Even when another crisis was precipitated by his unwillingness to consider anyone else's sufferings or problems, he still felt that *his* needs were all important. When he felt bad, regardless of the cause, he interpreted that to mean that he needed to go away and do something to make himself feel *good* again. His selfishness became more and more extreme, leading to an emotionally and physically abusive family life, which ended in divorce. Even after the divorce, in spite of counseling, therapy, and numerous court actions, he continues to behave with an unwavering concern only for himself.

The power of selfishness can be all-consuming, and there are many, like the young man in this story, who act in self-destructive ways, all the while believing that they are doing what they really want and need.

In order for a relationship to grow in beauty and joy, each person must begin to recognize the individuality and equality of the other, and then learn to give to the other with unselfish love.[8] Through the pouring out of love, one begins to see that the true fulfillment of one's own deepest desires comes through giving selflessly to the other.[9] Contrary to the fear of many, this does not mean that we must become passive and allow ourselves to be used by the other person. It means that we recognize the fulfillment of our own highest development in giving to the other person rather than in trying to satisfy our own desires. We find that instead of acting automatically out of selfish motives, we can choose to give to the other person, willingly and lovingly. Through intense love, one cares for and values the welfare and growth of the other person, **as if these were one's own!** Meher Baba understood this so well and wrote about it so perspicaciously:

The disease of selfishness in mankind will need a cure which is not only universal in its application but drastic in nature. *Real peace and happiness will dawn spontaneously when there is a purging of selfishness. The peace and happiness which come from self-giving love are permanent.*[10]

However, today in a world virtually ruled by self-interest we are often told that our own growth is stifled if we place others before ourselves. We are encouraged to express ourselves and our preferences, to discover what it is that we want, and then set all our energy towards getting it. Particularly in our American society, we are disocouraged from doing what others want us to do, or from doing anything for others unless there is a visible and tangible compensation in it for us. This approach to life develops selfishness, and ultimately brings isolation and loneliness into our being and into our relationships to others.

Performing one's obligations, doing one's duty, doing what others want us to, doing things for others, even living one's life for others, do not of themselves stifle a person's expression and growth. It is the fear, resentments and anger associated with these acts and the a lack of love in the actions, that stifles a person. Contrary to what we have heard from some authors, you cannot "love too much," but you can certainly *desire* too much from others. If we care deeply for another person and consciously choose to give selflessly, we enter a realm of beauty, joy and communion. This is not co-dependency or pathology, for love never diminishes us – it is the deepest fulfillment of our destiny as men and women. Indeed as Teilhard de Chardin has emphasized throughout his writings: "The give we make of our being, far from threatening our ego must have the effect of completing it."[11]

A simple way to reduce selfishness and bring more love into your relationship is to practice the expression of love in your daily life. Most of us do not do this because we have never thought or been taught that it is possible to intend love. We think of love as something that "happens" rather than something we "do." We are not accustomed to the idea that we can consciously and intentionally blend the quality of love into our actions, feelings, and thoughts—**we can will to invoke love to come into expression in our lives.** Our relationships are often characterized by the familiar patterns of "attack" and "defend"—the instant and seamless expression of our selfishness. Just because our selfish actions are comfortable and seem automatic, doesn't mean that they should be seen as unchangeable or fixed for life; indeed these patterned habits, which lock our lives into endless cycles of conflict, can be changed.

It is well known that the affective state of the 'atmosphere' around you is influenced by the qualities you express through your speech, actions, and emotions. When you are tense and angry, the 'atmosphere' around you is agitated and dark. When you are gentle and easy going, it is relaxed and when you are affectionate and playful it becomes lighter. We also know that it is possible to intentionally choose the qualities which you wish to express in your life.[12] If you consciously focus on bringing unselfish love into your actions, feelings, and thoughts, and you persist in this practice over a period of time, the quality of love will eventually come to permeate all the regions of your life. If you put your energy into thinking of ways to express love in your intimate relationships, and you develop and practice loving actions and loving thoughts, your whole life will radiate the quality of love.

The conscious practice of love stimulates the flow of a beautiful exchange in a relationship. True love is a practice. As Franz von Baader said, "To know the truth and to love and do it are one and the same thing."[13] Love grows as each person pours it out to the other. By intentionally practicing unselfish love one discovers a hidden law: "the more love you give out, the more love there is flowing into you and through you." The conscious practice of love can also stop and reverse a friction-filled, negative relationship. As soon as even one person in the relationship changes from a mode of negativity to an expression of love, the door is open for understanding and growth.[14]

The awakened heart says, "I must give, I must not demand."
Thus it enters a gate that leads to a constant happiness.
—Inayat Khan [15]

• A PRACTICE FOR DEVELOPING UNSELFISH LOVE •

Here is a simple and direct way to stimulate and develop the quality of unselfish love in your relationship:

Sit quietly by yourself and think about your beloved partner and of your love for him or her. You might do the Invocation of Love. Focus for a moment on your sincere desire to increase and intensify the love in your relationship. Remember that no matter what else is going on in your life, your beloved partner is the most important person in your world and needs your attention, your care and, above all, your love.

Then reflect on what you might be able to do, that would demonstrate and express your love to the other person—something that you know would truly please him or her. Think of several SPECIFIC things, like something you could say, or refrain from saying, something that you could do, or refrain from doing, things that you know will touch the other person and bring more love and harmony into your relationship. These things do not have to be large and important, but they should not be too vague, abstract or general.

You could choose something as simple as closing the kitchen cabinet doors because it bothers your partner to see them open. Or you could prepare a favorite meal for him or her, or buy a gift for no special reason, or pick up the socks that are always left in the middle of the living room without complaining and making a big issue of it. You could also do something more significant, such as showing special interest in his or her current "project", even though it isn't one of your own interests; or not acting withdrawn and angry even though you feel that way, when he or she watches the basketball game on T.V. Do not spend time and energy evaluating or wondering if something is the right thing or if it is a big enough act. Robert Sardello tells us that "The phenomenon of love works in such a way that the small acts are the big consequences. That is to say, the smallest acts of love each encompass the whole world."[16]

Most people are flooded with ideas as soon as they turn their attention to finding more loving ways to interact. We know our partner well enough to be familiar with what will make her or him happy. But if you do have difficulty choosing something, just watch and listen to the other person. Observe what your partner does and says. It will not take long to find many things that you can do to bring him or her delight.

Whatever you choose to do, decide to do it with love and for the specific purpose of giving love, and **NOT FOR ANY OTHER REASON!** An unselfish act done with great love can create an atmosphere in the relationship that is charged with harmony and gratitude. But if you do something for the other person because you think you'll get a reward or because you think it will get you into a better position to ask something in return, you are trying to manipulate your interactions with your partner to your own advantage. Or if you do something "nice" because you are afraid of your partner's anger, you are not practicing unselfish love.

However, if you are feeling indifferent or even negative (unhappy, disturbed, worried, etc.), and you decide to do this exercise anyway, your effort and intention to express love will invoke love's power to come through you to your beloved one—thus helping you to overcome your negativity. It is your motive that counts. Any motive other than love will not accomplish the aim of this exercise.

DO NOT LOOK FOR ACKNOWLEDGEMENT

You are doing this practice out of love for this person, and because it would make a difference to her or him, and not because you expect recognition, or appreciation, or love, or indeed anything, in return. This is a special effort that you are making for the sake of love. The spirit of the exercise is to do as much as you can, without expecting anything from the other person.

DO NOT SEEK TO DISCOVER WHAT
THE OTHER IS DOING FOR YOU

Trying to find out what your partner is doing would be in contradiction to the spirit of the exercise. Nontheless, for many the patterns of competing and battling are so ingrained that they are unable to *let it be* and this constant *wrestling match* is not something that they are seeking to change—they believe that it is the way things *have* to be. A good friend presented such a situation:

> Ann was a recently recovering alcoholic and she was energetically trying to change the negative responses she had practiced for a lifetime. She told us that she could not come up with anything to do for her husband of nearly 40 years. As it turned out, the exercise had activated her powerful sense of competition which had been characteristic of their relationship since its beginning. She became so involved in trying to figure out what her husband was doing for her in order to "one-up" him or to "win the guessing game," that she never found anything to do for him. The simplicity of just giving joy and delight to him was something she could not comprehend. She had become locked in a petty self-centered attempt to show how well she could second-guess him.

If you should come to know what it is that your partner is doing (or not doing) solely by the joy and delight you feel, then the exercise is producing the intended results. And most likely, you will also notice that your partner feels something, too. Perhaps you will be able to see that he or she is feeling more loved and appreciated because of your freely offered expressions of love, whether or not she or he can identify exactly what you are doing.

෨ ෬

As a daily practice, this exercise can change the character of your relationship. Many couples who have taken the Way of the Beloved course, have told us that this exercise has changed their whole attitude and approach to life. Frequent comments are, "Why haven't we done this before?"; "Now we get up in the mornings and think about giving to each other"; "Not only do we love doing it, but everything else that we do is enriched, whether we are together or apart. What a difference!" Many are continuing to initiate loving actions on a daily basis, even years later; for them, "It has become a way of life!"

This practice brings joy into your life because it is a concrete and practical way to blend the quality of love into your thoughts and actions, and to invoke the quality of love to enter the very fabric of your daily life. By initiating loving actions, love gains direct entrance into every corner of your relationship. It is important to pick one thing to do or to refrain from doing, each day, and **DO IT!** It can be the same thing or something different, but do something every day.

The biggest problem that people have with this exercise is that they do not sustain it over an extended period of time. If we are having difficulties in the relationship we feel negative, so we think we have a good excuse not to do something loving. And if things are going along smoothly, we don't get around to thinking about doing something special or extra. We take it for granted that we must be doing everything that is 'necessary', and that all will continue to go well. It takes a conscious effort to become more loving, it does not happen on its own.

Begin today to think of giving to your love relationship instead of getting from it. Focus on giving to your partner instead of getting something from him or her. Do not think of what the other person should do, but think instead of what you can do! Every day, think of how you can give to the other, to the relationship, and to your goals of love and fulfillment with this other person!

> *Faithfulness to the little things will help us to grow in love.*
> *We have all been given a lighted lamp and it is for us to keep it burning.*
> *We can keep it burning only if we keep on pouring oil inside.*
> *That oil comes from our acts of love.*
>
> —Mother Teresa[17]

• 3.2 IDENTIFYING AND TRANSFORMING NEGATIVITY •

Life brings all sorts of difficulties, but the biggest problems are the inner ones: they come from our aggressive and angry attitude, our desires and attachments, and our lack of insight. So in all our life situations and circumstances, we must practice the discipline of working with the passions or afflictions.

—Kalu Rinpoche[18]

Why, when two people are trying their best to live in love and harmony, do problems and conflicts arise to separate them? The greatest blocks to love in human relationships are the habitual emotional reactions[19] we have towards other people. Every person has what seems to be automatic, positive and negative responses to others. A positive response, such as attraction or approval, can be enhancing to the development of love. However, the negative reactions, such as anger, jealousy, resentment, criticism, or irritation cut off the flow of love and start the downward spiral of conflict and separation.

When a man and woman "fall in love"[20] everything about the other person seems thrilling and wonderful. Everything that they say to one another or that they do together, brings a sense of beauty, excitement, and joy. As they embark upon living their lives together as a couple, they become closer; they spend more time with each other and see more and more of each other. They get to know each other better and better, and then they usually find each other harder and harder to love. We are all familiar with this sequence of events. What has happened? Where has the love gone?[21] What has corrupted its beauty? Why is it so inevitable that problems and conflicts should arise?

In the beginning of a love relationship the patterns of negativity within each person are suspended by the intensity of a new love. Intense love makes us want to be with the other person all the time, and it makes us spontaneously caring and kind. Love makes us appreciate everything about the other person, and we want to please the one we love. But as two people live together, the other elements within their personalities emerge and become more active. Every person wants to assert his or her persona or personal self in his or her own way, and each wants to be satisfied and to do as he or she pleases. For this reason, people do not blend naturally or easily with another in love.

The very attempt to grow closer to another person and to build a creative relationship together, can stimulate the negative elements to come to the surface. These powerful forces of separation and alienation are largely unconscious, but when stirred-up by the new streams of psychic energy pouring in from the relationship, they will erect barriers between the two people trying to love. Often when two people first fall in love they seem miraculously different from their "old selves." This is a *honeymoon* period where the negative patterns of response seem to have disappeared, but actually are only temporarily suspended. As the relationship moves into a life rhythm of commitment and responsibility, the previous difficulties reemerge with even more intensity and negativity. When you commit yourself in love to another person, it is more than a decision: the psychic current flowing through you changes direction and begins to flow towards your ideal self. The glow of love is born in your heart, and this is the time when your nature gets stirred-up and your blocks assume greater resistance to the challenge of loving another.

This is a very difficult period in a relationship, because, not only are the lovers overwhelmed with their own reemergent negativity and the unfamiliar problems of their partner, but also because so many begin to experience a profound disappointment. Most of us enter into an intimate relationship with the expectation that it will end our loneliness and "make things better," only soon to discover that things are a lot worse. Many relationships do not survive the storm of conflict and the disappointment that follows, but this crisis is the beginning of the "real work" of learning how to love.

Every one of us has these negative emotional response patterns. Most of the time we act and react automatically, without thinking. Then we believe that this is truly who we are.[22] The identification with these emotional states is often temporary and partial, but in many people, it has become so habitual and continuous that it has usurped their whole identity. It is clearly necessary to know what we are feeling and to "own" these emotions, if we want to grow and to be a whole human being. However, to identify one's "self" as the emotions is to give to that haphazard collection of likes and dislikes a role which brings only chaos to our life.[23]

It is not true that we are only our thoughts and feelings. Human beings are more than a collection of emotional reactions—positive or negative.[24] This affective nature is part of who we are, it is not the sum total of our being. As Thomas Keating has put it, "The emotions have no way of knowing what is good and what isn't good for the whole person. They only report what they feel. They simply record what feels good or not good. This is not the kind of judgment that is suitable for adults."[25] Thus, we do not have to be ruled by our emotions. We do have the ability to make a choice. We can learn to change even our most deeply ingrained response patterns.

So, what do we do with them? If we give them license, if we let them rule us, then we are at their mercy. Expressing negative emotions stimulates them and gives them energy. It makes them stronger, increasing their intensity and hence their control over us. Also expressing negativity is hurtful to others and does not lead to loving relationships. Today many are taught to express negative emotions and they can become very good at it, but is that a useful skill? However, repressing our negative emotions is not a solution either. The physical and psychological results of living in a constant negative emotional state, or of pushing our emotions back into the unconscious (repression), are well known.[26]

Emotion is a power, and it can be channeled by us into more constructive paths of expression. There is a creative alternative to the indulgent expression of negativity or the repression of these dark emotions.[27] We do have a choice in the expression of our emotions. We can learn the skills of screening and evaluating our thoughts and emotions and of choosing to express only those which are constructive to a loving relationship. Consciously willing to stop the expression of a negative emotion is not repression. Intentionally changing our negativity is neither expression nor repression. These are purposeful decisions which can be implemented by any person who wishes to change her or his habitual responses.

Our goal is to *transform* negative emotions through love. Rather than suppressing our emotions or indulging in them, we can learn to "view" them for what they are, with the intention of directing their energy into more constructive pathways.[28] We can learn to dissolve our negativity by replacing it with love. To some this may sound impossible, but it is a process that has been used by many people before us, and every one of us has the ability to make use of it. People have the power to change their negative responses if they are willing to do the necessary work involved. No matter how powerful or well-entrenched a pattern may seem, it can be changed. It is possible to become more like the person we choose to be. It is possible to transform the negative elements and become capable of a greater expression of love.

•EXERCISE TO TRANSFORM NEGATIVITY•[29]

PRELIMINARY INSTRUCTIONS

The first step in changing our negative responses consists of observation and identification. We must observe ourselves carefully to become aware of our reactions. The patterns of our negative responses can become clear to us by candidly (mindfully) watching what we actually do in our interactions with others, especially with our partner. And we must observe and become familiar with the situations that produce these negative reactions. It is useful to remember that our habitual response patterns are mostly unconscious and operate automatically, and that we will, as a rule, strongly resist even knowing *what* they are. We have learned these ways of reacting to others over our whole lifetime; they are an integral part of our "identity structure" and they will not be easily transformed.

The second step is the crucial one. It is the *moment of choice*. We must make a sincere decision to change our negativity into something better, more beautiful, more loving.

Even though we have decided to change our self, the change will not occur without effort. We must have a strong heartfelt commitment to follow through on our decision, and we will have to use discipline and will to carry out the specific practices and techniques which can transform the negative elements within us.

The fruits of this work will be demonstrated to us when we actually respond in a positive, constructive, and loving way, to a situation that, in the past, evoked a negative response.

• THE EXERCISE •

Write down the events of your day, particularly the interactions with your partner, hour by hour, **backwards.** Do this in the evening, individually, in a quiet, peaceful place. Start from the hour in which you are doing your writing (say 8 PM) and write about what happened from 7–8 PM, then 6–7 PM, then 5–6 PM, etc. Write short notes without details, i.e., an outline of your day.

Look through the events involving interactions with your partner as if you are an objective observer watching the scene, and notice **your own part** in each event. Think about what happened, how you acted, what you experienced, what you thought, and what you felt during the incident. Then decide for each situation whether your actions and emotions were **POSITIVE** (i.e. constructive or wholesome) and leading to a greater flow of harmony and love, or **NEGATIVE** (i.e. separating or unwholesome) and leading to disharmony and pain.

- Be careful here. Try not to explain, judge, criticize, condemn, change, justify or analyze yourself or the other person. Just **observe** in the spirit of impartial inquiry with the intention of seeing and knowing your own self more deeply. (To aid in the process of identifying your specific emotions, see Appendix #1, for an extensive list of positive and negative emotion-words.)

When this is done, pick one event that has some negative emotional charge for you. On a clean sheet of paper write down a detailed account of what happened as if you are an objective observer of the scene. Look at the people, including yourself, as if you are watching a play or a movie. Observe yourself carefully, becoming aware of your own thoughts, emotions, and reactions, and write down how YOU acted, felt and thought.

Then draw a line underneath what you have written. This line is a symbolic way of putting the event as it occurred into the past. You can now begin the work of changing yourself.

Rewrite the event, keeping everything the same, except for **your own** responses, thoughts, emotions and actions. Revise your own part in the situation, changing yourself so that you act and think and feel according to the best and highest spiritual understanding conceivable to you. If you can think of several positive, loving, and compassionate, ways you can meet this situation, write down a number of new versions of the event.

Sit quietly and close your eyes. Visualize the new scene, like a play or a movie within your mind's eye from beginning to end. Imagine yourself responding, feeling, and acting in the new, positive, more loving way. Take plenty of time to do this. The more vividly you see and feel the new response, the more potent the effects of the exercise.

Rehearse the previous step over and over again. Do it day after day, until you begin to feel some "truth" in the new version of the event.

Sooner or later, a situation similar to the one you have been working on will arise again in your life. When it does arise, observe yourself. Notice any changes in the way you act, speak, feel or think. Keep a written record of your observations and changes.

DISCUSSION OF THE EXERCISE

The purpose of this exercise is to practice changing your negative responses through love and gratitude, regardless of what you see in the other person's behavior or character. This is not easy for anyone. Everyone has resistance, conscious or not, to doing this work. We each approach the world through perceptual screens that we have developed over many years of living, and it has become "natural" for us to believe that our own way of seeing things is correct and valid. In addition, we have developed dozens of reasons and feelings by which we explain, justify, and excuse ourselves for being the way that we are. We may say that we want to change and grow, but when it actually comes down to it, we find it very difficult to **do**!

Many of the people in our classes simply don't get around to doing this exercise. We all seem to need a very strong motivator, usually an intense emotional crisis, to even start. (Pain is the way "life" gets us to do the work of growth.) But the work can be just as potent when done without a crisis, in an ongoing and disciplined rhythm. Of course this requires a strong commitment, and the discipline to follow through.

Doubt or ambivalence about beginning the exercise is a form of negativity, inertia, or resistance —a way that we use to try to get out of doing what needs to be done. For example, "This will never work," "I'll never be able to change this feeling," "I'm much too busy right now, I'll do it later." These are typical excuses that we will need to overcome in order to begin. But the resistance can be very strong, even when we think that we don't have any and even when we believe that this exercise sounds like a simple and direct way to change our negative reactions.

> One woman who had been a student for a few months, told us that when we presented this exercise she immediately thought that it was a "wonderful" technique to use to change her negative responses. She was naturally a loving person and was glad to have a new tool which she anticipated "would be a pleasure" to apply. However, shortly after receiving the exercise, she, and her husband of more than 30 years went on a vacation with their two grown children. It is well known that family vacations are 'special' opportunities for exposing our negative patterns and for arousing strong negative emotions. They had only been at the hotel for one night, when she and her husband got into an argument and she left the room, intending to seek some solitude, to do the exercise and to change her anger. But

she had not taken 3 steps outside of the door, when it hit her that she did not want to transform the anger into love; she really wanted to keep it! She felt righteous in her anger; after all, "He was the one who was wrong!" More than anything, her realization was a shock and called into question her sincere desire to transform her negative emotions. She also saw that she was not looking forward to doing the hard work necessary to change her habitual negative responses in the relationship. Indeed, her initial expectations of it being easy and pleasurable became false in the face of her powerful feeling of justified anger. To change the anger felt like it would be a surrender, a loss.

Through this incident, she gained some respect and insight into the difficulties encountered on the road to self-transformation.

Once you have begun, you will need to become scrupulously honest with yourself as you practice identifying your negative responses. Some of us tend to be too hard on ourselves (this itself is negative), and some of us like to remain blind to our own flaws. It takes practice to be candid and frank. This is why this exercise is done privately. You never need to disclose anything about your work to anyone else. It is for you and your own growth. As you practice observing yourself without judgment, you will become more aware of your reaction patterns and you will be more able to see yourself with clarity.

You may decide whether it is best to start with a small irritation or a deep and significant problem in your relationship. Small problems are often indicative of larger issues. They may not really be small at all. No negative response is too insignificant to work on, and to change. If you can respond in a new way even once, you have proved that you can do it! Any success is a great encouragement to continue the work and tackle another problem area.

A young woman in one of our classes was surprised at how encouraging a little success can be. She had been through an unhappy first marriage. Newly remarried, she was very much in love, but somewhat wary because of the disillusionment and hopelessness she experienced in her previous relationship. She was sincere in her desire to make her new relationship a good one, so she put her whole heart into trying this exercise. She had a remarkable story to tell at the next class meeting: She had worked for a few days to change her irritation and fear, in response to something that her husband did. (She never even told us what it was!) Then one day her husband did "it" again and she actually responded in the "new" way. She felt and thought the way she had visualized herself feeling and thinking while working on the exercise. She felt like she had become a new person. She was exhilarated! It was a small incident and a small change compared to the great dramas that a relationship can produce, and yet it was meaningful in its implication for conscious change in her life. This was thrilling to her and to all of us who heard her tell about it.

After you have chosen an event to work with, have written it down as it occurred, and have drawn a line under it, you can begin the work of changing yourself. In many cases you may find that you can easily think of a new way that you can feel and act in the situation. You may even be able to think of several better ways that you could respond. Write all of these down while they are fresh in your mind. There will very likely also be a time, or times, when you will not be able to think of a different way that you could respond in that situation. Should this happen, try the following: Believe that you can change your negative reactions into something better, and that this would be desirable and beneficial for yourself and every other person involved with you. Know that this change will bring more love into your life and will help you to move closer to beauty and fulfillment. If you are not really convinced, or if you are still ambivalent about this, divide a piece of paper in half vertically. On one side write a list of reasons why you should continue responding in the old way in this situation, and on the other side write a list of reasons why you should change the negative response to a positive, loving one. When you are finished, thoughtfully go over both sides. You will see more clearly where you stand; and you will then be more able to make a decision.

Recently, a couple in their early forties found themselves in a situation that is not uncommon in the "two-income-nineties." The husband was staying home and studying for a major career change, while the wife worked full-time in a high-pressure professional position. For months she had been returning home in the evening to find the house a mess. Her husband was not a messy person, but during his days he prepared his meals in the kitchen and spread books and papers throughout the house. The wife was angry when she came home every day, often after dark, and had to clean-up the kitchen before preparing dinner. One evening, as she negotiated the icy streets on her way home, the wife was anticipating a sink full of dirty dishes and she felt the usual anger rising up in her. A great dread of what she knew was about to happen came over her. Just as she approached the house she remembered the exercise on changing negativity. She stopped in the driveway, and in the midst of the growing inner turmoil, asked herself, "What do I really want to happen in this situation?" She realized in that moment of self-generated crisis that the love for her husband was the most important thing in her life and that she wanted to nurture that love more than hold on to her anger—as justified as it was. The new clarity of her options and of what she really wanted made it possible for her to make a choice. She entered the house with a different attitude and in a different state from the anger that had dominated her a few minutes before. Her husband, perhaps sensing this change, began spontaneously and energetically to clean the kitchen while she was changing clothes. They had a very different dinner and evening together from what had seemed inevitable that afternoon.

At this point, try the following strategies even if you are still ambivalent about your commitment to change. *FOR INSTANCE,*

- Realize that it is possible for a person to have many different responses to any situation.
- Think about how you could reinterpret or reframe[30] the event.
- Think about how you might give a different meaning to the other person's behavior.
- Try to imagine how the situation may look from the other person's point of view.

This may take some effort and the use of your imagination. The imagination will help you to write down several different ways that a person could respond in this situation. It may be helpful to pretend that the scene is happening not to you, but to someone else. *FOR INSTANCE,*

- How would … … … feel and act if she or he were in this situation?
- Imagine how someone whom you greatly admire, would respond and meet the situation.
- Imagine how one of your great heroes would respond.
- Imagine how a great spiritually illuminated being would respond.

Sit quietly, close your eyes and relax. Visualize the event with which you are working. Imagine yourself having a different response to the situation—as you have rewritten it. Imagine yourself responding according to the highest moral or spiritual principles that you know about.

It may help to begin with the Invocation of Love. Then, as you see the scene unfolding before you, you may repeat silently *STATEMENTS LIKE,*

- "I love you now, even though you are doing … "
- "No circumstance can diminish my love for you. I will love you even as you …"
- "I love you no matter what!"

Speak to yourself as you visualize the scene. *FOR INSTANCE,*

- "When … (name of partner) … does … I AM tolerant, loving, and compassionate."
- "I reject the negative attitude." Feel yourself turning away from the negativity and *REPLACING* it with the new response.

Repeat over and over again. *STATEMENTS LIKE,*

- "I turn from the negative element and express love and compassion."
- "When … happens, I feel grateful and loving."
- "I choose love."
- "I feel compassion. "
- "I am not a victim of … (negative feeling). Love is flowing through me."

Visualize the scene again and again. See yourself acting, feeling, and thinking in the positive, loving way, until you actually feel it! If your imaging is intense enough, you will feel the reality of the new experience. Take plenty of time as you do this. The more vividly you see and feel the new response, the more potent the results will be.

Be sure that you rewrite only your own role. Don't alter what you remember of the other persons' actions or any of the events. Change your own words, feelings, and actions.

This practice begins to weaken the hold of destructive patterns. You are rejecting, or turning from the negativity, and at the same time affirming a new and positive response. In effect, as you read over the new version(s) that you have written of the experience, you are reading your own "solution" to the problem. And as you visualize yourself acting in the new way, if you do it with some intensity, you are impressing upon yourself a new pattern.

Don't be discouraged by the tenacity of the old patterns. They took years to become established and cannot be transformed in a minute or a day. Even if we faithfully persist over a period of time, it is normal and one can expect to experience difficulties. The negative elements within our personalities do not want to leave! We have given them a good home for a long time and have even considered them to be a part of ourselves. They will not give up easily!

Here are some common ways that our personality tries to convince us to keep our negativity, and some possible ways to overcome them. Use these examples to create your own ways to overcome resistance.

• YOU FEEL THAT YOUR NEGATIVE RESPONSE IS JUSTIFIED, SO YOU THINK IT IS NECESSARY TO KEEP IT •

You may see that your partner is doing something hurtful, destructive or even immoral. Therefore, you feel justified in having a negative response. Though your observations may be legitimate and correct, and you may have to take a strong stand in opposition to your partner's actions, it doesn't follow that you have to do this with negativity. You can do what you have to do, with compassion and with love in your heart, no matter how serious the issue. For example, if your partner has been drinking too much, losing time from work, and narrowly avoiding car accidents, you can't sit by and act as if "it's all right, dear". It is not all right! You must do something! But you can try to overcome and change your fear and anger, and speak out with compassion instead of negative recriminations. If you make the effort to speak with love, you will find strength pouring through you, and you will be grateful for the opportunity to try to help the person you love.

Two young couples that we knew had this very problem. In both cases the husband had a serious alcohol problem and refused to seek any help. In fact, they both blamed their wives for the troubles in the relationship and denied that they had a drinking problem. This was an example of the common, "I can quit anytime I want" rationalization. These couples never met each other and took the course some years apart, but both of the wives discovered by trying to transform their intense anger and resentment, that the source of their negativity lay in their sense of helplessness and victimization. They also became aware that to be angry with their husband *enabled* him to better justify his drinking, thus creating a vicious circle. The more angry and helpless they became, the more they complained; the more they complained, the more the husbands went out drinking, etc. Both of these women subsequently joined Alanon and gained the strength and clarity to be able to confront their husband's drinking from a more positive and constructive state of heart and mind.

• YOU FEEL, "WHY SHOULD I CHANGE?" "WHY SHOULDN'T THE OTHER PERSON MAKE SOME CHANGES?" •

"Why is it always me; why am I always the one who has to change?" How often do we feel this way? If we want something in our life to be different, it is only ourselves that we can change.[31] We cannot be responsible for anyone else's decisions and actions, but we are indeed responsible for our own! We cannot force anyone else to be different from the way that he or she is, but every change that we make, which diminishes negative expressions opens up the possibility for a more loving interchange. It is best when there is a mutual commitment to dissolve negativity and to intensify the love in the relationship. But even if you are the only one who is working to change and grow, the relationship will be different because of your efforts. If one person makes a change your interaction will be influenced.

From time to time, one member of a couple attends our classes alone because his or her partner refuses to participate. These people tell us that their relationships have become entirely different because of the changes they alone have made in their attitudes and actions. In her excellent book Michelle Weiner-Davis, has a Chapter titled, "It Only Takes One to Tango," devoted to unilateral changes in a relationship. She writes, "Years of experience have taught me that both partners need not be present during therapy sessions for the marriage to change. In certain situations, both parties' presence hampers the change process. I have observed hundreds of people change their relationships without the presence of their spouse in therapy and without a formal agreement from their spouse to work on the marriage."[32]

One afternoon as we were talking to a friend of a friend the idea that one person can change a relationship was made more concrete to us. He told us of a concept that he had found very useful in those instances when he was feeling that he was doing all the work in his marriage. His AA Sponsor had given him this example several years prior to our conversation, but he had never forgotten it: "Think of a ping pong game; as long as you keep hitting the ball back over the net, the game will go on. You can choose **unilaterally** to put your paddle down!"

Admittedly, it may be quite difficult to "put your paddle down." Michelle Weiner-Davis gives us an example under the heading, "You Don't Have to Like It, You Just Have to Do It":

> Several years ago my friend Denise told me how she resolved an ongoing marital struggle once she recognized what worked and let go of the idea that she shouldn't have to do it. As a saleswoman, she has to do a significant amount of traveling. Initially, her absences put a great deal of pressure on her husband, Cal, who then had to balance his high-pressure career with caring for their two children. Since Denise regularly balances motherhood and career she could empathize with his feelings, but nevertheless felt he should just grin and bear it and be grateful for the times he is not on duty.
>
> Each time Denise prepared herself for a trip, she got tense, anticipating a negative response or complaints from Cal. Sure enough, when he complied, grousing about having to take their daughter to school the next day, she used to accuse him of being unreasonable, unfair or sexist. Needless to say, he didn't thank her for the feedback. Instead, he would defend his position and they would get into a huge fight, hardly the response Denise wanted as she packed to leave her family.
>
> Then someone advised her, "Denise, Cal doesn't have to love your traveling, he just has to agree to manage things when you're gone." This, she was soon to discover, was very important advice. From that point on, every time Cal mumbled under his breath something about being left alone with the kids, she remained quiet. Remarkably, within minutes, Cal would turn to her and start a completely unrelated, amiable discussion. Apparently, Denise's silence did not provoke him to justify his position.

At first she thought, "I shouldn't have to control myself in this way. He should just be more reasonable." But now, after many years of peaceful and loving departures, she knows better.[33]

Remember that there are many negative reasons to stop playing the game—cowardice, withdrawal, revenge, anger, fatigue etc. Whatever one's motives, the relationship will change if you put your paddle down, the changes may even be beneficial. However, as you change yourself through the motive and quality of love, you will also discover that this process brings you happiness. Even though it may seem otherwise, it is really our own negativity that makes us unhappy. As we begin to transform our negativity and replace it with love, we find a tremendous pool of joy and happiness flowing through us, despite what anyone else is doing, or whatever is happening in our life. It never profits us to resist changing ourselves because someone else is negative or something in our life seems to be an obstacle. When we develop a positive attitude of gratitude and love, we unlock the door to a new life.

• YOU BECOME OVERWHELMED BY A WHIRLWIND OF EMOTION •

Becoming overwhelmed by emotions happens to all people from time to time, and to some, quite frequently. In this state you are not in control; the emotions are controlling you, and you cannot think or act clearly. You are so involved in your feelings, that it seems impossible to feel any other way. You feel trapped by the impossibility of the situation and think that it is useless to even attempt the exercise. You don't even want to try.

If this is happening to you, notice it, and observe it. Become aware of what is going on within you and be able to say, "I am overcome by ... (emotion) ..." You may have to wait until the worst part passes before proceeding. As soon as you are calm enough, recognize that being caught like this can become a block to your growth in love. Self-observation, identification and recognition of your hyper-emotional state, are the beginnings of the process which can extricate you from the whirlwind.

Some people take a strong, determined approach, and say to themselves, "I will not let powerful emotions stop me. I will work on this in spite of my feelings. I will find a way to change. I accept this challenge. It is my opportunity to make a step in growth." Others who function differently, may use the Invocation of Love over and over again, until they can feel calmer and have some love flowing. When they are in a better state, they can then think more clearly about making a change. Some need to be alone to meditate for a while. Many pray for spiritual help.

It is never useful to feel vanquished or defeated. It is essential to persist in your efforts to gain clarity. You may not be able to gain control in twenty attempts, yet on the twenty-first you will do it.

• YOU THINK YOU ARE RIGHT •

This ego-centric attachment to our own view of life can be very subtle, because we are so comfortable with our own ways of seeing and doing. You can recognize that this block is active when you think that you know "better" than your partner. We saw an example of this in one of our evening classes, which illustrated how such an attitude can blind a person to love, and prevent her or him from realizing the need to make a change.

> Two women in the group had shared the problem of feeling hurt when their husbands criticized them. One of them was a very gentle, sensitive person, and tears came to her eyes. She said, "Sometimes I can be doing something and enjoying it, and Roger will come by and tell me to do it differently." Her husband was a good man who had no wish to be unkind, but his manner was strong, self-confident, and a little arrogant. He said, "But I'm just trying to show you the best way to do things. You should see it as me helping you to improve."
>
> Other people in the room tried to tell him that his attitude was superior and egotistical, that it was insensitive and demeaning to his gentle wife, and that it did not allow for her to do things her own way and be appreciated.
>
> He responded with disbelief and said, "You mean when I see her doing something the wrong way, I should just go by and not tell her how to do it right?" He could not believe that there might be other ways to do things than his own. Or that it might be more loving to leave his wife alone to do it her way, even if it wasn't the *best* way.

We must decide whether we would rather be right or rather be loving. We often have to face this choice. The man in this example could not see it at the time, but many of us do understand that in order to become more loving, we must overcome our need to have things done our way, and to grant others the freedom to do things differently. Which is more important: to be right, more efficient, superior, etc., or to be loving?

• YOU THINK YOU ARE WRONG •

If you think too little of yourself and are always feeling that you are not good enough, you will not do the exercise correctly. Instead of invoking love, you will tend to feed your low opinion of yourself and intensify your poor self-image. You cannot be in a loving state if you always belittle yourself and allow yourself to be stepped on.

There are many people who truly believe in their own weakness and feel that they cannot do anything right. They see themselves as always inept, never looking 'right,' not dressing 'right,' never speaking or expressing themselves 'correctly,' and on and on. Believing in one's own weakness becomes a self-fulfilling prophecy and a vicious trap: one is constantly accumulating evidence to verify one's inferiority.

Also many people have the mistaken idea that being loving means to put themselves down, to be self-deprecating, and to act in a self-effacing manner. They defer to others' decisions and do not speak their own truth, acting as if they were really inferior to others. They may or may not be aware that this is really a pretense which covers their true motives and feelings. They believe that their show of self-effacement means that they are superior in the art of unselfish love, while, in reality, they may be filled with anger, resentment and self-pity. Prideful self-effacement is as egocenteric as self-aggrandizement, and no less a block to developing a loving relationship. This attitude often creates a false semblance of harmony in a relationship.

> We knew a woman who became fixated on her interpretation of the meaning of gratitude. She thought it meant that she should allow her husband to treat her inconsiderately and to take advantage of her. She thought that *being grateful* had to mean that she must accept her husband's behavior as it was, without protest, even though it was negative and hurtful. She wasn't able to see that she could be in a state of gratitude and express her point of view at the same time. Of course, she was really full of resentment towards her husband for his attitudes and actions towards her. Before long, she angrily divorced him, and rejected the concept of gratitude too!

If you discover that feeling incompetent and in the wrong is your problem, recognize it as a major barrier to your work in becoming more loving. When you see it as a block and really **do** this exercise, beginning to replace the negativity with love, you will feel an inner strength and determination to change your attitude and move in a positive direction. **Would you rather be wrong all the time**, or would you rather be loving?

Love is a great power. "Love is not unarmed." When you are filled with love you are filled with creative energy. In a state of love, your ego's concern with being wrong or right diminishes; you are less focused on yourself and you care more about loving others and saying and doing what is best and helpful for them.

• YOU THINK YOU ARE GIVING UP SOMETHING VALUABLE •

Believing that to change our emotional habits is to give up something of value may be a universal and inevitable human experience. We are so identified with, and attached to, our emotional states that we feel we are losing something when we try to change them. Just one experience of changing a negative response is proof enough that we move into a better state through this process. Nevertheless, we still have to overcome the inner feeling that we are going to lose something each time we decide to make a change. We have to make the choice each time: "Which path shall I take, the one of negative expression which I have used for many years, or the path of love?" The force of our commitment, persistence and consistency in the practice of the exercises, and the sincere desire to become a more loving person will carry us past this block.

ကာ

It is impossible to predict when or how you will see the results of this work. It is unusual for a change to be demonstrated in a only a few days, but it has happened to some people. Most issues have to be worked on over a period of time. If you have plunged right in to working on a serious problem, you may not see results for quite a while, and you may have many difficulties and resistances to overcome on the way. Sometimes it takes months or even years to change a strong negative pattern. And then it may rise up again from time to time, even after you think it's gone. We must not get discouraged or feel inadequate before the task. Discouragement is a negative response and can be a potent block. Your attempts and your decision to change are already a step

75

in the right direction. Remember that the very effort to make a change leads to the awakening of new love. You will feel a difference.[34]

The "real test" is in the life events as they occur. As you encounter situations similar to the ones you have been working with in the visualizations, you become more keenly aware when you start to react in the old negative way. Sometimes you can feel an interval before you actually react. It is in this space that you have an opportunity to choose your response, and to will-to-love in that moment! You do not have to wait until evening when you plan to do a visualization. And the day will come when the tendency to react in the old way will not be there, and instead the response of compassion and love will flow through you.

The practice of transforming negativity could become a part of your daily life, as much a part of you as your negative responses used to be. This would have profound and long term effects on your inner life, and your relations to others. Transforming negativity is a powerful tool which can lead to a transmutation of your whole being. Imagine the potential for love and harmony that a man and woman can realize together.

· PART TWO ·

ENTERING THE WAY

Personal love is of a strongly emotional nature and is experienced on the level of the personality. But compassion is an octave of love from which a person completely enfolds another without reservation or thought of reward. It is not based upon the attraction between personalities. Compassion is an impersonal love which embraces all people selflessly. This octave of love is so greatly needed on the Earth today.

—Herman Rednick[1]

To be a *beloved* couple means more than having a satisfying and meaningful marriage, more than being willing to listen, and more than being caring and attentive. The name, "beloved," is not just a new affectionate term that one can call one's partner. The Way of the Beloved requires a leap to a new orientation towards one's partner and one's relationship which transcends what is normally accepted as possible in married life.

To enter the Way of the Beloved, a more intense focus on the relationship and a greater commitment to love is necessary. One begins to recognize that there is an inescapable necessity to transform oneself in order to reach a state of higher, more selfless, love. One also realizes that it is necessary to reach out beyond the emotions and the mind to a universal spiritual aspect and to aspire beyond the level of the personality to a love and union that transcends the ego.

Along with this recognition comes the avowed willingness to diminish one's sense of a separate self through the commitment to love another, **no matter what!** Therefore, one becomes willing to give all of oneself in love to the beloved one and to embrace through love the other's whole being as part of one's own life expression.

The Chapters in Part Two develop and illustrate the concepts that reorient a couple towards a more selfless loving, which prepares them for greater spiritual aspirations. Through integrating these concepts and practicing the exercises, a man and woman begin to see their relationship in a completely different light. The vision of the "beloved" unfolds, and they begin to actually experience what it means for a lover, a partner, a husband or a wife, to become a "beloved."[2]

CHAPTER 4

• 4.1 RESPONSIBILITY •

We cannot change people directly. We can change people by changing ourselves. Our beauty and love evoke change within the other person. This is what the sun does. The sun loves the seeds so much that they sprout and become flowers.
—Torkom Saraydarian[1]

When you want to see a change in your life, the way to bring it about is to change something in yourself, and that difference within you will be reflected in your outer world. If you feel that there is something in your love relationship that needs to be different, look within yourself to see how you can change your outlook or attitude in order to bring about a difference. When you see aspects of your relationship that you would like to improve, or you see traits in your partner that you would prefer to be different, this is your opportunity to take responsibility upon yourself to make a change. To take responsibility means to make an offering or a solemn promise—for couples this means to be a loving *spouse.* [2]

Do not blame your partner for a difficult situation, and do not take blame upon yourself either. Blame is a negative attitude which cannot produce positive results and is a useless and wasteful drain of energy. The futility and circularity of blame is revealed very well by Michelle Weiner-Davis:

> Rather than thinking about actions and reactions as being causally related (A causes B), "If Steve spent more time at home, Ann would feel like having sex more often," SB [solution based] therapists think about actions being related in a circular fashion (A leads to B leads to A and so on), for example, "She is less interested in sex because he's not part of her life *and* he is not part of her life because she isn't

79

interested in sex." Clearly, it is not an either/or proposition; it is both. According to this view, it is impossible to determine blame or fault because there is no beginning or end to interactions. Attempting to assign blame results in the ultimate chicken-and-egg debate.

Think about the countless number of times you and your spouse have angrily tried to figure out who started a fight or who's to blame for a particular problem. "You started it" are words echoed throughout living rooms everywhere. The process of determining blame rarely yields a consensus because although we are aware of our partner's impact on our own thinking, feeling and behavior, we are not conscious of how we impact on our partner.[3]

You will see real differences when you make creative changes in your own attitudes and actions without looking for reasons or causes or conditions or people to blame. If you have a thought like, "If she would only stop …, things would be O.K.," or, "If he would only do …, I'd feel so much better," this is your cue to take responsibility and to change yourself. When we approach life this way, we discover that it is our state of mind and heart that centers our sense of self, and not external situations or conditions.

To take responsibility and make an offering to your beloved, first adopt an attitude of gratitude for the condition. This will dissolve your resistance and give you a positive approach. Intentionally shift in the direction of greater love, more giving, and less selfishness. The movement in your attitude will have an influence in your demeanor, and will affect what you say and do. Although it may be subtle, any change in your attitude will eventually be registered in the atmosphere around you, and the relationship with your partner will be affected. When one member of a couple takes the responsibility to modify his or her attitude and to work on the relationship, even if the other person refuses to do anything about the problems, there will be a difference in the relationship.[4]

If you are looking for the other person to do something, to change an attitude or be different in some way, you are using the "I need to get something" approach, rather than the "I will give" approach. Also if you think that your partner should meet you half way, or if you think there is a need for compromise, recognize that you are negotiating instead of choosing to love. As useful as they may be at times, negotiating, competing, and winning do not increase love in a relationship. You will find it much more useful to think, with love, of ways that you can speak and act differently that are consistent with what you truly want to achieve in the situation.

The best way to solve a problem and move into a state of greater love is for each person to take 100% of the responsibility for bringing about a change within himself or herself. There is no compromising in the world of love. A halfhearted effort can only result in shallow, half baked solutions. A willingness to give wholeheartedly is a movement away from being self-centered and competing, to being centered in love for the beloved. Any problem between you becomes the problem of both, and each one takes 100% of the responsibility for transforming it into an opportunity for growth in love for one another.

We are so afraid that if we give to the other wholeheartedly, we will lose something that we really value. But if we can commit ourselves to not limiting the changes we are willing to make for the sake of love, we find that we have lost nothing but our fear. And we have gained the beauty and joy of a greater love.

Once there was a Master who sat through the complaints a woman had against her husband. Finally he said, "Your marriage would be a happier one, my dear, if you were a better wife."

"And how could I be that?" she asked.

"By giving up your efforts to make him a better husband."[5]

• 4.2 ADMIRATION •

it therefore seems to me that admiration is the first of the passions, …

—Descartes, *Les Passions de l'âme.*[6]

For Descartes, admiration is related to our most basic apprehensions of the world. Four hundred years ago, he noted that in order to be aware of the world at all, we need admiration. Admiration is seldom spoken about, but serious reflection has revealed its most fundamental nature through a link between admiration, perception and cognition. In his last book, Gaston Bachelard observes: "one enters the world by admiring it. The world is constituted by the totality of our admiration … admire first, then you will understand"[7] And he ties the "dynamism" of the poet's "exaltation" (i.e., Love) to our "understanding" of the world. Thus, admiration is a form of love, without which we would not perceive the world, nor comprehend it.

In reaching for the high goal of unselfish love, a couple cannot be satisfied with merely reducing conflict and learning to get along better. Acceptance of one another and being kind and considerate is not enough! There must be something more. A powerful, active flow of love pouring out from each to the other is an utter necessity if the relationship is to move beyond the ordinary stresses of living together. This powerful and active love begins in that spontaneous admiration which all lovers know in the beginning. Indeed, when we first fell in love, when our relationship was fresh, we could see the inner spark of beauty shining through the other person. At the dawn of love we were given a glimpse of "the light beyond the form"[8] and unbounded admiration involuntarily appeared in us. We spontaneously looked toward the person we loved with wonder and delight—and utmost admiration. Initially, admiration for our beloved-one arose effortlessly, for it was in the nature of that new love itself.

Admiration is a precursor to the ennobling quality of devotion. It is an affirmation of the highest and best qualities in your loved-one. Criticizing and belittling another person cuts off even the possibility of love. Admiration always evokes and expands love. The more you admire your beloved, the more you feel love flowing through you to him or her. In addition, your continued admiration will stimulate and inspire love and creativity in the other person. Admiration encourages mutual respect and intensifies the positive, elevating emotions. It inspires both people to reach for greater heights of love. As Torkom Saraydarian said so precisely: "Let us show our admiration for each spark of light, love, and beauty expressed in our partner. Every time you admire a good deed, you increase the energy behind it. Admiration is like watering your garden … To admire means to see the highest in your partner."[9]

Indeed, when your relationship is harmonious, it is a joy to find qualities to admire in the other person—it is easy to do. But when difficulties arise or circumstances change, negative feelings may come to the surface, and then you may not be able to think of any characteristics that you admire in your beloved-one. Sometimes the very attributes that you used to admire look negative to you.[10] For example:

> A woman told us how she felt 10 years ago when she first met her husband. She was filled with admiration for his heartfelt generosity, his willingness to share money and to help others in need, his very delight in giving gifts. Now with four small children and a limited income, she became frightened and angry when he gave $20 to an indigent stranger.

> Another woman told how she used to admire the creative work of her craftsman husband and his consistent principle of artistic excellence. Now, after a few years of marriage, she resented having to work to support him while he took "his own sweet time" perfecting the smallest detail of every job. Her resentment made her forget that she had ever admired him at all.[11]

•An Exercise to Restore Admiration •

The admiration you once felt can be renewed. This may be accomplished if you will recall the original feelings and circumstances and bring them to life in the present context of your relationship:

1. Start by recognizing the qualities that you admire right now in your partner. Write them down, and visualize the other person, with love, as you think of each quality.
2. Then make a list of qualities that you *used* to admire, but have forgotten about, or for which your feelings may have changed over a period of time, or because the circumstances are different.

Recall the admiration that you had for each quality. You may have to recollect the context of your relationship at that time in the past. Then interpret each quality in a positive light, the way that you used to, instead of in the present negative way. (For instance, the woman in the first example would remember how she used to admire her husband's generosity, and then she would endeavor to see that his generosity is still a positive and admirable quality, even in the present context of their family life.)

Work to admire the positive aspect of the characteristic, even if some consequences of it seem undesirable to you. (Remember that at one time you did admire this very trait.)

3. Practice these steps until you feel that you have resolved your negative response to those aspects of your beloved that you once admired. You may also use the Transforming Negativity Exercise (Ch. 3.2)

ഇരു

In restoring admiration for your beloved-one, be careful to not fall into the common trap of thinking that you must admire your partner's negativity. Many people today are taught that we must love the *whole person*, but this does not mean that we should passively accept his or her negativity. It may be necessary to express your viewpoint and discuss the issues when they arise. {We mention this problem in the section on Gratitude (1.3).

Another difficulty faced by many in our competitive culture is the idea that to admire another person implies one's own inferiority to him or her. To admire another may even be viewed as humiliating. We all know persons who only feel secure and "in control" when they are "putting others down." The French, existentialist philosopher, Gabriel Marcel cited an interview in which a noted public figure admitted that, "admiration was for him a humiliating state which he resisted with all his force." Marcel was concerned that this attitude "embodies a state of mind which is becoming more widespread."[12] In order to explain the increase in this attitude, Marcel alleged that "subjective psychology" and "realism" were largely responsible for this problem. He says, "the ideas of admiration and revelation are correlative and a subjective psychology is bound to misunderstand completely the nature of admiration ..."[13]

Marcel also clearly saw that, "the function of admiration is to tear us away from ourselves and from the thoughts we have of ourselves."[14] It is certainly the very nature of admiration that it "tears us away from ourselves." Only when we are torn away from our ego-concerns, our selfish absorption in our self-interests, can something greater, something more of love, open in us. This is the nature of revelation through love; how else can a true revelation come to us except through love? Thus, as Marcel also said, "admiration is related to the fact that something is revealed to us."[15] Eventually, love will reveal to us the true nature of God, of ourselves, and of the whole cosmos. And at the beginning of this process, admiration reveals love. Thus, "Admiration is a transformation process ..."[16] Rekindling your admiration for your beloved reveals the way for a whole-hearted rededication of your love and devotion to your beloved.

• 4.3 RADICAL TRUST •

Create for yourself a new, indomitable perception of faithfulness.
What is usually called faithfulness passes so quickly.
Let this be your faithfulness: You will experience moments—
fleeting moments— with the other person.
The human being will appear to you then as if filled, irradiated
with the archetype of his spirit.
And then there may be … other moments, long periods of time,
when human beings are darkened.
But you will learn to say to yourself at such times,
"The spirit makes me strong. I remember the archetype. I saw
it once.
No illusion, no deception shall rob me of it."
Always struggle for the image that you saw.
This struggle is faithfulness.
Striving thus for faithfulness, we shall be close to one another,
As if endowed with the protective powers of angels.
—Rudolf Steiner.

When love is strong we feel emotionally safe and secure in our beloved relationship. Yet this feeling— that the relationship is a haven of safety and support for us—is only one aspect of the many emotional cycles that ebb and flow within a relationship. The feeling of safety cannot be grasped and held on to because life is ever flowing and changing. Even though it may last for what seems to be a long time, it is always temporary. We are never truly safe when we put our trust in the emotional or personality level of the relationship.

Putting one's trust in another's personality inevitably leads to disappointment and eventually to disillusionment. No person is perfect. Every person's nature is a complex and unpredictable mixture of conscious and unconscious states, positive and negative qualities, patterns and moods, and selfish and unselfish motives. No one can satisfy or please another person all of the time.

Yet we need to have trust in *something* which can sustain our relationship through the uncertainties of life's events. We must have some concept or belief that gives us a sense of purpose for our life together. Thus, we must reach out to put our confidence and trust in an idea or principle that is greater than the individual personality of our partner. We must find an over lighting principle which can sustain the love in our relationship and stimulate our continuing efforts to strive for greater fulfillment and harmony.

In human relationships, it is usually the power of habitual patterns that rules our thoughts, perceptions, and feeling life. What we *see* in our partner is actually what appears to us to be going on. This appearance is colored by the filters of our own vision and viewpoint and is therefore a relative or contingent reality—it is true only for *us*. We "see as through a glass darkly"—the greater actuality of our life is veiled from us. Therefore, when we look for a concept or belief to sustain our love, we must seek for something beyond appearances, in which we can place our trust. And when we do this, we find that we must make a leap of faith. We must leap to a higher principle in which we can believe and which can sustain and nurture the love in our relationship even when all our reasonings, feelings, and perceptions seem to tell us otherwise.

For example, in a marriage where the man and woman are trying to become beloveds, each person will have made a definite commitment to try to bring more love, joy, and fulfillment into their life together. And yet there will be times when one partner will do and say things that are negative, which appear to the other to be the opposite of a commitment to love. It is at this very time that one can believe—even though it does not look like it can be so—that the other person is trying his or her best, in his or her own way, to honor the commitment. It is possible to recognize that the other person is doing the best to love that she or he can, within the surrounding circumstances as he or she perceives them. Our partner's way is unique, not a copy or mirror image of our own.

What usually happens, however, is that our instant impulse is to criticize and judge the other person. When our partner is behaving in ways which we judge to be outside of what is proper and legitimate, we automatically condemn him or her because those ways do not fit our standards of appropriate behavior. But if, at that very moment, we can accept that the other person is, in truth, trying his or her best, even though we think that he or she could or should behave differently, we will make a movement towards becoming less critical, more tolerant and more loving.

A man in one of our classes told us how the use of this exercise had changed his perceptions. In the past, his very sensitive wife would often become emotionally distant and withdraw from him. He believed her behavior stemmed from meanness of character and a desire to punish him. Working with the concept of seeking for a higher principle on which to base his perceptions of his wife's behavior, he was able to momentarily suspend judgment and to disbelieve what he "saw" her doing. In that moment he was able to listen to her in a fresh and new way, and he realized that what he believed was her meanness stemmed from hurt feelings caused by his own actions towards her, and she was withdrawing in an attempt to protect herself. He then came to the understanding that what she needed was his love and not his righteous judgments and defensiveness.

Each of us knows that there are times when we become angry or hurt, confused, or belligerent, and that we act in an unloving or even hurtful way. According to our own patterns and habits, we may attack, lash out, or withdraw and blame; yet we firmly believe that we have not given up our commitment to try to bring more love into our relationship—we have *slipped* or momentarily succumbed to negativity. We *know* that we are still trying! ... But when our partner acts in a negative or hurtful way, we apply a different standard. Our partner's negative behavior looks foreign and unreasonable to us, and we feel that his or her actions are indisputable signs that he or she is betraying the commitment to the relationship and to our love. Thus we feel hopeless about the relationship!

Without realizing it we have been applying a DOUBLE STANDARD— one standard for assessing our own unloving and hurtful actions and a different one for the other person. We know that it is possible for us to make a mistake and still be committed to the relationship. Yet when the other person is overcome by negative emotions, it seems to us that the relationship is over. Can we not grant that our partner has times of negativity just as we do? It is inevitable that another person will express negativity in ways that are entirely different from our own. Can we not allow the mistakes and failures, without questioning his or her commitment, even though it looks to us like a betrayal? Our belief and trust that our partner is trying his or her best—in spite of appearances to the contrary—will help to rekindle a flow of love in both people, especially when it is needed most.

After Terry had been working with the concepts and practices of the Way of the Beloved for several years she told us how valuable the concept, "Don't believe what you see and hear," had been to her. She had mentioned frequently that her sense of individuality and of personal strength was connected to a recently developed ability to "stand-up for herself" in intimate relationships. Therefore it was very important to her sense of personal coherence to believe in the "truth" of her own perceptions, and not be pressured by others into denying her comprehension of events.

Terry's husband was an energetic man with numerous interests in his busy life. She often saw him choosing to pursue his own activities rather than spending time with her. She felt that other things came first to him and that she was secondary in his life—i.e. he did not really love her or value her presence. This created constant conflict and pain in their relationship.

Through a deep desire to resolve this fundamental conflict, Terry was able to start questioning the truth of her perceptions. She gradually began to recognize that what she was seeing and hearing might not be the whole story of their interactions. It became possible for her to really believe her husband when he told her that he loved her and did not want to lose her and that he was truly trying to be less selfish. Then, when he seemed to ignore her and chose other activities rather than being with her, she was able to disbelieve that he had stopped loving her. Even though what she saw and heard and felt was his rejection of her, it became possible for her to speak to him in such a way that he could better hear what she really needed and wanted. She had found a key that opened the door to a future of love and closeness in their marriage. She was able to talk to him without condemning, accusing, or judging as she had for years, and this in turn freed him to be able to respond to her real need for him to choose her first and to lovingly affirm her primacy in his life.

• Radical Trust Exercise •

If we do not put our trust in the personality of our partner or our perceptions and judgments of her or his actions, what are we to put our trust in? Here are some examples of principles that we can remember and repeat to ourselves when put to the test:

- My perception is partial and limited; what I see and hear is not the whole. — Things are not what they seem!
- Regardless of what is happening right now, we truly love each other.

- Both of us are deeply committed to this relationship, and our commitment is greater than the present moment.
- Each of us is trying to be the best person that we can be.
- My beloved needs my love, not my criticism, especially now!
- We have come through stormy times in the past, and we can come through this one too.
- Despite hard times, we have had many years of growth and progress in loving together.
- We are committed to doing our best to love each other, though it may look otherwise.
- We can remember the power of the love that brought us together.
- There is a goal, a future, and a purpose for our relationship.
- There is a solution to every problem when it is met with love.

In addition to these somewhat immediate facts of our life, we can also put our trust in something *higher* than what we can understand or control.[17] We know many couples who, from the first moment that they saw each other, felt a powerful sense of recognition. Both people seemed to *know* that they were meant for each other and that they were *destined* to be together. When difficulties arise between them, regardless of how bad things seem at the moment, these men and women can recall their conviction that they are a *destined couple*. The belief in their experience of a *recognition* which goes beyond anything that can be rationally assessed, becomes a sustaining force in difficult times. In this regard, couples who practice a religion or follow a spiritual path often use principles which are part of that belief structure.[18] For example, one woman told us that when things were rocky in her relationship, she would remind herself that, "God brought us together for a spiritual purpose. This is a *test* of our love."

We could also remember that we are seeking for a love with this person that is not shattered by or contingent upon the way that he or she acts or does not act when he or she is under pressure or in distress—a love based on something that reaches beyond personality characteristics.[19] In a relationship where both people have made the commitment to become more loving, each must believe that the other person is trying her or his best to honor that commitment, **NO MATTER WHAT ONE SEES OR HEARS TO THE CONTRARY.** Even though what we perceive appears to be a betrayal—the opposite of what a loving commitment is—we must remember that things are not what they seem to be. No matter what you see or hear, your beloved partner is, in truth, trying his or her best to bring more love into your life.

• 4.4 DEVOTION •

Wholehearted devotion between beloveds is felt as an up-welling aspiration to blend in love on all levels of life—physical, emotional, and spiritual. Because of your great love for one another, you strive to become more and more interconnected. Through devotion, each looks to the other to bring and share fulfillment on every level of life.[20]

Few of us indeed have reached a level of constant and unalloyed devotion toward our beloved partner. We know that our relationship is not a complete and pure exchange of love. We must acknowledge that, although we deeply desire an unlimited expression of love, each of us feels at least some degree of unfulfillment in our relationship. We may experience a restlessness that is disconcerting. Or we may feel that there is a veil between us—an invisible barrier separating us.

The pain of unfulfillment and separation drives many to look outside their relationship for the missing quality. When we feel a lack in our relationship, we search elsewhere for satisfaction. And when we experience pain or conflict in the relationship, we try to get away and go somewhere else for relief and solace. In our one-track individual-centered culture, this is the most natural path to follow when tension builds and the going gets rough.

Whatever the reason, this turning away will dilute love and closeness with our beloved. We are trying to reduce our anxiety by distancing ourselves from the situation, but in doing this, we siphon off energy that is necessary to the relationship. We are moving away from the path of intensifying love.

Here are some common ways that people take energy away from their relationship:

- A woman finds that she is unable to communicate with her husband about certain meaningful areas of her life. She confides in her friends. She feels more comfort, more understanding, and more communion with them than she does with her husband.
- In order to avoid the difficulties and tensions of building the relationship, a man or a woman may become a workaholic. This provides her or him with a "good" reason to spend less time and energy building the relationship.
- Many couples take great pains to see that each has plenty of "individual space," including, perhaps, separate bank accounts, individual vacations, different leisure activities, even twin beds.

- A married couple may put all of their life energy into their children, their home, their business, and/or some other project, and they never seem to *find time* to cultivate their relationship.
- And, of course, the most extreme example of looking elsewhere is to become emotionally or sexually involved with another person(s).

Everyone can recognize that there are a myriad of these patterns which function as *escape hatches* and lessen the intensity of both positive and negative encounters in the relationship. When we feel that interactions are getting too heavy, we think we need to relieve the pressure and tension to protect ourselves and escape. The use of escape hatches as a way to *cool* down when emotions get too intense is a common recommendation in our society.

It is true that there may be occasions when both people are saturated with the intensity of their struggle, and it becomes necessary, appropriate, and constructive to take time-out. Each person may benefit from being quietly alone for a while, or from going to talk to a trusted friend or advisor in an attempt to gain a new perspective and to see things differently. The motive is not to escape and look outside the relationship, but to find new pathways for the growth of love. Then energy is not being taken away from the relationship—in this instance, both people are searching for new ways to bring a positive flow into their interactions.

More devotion may reveal the blocks between us. Thus, when a woman and a man become aware that they are stifling or diverting the energy that they need for the relationship to grow, they should also realize that only more love will move them through the blocks that keep them feeling separated. In our work we often speak about intensifying love. What do we mean, and how can that be done? Through our sincere aspiration to become closer and more devoted to our beloved, we can intend to focus, concentrate, and direct our energy and awareness toward our partner. Just like a magnifying glass focuses the rays of the sun to an intense point, we *can* gather the energies in our lives and focus them more intensely into our beloved relationship.

Many of the techniques that we have worked with so far can change the quality of our energies by neutralizing or transforming negativity and infusing love into our interactions, attitudes, and feelings toward the other person. But if every time pressure builds up in the relationship, we seek to open a safety valve and let off the steam, we will never build up enough intensity to overcome our blocks and break through to a new level. If we want to effect an intense focus of our energies toward our relationship, instead of *turning away* to seek relief from the difficulties, we can try a different approach. Motivated by the desire to develop a relationship of greater depth, closeness, and love, we can see the build-up of tension and anxiety as an opportunity to increase the depth of our understanding of the other person and to intensify our love. Instead of interpreting anxiety as always destructive to our relationship, we can see it as a means for the relationship to grow. If we use our will to invoke a strong focus on the power of love and devotion to move us through the conflict, tension can be a stimulus toward deeper and greater loving.

• Exercise •

Ask yourself the following questions:

- How important to me is our love?
- How much of myself do I give to it?
- How much of myself, my life, my interests, my concerns, do I share with my beloved one?
- What areas of my life do I share with others rather than my partner?
- How much of my life is separate from my beloved?"
- When something happens in the relationship that is disturbing, what do I do?
- What are my escape hatches?
- Am I willing to give up any escape hatches, to try to use this energy in striving for more love?

If you decide not to turn away, escape, or use a safety valve, but to work through the barrier or pain with your beloved, then you will feel like you are in a *pressure cooker.* Staying in the pressure cooker for the sake of love is an act of devotion; turning away is a lost opportunity. However, staying in the pressure cooker is not in itself a guarantee that you will grow in love. There are many couples who are confronting each other all the time. They are always in an emotional pressure cooker, and they seem to have no escape hatches. Yet, instead of growing in love, they appear to be locked in an endless battle—a nightmare of negativity. Love is not the only way that a man and woman can be bonded to each other. Rejection, negativity, and hatred can be powerful bonding agents, but these bonds are chains and they enslave, where the bonds of love lead to freedom. Using the pressure cooker is an intentional way to build tension and energy for a breakthrough to more love, not a life-style based on the unending indulgence of negative emotions.

When a couple decides to stay in the pressure cooker, they can face each other in love and meet the blocks together. The relationship becomes a giving of all to the Beloved, and an asking of all from the beloved. The commitment becomes to love, despite anxiety, fear and unfulfillment and the desire for flight and relief. Thus, we can make the commitment to bring our creative energy into the relationship. This will build the intensity necessary to move in consciousness, for there can be no growth without tension and anxiety.

Our faith, love, and commitment are tested when difficulties arise—a true love is a tested love. At a recent retreat students were asked to write, as an offering to the other participants, a paper about what had been most helpful to them in their beloved work. One student wrote about the pressure cooker:

> My "beloved offering list" begins with, and ends with: STAY WITH IT!!! … Stay in the pressure cooker. Life together as a couple really changed for us once we stopped making dramatic exits and entrances, once we stopped being afraid of what would happen if we let the anger boil-over and explode, or lose its steam altogether. We discovered how funny some of our fights were, and how much the same we were about feeling unloved, unheard, unspoken to. …
>
> With all of the experience we have had to date with fear of commitment to each other, with trying to reject the things about each other that we feel that we did not sign-up for, with tempers, personality hell-realms, and intellectual blueprints for how a relationship *should* look, we nearly lost each other ten thousand times.
>
> I believe that we were absolutely intended to be with each other, and that learning to commit to stay with it—to not leave each other—is a very important part of our path. I have seen my ego, frozen with pride, insisting that, "This is it! I don't have to take this anymore." As I have learned to receive love more easily, I have been given the courage to say out loud, that I really want this marriage of ours to continue and flourish with love. I cherish this union.[21]

If a couple makes a mutual commitment to stay in the pressure cooker and work through their blocks together, each is saying something like the following within his or her own heart: "I turn to you, my Beloved, with all that I am and all that I am striving for." And with this, there are further implications: e.g., "I will not withdraw"; "I will not turn-away"; "I will not look elsewhere"; "I will not coast"; "I will not be content with less than love!"

If you are willing to focus more and more of your energy into your relationship, then it can become the great arena for spiritual growth for both of you. When you are committed to greater love, you become ever more connected and devoted to one another in a positive way. Every lack in the relationship becomes an occasion for intensifying love. Thus, in meeting difficult experiences constructively and consciously, the relationship becomes a path of spiritual growth.

CHAPTER 5

• 5.1 FORGIVENESS •

We must make our homes centers of compassion and forgive endlessly.

—Mother Teresa[1]

No matter how hard we try to love another, we are all still mixed beings who cannot simply will our perfection in love. We unavoidably hurt one another; it is an inescapable part of life and of interpersonal relationships. Even for couples who want to intensify their love, pain is given and received. This happens unintentionally, arising out of our negativity and ignorance, and we are usually unaware that we are doing it. Mother Teresa's statement that we must forgive endlessly is not just a poetic or ideal injunction; for couples trying to grow in love it is a practical necessity. Without forgiveness in a relationship, the flow of love is blocked and a couple is unable to move into expressions of more selfless love.

To embody forgiveness means that in the face of our own and our partner's faults and errors we can invoke a commitment to love "no matter what." We can bring into our relationship a more intense and inclusive love than we have known before. The commitment to love *no matter what* does not mean that we excuse or condone our partner's negativity, but that we learn to love even though it is there. Through this learning process our love increases. We can now love where we have not been able to love before.[2]

In our beloved relationship, most of us would like to be able to forgive and be forgiven, but as C.S. Lewis observes, "Everyone says forgiveness is a lovely idea, until they have something to forgive, …"[3] It is not so easy to do. Our past hurts and injustices have a strong grip on our consciousness and convince us that we are "right" and "justified" in holding on to them. In addition, the ways of the world teach that we should try to get back at those who hurt us in order to even the score.[4] Lack of forgiveness is an ancient and great obstacle to the flow of love between people. The inability to forgive keeps us chained to the past and to our own and the other person's negativity. This is explained succinctly by Torkom Saraydarian: "Unforgivingness forces you to focus your energy on events which hurt you or others. These events are now within your mind as living images. By dwelling on them and channeling energy to them, you perpetuate their existence, not only within you, but also within the world, through constantly broadcasting these events via your thinking."[5]

What do we mean by the word "forgiveness?" In *The Roots of English: A reader's Handbook of Word Origins,* Robert Clairborne states that the word "forgive" originally meant to "give up" one's anger.[6] The practical question of forgiveness for those striving to be more compassionate must be, "how can I bring in enough love to clear the reactive and negative blocks in my nature which prevent me from loving this person now?"[7]

Confusion gains entry into this transformative process when we forget that forgiveness is not granted by one person to another. A person cannot forgive. Only the power of a higher love can forgive.[8] Jacob Boehme, the great 17th century Christian Theosopher, said that "No man can forgive the sins of another man; the sinner himself must free himself of his sins. Sin is like a shell, out of which the new man grows, and he then throws the shell away. This is called 'forgiveness,' because *God in man* gives that which is sinful away."[9] A recent statement of this aspect of the meaning of 'forgiveness' is given by Tsogyel Rinpoche in his popular book, *The Tibetan Book of Living and Dying*: "Forgiveness already exists in the nature of God; it is already there. God has already forgiven you, for God is forgiveness itself. 'To err is human, and to forgive <u>divine</u>.' ... In order to clear your guilt, ask for purification from the depths of your heart. If you really ask for purification, and go through it, forgiveness will be there."[10]

Thus, true forgiveness dissolves *our* negative bonds that chain us to our past hurts and is not related to redeeming the person who has injured us. If we think that we are forgiving the other person or being magnanimous by conferring a favor on her or him, it is our ego puffing itself up. Some people feel that they are doing a good thing when they can say, "I forgive you," but unless they have grown into a state of greater love and have true compassion for the other person, the words do nothing but subtly feed their ego. True forgiveness makes us more humble and fills us with compassion.

There are two aspects to the meaning of "forgiveness." In the first sense we actively work to give up our own blocks to loving the person who harmed us, regardless of what he or she does or does not do. In the second sense the consequences of our harmful acts (sins) are taken from us by the power of love (the "God in us").[11]

No matter how badly we have been treated, or have treated another, it is our own negativity, the anger, resentment, or guilt that we are holding on to, which poisons us and prevents us from loving in this moment. We feel justified in our attachment to our grievance and we avoid forgiveness through our ego's pride or through the fear of being hurt again. Even though the other person caused us pain and our responses seem legitimate under the circumstances, unforgivingness keeps us in the bonds of negativity and stops us from moving toward greater love. The following story of Tim and Angela is an example of this:

> When Tim and Angela met, they were in their early 40's. Neither had ever been married and they had been satisfied with their single lives and the "single scene." Tim believed that someday he would meet the "right" woman and get married, but Angela had a history of being betrayed by men and had developed a conviction that, "no man can be trusted." On the very first date there was a mutual, magical recognition that they were "the one" for each other. They firmly believed that they "belonged to each other and that they would be together 'forever.'" Tim moved in with Angela, and everything was bliss. However, about 3 months after they had gotten together, Angela went out of town to some professional meetings, and while she was gone, Tim had a one- night stand with an old girlfriend. It is not clear why Tim told Angela about it when she returned. At any rate, this casual betrayal of what Angela took to be an informal, but binding, "lifetime" commitment between them, convinced her, beyond reason that "even 'Mr. right' cannot be trusted." Tim and Angela continued to live together and, despite this impasse, Tim was convinced that Angela was his destined wife. But Angela made it clear that Tim had committed an "unforgivable" treachery and, despite his contrite promises of faithfulness and his continuous proposals, she would not marry him. Part of her reasoning was that, if he had betrayed her after just 3 months, it would be much worse after they were married. Angela continued to believe that Tim was her "soul-mate," but she was afraid of entering into a deeper relationship or of loving Tim any more than she already did. She felt that Tim had

devastated her trusting heart at a time when she was most vulnerable, and she would not give him a chance to do it again. Tim faithfully kept all his promises, and he pleaded; he wept and he proposed to no avail. There was nothing he could say or do that would prove to Angela his continuing faithfulness and love. Angela went with him to some couples classes and to a therapist, but she could not become free enough of her fear to forgive Tim and place herself in that vulnerable position again. After 4 years, still believing that Tim was "the one," Angela left Tim and moved to another city.

This case is an illustration of Michelle Weiner-Davis' sage observation that, "Even the best problem-solving techniques in the world won't penetrate the resentment one feels from the lack of forgiveness."[12] The story of Rob and Janelle presents a comparable situation with a different outcome.

Rob and Janelle also met in their 40's, but it was a second marriage for each of them. They had 5 children between them, and 3 were still teenagers. Some months after they were married Janelle found out from a casual comment by Rob, that he had occasionally been going over to visit with his ex-live-in-lover, Karen. (The relationship was from years before and Janelle had never even met Karen.) Janelle was devastated. She was shocked beyond belief and felt that Rob had betrayed everything that they had worked for in their relationship. She kept asking herself over and over again, "Why would Rob even want to ever see her again, if he loves me?" To Janelle it was as if Rob had gone back to Karen, as if he had already "left" her. She was so deeply wounded and inconsolable that she believed she might have to leave Rob. Janelle also felt that the fact that Rob did not tell her that he had been seeing Karen was proof that his betrayal was intentional. For his part, Rob felt that he had done nothing wrong. He maintained that he was doing the "right" thing by being warm and friendly to Karen, and since there had been no "hanky-panky" his visits were "proper" and "good" for Karen. Rob could not really understand why Janelle was in such a state of deep hurt. In fact, he said several times that, she shouldn't feel hurt because his motives were 'good' and therefore he was innocent of wrong-doing. He explained that he did not think it was necessary to tell Janelle everything that he did. He was, after all, a mature adult and an 'independent' person.

Besides the idea of "asking her permission" for his various activities felt to Rob as a serious abridgement of his freedom.

Janelle's unremitting pain erected a protective wall within her which prevented intimate and loving contact with Rob. And the future of their marriage looked doubtful. But both of them desperately wanted the relationship to continue and to provide that fulfillment and companionship they were looking forward to as they got older. At this point they heard about the Way of the Beloved program and decided to give it a try to see if there was any hope for them. Although he could not understand why Janelle had had such an "extreme" and "unwarranted" reaction to what he had done, Rob was really afraid that Janelle would leave him because of the situation he had created, so he agreed that he would never see Karen again. They were both very sincere in working toward a resolution and the restoration of their love. Over a period of 2 years they gradually broke down the separating wall between them. They began seriously to use the Gratitude Exercise (Section 1.3) that they learned in the Way of the Beloved classes. As they became closer and more grateful for each other's presence in their life together, they began to share more time and experiences than they had before the crisis. Janelle slowly realized that she was gratefully accepting many of Rob's thoughtless and selfish traits and that she was loving him, including all these "faults." The sense of betrayal faded and one day Janelle knew that she had forgiven Rob because their love was alive again. Rob has never understood "why" his actions were so hurtful to Janelle, but he does know, beyond question, that his actions were the cause of her hurt. He has also learned that he must acknowledge the reality of her hurt and not try to dismiss it or to excuse himself of wrong-doing. Rob is now placing his love for Janelle before his need to defend or justify his ways of acting, even though he does not understand the causal links to her feelings.

Of course it is much easier for most of us to feel indignation or righteous anger at being hurt, than to become aware of how we may be hurting another. When we realize that we have hurt the other person, we must recognize what we have done and accept responsibility for our actions. Some people feel so terrible at the very thought that they may have hurt their loved one, that they become overwhelmed with guilt. This guilt can be paralyzing and it will block any love from coming through. In contrast to this reaction, many others find it too easy to excuse themselves or rationalize their actions and they go on as if nothing has happened. It is important to know that when we have hurt another, remorse and sorrow are constructive emotions and are not negative. True remorse leads to "redemption" or the changing of our hurtful ways. Remorse and sorrow for our harmful actions can lead us to apologize sincerely, to make amends for what we have done, and to resolve not to do the same thing again. As Martin Luther King, Jr. once wrote, "Forgiveness does not mean ignoring what has been done or putting a false label on an evil act. It means, rather, that the evil act no longer remains as a barrier to the relationship. ..."[13]

Someone asked us, "Is it all right to ask for forgiveness?" If you are truly remorseful and determined not to hurt the other person again, you will make amends willingly, and thus be free to love again. The experience of being forgiven comes from the power of love itself, not from the other person. Otherwise, another could hold your forgiveness and, therefore, your freedom hostage to their anger, conditions, revenge, etc. WHEN YOU ARE IN A STATE OF LOVE, YOU KNOW THAT YOU ARE FORGIVEN, whether or not the other person is free of negativity or able to forgive you. Forgiveness is inherent within the love that is flowing through your being and does not come from something that the other person must say or do. This is illustrated by Christ's teaching that, "your sins, and they are many, are forgiven you, because of the greatness of your love. Go and sin no more" (Lk. 7:47).

You can become free from the grip of negativity through compassion and forgiveness. Forgiveness is a natural outflowing and consequence of deeply experienced love. "Endless forgiveness" is the foundation upon which a loving relationship is built and upon which it must rely if it is to be filled with living force and the energy to grow. It would be a pretense to think that you are trying to intensify the love in your relationship if you keep a mental list of your own or your partner's faults and errors. As long as you hold on to fears or resentments of the past, you are blocking the flow of love in the present.

Since forgiveness emerges from the very nature of love itself, its living force sustains the life and love of a devoted couple. It is an active pouring out of love freely offered from one to the other. Thus forgiveness is much more than a way to end an argument or neutralize resentments and hurts. As important as those might be, forgiveness sees through the eyes of love that what has already happened is in the past, and that love is flowing now, creating a new potential in this present moment.

Forgiveness is not a passive capitulation of one person to another. In forgiving, one chooses to love the other person above the pride of one's own ego. When we forgive, we cancel within ourselves any debt that we may think is owed us. Thus we reduce the power of our egos' demands for satisfaction and for evening the score. We have chosen LOVE over the further expression of our ego. In this direct way we are transmuting the ego's pride and self-concern into selfless love for the beloved. Frederic Wiedemann describes this process in his book, *Between Two Worlds: The Riddle of Wholeness*:

> Being brought face to face with the ego that refuses to forgive, yet also with that transpersonal side of ourselves that wants to forgive, we experience a kind of crucifixion. Forgiveness is such an extraordinary process because it cancels out the ego's demand to extract the debt we are owed. Forgiving is deciding to forsake the repayment and totally releasing the offender from having to make it up. To break through the hurt and actually forgive the wrong requires a constructive breakdown of human pride.[14]

Some people ask, "How can I ever forget what was done?" Forgiving does not require that we forget what has happened to us.[15] Forgiving requires that we find a way within ourselves to have compassion for the *person* who has hurt us even as we are aware of the harm done to us. The power of compassion will dissolve our attachment to the negative effects of the harm; and the resentment will no longer be alive in our psyche. The negativity becomes part of our emotional past even as we remember the event.

A direct path to a heart of endless forgiveness is to invoke the power of love and gratitude (Sections 1.1 and 1.3) and to work on transforming your negative reactions (Section 3.2). A specific exercise for forgiveness follows:

• Forgiveness Exercise •

PART ONE
WHEN YOU HAVE BEEN HURT BY THE OTHER PERSON
Recall a situation in which you have been hurt, wronged, misunderstood, criticized, or the like, by your partner. Observe how you feel and how you respond. Specifically, what do you do and say (or not say) to the other person? It is helpful for clarification to make notes of your responses.

Within your recollection of the event, your work is to love now. Remember that to forgive does not mean to indulge others. It does not mean that you affirm or support or approve of what the other person has done. Nor does it mean that you will be passive and allow it to happen again. The other person is responsible for his or her own actions. Your work is to love the other person, NO MATTER WHAT, i.e. regardless of what happened or how you feel about it. Love will bring forgiveness into your heart and mind.

To intensify your state, do the Invocation of Love, thinking of a time when love was spontaneously flowing between you. When you have recalled this love and begin to feel it, visualize your beloved as he or she is now, and say (silently, over and over again):

"I love you and my heart enfolds you."

"I do not ... (hate, resent, fear) ... you; for that is in the past and I was hypnotized by misunderstanding."

"Now compassion and forgiveness fill my heart and mind, and I can only love you."

PART TWO
WHEN YOU HAVE HURT THE OTHER PERSON

Think of a time when you have hurt your beloved. Recall the event as it occurred and the specific way in which you hurt the other. Vividly reliving this incident will evoke feelings of sorrow and remorse for what you have done. As these feeling well up, visualize your partner and offer her or him your apologies and your desire to make amends.

Think of specific ways that you might apologize and make amends for what you have done. It is best to write them down at this point because writing brings them into concrete form and increases the likelihood of acting upon them.

Do the Invocation of Love, thinking of a time when love was freely flowing between you. When you have recalled this love and begin to feel it, say within your heart to the other person:

"I love you and my heart enfolds you."

"The sorrow that I feel because I have hurt you shows me how I have been hypnotized by negativity and lack of awareness."

"I shall make amends by ... (doing a/b/c) ... and by not doing ... (the same act) ... again."

"I know that love is stronger than my negativity. Therefore, I feel only love andcompassion for you."

It may take a hundred repetitions, or three hundred, but if you do this exercise with sincerity and intensity, you will feel a difference. As you pour out love to the other person, forgiveness will free you from the hurt, anger, fear, resentment and guilt that cause you pain. And it will remove the blocks between you and your beloved, creating an atmosphere in your relationship that is conducive to new possibilities of love.

෴

To the extent that there are unforgiven hurts in a relationship there is an underlying lack of loving closeness; the ego grows large with fear and resentment. Practicing endless forgiveness is a powerful way to reduce the grip of the self-centered ego and indicates a movement toward a higher, more inclusive, or spiritual love.

Spiritual love is attained in a couple's relationship through the shared commitment to *Love No Matter What*. Implied within this commitment is an orientation of "pre-forgiveness." A man and a woman working together toward spiritual love have the realistic expectation that because of continuing ignorance and negativity there will be errors, misunderstandings and hurts. Accepting this knowledge and being committed to loving regardless of what happens, both people become willing in the present, to forgive whatever hurts may befall them in the future.[16] Pre-forgiveness is a step in loving that prepares us for the sacrifice through love of the separative ego.

• 5.2 SACRIFICE •

A living love hurts ... If you really love one another wholeheartedly there must be sacrifice. Sacrifice, to be real—it must hurt. It must empty us of self.

Mother Teresa[17]

One evening as we were introducing the concept of sacrifice to a group of couples, a man jumped up suddenly and nervously asked, "Did I hear you say 'sacrifice'?" When we nodded, "yes," he said, "I'm getting out of here!" and headed for the door with a mock frightened expression. Just as quickly, however, he sat back down and said with a laugh, "I knew this was coming. I guess there's no way out of it."

This man was expressing the fear and aversion that so many of us experience when it occurs to us that in order to move into a state of more intense love with our partner, we really must change, transform, give up, or sacrifice some of that substance which we have always thought to be our very "self."

Sacrifice means to "make sacred" or to "transform into a spiritual form."[18] When we choose to love, we freely offer some part of our 'self' to be transformed into the substance of love. The sacrificed aspects of our self become purified, made transparent to the personality and the forces of the world, and consequently, we come to be a clearer vehicle for the embodiment of a higher octave of love. This kind of love transcends the personality. It is pure giving— unqualified, and unreserved. It flows freely, neither asking nor desiring anything in return. It is a radiation of the true heart that pours forth like light from the sun without conditions and without expectations. This love is also called compassion.[19]

When a woman and a man are committed to giving love to one another, they are constantly faced with the choice: "Do I defend my own ways, or do I choose love?" The individual's personality, or ego, cannot partake of a more selfless love because its nature is to seek only its own well-being.[20] In the attempt to satisfy the needs and desires of the personality, one inevitably encounters friction or confrontation with the needs and desires of other personalities —often they oppose one another. Conflict with our loved one, or with anyone, will continue to occur until we realize that only sacrifice in love and the consequent purification of our ego will bring us peace, joy, and spiritual fulfillment.

However, since the ego is concerned only with what it defines as its "self-interest,"[21] as broad or narrow as that may be conceived, the very idea of sacrifice is threatening. Sacrifice is always painful to the personality. To choose to love another person is to choose to change patterns of thought and ways of acting that we have found, in the past, to be in our self-interest, for the sake of that love. The pain we feel is the pain of attachment to our old patterns and ways. Torkom Saraydarian explains that overcoming attachment is always painful:

> When you are attached to glamours, Maya, illusions, and other negative things, you feel pain when they are removed because you identify with them. For example, you say, "I am my jealousy. If you take jealousy from my emotions, you take the 'soul' out of my body because I am identified with jealousy." That is where the painful meaning of sacrifice comes from ... That is why it is difficult for new ideas to penetrate into the minds of people; people are cemented to old ideas ... If such an attachment exists, you cannot accept a new idea.[22]

Love requires that we become larger than our individual selves through sacrifice.[23] When we overcome the clinging attachment to our habitual emotional reactions, perceptions, and ideas of who we are, we experience pain. However, when we replace self-centered emotions, perceptions, and ideas with selfless love, we also experience joy. When we knowingly sacrifice self out of a heart full of love, the pain may be acute, but the joy and exaltation that fills us is much greater than any personal satisfaction we have ever known.

A woman and a man who are reaching to fill their relationship with higher love must be willing to transform through sacrifice those elements of their thoughts, feelings, and actions which are concerned with individual satisfaction and self-interest. A life lived in service to the 'individual self' directly inhibits the manifestation of a greater, more selfless, love. When a woman and a man make a choice to love instead of satisfying the preferences and desires of their individual personalities, they have chosen to approach a higher octave of love. When they are committed to giving love to one another no matter what difficulties they may have to confront in their relationship, they are beginning to make their relationship "sacred." Their life together can now become a spiritual path.

Therefore, this is not a casual decision. Entering the spiritual path of the Beloved means that a man and a woman are embracing a greater responsibility toward one another than they anticipated or "signed up for" in the beginning of their relationship. For through the commitment to pour out love *no matter what*, each becomes willing to give to the other her or his own life-substance or essence. Thus, their life energy is shared and each embraces the other as part of his or her own *life-being*. When a woman and a man become beloveds each becomes linked to the sum total of the other person's actions and their results. A friend once asked us, "Do we marry each other's karma?"[24] Yes, we do! When we are committed to our beloved through deep love and devotion we accept the weight of her or his karma (and the influence of her or his light) into our life as if they are our own. In fact, each person experiences the consequences of the negative and positive actions of his or her beloved as they both struggle to grow in love and increase in light and spirit. Each assumes whatever burdens the other may be carrying and seeks to pour out love at every moment. In the spirit of sacrifice each gives selfless love without reservation or thought of reward.

Twenty years ago, when we first saw Mother Teresa's statement that a "living love hurts ...," we were baffled and dismayed. We had recently found a "living love" with each other and could not comprehend how it could be anything but glorious. It did not take long, however, to realize that in a relationship where each is giving love wholeheartedly and without expectation, there is still pain. As much as we may wish it to be otherwise, the negativity we embody and express affects our beloved one even as we are trying our best to love. We generate negativity as we misunderstand, resent, or rebel against the process of growth in love and consciousness. This is a natural and unavoidable process, and only when the love that we live becomes an unreserved, selfless love, will our nature be purified and our ego transformed.

It is essential to remember that if our motive in sacrificing is anything other than love, then nothing is made sacred and the pain is for nothing. Purification and transcendence cannot be accomplished by will alone. To sacrifice for the sake of love is a state of mind and heart that indicates a *metanoia*, a deep turning about, or a reorientation of our whole being toward selfless love. This can only come about as a radical free choice. A beloved couple makes this choice, and to demonstrate the truth of it, translates this greater commitment into the words and actions of their daily life.

In our individualistic times it is not surprising that many interpret sacrifice as embodying some form of coercion. But love by its most fundamental nature cannot be coercive. To say, "to choose love is to choose sacrifice" is to comprehend that once we have committed ourselves freely to love another, a logical and existential consequence of that choice will be sacrifice. Persistence in loving inevitably leads to purification by sacrifice and a transcendence of our old nature.[25]

Since the word "sacrifice" is so threatening to many, we have found that some people need to adapt the concept into terms that make it possible for them to use it. Recently, a man in one of our classes was able to make this connection without using the *scary* word "sacrifice."

> Gene, a professional man in his 60's, clearly understood the concept when it was presented and he recognized the validity and necessity of sacrifice in a loving relationship, but he had an *allergic* reaction to the word sacrifice. At our next class, Gene gave a lengthy preamble in which he described how he had analyzed and worked with the concept in order to determine how he could use it in his marriage. He had decided that if he saw that his wife had a need or that the relationship would benefit from his making a specific change or by his giving-up something, he would *choose* to do it because he loved her so much. The key for Gene was that he (as a free, loving and independent person) would be making the choice; and as long as he focused on the free choice aspect of the concept, he was willing to accept the consequences of his decisions—e.g. pain, inconvenience, discomfort, or more closeness and love. Gene never mentioned the word "sacrifice."

ഇരുഃ

• Exercise •

In the spirit of self-exploration consider and write about the following questions:

- How can I sacrifice for the sake of my beloved and for our life together?

108

- Am I *willing* to sacrifice for the sake of my beloved and our life together?
- If not, why not? What is holding me back?
- What is my beloved sacrificing for me?

(Begin to keep an ongoing list, adding to it over a period of time.)

This exercise will help you to clarify and stay up to date with the ever-changing tides of loving give and take in your relationship.

• 5.3 AFFIRMATION •

*In an ancient Tibetan Scripture seven forms of love are enumerated, four belonging to the gods and three to men. The lowest of the three human forms is mere physical attraction, shared also by atoms and molecules. This exhausts itself as soon as satisfied. A higher form may be called psychic; it is on a reciprocal basis: I will love you if you will love me, and you owe me something for loving you. This form holds within itself the seed of its own death. The third form already borders on the ways of the gods and is a little difficult for men [women] to achieve and so must generally be learned. **This is to so love the beloved that we desire only his [her] highest good and in his [her] own terms. Such love is immortal and the ages cannot quench it.***

—Clara Codd[26]

Love, if it is deep and intense enough, is a power that is greater than our own egotism. Vladimir Solovyev, Russia's great Christian Philosopher, understood the dynamic power of love to be the liberator of the true individuality from the entanglements and attachment to the ego. In 1892-3 he wrote *The Meaning of Love*, which is still one of the most profound treatises on the destiny of love between the sexes. In that work, Solovyev tells us that,

> Truth, as a living power that takes possession of the internal being of a human and actually rescues him from false self-assertion, is termed love. Love as the actual abrogation of egoism, is the real justification and salvation of individuality. The meaning and worth of love, as a feeling, is that it really forces us, with all our being, to acknowledge for another the same absolute central significance which, because of the power of our egoism, we are conscious of only in our own selves.[27]

If the truth of our love for our beloved becomes intense enough, then it causes us to enfold the beloved one with the same care and concern that we ordinarily reserve only for our own individual self. We begin to support and affirm the other person's happiness and the fulfillment of his or her desires in the same way as we do our own.[28] And what we come to know by experiencing this shift in our self-concern, is that we are also nurturing and intensifying the love that enlivens our relationship. Through such love, a selfless reciprocity begins to develop in our life together.

A mutually willed and loving reciprocity means that we love our beloved with such intensity that our deepest desire is for his or her highest good. We recognize that this must manifest in his or her own terms and forms and not ours. Therefore, this can not come into being by asserting our own terms and forms (our ego-self), but will be evoked only by affirming our beloved with a selfless love. Franz von Baader, the "professor of love," said it so simply, "the giving of love is … the affirmation of the … [beloved] through a denial of one's self."[29]

In this day and age many react to the very mention of self-effacement, or to the denial of self for the sake of another, with apprehension and a rising fear that loving means losing their awareness of individual existence. The identification with the separative self is extremely powerful and all-encompassing in the modern world and, without a clear spiritual focus, it is very difficult for people to accept that they could become a higher or truer self. However, the process of developing or growing through love necessarily involves "overcoming what we have been to become what we might." And all the great spiritual teachings tell us that as we grow into our destined potential as spiritual beings we shall not lose anything that is real.[30]

However, as long as we are living in the *thrall* of the separative self, it will appear to be in our "self-interest" to reject or disaffirm others in order to assert our own independent existence. The personality, by nature, tries to avoid, negate, or otherwise distance itself from other people in an attempt to prevent entrapment in what it believes is not itself. The effort to become invulnerable is an important part of the illusion of the separate self and it can only be maintained by negating or saying *no* to others. Many people seem to believe that if they continually criticize and/or reject what they do not like in another that she or he will change to more closely fit with what they think they want. Our ego cannot recognize, and it is totally surprised to find out, that in rejecting others we do not change them, nor do we free ourselves from them; in fact, we create bonds—negative bonds.[31]

Most of us are not very good at recognizing the negative bonds of rejection in our relationship. Instead, we may be aware of discomfort; or, perhaps, we have a feeling of being limited and restricted by the relationship. Or we may feel frustrated or thwarted by our loved one, as if he or she were an adversary. Or we may become irritated by our partner's "faults" or "negativity," or discouraged by the many "differences" between us. What we do not realize is that the feelings aroused by these negative bonds in action are not being caused by the other person or by the relationship. They are arising within us from *our rejection* of the independent or existential reality of that other person. We affirm or reject another, not because of who she or he is, but because of who **we** are.[32]

Love is the power that bridges the gap of our separation and connects us to our beloved one on a level that is beyond the personality. If we are following the beloved path we are already committed to love no matter what we encounter in each other or our life together. A further commitment emerges as we recognize that we must use the "will-to-love" to break through the negative bonds. The will-to-love impels both a woman and a man to reach for a more inclusive love which becomes a true affirmation of the beloved other.[33]

We meet many couples who ask sadly, "We are so different, how can we ever get along? How can we ever work it out?" Our world today certainly conditions us to see differences between people as indicating incompatibility. For most people love is strictly on a personal level; therefore, it is a widespread notion that we can love another person more easily when we believe that he or she is similar to ourselves. We consider it an advantage that the other person likes the same things we do, that she or he enjoys the same activities and has similar ideas about life, etc. Differences are viewed as *problems*. If a man and a woman discover that they have different personality types, they think that they are unsuited to one another. If they find that the other person has a different way of doing something, they feel separated and contradicted. To these people, the differences indicate that the other person is in opposition to them. Thus it becomes very important to learn how to negotiate, to defend one's personal rights, to stand up for one's own beliefs and to make one's individual preferences clear. It then becomes a persistant and negative habit to feel limited, restricted, injured, and in competition with our partner. Personal differences are almost always seen as a deterrent and an obstacle to loving. In view of this, Michele Wiener-Davis was surprised by the following incident which she relates under the heading, "IS DIFFERENT BAD?":

> Paula, a woman in her thirties, was having difficulty resolving a marital issue. She began by telling me, "My husband always wants to go out and do things but I'm a homebody. He is very athletic and I love to read. He loves entertaining people in our home but I prefer

to be alone. He loves to laugh but I am more serious." As she spoke I thought she was building a case for divorce. I was convinced she was about to say, "There are too many irreconcilable differences." Instead, she concluded her soliloquy with, "We are different as day and night—we're perfect complements.[34]

Whatever her other problem may have been, this woman knew something very valuable about relationships: If we say "yes" to the differences, if we affirm them, they enhance and expand us. Couples are surprised when we tell them that they are indeed fortunate to be so different because they have a greater incentive to grow in love than a couple who blends naturally on the personality level. Most people do not understand that one of the beneficial purposes of marriage is to provide an arena where we learn to love and affirm another regardless of any differences—no matter how "unlike" us they may seem to be. Our spiritual ascent in love begins with that great creative difference of male and female. These two different genders that are inherent in the very definition of humanity constitute a differentiation at all levels of our being and challenge us to love the opposite enough to harmonize our polarities into a new symphony—a new synthesis. To love only what is comfortable, familiar, and the same as ourselves is to perpetuate our egotistical view of the world. Here are examples of how two beloved couples have creatively affirmed their differences:

Maggie liked to go to garage sales, flea markets, and thrift shops where she would buy used kitchen equipment. She then took considerable delight in refurbishing and fixing these things up for her gourmet kitchen. Her husband, Paul, on the other hand, preferred to go to the mall and buy whatever they needed 'brand new,' with no "hassles" involved. Maggie disliked the mall and sometimes called it a "consumer ant-hill;" Paul has always considered garage sales to be dreadfully boring. Maggie and Paul are a congenial couple, and it cannot be said that this was a very contentious issue. But there was an edge of criticism or impatience with each other's way, and this sometimes led to Paul stalking off to the mall by himself or Maggie going alone on Saturday morning to the flea market at the fairgrounds.

When Maggie and Paul heard of the Affirmation concept, they realized that they could apply it to this conflict. As a result, their activities did not change, but their attitudes did. Each began to see the advantages in the other's way. For instance, even though finances were not a big concern, Paul could appreciate that Maggie was saving them a considerable amount of money by not shopping at the local gourmet shops. Maggie saw that Paul was right to purchase new the things that were not part of her hobby. She had bought a lot of stuff in the past that was not for the kitchen and never got around to using it. It was not that these mutual advantages were so great, but their change in attitude toward each other's way made it possible to be more sympathetic and even to admire what the other did and not to be critical. They began to share in the satisfaction and happiness that was derived from doing things the way that best suited each one's disposition. They began to enjoy their differences as an expansion of life and not as a reason for conflict.

There was another couple whose temperaments and dispositions could not have been any more divergent. They used to say that they were like Summer and Winter. Trish was all action, she played soccer and racquetball, she liked to go skiing and swimming and attended the local basketball games. Her husband, Ted, was a technical writer and worked at home; he was considered a semi-recluse by their friends. He liked to read and do research for his books. Ted and Trish told us that in the beginning they were apprehensive about their marriage because they were so different from one another, but now they realized what an advantage their differences were to their children. Trish could give them all opportunities for sports and an active life, where Ted was always there to read to them, help with homework and to tell stories. He stimulated their intellectual life, while Trish balanced that with an active social and physical life. Their beautiful children are a testimony to this unusual complementary parenting style.

The preceding stories illustrate how affirming differences actualizes their complementarity, reducing conflict and creating greater harmony and flow of love in a relationship. We realize a more profound aspect of *Affirmation* when we see that it is really a deeper action than the affirming or negating of the other person's personality. In fact, "affirmation of the beloved" transcends the limits of our conventional and habitual thinking, feeling, and acting. It is an unconditional action that is not bound by our judgment or emotional predilections and is not dependent upon any likes or dislikes, similarities or differences, or even the positive and negative characteristics of our partner's personality. It is based instead upon that more inclusive loving which, similar to pre-forgiveness, emerges naturally out of the intensification of our love and devotion to our beloved. It is a manifestation of a more spiritual love.[35]

As the love in our relationship becomes more intense and more inclusive, we are strongly supporting, validating, and affirming the "higher spiritual aspect" of our beloved. In affirming the beloved out of deep love, we help to reveal and actualize his or her hidden spiritual nature, allowing the "True Self"[36] to shine through the personality. Love is a power which transforms and elevates the beloved into a more spiritual level of being. And as we invoke the higher spiritual aspect of our beloved to come forth, we evoke our own Spiritual Self into greater expression. Through *affirmation* we find the true being of our beloved and at the same time we become our own *higher self.*

In daily, practical life, a more inclusive love leads to a state of such harmony and closeness, that there is no longer any reason to say "no" to the other person for the purpose of asserting your own individuality. Indeed, "even as Freud said, the little word 'no' is the hallmark of Death."[37] The ego's need to say "no" to the other is superseded by an unprecedented desire to affirm him or her in every little thing. It is not only that you are just "willing," it is that you "want" to affirm the other person's way. Your attitude or orientation is, therefore, to say **"yes"** to your beloved because you now identify your own self-interest with her or his continued happiness and fulfillment. This becomes a commitment to love on a higher, more spiritual level, and is not in any way a capitulation to the other's personality. You are freely choosing from a heart full of love, to validate and support the other person's ways. It is not a *yielding* or a *giving-in*, which is a contraction of love—i.e. acquiescing is usually undertaken out of fear—but this free choice is an all-encompassing affirmation, moving us beyond the "no" of egoism to the unrestrained "yes" of unselfish love.[38]

Saying "yes" to our beloved may very well take the form of choosing, in daily activities, to do things the other person's way instead of our own. Some couples begin by ceasing to make "issues" out of small preferences. They stop trying to assert their own way and just "let it go." Others begin to experiment with actually trying the other person's way. For example, one couple told us that have always taken turns cooking dinner for each other. In the past the cook would, as a matter of course, fix what he or she liked to prepare and eat. In working with Affirmation, however, they agreed that it would be more "loverly" to prepare what the other liked. Now they report it is much more fun, and cooking for the other person has given each a greater insight and understanding of the other. A second couple found themselves having a "serious" argument about the "correct" way to put the toilet paper roll on the holder. He maintained that, obviously, the paper should unroll over the top. But she countered that she had always put the roll on the other way so the paper would unroll from the bottom. In working with Affirmation each decided, unbeknownst to the other, to put the toilet paper on the way the other preferred it. It took two weeks for them to realize what was happening, and then they had a truly loving laugh together. We do not know which way they decided to put the roll, maybe either way is just fine, but it was never a problem for them again. On the contrary, the memory of the "TP War" became a symbol of how they could resolve any difference.

These simple acts done in the spirit of loving affirmation of the beloved other make a big difference. Some people have found that this practice can be extended to larger and more important issues. For example, one couple, who loved to take car trips, encountered an almost archetypal man/woman difference which often causes marital conflict. It has been observed by many that men strongly resist asking for directions when they get lost. It may be an expression of male pride, but for Aaron and Elizabeth it was a constant source of arguments and hurt feelings. Sometimes they would drive in circles for, what seemed to Elizabeth like hours, while Aaron claimed that he knew where they were, and he refused to stop and ask anyone. Elizabeth would become furious when this happened and she would feel powerless to stop "the nightmare," as she called it. In working with the Way of the Beloved concepts Aaron and Elizabeth first realized that they were not using Gratitude in this situation. As they became more grateful for each other, they could appreciate the other's viewpoint in this recurring conflict. So they decided in the spirit of "Affirmation" to switch roles on their next trip. Elizabeth would drive and not ask for directions, and Aaron would sit quietly in the passenger seat. To make a long story shorter, it only took a week for Elizabeth and Aaron to make a radical change in their attitudes about their different ways of dealing with this situation. They never argued about it again. Since Elizabeth had a better sense of direction than Aaron, she wound-up driving most of the time, and Aaron became the one to ask for directions when they 'occasionally' needed them.

ଽଓ୯ଽ

• Exercise •

It will be helpful to identify some negative and positive *bonds* in your relationship. These bonds are related to habitual emotional responses, but often they are veiled, covered-over and clothed in such a way that we have difficulty in recognizing them. They can be more easily recognized by thinking of them as encounters which have a noticeable and potent effect on one or both parties. Write brief descriptions of your encounters with your beloved, looking for key emotional words: e.g., I was complaining, criticizing, judging, competing, rejecting, witholding, withdrawing, etc. or I was approving, admiring, caring, nurturing, enfolding, etc. (See Appendix 4 "Emotion Words"). These descriptions will inform you of the quality and tone of the connecting bonds between you and your beloved.

Affirmation transcends both negative and positive bonds. You can increase your awareness of the extent to which you Affirm (or negate) your beloved by doing a daily retrospective. In the evening recall backwards (see Section 3.2 "Transforming Negativity"), the interactions with your partner and note whether you had the attitude of saying "yes" or whether you denied or said "no" to her or him. Write down your observations. For example, one woman wrote: "I always want to leave meetings, parties, and other social gatherings long before my beloved does. This evening, however, I was able to *affirm* my beloved by staying later with him, without feeling an inner resistance and resentment; and I delighted in seeing his enjoyment of a visit with friends." And a man told us:

> I really don't like sitting on the ground outdoors listening to a jazz concert, but my wife loves it. I have never liked jazz or the bugs in the grass and I get leg cramps. This afternoon, in contrast to past experiences, I found myself supporting and encouraging my wife to go to a local concert. I was definitely glad for her to have this opportunity and later I *affirmed* her satisfaction in the music. I believe that she felt the difference in my attitude —there was no disapproval or put-down like there used to be.

You can also explore your attitude toward the concept of radical Affirmation. For instance, if you experience resistance to the idea (as many do) or are in conflict about whether or not you want to use it, do not try it. If your motives are mixed and your willingness is not clear, doing this exercise will cause resentment, which, of course would be in contradiction to the spirit of the concept. However, do consider *experimenting* with acts of Radical Affirmation on those occassions when you feel it is possible. These experiments may lead to experiences which will open a door to more experiments, etc.

One woman reported that, "Saying yes to my beloved is a never-ending process, in that just when I really feel *yes* in one area, I discover a deeper area somewhere where I need to say yes." It is important to realize that Affirmation is a process which inevitably moves to deeper and deeper levels. No one can affirm another in her or his most profound *other-ness* without starting at someplace and growing by practice toward those regions which we never even knew were there.

Some couples have found this exercise to be a great eye-opener. Recently when we presented the idea of Affirmation in class, one couple felt very receptive to it and they put a lot of effort into trying to use it as an approach to their many differences. During the 2 week interval between classes, they began to look at other couples in a new way, and they saw the divisive competition, the defensiveness and the constant pick-pick-picking that was taken for granted in many marriages. They realized just how important it was for them to make a conscious effort to say yes to each other. Like no previous exercise had, this exercise struck a chord in them. In just 2 weeks they were visibly changed by the practice. As the woman has said more than once since then, "Why would I ever want to say "no" to my beloved?" For this couple Affirmation became an important stimulus and inspiration to a greater love in their relationship.

℥Ω

Using the concept of radical affirmation can build intensity in your relationship. Saying "yes" to your beloved is a commitment to love on the spiritual level. It can move you toward a deeper understanding of the transformative potential of the Way of the Beloved and to a spiritual "vision" of your own beloved. When we really affirm our loved one, we begin to experience the truth of the oft quoted aphorism: "Only by losing yourself in love do you find your True Self." [39] Thus through the loving affirmation of our beloved, we stand at the threshold of a new life and a new reality.

Martin Buber is one of the few thinkers of any age who truly understood the spiritual potential of affirmation in the intimate loving relationship of man and woman:

> That the men [and women] with whom I am bound up in the body politic and with whom I have directly or indirectly to do, are essentially other than myself, that this one or that one does not have merely a different mind, or way of thinking or feeling, or a different conviction or attitude, but has also a different perception of the world, a different recognition and order of meaning, a different touch from the regions of existence, a different faith, a different soil: to affirm all this, to affirm it in the way of a creature, in the midst of the hard situations of conflict, without relaxing their real seriousness, is the way by which we may officiate as helpers in this wide realm entrusted to us as well, and from which alone we are from time to time permitted to touch in our doubts, in humility and upright investigation, on the other's "truth" or "untruth," "justice" or "injustice." **But to this we are led by marriage, if it is real, with a power for which there is scarcely a substitute, by its steady experiencing of the life-substance of the other as other, and still more by its crises and the overcoming of them which rises out of the organic depths, whenever the monster of otherness, which but now blew on us with its icy demons' breath and now is redeemed by our risen affirmation of the other, which knows and destroys all negation, is transformed into the mighty angel of union of which we dreamed in our mother's womb.**[40]

• 5.4 CONSPIRATION •

A lasting marriage is not the "two of us trying as two individuals to survive side by side." It is "the total union of Us creating together ..."

—Paul Pearsall[41]

The idea of *conspiration* or breathing together is not something that is part of our everyday thoughts and conversation. Yet on the physical level, moving together and breathing together are common experiences and they are known to be beneficial physically and emotionally. Conspiration may be experienced in sex or in dancing the waltz or it may be consciously initiated as a relaxation technique or as a technique to encourage deeper "bonding."[42] The conspiration of a beloved couple extends also to a less visible level.

When a man and a woman choose to merge or blend their lives through deep love and devotion, they begin to experience a transformation of their sense of personal identity. Before becoming a beloved couple, each believed himself or herself to be a separated individual, moving alone through the sea of life. Now, however, through their devotion and love for each other, they have become psychically blended, and they "breathe" together on a mutual path toward spiritual fulfillment. This is a creative convergence taking place from the inside out, and it is a natural result of the intentional intensification of love.

Perhaps in the past, even though they were *married*, each saw herself or himself as still in the *marketplace* of the world searching as an individual for fulfillment wherever it could be found. Now, as a beloved couple, they look only to each other for fulfillment in love on the physical, emotional, and mental levels of life. The arena for spiritual growth has become focused within their relationship, and the opportunities for evolving and expanding consciousness are now centered in their loving interactions. Paul Pearsall says that this "is taking on the most important life challenge—to silence the search for the self and try instead to make a whole new searching and growing loving unit."[43]

Thus each individual has become part of a new and larger whole—a beloved couple. Awareness of this new identification means that each intentionally approaches the world as a *representative* of that greater unity. Each begins to think of herself or himself not as an "I," but as a "We."[44]

When we meet the world as a we—i.e., a team—all our interactions with other people change, and the events and conditions of life take on a new tone and meaning. Indeed, "we share in a give-and-take of the world's loving. Our unqualified caring for one another ... helps make us better and helps make the world a better place."[45]

Thus, when we say that the united couple "breathe" together we do not mean that they synchronize their inhaling and exhaling, although that has been observed to take place.[46] What we mean is more like what takes place in a string quartet. In a string quartet's performance each musician plays a unique line of music. Sometimes the bows of all 4 players move together at the same time (like breathing together physically), but most of the time the bows move differently, each one going in its own way, in or out, short or long sweeps, sharp or smooth motion, according to the particular phrase of music written for the instrument. And yet all 4 players are *breathing* together to the rhythm and structure of the musical composition. They are all playing ONE piece of music. Thus it is with the *duet* of a beloved couple. Each must play his or her part, in his or her own way, yet blending and harmonizing in a greater rhythm. They are each *playing* a melody of music of their own and simultaneously they are conspiring as ONE in the same composition—the activation and manifestation of the unity of their love.

It is not uncommon to see couples all around us who live as *married-singles*, or worse as two single people occupying the same house. We also know of many couples who wish they could be really together and become a *we*. However, without models or wiser guidance than our society readily offers,[47] they can only fill their relationships with selfish desires, individual goals, attempts to obtain momentary satisfaction wherever they can, and vain pleas for true fulfillment. Thus, what is carried to the world from those relationships—from their potential "we-ness"—is more "me-ness." People in this prevalent kind of marriage encounter the world as individuals with all their personal wants and frustrations. And again Paul Pearsall gives us an appropriate observation: if "we seek *only* 'self'-fulfillment through marriage, our marriage can end up burdening instead of helping society."[48]

When a couple enters the Way of the Beloved, they have chosen to move in a spiritual direction toward a more complete union in love. This means that their relationship is becoming alive with the qualities of gratitude, devotion, sacrifice, beauty and unbounded love. When a beloved couple becomes a "we," they encounter the world together in the spirit of love. Each individual becomes a carrier of the love that is shared in the relationship—i.e. each carries the other to the world. Everything that one of them does becomes an extension and expression of the love for the other. Thus, whatever they do and wherever they go, the loving atmosphere of their union permeates everything. And concurrently each person feels more complete and alive as a true individual.[49]

Approaching life together as a unity, couples meet problems as a "we," instead of as an "I." Their moving together is a conspiration, and they no longer feel alone. For the beloved couple, the problems of each become the mutual problems of both, and also the joys of each become the joys of both.[50] In this blending they discover that the sharing of delights and burdens has amplified and elevated them both. As Herman Rednick said, "Of course ... [beloveds] will share each other's burdens, since you are One psychically. Remember that this is the treasure that you can reap in this world ... **move together**, in every and any direction you may go, whether you take a trip or visit a relative, go together as one Spirit."[51] Two friends of ours recently found out how different their life could be when they learned to approach family crises as a team:

> Greg and Pam were in their early 50's. They had been married for 11 years, and they had 5 adult children from first marriages, who still needed a lot of help from them. The *dreaded* Fall holiday season was approaching and, as usual, they were planning to go back East, not just to visit, but to try to resolve some of the *family stuff* that had been building up since the previous holidays. Their dread was based on several years of seeing their own relationship deteriorate as they tried to help their respective families. In the past, each had taken the attitude that "it was the other's family" and that "backing off and not getting involved with the other's problems, was the *right* thing to do." They believed that helping with family problems was an "interruption" and a "drain" on their relationship. Each knew that dealing with their respective family was unavoidable, but each felt the strain and thought that the continuing necessity of having to care for others was separating them. However, since they were in a Beloved Class, they tried to approach the Fall ordeal with a new attitude. They thought that they would try to go as a team, as a couple who were lovingly united.

When they returned home to Albuquerque that year, they reported that instead of being exhausted and needing "marriage repair work," they had never felt closer and more in harmony with each other. When they were with Pam's chronically ill son and the 3 neglected grandchildren, instead of feeling that she had to do everything alone while Greg went off and played golf, Pam felt that he was right there helping and supporting. And when they went to see Greg's extremely difficult sister, Pam was able to give Greg the emotional backup that made their visit almost pleasant—a first in Greg's life. This trip was a milestone for Greg and Pam. It convinced them that they were united as a couple and that they were able to move in the world as a unit to the benefit of themselves, their families, and others.

The conspiration of a beloved couple will not go unnoticed by others. Sometimes the love and blending of a beloved couple is appreciated and admired. One woman told us that on several occasions after her husband had visited her at her office, her co-workers remarked that she had "lit up" when he arrived, and continued to "glow for hours." However, today's world is not always sympathetic to the togetherness of a beloved couple. Two PhD. psychologists, who are a beloved couple, told us how disturbing it was to attend a professional meeting to deliver a joint paper and afterwards be openly scorned for wanting to sit next to each other at the dinner table. They were viewed by their colleagues as negatively over-dependent. "We like to be together," they told us.

Another friend, in response to constant criticism from others for her desire to spend so much time with her beloved, defended herself by writing, poetically:

> I am walking upon my destined path ... and I meet my
> true love and I love him. I want to walk with him because I
> love him ... Our destined paths are one. Some think I want
> him near because I am not strong, but the fire within me
> is strong. Some think I want him near because I have no
> direction, but the purpose within my heart is clear. Some
> think I want him near to be contrary to the way they are,
> but I have no quarrel with another's life. Because I love him,
> I want to be near him.[52]

ഇൻ

To know more about where you stand or how you are "breathing" (conspiring)[53] with your beloved, think back over the events of each day and ask yourself the following questions:

- As I go about my activities, how do I present myself to others? What kind of messages am I broadcasting about the quality of my love relationship?
- Am I vulnerable to entanglements in the drama of other people's lives?
- Am I looking toward my marriage as the arena for emotional processing, or am I "looking around," elsewhere?
- Am I "available" emotionally and/or sexually?
- Do I look toward the relationship with my beloved as the source of love, fulfillment, and spiritual growth, or not?
- Do we work together as a couple to meet the problems in our lives?
- Do we (both) believe that we can meet any problem together with love?
- Do we believe that through a truly loving heart there is an answer to every problem?
- Do I carry my beloved with me in my heart as I move through my day? Does my beloved carry me in her [his] heart as she [he] moves through the day?
- Do we really believe that we are both parts of a greater unity?
- Do we move together in the spirit of love?

ഇൻ

There are four levels of the concept of conspiration. These levels are not clearly separate; they interpenetrate and have overlapping edges; they can, however, be hierarchically ordered—from physical breathing to spiritual communion.

The first level is the physical-emotional, as briefly described in the first paragraph at the beginning of this Section. The second level, which has been the main topic of this Section, can be called "psychic" conspiration. It is exemplified by a mental and emotional unity through love of a beloved couple. The third level is described by Teilhard de Chardin when he characterizes the future unification of the whole of humanity as a "conspiration," a great *collective soul*.[54] And the fourth level of conspiration involves the relationship of the concrete (i.e., manifest) human form with its higher archetype, the Soul, existing in spiritual realms—i.e., the physical with the spiritual, the visible with the invisible.[55]

In the last chapter we show how a beloved couple can realize the third level of conspiration, e.g., "Copresencing" (7.3.2); and the fourth level is presented under the title "Visioning the Divine" (7.1).

· PART THREE ·

SPIRITUAL UNION

The following is a personal statement of one man's realization of the Way of the Beloved as a path to spiritual enlightment:

> From yoga to yoga and practice to practice what motivates me in spiritual work is a longing for completeness, a longing for an unmediated intimacy with the whole field of life and experience, its source and its process. I long for an unmediated intimacy with the original light of consciousness that apprehends this shady spot we write in
>
> > that sees the grasses move in the up-hill breezes of afternoon
> > that hears the humming birds zip and whir in the trees above us
> > and that quietly smiles at me from the other chair here.
>
> For many years I have sought to discover this intimacy
>
> > through introspection;
> > through deep, quiet breathing;
> > through floor-gazing, wall-gazing, sky-gazing, mind-gazing;
> > through watching the hand pull,
> > > the toes point,
> > > and the sock slide up.

Windows on real intimacy have opened for me in these ways, but only through

> extrordinary grace,
> extraordinary pain,
> and impossible-to-maintain effort.

Most of the time I remain separated from the intimacy I long for by noise and confusion I do not understand.

I have made intense inquiry of many floors and walls and ceilings in the rooms of myself, but I find that I am permitted exit and entry only reluctantly. I have not worked as hard as I believe I could—I know—but I continue to work, to sit and to long for the love I have only but rarely known. The Love that makes these oaks grow and this mosquito buzz from ear to ear.

Here now—in the middle of my life—I have learned of a new possibility—an old possibility—one I have overlooked:

I feel Elena's feet lying over my knees in this green and grey and brown and blue place as we sit on our fold-up camping chairs with the ants. I look over at her intently pouring her heart out in her writing. I wait there. Watching her. I feel love moving when I notice that her eyes are wet. She feels my eyes upon her and returns my gaze. Smiling, she is in no hurry to look away.

Here is possibility. The Path of the Beloved. An access to love, to unmediated intimacy, to spiritual completion through relationship with this beautiful, loving woman, my wife, my Beloved. I have only just begun to appreciate her. The possibilities open out in amazing grace.

Unlike the plywood floor of my little meditation hut at home, she responds to me immediately. I do not have to sit all night to make the floor open. She opens her eyes and admits me gladly into her heart. A vast and timeless world is there—an infinite receptivity.

I am beginning to learn how to get lost in this place—how to lose myself in Elena, to pass into and through her heart—as she opens her heart for me to pass through into the original light and love I have longed for all my life.[1]

In Part 3 we unfold the concepts for the spiritual *yoga* of the Beloved. We will explore the beginning steps that a couple can take to make the spiritual path of the Beloved a reality in their life. These Chapters are written for couples who want their love for one another to become their spiritual path, their yoga, their way to the heights of spiritual consciousness. To walk the path of the Beloved, a man and a woman reach out to the higher, spiritual aspect within each other through deep love and devotion. They reach out with love to see the Light beyond the form—the True Self, the Divine, the God within—manifested through the actuality of the other. When, through intense love, a man and a woman blend and unite on all levels with the divine spirit in each other, their union becomes a door to the higher worlds. Together they can ascend in the beauty of a dedicated spiritual life. The Way of the Beloved is a straight road to spiritual fulfillment.

The Way of the Beloved is an inner walking; it is invisible to the world, thus there are no special rituals required. The practices of the path are meditative in nature. In addition to the exercises presented in the first 2 parts of this book, we recommend 2 forms of meditation practice. The first is the practice of sitting quietly, concentrating on a spiritual concept related to the beloved path for 10-20 minutes every day. The second is the silent use of a mantra (a short phrase which recalls the seed-thought of the meditation)[2] all day long while engaging in daily activities.

⚛

For sitting meditation you can be alone or together. It is good to meditate at the same time each day, if possible: early in the morning or before sleep in the evening. Beloved meditations can be done on their own or can be incorporated into other practices. Here is a good procedure to follow:

- Read through the entire meditation text.
- Then focus on one sentence at a time, reading each one aloud or repeating it silently, mentally concentrating your attention on the meaning.
- Form an image in your mind's eye of the spiritual concept being expressed in the sentence. See it as clearly as possible.
- Place yourself within that image and feel its reality.
- Follow the same procedure with the mantra.
- Then, with eyes closed, hold the image within and repeat the mantra silently for a few minutes.
- When your sitting meditation is over, continue to repeat the mantra with the image.

128

Do this throughout the day and before sleep at night.

We can begin with the following meditation:

Meditation:

THE PATH OF THE BELOVED[3]

> *The path of the beloved has a transcendent potential,*
> *It is through my beloved that I learn to love;*
> *I look beyond the personality to the spiritual aspect*
> *   and I see divinity within my beloved;*
> *Through deep love and devotion, we ascend to spiritual heights.*

Mantra: *In deep love for my beloved, we ascend to spiritual heights.*

Using a mantra all day is a way to impress the image and the concept into your consciousness and to keep you focused on the spiritual work as you go about your activities in the world. As you move through your day, your mind and heart are infused with the energy and substance of the mantra and the image. Thus whatever you are doing in the outer reality, at the same time, you are aware of your love for your beloved and its spiritual purpose.

If your work requires your mental attention, just having the image with you will produce the desired effect. It is normal for the focus to often slip away from us. Turn again and again to the mantra and the image. In this way every hour is used to walk the path. In the Bible we are told to "pray without ceasing;" when we use a mantra with love, it becomes a continuous prayer.

· CHAPTER 6 ·

6.1 THE CIRCLE OF LOVE

The ring is an ancient symbol of a circle of force that surrounds a couple united in love and devotion.

—Herman Rednick[1]

When an intense, living love is flowing between a man and a woman, there is no sense that one person is active and the other receptive, there is no distinction between who is giving and who is receiving. There is a flowing circle of energy which is like a dynamic ring permeating, penetrating, and enfolding both people as one. It is not limited by time or space, for the flow of love-energy is continuous and boundless. One cannot distinguish cause and effect or tell from where or whom it originated. Within the circle, each person feels as if he or she is the whole circle as well as a whole individual, for the flux of giving and receiving, active and receptive, has become a limitless flow. The *circle of love* is a sublime exchange. It carries both people into a trans-temporal, eternal realm, wherein a man and woman are always "present" to (copresencing) and "with" (coinherent in) each other. In the circle of love each lives within the other. Each embraces the other as part of his or her own self. Each is united with the other as a pure polarity in a transpersonal field of encompassing, transcendent love.

Words can only suggest what this ineffable experience is like, for the circle of love is a glimpse of the eternal, a fleeting taste of the nectar of the Gods, and even a brief moment of it will kindle an unquenchable longing for more. As they were about to ascend to the second sphere of Paradise, Beatrice tells Dante, "Well do I see how the Eternal Ray, which, once seen, kindles love forevermore, already shines on you."[2] A couple who has had this experience knows that the circle of love is more than just a metaphor. It is a tangible reality that may be *seen* by one who is psychically sensitive and has some vision, appearing sometimes as a ring of light and sometimes as a sphere.

A man and woman enter the circle of love when they blend through intense love on all the levels of their life. Entering the circle is a "meeting," a "joining" or "merging," which may take place in the first burst of love between them, or it may occur after many years of marriage, or it may not happen at all in an entire lifetime of living together. It is not just a physical event—it is a spiritual one. When a man and woman enter the circle of love they rise into a world of heightened consciousness. The event is initially an experience of intense joy and fulfillment and it can be ecstatic and transcendent. The power of a single experience can sweep a couple along in its stream of spontaneous, seemingly unending bliss.

Immersed in this stream, a man and a woman feel as if they are in an atmosphere of eternal light which will never disappear. And yet it does dissolve and disappear. It is not self-sustaining. Indeed, if a couple experiences even a few moments in a whole lifetime it is like a great gift or a grace. The circle of love seems to come and go according to its own mysterious and occult laws. And just as it feels like forever when it is here, when it is gone, it feels like it is gone forever. Initially, love seems to enter our life gratuitously, as if by magic. And, perhaps in part because of this, we find that we are not able to sustain that elusive state. We may have an intense desire to do so, but how can we pour out love steadily through the cycles of growth and change which we all encounter in life? The negative patterns within each one's personality and the negative forces throughout the world, disrupt the flow of love, effacing time and again the beauty and transcendence it brings to our life. Our work on the Path of the Beloved is to learn how to re-create the circle of love.

∞ ∞

There are two universal principles or energies that manifest at all levels of creation— the masculine and the feminine. These principles are "polarities," i.e., polar opposites, which, when they merge, "form indivisible unities or wholes at all levels of existence."[3] Both women and men have currents of masculine and feminine energy flowing through their psyches. Thus one cannot say that a woman has "these" characteristics and a man "those," but we can say that the masculine principle is one thing and the feminine principle another. Although it is a widespread notion today that both masculine and feminine currents are present in the psyche of each human being, "a holistic understanding would not ignore the mutual influence between the physical body and the psyche,"[4] i.e., embodied humans are male or female. Since the beginning, humanity has been composed of two genders.[5] Part of the definition of humanity is that it consists of two sexes which are not reducible one to the other, and being a "gendered" being is essential to the experience of being human. Thus man and woman are polar opposites, i.e., they are different embodiments of universal principles, indeed they are asymmetrical and complementary.[6]

The fact that man and woman are not reducible to one another indicates that the experience of the life-world is not the same for a man and for a woman. Indeed, John Gray has based his very popular book on this observation: "men and women differ in all areas of their lives. Not only do men and women communicate differently but they think, feel, perceive, react, respond, love, need, and appreciate differently. They almost seem to be from different planets, speaking different languages and needing different nourishment."[7] One of the most important differences between men and women is that they participate in the realm of love in very different ways. It is particularly in the attempts made by men and women to love one another that our bipolar human nature emerges and presents us with, what could be considered, the central problematic of our times.[8]

In the realm of heightened consciousness which we call the "circle of love," the man's experience reflects the rhythms and qualities of masculine energy and the woman's experience reflects those of the feminine energy. Thus, we find in our classes and seminars that, in their love relationships, the women overwhelmingly identify with the feminine principle and the men with the masculine (male) principle. The identification of women with the feminine energies and men with the masculine energies in the "world of love" seems to take place regardless of the person's profession, job, or other roles in the world. For example, a man or a woman may be an operator of heavy machinery, or in the armed services, or in business, or a parent who cares for small children, or a professional teacher, or a medical doctor, or a pilot of an airplane; in his or her "love-life" a woman identifies herself with the feminine aspect and a man with the masculine. On the very rare occasions, when a person or a couple has felt that they do not make this type of identification, we have said, as John Gray has done, that since each person and each couple is unique, this is not a problem, "either ignore it ... or look deeper inside yourself."[9]

To help in the understanding of the polarity and asymmetry between men and women in the world of love we can observe that the directional flow of the energy of the feminine aspect is *magnetic* or *centripetal* (interiorizing, converging, attracting or *yin*), and the directional flow of the energy of the masculine aspect is *precipitating* or *centrifugal*, (exteriorizing or expanding, or *yang*).[10] Thus we can describe woman's fundamental mode as being magnetic in nature, i.e., when a woman in love reaches for her polar opposite, it is an invocation, a magnetic force seeking to draw him toward her. The mode of man's energy, on the other hand, can be described as precipitative or outward moving. When a man reaches out with love to his polar opposite, his energy flows out toward her as an offering.[11] We can use these descriptions as an overview or a larger perspective to help us see more clearly the different modes that men and women embody when they express themselves in the "world of love"—or in a conflict.

What happens when the flow of love stops between a man and a woman? Since man and woman are not reducible to one another and their experience of the life-world is different a true understanding or *comprehension* of the other cannot be achieved by means of ordinary communication, empathy and identification. The disparity between man's and woman's perception and experience of love is the major cause of the conflicts and misunderstandings that dominate male/female relationships today. When love is lost, men and women have very different ways of coping with the situation and most of the time their attempts to reestablish the circle of love are not effective. The so-called "natural" or "spontaneous" ways that the personality seeks for love when it has been lost, actually produce more misunderstandings and adversarial interactions. The "ways of the personality" create a movement away from the other person and from love, producing exactly the opposite situation from what both men and women claim to be seeking, and indeed, what most of them desperately want. If a man or a woman in an intimate relationship expresses his or her fundamental gender mode only through the grasping and self-protecting aspects of the personality, then conflict and a "spiral of separation" will characterize their life together.

The seven parts of Section 6.2 are portrayals of some of the ways that the different experience of love for man and woman produce conflict, disharmony and divisiveness between them. Each portrayal is focused around a particular theme, and the germ of each is found in the **bold**, ***italic*** headlines. These italic sentences form whole paragraphs that summarize each portrayal. Read through the italics of each portrayal first, and then go back and read the more detailed expansions under the headlines.[12]

6.2 THE SPIRAL OF SEPARATION

6.2.1 THE VICIOUS CIRCLE [13]

The directional flow of the field of masculine energy is precipitative or outward moving.

When a man seeks to love, seeks to connect with his beloved, his love is a stream of centrifugal force, a flow of energy that spirals outward from him towards her. He feels that he is moving freely out of his own choice and that his love is an offering to her.

Feminine energy, on the other hand, is magnetic in nature.

When a woman reaches out or seeks to touch her polar opposite it is an invocation, a magnetic, centripetal force seeking to draw him to her, so that she will be filled and sustained by the current of his devotion and love.

In order to know that the Circle of Love is alive, the woman must feel the flow of love energy coming toward her from her beloved.

Woman needs the continuous contact of the love-energy from her beloved or she does not experience the living reality of the circle of love. She desires and needs the love-energy that her beloved gives to her in order to feel that their love is alive.

On the emotional level, she thinks of the circle of love as "being loved" and she will describe her experience of the relationship with her beloved as one in which she "is loved." A woman may say that her desire is "to be cherished," for to be cherished by her beloved is to experience their connection in the circle, or world, of love. "Being loved" is the necessary sustenance for the circle of love. Without the sense of "being loved" she and the circle of love itself will starve.

Therefore, a woman feels the necessity to know, at all times, that her beloved loves her and is *with* her. This is true, despite the fact that she has been assured in a thousand ways by her beloved and has had many confirming experiences; she still must be shown, told, constantly affirmed anew that she is loved by her beloved. This aspect of a woman's functioning is not some kind of psychological insecurity, as it is often mislabeled. Nor is it, as so many think, a particularly female, neurotic pattern. Indeed, it is a psychic reality of the feminine principle in manifestation. It could be said, that this seeming insecurity is an "archetypal mode" of expression for the feminine aspect within a love relationship. Therefore, it is the "natural," "appropriate," even "legitimate" functioning of a woman in love.

Masculine energy tends to go out in all directions. In the Circle of Love, a man turns to his beloved and directs his energy towards her.

In the intense state of the Circle of Love a man "wants" to turn his love and devotion towards his beloved. He sees his beloved as the spiritual treasure of love for which he has been longing and seeking.

It is necessary that the man feel that he is acting freely, that his love is a free gift. He is repelled by the thought that he "has" to love, that he is "obligated" or "coerced" in any way to give love for any reason other than his own desire and unfettered choice. This is not because men are constitutionally against love and intimacy, as they are so often accused of being, but it is the "natural," "appropriate," mode of male functioning in love relationships with the polar opposite.

When the Circle of Love is broken, a woman will urgently feel that she must reestablish the contact and restore the flow.

If the relationship has been intense, the woman's need to restore the contact with her beloved can be very powerful and urgent. If the relationship has also been deep, the woman feels bereft and seeks desperately to make contact by any means.

She will often attempt to make the contact directly by asking, "Do you love me?" She may ask repeatedly, much to the man's consternation, "Do you still love me?" It does not matter how long they have been together, it could be 3 days, 3 years, or 30 years, when the woman feels a separation, the need will be undiminished by time.

We remember one woman, for instance, who had been married 5 years, yet felt the necessity to call her husband at his office to ask if he loved her. He thought that there was something seriously wrong with her and was annoyed that she should interrupt his work in this fashion. He never suspected that he had anything to do with *her insecurity*. He did not have any idea at all that it was his withdrawal of love-energy from her that was the direct cause of her conduct. This is far from an isolated incident.[14] Many men have come to us convinced that their wives were in immediate need of counseling or therapy because they were "pathologically insecure." Even the wives wondered why they were always asking for the man to say that he loves her. When this is the case the man invariably believes that there is something wrong with his wife, and often the woman agrees. They are both surprised when they hear that many other couples have the same experience. The woman is delighted and feels vindicated when she hears that her *need* is valid and justifiable. The man is usually somewhat chagrined and confused to hear that his wife is not sick.

The woman's response to a sense of separation may also take the form of asking that they *talk*. Men often have an immediate negative visceral response to the request for talk. However, men must come to the recognition that a woman's asking for an affirmation of love or a request for talk are all *appearances* on the emotional level of the fundamental polar differences of gender. What a woman really wants is *loving contact*. Usually, true expressions of love from the man will accomplish the connection that the woman is looking for, and actions are better than words. However, any kind of contact or sharing of emotions or experience, even an argument, may be necessary to assure the woman that they are still connected in some way.

Since a man's energy flows outward, expanding in all directions, as he projects himself on this flow, he will feel a longing to be free.

Men experience and suffer from the illusion that "freedom" means the unrestricted exercise of an autonomous personality.[15] Consequently when his beloved asks for anything at all, he senses a threat to his *freedom*. He begins to feel trapped and stifled. Many men experience a feeling of suffocation and turn away to catch their breath. A man seldom has any awareness that his responses are, not only hurtful to his partner, but that they reinforce her desperation to restore the flow of love between them.

For his part, if he has reconnected with his beloved even once, a man thinks that the job is done.

The man knows that he has told his partner that he loves her. He knows that he has expressed affection to her, perhaps even recently. And it seems obvious to him that he has not given his beloved any cause to feel separated or unloved. He truly believes that he has already "done it"—i.e., conveyed to her that he loves her. And in his world of love he has. Now he is ready and wants to turn his attention and energy elsewhere. At this point when asked about the direction of his affection, he may well say, "Of course I love you. I married you, didn't I?" or "I'm still here, aren't I?" From his perspective as a man, he really believes that these responses are valid, and that they should certainly satisfy the woman's need.

Thus the circle of love may disappear from one instant to the next because of this fundamental difference in the way a man and a woman experience love.

Indeed, at the first indication of separation the woman may ask for contact. If contact does not occur she may become disturbed, anxious and demanding.

If contact is not made, the woman may pull harder. In her frustration she may become desperate and begin to demand, then to demand more and more, and eventually resort to nagging. This may well be the origin of that well-known archetype of the shrew. Even when the dynamic of the vicious circle is exposed, it is difficult for men to accept that a nagging wife is the result of a break in the circle of love. Of course, many couples have never had the experience of the circle of love, but nonetheless, the woman's nagging is the only way she knows how to search for that which is essential to her life as a woman, even if she has yet to experience it or would not know how to name it.

The man will then feel caught and imprisoned in a situation which he sees as becoming incomprehensible and unfixable. Indeed, he may be totally convinced that to be "truly" himself his only resort is to withdraw or escape from the situation altogether.[16]

Faced with the conviction that his freedom is being denied by the woman, the man will withdraw when she asks for his love.[17] He turns away psychically and he may also physically remove himself from his partner because he believes that the only way to *survive* as an independent agent is to work out the problem alone or to turn in another direction.

The woman interprets the man's turning away as an utter rejection. She is convinced that her beloved doesn't love her any more, and her distress is multiplied.

Feeling that her beloved is rejecting her, the woman construes everything that the man does as exactly the opposite of what she is clearly asking for and which she wants and needs for her *survival*. It may be difficult at this point in the cycle for the woman to consider anything other than that the man is just refusing to love her, and that this is seriously undermining the relationship.

The man perceives the woman's anxiety at his withdrawal as a wish to entrap him and his usual response is to further increase the distance between them.

The man's fear, which may now rise to the surface, is that the woman may be, or is actually, trying to *absorb* him or take away his autonomy and independence. This fear becomes his motive and justification for becoming even more absent from the arena of the relationship. The man may feel a powerful and urgent desire to escape, to get away completely from such a dangerous situation which, in his perspective, threatens his existence.[18]

When the man thus turns away psychically, the woman experiences a sense of abandonment which is terribly painful.

The woman experiences a literal *tearing away* of the connecting love-energy between herself and her beloved, hence the consuming pain of separation. The anxiety, apprehension, and primary fear of woman finds its consummation in the "fear of abandonment." The fear of abandonment is a universal experience of the feminine aspect, whether it is acknowledged as such or not.

For the woman, the expectation of being abandoned by the man is that deadly harbinger of the *failure of love*, i.e., of all her hopes, dreams, and the very blood of her inner life. It is a justifiable fear because of the man's conviction that, if he gives in to her demands, the vicious circle he is caught in with his partner will threaten his *independent life*. Today, for the woman, the anxiety and threat of the man's turning away is acute. For most women in our culture the primal fear of abandonment has risen to the surface and casts a shadow over almost all love relations. On the emotional/personality level this fear finds expression in a variety of ways, ranging from the avoidance of intimate relationships with men to intense anger and a desire for revenge against all men.

Thus, the man and woman become ensnared in a web of conflicting energies and contradictory interpretations of their actions toward one another, intensifying fear, killing love, and spiraling them out of "sight" of each another.

Thus, the circle goes round and round with increasing intensity. Locked into a reactive cycle the lovers spiral away from each other and the love between them is lost. Unless this vicious circle is cut through, its force will spiral the man and woman toward greater and greater divisiveness, until in the end, the relationship is terminated.

The spiral of separation can take on the aspect of a destiny, an unstoppable force of nature, inevitably resulting in divorce. Given the structure and mood of our individualistic culture, divorce is usually seen as the only solution to the spiral of separation. It is the institutional recognition of the psychic separation and loss of love between a man and a woman.

6.2.2 ARE YOU WITH ME?

Since woman is magnetic and her energy is centripetal, she naturally tends to be inclusive.

When she is physically apart from her beloved, a woman *takes him with her*. Indeed, she cannot help taking him with her because the magnetic dynamics of her energy-body do the job for her.[19] It feels easy and natural for her to include her beloved in her plans and activities. For the woman in love, her beloved inevitably becomes an integral part of, not only her outer life-world, but also the normal flow of her thinking and inner life, in general.

A woman will often assume that a man functions inclusively as she does.

To a woman, *inclusion* at all levels is a part of what love means. Her experience of *how to love* makes it apparent to her that her beloved, if he loves her at all, would include her in his inner and outer life as she does with him. If she does not assume this, she certainly wants, and probably hopes that he will include her in her outer and inner life. Since this is how she experiences love, she believes that the man should now or will eventually have the same experience.

But man's centrifugal energy tends to flow outward into projects and "doings" in a way that does not include his beloved.

Man's energy moves outward and relates to whatever, whomever, wherever he is at each moment. Because of his unilateral, precipitative, "I" mode, and his desire/need to feel independent, a man either does not, or appears to not, include his beloved in his everyday activities or in the flow of his inner life. He does not take her with him into his world of action; indeed, many men still believe that "women don't belong there." In his inner life, a man is usually caught up in self-focused activity and it would seldom occur to him that he might bring a consideration or image of his beloved into that process.

The man and woman can be together in the same room, yet the man will not be including his beloved in whatever he is about. For instance, a man will usually say, "I am doing thus and so," even when he is engaged in a project together with his partner. Also a man often will tell others that, "I am going to such and such a place" or "on vacation," when it is obvious that he is not going by himself. On the other hand, women almost always use the inclusive "we" in the same situations.

A man is seldom aware that his exclusion of his beloved is hurtful to her, indeed, he is just being himself and certainly not intending any harm.

Indeed, a man may well think that "everything is fine" in his relationship. He is oblivious to the fact that he is constantly taking away his love-energy from the one he loves. Thus he is totally unaware of anything being wrong in the relationship.

The man characteristically does not know that his beloved includes him in her very being, or that she sees it as a problem that he does not function as she does.

Since as a rule, the man knows nothing of the *inclusion gap* he may believe that things are smooth in the relationship. He does not perceive or even conceive of the woman's mode of inclusiveness. However, women usually are very much aware of not being included and interpret this as a problem in the relationship.

Since the woman experiences the man's lack of inclusion as a withdrawal of love and caring, the issue of inclusion may arise as the initial step toward the spiral of separation.

As the woman becomes aware that she is excluded much of the time from the man's inner and outer life, she may begin to doubt his love for her. From her perspective, if he does not include her, in much the same way she does him, then he *must* not love her. When a woman feels that her beloved is "not with her," that his love is not flowing out to her, she feels separated, cut off, and perhaps even abandoned by him.

It may come as a shock for a woman to discover that man's centrifugal energy flows oppositely from hers. And, even if a man becomes aware that this situation is a problem to her, it will still take a great effort on his part to overcome his outwardly flowing and fragmenting energy. A man must make a very conscious commitment to give out love, to intentionally direct his love-energy to his beloved, if he is going to include her.

Thus, following her mode of feminine expression, the woman will ask her beloved for more inclusion and consequently, a greater depth of commitment.

The woman needs to ask in order to feel that the circle of love is still alive. She feels that in order for the relationship to grow there has to be progressively more inclusion. If there is not, she begins to believe that her partner is "not coming through" for her. This is such a common experience of women today that it has entered the popular culture as a standard metaphor for "men in relationship." However, when a woman becomes convinced that the man is not coming through for her she may react negatively, becoming grasping and possessive which is a degenerate and injurious state of "love."

The man, however, following his mode, perceives her asking for greater inclusion and commitment as a threat to his independence and autonomy.

A man's primal fear of losing his freedom leads to the manifold stereotypes that depict marriage as a trap for men. Some common phrases and popular negative images which arise from the man's reaction to the woman's inclusive mode would be: "She finally *caught* herself a man" "So, the wife's got you on the ol' ball and chain, has she?," "Well, you better go home and check with your boss before ...," and many other phrases heard at bachelor parties and in locker rooms.

Men often interpret the woman's desire to be included to mean that she wants him to ask for her "permission" to do "his things." He may feel that his partner wants to manage him and his life. Indeed, he might be convinced that his marriage is a prison and that he has already lost his freedom.

Thus the spiral of separation can intensify without either party being aware that the issue is one of including the person you love in all areas of your life.

Including the other is virtually automatic for the woman in love, yet it is quite difficult for the man.

6.2.3 A DIFFERENT DRUMMER

In relation to the dynamics of loving, men and women live in different emotional realms with different temporal rhythms.

Since a woman is centripetal and magnetic, she holds the hurts and unresolved conflicts in the relationship within her. A man characteristically drops an issue and goes on.

Torkom Saraydarian says that "a woman's aura takes at least three days to settle and become calm after being upset. A man's aura settles in two hours."[20]

Men tend to think that women obsess on past hurts and that they unnecessarily burden themselves with the accumulated memories of wounds, but to women this is just the normal way to be.

A friend had just spoken with her partner about conditions that needed attention at her work and, in addition, about some issues arising in their relatively new and intense relationship. With disbelief she told us, "He didn't want to get into it. He thinks I burden myself with these things." And then she added, "But I think I'm just living life."

A woman usually wants to talk, and perhaps receive an expression of love from her beloved in order to get resolution. The man thinks that she is dwelling on the issue, deliberately prolonging the uncomfortable and hurtful situation.

When a woman feels that her efforts to talk and resolve the situation are unsuccessful, she becomes even more hurt, wounded, and rejected. She may either withdraw or get angry, or both. The man often interprets her anger and withdrawal as her way of *punishing* him or getting *revenge* for his unwillingness to engage. This is the furthest thing from the woman's mind. She thinks that she is withdrawing to protect herself and perhaps to nurse her wounds. She may also think that her anger is justified and that she needs to "stand up for herself" and not allow herself to be rebuffed, ignored, or treated that way. The man, however, is sure that she is deliberately trying to get back at him for *something*.

Not understanding how the woman's psyche functions, the man believes that his beloved is **purposely** *keeping a list of all the bad and hurtful things that have ever happened between them.*

The man may even regard the woman's *list* as her carefully collected stash of ammunition being saved for their future conflicts, and he may feel at a disadvantage because he can not remember much of "that stuff."

In relation to this response pattern, Torkom Saraydarian says that, "a woman's husband may say a word and never notice that it hurt her. That hurt can remain ten years in her aura; ten years later, she may turn to her husband and say something nasty because the wound is still there."[21] In this, not infrequent encounter, the man hasn't a clue about what is going on, and in confusion or pain, he will withdraw, setting in motion the spiral of separation. He may feel deeply hurt that his partner "chose" to remember his hurtful act (for which he may feel guilty and truly remorseful), or he may be convinced that she is seeking vengeance for something that she only imagines has happened; he certainly can not remember any of it.[22]

The man finds it painful to talk about difficult issues. The woman finds it painful not to talk about difficult issues. A vicious circle indeed.

6.2.4 THE REAL THING

A man experiences his love as "real" only when it is offered freely.

A man feels that the love he has to offer is not the "real thing" unless he can express it *when he wants to* and *in his own way*. He believes it is necessary to give out his love when and how he decides to, otherwise he loses his freedom, becoming a slave to forces outside himself, and then his love is not "love."

A woman also experiences her beloved's love as "real" only when it is offered freely.

A woman needs to know that her beloved gives her his love because it is his own desire that he do so. A woman in love wants and needs the man to value her presence in his life, to want to be near her, and to cherish her. She needs to know that he is giving her his love because he wants *her*, because he desires *her* and because he sees their love and life together as his great fulfillment. In other words, she needs to believe that he perceives what she is offering him as the culmination of all that he desires in the world of love.

To a woman love must come from her beloved spontaneously, without her asking for it. If she has to ask for it, it is not the "real thing."

A woman does not truly know that her beloved loves her unless he offers her his love spontaneously, as his free choice. Only if it is his free gift to her does she actually identify and interpret his actions as loving. If she has to ask him for love, it appears to her that what he gives her is a token, a shell, which does not contain the genuine living substance of love. Even if he responds smoothly and quickly to her request, she, nonetheless, feels that it is done as an obligation. She sees him as acquiescing or doing his duty, or worse, that he is giving-in and "following orders," none of which is a gift of love.

The man feels that he should not have to be asked. "Asking" is seen by him as coercion and a constraint on his offering of the "real thing."

When the woman "asks" for love, she believes that she is asking for the "real thing," even though she may have a vague suspicion that she will not get it by asking.

When a man is asked to give out love to his partner, or to "do the loving thing," or to do what his beloved wants in the arena of loving, his immediate impulse is to hold back and withdraw. He resists meeting her needs and expectations because he perceives them as her way of defining for him what love is. This violates his sacrosanct freedom to choose to love in his own way and in his own time. The woman, of course, interprets his resistance as a rejection of her, yet she may not know what else to do but to keep on asking. Indeed, at some level most women believe that if they persist, the man will change. She cannot recognize that the man's choice to love in his own way is essential to the continuation of the circle of love. She may even believe that, "he is not in touch with his feelings, and doesn't know how to love!" Consequently, the man feels frustrated, thwarted, and that his love is not accepted.[23]

Both man and woman are seeking the "real thing," but since they experience and understand love in entirely different ways, they seldom recognize the other's efforts as contributing to its increase and enhancement—quite the contrary. [24]

Often we see men acting in ways that they believe are loving, but that women do not recognize as such. For example, many contemporary writers are aware of the misunderstandings that constantly occur because women simply want to talk and be heard, while men believe that they are being asked for a solution to a problem. In his enormously popular book, *Men are from Mars: Women are From Venus,* John Gray writes that, "the most frequently expressed complaint women have about men is that men don't listen. Either a man completely ignores her when she speaks to him, or he listens for a few beats, assesses what is bothering her and then proudly puts on his Mr. Fix-It cap and offers her a solution to make her feel better. He is confused when she doesn't appreciate this gesture of love. No matter how many times she tells him that he's not listening, he doesn't get it and keeps doing the same thing. *She wants empathy, but he thinks she wants solutions.*"[25]

Some social scientists also are aware that the inability of the woman to recognize the man's gift of love is not just individualistic and psychological. They refer to the very potent and active forces in our society which label only certain actions as loving. Francesca Cancian cites a case where psychologists were doing a study in which "they labeled practical help [e.g., Mr. Fix-It] as 'instrumental behavior' and expressing acceptance as 'affectionate behavior,' thereby denying the affectionate aspect of practical help. The wives seemed to be using the same scheme; they thought their marital relations were pleasant that day if their husbands had directed a lot of affectionate behavior to them, regardless of their positive instrumental behavior. ... One husband, when told by the researchers to increase his affectionate behavior towards his wife, decided to wash her car, and was surprised when neither his wife nor the researchers accepted that as an 'affectionate' act"[26]

Another well-known example, is the fact that many men believe that the most direct and convincing way of showing their love is through sex.[27] Men often see sex as "the universal solution," when even a sexually responsive woman *also* wants affirmation and affection, emotionally and verbally.[28] If he is rebuffed, the man feels rejected and the woman may conclude that, "all he wants is sex, not love."

The woman does not recognize the man's offering of love because it does not look like what she expects love to look like.

The feminine experience of love leads the woman to envision, often in vivid detail, the ways that her beloved could communicate his love for her. Her definition of love may include certain gestures of affection, words of appreciation, indications of caring, talking about issues and sharing feelings. Her beloved's offerings, since they originate in the masculine mode of an individual man, are seldom what she expects. Indeed, she may often consider his efforts as inappropriate or as something less than what she would call love—i.e., "too little, too late."

If the woman is not able to accept her beloved's gift as the "real thing," she will probably let him know, in one way or another, that he did not "come through for her" thus expressing her disappointment in him and their relationship.

The man seldom recognizes the woman's efforts toward greater love as she intends them.

We are reminded of a young couple, who had a very harmonious relationship and no great crisis was looming, but the woman, Jean, remarked to us curiously, that every evening when her husband, Lionel, came home from work and she asked him how his day had been he flatly refused to talk about it. Indeed, Lionel's job was very technical and his work environment was quite dysfunctional, even toxic. He told us that when he got home in the evenings all he wanted to do was to go upstairs and rest for a while. At that time in his daily process Lionel was quite unable to view Jean's intentions toward him as anything but an annoyance and an interference in *his* need to recover himself. He was worn out and didn't want to have to repeat, verbally, his whole, difficult day all over again. However, Jean had been persisting until there was an "issue" developing and Lionel was becoming quite peeved at her determined efforts to get him to talk. During our conversation, Jean suddenly realized that she did not really need to hear about Lionel's work the minute he came home, but that she just wanted to make a connection with him after not seeing him all day. It became clear to her that when he came home from his always stressful day it was not the right time to reach out for contact. This insight made it possible for her to make a constructive change that Lionel could, in fact, recognize as an effort toward love.

Jean reported some weeks later that she never again asked Lionel about his day after he came home in the evening. Instead she found other times to show her interest in his job, and other occasions to reach out for meaningful contact.

The woman's attempts to get love from the man often produce exactly the opposite effect. They turn him off and make him want to get away. Men are rather fragile in these matters and their need for self-preservation and the fear of losing their independence can easily take precedence over any other prospect.

When the man believes that he has offered the "real thing" and has been "burned," he withdraws.

If the woman refuses the man's offering, he feels this to be a direct and obvious rejection, and he may believe that he can never be "good enough" for the woman. Men refer to this situation as "getting burned," and when a man believes he has been burned he feels a great reluctance toward making any more offerings, now, or in the foreseeable future.

When the woman feels that she has been asking for the "real thing" and the man withdraws as a result, she feels totally rejected and deeply hurt.

The woman believing that she is making an affirmative movement toward the "real thing" (which may even be an explicitly shared goal), will interpret the man's withdrawal as a direct rejection of her and their commitment. She cannot conceive that her *requests* for love could be interpreted by the man as anything other than what she intends them to be.

This mutual perception of rejection drives the two of them apart, all the while each firmly believing that she or he is doing what is necessary and sufficient for the "real thing," the circle of love, to blossom again between them. This is indeed a "vicious" circle.

Thus, in the perpetual search for true love a man and woman play out the dance of polar differences. The man interprets the woman's actions to seek greater love between them as attempts to control him. And the woman interprets the man's efforts to express his love for her as inappropriate and inadequate.

6.2.5 THE LAMP AND THE FLAME

Metaphorically speaking, the man is the lamp of a relationship and the woman is the flame.

The man's precipitative force constitutes the outer substance and form of the relationship—the lamp. The woman's inner light, her centripetal energy, is the flame in the lamp.[29]

It is the woman's job, as the flame in the lamp, to strive for greater light.

The woman is ever seeking improvement and the evolution of the relationship. She is always seeking upward movement, input of energy and the living "real thing." She tirelessly tries to develop, improve, nurture and deepen the love and intimacy in the relationship. She is looking into the future, desiring to bring about the changes she can envision as the fulfillment of their love.[30]

When the circle of love is active, this striving is a beautiful exchange.

As the flame burns brighter the lamp expands its brilliance. The woman's love creates an atmosphere in their relationship that evokes, enhances and expands the man's life expression. Thus, she becomes an inspiration and stimulus to her beloved to develop his best and most lofty qualities. The man knows that the woman is *in love* with him because she admires and supports what is important to him. Her admiration for him and her love for him make him feel that he can attain his goals and that he is succeeding in his quest. This, in turn, makes it possible for him to to express to her that he loves her and values her presence in his life. She appears ever more beautiful and inspiring to him; she becomes like his muse. In the circle of love the man sees that his own greater fulfillment comes with meeting and exceeding the woman's vision and expectations; as he strives to fulfill her vision for their love, the scope of the lamp expands and its substance becomes more luminous; the woman feels with all her being that her love for her beloved will bring about his transformation.

When the circle of love is broken, and the spiral of separation begins, the woman's tendency is to try to bring into reality the potential that she envisions by advocating for a "better" lamp.

The woman, seeing the potential for greater love, believes that a brighter flame will need a better lamp. Almost as soon as the honeymoon of the relationship is over, she begins to bring her vision of their future into reality by promoting improvements in the relationship and in her beloved. Her burning desire for him to realize his "potential" leads her to want the man to change—to be more like her vision of who she believes he *can* be. She wants him to grow and her great wish is that she will be the influence that changes him.

On an emotional and physical level this desire for a better lamp is translated by her to mean that the man should begin to "clean up his act" and "settle-down" and give her that which she needs and desires.

The man begins to view the woman's expectations for him and their relationship with alarm and fear. He is repelled and feels that he is being forced into a mold of her design.

The man will almost always mistake the woman's intent and meaning when she advocates for changes in the relationship—i.e., a better lamp. He cannot see that his own greater fulfillment and evolution is at stake. He may see that it is not just his paranoid fantasy that she wants to change him—indeed, she really *does* want to change him! The woman's efforts to bring her vision of greater love into reality are interpreted by the man as criticism and as a rejection of who he is right now. He often feels, "She doesn't love the *real* me! No matter what I do, it is never enough."

When confronted with the difficulties that inevitably arise in life or with a greater awareness of the man's limitations and faults, the woman feels disappointed and let down.

She reacts by becoming intolerant of her man's limitations and failings and blames him for not *delivering* and coming through for her.

The man feels put down and criticized. He may feel that her demands are endless and that even his best efforts are unrecognized and unappreciated. For example, he might think, "No matter what I do it is never good enough." Thus he becomes reluctant to keep trying because, "he is bound to be rejected anyway!"

This leads her to become even more disappointed in him and more frustrated, judgmental and intolerant. She does not realize that she is not loving him "as he is." She does not accept him as a complete human being with positive and negative characteristics. She wants him to be *better* than he is. And she can certainly enumerate all his faults and lacks very clearly. She lets him know, in no uncertain terms, how he is letting her down.

This makes him feel even less like giving her anything at all, especially love.

The woman may believe that she still loves him, but, at this point, there is no way that the man can recognize it. In his view, she is not providing the positive, admiring love that enhances his life and makes it possible for him to express love to her.

Back and forth, feeding on itself, the negativity grows.

Even when both the man and the woman are sincerely working towards greater love, the spiral of separation can continue.

When a sense of failure rises up in the man his centrifugal nature tends to externalize his fear and anxiety by blaming others. On the other hand, women usually blame themselves. This often leads to a vicious circle where men blame women and women accept the blame. The woman takes the responsibility on herself and feels, "If I were a better woman, if I were more beautiful, more attractive, more inspiring, then I would be able to make it better for him and he would be happier, more productive and more responsive." A man may say, "I'm just not a very good husband," and want to get out of it, which almost inevitably triggers the woman's fear of abandonment and the death of love. Her fear of abandonment may lead to desperately grasping at the man which increases his fear of being "taken-over," "absorbed," "caught in the spider's web," etc …

If the lamp cannot sustain the flame, he becomes cold and dead.
If the flame consumes the lamp, she also perishes.

6.2.6 YOU JUST DON'T GET IT!

The centripetal structure of the energy-body of the feminine is more attuned and receptive to psychic and spiritual impulses than the masculine.

Usually, women's "auras" are more transparent than men's. Women are more sensitive and more affected by the subtler streams of energy flowing through them. Therefore, women in general, have a greater "affinity for working with energy and vision."[31] Indeed, virtually all spiritual traditions affirm that every woman is a specific locus for the embodiment of divine wisdom, and that on the higher levels She is, e.g. Mary, Holy Mother, Sophia, Shekinah, Isis, Tara, etc., a being "of mystic power ... containing all the mysteries of the heavens and the earth."[32]

Masculine energy, being centrifugal, is more focused on the concrete and physical.

The masculine energy-body acts as more of a barrier to subtle vibrations than the feminine. Since masculine energy has been dominant in nearly all cultures for the last 2,500 years, it is not surprising that mankind is generally focused on the development of concrete knowledge and power only within our physical/material existence.[33]

The woman knows that she has an intuitive grasp of the deeper levels of human functioning. She believes, with some justification, that she "knows" about the "important" things in life.

Because she is more open and receptive to psychic and spiritual impulses, a woman often feels that she *knows* how to strive and work on the spiritual path in a *direct way.*[34]

Her intuitive and empathetic approach is clearly an advantage in the areas of personal relationships with her beloved, children, family, friends and co-workers. Most women feel that they can function better than men in these areas because, in general, they are more sensitive, compassionate, caring and enfolding. Historical and economic events in the last 200 years have reinforced this assessment as men have been drawn further into a cold, competitive world of work from which women, until very recently, were excluded and "women's ways" were anathema.

Yet when the circle of love is broken, negative emotions may arise and set the spiral of separation in motion ...

A woman might realize for the first time that her beloved is not functioning as she does, and to her it seems that he is not doing what is necessary to develop the "important" aspects of life.

Indeed, most women believe that they really know how to do "it" and men do not. Faced with this situation, women say, "men just don't get it." Women believe, and rightfully so, that they are more intuitive when it comes to relationships and interpersonal communication, but this leads them to be intolerant of the way a man characteristically participates in a relationship. Men do not interact in the ways women regard as "the way" to nurture and conduct intimate relationships. Women often believe that if men were more like women, many relationship problems would be solved. They have little insight into how the man does "it" and because of their greater ability in the area of relationships, they become convinced that the man is not doing "it" at all. Women do not see the man's "walk" anymore than men can enter into women's "ways."

A woman may look at her beloved's actions, and sincerely believe that what she sees could not possibly be efforts to be loving or caring for her. This occurs so frequently and on such insignificant levels that, although it goes unnoticed most of the time, it can color the whole atmosphere of the relationship. For instance, in our couples classes we constantly hear complaints from women that the men are not doing the assigned exercises. The women do not see the man engaged in certain systematic and visible practices which they can recognize, so they think that the man is not really doing the Beloved work. They become convinced that the man does not want to develop the relationship and is not truly committed to spiritual growth. The woman's inability to recognize the masculine mode can quickly lead into the spiral of separation.

For his part, the man does not constantly question his own way of functioning.

Men know that they can work with strength in the physical world. They know that they can solve intellectual and concrete problems. They believe that it is their job to act assertively and creatively in worldly situations. They have seen the effectiveness of their way and they have been able to produce great achievements in the world. Indeed, man's ways have dominated humanity's approach to life for, at least, 2,500 years and are responsible for the wonders of our modern technological world.

Arising out of this historical context is the male myth that women's ways are weak and ineffective. And yet in the world of "feeling" they cannot but acknowledge that women "know," in a way that they do not. Thus it may be difficult for a man to justify himself. But men recognize no way to function but their own, and the only other option being presented to them, in the USA today, is to imitate the woman's way. This current predicament has resulted in the, so-called, "men's movement" and the desperate attempt by many men to re-validate traditional male values.

For millennia men have considered themselves as superior to women. Even today, most men retain an inner conviction that they are superior to women, just by virtue of being a man.

As we enter the twenty-first century an overwhelming worldwide majority of men characteristically and stereotypically, still believe that women are weak, overly emotional, irrational, unpredictable, and even dangerous.[35] Feeling superior and critical of women, yet at the same time confused, men will say to each other such things as: "can't live with 'em and can't live without 'em" or "never trust a woman" or, now that women are making their voices heard, the oft expressed, "what do women want?"

Many men still regard their inability to understand women as a badge of manly honor and pride. This attitude sustains the crumbling myth of male superiority, which leads men to stereotype women as overly emotional, inscrutable and irrational. The constant repetition of these labels for women reinforces men's denigration of women and women's ways. Thus men fall into the trap of constantly criticizing women. Even when a man is strongly committed intellectually to women's equality, when he is in an emotionally charged conflict with his partner many remnants of misogyny are likely to surface and he may revert to criticisms of his beloved that are based on atavistic attitudes of female inferiority.

But almost all women have an inner sense that it is really they who are superior because of their greater spiritual and emotional sensibilities.

From time immemorial women have been aware of their connection with the rhythms and cycles of the earth and their greater sensitivity to the spiritual realms. In the last few decades millions have become painfully aware of the degree to which the myth of male superiority and its concomitant worldly dominance has been oppressing them socially, politically, economically and sexually. This has given rise to the much needed "feminist movement" and also to its excesses, including the separative trend of advocating "women's power," of goddess worship groups, and of those who say that women do not need men at all, i.e., they are sufficient unto themselves. This trend exerts a negative influence on women who are on the spiritual path, particularly the path of the Beloved. We have seen a tendency on the part of some strong women in our classes to look down, as if from superior heights, on men, which, of course, prevents them from loving their husbands and doing the Beloved work.

When the woman talks to her beloved about the ways she perceives others and how she knows things, the man hasn't any idea what she is talking about.

To the man, what the woman says about how she perceives, learns and loves, does not make any sense. No matter how perceptive a person he is or how close they are as a couple, the man usually cannot "relate" to the woman's description of her ways.[36] Many couples have told us about this situation and we will give three examples:

A woman that we know very well, and who is in a close and long-standing beloved relationship, has told us that when she walks in a building or room she always senses the particular vibration or quality in the atmosphere of that place. Yet she is constantly surprised when she tells her husband what she feels because he invariably says that he doesn't notice anything in particular and, "doesn't know what she's talking about."

Many couples over the years have told us about the circumstances concerning the cycles of the moon. Women often feel the stimulating intensification of energy before and during the full moon and a waning of energy afterwards. In commenting on this monthly cycle to their husbands, these women usually have found that, even if the man knows intellectually about the rising and falling of Lunar energies, he will respond that he never feels any energy changes during the moon's cycle.

Once we met with a couple who were considering purchasing some buildings and land from us for a group center. At one point, the man wondered where his wife had gone. He looked out of the window and saw her pensively walking around outside. He told us, with obvious admiration and appreciation, "She is probably *feeling it out* "and then he confided, "That's not something that I can do!"

But when a woman talks to other women they understand each other perfectly. This constitutes a powerful justification for saying that, "men just don't get it." A woman may then fall into the trap of intolerance.

When a woman becomes convinced that the man just "doesn't get" what is perfectly natural to her, she may join the growing chorus of modern women who say, "men always let women down," "men cannot give women what they truly need because they are emotionally unavailable and won't talk about their feelings," "men won't talk about or face the 'real' issues in the relationship," and finally, "men's ways are inept, mechanical and harsh—I don't have to take it anymore." Intolerance and misunderstanding of masculine ways often blinds a woman to a man's sincere attempts to admire her and to accept and respect her feminine ways.

In the activities of the world, women still find that they have to act like a man in order to succeed. But they may have an underlying attitude that it would be for the good of all, "if men were just more like women!" On the emotional and personal level, a woman often translates this belief into efforts to convince a man to *try to function in the way that she does.* She would very much like her beloved to become more sensitive, to talk about his feelings, to communicate and share in the way that she has demonstrated to him so many times.[37]

Operating out of different psychic spheres, neither the man nor the woman is able to comprehend how the other functions in the world of love. Therefore, if they follow the path of least resistance, the selfish personality and the negative emotions will rule their lives. Indeed, the spiral of separation will continue as a dominant factor in all human relationships as long as men and women reinforce and maintain an atmosphere of egotistical self-assertion and competition.

6.2.7 THE FEAR THAT HAS NO NAME

When the heightened state of the circle of love is lost and the separative personality resumes dominance of the consciousness, a couple enters into a "between" state.

Once the world of love is experienced or known, when it disappears and we are again in our mundane state, there arises a profound sense of grief at the loss of something wonderful. We are plunged into the "between." How can a man and a woman who have experienced the union of their two hearts in the circle of love ever be really satisfied with that previous illusory state of separate personalities? "One glimpse of the 'eternal ray' kindles the desire for that light 'forevermore.'"[38] Yet, for all their longing for a return to that blissful unity, no amount of will or desire, of itself, can restore the circle of love. Even truly loving couples live most of the time in the "between."

Both man and woman desire fervently to reenter the world of Love, but paradoxically and inexplicably, this desire is accompanied by a profound fear.

Once the experience of a higher state of love is lost and we are in the "between," there is the awakening of a new and heretofore unknown "fear and trembling."[39] No matter how much a couple wants to reenter the circle of love, concomitant with this desire is the loud voice of the personality crying out in fear of annihilation. Sometimes this fear can be so intense that it becomes a sickening terror and panic. Or it can be experienced as an overwhelming sense of dread or impending death. Strangely, the fear increases the more often one enters into, and then loses again, the circle of love. Initially, loving union is like a grace and one is drawn-in unknowingly, but the more one knows and experiences it the greater the personality's apprehension and fear.

This is the personality's fear of the loss of identity as it approaches the threshold of a spiritual Love, which is a higher state of consciousness.

The fear of losing one's individual identity through love of another person is probably at its highest in all of human history. Both men and women fear that an intense love relationship can be a real threat to their independence as self-willed beings. This is not surprising since humanity, as a whole, is at the extreme expression of individualization, the sense of separate selfness. And the current Western view of humans as only bio/physical mechanisms certainly reinforces our sense of unbridgeable aloneness at every level.

Many people experience the fear before the "threshold" when a new step towards more commitment and love is at issue in a relationship. It may be felt intensely by a sensitive person at the time of impending marriage. The fear of loss of individuality is triggered, at least to some degree, in a relationship every time greater love becomes possible. These can be life-changing experiences and they can remain vivid memories for decades:

> One woman told us that in 1957, when she was just 20, she was engaged to soon be married. As a serious, creative and introspective person, she always thought deeply about her life and, since something big was approaching, more so than ever. Just weeks before the wedding, while traveling on the NYC subway to meet her fiance, she was reflecting on the coming changes in her life, and very suddenly she was overcome by a huge wave of dread. She felt as if the shadow of death had descended upon her. Instinctively, inexplicably, she felt as if her death was immanent. As the train whooshed through the dark tunnels the dread deepened and all she could focus on was to somehow get to her fiance. When she arrived at his apartment, she wept and wept for what seemed like a very long time. He, of course, had no idea what was going on, and was just a vague and puzzled presence until her weeping subsided somewhat. Neither of them had any idea of what had happened and it was 30 years later before she had any understanding of the nature of the experience.
>
> Not too many years ago, a couple in a great crisis came to see us. They were in their mid-forties, very successful professionally and had no children. They had been doing the Beloved work for 2 or 3 years and were sincere spiritual seekers. Yet, suddenly one day, totally "out of the blue," the man told his wife that he had to leave—that is, her, their marriage (of 7 years), their life together, their past, their future, all of it! She, of course, went into shock and with some hysteria begged him to, at least, come and consult with us which he agreed to do, but he offered no hope that he would change his mind.
>
> The very next day they came to see us and the man gave us the following explanation: Before they were married he experienced a great, almost overwhelming fear and he had felt it once or twice over the years, but this time it was much stronger. On the day in question, all of a sudden, with no warning that he could discern, he became overcome with a sense of being strangled psychically and he was

terrified. It was like he was being forced, against his will, to be there in his house, with his wife, and in his marriage. He felt that he had to get away or be psychically suffocated!

It turned out that this particular fear and feeling of choking had been discussed with his therapist some years previously, but without any new insights. The four of us together were able to reframe his experience in terms of "fear before the Threshold"—the fear of losing himself by loving. After about three sessions he told us that he had realized that he could make a *free* decision to stay with his wife and to love her. He said that he could not have stayed in the relationship as long as he felt he was being "forced" to be there. He became able to "decide" for himself that the beloved relationship was what *he* really wanted in life. At this point the fear began to dissipate and it eventually left him, and as far as we know "they are living happily ever after!" ...

From a psychological or emotional perspective, this fear is often labeled, "fear of intimacy," and reasons for its disturbing presence in a person are supposedly to be found in the traumatic experiences of childhood. But focusing entirely on a person's life experiences of rejection, loss, etc. misunderstands that the deeper origins of this "fear and trembling" lie in the illusory nature of the personality or ego itself. No amount of conventional *therapy* can dispel this fear in a spiritually sensitive person because its source lies beyond the personality in transcendent realms not recognized by Western science and psychology. We have spoken with many people who have told us that as a result of their therapy they gave up their search for greater love, and instead tried to strengthen their separative ego. This choice of direction contradicts the spiritual quest of the Beloved path. The realm of the circle of love lies beyond the *separative ego*, indeed, it is its transmutation and transcendence.

Both man and woman know this fear, but at this time in history, man's fear is greater, more acute and more public.

It is very difficult today for a man to have a clear understanding of who he is in relationship to women and to the world. Men do not see where they fit in, who they are, or who they must become in the "new order" of things. It is becoming commonplace to say that, "men no longer know what it means to be a man."

Therefore, through his every experience in the world, a man is confronted with a loss of identity, a loss of sense of self. In regard to love relationships, men do not know how to love in a context of equality with women. In regard to the transcendent, spiritual love promised in the beloved path and the requirements and commitments involved in the beloved relationship, the man's fear of loss of self has become a dreaded terror.

Many men in our classes have written about their own experience of this fear. Here is one example:

> The male perspective of the path of the Beloved, is, in my experience full of fear. I know that the "Ego path," the battle for superiority, for justification, for explanation and for the struggle to be right is exhausting, painful and stands in the way of love and acceptance. I am aware of a long standing terror to even contemplate total surrender to love with my beloved. I come close, I want to, I find reasons not to. The fear of being dominated, losing my boundary, of being overwhelmed is like the fear of death. It makes me reluctant to even say, "I love you." I stay in the outside world, I am comfortable there. I am in control most of the time; risks are few.
>
> I resent the unrelenting demands to look at my life, to search for meaning, to grow, to love. "Leave me alone," I say, "don't rock the boat. I am just fine!" …

The "fear before the threshold" is the deep, underlying source of the, so-called inability or reluctance to *commit* that so many men exhibit today. Now that women are coming forward into greater expression, men's fear has escalated into a force of enormous intensity. The 2,500 years of suppressing and denigrating women have not provided men with the attitudes and tools for meeting women on a "level playing field" in the area of work, and much less in the arena of love. Many men have come to believe that it is impossible for them to be a good husband. A history of failed relationships leads them to give up on women—in other words, to give up on love.

The woman's fear takes a form that is different from the man's. It emerges at a different time and in a different way.

A woman knows beyond a shadow of doubt, that there is a great fulfillment in the attainment of the circle of love with her beloved. She may feel no resistance to moving toward this high state. But once she has experienced the blending and merging within the circle of love she has been transported to a different state of being, and she becomes acutely aware of the necessity for her beloved's love-energy to be present in order for her to *be* in that realm. In the circle of love, the expression, "you are necessary for my life" takes on a living reality for both people. Yet, for the woman, to awaken in this wonderful state is also to become subject to the hovering, dreaded potential of what her existence would be like if it were taken away. Thus the terrible apprehension and horror of the the prospect of her beloved's *absence*. Her very life of love is now at stake in the relationship with this man. If he were to leave or turn away from her psychically, she will experience a *psychic chill* akin to an apprehension of death.

We have spoken with several women who have experienced this surge of a chilling psychic fear and identified it for what it is.[40] Their accounts of the way this psychic feeling would come upon them, suddenly, without any visible cause, are similar:

> One good friend, who suspected that the man she loved was about to leave her for another woman, would just be driving her car along when suddenly she would feel a cold chill, "tearing her *self* from herself," and strange images would pass before her mind's eye.

> Another woman would be going about her usual work day and abruptly feel a surging wave of psychic cold pass over her. She would *know* immediately that, some-way or another, her husband had turned his psychic love-energy away from her even though he could be miles away. At these times the urge to contact him was almost irresistible and, if it was at all possible, she would try to phone him. Initially, he was totally unaware that anything happening within him could have caused her behavior. Indeed, he thought that she was probably overly imaginative. It took a few years for him to recognize the validity of what she was experiencing.

Because of the uncertain state of manhood today and men's consequent lack of ability and skills in relationships, woman's fear of abandonment is nearly omnipresent. A woman must constantly face the possibility that the love-energy flowing from her beloved may be taken from her. She will undoubtedly feel pain if her beloved turns the flow of his love-energy into his work, his leisure time, or toward activities which explicitly exclude her. But for a woman who has been in the circle of love with a man, nothing can compare with the total devastation she will feel if her beloved turns the flow of his love towards another woman. It is like a violent tearing away of the living energy of her psychic body. Thus, this is the ultimate betrayal of love.

Woman's fear arises with maximum intensity when love is most alive, most actively pouring out in all directions from the man. Thus we have the paradox that, in order to really fear the loss of love, a woman must unquestionably experience its presence. Living with this dreaded possibility is like an incessant confrontation with death. In the feminine experience of love, the loss of the circle of love is the loss of "life." Those who have never known this love have only vague or theoretical fears of its loss.

Many women today have actually experienced abandonment so often that their increased expectation of it prevents them from entering into meaningful love relationships. A woman's experience, that men do not "come through for her," becomes a generalized apprehension of intimate relationships. Many have had such an extensive history of being "let down" by men, that they describe themselves as having, "given-up on men," i.e. given up on love! This is not entirely a result of the *therapeutic mode* which is dominant in our society; it also stems from a rather realistic appraisal of the current state of man's dilemma. The cumulative impact of a history of disappointments with men can lead a woman to see any romantic interactions as, nothing but, potentially painful.

Both men and women fear the vulnerability that is an essential aspect of a transcendent love and the loss of identification with the selfish ego which is its result.

For both men and women today there is a background state of inchoate fear which expresses itself as a whispering, small voice telling them that they will lose something very valuable if they give themselves in love to another. Nevertheless, there is also some recognition that surrendering to love is essential and unavoidable if they are to enter the transcendent circle again. Herman Rednick expressed this double-bind as follows: "So many are afraid of losing their personality. They think if they lose their precious personality, nothing will be left ... If you want to move up the spiritual path, the personality [ego] must be sacrificed. You might think you are losing life itself, but in reality you are dropping a ton of blocks."[41]

Thus, on an emotional level, both men and women feel a wide range of unwillingness to enter into deep relationships, a lack of desire to develop the love in a relationship or a resistance to seeking and surrendering to the "call" of love when it appears. Many even experience a variety of sexual inhibitions and the distortion of healthy desires.

Women can become vulnerable to overwhelming and paralyzing fears of betrayal and abandonment, and also, to a lesser extent, to male indifference, dominance, and abuse. Men, on the other hand, can become subject to varied extremes of immobilizing fears of the rejection of their love offerings, their ultimate failure as a man, the exposure of their irrational guilt, and the loss of self through absorption into the feminine.

Thus, love, vulnerability, and fear are intertwined. They are co-inherent aspects of the beloved relationship and, if the fear becomes stronger than the desire for love, the relationship may remain in stasis—suspended between the promise and the failure of love—never reaching transcendence. However, if one of the parties persists in seeking the circle of love and the other is too full of fear to continue, the spiral of separation will begin, and quickly reaching terminal velocity, fling the former lovers into separate life-worlds.

• 6.3 LEAPING THE CHASM •

The following Fantasy was written by a woman who had just been introduced to the Way of the Beloved. It was her creative *vision* for the Goals and Commitments exercise described in Section1.2.

A FANTASY

I. The Dream

> I am the goat, you the eagle.
> I leap among the rocks, climbing ever higher to reach the ultimate goal.
> You soar, free, through the skies, unaware of the labor of climbing.
> And I, I do not know the freedom of soaring unfettered.
> Each a half, never understanding the whole—the need to be anchored to the solidity of earth, and the equal need to fly free of any entanglement.
> You, the eagle, tire. You come to rest on my shoulders; for a while I carry you while you gather strength.
> And it is your turn; gently, but strongly, you lift me up.
> Together we soar over the beauty of this God-given earth.
> Again you tire. We reunite with the mountain once more— and the cycle is ever repeated.
> I am the goat, you the eagle.

II. The Awakening

> The dream cannot fuse with the reality!
> The eagle cannot rest for long with the goat; he weeps for the freedom of his skies. The goat's tender flesh bleeds from the weight of the eagle's talons.
> Nor can they dwell in the eagle's world, the goat soon a fetter for the eagle. At the same time the goat longs for the earth's security and the challenge of a new boulder to scale.
> We are so different, my love; you, the eagle and I, the goat.

III. Reality

> Where can we meet, my love, my eagle?
> To rest in the sunwarmed mountain meadow dappled with
> spring flowers.
> To seek refuge from the storm under a craggy outcropping.
> To share the beauties, strengths, joys, gifts of the mountain as
> each perceives—the same mountain through different eyes,
> each striving for the ultimate experience of the mountain's
> peak.
> You are the eagle, I am the goat.
> And the mountain? The mountain is the Way of God.

A *mystery*, in the true sense of the word, is before us. The realization of the meaning and purpose of the existence of the polar opposites has been the goal of spiritual seekers and philosophers in all of humanity's known history. On the one hand, the pull between male and female towards each other is one of the most powerful forces we know; on the other hand, it is painfully apparent that conflict, misunderstanding and the spiral of separation characterize the relations between men and women today. Thus we are faced with an intolerable dilemma: what we want most in life is so elusive, so cloaked in mystery and so seldom attained, that many have totally given up on it. The old blueprints and maps no longer work and most contemporary advice is inadequate or contradictory. For a couple on the path of the beloved, the mystery of polarity is enacted every day in the very fabric of their life, in the world, with a real other person. Their task is to reveal and manifest the purpose of male and female—to leap over the chasm of separation and enter the mystery, the transcendent Circle of Love.

୫୦ ଓଃ

In our extremely secular, technical and psychologized society there are several popular techniques being recommended for increasing the *understanding* of sexual differences and answering the "gender question."

- **Understanding gender differences by separation**

In the search for the understanding of the mystery of sex and gender, some believe that they must find their own identity as a man or woman through the identification and association with others of the same sex. There are numerous men's and women's groups whose goal (aside from certain social and political agendas) is to "raise the consciousness" of gender identity. Some of these groups attempt to unearth and bring back into activity, ancient mythologies and traditional rituals and values.

To be in an unmixed group of one's own gender can bring a sense of kinship and comfort. We can *relax* emotionally and feel that we are affirmed and *understood*. It is a relief not to have the tension of polarity. But unless the express purpose and practices of the group include the development of greater love and harmony, there is a real question of what is being learned that will reduce the friction between the sexes. Indeed, the sense of security found with one's own gender often enhances the feelings of separation from the *other* sex. It may bring greater personality expression and satisfaction, but it does not help us to bridge the gap between man and woman.

• Balancing polarities

Many people believe that since each of us is a *mixture* of the male and female principles, we should try to "balance our nature" and thus become more complete, or whole human beings. It is thought that through the practice of imitating the traits of the opposite sex one can, by a conscious effort, become balanced and integrated. There is a growing movement towards the idea of "androgyny" which is usually thought of in terms of an equal internalization of those culturally defined *traits* which are considered masculine with those which are considered feminine. This approach, of course, denies that gender— the polarity of personhood—goes deeper than psychological dispositions and socially acquired roles. It denies the spiritual origin and purpose of the polarities and of gender.[42]

One of the most common expressions of the "balance the nature" approach is the idea that men should "get in touch with their feelings" and be able to talk about them in the way that women do. Another expression is the idea that women who enter the workplace must imitate male aggressiveness, male dress, male insensitivity, etc., in order to succeed in the "man's world."

However useful these attempts may seem, they almost never bring about a movement toward greater understanding between men and women.[43] In fact, the denial of a deeper meaning to gender differences and the attempt to balance male and female psychological traits leads to a confusion and distortion of gender differences, and often we see a sad caricature of a man or a woman. The attempt to mechanically "balance" lists of current gender qualities just diverts us from the heart of our spiritual identity. It does not lead to synthesis, complementarity, conspiration, interdependence, or even the harmonious interaction of men and women. The heart of love is missing.

- **Scientific rationalism**

Many people today believe that the fundamental conflict between man and woman is the result of a lack of a clear, "scientific" understanding of each other. This comes, perhaps, from the false assumption, which is deep-seated in our very literal and rationalistic culture, that to know and to understand something is to act and change our behavior because of that new knowledge. It is a wide-spread erroneous belief that people will be motivated to change their patterns of behavior if they know what the *true* nature of a situation is.[44]

Trying to understand one another through discussion and sharing is, no doubt, a step in the right direction. There is a growing trend toward a true dialogue between men and women about their differences. For instance, Cornelius Murphy says that his book, *Beyond Feminism: Toward a Dialogue on Difference*, is a reflection on the fact that,

> the movement toward emancipation has now reached a point where collaboration, rather than antagonism, must characterize the relations between the sexes. There is a growing recognition within the women's movement that further progress toward a new humanism requires the development of an equality that affirms the differences, as well as the similarities, between men and women.[45]

The investigations into gender differences by the popular psychologist, John Gray, and the linguist, Deborah Tannen, are also very insightful and helpful to their many readers. Deborah Tannen gives a positive prognosis for these attempts at the end of her popular book, *You Just Don't Understand* :

> If you understand gender differences in what I call conversational style, you may not be able to prevent disagreements from arising, but you stand a better chance of preventing them from spiraling out of control. When sincere attempts to communicate end in stalemate, and a beloved partner seems irrational and obstinate, the different languages men and women speak can shake the foundation of our lives. Understanding the other's ways of talking is a giant leap across

the communication gap between women and men, and a giant step toward opening lines of communication.[46]

Honest and genuine "dialogue" may, in general, have the effect of neutralizing negativity, but it does not necessarily lead to greater love, therefore its effect is usually temporary. Since the experience of the life-world is different for men and for women, neither is able, in fact, to comprehend the true nature of the other's way of perceiving and expressing love.[47] This is, of course, especially true in intimate relationships—that area of life which is, for the vast majority of people of both sexes, what they want most.[48] And it is, paradoxically, where they are most vulnerable and subject to the deepest hurts. Men and women frequently find it impossible to "identify" with the "other" and therefore they feel alien and estranged. In truth, each *cannot* know the nature of the other's path. Indeed, this is the great mystery of the polar opposites and sex.

It is interesting to see that the closer two people become, the more they are aware of the difference in their paths and the chasm between each of them and the "other." This phenomenon is illustrated by a friend in a long-term, very close beloved relationship, who wrote:

> I imagine that my journey through life is like walking on a path. ...
> I know I have met my true beloved and walk together with him. I
> know that I want to be with him forever and love him forever ... But
> there is something I do not understand. His path, which I believe
> and feel to be one with mine, must take him upon a trail I cannot
> see. I hear him describe it as he walks along, but I cannot walk with
> him. My one true love, I feel him close to me and I can not see him.

Thus, "understanding" or intellectual analysis of the polar opposite is not a true resolution of separateness. "Understanding" does not require love of that which we are seeking to understand, often quite the contrary. It does not, of itself, bring forth greater love between a man and a woman. In the past 100 years psychology and the social sciences have collected enormous amounts of information about us, yet men and women seem to occupy increasingly separate "planets."

೫ ೫

WHAT WE TRULY WANT AND WHAT WE ARE TRULY LOOKING FOR ON THE PATH OF THE BELOVED, CAN ONLY BE ACHIEVED BY A *LEAP OF LOVE*.

The following composition was inspired by the Fantasy at the beginning of this Section. It was written by another woman, four years later:

IV. At-One-Ment

You hover near the threshold of my Heart's Door. Stilled
momentarily in your flight. Your strong wings eager to soar
the skies of my Inner Space, the Beloved Heavens of my
Soul.
Your keen eyes searching, searching.
You, the eagle.
I, the goat, await your moment of decision with infinite
patience, with ultimate care, with the Sacred Fullness of
Love.
In quiet strength I watch you from the sweet grass near my
Heart's Door. Poised. Ever awake. In Love, I wait.

The feathers on your breast part as you dive, true and
straight to the mark.
Never a being as fleet as I in that moment. Aligned suddenly
and perfectly with your Heart's   Open Door as you soar
through my own.
Never a sun as brilliant as the Light flooding our senses.

And what did we expect? To find the inner-scapes of each
other's Being?
To discover some aspect of our Selves sacrificed in the choice
of [commitment]?

Lo, I passed through your Heart's Door and you through
mine, only for each of us to find our full Selves   residing
therein, unchanged in our Beingness.
The realization of At-One-Ment. The Knowledge that our
Essence is One.

What we truly want and what we are truly looking for on the path of the beloved, can only be achieved by a "leap of love;" a leap over a chasm which may seem like an unfathomable, threatening abyss; a leap into a totally unknown area with no guarantees of any reward at all, not even of safe passage; a leap based only upon a trust that the power of love will carry us to the higher levels that we seek; a leap which can take place only through the faith that if we seek love only and first, above all other considerations, we will become clothed with its substance and protected by its power. This love is not a metaphor, but is a practical and available energy which will stream through us, as from an infinite source, as long as we pour it out to our beloved.

If we seek love first, we are walking in the Way of the Beloved. On the path of the beloved, the task for man and woman is to love that which cannot be understood, i.e., the truly "other," the polar opposite. Each must love the other person *without* understanding or being understood by the other. One must love without the conventional supports of "worldly logic." One must leap "beyond" "common-sense," indeed beyond anything that is "known," into and over the chasm of separation. Only an intense spiritual love and devotion toward that mysteriously unknown and seemingly unknowable polar opposite embodied in the tangible person of our beloved, can carry us across the chasm of separation.

To leap over the chasm of separation means that each person must overcome the numerous objections, resistances and fears that rise up from the ego/personality to prevent the expression of greater love. Each one must overcome the blocks in the personality toward unselfish loving without any support but faith in the power of love.

Thus our love must seek to do what the other person will recognize as being loving and not what we ourselves think or feel is the loving thing to do. To us the action may well seem *unreasonable* and we may not understand how it could possibly be construed as *loving*, and indeed, we may not be able to fathom the meaning of what we are doing, and we may not even like what we must do. Our love must have the purity and power to leap beyond *common-sense* into and over the dark abyss of interminable interpersonal conflict and to penetrate the mysteries of transcending personal self-centeredness. Transcending the ego is the greatest challenge facing the beloved couple (indeed everyone, for all of humanity is facing this transformation!), and holds the promise of the greatest fulfillment of spiritual Love.

The Circle of Love is a goal in the beloved relationship, an achievement, and not at all an automatic daily reality. The Way of the Beloved teaches that "love is the key," love is the way to dissolve every problem. For example, in response to those who thought they had to "balance the nature" through immitating the polar opposite, our Teacher wrote:

> There has been some misunderstanding about developing the feminine and masculine nature within. The woman does not try to analyze the qualities of the male aspect, nor does the man try for the feminine aspect. This development is more on an unconscious level. The conscious effort you make is to concentrate on … [one's spiritual ideal] with love. Love is the conscious force flowing through. Love is wisdom, and as this principle pours into your system, the qualities you need will be given to you.[49]

If for the sake of love one can bypass the demands of the personality, there are ways for a woman and a man to create conditions that move their love into a more spiritual domain and make the rejoining of the circle of love much more possible. Since women and men experience love so differently, the concepts, "to intensify love for each other" and "make a leap of love over the chasm of separation," mean one thing for women, and something entirely different for men. Therefore each requires his or her own meditation practice.

ℝ℞

Seeking to restore union in love, a man reaches out with a stream of force, willingly and freely pouring out love to his beloved. The woman, on the other hand, aspires upward to embody and manifest the light essence that both are seeking. She reaches deeply within the heart and from a state of poised and loving receptivity, magnetically calls the man to union. Thus, the circle is joined again, when each becomes an *active* principle, charged with the living current of love. Both are actively loving, yet from opposite states of being.

The most direct way for a beloved couple to affirm and recreate the circle of love, is for each person to focus his or her whole being toward the beloved through the use of a mantra. This practice can be done at any time and anywhere, when together and when apart, day and night, while working, resting or playing. Seeing the image of the beloved and feeling his or her presence, with love, has the same effect as repeating the words of the mantra. The mantra and the image work together.

- **For the man**

    Repeat the words—"I reach out to my beloved with love" or, "I pour out love without ceasing to my beloved."

- **For the woman**

    Repeat the words—"I am poised, loving and receptive to my beloved" or, "I am in a state of love, receptive to my beloved."

These mantras are not designating *roles*. They are concepts which impress our consciousness with a certain quality of vibration if they are practiced with sincerity and spiritual aspiration (for the usage of a mantra refer to the Introduction to Part Three). They can call forth a quality of love that helps us to leap over the chasm that separates us from our polar opposite. They evoke from us an energy that can bridge the gap of not being able to "see" and comprehend the polar opposite. Thus they stimulate us to awaken from our illusion of separation. Fifteen or twenty years ago, when we introduced these concepts, we were concerned that "modern" men and "liberated" women would react negatively because they would associate these mantras with "sexism." However, the opposite response occured. The women were virtually unanimous in their enthusiasm. They told us in a variety of different words, "This mantram was wonderful! When I would use it, I'd begin to feel that, at last, I could really be *myself*." We often suggest that people experiment to see what effects the mantras have, and then decide what to do.

In order to reap any benefits from the use of a mantra, one must use it constantly and with sincerity. Thus both persons intensify their focus on loving each other as expressions of opposite polarities. And in aspiring to enter the transcendent circle of love, they become willing to leap over the chasm of separation.

ॐ

• MAN'S WORK •

The task for the man in the Yoga of the beloved is to pour out the love energy to his beloved continuously. His work is to become a steady beacon of love for her, thus continuously reestablishing the heightened state of the circle of love. Through his work to reach out to her, he will carry her with him everywhere he goes and in everything he does. His attempts to do this are a real struggle, for when he makes the effort to do the work, he is confronted with the potent and unconscious barriers in his personality that rise up to stop him. Each and every time he tries he must call forth the power of the will-to-love to overcome the blocks and leap over the chasm of separation.

WHAT MAN MUST OVERCOME

Unawareness & Emotional Withdrawal
Perhaps the most common obstruction to the man's work is that he is unaware of (and very surprised when he finds out about) what is needed to keep the love in his relationship alive. The idea that he could pour out love continuously is, at first, inconceivable to him, and that it is *required* of him, makes him very uncomfortable. He may well be engrossed by the pressures of his work and distracted by his other activities in the world and his own busy mental processes. Thus he thinks he is "too occupied" to maintain a focus on loving his beloved. This may manifest as resistance and protest against the very legitimacy, importance, or necessity of giving love, at all. Very often we see men manifest an attitude of vagueness and inattention to the needs and work of loving relations. They have become mentally and emotionally numb to the demands of a love-relationship and to their partner.

Since the man's basic mode of defense is to turn away when difficulties arise in his intimate relationship, this becomes manifest at all levels of his being. A man may retreat, not only physically, but also by dulling or numbing his emotional, mental and even sensory responses to his experiences. John Gray has popularized the metaphor of a "man's cave" to illustrate this type of withdrawal.[50] The cave is the place where a man retreats from his love relationship when he feels a pressure or a threat to his sense of individuality and personal freedom.

However, even as they depart into their caves, many men would agree with Thomas Merton when he says that "To be thus the prisoner of one's own selfhood is, in fact, to be in hell."[51] And even though they may know that withdrawing into the cave of unawareness is a state of isolation based upon a false conception of self and of true individuality, understanding of a phenomenon so deeply rooted in the very ontology of the personality is never enough to overcome it.

Although to get away is the *natural tendency* of the male centrifugal energy, a man who walks the path of the beloved has made a commitment to intentionally focus his mind and heart on loving his beloved. A man on the beloved path uses the mantra so that he will be *present* to his beloved even when he is diverted by his lack of focus or the desire to be in the cave. His commitment includes that he take on the responsibility of increasing his awareness of what it means to pour out love to his beloved continously. He overcomes his unwillingness by drawing upon the power of his "will to love."[52] Thus he can overcome the tendency to space-out or turn away and instead, purposefully make a "leap of love." Through the use of the mantra, he overcomes his predisposition to withdraw and deliberately turns his attention towards his beloved. This act of will is motivated and inspired by a man's deepest spiritual strivings. He leaps over the chasm of separation through the will to love and the practice of the mantra.

Fear

The greatest barrier for men is fear—"the Fear that has no name."[53] As we have described it in several places, this fear takes many forms: the fear before the spiritual threshold; the fear of ego-death; the fear of losing the sense of the individual self; the fear of being *absorbed* or *gobbled-up*, the fear of losing personal freedom and potency; the un-named fear which stops men from *giving* themselves and *surrendering* to love of the beloved.

Despite vigorous denials, this is a prevalent and *real* terror for most men today, especially those who have a spiritual yearning. Many will repress or suppress their fear and attempt to go on with life as they know it. Most will try to protect themselves from the disintegration that they fear love represents. Thomas Merton described it well when he wrote, "Love demands a complete inner transformation ... and this involves a kind of death of our own being, our own self. No matter how hard we try, we resist this death ..."[54] The man's almost instinctive impulse to protect himself means that he has some sense of what is at stake in loving another, but he has, as yet, been unable to act in a more enlightened and loving manner.

A man cannot rise into the circle of love unless this fear is recognized, confronted and overcome—not just once, but many times. A man must integrate, into his psyche, the concepts that, not only is the path of love truly in one's own higher self-interest, but in addition, love is a power that is greater than any fear.

In the way of the beloved a man makes a commitment to choose love *first* above all his reservations and resistances, including his fear and terror. As the intensity of his beloved relationship builds and a man gathers the courage to *leap* into greater love, he may feel that he is putting his whole life on the line. At that moment he may feel that he is risking everything he is, everything he has and everything he knows. He cannot even tell if there really is another side to the yawning chasm between himself and his beloved or whether or not he might plummet into the dark abyss to total annihilation. It takes enormous courage not to turn away when faced with this fear. When a man actually does face the fear and move through it to pour out love, it is very likely to be a life changing experience. Indeed, he may actually experience the intense light of ecstasy and transcendence. But true freedom has not yet been attained, for, often to his great dismay, this passage has to be made many times, over and over, until the man dwells continuously in the light of transcendent love.

Thus a man must develop the inner strength and unshakable faith in the power of love to leap through the fear over the chasm of separation. His spiritual strength develops and grows every time he turns to the mantra and pours out love to his beloved. Using the mantra is the most effective way to transform the primal fear of the beloved *other*. The use of the mantra along with a stream of love sent out from the heart becomes an offering to the spiritual treasure that is the goal of the beloved path: to dwell in the light of the transcendent circle of love.

After a few years of following the path of the beloved, we ask our students to meditate on the question, "What am I willing to offer for the Spiritual Treasure of the Beloved"? Here is one man's response:

> I am willing to offer my little self, to surrender that part of me that insists on thinking I am a separate being that can go my "own" way.
> I am willing to offer up the fear that plagues me at every turn as I try to do this.
> I am willing to offer all the love I can cut loose, to give it to you as fast as I am able, trying to realize that there is always more and more.

I am willing to surrender the anger that I use to protect my ego and
to explore the fear and pain that lie beneath it.
I am willing. Yes, I am willing.
I am willing to offer my ego's need for ego-stroking, ego-gratification.
My desire for the fullness of love is greater.
I know that my ego is often <u>not</u> willing, so I am willing to offer it,
too, in exchange for Love.

Pride

To become a steady beacon of love to his beloved, a man must act against
what has been variously called, "male vanity," or "a man's pride." This is the
personality's identification with its own idea of being a *man*. It is composed of
largely unconscious, culturally defined characteristics and patterns of action
that men consider to be "manly" and which define manhood as opposed to
womanhood. Those characteristics which men prize and with which they
identify their *maleness* vary from culture to culture and have been changing
rapidly in the modern western world.[55]

Many men in the U.S. today still cling to the ideal of the "Rugged
Individualist"[56] as the only true way to be a real man. This idea, outdated
by100 years, is used by them to intellectually ratify their acting out of an
irrational fear-of-loving and as a rationalization for characterizing love as self-
annihilation. It certainly is a protection from having to admit to vulnerability
or fearfulness of any kind, which is considered *unmanly*.

In simply desiring to be on the path of the beloved, a man works against
the dominant societal thought-forms of separation and isolation. When he
begins the path of loving his beloved he discovers that to choose to isolate
himself from her is, as Thomas Merton says, to choose "to be in hell."
Intensifying his love-focus leads him to the realization that the isolation of
one's cave of individuality provides only an illusion of independence, and
that the love of his beloved is in his own true *self-interest*, for it is a door to
true freedom. He discovers that giving love—no matter what, to his beloved
counterpart is a direct way to enter the world of light and authentic being.[57]

It is not easy to overcome the precious image that a true man is one who
"stands alone, against all assaults to his independence." But through the will-
to-love it can be done. Here is an example of a paper written by a man who
has spent most of his working life in the outdoors, a self-professed *rugged
individualist*, who has recently learned of the circle of love through doing the
Yoga of the path of the beloved:

As our life becomes more centered on each other, the security of our togetherness becomes more important than anything else; the sanctity of our relationship has priority. Despite outside pressures and impacts, I can think of nothing that should come between us and weaken our union, whether friends, family or famine. I have come to believe completely in the primacy of our love and rely upon it. At the same time, while I may not better understand others and my relationship with them, I have become more willing to accept others for who they are.

I have long aspired to rugged individualism as my guide and strength. Loving Gina has made that aspiration at the same time both less important and more achievable. In being secure in my love for her, and in being loved by her, I don't have to prove my individualism, I have it.

Negativity toward the feminine aspect

A more subtle barrier that arises when a man is threatened in a relationship, is the ancient complex of attitudes that characterizes the whole of womanhood in a negative mode. Misogyny runs so deep in the male psyche that, even today, many men still believe that there is substance to the belief that the essential nature of womanhood is an irrationality and emotionality which inevitably leads to their necessary dependency on men.[58] Even in *enlightened* men, this fallacy can prevail on an unconscious level, and when a man is caught in the spiral of separation, it may emerge in subtle forms. Some men, trapped in a kind of a self-serving male perspective of inherent superiority, may not acknowledge the value and necessity of sustaining the love-flow towards their beloved. Some will act as though they must never *back-down* or retreat in an argument, because they are superior and will someday win the battle. Others find that, when the pressure is on, instead of seeing the equal partner and companion they recognize as their beloved, they see a representative of *womanhood*, who is inferior and dependent, yet domineering and irrational. Thus they shift responsibility for difficulties in the relationship from themselves to what they believe are manifestations of inherent feminine inferiority and negativity in their beloved.

A man on the path of the beloved, has already decided that love is in his own true self-interest; thus he will recognize, identify and consciously change his deep-seated negative attitudes and beliefs about women. For example, through the will-to-love he can leap from interpreting her needs and desires as

177

negative, to intentionally seeing them as legitimate. Through the will-to-love, he realizes that he perceives his beloved's needs (and even her demands) as negative only when he resists fulfilling them. Because of his intense desire to reestablish the circle of love, he knows that he must overcome his resistance—whatever form it takes—and through love, strive to meet and even surpass her expectations and desires. He makes the leap of love without comprehending or understanding the validity of her attitudes, actions and needs. He chooses to use the mantra and pour out love, *anyway*. Through the Yoga of the beloved, he affirms the truth of Torkom Saraydarian's statement that, "Woman is a challenger ... she evokes from man the best that he is. Men must be grateful to women who do this."[59]

Saraydarian also says, "A man must always direct attention to the jewel inside the woman, never to her wrong behavior or her weaknesses. Whatever is concentrated upon will increase."[60] Therefore, whatever he sees in her, he puts aside his [distorted] view and makes the *leap of love*, knowing that whatever he focuses on will expand and grow in spirit. Through the will-to-love, instead of belittling his beloved and *putting her down*, he can love the mystery that she embodies. He realizes that when he sees the beauty and love within her feminine nature—and truly appreciates it, it can manifest outwardly. Thus, by seeking in her for inspiration, encouragement, solace, comfort, and the highest earthly manifestation of spiritual wisdom, he can enter the great mystery of the feminine through the being of his beloved. He embraces the mystery of the feminine as the door to his highest fulfillment.

The Tendency Toward Conditional Love

To pour out love continuously means that a man must give out love to his beloved even when he is met with negativity or rejection. A man is usually so devastated by rejection that it takes a very strong commitment for him not to withdraw when he encounters it. But if a man's love has the condition of needing an immediate, positive response, it will surely be very limited. The woman's refusal of his gift of love is a *test* for the man—it makes it harder for him to persist in loving and thus requires that his love become greater than it has ever been before. In the Yoga of the beloved the man uses his focused will to pour out love without condition, no matter what the response or lack thereof. Whether his beloved receives or rejects his overtures, whether she reacts negatively or retreats, it does not stop his efforts to reestablish the circle of love.

Not only is this process painful and difficult to do, conventional attitudes look down upon such a relationship and consider it to be co-dependent. But we have seen otherwise, indeed sometimes the man will be tested beyond all reasonableness and expectation:

A mid-thirties man and woman met in graduate school and the *chemistry* was so strong that they *knew* that they were destined to be together, despite many failed and contentious past relationships on the part of them both. They could hardly believe that they had, at last, found the *destined* love for which they had been seeking. Within a week they were living together. Three months later the woman, Sylvie, somehow found out that the man had not yet told his former girl- friend about her and was still meeting with her frequently. She was devastated. She was totally unable to make any sense out of his infidelity and felt betrayed at the deepest level of her being. Even though Seth immediately ended his relationship with his former girl friend, and didn't see or speak to her afterwards, Sylvie felt that she could never trust him again, ever. She had been betrayed in former relationships and could not subdue or reconcile the fear that Seth would do it again.

One might expect that that was the end of the story and the end of a promising relationship, but that was not the case! Sylvie did not move out, although she frequently threatened to, but she was unable to get over her fear and anger and regain the love and closeness that she and Seth had had before. She was confirmed in her resistance to his loving, she would not sleep with him, and rejected all of his invitations to be close emotionally. One would think that Seth would clear out pretty quickly when faced with Sylvie's continuous rejection, but he did not! Instead, he decided that he had committed a grievous, albeit foolish, error, but he still believed that Sylvie was *the one* regardless of how she was now tearing him apart on a daily basis. He apparently took the teaching seriously that his job was to pour out love regardless of the response of his beloved. Being strong-willed and somewhat taciturn, Seth quietly loved Sylvie no matter what. However, Sylvie's resistance did not abate. Indeed despite Seth's best efforts to be loving, nothing changed. After a couple of years everyone, including us, began to think that it was a hopeless situation. But Seth persisted. Even though his friends said that he was "nuts" or "codependent," he continued faithfully to pour out love as best he could, and he held on to the belief that eventually

Sylvie would forgive and trust him again. The years painfully passed by without any change in Sylvie's attitude. But she did stay with him and he with her. It really seemed ridiculous to everyone except Seth.

Miraculously, after about 5 years of no encouragement or signs of movement on Sylvie's part, one day she began to relent and to respond to Seth's overtures of love. She told him how thankful she was to him for staying with her all those difficult years and once again affirmed their "destiny" together. She said that she believed now in his love for her and they were married within 4 months. Now, 6 years later, they have continued to be a very close and loving couple.

This is indeed an example of the power of a man's will-to-love to overcome seemingly unsurmountable obstacles to find mutual love with his beloved.

As a man becomes willing to make the leap of love no matter what the response, he pours out the stream of love-energy to his beloved *without her having to ask for it*. This takes effort on his part, but it is the greatest gift that he can give to her. When beaming out love becomes the tone of his life, he will receive, spontaneously, as a gratuitous reward from his beloved, an incalculable blessing, that only selfless love can elicit from the Feminine. As Torkom Saraydarian says, "A woman is a man's greatest asset in this world if the relationship is correct … A woman will encourage her husband, she will sacrifice for him, and at the most critical times in a man's life, she will be the one to reach out, grasp his hand and pull him up. She will give him spiritual power and everything that he needs."[61] Thus through the sustained practice of pouring out love, a man becomes able to leap the chasm of separation and rise into the transcendent circle of love. This is man's true power in the relationship with his beloved and it is to this that a woman responds with the offering of all her treasures.

ಶಿ ಚ

• WOMAN'S WORK •

The woman's work on the path of the beloved is to remain poised in a state of intense love and receptivity, reaching upwards to the spirit for her sustenance so that she can manifest to her beloved the light of the transcendent circle. Her work is to be poised in her center, ready to receive him into her heart by responding to any and every offering of his love. Her work is to meet the condition given to her by her beloved—no matter what it is, with the power of love.

Her attempts to do this are a struggle for, at every turn, she is confronted with the barriers in her personality that rise in front of her, blocking her movement. For her to cross the chasm of separation she must leap upwards into a state of love. Remaining therein and radiating that love, she will see the chasm dissolve.

WHAT WOMAN MUST OVERCOME

Disappointment, frustration and anger
The greatest barrier that a woman of today must overcome is the tendency to allow her disappointment in her beloved to eclipse her love for him and place a cloud over their relationship. When she sees that her hopes and expectations are not being fulfilled, she becomes frustrated and angry that he isn't coming through for her.[62] She may be overloaded at work and/or at home and he is not there to help. And when he is there, he is not *present* much of the time. She becomes disturbed, sometimes distraught, because she feels that she is not receiving what she needs physically, emotionally and spiritually.

When a couple is committed to the path of the beloved, the woman discovers that if she wants the circle of love to be active, she will have to learn to love even while she is not receiving what she needs from her beloved. This does not mean that she passively accepts his withdrawal or that she becomes submissive and allows herself to be used or dominated. It does mean that she makes a conscious decision to reach for a higher love, based on their committed relationship and her radical faith[63] in the truth and effectiveness of the Beloved Yoga. Although to some, this arrangement may appear as co-dependent, in actuality it is not. The woman has made an independent and conscious choice based on the spiritual teaching of the primacy of love. It means she is striving to embody and make manifest in her relationship, the truth that love is a cloak of power!

181

Her work is to *leap* into a state of love no matter what condition she meets in her relationship, no matter what her beloved says, thinks or does. She leaps by consistently using the mantra, "I am poised, loving and receptive to my beloved," with the power of the heart. She will leap into love if her efforts are genuine, constant and intensely focused on breaking through to a higher level of love.

The leap into love raises her into a region wherein her negative emotions are suspended; she is able to bear the pain of her beloved's absence or lack of sensitivity and pour out love, regardless. From this state, she can recognize those times when she should not *ask* her beloved for contact—and then, in the pain of living *without*, pour out love to him. From this place of higher love, she can find a way to bear the painful experience without frustration, disappointment, resentment or anger.

To leap into the region of love that dissolves the chasm of separation, a woman must use the mantra all the time. In times of stress she can, in silent meditation, repeat the mantram, "I look to … (my higher power, our commitment, the Spiritual Ideal, my higher self, the power of love) to sustain me even though I don't receive what I need from my beloved." She can also focus on the concept that the power of Love is greater and stronger than her own weakness, vulnerability and feelings of deprivation. And she can make use of the Transforming Negativity exercise along with the concept: "I will not be angry, frustrated, & demanding. Through faith, I love and thus I am receptive to my beloved."

Fear

In the beloved relationship, a woman who has known the intensity and joy of the transcendent circle of love, also knows how vulnerable she becomes when she gives herself completely to unreserved, unqualified, sacrificial love for her beloved. Along with this knowledge can come a feeling of apprehension that she will be *lost* or *shattered* if she gives herself fully to that love. This feeling may even increase, along with a euphoric sense of anticipation, the closer that she and her beloved come to transcendence. This is the woman's "fear before the threshold." In women today, this fear, almost always, dissolves with an offering, even a simple gesture, of deep love from her beloved. If love is present in a situation, a woman will *melt* as the possibility of the *circle* is offered to her.

But the most prevalent and intense fear that women today experience when they love a man deeply, is the fear of abandonment—the fear of the loss of their circle of love because the man will turn his love energy away from her and give it to some other activity or some other person. As we have said, this fear can be extraordinarily painful, and so intense that it produces a paralyzing anguish. If she is overcome with the fear, she may desperately grasp at her beloved to try and keep him close to her. And as long as fear is dominant in her consciousness, it can lead her into jealousy and possessiveness which, as she may well know, always stifle love.

A woman, who is on the path of the beloved, has to be willing to leap into love regardless of the fear and the very real risk that is involved. She may feel that she is on the brink of imminent annihilation, but she must have the courage and the power of the heart to choose the primacy of love over her fear. She must have the courage to make the leap whether or not her beloved can fulfill his promise of constancy. She must dare to leap into the realm of selfless love with or *without* him, and remain there, no matter what. Indeed, she can not wait around for him to move before she enters into a loving state. And she must be willing to dwell in the realm of love, seemingly alone, and to pour out love to her beloved no matter what his response is. She must enter into a state of love while facing the possibility that she will be lost and shattered if he does not meet her there. She realizes that she must trust completely in the power of love, and not in the conduct of her beloved, to sustain and protect her. Most women are mightily capable of maintaining this trust because they intuitively know the truth that there is no fear as great as the power of love.

On the spiritual path, working to overcome the fear of abandonment, whether it is active or dormant, is a very intense practice. It is a seemingly impossible task to face the fear of abandonment without criticizing or condemning and without putting enormous pressure on the man, relying solely on faith in love and the sustenance of the spirit. But this is the woman's work: through her intense dedication, she develops the spiritual qualities of courage, selfless love (compassion) and divine patience. This is what she has been striving for all along.

Pride

Even with a strong desire to remain poised in a state of love and receptivity, a woman often meets the resistance of pride. Woman's pride may be expressed as *intolerance* of the way her beloved approaches and acts in personal relationships, in general, and especially, the way he is with her. Her pride also takes the form of *rigidity*. A woman will hold on to her ideas of how her relationship should look and feel and take it for granted that her way of being in a relationship is the right way—perhaps the only way for a relationship to be a *good one*. She knows she is *right*, and will not be shaken from her view.

A woman, who is doing the work (for example, using her mantra day and night), gradually becomes aware of what her unconscious assumptions about love have been, and she may see how they have affected her relationship. This realization expands her view. She examines the ways that she imposes her own ideas of what love should look like, on to her beloved, and how she has pressured him, verbally and otherwise, to do "it" like she does—i.e., the right way. She becomes aware of how she has been hinting or even blatantly suggesting that he should be relating to her the way she does toward him. Indeed, she realizes that she has only recognized his ways *as loving* if they match her own various preconceptions and expectations.

Her most important realization, however, is that only with *eyes of love* will she be able to overcome the prideful assumption that love from her beloved must look a certain way in order for her to recognize it. She must put her viewpoints and expectations aside and make a leap of love, in spite of being convinced that she knows what is right. She must make a leap based upon nothing but her faith in the encompassing wisdom of a higher love. She must make the movement into love without seeing or knowing what the outcome will be. Only when she enters a state of love will she be able to counteract her attachment to her viewpoints as the right ones, for only from a state of love will she see and hear and recognize her beloved's offerings of love as **he** intends them.

The leap into a state of love makes it possible for her to recognize and receive her beloved's offerings, no matter how they have appeared to her in the past. Instead of expressing to him, "love as I love," she feels grateful for his gift and can accept it as love. As she uses the "woman's mantra," she becomes poised in readiness, but not asking or needing. The power of the mantra helps her to neither expect, nor ask, nor desire anything from the man. It helps her to love him freely, wanting for him only what is in *his* highest good and in *his* own terms. And as she continues the practice of the Beloved Yoga, she discovers that when she is in a state of poised, loving receptivity, she is creating an atmosphere in their relationship, that makes it most possible for her beloved to offer her the *real thing*—his true love, which is the only thing that she has ever really wanted from him!

Unworthiness

Any woman, who wants her relationship to grow, learns very quickly that asking directly for love is never the best way to make a contact with her beloved. As we have said, because of her greater sensitivity to the quality of the energy flows in their relationship, a woman has much less capacity for tolerating psychic separation than does a man. Thus she will feel the urgent need for contact when he doesn't even notice that it is gone. But she knows that "asking" or "grasping" at him rarely brings the result she desires—that it usually turns him off. And she also knows that if she seems "needy," that that, too, can put a pressure on him that will augment the spiral of separation.

If a woman is reaching beyond the emotions for a higher love, her work is to transform her natural impulse to "ask" directly and, instead, initiate the contact of love by becoming actively magnetic. Out of critical necessity, combined with her deep desire for a true expression of love and faced with the undeniable evidence that her usual approaches do not work, she uses the mantra and thus can move into a state of love. Through "being-in-love," she becomes magnetic, radiant, poised and receptive to her beloved's true offerings. She "asks" and invites his expressions of love through the magnetism of her love-radiance. From her center of love, her radiance evokes from him the loving contact that she seeks.

Every woman knows how to be magnetic, but often, after a period of being together with a man, women stop paying attention. There is a strong tendency in many women to feel that once their relationship is *established*, they shouldn't have to reconstitute it constantly. To them, the work of becoming magnetic has already been done. Now they take it for granted and assume that their beloved should continue to respond as he did in the past. It may come as a great surprise to these women to discover that, if they aspire towards a higher love in their relationship, or even if they want to have any love at all in their relationship, they must consciously and intentionally be as radiant and magnetic as when they first fell in love.

Unfortunately, there are many women who believe that they cannot become truly magnetic anymore. Indeed, many are not aware of ever having been magnetic, they have never thought of themselves that way. Many have never thought that being magnetic is a quality that could be acquired or something that they could *do*. They may think that they do not know how to, and that they are unable to, perhaps because they have grown older, or have had children, or that they are not good enough, not beautiful enough, not deserving enough, or not worthy. The conviction that one is inadequate and unworthy is a very difficult barrier to overcome, and so many women suffer deeply because of it. But if a woman truly wants love enough she must make the choice to overcome this, all too common, emotional dead-end.

In the way of the beloved, a woman has already made the commitment to choose love, first, above all other factors and influences. Thus she must not let her feelings of inadequacy and unworthiness control her. Her work is to reach for a higher love in which her (supposed) inadequacies are "sacrificed"—that is, dissolved in the sea of that greater, encompassing love. She must reach up to become the highest spiritual self that she can imagine—even unto the "eternal feminine!" She must make manifest the *mystery* of the eternal feminine which in her deepest heart of hearts, she has always felt to be her secret true self. She must become and make manifest the divine feminine qualities that her beloved, in his heart of hearts, truly seeks. No matter what her blocks, every woman can do this; indeed, just the thought of this possibility will set most women aglow.

The Tendency Toward Conditional Love

A woman in one of our retreats wrote the following candid response to the question: "Is there anything that can keep you from crossing the spiritual threshold?"

> Yes, there are barriers that keep us from crossing the spiritual threshold, and while it would be far simpler for me to enumerate those of my beloved, I shall delve a little deeper and expose a few of my own.
>
> The first for me is the persistent thought that I am doing more spiritual work than Mel and thinking we cannot progress until he … (fill in the blank, blanks). As soon as I think this, love stops, I stop pouring out love and even when I don't say anything, my beloved keenly feels the loss and ever so slightly pulls away. A barrier has been erected.
>
> Another for me is a mental criticism, no matter how subtle or slight … And impatience is a barrier I know I create, allowing other love-destroying elements to enter …
>
> The biggest one is thinking I know how love looks or how *things should be* before I can or will love, and I know that this keeps us from crossing the threshold. To love no matter what is a tall order … It is so easy to feel irritated or superior or even unworthy—all just tricks of the wily ego/personality to keep us from our spiritual goal.

Torkom Saraydarian says that it is the "responsibility of a woman to evoke the highest latent in man … "[64] It is the woman's work in the beloved relationship to light the way, to constantly strive towards greater love. Usually a woman feels that she is "working on herself" to grow spiritually all the time and she wants her beloved to share the path with her. She wants him to grow, too, to become *better* than he is, to achieve his highest goals. Indeed, she feels that it is her *mission*, to see that this comes about. To her, it is one of her most important "purposes" or "assignments" in their relationship.[65]

The barrier that blocks her path to higher love is that she wants her beloved to change *before* she loves him. She wants him to fulfill her vision for him first, and then she will love him. She does not love him wholeheartedly and freely the way he is now. After all, he is not actualizing the fine potential that she sees in him—he is not yet what she wants him to be. If this is her approach, she does not love the person, who is her beloved. Her love is therefore conditional: it is limited and colored by her expectations, by her viewpoints, by her hopes and desires.

Thus a woman who is on the path of the beloved is faced with a formidable challenge. For her to leap into love means that she must, in the same breath and simultaneously, hold the lamp that leads towards the realization of her beloved's highest potential while loving him completely and unreservedly *as he is right now*. And in addition, she must embrace with immense gratitude, their relationship and their life together as they are in this moment.

Her great realization as she does the work of the Beloved Yoga is that the very leap into love gives her the ability to create this miracle. She discovers that her power of evocation toward spiritual fulfillment in the circle of transcendent love comes about through the radiance of her love, alone. Through this radiant love that asks for nothing in return and has no conditions, she inspires her beloved to reach for greater heights. She influences him and causes changes in him through the light of the love-wisdom that flows through her. Simultaneously she is appreciating and loving him in the present.

As she intentionally dwells in a state of love, a woman finds that she is no longer just enduring or tolerating the limitations of her beloved. Instead, her inspiration and faith in her beloved's potential invoke the best from him and make it possible for him to "come through" with love for her. Her desire to change him is transformed into an inspiration, and she feels that she is now a *muse* for him, instead of a critic. As his muse, she trusts, admires, affirms and loves him, now. Indeed, she flies *with* him to the heights of a sublime love

ॐ

Thus through the circle of love, we see that if you want to know what it means to be a man or what it means to be a woman, if you want to know *how* to be a true man or *how* to be a true woman, the way to find out is through love of the polar opposite. Through the circle of love, the truth of the *other* can be revealed.[66]

In the circle of love a man knows that his beloved will receive the *real thing* when he continuously demonstrates to her:

- that he loves her no matter what
- that he sees and appreciates her beauty
- that he "values" her, that she is "important" to him
- that she comes first in his life
- that he desires her and wants to unite with her

He finds out that if he gives his beloved the *real thing*, all else in her life is eclipsed by his gift. Torkom Saraydarian writes,

> People think that a woman feels secure if she is beautiful and successful. This is a wrong idea. A woman's security does not come out of her personality existence, but out of her man's love for her. If a man gives love to her, she can feel secure in any condition.[67]

When a woman is offered the *real thing* from her beloved, rarely will she not *melt* and receive him into her heart. For when the circle of love is alive and glowing, everything else seems possible and solvable.

In the circle of love a woman discovers that her beloved will feel the truth of her love for him:

- when she accepts his offerings of love as he intends them
- when she radiates the beauty and the love that he desires
- when she manifests to him those higher qualities which inspire love and creativity in him
- when she loves him NOW, as he is, while inspiring him to grow further.

Paradoxically, it is true that, most of the time, a woman must leap first, before her beloved. Indeed, one of the great secrets being revealed today is that woman is the one who must take the lead in transforming humanity.

Torkom Saraydarian summarizes in a few words the essence of the woman's work on the path of the beloved:

> Woman has a certain magical, mysterious way in which she evokes the best in a man. Woman is more advanced physiologically and spiritually than man, but the best the woman can bring out of the man is the best the woman has in her ... A woman must have greatness in her to bring greatness out of others. Woman must build that greatness, build that beauty, build that creative mechanism within herself so that her creative magnetism pulls the beauty out of man.[68]

❧

The Circle of Love

Through pouring out love the man grows spiritually,
And the woman flowers in radiant love-wisdom ...
Her love inspires him, thus she becomes his muse ...
His love pouring to her evokes the beauty and power latent in her,
Then her love magnetizes and evokes the best and highest to manifest in him ...
And she becomes that divine counterpart which he has been seeking ...
Together they rise to spiritual heights.

CHAPTER 7

• 7.1 MUTUAL EXALTATION •

If you treat an individual as he is, he will stay that way, but if you treat him as if he were what he could be, he will become what he could be.

—Goethe[1]

• INTRODUCTION •

It is commonly accepted that the words and thoughts which are expressed to a child can have a profound effect on the person he or she becomes—i.e., how the adult person will act, think and feel. If we consistently emphasize the positive aspects of a child's personality in words and tone, we encourage the development of those qualities. Moreover, if we speak of the best and highest qualities of his or her essential being, we evoke these qualities to come into manifestation. This process, although we seldom give it broader application, is also true for adults, especially for those who are closely connected to each other, as are a man and woman who are a beloved couple.

When a couple makes the mutual decision to walk the Path of the Beloved their wish to move towards a higher consciousness necessarily includes a great aspiration to see and evoke the highest within the other person. Through the intensity of their deep love, they want to raise the beloved *other* to spiritual heights even more than they want to attain to the heights themselves. Their work on the path changes. It moves from the work of striving to love the beloved *no-matter-what* to also include the work of *exalting* the beloved-one in thought, feeling, speech and action, thus invoking the higher aspect of the beloved's being to come into expression in their life. This is true compassion or spiritual love, which does not in any way diminish individuality—rather, it augments and enhances the being-ness and individuality of each. In the beloved relationship, the awakening of compassion within each person, is expressed in the practice of *Mutual Exaltation*, which has as its goal the appearance and realization of the divine in our beloved-one.

We have seen it expressed over and over again in the Perennial Wisdom, that the practice of intensifying selfless love will awaken the individual seeker's spiritual nature. In the Way of the Beloved this becomes a double or reciprocal action, a *mutual* exaltation, which purifies and transforms *both* people. When the lives of a man and woman are thus joined together in love, devotion and spiritual aspiration, the physical and emotional nature becomes lifted up to a higher octave of expression. As they intensify their love and devotion to the highest in each another, each person will gradually become aware of and infused with the other's higher aspect, as well as with their own. The bond in their physical marriage will be strengthened and the integration within each will become a tangible reality.[2] In this way, as beloveds move together on the path of love, they bring into manifestation the highest spiritual being in each other.

Meditation Practice

Spiritual Wisdom teaches us that within the heart of every man and woman "is a spark of divinity, which is the highest life-principle in the entity. This is the Light of God within the person."[3] A mantra of love is the most powerful practice and the most direct way to fan the spark of divinity within our own heart and the heart of our beloved. Using the love mantra concentrates the spark within the heart into greater activity. Through this practice, a beloved couple can enter into a state of mutual exaltation. "The spark becomes a flame, and the flame, a force which permeates the whole body and mind with the Light of God."[4]

Many couples begin the day with a meditation practice. Your practice can begin and end with the Invocation of Love (Section 1.1). See the image of your beloved in your mind's eye and silently say, *I enfold you with love, my beloved.* Continue for a minute or two after the end of your meditation practice. Then carry the image and the mantra of love with you as you move into the activities of your day. Or, use the mantra, *I touch your heart with a beam of love* while seeing and feeling a beam of love streaming out from your heart to your beloved's. Use the love mantra all day long!

• EXALTING THE BELOVED •

To exalt each other, we reach out to commune with and blend spiritually with the higher aspect of the other's being. We reach out for the highest we can conceive of in the other person, even as we know that he or she is an ordinary human being who is far from perfect. Thus our love must be intense enough to reach beyond the emotions and the personality.

For most people today, love is believed to be just another feeling—a mysterious force of unknown origin, within the personal and emotional sphere of our existence. But for beloved couples and spiritual seekers everywhere, love is a great spiritual power that goes far beyond our limited personal life. Beyond our personal life and its capacity to love emotionally is a limitless Sea of Universal Love. This *sea* has been recognized and sought all over the earth by those who seek a spiritual awakening. We may hear it referred to as the "ocean of love" or a "higher octave of love," or "Divine Love," "God's Love" (*Agape*), or, simply, *Compassion*. It is a realm of unconditional, unqualified, unreserved, pure love, which is universal and therefore, non-personal—free to expect nothing and to defend nothing. It is a radiation that flows forth like light from the sun, without reservation, upon all that exists.

Dwelling within that sea of universal love is the radiance of our own higher self and that of our beloved. The higher Self, or soul, is our true, Eternal Self (*Atman*), who is working through our personality and physical equipment to bring more light and spiritual expression through our form. When we reach out to grow spiritually, we continuously evolve towards that higher state. Each person is constantly evolving towards that eternal Self as his or her mind and heart increasingly identify with that *life* and Reality.

We live now as personalities, centered in our individual ego. In our best attempts to meet in loving communion with our beloved, our ego-centered personality comes into conflict or friction with the purposings of our higher Self. The nature of the personality is that it wants to express its limited self. It wants to be acknowledged, accepted, understood, and validated as a separated individual and only on its own terms. Our Higher Self, however, as an embodiment of universal love and compassion perceives its union—or one-ness-in-love—with the higher self of the beloved, and thus, gives out spontaneously without regard for any personal interest. It cares only for the spiritual well-being of the beloved *other*.

Both our own higher self and that of our beloved are without boundaries in the sea of universal love. Thus, once our consciousness opens to the realm of the soul, we are simultaneously in touch with our higher self and that of our beloved. As we reach out to a higher octave of love, we enter a new realm of communion with the true being of our beloved. This is a state of spiritual union centered in Divine Love. No interaction on the physical, emotional or mental level can compare to the heights of joy and ecstatic love that touch us in this realm. Once this contact is made, a couple knows something of the potential that awaits them on the spiritual path of the Beloved.

Inner Silence and Attunement to the Higher Self

To invoke the soul vibration we must be inwardly silent. Our mind must be quiet so that thoughts do not intrude to block our attunement to the soul quality. And our emotions must be turned toward the soul level through aspiration and love. In this way we become receptive to the higher vibration. And through deep, intense love for the highest being of our beloved, the power of our Soul can truly flow through our mind and heart. Through this Love, we can turn from the ego-expression, and become an expression of the unconditional, spiritual Love that is our own higher self.

This does not happen quickly or easily. We must go through a process of choosing that love, the love of the higher self over and over again. We choose that love by remaining inwardly silent and consciously pouring out love and compassion. Even when our aspiration is strong, the process requires will and discipline and much testing over a long period of living through changing moods and events. Only when we have tried it many many times with intensity of dedication, can we begin to feel a new vibration entering our life.

Through invoking the soul quality over and over again in the seemingly interminable and relentless daily situations of our lives, the higher vibration will gradually become impressed into every level of our life. Then the relationship becomes centered in the living presence of a love that is pervasive and universal. When a couple, through mutual exaltation, reaches for this universal love, it becomes possible for them to experience a true security in their relationship, because their security is anchored in the Spiritual Presence. Without the focus on the universal, Divine Presence, they are still subject to the psychic storms that well-up from the unconscious levels of the personality.

• The Exercise •

A good way to prepare for the exercise to develop mutual exaltation, is to use the format of the Listening Exercise given in Section 2.2. To be in communion with the higher Self of our beloved through love, we must be in an intense state of clear and unconditional listening. This is a state of meditation in which we are inwardly silent, but acutely aware and receptive to the other person. All of our being must be reaching out to attune to the soul, the Eternal Self, the higher spiritual aspect of our beloved. We must listen with all that we are: our ears, our eyes, our mind, our heart—our whole being. Once we are truly *listening*, we have the ability to turn from the demands of the personality and choose the ever present compassion pouring down from our higher Self. Using the listening exercise format will provide an opportunity for concentrated self-observation in a structured, safe setting.

We have divided the following exercise into 2 parts: part 1 consists in suggestions for watching and changing your inner focus, and part 2 suggests ways to apply the exercise to daily life.

Part 1:

As your beloved speaks to you and you are inwardly silent, yet aware, observe whether you are actually answering the demands of the personality, or not. Assess whether you are truly desiring only to *hear* the other. Seek to determine whether you sincerely want *nothing* in return. Be aware of *consciously* pouring out love, understanding and compassion to your beloved regardless of what he or she says or does. Do not express your side—try not to even *think* of your side. Even allow yourself to be mis-understood or mis-quoted without trying to correct the other or to defend yourself in any way!

As you are silent, you will have the opportunity to observe your own personality patterns that screen you from the higher consciousness of love. For instance, ask yourself:

- *Do I really turn from the selfish impulses of my personality, without repressing them, yet at the same time maintaining awareness of what I am experiencing?*
- *Do I feel that I really don't want to do this? Or that I'm not ready for this? Or that this is bound to be ineffective?*
- *Can I LOVE the other person when he or she disagrees with me and even hurts me?*

- *Am I attempting to avoid seeing and hearing the other person, in any way, for any reason?*
- *Do I think that I'm trying my best, even though I don't actually* feel *love?* (*Trying* means that you know what to do and you're not doing it! You're finding *good* reasons, justifications, or obstacles, to prevent a flow of love.)
- *Can I reject these old patterns and* love anyway? *Can I generate love for the other person,* anyway?
- *Am I, in truth, expecting and wanting nothing in return?*
- *Am I truly free, in a state of love and listening, or do I really have expectations that the other person will perform differently at some other or future time? Am I secretly hoping that I'll get some acknowledgment or some reward, or something, in return for my efforts?*
- *Am I trying to do the exercise correctly, but actually only temporarily suspending my desire to respond, or waiting for the other person to react in the way I want?*

Here are some possible examples of what you might be waiting for or expecting in return: After *listening*, you would like the other person to: acknowledge your efforts to listen; or acknowledge your efforts to be loving; or be "present" for you, to help you, love you, understand you, appreciate you, admire you; or change some behavior and do it the way you want; or even let you be, leave you alone, or stop bugging you.

The more intense and pure your state of *listening*, the easier it will be to answer these questions and move beyond the concerns of the self-focused ego. Some people think that they are doing it and not getting results. But they are actually not doing it at all! The results of this exercise are inexorably *disclosed in the existential process of doing it!*

Part 2:

For a dedicated beloved couple, the purpose of this exercise is realized by practicing it whenever you are together, and whenever you think of each other, as you live through the hours and events of your daily life. The spirit of the practice can be carried into all your interactions as you reach for the highest inspiration of love with your beloved. You will find that if you practice the exercise in your ordinary interactions and listen to your beloved with your whole being in a state of love, you will begin to *loosen* yourself from your ego-identification and dwell instead, in a realm of intense love for your beloved. Thus you will begin to experience the spiritual truth that "only in losing your life, do you gain eternal life," (Jn. 12:25) for this path leads us to transcend the life of the personality and enter a higher realm of consciousness.

Whenever you are with your beloved, sustain a quiet mind and a heart of love. Use the following mantra to keep centered and prepared, in a state of readiness to hear your beloved:

With a calm mind and a heart full of love, my Soul comes forth to blend with my beloved.

Meditation:

> In the new age, beloveds will pour out love and lead one another on the path. Through awareness, they intensify the flow and keep it alive every hour. They see the highest that they can conceive in each other. When they love the God in each other every hour of every day, this becomes a great path toward spiritual liberation.[5]
>
> Mantra: *With a calm mind and a heart full of love,*
> *my Soul comes forth to blend with my beloved.*

₧₧

• VISION THROUGH LOVE •

All spiritual teachings tell us that the way to wisdom and truth is through love, that love and wisdom are one, that love reveals the invisible truth hidden behind our ordinary seeing and that love opens our vision to a higher reality. In Western esotericism, Love-Wisdom is a hyphenated word, one term.[6] To the Tibetan Buddhists, the center of the mind is within the *heart* and the heart is referred to as "the Heart of Perfect Wisdom." And yet, in most of the world today, love is not recognized at all as a source of wisdom or knowledge. To the contrary, love is considered to be only an ephemeral *emotion*, quite suspect, and extremely unreliable. Thus, underlying all the attempts to open our eyes to the wisdom of love, the attitudes and assumptions of our very secular society subtly influence and inhibit our efforts. These rationalistic and psychologistic concepts, which deny that love is a source of wisdom or truth, have brought uncertainty and confusion into the minds of many people and have effectively prevented them from *trusting* in the power of love, which is an essential element in the relationship of a beloved couple.

The first assumption is the well-known and oft-quoted maxim that "love is blind." This very popular saying equates the distorting, emotional attachments that are naturally and unavoidably mixed in with our present experience of love, with the *love itself.* The philosopher, Max Scheler says that the person who believes this proverb, "thinks of love in terms of a mere impulse of sensual passion ..." And "The blinding element in an ... infatuation is never the *love*, but the sensual *impulses* ..."[7]

Thus it is not the love that blinds us, but the illusions which permeate our consciousness and cloud the purity of our love, i.e., desires, attachments, negativities, limitations, etc. Indeed, the love that we know now is far from a pure love—it is a veiled reflection of that higher, divine love, which we aspire to embody. Our work on the spiritual path is to intensify and purify the love that we have until it becomes more like that greater divine love— Compassion. One can only express *pure* love after a high state of illumination has been achieved. If we start by working sincerely with the best that we have, we can use that as a basis for a gradual ascent to the higher levels of love-consciousness.[8] When we love with the limited, relative love of the personality, we are preparing our heart for the unlimited Love of the divine. Indeed how else can we begin except from where we are, working with aspiration and dedication in the faith that from the love we have now can come the greater love we are seeking. That greater love is the wisdom we seek, and it is through the eyes of *that* love that we can see our true Beloved.[9]

The second assumption that discounts the value of love, claims that because love invariably idealizes the beloved, our vision is distorted and therefore cannot lead to *objective knowledge.* The extreme materialistic orientation and methods of our society dictate that *real* knowledge can only be derived *objectively.* Thomas Merton answered this *scientific* objection definitively: "On the contrary, the subjectivity essential to love does not detract from objective reality but adds to it. Love brings us into a relationship with an objectively existing reality, but because it is love it is able to bridge the gap between subject and object and *commune in the subjectivity of the one loved.* Only love can effect this kind of union and give this kind of knowledge-by-identity with the beloved."[10]

The fact that love idealizes the beloved does not necessarily mean that *objectivity* is absent and that our vision is distorted because of our love. There is difficulty here only for those who assert that the idealizing aspect of love does not lead to *true* knowledge. As Max Scheler says, "The blindness ... is all on the side of the detached observers ... "it is the lover who actually sees more of what is present than the others, and it is *he* and not *others*, who therefore sees what is objective and real." ... Love is the most personal of attitudes, but a thoroughly OBJECTIVE one nonetheless, in the sense that we are *objective* insofar as we free ourselves (in an unaccustomed fashion) from bondage to our own interests, wishes and ideas."[11]

The idea that an observer must be detached to be objective is not only being questioned by modern science itself, but those with spiritual insight and sensitive vision see that this so-called, objective knowledge is actually a limitation that restricts us to only the material, physical level, and thus ignores, even denies, the deeper, higher, or *invisible* realms of being and consciousness. Indeed, Vladimir Solovyev asserts that, "It is well known to everyone that in love there inevitably exists a special idealization of the beloved object, which presents itself to the lover in a completely different light from that in which outsiders see it. I speak here of light not merely in a metaphorical sense ... but also of a special sensuous perception: *the lover really sees, visually perceives, what others do not.*"[12]

Thus, although the lover may be the only one to see the "light" in his or her beloved, this does not diminish or compromise the REALITY of the apprehension. A delightful answer to both of the objections to love as a source of knowledge or accurate perception can be found in a wonderful book by the Jewish mystic, Allen Afterman: "A detached observation of a couple pressing their mouths together does not reveal their purpose nor the nature of love. Nor could they prove to such an observer that love objectively exists, nor even describe it. And although they convince him that they feel "love," he might offer alternative psychological or behaviorist interpretations of this experience. The objective observer who rubs his mouth against another person's may prove to himself that love does not exist. Only if he yields his "objectivity" will he eventually love."[13]

For a beloved couple who has been striving on the path, these assumptions may not emerge into consciousness as such. But they may be experienced as feelings of doubt or skepticism about the ways and methods of the path. When problems arise, the efficacy of the power of love may be questioned. A person may become discouraged and think,"I don't see how this can work." "Where is it that we are going?" And the tendency to analyze and rationalize, rather than love, is always a great temptation.

But when a beloved couple becomes willing to consciously and deliberately replace these tendencies in favor of love and mutual exaltation, their faith in the power of love becomes an active force orienting them towards the realization of the Spiritual Teachings. They begin to see that love brings clarity to the mind and gives us insight that can come in no other way. They see that through love, the mind becomes clear and we are open to the influence of energies from the higher realms. Thus love gives us the ability to evoke the highest in our beloved. Perhaps the greatest discovery that comes, is that love is the perceiver of knowledge beyond the intellect and is the door to the higher consciousness.

Indeed, love, intensified by mutual exaltation, is the power that opens our eyes so that our perception is clear and we can see the true, divine image in our beloved. It is only through the eyes of love that we will *see* and *know* our true beloved. When we love deeply and with great devotion, we become able to see beyond the sheer physicality of the manifest form. Our vision gazes beyond the personality, and we apprehend the spirit in the form. This is not a dream or a fantasy or a projection, but a *greater reality* that has thus far, been veiled from us.

Meditation:

Through deep love and devotion, I look beyond the personality and I see the true, spiritual aspect of my beloved's being.

Love gives me vision.

Through intense love for my beloved, the door is opened to a world of light.

Mantra: *Through intense love for my beloved,*
the door is opened to a world of light.

ഇ൫

• VISIONING THE DIVINE •

For now we see through a glass, darkly; but then face to face.
—I Cor. 13:12[14]

It is through our intense desire to exalt our loved-one to spiritual heights that we bring the highest truth of our beloved into manifestation. The will-to-exalt the other is an invocation that brings forth the divine aspect of our beloved's being, the spiritual truth of our beloved-one. A man and woman who aspire to transform their marriage into the path of the Beloved must know and trust that the power of love, if it is intense enough, will open them to the vision of regions beyond the material world. And they must have an unwavering faith that through the pouring out of that love to each other, they will experience the vision of a Divine Spirit in their beloved.

Since time immemorial visionaries have testified to the existence of spiritual worlds of higher consciousness, beyond any description that words can give: worlds that are beyond time and beyond space, wherein Divine love and spiritual beings may be directly perceived. They tell us that these worlds are actually more substantial and richer in images and forms than the sensory world. Yet these worlds remain a total mystery to the modern Western mind buried, as it is, in materialistic thinking. Still, there are many in the West who experience a sense that there exists something more than the material world or feel an inexplicable longing for some undefined and unknown fulfillment. Some have had a glimpse of something other or higher or an experience that cannot be understood by our accustomed secular modes of explanation.

Through following the practices of the Way of the Beloved, we can develop the abilities needed to experience the reality of the worlds of higher consciousness. On this Path, we discover that through loving deeply and exalting our beloved one, our vision begins to change. As we look-again or re-vision our beloved with the eyes of a greater love, we begin to see in a way that is not habitual or familiar. We find that we can vision or envision our beloved as the divine being he or she truly is. Seeing the divine Spirit of our Beloved "face to face," is to look at him or her through the eye of the heart.

The intensification of love and the consequent purification of our being activates the heart center, thus awakening what might be called the "perceptual capacities" of the heart. The eye of the heart opens our senses to the vision and perception of levels of being that are beyond reason and which surpass all the concepts of the mind. It is by means of this faculty, the eye of the heart, that we begin to see our beloved as an embodiment of a higher Being or Spirit. It is the eye of the heart which sees what is invisible to the eyes of the modern mind.

That ability of the heart which leads to greater vision has been called the "creative imagination."[15] The creative imagination is the actual eye of the heart which sees into the other, higher worlds of light. The creative imagination, infused with Love, will open the doors to the higher realms of consciousness.

Many Westerners have a negative attitude toward the imagination. It is commonly thought that the imagination only produces images and thoughts that are not real.[16] However, seekers on the spiritual path can benefit greatly through cultivating the ability to create and sustain images. When we concentrate on, and visualize, the image of a divine being, the Spirit, within our beloved, we attract the higher forces associated with that Image. We also become sensitive to images impressed upon our consciousness from other planes. When used correctly, the creative imagination makes us more receptive to Forces and Ideas from the higher realms.[17] The creative imagination is the entrance to the higher, nonmaterial planes. This idea is not entirely unknown in Western cultures. For instance, in Bernard Shaw's Saint Joan, the Inquisitor challenges Joan with: "Your voices are only in your imagination." She replies: "Of course. How else does God speak to us?"[18]

• Meditations/Exercise •

To entertain a vision deeper than surface permits, and thereby to revision the world, is to begin envisioning God himself ... We need a method having the power to overcome our feeling of being cut off from the supernatural, power to restore the knowledge of God. ... [19]

We can, indeed, move toward the ability to look beyond the manifest forms into the realm of invisible spiritual realities. Through the use of the creative imagination, blended with and empowered by love, we can invoke the vision of the divine in our beloved.

Exercise

Visualize the divine spark of love within the heart of your beloved. Imagine this spark increasing until it is a radiant blue light permeating and surrounding his or her physical form. Imagine that this is the light of divine love, the higher

201

Self, Soul or Spirit of your beloved. See this Image before you as you pour out love to your beloved. Use a mantra, e.g.:

- Through love I see the divine in you, my beloved.
  or
- Through deep love and devotion I see ... the Divine ... in my beloved.

> ... the True Self ...
>
> ... a Spirit Being ...

  or
- Through the will-to-love, I see ... the Spirit ... in my beloved.

> ... the highest aspect ...
>
> ... the Spiritual Ideal ...

We know that the beloved we see with our ordinary, limited vision, is not the True Self, the divine being of our beloved-one. The True Self of our beloved exists on another level, as does our own, yet it subtly and simultaneously interpenetrates the material manifestation. It is our intense invocation of love that causes the invisible spiritual realities to descend into our heart and, thus, open our eyes to the truth of our beloved's being. Indeed, the "[creative] imagination transmutes the sensible world by raising it up to its own subtle and incorruptible modality."[20]

Since ancient times, the practice of re-visioning has been highly developed in both Buddhism and in Sufism. The Buddhist tradition has, from its beginnings, incorporated the practices of creative imagination and visualization.[21] For the Sufis "love is the teacher," and a celestial love, (which we have been calling "compassion") will open the door to a vision of the Spirit. A vision of the Spirit, called a theophany, is a physical presentation of a divine being, that something, that Image, which manifests or reveals divinity. Henry Corbin, who has written extensively about the "theophanic image" and the "theophanic imagination" in Sufism gives us a detailed description of this magical process:

> Thus it is the Active Imagination which places the invisible and the visible, the spiritual and the physical in sym-pathy. It is the Active Imagination that makes it possible ... to love a being of the sensible world, in whom we love the manifestation of the divine Beloved; for we spiritualize this being by raising him[her] (from sensible form)

to incorruptible Image (that is, to rank of a theophanic Image), by investing him[her] with a beauty higher than that which was his[hers], and clothing him[her] in a presence such that he[she] can neither lose it nor cast it off.[22]

Thus, by opening the eyes of the creative imagination, we love our beloved as the physical-emotional-mental being whom we see with our ordinary physical perception and at the same time we love the spiritual, i.e., theophanic, being who is his or her True Self. This "ascending" and "descending" movement of that love which aspires to see the divine, transforms both ourself and our beloved-one and leads us to the vision of the higher worlds.[23]

• Meditation/Exercise •

Choose a photo, painting, statue or symbol of a divine being with whom you feel a connection. An image of a universal being from any spiritual tradition, such as the Christ, the Divine Mother, Tara, Krishna, Sophia, the Virgin Mary, or Quan Yin embodies in a visionary or artistic form the divine qualities toward which we aspire. The image can become a focal point for our aspiration. Since in our present state of consciousness, we do not directly perceive divine beings, we can, however, invoke and align ourself with the radiation pouring forth from the portrayal of the universal being. And as we concentrate with reverence and devotion and love on the image, our consciousness is influenced by the divine qualities of the spiritual being. Thus the image becomes a means to contact the divine qualities we seek to envision in our beloved.[24]

Visualize the image of the divine being within the heart of your beloved or surrounding your beloved's form. As you pour out love, use a mantra:

- Through love I see the divine image in my beloved.
    or
- I see the ... Christ ... in my beloved
                    ... Holy Mother ...

A woman we know had been working with this meditation devotedly for several years, when she told us the following story:

This is a hard story to tell, because for most of what happened, I don't know if I can find words. It was the end of the day, and we were both very tired. My beloved was hurting—his back and neck were painfully sore. He asked me if I could rub them, but I was exhausted and wondered if I had the energy to do it. I remember thinking that I loved him so much and wanted so much to ease his pain and help him to feel better that, maybe, I could call up enough energy to work on him. I called upon my will and felt myself overcome my exhaustion. I said OK. So he lay down on the bed and I sat on him and began to massage his back. I did it with a lot of love and the room was very quiet. Then something changed. The atmosphere opened up and as I looked down on my beloved's back I saw that I was touching the Body of Christ. My beloved didn't look any different, it was still his back and his muscles that I was rubbing, but it was the Body of Christ that I was touching. There was a feeling of great love, a pure kind of love, that seemed to glow in the room. Time became elongated or maybe suspended, like we had moved to a different place, although we were still on the bed in our bedroom. While this was happening, wild and intense thoughts were moving through my mind in bright and vivid colors. I thought, "Oh my God, this must be what Mother Teresa sees when she says she sees the Christ in the people she works with." And I saw and felt in myself how she must feel when tending to the poor and sick and dying. And then, "Oh God, this must be what the great artists saw and felt when they were painting the Christ." And I saw images from Michaelangelo and El Greco move before me and felt the intensity of the contact they must have had with the Christ as they worked. And I also thought, "Why am I thinking all this?" The love and vision that is present in our room is so far "above" all these thoughts. At some point, it all began to fade and I saw my beloved "as usual," again. But some of the feeling remained and it was very beautiful and sublime for a long time afterwards.

Thus through seeking the divine in our beloved, we acquire the ability to actually see in another way. Through the use of these exercises we can come to see our beloved as a manifestation of the Divine. The invocation to the spiritual being blended with the power of Love can break through the veils we have erected between us and the luminous Divine Realities which remain invisible to the ordinary consciousness. We begin to see the transmutation of the physical form of our beloved into a theophanic figure embodying the

Presence of Divinity. To see the Divine in our beloved through the eye of the heart is to know spiritual love without any loss of ordinary love. However, we will have transcended the possessive aspect of mundane and emotional need-love which has heretofore blinded the eye of the heart.

• Three Obstacles to Revisioning •

This life's five windows of the soul
*   Distorts the Heavens from pole to pole,*
And leads you to believe a lie
*   When you see with, not thro' the eye.*
          —William Blake *Auguries of Innocence.*

I

In our age, dominated as it is by materialism, the idea that truth can only come from so called, objective perception, i.e., the five physical senses, narrows the socially and scientifically approved mode of visual perception to that which includes only physical objects. The dominant materialistic belief or orientation excludes anything from reality which is not material, therefore, all perception of the non-material is regarded as hallucinatory. Consequently, we not only reject as invalid any other mode of visioning but, in general, our culture specifically does not condone any alternative ways of seeing. Indeed, our civilization is currently locked into a mechanical model of visual perception involving "sense organs," "external stimuli," and "neural pathways."

Some students in our classes encounter difficulties in doing the beloved work because their cognitive faculties are so educated and habituated to the modes of thinking and perceiving that dominate our modern world. Their scepticism about the idea of any Greater Reality is usually unspoken, nevertheless, it acts subtly to dim their enthusiasm and diminish their efforts on the path. Sometimes we encourage a student to suspend his or her disbelief or doubt long enough to persist on the beloved path. Most of the time, if a student continues to do the work of loving, the changes in his or her life brought by the power of love, convince him or her to continue. One man was forthright enough to write:

I still can't say that the concept behind this path is true and valid. However, all I have to do is look to my growth and the growth in my

205

relationship over the past two years to know that it has worked thus far. We have raised the vibration of love in our relationship many fold, and this vibration of love has been noticed by those around us. It has escaped the confines of our personal lives and the walls of our home and spread out beyond our neighborhood into the universe. I continue in devotion to this path and look forward to the new areas it will uncover and the spiritual growth it will nurture.

Meditation:

VISION

When you started your relation with your beloved, you reached out to her[his] higher nature. You could see in her[him] a glimpse of the light beyond the form. But this concept was lost, and negative emotions arose. Every hour we have the choice to transmute Maya or to be carried along the stream of illusion. The vision of love is regained by turning from our personality and seeing our beloved as an expression of Soul. See in your beloved the highest you can conceive in an individual. See the Divine in her[him] trying to work through a form not yet perfected. When you keep your focus, and see with eyes full of love, understanding and vision shall flow like a river of light through your heart and mind.

Mantra: The veils of Maya are lifted,
              I see the Divine in my beloved.[25]

II

Many of us are not subject to the belief that all of existence is material in nature and we realize, at least to some extent, that our perception of the world is somehow illusory, i.e., "not what it seems." Yet there is a much older religious tradition, which underpins the current world view of spirituality in both the West and the East that causes confusion and difficulty for many. This potent tradition leads us to believe that spiritual Reality is a world that is other or separate and apart from this world.[26] Eastern religions as well as Christianity, in the West, contain world-denying, ascetical ideas which posit the world of all physical manifestation as negative or evil and thus, totally separate from God or anything connected to Spirit.[27] Many students come to us after having spent years in a Zen Monastery or a Christian Seminary or an Ashram in India. They have devoted themselves to meditation in an isolated environment, apart from the world and all the entanglements, concerns and responsibilities of daily life. They believe that spiritual enlightenment can only be achieved away from all worldly-life situations.

Thus, when such Western seekers are married, leading a family life, and working in a business or profession, as is usually the case, they are constantly plagued by the feeling that to really be following the spiritual path one should be in a place apart meditating all day long. When a student approaches us with gnawing doubts regarding the actual possibilities and potentials of the beloved path, we often recognize that it is a manifestation of this particular conflict. These seekers cannot get past the feeling that they must choose between living with and loving their beloved OR living with and loving God. We know students in whom this conflict has persisted for years.

And yet, at this time in history, that stream of thought which teaches the simultaneity and interpenetration of the physical and the spiritual worlds, which in many traditions has been submerged for hundreds of years in institutionalized misogyny and erroneous ideas of asceticism, has begun to reemerge.[28] Historically, in all three of the Western religions there has been an explicit and prolonged turning-from their original revelation that the higher worlds are not separate from this material manifestation, and that the higher, spiritual worlds are made manifest in this world, albeit distortedly mirrored. The founding revelations of these religions assert clearly that humanity is a Divine manifestation, as is the Natural world, and as such is not actually separate from God, indeed, we are only hypnotized by the distorted image of the Spirit that is revealed to us in matter. Putting these erroneous doctrines of a world-denying asceticism behind us, we are now beginning to understand the validity and necessity of leading the spiritual life in this world. And Western seekers are faced with the prospect that our true work on the Path is to intensify the spiritual vibration in this level of existence, not only for our own individual betterment and growth, but to serve and touch others with the light of the Spirit here and now.

Our teacher writes: "When we have thoughts about God the tendency is to look up into space at the stars. But this room, this hour, is full of Spirit. The statement that 'We live, move and have our being in God' is a spiritual fact … The holy spiritual vibration of love and beauty and wisdom fill the atmosphere around us … We develop our ability to become one with the … [divine spirit] … through the substance of love."[29] Thus, on the Beloved path, "human and divine love are by no means opposed to one another ... They are two forms of the same love: passages in one and the same book which one must learn to read with 'eyes of light' ..."[30]

Thus, through "eyes-of-light," that is, the "eye-of-the-heart," the greater Reality that we enter is not a place that is separate and apart from this world—it is this world seen within the higher world, both worlds experienced simultaneously through vision transformed by love. To see the Divine in one's beloved is to unveil the spiritual Reality of her or his being which has been right in front of us all the time, but which can only be seen through the eye-of-the-heart. The Sufis describe this situation with one of the many stories of Majnun and his beloved Leila: "When someone said to Majnun, 'Leila, your beloved, is not so beautiful as you think,' he said, 'My Leila must be seen with my eyes. If you wish to see how beautiful Leila is, you must borrow my eyes.'"[31]

Meditation:

MOVEMENT ON THE PATH

How do we move on the path of the Beloved? It is through the power of love that the transmutation of the personality takes place. Thus the spiritual fires rise within and awaken the higher forces.

Worship the divine being in your beloved very intensely. You are both working out your natures and your destiny together. The divine being is there—she [he] is right HERE! You work it out with her [him] in everything you do—in your home, in your kitchen, in your work, in your philosophy, in your meditation—all working together as one. When, through intense love, you see the divine in your wife [husband], then does she [he] become your "Beloved." And you have crossed a threshold on the path.[32]

Mantram: *What greater treasure is there than my beloved?*
> *or*
> *I see God in my beloved.*
> *or*
> *Through love I see God in my beloved*
> *or*
> *Where shall I look for God, when close at hand is my beloved,*
> *All I need is the love to have the vision to see God in my beloved.*

III

Many couples, who aspire to transform their marriage into the Path of the Beloved, initially believe that as they use the exercises and repeat the mantras they are having the vision of God in their Beloved. But just saying the words, "I see the divine in my beloved," does not mean that we are having the experience of seeing the spiritual being of our beloved-one. When we use the mantra, I see the divine in my beloved, it means that we are seeking, imagining, aspiring towards and invoking that experience. Apprehending the theophany is an achievement; it is much more than a repetition of words, a wishful imagining, or even an intense emotional experience. It is a true opening in consciousness. The seeing of the divine Image in our beloved is a parting of the veils of Maya, an unforgettable psychic event, indeed, a profound experience of a greater Reality. We actually cross a threshold in consciousness and see with a transformed vision into another world of Being.

Often we encounter people who, when they are able to rephrase the statements of a spiritual teaching or successfully repeat a mantra for awhile, think that they know the true meaning and have learned and accomplished the teaching. They seem to believe that becoming acquainted with the concepts intellectually, i.e., having the "information," is the end of the process. They mistake the purely linguistic "abstraction" for the Reality.[33] There is a Buddhist saying which is appropriate here: it cautions the student not to mistake "the finger pointing at the moon for the moon." The teachings, the meditations, i.e., the words, are the means to vision, not the vision of Reality itself. A spiritual concept must become a reality in the heart & mind, i.e., the concept must be realized, integrated into our very depths, so that it becomes part of one's whole being.

We do not want to minimize either the difficulties inherent in the transformation of all our habitual cognition and vision, or the barriers to a mere belief-in, much less to an experience-of, the spiritual realms. Nevertheless, the step on the ladder of love that we are reaching for is consummated by the actual vision of the Divine in our beloved. The simultaneous activity of natural love (Eros) and spiritual love (Agape)[34] in the material presence of the physical form of our beloved is the key to the experience of seeing the divine in our beloved—the theophanic revelation. Yet, even if we believe this with all our heart, belief alone will not confer upon us the Vision.

However, **seeing the divine in our beloved is achievable.** Indeed, through continuous intensification and transformation of the love for our beloved and devoted practice, we can attain to it.[35]

A man told us about an experience that came to him only a few years after he and his beloved had found each other and the beloved path:

> We must have been getting ready to go to bed, it was evening and we were undressing. I just saw her walking across the floor. That's all. But there was an electrical charge in the room, like a light, and she was more beautiful than the most beautiful being I have ever seen or could ever imagine. She was the Goddess, she was Tara, she was the Holy Mother. I was seeing God walking across the floor.

And a woman told us the following story:

> Our relationship was so volatile I never knew what could happen at any moment. For months I had been saying, "I see the Christ in my beloved." One day I was standing in the kitchen, looking out the window, watching my beloved cross the bridge over the little brook between the parking area and our house. I was saying "I see the Christ in my beloved" over and over again, and then, just for a second, I saw it. I saw my beloved walking through a great span of the ages of time, moving toward the Christ, becoming like the Christ, becoming that great spiritual Being that was already within him right now. I don't think I'll ever forget what I saw that day, even though it lasted for only a split-second!

Thus, a man and woman, who are seeking the divine and who have intensified and purified their love for each other, look for and find the Face of the Spirit in the face of their spiritual counterpart, their beloved of this world. For modern Western couples, this practice of visualizing the Divine, which, in the past, was thought to be possible only for ascetic monks and isolated mendicants, can become part of their daily life as seekers on the spiritual Path of the Beloved right here in the world of dense Maya.

When we see the Divine in the form of our beloved, the true Beloved is disclosed to us and we realize that this is the One we have loved all along. Indeed, it is the Divine that we have always loved in the other person and toward which all our love has truly been directed.[36] And yet at the same time we love the person as one human to another. To quote Corbin again, "Love tends to transfigure the beloved earthly figure by setting it against a light which brings out all its superhuman virtualities ..."[38]

Meditation:

> For a couple on the beloved path, the love we share is not just a strong emotion. Love is a great spiritual energy that comes pouring through our being, giving us the vision to see the divine in our beloved. When we love deeply and see the divine in our beloved, this will do away with the veils of illusion and separation. And when we love God in our beloved with intensity and devotion every hour of every day, this becomes a great path toward spiritual liberation.[38]

> Mantram: *You are my beloved,*
> *I bless you with light,*
> *Through your form I see the face of God.*

On the path of the beloved, the "ladder of love" leads us gradually from one level to the next, from sense perception all the way to the vision of the true Beloved and even of the "Over-lighting Presence." Love brings clarity to the mind and gives us the ability to evoke the highest in our beloved-one. The power of love will bring forth the vision of the Divine in our beloved. Through love we see and, therefore, live in the Divine.

ၸဢ

• 7.2 THE TEST OF FIRE •

The heart sleeps until it is awakened to life by a blow;
it is as a rock, and the hidden fire flashes out when struck by
another rock.

—Hazrat Inayat Khan[39]

Is it not commonplace in today's world that in the relations between men and women we often see a dread fire flashing out? Not infrequently, we see couples, even very devoted couples on the path of the beloved, interact like two impervious rocks smashing together, creating a fire-of-friction which threatens to erode their relationship and seriously damage their potential for love. Indeed, many a man and woman are already "burned-out" from their contentious encounters with the opposite sex. We all have ample evidence to discern that a man and a woman do not become a beloved couple, or even a loving couple, simply by declaring that they are *beloveds*, nor do they attain that state by intending it to be so, or by ardently desiring it. To become a *beloved couple*, a man and woman must have the mutual aspiration to reach for a transcendent love and union that is as yet unknown to them. When they make a commitment to work together toward this achievement, they realize that their relationship must become a yoga, a path, a conscious *practice* which can lead them to the actual realization of their goal. And as they move together on this path, they discover, oftentimes to their great distress, that their path does not unfold naturally and smoothly in front of them.

In order to move from the love that they already know to that higher love toward which they aspire, a man and woman must go through a gradual and arduous process of ascent, both as individuals and as a couple. The love that they share must not only expand and glow with ever greater luminosity and intensity, but it must also be refined and purified until both people rise to the higher levels of love-consciousness. And in this process of purification, their love must be continually challenged and tested by fire.

In our ordinary life of worldly affairs, we accept as necessary, the process of gradual growth through ever greater challenges. In learning mathematics or a sport or how to play a musical instrument or how to sing, a person is first given simple exercises and then, after becoming proficient at that level of skill, is gradually faced with more difficult practices to master. In this way, the student's skill is developed and refined. However, we are not accustomed—nor are we taught—to think that a similar process of growth is necessary or desirable in our love relationships. And yet, how can we achieve a greater love without being faced with challenges to our current capacities? A relationship that is not challenged becomes stagnant and complacent. It cannot grow or prosper. It cannot demonstrate its worthiness nor can it transcend itself. That which stands still decays and dies! Indeed, there can be no growth without effort and struggle. In looking back on our relationships, can it not be truthfully said that it was the times of struggle, perhaps even the times of chaos and crisis, filled with disturbance, confusion and pain, that mark the turning points in learning how to intensify love for our beloved? Is there not an inherent and ordained connection between our growth in love and the challenges, crises, and sufferings that we have overcome?

When a couple makes a commitment to intensify their love and to consciously enter the beloved path, they do not expect that their life may actually become more difficult.[40] However, as the mind and heart turn towards the light of higher love, the negative elements within each person are stirred into activity. The dynamics of truly loving another person and of sharing a life together stimulate the latent patterns of the ego-oriented-self and bring them into painful awareness so that in the struggle to overcome them a person may be processed and purified. When life together becomes more difficult, it means that this process of purification is taking place.[41]

There is a common misunderstanding that if things are not going well in one's life or if one is going through a period of painful emotional storms, then something is "wrong," or one is doing poorly—even failing. However, this evaluation does not reflect an understanding of the process of true spiritual growth. Contrary to the accepted dogmas of our popular pleasure oriented culture, a smooth life together is *not* the measure of a couple's achievement and progress on the beloved path of love. Trials and tests of a couple's commitment to love, *no matter what*, will sooner or later come to all couples and especially to those who are sincerely committed to one another and are doing their best to be loving. Continuing challenges to the very idea of "what love is" must arise out of the inevitable tensions of a shared outer and inner life. It is through this continual dialectic of conflict and resolution that we become the active agents of each other's growth. The will-to-love our beloved evokes in both of us the qualities we need to move on the path towards a higher love—a love, presently inconceivable.

Through loving our beloved, our polar opposite—a truly *other* person— we come to realize that, if we are to be purified and to grow spiritually, it is inevitable that we must confront and overcome those influences that obstruct our realization of the Greater Reality we seek. Thus we must conquer those forces which are preventing us from embodying a more *self-less* love, a higher, purer love which we call *divine love, Agape,* or *compassion.* We also come to see that this process must take place over some period of time—the ego cannot be transformed overnight—and thus it is a painfully difficult struggle.

The following Meditation expresses these ideas in a concise statement and provides a mantra to help achieve a useful orientation to the struggle for a higher love:

Meditation:

STRUGGLE ON THE PATH[42]

Man and woman reach out for a higher aspect or principle when they go into marriage. The polar opposite evokes in them the qualities necessary for their spiritual growth. It also acts as a catalyst and awakens the thought forms that are dormant in the unconscious. They are brought to the surface to be transformed, so that the individuals will be purified.

Mantram: *Through love for my beloved,*
         I ascend to greater heights.

ॐ ॲ

In a lecture given on November 8th, 1906 Rudolf Steiner said that "suffering … seems to man sometimes to grip so deeply into life as to be connected with its very greatest problems. Hence the problem of suffering has occupied the human race since earliest times and whenever there is an endeavor to estimate the value of life and to find its meaning, people have above all tried to recognize the role played by suffering and pain."[43] Wisdom traditions throughout human history teach us that pain and suffering are an intrinsic and imperative condition of our very existence as incarnate human beings. Indeed, pain and suffering are inherent in the nature of existence and unless and until we become one with the Infinite they will be with us. We may have heard that the Bible states that, the whole created universe groans because it is separated from God (e.g., Ro. 8:22-23 & II Co. 5:2-4). And the first Noble Truth of the Buddha is that, *Existence is suffering, beginning and ending, change and variation—whether their essence is pleasure or pain—these are suffering.*[44] Thus, suffering is that which we experience as an element of our sense of separation and estrangement from the Spirit, our banishment from our true Home in God. Human beings at this stage of evolution almost universally suffer from the conviction and experience of a profound isolation which extends to our personal separation from other human beings, from nature, from all the other parts of the created universe and, most poignantly, from our beloved-one. The experience of separation is what is named the "cloud of illusion," or *Maya*; it is the result of humanity's descent from a spiritual existence into material life.

The idea that life-in-form and suffering are somehow inseparably linked was known and accepted from ancient times, but recently our secular culture has reversed this truth and now claims that our purpose in life is to feel pleasure and enjoyment. Thus, despite the fact that the necessity of pain and suffering is a universal spiritual teaching, it is neither popular, nor well accepted, in secular Western societies. Our post-modern psyche seems baffled by the undeniable experience of pain and suffering. We have lost the comprehension that joy and suffering, happiness and pain, are polarities—like light and dark, male and female, life and death—and that one is meaningless without the other. Indeed, we seem to have forgotten that if there was no suffering there could be no joy, that they are relative to one another like "up" is to "down." We are deceived by the modern, rational mind, which considers polarities to be opposites instead of complements, implying that it is possible to have one without the other and leading us to think we can have a life of happiness without experiencing any suffering.[45] We no longer seem to comprehend that even though true polarities appear to be, and do function as opposites or contraries, they are actually necessary and thus complementary parts or aspects of a greater whole, a greater Reality.

The inability to see the connection of life and suffering and the necessity of polarities as united "spiritual wholes" is part of a common myth shared by Western cultures: i.e., civilization and technology have brought, or will eventually bring, relief from suffering to the whole world.[46] In our culture of material abundance and comforts and with the achievement of a relative freedom from infectious diseases we have created the widespread myth that pain and suffering are accidental or arbitrary. And the dominant belief is that suffering would be unnecessary if we were just to develop the proper technology and greater skill in controlling Nature. Thus, in Western secular societies, life is dedicated to the pursuit of individual pleasure, and there are many today who believe that if they do everything "right" they should not have any illnesses or serious suffering in their life.[47]

Given the pervasive power of the myth that we can eliminate suffering, many contend that illness and other problems in life must be the result of some *personal* failure. Thus when suffering comes to them, people feel guilty! It is extremely common to blame the victim for bringing the condition upon himself or herself, even if the victim is oneself. How often do we hear that "I, or you, must have done something *wrong* to bring about this painful condition"?[48] Or if we do not blame the individual, we see suffering as a sign of the failure of our social/political structure or of the incomplete knowledge of science and technology, e.g., "The government needs to fund more research into this illness/problem so that we can *conquer* it." Our recent history amply demonstrates that, even when faced with a constant stream of actual situations to the contrary, elements in our culture are quite capable of constructing purely abstract theories of how we should live and grow which involve no unpleasantness at all! From such an erroneous perspective, when we inevitably encounter difficulty and pain in our life, we will likely protest vehemently and stubbornly resist the experience. Tragically, this resistance increases the intensity of our pain and causes greater suffering. An American Zen teacher tells us that, "suffering is a function both of the pain and the degree to which the pain is being resisted."[49] And Thomas Merton says that "the truth that many people never understand, until it is too late, is that the more you try to avoid suffering, the more you suffer ... the one who does most to avoid suffering is, in the end, the one who suffers most."[50]

Resistance to the truth that suffering is an essential element of our real manifest cosmos and a condition of our very existence on the physical plane is why so many in the Western world fail to move with a sense of purpose through the inevitable painful experiences that are such an important part of their life path. We live in an atmosphere that is so permeated with the idea that suffering can be avoided, that the question of why the process of spiritual growth is always so painful remains unanswered. It has become difficult for people in our Western world to believe that pain and suffering might have a deeper meaning and an important purpose in life.

Seekers on the spiritual path should quickly learn that the many experience of distress, affliction, tribulation, anguish, adversity, tragedy, misery and trouble have the innate potential to drive us into a new awareness, a deeper level of our being and existence. And that when pain and suffering come to us, there might be an otherwise hidden meaning to explore and an important purpose to be served in our life, i.e., suffering is a necessary part of the plan for our spiritual development.[51]

> For even as love crowns you so shall he crucify you.
> Even as he is for your growth so is he for your pruning.
> Even as he ascends to your height and caresses your tenderest branches that quiver in the sun,
> So shall he descend to your roots and shake them in their clinging to the earth.
>
> —Kahlil Gibran (1883-1931)[52]

This is one of the most famous of Gibran's testimonies to the mystery of love. Living today in the West, people have great difficulty in accepting that love is really a "purifying fire." Indeed, the sentimental and romantic notions of love common in our culture never reach to the reality of love as the most powerful force for purification and transformation available to humanity. Indeed, when a couple is being confronted again and again with a difficult problem or conflict, the tendency is to become deeply distressed and wonder why this keeps happening, i.e., "Why me?" or "Why us?" But even when both persons have given themselves fully to the beloved path and are doing their utmost to blend through deep love and devotion, the tests will come, for the love that they share is not yet what it must become.

On the spiritual path we are constantly being tested so that we can demonstrate whether what we have learned about the spiritual life is only a concept held in the mind, or whether it has been integrated thoroughly into our being and is alive and growing within as a force determining our thoughts, feelings and actions. The pain of moving through distressful experiences and conditions may impel us to make a serious effort to develop the inner qualities that will usher in a true resolution to our dilemma. We must creatively draw on our will and our love to create a solution.

Thus, periods of great difficulty are a necessary part of the path because they force us to exceed our current limits of will and love. We cannot make progress unless we creatively face the crises in our life. A crisis can serve to purify us of negative elements as well as to strengthen our faith in the work and in our will to continue with the difficult path to greater love. The more intense our thrust toward the light, the darker is the "Night of the Soul" when it comes. The reason for this is that as we strive spiritually, we are opening up to the vibrations from the higher realms and this influx of light exposes the dark and negative elements within and without. The negativity resists this exposure, and we may suddenly find ourselves in a state of utter futility and darkness.

Many couples on the beloved path do have a loving and harmonious relationship, and some have thought that because of this they might not be moving forward on the path. Over the years several couples have expressed to us that they had considered digging up some hidden or denied *emotional* problems in order to progress. Indeed, some couples have even asked us if they might not speed the evolution of their beloved relationship and their spiritual growth by seeking out conflict or suffering, even initiating it purposefully. Neither of these stratagems is necessary or desirable. We don't have to look for challenges or try to create them. As we strive on the path, the tests will come of their own accord. When we need them, and when we are ready, they will arise out of the very fabric of our life together. Indeed, the unfolding of the Will of the Divine (i.e., the Law of Karma) in our life of struggle will eventually bring into expression all the glamours and illusions which are part of our personality, and also the selfish and negative elements hidden within that are now beyond our awareness.

A man and woman who are truly committed to the path of the beloved usually have an awareness that at some other time and place they must have already gone through a process of growth and purification, both as individuals and as a couple. This must be so, or they would not be ready and willing to do the work that is required of them on this path. The intense and relatively unselfish love which they have experienced must have developed and evolved from states of lesser love. Yet, if they aspire to reach upwards to the more spiritual and transcendent qualities of the beloved-experience, their love must be further purified and tempered. It must be refined and *proven*. Indeed, in order to reach the heights of spiritual love, a beloved relationship must be confronted, not only by challenges and difficulties, but by a *crisis* that erodes and dissolves its very foundation. That foundation must be dismantled and seen from a totally different perspective so that it can be transcended and a new one realized.

Most of our students react with sadness and fear at hearing this concept. The idea that a devastating crisis in our relationship might be necessary to achieve our spiritual purpose is a disquieting thought—it is contrary to their assumptions of what a marriage can be and to their image of what a beloved relationship ought to be. Indeed, it often comes as a disappointing shock to realize that even after so much suffering and genuine achievement in the relationship, there is more work to be done, perhaps even greater horizons of suffering to be crossed.[53] This is a very crucial period for most seekers. Some do not want to hear that their struggle will continue and must necessarily intensify. And many others do not want to hear that the foundation of their relationship, which they evaluate as good and positive, must be overthrown and superseded, for a new and greater one to emerge. Indeed, the level of faith required at this juncture is daunting, for who among us would be willing to seek beyond a "good and positive" circumstance for the promise of something better which we cannot even conceive? This in itself is a test. And we must realize that the Way of the Beloved, as a spiritual path, is replete with such impenetrable choices.

☙❧

The fire next time. The revolution, or second coming;
he will baptize you with the Holy Spirit and with fire.
　　　—Luke 3:16[54]

Thou bringst forth souls and lesser lives,
Which from above in chariots swift thou dost disperse
Through sky and earth, and by Thy law benign they turn
And back to thee they come through fire that brings them home.
　　　—Boethius (C. 480-524 CE)[55]

To enter the valley of love, one must plunge wholly into fire. Yes, one must
become fire itself, for otherwise one cannot live there. He that truly loves must
resemble fire, his countenance aflame, burning and impetuous like fire.
　　　—Farid Ud-Din Attar (Fl. 1150-1200 CE)[56]

Trials will never be lacking in religious life, nor does god want them to be. Since
He brings souls there to be proved and purified, like gold, with the hammer and
the fire, it is fitting that they encounter trials and temptations from men and from
devils, and the fire of anguish and affliction.
　　　—St. John of the Cross (1542-1591)[57]

What meaning do these fire-metaphors have in our secular, post-modern culture? When Christ returns will He "baptize" us with fire? Will our souls return to God through fire, "by Thy law benign,"? Or "to enter the valley of love," must we "become fire itself"? Perhaps, many can identify with Attar, because love often resembles fire. And perhaps many may feel that God is pitilessly purifying us "with the hammer and the fire." These kinds of images are not current and very few modern Westerners, even those who profess a religious practice, would feel much receptivity to the idea that the very roots of their personality must be burned away by the refining-fire of the Holy-Spirit before the Wisdom and Love of God can dwell in their soul. Nevertheless, the fundamental laws guiding the evolution of the human soul have not changed, just because we are in a secular, humanistic and anti-mystical age.

What useful meaning might "test-of-fire" have for couples today? Clearly, we are not referring to the emotional conflicts and personality problems that a couple meets constantly in the day to day unfolding of their life together. What we are referring to are the kinds of crises that directly challenge us to question the inherent validity of our immediate experience. A test-of-fire comes as that dreaded situation which forces us to reevaluate the very roots of our being. It will suddenly call into question, who we think we are, what we are really doing with our life and our relationship, and the very reason and purpose for our existence—that is, the *why-of-it-all*. This is a circumstance that can be a frightful and shocking experience, one which legitimately terrifies and shatters our personality and may plunge us into the dark pit of despair. It is an experience that has the potential to expose a block or illusion or a hidden limitation to our present state of awareness. It is a sudden psychic trauma which could beat us down and limit our life expression or, if we can meet it creatively with love and will, it can lead to a realization that is so much greater than any insight or *aha*-experience we have ever had. Indeed, it can catapult us into a new, expanded, more inclusive level of awareness, wisdom and love-consciousness.

Thus, while moving through a test-of-fire we experience a blindness beyond which we cannot penetrate. Indeed, we are overcome by the darkness and we cannot see any way out. We think we are doing everything that a "beloved" *should*—as one woman we know cried out, "It's just not working! Is this the Dark Night of the Soul?"[58] Indeed, the soul must lose what it believes is the *light*. And before any new light or love dawns in our heart, we may also lose our faith and hope in the possibility of any fulfillment—even in the validity of the Path. We may find ourselves sincerely trying to follow all the practices of the beloved path, yet everything we do seems to produce the wrong or opposite results. We cannot find any way to love in the paralyzing circumstances presented to us. It is a most difficult and dark time for a beloved relationship, and a couple cannot move through the process without intense suffering and pain.

Since the effects of any particular event are different for each couple and for each person in the relationship, a situation that feels like a mere setback or difficulty for one couple, may be seen as a profound and insurmountable tragedy for another.

Here are some examples of situations which became a test-of-fire for couples we have known:

1. A test-of-fire can come as a totally unexpected, unanticipatable condition or event, like a serious accident; becoming a victim of a crime; the discovery of alcohol or drug addiction in either partner or in the family; or the sudden onset of a catastrophic or chronic illness in oneself or one's partner. For instance, one man confided to us:

   When Marcy first became ill, it brought us closer together. I devoted myself to caring for her for months, even to the detriment of my business. That didn't seem to matter much at the time. But as the months, and now years, have gone on, our relationship is so different, we can't see how to be beloveds anymore. We can't do any of the things that we used to enjoy that were part of our *togetherness*. We used to go backpacking in the mountains and to the theater, we'd have guests and parties in our home, you name it! We don't have that kind of life anymore. I'm a caregiver mostly, and that's all right for what it is, but are we beloveds? We can't make love like we used to, we can't go out like we used to, it's all gone. It's just not the same ...

2. For many people there is lurking in the recesses of their mind an event or situation that they fear as an ultimate ordeal, an "anything-but-that." Should that which they fear actually come to pass, it can become a test-of-fire. It can be almost anything, but events like the death of a child, sudden abandonment by a spouse, or an extramarital involvement are common anything-but-thats.

A woman once told us that she believed she could face any experience except for the death of one of her children. She even said to friends, "I can handle anything-but-that." It was only two years later that her 11 year old son died, very suddenly, from complications of an ordinary childhood illness. She went into a massive depression, boiling over with anger toward God and blame against her husband, none of which had been present in their relationship before. Her marriage ended, and she has never really recovered even though that was 25 years ago.

3. A test-of-fire can arise in the guise of an apparently new opportunity for one or the other member of a couple.

We know a man who loved the theater and had always wanted to be an actor. Ever since he was very young he passionately studied the thespian craft and dreamed of performing on stage with a repertory company. Shortly after he married his high school sweetheart they found the spiritual path of the beloved. They had just begun to devote themselves to each other and to raising a baby when he received the offer he had been waiting for all his life. This was a real opportunity to fulfill his dream and to go on tour around the world with a famous Shakespearean company. But, of course, this would mean being "on the road" nine months out of the year. How could they sustain a loving marriage with him gone most of the time? He was faced with the dilemma of deciding what was more important: realizing his individual dream of fulfillment or seeking to move on the path of love ... (We will tell the rest of this story later.)

4. A test-of-fire may also come in the form of an awareness that emerges gradually out of the normal progression of life. A couple may not even know that it is happening until, without any forewarning, they find that they are immersed in it.

Two common examples of this test are "The Empty Nest Syndrome" and Retirement. People may look forward to the time when their children will be independent. They may prepare for years for their retirement anticipating that they will enjoy a life of freedom in those years. Then, when the children leave, they find themselves alone together in an empty house and when they retire they don't know what to do with themselves. They often drink too much and argue about trivialities, becoming isolated, depressed and subject to numerous illnesses. They lose any sense of purpose for living and fall into the pit of aimlessness and despair. Many never regain a hold on life.

5. A little understood or recognized test-of-fire usually affecting spiritual seekers is the buildup up of fear, dread or terror before the *threshold* to the unknown. This can be the threshold of new knowledge about one's self or the world, or the revelation of a new possibility of greater commitment and depth in one's love-relationship, or the approach of the Sacred in a myriad of forms. Andrew Harvey captured the sense of this test-of-fire: "there is a violent beauty in revelation that the soul loves but the ego fears as death."[59] Indeed, the threshold is a harbinger of death, but it is the death of the ego, not the Spirit or love. However, we cannot know this at the time, and without adequate preparation we most likely will back away and never realize what happened.

Two examples come to mind: both were men and both were successful professionals. They both took to the beloved work with love and will. However, as their relationships approached those places where any continued movement on the path required greater commitment and sacrifice which would seriously call into question their basic assumptions of who they were as individuals and how they should live their life in a beloved relationship, both were overcome with dread and fell back. One divorced and the other stayed married, but left the beloved work. We will present their stories later.

ॐ

Are there ways to prepare to meet a test-of-fire? A couple dedicated to the practices of the beloved path is preparing continually in their daily life. All the work that they do to love each other "no matter what" is a preparation. Every day they face many smaller or larger tests which demonstrate whether they are falling into routines and taking each other for granted or are actively cultivating their devotion to the path of love. But since the test-of-fire covers them with a cloud of un-knowingness, apparently negating any way that they already know to follow, a solution seems *impossible*. It is at these extreme times that they often become discouraged and think, or even say to each other: "Why should we continue to walk this path?" "We are going nowhere." "Maybe we never loved each other anyway!" And many couples do give up. But for those who are willing to persist, despite the seeming impossibility of the task, there is always the hope and the real possibility that they can break through the darkness and doubt into a state of greater love.

There are two interrelated parts to any method which can help prepare us for the test-of-fire: *attitude* and *technique*. *Attitude* refers to our inner orientation and *technique* refers to the specific practice and resultant actions. Attitude as inner orientation means that we know which way our inner compass needle is pointing, e.g., the word "orientation" comes from knowing which way is East, the Orient.[60] Orientating ourselves within the world of love and thus, within a *spiritual cosmos* (i.e., heading East, the traditional direction towards "enlightenment"), is essential to meeting the difficult tests in our beloved relationship as precious opportunities for spiritual growth. As we have said so many times, since contemporary humanity has lost the compass along with the needle, our orientation is a first priority. It would seem that if our attitude toward our suffering is oriented toward the spiritual heights, our suffering becomes actually conducive to creativity and growth.

Each of the following concepts and exercises describes a reorientation in attitude and suggests a meditation practice:

1. SPIRITUAL PURPOSE

The test-of-fire gives a man and woman the opportunity to develop a Vision and a Faith beyond what they already know or have dared to conceive possible. To achieve this, they must find some purpose greater than any they have relied upon—e.g., the Radical Trust discussed in 4.3. They must reach for a spiritual goal and a higher concept than they have been able to see before. They must discover—or rediscover with a new understanding—a spiritual teaching that can become a guiding principle and a *sustaining* vision, one that will carry them through the painful process of purification by fire.

All Spiritual traditions tell us that there is order and purpose throughout this world and throughout the universe and that even if we cannot see it or know it, there is design and meaning to all our experience. Seekers are taught that the experiences of our life are part of a Great Spiritual Plan—for our own life and for *all* life. Moreover, Higher Forces and our own Higher Self have placed us in the environment that is best suited to our spiritual growth. We are Karmically placed in the conditions that we need to stimulate our spiritual development, and not in the conditions that the ego wants or thinks it should have. Thus there is a hidden manifestation of Divine Love in the very depths of our personal reality, which can provide a key to opening our comprehension of the spiritual potential within our everyday experience.

A couple on the path of the beloved comes to recognize that it is not an accident that they have been brought together with each other. They begin to realize that there must be an overlighting spiritual purpose for their relationship. Some comprehension dawns, or maybe some belief, that it is necessary for them to experience their conflict and the disturbing circumstances in order to grow in love and consciousness. They see their pain and suffering as an unavoidable part of their path and they believe that, with a creative spiritual attitude, they will be able to move through the difficulty. Through their intense aspiration to advance spiritually, they must focus on the divine purpose hidden behind the events that often overwhelm them. Thus they become oriented within a spiritual cosmos or framework of belief, thought and faith which gives them the opportunity and the ability to meet conflict, pain and suffering as a precious opportunity for their spiritual growth.

They also come to believe that if they continue and persist in faith through the dark time, reaching steadfastly for a higher truth that somehow, some way, a door will open to a resolution and a realization of new love and harmony. Through faith in the power of the Spirit, the will to sustain a focus on the Divine in our beloved and constantly abiding in love we will eventually see a break in the psychic storm and move into a realm of greater light and wisdom. The terrifying and seemingly hopeless internal struggle transforms the body and mind into a clearer instrument for the higher love to flow through. This is the process of purification by fire. Thus, rather than giving up, this is the time to intensify the thrust toward the spiritual threshold.

Some couples tell us that they are only able to persist because they recognize that if they do not do the work now, when the difficulties arise again it will be the same test all over and they will have to handle it anyway, perhaps under even more difficult circumstances. Indeed, if we fail to meet the test-of-fire it must return until we do! In order to reach the heights of love and a truly higher consciousness, no stone may be left unturned. To disregard this law or to detour from the path, inevitably leads one into deeper Maya and suffering. We must learn that all our experiences, and even our so called *environment,* are the result of *who* we are. Moreover, if we resent and resist the test we become tied to the very conditions we are so anxious to leave behind. These conditions will not change unless we radically transform the current state of our mind and heart.

The following meditation provides sustenance for this orientation:

Meditation:

STORMS ON THE PATH [61]

When you decide that the Beloved path is your way to the higher worlds, you make a commitment to the Spiritual Beloved, the divine being within each other. You realize that every experience comes to you with a purpose—to teach you and help you reach the spiritual mountain top. You recognize that you must meet all problems in your life together as opportunities to overcome the blocks in your nature. You keep intensely focused on the divine in your beloved, whether conditions are calm or stormy, whether your emotions are bright or dark. When you realize that all your experience is according to a plan, you will face it with courage. You will not resent it. If you resist the experience, it will repeat itself later, in more difficult circumstances. And if you persist through the storm with love in the heart, a psychic veil is lifted, and you shall be touched with the light from another world.

Mantram:
I am dedicated to the spiritual path of the beloved,
Through intense love, I shall break through the storm.

or

No storm or wind can move me from the path.
Love with my beloved is the way to the higher worlds.

or

The struggle on the beloved path leads me to the spiritual heights.
Through intense love I shall break through the storm.

or

Every experience is an opportunity for spiritual growth,
My beloved is helping me to move toward the spiritual heights.

2. THE ATTITUDE OF GRATITUDE

Knowing that there is a purpose behind the events in their life makes it possible for a couple to aspire toward a state of gratitude. Faith that their suffering has meaning, even if they cannot see it, shall provide the foundation for the light-of-gratitude to sustain them through a difficult test. Instead of complaining, resisting and resenting the purifying fire, trusting that their experience is helping them to grow toward the higher consciousness, opens the door to gratitude (refer back to 1.3 for the discussion on the nature and scope of gratitude).

All Spiritual Traditions have a way of offering the concept of gratitude or thankfulness. In the Bible, it is written: "We know that all things work together for good to those who love God" (Ro. 8:28). Trust in this truth will give us great power to meet the suffering and pain which is ours to experience. But even though many believe it and even may have had an experience of its truth, the modern Chasidic Rabbi, Adin Steinsaltz reminds us that, "there is a difference between theoretically knowing that God is always present and knowing it when one is crushed. To be sure, there are many saints and even ordinary men [& women], who are able to ... receive ... the evil as well as the good ... without complaint ... also with joy. The capacity to do so is a function of deeper comprehension as well as of faith or certainty in the wisdom of the hidden workings of God."[62] And Paul Tillich takes us further by showing that to be grateful for all our circumstances would be to consecrate or elevate our whole life, to "become a bearer of grace":

> In the letter to 1 Timothy 4:4 we read—"For everything created by God is good and nothing is to be rejected if it is received with thanksgiving; for then it is consecrated by the word of God and prayer." In these words, thanksgiving receives a new function. It consecrates everything created by God. *Thanksgiving is consecration; it transfers something that belongs to the secular world into the sphere of the holy ... It has become a bearer of grace ... Everything for which we* can give thanks with a good conscience is consecrated by our thanks.[63]

Thus a sustained and daily practice of gratitude for every experience[64] will develop an orientation or attitude toward our life-world which enables us to believe that it is at least possible to meet our circumstances with active thankfulness. This is a significant reorientation of our inner stance toward the vicissitudes of life. The invocation of a state of gratitude can be a powerful preparation for meeting the test-of-fire—it is a firm place to start and a rock to stand on when the inevitable tempest of raging fire threatens to drown us.

Use the following gratitude Meditation:

Meditation:

THE POWER OF GRATITUDE [65]

I walk the path of light that is full of struggle every hour,
But I am focused on the divine purpose all day long;
This struggle helps me to grow in spirit,
I am grateful for the struggle,
It has taught me to love in the golden presence of this hour.

Mantram:
*I am grateful for this experience
because I know it is helping me up the spiritual mountain;
I enfold my beloved with love.*

3. THE WILL-TO-LOVE

To grow spiritually means to learn how to love when and where we have not been able to love previously. It is for this purpose that the Beloveds have been brought together. The test-of-fire is their opportunity to develop the will-to-love, *no matter what*. Without a steadfast intention to love in all circumstances, without a deep, heartfelt commitment to reach for the power of love *first*, we cannot derive a true spiritual benefit when we are immersed in suffering. Love in this sense is the "will -to-love." Without the guiding force of the will-to-love, it is difficult, perhaps impossible, to sustain our faith in the process and purpose of seemingly insurmountable conflict and interminable suffering. Those who lose faith in the midst of suffering plunge into despair. Without love we will be unable to trust in anything. Thus the will-to-love gives us the power to reorient the habitual attitudes of our blind and limited ego-self. Suffering and pain alone are extremely effective in stripping away the arrogant illusions of the ego, but without the will-to-love they can lead us into greater bondage within an enlarged and more negative egoism fed by continuous *meaningless* suffering.[66] This is the underside of egoism which draws it's conviction of innate superiority from the sovereign measure of its suffering, and thus inflates itself by asserting, "No one has ever suffered as much as I must!"

To call upon and make use of our will-to-love requires that every day, every hour, we use a love Mantra with an unshakeable faith in its effectiveness to change our inner state. It takes enormous courage and perseverance to walk the Path and meet a test-of-fire. Every morning and throughout the day, actively renew the will-to-love. For example continuously use one of the following mantras—saturate your mind with the invocation:

> *I will love today.*
> *I will persist on this path today.*
> *I will love, no matter what the test.*
> *I say, "Yes," to the struggle, I will follow this path. I will love.*
> *I will not give up. Today I will love!*

To be in a state of love is the best preparation for meeting a test. If our attitude toward our suffering in a time of great confusion and darkness is oriented by the unshakeable will-to-love, the experience becomes conducive to creativity and growth. Through the will-to-love all experience may bring us into a new awareness of deeper levels of our being and existence.

4. SACRIFICE AS A NECESSITY
When a couple has made the commitment to move towards a higher realm of love, they realize that they must be willing to sacrifice whatever attitudes, ideas, beliefs, habits or opinions stand in the way of their vision and spiritual destiny. Thus they become willing to "give-up" or *transform*, that which blinds them from seeing the Divine in their beloved. A man and woman cannot blend in love to become a Beloved couple, unless attachment to the separative tendencies of their egos is intentionally and consciously sacrificed for a more selfless love. We cannot ascend the mountain of Spirit unless we sacrifice the lower in order to attain the higher. And the painful, disabling test-of-fire requires a greater sacrifice than we could have ever imagined— i.e., *who we believe ourselves to be.* Thomas Merton writes: "Love demands a complete inner transformation ... And this involves a kind of death of our own being, our own self."[67] And in speaking with a student, Thuksey Rinpoche had this exchange:

> Q: "Is the process toward enlightenment painful?"
> A: "Yes."
> Q: "Is this pain necessary?"
> A: "Yes. One life has to end for another to begin. The ego has to die for awareness to be born. The ego does not die fast." Then he said, "The misery you will have to endure in realizing enlightenment is nothing to the misery you will endure in life after life if you do not realize it. To get an arrow out of the flesh, you have to probe the wound. That hurts. But be grateful that you have understood enough to choose this misery."[68]

The Buddhists have always had a firm grasp on the necessity of ultimately sacrificing, "renouncing" or "abandoning" the very core of what we believe and perceive. Buddhist practice is founded on the notion that our current state of consciousness is submerged in the illusions of Maya and, therefore, everything we believe and perceive is in error and only constitutes a *shadow* of the Truth. The Buddha taught that in order to overcome the illusions of the selfish-ego and of Maya:

> We must be still within ourselves, still and calm, and yet we must also, at the same time, be moving forward, moving further and deeper towards each other, towards the world. What is not useful for this endless transformation must be abandoned; anything that prevents a finer flowering of our spirit must be left behind; anything that hinders us from dealing with the world as it is, with ourselves as we are, in this place and in this time, with all the dangers and fears and sadnesses of this time and this place, must be renounced, and renounced, if possible, without grief and without nostalgia. Every truthful transformation takes us closer to the world, closer to things, closer to each other; the clearest and wisest man becomes the world, becomes Buddha, becomes "awake," enters without fear and without hope, and without any consolation or protection, into the full presence of Reality.[69]

Indeed, a beloved couple must realize that the path lies precisely in the sacrifice of their *attachment* to their selfish-ego, even as they resist those painful changes that appear to make them "less" than who they think they are. It is attachment to the selfish ego that "prevents a finer flowering of our spirit." It is our absorption in self-interest, our self-love, and our illusions of self-sufficiency and separateness, that prevents the vision of "ourselves as we are" in Truth. We must even renounce all our negative *and* positive emotional responses to our time and place and it would be best if we could do this "without grief and without nostalgia." This may indeed seem an unachievable goal, but when we are truly on the path of love, we will not even *think* of the separated ego-self, much less be attached to it. Yet, to move closer to each other it is essential for Beloveds to become "awake" and enter "without fear and without … protection, into the full presence of Reality." Indeed, this is only achievable through the sacrifice of one's precious thoughts, feelings, opinions and beliefs for the sake of a higher love. Thus, Beloveds enter into a state of mind and heart that denotes a *metanoia*, a deep turning about, or a selfless reorientation of their whole being toward Love and toward the Divine.

There is a common mistaken notion describing the process of seeking enlightenment which asserts that "we must give up the ego." We do not achieve a state of "egolessness" by abolishing the ego, despite what it sounds like. This is impossible! The Sufis say that the ego is the top rung of the ladder we are standing on, and if we believe that we must destroy it, where will we stand? What we must sacrifice is our *attachment*, our fondness for the selfish-ego. It is our attachment to self-love, self-aggrandizement, self-interest and the seeking of personal pleasure that is the problem. It is the "self-love" of the ego (i.e., *egoism*) which must be sacrificed, and thus, the ego will become transformed into a vehicle of love-for-others or compassion. However, this cannot happen as long as we are committed to, and identify ourselves with our selfish desires and personal self-interests.

What this means for us in practical terms of reorienting our attitudes toward sacrifice, is that, by relinquishing whatever egoism we are clinging to, through gratitude, love and faith in the Divine purpose, we will attain a higher state of consciousness and become more at-one-with the spirit-of-love. Gratitude, love and faith have the *power* to transform the selfish-ego, but they cannot do it if we are casual or lacking courage. We must passionately aspire with great fortitude and make faith and love our *way of life*.

Thus, no matter how painful and impossible the condition may seem at the time, we trust that when our attachments to the separative-ego are sacrificed out of love for our beloved we will move into a new world of love and a fulfillment of the promise of the Way of the Beloved. Sacrificing the separative impulses of our ego-nature opens us to a union-in-love that is centered in the Divine Presence. This would be a participation in a spiritual *whole* which is greater than the individual personality can encompass. When the relationship of a beloved couple is centered in this living presence of the Divine, it is no longer vulnerable to the powerful storms welling-up from the unconscious levels of the personalities or from catastrophic events streaming in from the life-world. It has been said that, "nothing shall be denied a couple focused and centered in the Spiritual Presence."

This is a meditation on Sacrifice in the context of the Beloved relationship:

Meditation:

SACRIFICING THE PERSONALITY[70]

Life with your beloved swings from joy to depression, from crisis to crisis. Through love without criticism, you know that your beloved is helping you on the spiritual path. But the ego is large and has a great fear that you will lose yourself.

When you are truly on the path of love, you will not think of yourself. You will know that only by losing your selfish-egoism will you find your True Self. When you are centered in the Living Presence, a greater Reality shall be revealed.

Mantram: *Through deep love for my beloved,*
I lose the illusion of my separate self
and I find my true spiritual self.

₧₨

Thus, for a beloved couple, the problems that emerge in their relationship, even the threatening crisis that comes as a test-of-fire, are not viewed as obstacles to their happiness and pleasure in life, but rather as signals that there is work to be done. They are seen as a necessary part of the path of spiritual growth.

Many beloved couples have lives that are filled with constant turmoil. Their relationship seems to be a constant series of one crisis after another. This condition often produces an intensity that can lead to breakthrough experiences, if the intensity is directed to the will-to-love and to sacrifice.

But there are some beloved couples who have an unusually harmonious relationship, and they often think that they have really achieved something and are doing well on the beloved path. This is a real trap that can lead to a complacency and lack of attention to the work of transformation. These couples are surprised and shocked, and often react with disbelief and puzzlement when they are faced with an unforeseen conflict or test. Again, as Rabbi Steinsaltz explains:

> the greatest hindrance to spiritual awakening is a certain smugness, a dullness of the heart and mind. In this case, all the books and all the messages of spiritual love will not avail. Indeed, self-complacency is a more serious obstacle than depression or stupidity. To overcome it, to smash through the barrier of "fatness" of soul, it is often necessary to pass through some sort of crisis or tragic experience. And this is often brought about by heavenly intervention, against one's own wishes and designs.[71]

Indeed, the process of purification is mysterious and involves purposings beyond our ken. We don't know how or why it happens that some couples can come through a difficult test or, as is so common in our turbulent times, one or both people give up the struggle. When both people feel that they "have" to do *it* and are committed to the necessity of "doing *it* together," there is more of a chance that they can come through to a new place. But what does it mean to "come through"? As we shall see in the following examples, just staying together is not a demonstration of "coming through." Only a greater awareness and activity of love indicates that a real movement has been made. Sometimes it is more constructive to break the connection and move apart. As our teacher said, "When a couple find that there is no love in their union and that they are caught in conflict which they cannot solve, they should try to see the divine in each other and dissolve the block. If this cannot be dissolved, they should seek another path that is constructive to their spiritual purpose."[72] If a separation should occur, each will enter another cycle in their spiral of life-experiences, hopefully, with an intensification of their hopes, strivings, limitations, sorrows and sufferings, any of which might become new opportunities for spiritual growth.

No matter what work a couple has been doing, no matter how much love there seems to be between them, no matter how *we* might feel about their prospects as a beloved couple, there is no way to predict the outcome of a test-of-fire. The following four stories describe how some couples have met their test-of-fire:

1. Here is what happened to the two men whose relationships suffered from their fear-before-the-threshold:

    Jeremy and Rachael were married in their late 30s. Rachael had been briefly married before, but had no children. Both were professionals in the field of Public Administration, and separately they had been searching for several years to find a spiritual path.

    Jeremy was plagued with fear right from the beginning of their marriage. We interpreted what we saw in him as fear of losing his identity, his *idea* of who he was: that is, his carefully constructed, independent and somewhat solitary personality. But both he and Rachael were sincere in seeking a Spiritual goal and practice. Rachael enthusiastically embraced the beloved path almost immediately. As the first 5 years went by, Jeremy alternated between reticence about the Beloved Path and tentative acceptance. Most of the time he would try this group and that group, going from one to another, i.e., Zen, Tibetan Buddhist, Hindu—always an Eastern ascetic discipline.

    In one cycle he did move more deeply into a commitment to the path of the Beloved and tried to adopt it fully as his path to enlightenment. He and Rachael became a beloved couple! But fear was always an underlying factor, a shadow on their life together. Twice during the time that we worked with them, there arose doubts on Jeremy's part as to "whether they should be together at all!" The first time that this happened he backed off and turned away psychically from the Beloved work and from his wife. The second time, with no warning or preparation, he declared that he was leaving the marriage, because he was overcome with terror at the idea of "just continuing." At this juncture, he somehow gained enough insight into his "fear-before-the-threshold" to stay and continue. However, it was not long before he began to drift away again from actively participating in the beloved work, even as they stayed together. Perhaps as a sign that the relationship was cooling, Rachael found a different line of work which took her away much of the time.

    It was 5 years after they stopped actively working with us that we heard Jeremy had left Rachael permanently, again with no warning or discussion—just the vague desire to no longer be a couple, and they were divorced after 12 years of being together. It seems as if Jeremy's persistent, unalterable view of himself continues to be one of a lonely monk, going it alone, "beholden" to no one. And it would seem that he considers the solitary life to be the only life he would consider as *spiritual*. We have come to believe that Jeremy is still not really aware that it is the threshold of the unknown and the necessity to transform his self-absorption into creative compassion that he fears.

Jonathon was an internationally known Professor of Neurophysiology in a prestigious university, and his research and teaching had always been of supreme importance to him, but the time came when he must retire! He and Andrea had been married for 36 years and had three grown children. It was a very good marriage, except that Andrea had always felt that Jonathon did not spend enough time with her, and she was looking forward to his retirement.

Both of them had been fruitfully pursuing the Beloved work for 4 years, but as the actual moment of Jonathon's retirement approached, his 50 year identification of himself with his profession was being threatened at its very foundation. He had been fearfully anticipating retirement for several years, but as it became imminent his fear expanded and manifested as skepticism toward the spiritual work itself. We believe that the work he had done to increase the love for his beloved, and thus to diminish his ego-focus, had magnified the possibility of "losing his identity," when he retired.

As a scientist, Jonathon was "born and bred" on materialist principles and considered a skeptical and thoroughly empirical attitude as healthy. Nonetheless, he had been able to regard love and love for his beloved, in particular, as a kind of absolute, i.e., an important area of his being and life not subject to scientific doubt. However, as his fear grew this fire-wall crumbled. Confronting the long-dreaded moment of retirement and, at the same time, approaching the threshold of a greater love with the possibility of becoming a less self-centered person, was just too much. Abruptly one day, Jonathon, in a paroxysm of desperate doubt, convulsively threw out the baby with the wash water and declared the work on the path to be nothing more than a hoax, a false and misleading approach to his inner and outer life—e.g., vague mysticism, a cult! The immediate relief brought by this turning-away seemed like a real resolution and, from then on, he could not turn back to the beloved work which had been creatively confronting the frightful dilemma that had plagued his life for many years.

Jonathon soon retired without having resolved his basic fear. He stopped doing any spiritual work and he plays a lot of golf and often takes trips away from home by himself. He and Andrea are still married, and she has continued to be "interested" in the spiritual life, but neither of them pursues any further growth on a path of love.

2. Sometimes a test-of-fire will send one person in the relationship spiraling off, or even downwards, back into the world he or she knew before doing any of the Beloved work. This may happen after many years of a congenial marriage and sometimes even after doing the work and seeing some movement on the path.

Roberto and Mariana always had a rocky marriage, yet they had been working on the beloved path for several years and had made some progress. For instance, they seemed to have developed a strong commitment to "stay the course, no matter what." Many crises had come and gone, but they had hung on and continued to love each other with a remarkable tenderness and fortitude. However, Roberto was wrongly accused and convicted of a crime. The whole thing seemed like something out of a cheap novel. But no matter how bizarre and ridiculous the situation became, it was one with catastrophic consequences: A whole year of degrading jail-time, followed by an egregious and lengthy parole under corrupt officials was devastating to Roberto's rather tenuous grip on the spiritual path.

Throughout it all Mariana never wavered and stood by Roberto with love and devotion. However, Roberto emerged from his test-of-fire a beaten man. He was truly broken by the experience and, when it was over, all love and faith had been drained away. He could no longer relate to Mariana as a beloved, or even as a friend. He reverted back to his way of life and his attitudes of 20 years before, prior to knowing about the spiritual path, and he seemed to blame Mariana for everything! They did divorce, but it took several more years of intense conflict and heartache before they could bring themselves to it—it seemed a great failure to both of them. Roberto now drinks a lot and wanders in the world, a lost soul. And even though they are in touch, it cannot be said that he and Mariana have remained close in any way.

Eventually, Mariana felt that she was free from her commitment to Roberto and, though deeply saddened, she has never left the Path. Now in middle age with the children grown and out on their own, Mariana has remarried and with her new husband is continuing on the path-of-love.

3. There is not much hope for a couple to come through a test-of-fire unless they believe that they have been brought together for a spiritual purpose. Being together only "for themselves," i.e., a *partnership* or an *alliance-a deux*, will not provide a couple with the faith, love and will to meet a test-of-fire. As long as two people are with each other for personal satisfactions, their life together can only be sustained if the road remains relatively smooth. Of course, very, very few have a smooth road in life!

    We knew a couple who approached their marriage as such a *partnership*. Indeed, from the start of their relationship they decided to do everything "right," according to what the latest scientifically verified evidence indicated a "successful" intimate relationship should be.

Teresa and Nicolas had both been married before, and there were several children—his, hers and theirs. They were both physicists, and similar to most scientists today they truly believed that empirical science had answered most all of the "important" questions about human behavior, about our human nature as "hairless apes," about our inviolable instinct toward pleasure and avoidance of pain, and about the satisfaction and enhancement of the individual personality as the only true meaning of human life. They were convinced that the process of "self-actualization," in a kind of behavioral sense, *was* "spiritual growth."

Proceeding from their shared humanistic assumptions, they knew that they could enhance their professional careers through the combined power of their alliance. This was not so easy in the 1960s because science still deferred to males and regarded women as intruders on their turf. Nonetheless, they pursued together the same research, delivered joint papers and were co-authors of all their

Journal articles. They wrote a book together and even taught their classes as a couple. This presentation of all their professional activities as a mutual enterprise was actually a laudable achievement and may have helped to establish, in some small way, the legitimacy of women in hard science.

Perhaps it was only because of the continuing struggle with the entrenched male establishment in their professional life that their personal life seemed headed for success and continued harmony. Indeed, they treated their marriage like one of their favorite "projects." Every week one full day and evening was spent alone together, talking and "working on" their relationship. They thoroughly discussed and resolved every issue, shared all their ideas and belongings and planned every move they made together. They even wore matching outfits and were always seen together, like twins.

However, after 25 years, as their "two against the world" stance became less and less a necessity in their work, a major fissure began to develop. Perhaps the struggle to display a united front in their work had been holding them together and had prevented other conflicts from emerging. The real test-of-fire came when the children were all grown and Teresa felt that she needed more time for her "own" projects. Often this left Nikolas alone, doing the work of two. Then, out of some obscure motive, she began to drift back into the conservative Protestanism of her youth. (Nikolas had been Greek Orthodox in his childhood.) She began attending a "community church" and spending more and more time with a local preacher and his followers.

Nikolas was nonplused—it might be said he was flabbergasted! Never in a million years could he have imagined that such a radical change could take place in his partner or in their relationship. For more than two decades they had devoted themselves to a strictly empirical science. Nicolas was bewildered, he could only think that Teresa had somehow, "done-a-180." He felt that she was, without good reason, throwing away everything that they had worked for and everything that they "stood" for —i.e., the empirical method and exact science, even reason itself. In addition, Nikolas saw that Teresa was turning away from all their close colleagues and personal friends, even their children. In his very bones, Nikolas was unable to accept or understand what was happening to Teresa.

As Teresa entered more deeply into the rigid and patriarchal orientation of her religion, the conflict in their relationship escalated until it reached epic proportions. She began to insist that Nikolas must adopt her viewpoints, "or else." Within two years, Teresa declared that she "could never love an 'atheist,'" and she abruptly divorced him.

Teresa moved into a small community of "true believers" and has remained single. Nikolas has remarried and has a loving and rewarding relationship with an Archaeologist, but he remains troubled and puzzled by what happened with Teresa.

The following are two examples of couples who have "come through" a test-of-fire to a new level of spiritual love and understanding.

1. This is the story of the man we mentioned above "who loved the theater and had always wanted to be an actor."

    Carl was a body-builder and had emigrated from Austria as a child. His wife, Tina, was Hispanic, and her family had lived in New Mexico for centuries. As we have related, just as they were beginning their life together as a family, Carl was offered the chance-of-a-lifetime to tour with a Shakespearean Repertory Company. The problem was that he would be away for 9 months out of the year and they both knew that they could not build a loving and intimate relationship under those conditions. Both Carl and Tina are very reserved people and they find it difficult to talk to each other, family or friends. It became clear that they were not going to talk openly with each other about the looming crisis. Indeed, each preferred to look within and work alone to find a solution. Carl was given only two months to make a decision and, as the weeks passed, the tension between them became all-consuming.

    From Carl's perspective, he believed that, "I've been waiting for this opportunity all my life, if I don't take it this time, it will surely never come again. I do love Tina and the baby, but I also don't want them to 'hold me back.' Maybe I can continue to follow the spiritual path while travelling and performing, I just don't know ..."

    Tina said to herself over and over again, "I'm afraid that it will be the end of our marriage if he goes. How do I know what will happen to him on the road, all sorts of distractions, including other women. How will I manage here alone with the baby? Yet I know how deeply he wants to take this opportunity, it would be the fulfillment of his dream and I do, so much, want him to be happy and fulfilled …"

This was truly a dilemma for both of them. They were each confronting deeply conflicting goals which could only be resolved by some kind of sacrifice. Carl was caught in the predicament that if he followed his dream for a profession he would lose the love of his life; while Tina was facing the choice of gaining what she wanted most of all at the price of denying Carl his dream. The test-of-fire was upon them before they had time to prepare— they had no idea of what of what to do!

Finally about two weeks before the deadline, Tina tearfully told Carl that she knew how important his acting career was to him. She tried valiantly to convince him—and herself—that she would be OK living alone with the baby, "for as long as he would be away." Indeed, she said she "wants him to go, if that is his desire," and "she will be there waiting for him when he gets back."

Then, just as emotionally and tearfully, Carl confessed to Tina that he had already decided: he was not going! He told her that his love for her and their path together meant more to him than an acting career. Indeed, it was *she* who had become his dream!

Miraculously, Carl soon found that the local Community Theater Group needed a manager/director and his career has been in the theater after all. Carl and Tina went on to have five children and they pursued the path of the beloved with much intensity and joy. Their home life became their "path," and for many years they were a model to their friends and the community of what a loving couple and family could be.

2. The following situation actually happened in a very similar way to two couples we knew well. We have combined their stories into a single example.

Martin and Claire had been married for about 5 years and had two small children. They were both spiritual seekers, following the Path of the Beloved, and were devoted to each other. They were responsible parents and stable members of their community. Martin came from a wealthy family and owned a small, but profitable, business. They had no money worries, indeed their life seemed blessed. However, one evening, totally out of the blue, Martin revealed to Claire that he had had a "psychic" experience of intense love and communion with another woman. She seemed to Martin to embody his ideal woman, at least in a physical sense. They had never slept together, but he had been emotionally involved with her for several weeks. He was in terrible conflict about "what was happening" to him and frightened about the danger that this posed to his otherwise charmed life and marriage.

Claire was absolutely devastated, she felt shattered. And yet, her response to her beloved surprised him and even herself. She said that because she loved him so much, she truly wanted him to have this beautiful experience. She would not want it to be denied him. But what now?

Some very painful and distraught months followed. Martin tried to avoid the other woman but she was an important member of his small company. Despite her apparent magnanimity, Claire felt that her whole life and very existence had been destroyed, blown apart. She didn't know "who she was" anymore and felt that she had nothing left to rely on. All that she had believed about her marriage was gone—except for her love for Martin which actually was stronger and brighter than ever. Martin could not help but notice this corrosive effect on Claire, but he did not know what to do about it.

After much suffering and much meditation on her predicament, Claire had a realization: She said to Martin that she knew she was "One with the Divine Feminine" and that this could make it possible for him to discover in her all that he had experienced with this other woman—and more besides. Martin was quite doubtful. He had never heard of such a concept, but his love for Claire had never diminished during this whole episode, and because of his commitment to the beloved path, he thought to give the idea a try. Gradually, miraculously, over a period of months, the love between Martin and Claire took on a new quality. They began to have unusual experiences of communion and a new intensity of love was born between them. Realizing that his so called "ideal woman" was a delusion created out of purely socially conditioned images of *those women all men desire most*, Martin was able to turn all of his emotional energy toward Claire. He began to realize that Claire could actually give him everything that he truly desired—she could be literally *everywoman* for him. Claire blossomed, her friends thought she had become a new person, as indeed she had. Neither Martin nor Claire had ever thought that life could be like this. The other woman is still there, but Martin's "psychic" energy goes all to Claire and she has become the Universal Feminine for him.

Thus, only if a couple has a deep and abiding faith and a powerful spiritual focus, and they are able to persist with Love and Will through the test of fire, will they move through the dark and stormy night to a new level of love and spiritual fulfillment. It is only then that they can see in truth that the process was necessary for their growth and part of a spiritual plan for their life. No one *comes through* the test-of-fire without being *reborn*. William James long ago asserted that

> *Those who survive great illness or great loss are twice born—they have drunk too deeply of the cup of bitterness ever to forget the taste—and their redemption is into a universe two stories deep.*[73]

ഇരു

• 7.3 STATE OF THE BELOVED •

7.3.1 LOVE AND PERSONALITY

The personality is just a bunch of inherited ideas and stubborn opinions, which is really a block in the Divine Nature within. But the personality puts up a fight for survival and will give you all kinds of reasons why you should hang onto it. If you want to move up the Spiritual Path, the personality must be sacrificed. You might think you are losing life itself, but in Reality you are dropping a ton of blocks.

—Herman Rednick[74]

The greatest barrier that stands between us and the spiritual consciousness is the ego or personality. And yet, most people today identify themselves solely and completely as a separate personality. Even the most ardent spiritual seekers and the most devoted beloved couples cannot avoid this identification, for it is the state of consciousness of humanity at this time. Our whole civilization persistently commands us to acknowledge our own ego as a self-sufficient individuality. The inherent bond of love between people is generally denied and is replaced by an identification with a fragile, indeed an illusory, sense of separation and independence. This absolutization of the individual personality produces a fear and mistrust of others rather than bonds of love. Vladimir Solovyev writes that "the falsehood and evil of egoism consist in the exclusive acknowledgment of absolute significance for oneself and in the denial of it for others."[75] The conviction that the false self, the personality, is a sovereign aloneness and that it is forever separate from the rest of the cosmos, sealed as it were in an inviolable envelope of subjectivity, has led to the ubiquitous obssession with one's own self and the pursuit of one's own self-interest— for most this has become the highest goal of life.

Therefore, for the majority of people today and in most couple relationships, the experience of love is a purely personal and largely emotional concern, a feeling state of the personality or ego. Unavoidable differences between individuals have become indications that another person is in opposition to one's own needs or desires. Indeed, modern relationships are characterized by feelings of limitation and restriction. Instead of looking toward a geater experience of love through a relationship with another real human being, many experience the anticipation and fear of being hurt—and the more intimate the relationship, the more potential hurt. Utter selfishness has led us to so much individual unhappiness and meaninglessness, and it is this that seems to underlie our current social strife and violence.

Thus, in the modern world, we are faced with a painful paradox: the individual personality, with all its likes and dislikes, has become absolutized, yet we all still strive desperately to love and to be loved. This is certainly one of the greatest sources of pain and suffering in our age. We want desperately to love and to be loved, but the power of egoism waxes strong, sustained and backed by the instruments of our culture which have been created to support and enhance our natural human inclination toward selfishness and self-absorption.

Indeed, the power of love threatens the personality at the roots of its illusion, for it is the only force capable of transforming it. The norm today is to experience the personality as *life* itself, and any diminishment of its grip on our consciousness—that is, any lessening of our egoism—is felt as a sign of imminent death. The psychologist, Robert Sardello writes that "Even the *thought* of relinquishing egotism produces fear because egotism seems to provide a secure foothold in the world."[76] Our whole materialistic culture constantly bombards us with the erroneous dictum that there is no life "beyond the limits of our empirical personality" and, therefore, we must try again and again to save our own *life* (personality) at all costs. Thus, even though we seek love with all our heart, when confronted with loving interactions with another being, the personality will fight for its survival with defensive, isolating reactions.

It is not that the path of transforming the personality through love of others has become unknown in the last 2,000 years, but in our narcissistic age the transformative power of *Agape* is either ignored or expressly denied and Christ's commandment to "love ye one another" is mostly forgotten. Yet, as Teilhard de Chardin said, "Love alone is capable of uniting living beings in such a way as to complete and fulfil them, for it alone takes them and joins them by what is deepest in themselves."[77] Only selfless love has the power to transform, unite and transcend all the limitations and fears of the personality. The power of love is the alternative to a life trapped within the narrow confines of egoism and its loneliness. By intensely and deeply loving another, with great *compassion* or *Agape*, we can transform the inherently selfish personality into a transcendent heart of love.

And the relationship between human individuals that is best constituted to fulfill this transcendent purpose is the love between a man and a woman.

Thus the beloved relation provides us with the most powerful, most complete, most experiential opportunity to realize transcendent love—embodying, as it does, the greatest potential for the union of opposites on every level of life. The potential of the love between a man and a woman offers each of us the most powerful opportunity to "radically undermine egoism"[78] at its root.

Through blending and uniting in love with another human being who appears to have a completely independent existence from our own and who seems to be different from us on every level of existence and in every expression of form and life, indeed, one who is our *polar opposite*, we develop the capacity to "recognize for ourselves the absolute significance of another."[79] Thus, when love flows through every aspect of life on all levels of our being to our polar opposite, we can see and know the truth of the other's being as well as our own and there is no longer any room for egoism. Our own identification has expanded from a limited, individualized, separated self to include the life and being of another. Thus our egoism, our sense of being a separated personality, has been transcended and transformed into the substance of a higher, more universal, spiritual love.

This transformtion of the personality through love is the express intent of the Way of the Beloved and what actually does happen in the Beloved relationship. Every beloved couple has this opportunity and can realize its truth through the intense love that they express to one another. This is the ageless description of the Truth of the man/woman relationship, encapsulating the spiritual purpose of marriage in all its myriad manifestations since our beginnings.[80]

In the Bible, it is written, "He that loseth his life for my sake shall find it."[81] What does this mean? Teilhard de Chardin says: "At what moment do lovers come into the most complete possession of themselves if not when they say they are lost in each other?"[82] If a beloved couple, through deep love and devotion to each other, give themselves completely on every level of their life, it will open a channel within each so that the Soul may emerge into consciousness. Thus a man and a woman can become aware of the True Self—that spiritual being who we truly are. The *fire of love* burns away the selfish personality. The personality is sacrificed and transmuted, through intense love and devotion to the beloved, and the lovers become conscious of their Soul Nature. Thus the personality is transformed and transcended and they rise together to a higher level of consciousness. This is the essence of the *Spiritual Path*, the *Path of Love*, or by whatever name humans have chosen to call it over the millennia.

Thus within the union of beloveds lies the spiritual potential for the future of humanity. If we can give our whole self completely to the love of our beloved—that concrete other being, who is so close and yet so different from our own self—we can also learn to accept all others with a heart of compassion. Transmuting ego-consciousness through love awakens Soul-consciousness and it is the Soul that perceives the actual unity, copresence and coinherence, of all men and women, of all humanity and of even the whole Universe. Thus the state of brotherhood for all peoples can become a reality—as our Teacher said, "the path of the beloved has the potential to transform the earth."

Meditation:

The Key is Through Your Beloved.[83]

When you lose yourself in intense love of your beloved, the ego will dissolve and the soul vibration of your being and your beloved will merge in pure joy.
Thus as you give yourself completely, you become conscious of your True Self.
This is a path of Spiritual growth and freedom.
This is a path to the higher worlds of beauty and light.
Hold on to this stream of vibration and every other problem will fall into a harmonious pattern in your life."

Mantram: *I* lose *myself in my beloved and I* find *my True Self.*
or
Through deep love for my beloved, I find my true spiritual self.

80 CR

7.3.2 COPRESENCING

I searched for God for many years. I reached out to the stars and all was cold and speechless. I looked into the wonders of nature and the microscopic structure of plants and I was filled with awe. But my heart was vacant.

Then I heard a voice that said: "God is in your home." And I looked into the face of my beloved and there I beheld the radiant wonder of a soul divine.

And I heard again, without voice: "Become one with your beloved." And in deep love and devotion, I united with my beloved on all levels, the physical, emotional, mental and spiritual levels. In our ecstatic embrace the universe became alive. The vast stellar spaces were no longer voiceless, but streams of holy energy descended upon us. And as I looked on nature around me, it was filled with a thousand voices of love and beauty. When my heart opened I found God everywhere. Through deep love for my beloved, we ascend to the spiritual heights.

—Herman Rednick[84]

For millennia there has been a pervasive belief that, when two hearts burst forth with the peerless euphoria of new love, the madness of the gods has come upon them and they have been touched by a ray of timeless eternity. Such exalted feelings of fulfillment and completion bestowed by a newly found communion-in-love seem to abrogate all those wedding vows which declare: "'Till death do you part!" Indeed, enfolded in sweet love's embrace the lovers exclaim: "Surely we shall be together forever in the heights of each other's loving presence, rising forever into ever higher reaches of love and light. For beloved couples, today, here in the world, copresencing can be a step on the way to attaining an experience of this great potential which, on the higher planes, is a reality now. As one of our students wrote, " ...there is a love that connects us, binds us together, reveals us whether we are together or apart. When it seems tenuous, we later realize it was only hidden, and that the Light was there all along."

What do we mean by *copresencing*?[85] Copresencing is a mutual communing between those who love, with or without their physical proximity.[86] To truly commune or *be-with* one another occurs on an invisible level. Thus, even though we may be physically together, we may not actually be-with one another. It is so common today for people to be physically together but to not *be-with* each other. As Herman Rednick puts it: "You could live in the same house and be a thousand miles apart. You could be a thousand miles apart and your heart will sing with your beloved."[87] Copresencing with our beloved-one is an experience of mutual *being-with* one another—through love. When you are aware of your beloved in your heart, wherever you are, whatever you are doing, you are co-presencing.

We are definitely accustomed to thinking of and perceiving ourselves as separated physical bodies in space, but this is a very limited vision. Indeed, recent scientific studies demonstrate that even physically we are interconnected with others.[88] Through Love we see with different eyes! The experience of separateness is a consequence of a focus solely on our material manifestation, which leads us to perceive, conceive and believe that we are individual bodies localized in a space that is spread out around us and that all events, bodies, and beings existing in that space that are not within our unique location are "other" or "not I." This is our common human experience in the Western world today. The conviction of our ultimate separateness rests largely on the scientific doctrine of a *discrete* and *localized* time and space. Indeed, ever since Newton, in the seventeenth century, until the discovery of the quantum in the early 20th century, this was the scientific viewpoint. However, the revolutionary ideas of Quantum Mechanics and Relativity Theory have radically changed science's view of the universe. Indeed, even though most of the public does not know it yet, the Newtonian image of the cosmos is obsolete.

Copresencing is the experience of the underlying "nonlocal" nature of the universe. We begin to see that we live in a complexly interwoven psychic sea of subtle energies, with many levels of vibrations, flowing all around us and through us. Our thoughts[89] and emotions are currents in this sea. Thus our human-being is in truth not confined within a discrete container in a static location. We are composed of streams of living energy, continually flowing and weaving in and out of our mind and body, riding within the ever-flux of time and connecting us to all-that-is.

We can see or visualize our thoughts and emotions as streams of energy, as beams or living threads which connect and interweave us with other beings, especially those to whom we feel closely related. These interconnecting energies are not limited by time and space—the interconnection of the subtle energies is simultaneous and non-local. Every thought and emotion, every act, creates a stream of energy or vibration which goes out from us like a beam into the subtle atmosphere. This process has been graphically described by the Theosophist, Clara Codd: "Everything is really a matter of wave-length or vibration. As we act, as we speak, as we think, we set going an ever-widening circle of vibrations. The voice makes rhythmic wave-lengths on the air, thought makes rhythmic wave-lengths … on a still subtler form of matter. These all set up synchronous, though vastly subtler and quicker wave-lengths in the surrounding and permeating planes of ever subtler matter."[90]

A beloved couple is interconnected by many streams of these subtle energies, continually touching and weaving like the sounds of a great symphony entwining them in a vast net of sympathetic vibrations. At any moment the streams can be positive, beautiful connecting threads, or potent, negative bonds, like dark iron chains. When a man and woman love deeply, their forces are blended together. This happens on all levels of their existence, creating a gossamer net of interweaving strands of living light. The two become so attuned that they are continuously receiving, reflecting and influencing each other's vibrations.

It is the intensity of the love in the relationship that can bring this attunement into conscious awareness. When the relationship is casual, the connecting cords are weak and fluctuate—they come and go without much force. When the relationship is full of intensity and spiritual focus, the connecting streams of energy are brilliant with force, color, and activity. As we intensify the flow of love in our relationship, these interweaving strands become more potent and more vivid and we begin to become aware that, in truth, we are in touch at all times, whether we are physically together or not.

Thus, when the loving connection with our beloved is strong we may begin to perceive how we have a much greater responsibility than we had thought before. Indeed, every thought and emotion that we have towards any other person, but especially towards our closest beloved-one, affects that person. The greater the intensity the greater the impact. Everything that we do and think and feel affects the other person when we are physically together and when we are not together. When we do the Invocation of Love, we are sending out beams of living substance, which instantly touch and enfold our beloved wherever he or she may be. If we have a negative thought or feeling, it hits them instantly like an arrow penetrating to hurt and harm the one we love. It doesn't matter whether we are aware of what we are doing or whether the other person notices or not, the influences are there anyway. One can commune in love—or negativity—without the other even being aware of it. But once we know that our thoughts and emotions have such a direct effect on others, we cannot but become more responsible for our own state of mind and heart.

Of course, a beloved couple wants to be connected only through love. So the aspiration to fill all thoughts and emotions with love intensifies. A woman we know wrote the following paper:

> I remember when the realization began to dawn within me, that to follow the path of the beloved, I would have to be psychically there with my beloved at all times and through all experiences, and that if we are to move on our path toward the spirit, I must be there in a state of love, nourishing the divine aspect within him. I couldn't allow myself to have a negative thought, because I knew it would hurt him.
>
> This concept has grown through the last few years, so that now there is no time or place that we are not working together on our path. I feel him with me all the time, mostly as a feeling of love surrounding my heart.

There is no need to focus directly on working toward co-presencing. It appears as an outgrowth of the intensification of love. When the connections between beloveds are more casual, the co-presence may come and go. The work is to become more loving. When we are loving, and the love is deep and intense, the higher faculties open naturally. Through love we become aware of the links that are already there. Then we can consciously and intentionally intensify the connections of love. Thus there is no need to focus toward becoming aware of co-presencing. Love is the power that overcomes the illusion of "personal locality." Through love, it is possible to develop, enhance, and thereby become more aware of the fact that we are never alone, and that through our intense love for an other real person, we may awaken to a constant communion, an unbroken copresence, with our beloved-one.[91]

⚘

Lasting love that comes from the union of two souls transcends space and time. It is not bound by our bodies, diminished by distance, or blocked by barriers of any type.
—Paul Pearsall[92]

Copresencing is the inevitable result of the intensification of love between a man and woman and is part of the process of transformation from ego-consciousness into Soul-consciousness. When you are loving, when the love is deep and intense, you are opening up the higher faculties. The sense of communion with another person is an ability of the Soul, a perception, by the *organs* of the Soul, however vague or distinct, of the inter-weaving breath of all Life and Being. Communion with our beloved-one is a theophany, a presencing of the Divine and universal *breath* that inter-links the physical worlds (of time and space) and the Spiritual Realms in a seamless living whole. Indeed the *copresence of the I and the beloved other* is the true spiritual state of our being and of the whole cosmos. Through the path of the beloved, we discover that the experience of separation of one person from another and from Nature is illusory. This state of apparent separation—of everything from everything—is a particular stage in humanity's long evolutionary journey of consciousness and now we are beginning to emerge from its dark confines into Soul-consciousness, where a universal copresencing is the central mode of existence. Love is the power that will overcome our current illusion of separateness and open our spiritual eyes to the transcendent experience of true union with the One we love most, creating a radiance that ripples outward to include all of humanity.

The circle of love between beloveds initiates a kind of *creative convergence*[93] in which the personality is transformed and soul-consciousness over-lights and transcends the separative illusion of ego-consciousness. This becomes an experience of harmonious convergence with the whole cosmos, a transcendent experience emerging out of the spiritual union with our beloved one. The Soul lives in the experience of the unity inherent throughout the Cosmos and, thus, through soul consciousness, persons are in a state of constant communion— i.e., *copresent*, to one another and with Nature. Indeed, one day we shall all *consciously converge*, becoming copresent with all Life and All Being.

We have said before that communion is a spiritual breathing-together, a conspiration. That experience is a *soul experience*. To breathe as one spirit, breathing the same spiritual breath, is to enter the realms of the Soul— the subtle inhalations and exhalations of the Spirit. The very word *soul* comes directly from the Greek, *psuche* which originally meant breath.[94] For thousands of years the soul has been likened to the *breath*, it is the *breath* of the Spirit which permeates the whole cosmos and "bloweth where it listeth." When we are copresencing one another, we have entered into a state of soul-consciousness in which the simultaneity and unity of the subtle or etheric planes is the mode of our existence.

251

Thus through Soul-consciousness we enter into a realm of spirit-consciousness[95] in which we are actually copresent to one another all the time. Indeed, this sense of communing, touching, or being present with one's beloved can become the natural and everyday experience for a devoted couple united through intense love. Our Teacher told us that in the future, "The most important form of mass-communication, from the spiritual point of view, will be the flowering of telepathic communication between all the souls on the planet, and between men [women] and the higher beings. This will be far more significant and valuable than the present communication systems."[96] And, as we have quoted before, Teilhard de Chardin makes this very specific: "It is not in isolation (whether married or unmarried), but in paired units, that the two portions, masculine and feminine, of nature are to rise up towards God ... Spirituality does not come down upon a 'monad' but upon the human dyad."[97]

The idea that the whole, supposedly nonsentient, universe is, at some level, simultaneously aware of itself in all its manifold diversity and in all its times and spaces, is of ancient origin. Mystics and spiritual teachers in the East and the West have been affirming the underlying unity and consciousness of all existence for thousands of years and now modern quantum physics is presenting a rational, scientific basis for the actual experience of this unity. Those readers who are interested, may see the Supplemental Quotes on Copresencing at the end of this Section, for a wide ranging testimony to the temporal and spacial unity of the universe.

ॐ

Even in our modern world, it is not an uncommon experience for two people who love each other to feel that they are in "touch" when they are physically apart. This is particularly true when the circle of love (as described in Chapter 6) is flowing steadily and strongly between them. There are many accounts of lovers, separated by thousands of miles, sensing danger or a crisis occuring to a partner at exactly the time that it happens. This experience is usually attributed to some special power of intuition or psychism or ESP, but may these not be alternative terms being used to identify an instance of copresencing?

The visionary psychologist, Paul Pearsall and his wife, Celest, have shared many experiences of copresencing, especially when he was seriously ill with cancer.

Celest says:

"When Paul was in the hospital, I never limited my visits to just physically being there. ... I would send him messages all the time from home or when I was driving to see him or when I was driving home after visiting him. I gave him as many love transfusions as he ever got blood transfusions, and I didn't have to be there to give them."

And then Paul:

"I could always feel my wife's love even when she was isolated from me physically at the time of my bone marrow transplant to cure my cancer. Through the plastic walls of my isolated world, I could feel her love heal me no matter where she was ... I always knew when [she] was sending the "love transfusions" she mentionned above. I could feel them to such an extent that even some of the nurses seemed to notice. One of my primary-care nurses said, "I could tell even when you were sleeping when Celest was sending her love. I could see you sort of move, and there seemed to be an aura around you."[98]

It would be important to realize that the Invocation of love is never just words and feelings along with a visualized image. When we do the Invocation of Love and say in our heart, "I enfold you with a beam of love," we are sending a beam of invisible substance, a stream of living energy to immediately touch the other person. And when the love is strong and we are consciously visualizing beams of love substance flowing through our heart and enfolding the other person, we realize that "Love is not just an emotion. It is a great spiritual energy that comes pouring through ... [our] being"[99] and there is an instant connection in mind and spirit—no intervening space and no delay.

઼ ભ

Meditation:[100]

As I move toward my beloved through deep love and devotion, my heart is set afire. On this high level, my beloved enters my being and I hear his[her] voice within my heart. As we move together and blend spiritually, our hearts become One and all our activity carries an

253

atmosphere of love. Because we live within one another, a luminous and fragrant light surrounds us. I am grateful every hour as I walk the path with my beloved.

Mantra: *Together with my beloved, we walk the path as One.*

• SUPPLEMENTAL QUOTES ON COPRESENCING •

Here we have gathered together a diverse series of brief quotes, some aphoristic, from different traditions and from different times, to illustrate the notion that the whole universe and everything in it can be conceived of, and actually experienced as, *copresent* to itself. We offer these diverse statements because of the still widespread Newtonian view, often called "the billiard ball conception," of the cosmos as a vast, dead sea of separate and discrete material objects lost to one another in an infinite, featureless space.

The idea of cosmic unity was common among the Neo-Platonists:

> Everything is everywhere, anything is all things, the sun is all the stars, and each star is all the stars and the sun.
> —Plotinus (204-270 CE)[101]

> It needs must be that all things come into being, and that things are coming into being always and everywhere. For the Maker is in all things; his abode is not in some one place, nor does he make some one thing; no, he makes all things, and everywhere he is at work. The things that come into being have no independent power; to God is subject all the comes into being.
> —Hermes Trismegistus[102]

And we find it expressed often among Buddhists, from Tibet and China to Ceylon:

> This dust and that mountain, though one is big and the other is small, contain each other. ... Therefore the large is contained right in the small. ... an infinite number of lands and seas are always manifested in the dust [such that] one particle of dust universally pervades all lands and seas. ... When contracted, all things are manifested in one particle of dust. When expanded, one particle of dust will universally permeate everything.
> —Fa-tsang (643-712 CE)[103]

255

As soon as you know mountains are made of rivers and everything else and rivers are made of mountains and everything else, it is safe for you to use the words "mountains" and "rivers." In Buddhist practice, what is essential is for you to realize the nature of interbeing ...

—Thich Nhat Hanh[104]

Being is nowhere else than in the what-is, and with respect to our existentiality, this means that we are the whole and yet only part of it.

—Herbert Guenther[105]

We *are* the stream, source and flow, carrier and carried, the whole stream and yet only part of it—as a water molecule is the river and yet only part of it.

—Erich Jantsch[106]

The unity of the All, the manifest and the unmanifest, was also expressed by Christian thinkers:

In that abyss I saw how love held bound
Into one volume all the lives whose flight
Is scattered through the universe around;
How substance, accident, and mode unite,
Fused, so to speak, together in such wise
That this I tell is one simple light.

—Dante (1265-1321) The Divine Comedy

All things are "contracted" to form each creature ... To say that "everything is in everything" is the same as to say that God, by the intermediacy of the universe is in all things ... How God is without any diversity in all, since everything is in everything, and how all is in God, because all is in all, are truths of a very high order which are clearly understood by keen minds. The entire universe is in each creature ... with the result that in each individual the universe is by "contraction" what the particular individual is.

—Nicholas Cusanus (1401-1464)[107]

every individual substance expresses the whole universe in its own manner and ... in its full concept are included all its experiences together with all the attendant circumstances and the whole sequence of exterior events.

—Leibniz (1646-1716)[108]

The most familiar statement of copresencing is perhaps that of William Blake:

To see a World in a grain of Sand,
And a Heaven in a Wild Flower,
Hold Infinity in the palm of your hand,
And eternity in an hour.

—William Blake (1757-1827)
Auguries of Innocence.

Even in the twentieth century, some philosophers and many post-Newtonian, Quantum physicists, have expressed the idea of an omniscient, simultaneous and non-local cosmos:

... the body is the organism whose states regulate our cognisance of the world. The unity of the perceptual field therefore must be a unity of bodily experience. In being aware of the bodily experience, we must thereby be aware of aspects of the whole spatio-temporal world as mirrored within the bodily life. ... my theory involves the entire abandonment of the notion that simple location is the primary way in which things are involved in space-time. In a certain sense, everything is everywhere at all times. For every location involves an aspect of itself in every other location. Thus every spatio-temporal standpoint mirrors the world.

—Alfred North Whitehead[109]

each present reasserts the presence of the whole past which it supplants, and anticipates that of all that is to come.

—Merleau-Ponty[110]

In terms of the implicate order one may say the everything is enfolded into everything. This contrasts with the *explicate order* now dominant in physics in which things are *unfolded* in the sense that each thing lies only in its own particular region of space (and time) and outside the regions belonging to other things.

—David Bohm[111]

Photons are not localized at any particular position and time within the cavitylike fuzzy balls; rather, they are spread out over the entire cavity. In fact no satisfactory quantum theory of photons as particles has ever been given.

—Marlan Scully[112]

two physicists at the National Institute of Standards and Technology in Boulder, Colorado, recently ... managed to coax a single atom to exist in two places at once.

—JeffreyWinters[113]

Some of the thinkers that we have cited above are more concerned with the temporal unity, the *simultaneity*, of the Universe, e.g., Merleau-Ponty. Others are focused on the illusory nature of spacial separateness, despite the apparent perception of such a separation of objects in space, e.g., Plotinus, Fatsang,Thich Nhat Hanh, Herbert Guenther, Erich Jantsch, Dante, Nicholas Cusanus, Marlan Scully & Jeffrey Winters. It should be noted that, the concept of *non-locality*is firmly established in physics, yet its ramifications for our actual experience of the cosmos have not been explored very much to date.[114] Some of these quotes express both a temporal and spacial unity, e.g., Leibniz, William Blake, Alfred North Whitehead & David Bohm.[115] Thus, *copresencing* with our beloved is an experience of *mutual being-with one another here and now*—that is, in both space and time! Indeed, the Way of the Beloved could be viewed as the "Tao of Copresencing."

ଓ ଔ

7.3.3 ETERNAL FEMININE

The Eternal Feminine
Bears us aloft.

—Goethe[116]

For more than 2500 years the social and religious institutions of the world have neglected and denigrated the feminine aspect. In the Western world, the Universal Divine Spirit, God, has been thought of and described only in masculine terms. The spiritual teachings of the Divine as Father/Mother, both masculine and feminine, have been submerged and all but forgotten. Yet, in all the Wisdom Traditions, the Divine has always been known and recognized as comprising both principles and yet being beyond all duality.

Now, as we move toward the coming age, the Light of the Cosmic Feminine is drawing close to the earth and can no longer be ignored. All over the world, the vibration of the Divine Feminine is emerging into the consciousness of humanity[117] and the feminine aspect is coming forward into expression on all levels of life. Not only are women actively entering all fields of endeavor in the economic, social, professional, religious and political arenas, but the feminine aspect is being re-discovered and re-claimed and once again revered in humanity's approach to the world of Spirit.

In the Wisdom Teachings, the *Eternal Feminine* is the Force and Consciousness that sustains creation. She is the breath and power of all that lives. She is the embodiment of the essence of pure consciousness and Her *cosmic* Being is fashioned out of the divine fire of love. She is simultaneously manifest and unmanifest; She is in form and, yet, beyond form; She is in time, but remains Eternal.

The cosmic feminine consciousness is known in the world by a myriad of different names.[1118] She is worshiped by some as the Mother of the Universe, by others as Isis or Sophia or Mary or the divine Sakti. But behind every form and every name, there is one, singular Divine Reality.[119] She is One Power, the Wisdom of God, transcendent and eternal. Her holy presence bathes us with a magnetic purity and Her radiant light enfolds every woman and man upon the earth. Through Her presence, the Light and Love of God is descending upon humanity.[120] In the oldest sacred scriptures, the Rig Veda, She tells us of Her mystery: *"I am the Queen, source of thought, Knowledge itself. You do not know Me, yet you dwell in Me."*[121]

Despite the protests and actions of regressive forces, the world recognition of the feminine aspect is growing. Indeed, the coming age has been referred to as the advent of the incarnation of the "Virgin Mother"[122] and "the epoch of Woman."[123] And there is growing acknowledgment of the idea that the feminine aspect, Woman in form, is "the Torch of the Future"[124] that shall lead humanity toward its spiritual destiny. Thus it is beginning to be appreciated by spiritual seekers that, not only is the Divine Feminine a Spiritual Ideal or Symbol, but in her material manifestation, i.e., through the forms of actual women, She can be the guiding light of spiritual realization. Woman-in-form will come to be seen and known as the bridge between our incarnate life and the higher planes of consciousness[125] —e.g., as the *mediator* between heaven and earth. The great twentieth century Sufi Master, Hazrat Inayat Khan, taught that "Woman is the steppingstone to God's sacred altar."[126] And Sri Aurobindo, teacher of the Integral Path of Yoga for the coming age, expressed in his epic poem, *Savitri*, both the transcendent nature of the Eternal Feminine, and also her immanence and descent into our everyday life:

> *Incarnating inexpressibly in her limbs*
> *The boundless joy the blind world-forces seek,*
> *Her body of beauty mooned the seas of bliss.*
> *At the head she stands of birth and toil and fate,*
> *In their slow round the cycles turn to her call;*
> *Alone her hands can change Time's dragon base.*
> *Hers is the mystery the Night conceals;*
> *The spirit's alchemist energy is hers;*
> *She is the golden bridge, the wonderful fire.*
> *The luminous heart of the Unknown is she,*
> *A power of silence in the depths of God;*
> *She is the Force, the inevitable Word,*
> *The magnet of our difficult ascent ...* [127]

• The Eternal Feminine And The Beloved Path •

Man's Reorientation

From obscure places deep within, man reaches out to woman, seeking union with his polar opposite, the Divine Feminine in human form. He seeks the answer to the mystery that is hidden in "woman." He seeks to touch and know the spirit of beauty that dwells in her, that draws him so powerfully toward her.[128] He seeks the inspiration and stimulation of the heavenly Muse, who comes to him through his powerful love towards the feminine aspect, embodied in woman—his woman, his beloved. She will inspire him to fly to the heights. He yearns for the fulfillment of spiritual union with her, for he knows somewhere in his being that this union is a symbol and a pathway to union with his own soul, his own true, higher Self.

In the passionate intensity of the discovery of his beloved, man feels that he has found true joy and fulfillment, at last. Thus, it is a shocking surprise to discover that this is a fleeting experience, a brief respite from his ageless search. For even at the same time that he is exulting in this new union, he also experiences an uncomfortable restlessness, an agitation, and a growing reluctance. He has a vague sense that his *freedom* is coming to an end, that he is being caught in some kind of trap, subtly ensnared or chained down. He becomes suspicious and a strange fear of being profoundly restricted invades his psyche. With these experiences a man often begins to feel as if his very life is being smothered. And an ancient terror rises within him.[129]

When the initial grace-period in the relationship comes to an end, and the friction and strife of everyday personality adjustment increases, the man often feels that he now has concrete evidence that his wings have been clipped. Indeed, he comes to believe that he can no longer fly to the heights, and he thinks that it is "she," who has restricted him. It is apparent to him that the life of responsibilities brought to him by his relationship with a woman is unbearable, choking his very spirit, taking away his "real" life as a man. The woman has been transformed into the opposite of what the man envisioned in the beginning of the relationship. No longer is she his door to freedom and growth, the muse who will inspire him to rise above his old self, but she has become his restrainer, the one who would keep him chained to the mundane and trivial.

When these fear-driven, separating emotions become powerful enough, the man turns away from the woman. He may withdraw from her, finding it difficult or impossible to be "with" her, or even to express these fears of "losing himself." He may bury himself in his work, or he may blame this woman for his troubles and believe that he needs to seek a "different one" who will "really" give him what he was seeking in the first place. He may even go so far as to begin to believe that the problem lies with the inherent evil nature of women in general, and he will certainly find considerable support for this conclusion in Western societies. We see many men today who declare that they won't "fall into *that* trap again." And yet these same men confess to a sense of having "failed" some sort of critical, but inchoate, test.

The unfolding of this contradictory dynamic is rooted in the man's ego, which seeks to *possess* the eternal opposite seen in feminine beauty. He wants to *have* her for himself. He looks to this woman and to that one, but he can never have or grasp what he is seeking. Man cannot possess the Muse, indeed, he must abandon his attachment to his separated self through love to Her. Man's great illusion or error comes from his selfish ego that wants to have the feminine only on his own terms and make her subservient. But man can only have what he really wants when he surrenders to the Eternal Feminine, like the poets of old, who surrendered to their Muse. As William Blake put it:

> *He who binds to himself a joy*
> *Doth the winged life destroy;*
> *He who kisses the joy as it flies*
> *Lives in Eternity's sunrise.*[130]

In modern times, through the beloved path, the spiritual union of man and woman is possible on the physical plane. As man surrenders to the Divine Feminine in his beloved, she will manifest more and more the eternal characteristics he has always sought. He must overcome his desire to possess, and instead, give out great love, to receive the opposite polarity into his inner being. This is possible in the beloved relationship because of the sustained intent and commitment which develops into a deep enough love and security for the man to make a surrender of his selfish, possessive drives. When the love in his heart awakens, the woman will blossom and bring forth everything he strove to possess in women before, but could never grasp. Thus he makes it possible for his beloved to manifest the Eternal Feminine and blend with him spiritually. And they can move toward a spiritual union, the union of the polar opposites: masculine and feminine.

For a man, to *see* the Divine Feminine in the being of his beloved, is to see within her the divine vehicle which brings the ultimate, true, fulfillment of all his aspirations. He may see her as the Eternal Goddess, Sophia, or Mary or Tara. By whatever name he calls Her, and however he conceives of Her, he sees his beloved as mysteriously embodying, *for him,* the Presence of the *Sophia,* the Divine Feminine, the Wisdom of God in his everyday life. And as he sees and loves the divine in his beloved, he evokes those qualities of divinity—compassion, beauty, inspiration, understanding and healing—to come into manifestation through her person. And as a man pours out love unceasingly to his beloved, *his* devotion grows, and *his* love becomes more self-less and pure, a yielding of the grasping ego, a surrender of selfishness to the power of the Divine.

In practical life, as a man pours out love continuously to his beloved, whether they are physically together or apart, whether he is tired or not, whether she does what he likes or not, when she is appreciative and full of love and admiration for him, or when she makes demands on him and tells him what to do, that is, no matter what she does or doesn't do, he begins to perceive through the eye of the heart into the Divine within her. Thus he will begin to listen to the Wisdom within her and to *hear from her* the mysterious truths which can only be revealed by the feminine aspect. This is the path that leads him to that higher level of Soul-consciousness which is beyond male and female, and in which the truth of both is known.

The man's experience may be described by the following poem:

ODE TO THE FEMININE

Silver fire descended into the long night of my life
like sudden lightning illumines those proximate mercurial forms
that ages of blind stumblings would never touch.
Even as one flash revealing such Beauty should
kindle a wild love undying … yet by some
unknowable fate or grace, the Goddess has lifted that veil
more often than I would blushingly admit.
O, may I fall enraptured at Her immortal feet,
pledging with every breath, to love Her before myself
and wreathing my heart in utmost gratitude
for the eternal beauty revealed in Her glowing form.
That beauty reserved, not for Endymion alone, but for any man,
who has truly loved a woman with great intensity and devotion;
for he shall realize what men truly seek in women:
he will see God made manifest through feminine beauty,
and thus he shall know the spiritual fulfillment of all his loving,
for that Beauty becomes a power flooding the heart and mind
with Holy Fire.
Yet no man may reach out with his selfish ego
to grasp the sailing moon, for certain then
his yearning shall never cease and he shall go
from one woman to another, vainly seeking his completion.

And as he goes he becomes more empty, more selfish …
A man must surrender to the blinding sweet beauty
and soft calling voice that would lure him
into the depths of the trackless silent forest
or into the fathomless labyrinths under the earth
where he must suffer and wander for love of Her,
who would ever proceed his halting steps
upon a way he cannot know. 'Til overcoming
his sense he reaches a depth of dying to self,
consumed from within by the fire in his heart,
that Christ fire, Phoenix fire, that suddenly lights
the true form of his polar opposite, as his own complete being,
uniting the dual principles of creation within one breast.
Thus ancient man knowingly reached out to Artemis and
Deana,
and by other names, the Goddess of the moon,
the Muse and root of all true art,
the embodiment of the Eternal Feminine,
wherein each man must unite his soul with the Spirit
and fulfill the hidden purposings
of the varied forms of loving
between man and woman down the ages.
It is the same today for any man,
who would reach out with intense love
to the Goddess in his beloved, for She resides in every woman.
And by his love, a man may invoke her, whom he has always
sought.
But he may not possess her—no man binds the Immortal
Goddess.
Yet by great love and devotion he shall have her,
though he shall have ceased to be a man,
for he must become an immortal, as She.[131]

Woman's Reorientation

Woman reaches out for her polar opposite; she seeks through her *magnetism* to draw him to her so that she will be filled and sustained by the current of his devotion and love.

A woman feels the necessity to know, at all times, that her beloved loves her and is "with" her. Even when she has been assured in a thousand ways and through undeniable experience, she has to be shown, told, convinced ever and again, that she is loved by her beloved. This is not psychological "insecurity," as it is often mistakenly labeled. It stems from the psychic reality of the nature of the male and female principles. The male personality longs to be free and the woman feels this as a separation from herself. Her anxiety at his withdrawal is perceived by him as a womanly plot to entrap him. If it is the possessive or selfish part of her personality that rules and her needs are expressed as demands, that which she fears most will surely come upon her—the man will turn away from her.[132]

She must learn to overcome her tendency to feel abandoned, and, instead, center herself in the encompassing love of the Eternal Feminine. As she reaches out for the Divine Mother, her inner being will be sustained by spiritual power, and she will also be creating an atmosphere most conducive for the man to pour forth his love. If the woman can then *recognize* the man's gifts of love, she will feel his love coming forth to her. And her recognition of his love makes it possible for the man to overcome his fear of being trapped. This will reassure a woman and she will blossom as she is filled with the radiant love offered to her. The man's love invokes the spiritual aspect of her being, and she begins to manifest the divine qualities of the Feminine which he so passionately and ardently seeks.

Thus, the work for a woman is to *become*, out of deep love and devotion to the higher self in her beloved, the living manifestation of the Divine Feminine *for him*. Through her deep love and devotion to her beloved, she veritably becomes that for which he has always longed and sought in countless others. She becomes that radiant, Being who is the source of spiritual love and inspiration for all creation and is, in truth, the Image of his own Soul.

The Divine Feminine is *above all names and all worlds and all forms*. She dwells as a potential within every woman and Her power can come into expression on any and all levels of a woman's being. The universal Love of the Divine Feminine begins to flow through her as she consciously becomes the bearer and expression of *all* ways of love for her beloved. She is, at once, his wife, his mistress and lover, his closest and most valued friend and advisor, and his Muse, the highest inspiration for his lofty goals and spiritual aspirations—indeed, the very Mother of his Soul. Thus, the woman realizes her own Divine Nature as she becomes spiritually united in love with her beloved.

She accomplishes this in practical life by loving her beloved unceasingly, *as he is now,* seeing the highest aspect of his being through the veils of his personality limitations. She loves him unreservedly, even when he does not act like the man she wants him to be, or when he is not giving her the love and devotion that she needs and deserves. She recognizes his offerings to her as offerings of love, in whatever form he gives them, and she lets him know that she accepts his gifts in ways that he will see and understand. Thus, her experience of life is no longer one of toleration, endurance, exasperation or desperation, all colored by a lurking fear of abandonment, but it is transmuted by the power of a Patience and Love beyond space and time, and she can dwell *secure* in the Living Light of the Divine Mother's Presence within.

A woman recounted the following description of an experience of identification with the Divine Feminine:

> I had felt a deep connection with the Divine or Universal Feminine Spirit for many years and this particular week I was focusing on Her in my meditation practice. I loved to think about Her and this is what I was doing in the town Laundromat with my twelve year old daughter. When all the clothes were in the machines and my daughter was occupied, I inwardly turned toward the Divine Being of the Holy Mother. I was thinking about the week's meditation[133] and silently saying the mantra: *The Holy Mother fills me with love for my brother.* And as I was doing this, I realized that I was envisioning the Mother as something or some-One *other*, outside me, not "me." But then, the thought appeared to me: "Oh, but I have really *been* the different aspects of the Feminine described in the meditation." I know what it is to be that 'abstract, impersonal Mother Who is distant and part of the heavens.' And I know what it is to be the 'woman of power, with a vibrant blue being containing the Mysteries of the heaven and the earth.' And I know what it is to be the 'young woman with a sweet fragrance, radiating eternal love.' I feel that I have been all these women. I feel my identity with these qualities. I feel 'I am that' for each aspect." And then I find that I am repeating "I am that Radiant Mother," "I am that Radiant Mother." And there and then I *know* that, in Reality, She is that Great Divine Being of infinitely radiant compassion beyond any manifestation in form. And I *feel* "Oh, *that's* what I can be!" Then, with a simple, natural, flowing sense, I look around the room and *feel* Her Love everywhere. With

Her Love, I see three young men playing pool in the middle of the room and their forms, their movements, are like emanations of Her fingers. I "see" Her Presence like a great light everywhere around me, and my heart overflows with Love for Her. With a bursting heart I feel and I say, "I *LOVE* Her. And with gentle simplicity, I have a vivid sense of "knowing" that, "Oh, in my life I am Her messenger to my beloved." And then I see before me, the image of my beloved, and I see him with Her Love. I see that he, too, is within Her great light and that in our life together, he is truly Her messenger to me. And Her great light opened further, and I see that our life, the life that we know and *all* life, is Her Plan and Her Work. And I am filled with gratitude like an immense and powerful wave flowing through me. And it flowed so naturally, it felt like an eternal part of my being ...

Then I turned around and noticed, strangely, that everything was ordinary again. The experience was gone. I looked all around, searching physically and psychically for what had just been, thinking all the while, "But that felt like it would be *forever*, where is it now?" Yet everything had returned to its usual, ordinary, "normal" appearance, and the mantram was just the words of the meditation for the week.

Woman's Process

Part 1

A woman knows, in the central core of her being, that she is in touch with the *mystery of woman*, the divinity of the Eternal Feminine. She has a sense of knowing that she has within herself everything that her beloved needs and everything that he could ever desire. A woman may watch her beloved looking every which way—to his work, to his books, to his play or sports, even to his meditation practice —when she well knows that the secret of spiritual fulfillment for both of them is held within her Being. She invites him to look *to* Her, to look *into* Her, with the Love that will open his vision and cause her Spiritual Wisdom to manifest in their life.

It is her deep aspiration to be seen and recognized by her spiritual beloved as the vehicle and carrier of their ultimate attainment in the Divine, to be recognized by him as the one who can bring the spiritual love, light, beauty, wisdom and inspiration from the higher dimensions into their life. Her beloved's recognition, acknowledgment, appreciation and valuing of her essential divinity brings about the fulfillment of her spiritual destiny. Even if many others see and recognize her divine essence and beauty, it does not produce within her the effect of true fulfillment. She may be pleased, even flattered, but in her deepest, spiritual center it does not bring the realization she longs for. Accomplishment comes to her through the recognition and love that comes from her spiritual beloved.

Yet, a precarious balance must be maintained, for she cannot force the man's love and vision in any way. This is a great test of the constancy and steadiness of a woman's focus, of her love for her beloved and the Divine, and of her faith in their path. If she allows the possessive or critical part of her personality to rule and she pushes forward, this will result in the many forms of striving for union which are inevitably interpreted by the man as manipulative and which always fail to achieve what she truly is seeking.[134]

Many women face an inner conflict in pursuing the idea and attainment of identifying with their divine essence. Some are blocked by their own intellect, adhering to materialist, separating ideas, which prevent them from delving into the deeper areas of their being.[135] But we also see women who, even though they may entertain the idea that women are, or can be, the expression of the Universal Feminine, are controlled by those forces of separation and regression that support an expression of self-doubt and self-deprecation. They think, "Who am I to say, 'I am the divine'?" "I am not worthy, I do not deserve this," " This is not meant for me." Not realizing that their self-effacement is an expression of the ego, albeit a negative one, they believe that it is *arrogant* to identify with their inner divinity. Yet the very *opposite* is the truth. Not only does every person have the divine spark within, but the pure compassion of the divine expresses the essence of humility. Knowing its one-ness with all life, the divine consciousness is spontaneously radiant with love and has no need (as the ego does) to question its worthiness or to conceal or display or explain or justify itself. Identification with the divine is the opposite of "human pride." In Tibetan Buddhism it is called "divine pride." The Buddhist scholar, Miranda Shaw, tells us that:

> For women, the relationship with ... [the Eternal Feminine] is one of identity. Women must discover the divine female essence within themselves. This should inspire self-respect, confidence, and the "divine pride" that is necessary to traverse the ... path. Divine pride, or remembering one's ultimate identity as a deity, is qualitatively different from arrogance, for it is not motivated by a

sense of deficiency or compensatory self-aggrandizement. This pride is an antidote to self-doubt and discouragement ... When a woman reclaims her divine identity, she does not need to seek outer sources of approval, for a firm, unshakeable basis for self-esteem emanates from the depths of her own being.[136]

Occasionally, from the contact that she feels with the divine essence flowing through her, a woman will try to tell her beloved what she feels and what she *knows*. One of our friends, in an intensely emotional moment, told her husband, "I can give you everything you need and want." His reply, to her great dismay, was, "What a big ego you have." Thus, if a woman tries to tell in words "who she is" to her beloved, he may hear this as an egotistical expression of her personality. And, of course, sometimes this is exactly what it is. But if the woman is in a state of love and the man can not hear her, it is because *his own vision* is blocked. Herbert Guenther describes this interaction as follows:

> When man turns altogether too human, the goddess threatens him; when he unassumingly turns to her she lovingly goes near him. Then suddenly the tableau changes. The man submits to the world of the divine and the goddess displays her beauty in the world of man. The former partnership founded on expectations becomes a partnership grounded in values perceived. The goddess here becomes a bridge between man and his Being. Such a vision is not a mere abstraction, but is a tangibly perceived and felt situation ... [137]

Part 2

In the beloved relationship, when a test or a barrier on the path comes into activity, the feminine aspect is usually the first to become aware of it. A barrier often comes into a woman's experience as the feeling of "not being loved" or "not receiving what she needs," or of being "unwanted" or "left-out" by her beloved. This kind of response to a blockage is almost universal among women. These feelings are indicators of latent processes fermenting in the depths of the relationship, and thus they are legitimate and valid signals of the way that the feminine aspect holds the lamp for the relationship and leads the couple up the spiritual mountain. As the process unfolds in the woman: she must experience the painful spur of feeling unloved, in order to shake-up the relationship and cause movement in otherwise frozen situations.

Thus, when a woman in a beloved couple sees that something is "not right" with her beloved or in their relationship, she wants to do something to remedy the situation. And her impulse is to make the relationship and/ or herself *better*. When she sees her beloved failing or in trouble, if she is reaching out spiritually, her desire is to *love him more* in order to bring about his happiness and also cause him to fulfill his purpose. She *knows* that she has the ability within herself to evoke the highest in her beloved. If she is centered in love and can access the divine wisdom within, she will know what is right, what she needs to do, and how to proceed.

However, if she is focused in the personality, she almost always feels unworthy, inadequate and daunted by the task. Often she believes that what is happening is because of some lack that she must correct in herself.[138] And this may lead to some constructive changes on her part. But in truth it is happening because the beloveds are trying to grow spiritually and, in order to grow spiritually, it is necessary that they go through this process. They both are participating in a great, cosmic plan that exists throughout every level of the universe. The process of spiritual growth—the development of Compassion— may be painful, but it is life, itself, and it leads to the light and love of the higher consciousness.[139]

A Couple's Reorientation

As a couple devotedly follows the practice of Mutual Exaltation, a flowing exchange of living spiritual energies begins, creating a reciprocal, dynamic process: (1) In a beloved relationship, the woman is the representative and embodiment of the Universal Feminine Principle. Thus, she becomes, for both of them, the carrier and expression of Divine Wisdom. (2) As the man pours out love to her it is a powerful invocation for the woman to identify with the Eternal Feminine. As the woman becomes more like the Eternal Feminine, the man begins to experience and love the divine in her. Through his unceasing outpouring, the eye of the heart opens and he *sees* the Divine manifesting in his beloved. (3) And as he continues to pour out love to her, he evokes the divine to manifest more and more through her being. Thus she, in turn, increasingly uncovers the divine essence within herself, and she begins to acknowledge and manifest her true nature. Her vision opens and she begins to *see* the divine Lord of Compassion in her beloved. The fire-of-Love burns in her heart and she reveals more of divinity to him. (4) The veils of Maya begin to part for both of them as each *sees* the divine truth of the other's spiritual Being.

Thus, the dynamic, reciprocal process of mutual exaltation spirals the couple upward toward the true fulfillment of their spiritual union in love, the fulfillment of the divine purpose of love between the polar opposites. Both man and woman rise toward the realization of the destiny inherent in the very creation of the sexes.

• Seven steps on the Path Toward Fulfillment •

Since the Cosmic Feminine Principle is revealed by Her Presence, in and through the person of woman on the path of the beloved, the woman's relationship with the Eternal Feminine is that of *identification* and the man's is that of love, devotion, worship and adoration.[140]

Woman's Introduction
The work for a woman on the path of the beloved is to unveil and awaken the Divine Feminine Principle within herself. Through her identification with the Eternal Feminine Being she comes to the realization that she is an expression of the Divine. She embodies her divine identity through her deep love and exaltation of her beloved, through her intense aspiration and spiritual striving, and through her acceptance of its inexorable necessity for her work toward realization.

To accomplish this she must continuously uses a mantra:

> *The Holy Mother fills me with love for you.*
> or
> *The radiance of the holy mother pours through me to you, my beloved.*
> **or**
> *I am that Divine Mother pouring love out to you.*

Man's Introduction
The work for a man on the path of the beloved is to envision the Eternal Feminine in his beloved. Through his devotion to his beloved, as the living representative of the Divine Mother, he will experience the Sacred Presence in her form and manifesting through her whole being. And through his pouring out of love to Her, he will unceasingly evoke the divine presence which dwells within his beloved. Thus, the quality of his love intensifies until it becomes

a practice of worship and adoration. He offers to the Divine, the gifts of his heart, thus making sacred, i.e., sacrificing, and yielding, i.e., surrendering, his egoism to Her Divine Essence. In this way, his own vision is clarified, his being becomes purified and the eye of the heart begins to open. *Seeing* the Eternal Feminine being in his beloved becomes his spiritual path and purpose.

He must unceasingly use a mantra, for example:

> *Through deep love and devotion I see the divine in my beloved.*
> **or**
> *I worshp the Eternal Feminine in my beloved.*

• The 7 Steps •

There are several ways to practice the Seven Steps toward the fulfillment of the Way of the Beloved. They may be followed one practice at a time in the order given and then the entire series may be repeated. Or they may be practiced in any order, according to individual bent, each for an extended and variable time period. Or all the steps may be practiced simultaneously and continuously.

- Steps **1**, **2** and **3** are seed-thoughts which provide a theme for daily meditation and contemplation.
- Steps **4** and **5** describe the practice of offering gifts of the heart to the beloved. These are offerings to the Divine in the beloved-one, which cause one to grow in love and humility and to *make sacred* those aspects of one's personality which need to be transmuted. Through the practice of making offerings, one gives more and more of ones *self* in love to the beloved.
- Step **6** illustrates that which the separated personality experiences as an omnipresent, ongoing paradox in one's attempts to do the work. This step seems always to contradict and come into conflict with the previous 2 steps.
- Step **7** describes a way for the seeker to evaluate his or her movement on the path.

Man's Work

Meditate daily on one or all of the following concepts:

- **1** *My beloved is the living representative of the Divine Mother.*
- **2** *I worship the Divine Feminine through the being of my beloved.*
- **3** *Through devotion and worship my vision is purified, and I see the Divine Being in my beloved.*
- **4** Through his love, a man wants to make *Offerings* to the divine in his beloved. On the inner, psychic level, he offers his love, which, with full awareness, he pours out unceasingly to his beloved.
- **5** And in concrete ways, he presents to his beloved, gifts that she will perceive as offerings of his love. These may be actions that he knows she will appreciate or objects that he knows will be meaningful to her. Or he will present her with gifts that enhance her beauty or the beauty of their life together.

- **6** The **paradox** for the man is that, even though he knows the mandates of the practices, they must never be automatic or mechanical gestures. His offering must be given, not as a *duty*, but freely and willingly from the heart. He must give spontaneously and genuinely, even creatively. Overcoming all obstacles, especially fear, he must *yield* and *surrender* to the divinity within his beloved-one to *see* behind the veil that seems to obscure her divinity. Therefore, he must suspend his need to *understand* and instead follow the Buddhist precept: "Do not question woman ... Adore her ... [for] in her real nature she is [the] Perfection of Wisdom, and in this empirical world [She] has assumed the form of woman."[141]

  Thus the man becomes willing to follow *her* light, yielding to her divinity, *knowing* that She holds the mystery of his being and that She is the very *Mother of his Soul!*

- **7** A man may continually assess the maturity of his spiritual practice by evaluating the *self-lessness* of his love and his actual *vision* of his beloved as the Divine, the embodiment of the Eternal Feminine.[142]

Woman's Work

Meditate daily on one or all of the following concepts:

- **1** *The light of the Eternal Feminine pours through me to you, my beloved.*
- **2** *Through love, I become like the holy Mother, full of divine light and wisdom.*
- **3** *I am that radiant Sophia, (Eternal Feminine, etc.), pouring out love to you.*

We have introduced numerous women to the idea of identifying as the Divine Feminine. And we have seen many times that when a woman begins to feel the real possibility of identifying with the Eternal Feminine, a soft radiance will subtly infuse her being. Her eyes and her demeanor reveal an inner glow, a *knowingness* that she can, in truth, be an expression of the universal Divine Feminine. In a subtle way Her being reflects that knowledge that she can truly be *everything* for her beloved, everything that he needs and is looking for: e.g., the beauty, the love, the mystery, the spiritual fulfillment—indeed, she knows that she can be and reveal *all* for him.

- **4** *Offerings*: Through her love, the woman wants to give her beloved everything that is beautiful, inspiring and spiritually elevating. She wants to offer him a love that is pure and unqualified. Thus her first offering is to love him unreservedly *as he is now*, without wanting him to be better or different from the way he is. Through this love, she knowingly transmits spiritual energy and sustenance to him. With awareness, she remains poised in a state of divine wisdom and limitless, eternal patience—no matter what seems to be happening between them or in their life.
- **5** She also offers to him the acknowledgment and honoring of his total freedom. Thus, his creative expression is enhanced and she becomes able to *receive* his offerings of love when and how he intends them, recognizing his intention without condition, overcoming her own fears, judgments, and intolerance of his ways of loving.
- **6** It is the woman's **paradox** that while accepting and loving her beloved, *as-he-is-now*, she must simultaneously lead, magnetize, inspire, invoke and *evoke* the highest potential that is latent within him. She must hold the lighted lamp of their spiritual life and not settle for anything less than the highest truth. Therefore she must

live, not as a limited personality, but secure in the light of the Eternal. In this paradoxical expression, she brings the divine qualities of the *Creative Feminine* into manifestation: "The spiritual *creativity* attributed to woman ... concerns not the physical functions of the woman but her spiritual and essentially divine qualities, which 'create' love in man and make him seek union with the divine Beloved. Here we must think of the feminine human being, [as] the Creative Feminine. "[143]

- **7** A woman may continually assess the maturity of her practice by evaluating at once, the depth and the steadiness of her identification with the Eternal Feminine, the intensity of her exaltation of her beloved-one, and her actual *vision* of him as a being of Divine Majesty.

• Ceremony For Invoking the Divine Feminine[144] •

The following Meditation/Ceremony can magnify and intensify a couple's practice of Mutual Exaltation through a focus on the Divine Feminine. A ceremony is a symbol, or it can be thought of as a tangible reference, to that which is already happening on an inner, invisible level. It also can become an invocation to the living Spirit Presence when it is performed as more than a mechanical repetition of a prescribed sequence of ritual actions. With strong aspiration and intense love in the heart, a man and woman can experience the symbolic actions of this ceremony as a living reality. When this occurs, there is a descent of spiritual force and the participants cross a threshold in consciousness.

Preparations for the meditation:

- Set aside plenty of time in a private, secluded place. See that all responsibilities are taken care of, so that there will be no interruptions.
- Create an atmosphere conducive to meditation: Light candles and incense in front of the altar and around the room. Have soft meditation music playing in the background.
- Arrange the objects needed for the ceremony:
  There must be a chair or cushion for the woman to sit upon.
  There must be a place close to the woman (it can be a chair or cushion) where the man can perform his worship.

- The man must have a beautiful cloth or scarf, which he will later place upon the chair or cushion meant for the woman. This cloth will prepare the woman's chair as a seat for the Deity/Divine.
- The woman must have a tiara or crown. The tiara may be one fashioned out of diamonds and precious jewels, or it may be an inexpensive costume-party crown made for a child to dress as a princess (this may be easily obtained at any store that sells party supplies or toys). There must also be a mirror available to the woman.

• The Ceremony •

I

- With music, soft in the background, sit together. Meditate in silence for a few minutes, using a Love mantra.
- Read aloud the following 3 statements, together or in turn:

The essence of spiritual realization consists in a transformation of the inner life. The heart and mind become pure, and through that pure heart and mind comes enlightenment. It is through the power of love that the transformation takes place. As we join together in love and devotion, the physical and emotional nature becomes lifted up to a higher octave of expression. Let us meditate with intense aspiration so that this ceremony shall become a spiritual experience and a means to move to higher consciousness.

As we move into the coming age, the Light of the Divine Feminine is drawing close to humanity. We invoke the spiritual presence of the Holy Mother, who becomes the Feminine Cosmic Principle, in our meditation today.

Every activity in the world is touched by the light of the Divine Mother. With the Spirit of the new age she is now present among us.

- The Woman reads:
  As the embodiment of the Cosmic Feminine Principle, I shall see my beloved ... (name) ... as a spiritual being, the divine Lord of Compassion.

- The Man reads:
  Through deep love for my beloved … (name) … the doors of perception shall open and the divine perfection of her being will be revealed to me.

- The Woman then reads the Invocation:
  Divine Mother, I reach out to your holy being,
  May your divine radiance of love and light fill me with spiritual power,
  May my heart and mind be one with your great compassion,
  May I become one with your being.

- Both read:
  In our meditation, we will reach out to the Divine Spirit in the being of our beloved. …

II

(Silence, except for music …)

- The man prepares for his beloved the seat meant for the Divine Presence. With great reverence, he arranges the beautiful cloth on his beloved's chair. As he does this, he realizes that his deep, self-less love to his beloved raises them both to spiritual heights. He silently repeats the mantra: *Through deep love and devotion I see the divine in my beloved.*

- In front of a mirror, the woman places the tiara upon her head. (The tiara symbolizes the shape of a crescent moon, bordered with a myriad of brilliant stars—a fitting crown for the One Who is the *Queen of Heaven*.) With great aspiration and love in her heart, she sees the transformation in her reflected image. Within her dawns the knowledge that she is not only a woman but an embodiment of the Eternal Feminine, and that her beloved is a messenger and a carrier of the Divine to her—in truth, he is a Spiritual Being. She uses the mantra: *The Holy Mother fills me with love for you, my beloved.*

III

- Silently invoking and anticipating the descent of the Feminine Presence, they stand quietly together near the woman's seat.
- When they both are ready, the woman sits on the seat prepared for her.
- As the woman sits upon the seat meant for the holy Presence, in that act, she becomes AT-ONE with the Eternal Feminine, Mother of the Universe. She is transfigured and Her Divinity is revealed. With the eye of the divine, the woman sees in her beloved, the Lord of Compassion, her divine counterpart, the fulfillment of her spiritual destiny.
- The man offers his deep love and whole-hearted devotion to his beloved. He worships her divine aspect with his heart and mind, his hands & limbs; in his own chosen ways: for instance, sitting and looking at her, touching her hand, his hands folded in reverence to her (i.e., *namaste*), head bowed, or kneeling …

(He offers to the divine being in his beloved a heart full of love, giving to her the fruit of all his spiritual striving on the path. Through his love he becomes one with her divine radiation.)

- They meditate together AS ONE (Silently, for 5-10 minutes).
- Both use the mantra:
  You are my beloved.
  I bless you with light
  Through your form I see the face of the Divine!

- Then, after 5-10 minutes, the man reads aloud:
  Divine Mother of the world. Your beauty and radiance are the light of God.
  Your pure being dwells within the form of every woman.
  Thus all that is created by Your Love, through her, is infused with holy light.
  Holy being of Cosmic Fire we reach out to you.
  Pour your divine radiance upon us so we are risen into spirit consciousness to dwell eternally in the fire of your love.

- The woman reads aloud:
  Holy Mother, who is approaching the earth, Your cosmic being fills all space.
  Within you glows the Light of God. Your presence touches every woman & man upon the earth. And all that is created through love, in this world of form, glows with the light of your Spirit.
  O' Blessed One, who brings down the light of God to earth, Your divine radiance raises us to celestial heights.
  We are transmuted into spiritual substance and dwell eternally in the fire of your love.

- Here ends the ceremony.

Through the practices of Mutual Exaltation, a man and woman revere each other as Divine Beings and their relationship becomes a means to attain true spiritual vision and fulfillment. And when they are "both spiritually awakened—then it is in the woman that the man experiences human beauty as an epiphany of Divine Beauty, and it is in the man that the woman experiences in human form the Majesty of God."[145] Thus they experience the divine *counterpart* in each other.

But the achievement of one-ness in spirit is not yet established. Only through love and devotion and Mutual Exaltation cultivated over the years do a man and woman blend at the level of their divine nature and become as one-in-spirit. When the man and woman are together reaching for the spiritual heights, they become one light moving towards God. We explicate this goal of a union-beyond-the- personality, in the final section of the Way of the Beloved.

7.3.4 THE GOLDEN TRIANGLE

When the Love and Will of God descended upon the earth and took form, two great principles carried the Spirit of God. It was the creative Spirit of male and female, the positive and negative forces throughout creation, the two principles working together.

When man and woman become one through love, they are partaking of the universal creative process and they become one with the universal creative Will.

When man and woman blend in deep love in the physical, mental & spiritual body, this invokes the Spiritual Presence, thus lifting the couple to a higher plane. They become open to higher beings.

When man and woman love each other deeply, they move beyond the physical and emotional expression and move into a sea of Divine Light and Love.

The union of man and woman in a spiritual state, creates a magnetic field that opens the door to the higher Realm. When man and woman join in deep love, their whole being blends into a spiritual magnetic aura that sends out a note that is heard by spiritual beings.

This union makes it possible for man and woman to partake of the Divine Nature, to become part of the Spiritual Body of God.

Man's love for a woman and a woman's love for a man, blends into a fire that reaches out to another world. Love is the Golden Triangle: Man, Woman and God.

—Herman Rednick[146]

The Golden Triangle is the essence of the beloved path teaching. This triangle of man, woman and God has been known since ancient times,[147] but it is seldom spoken of or recognized in modern secular cultures. We have said many times that Love is the great power that connects the hearts of a man and a woman, that intense love is the bond that joins a man and woman on all levels and leads them to the spiritual heights. All Wisdom Teachings, Eastern traditions as well as Western religions, tell us that the Divine, by whatever whatever name called—the One God or the many Gods, the Spiritual Beings, the higher planes of Spirit, the Universal Spirit, Nirvana, Emptiness—all are fashioned out of "absolute" compassion, the transcendent power of Love. Thus, as Western religions teach, God IS love. Where there is love flowing between persons, there God is also. Where there is love, there is the presence of the Divine Spirit. And when this love flows between a woman and a man, the Divine Presence creates the reality of the Golden Triangle.

Any expression or level of love can invoke a spiritual presence. But even though every expression of love—physical, emotional or mental, brings forth and manifests the divine spirit in some measure,[148] on the path of the beloved we are seeking that mutual, aspiring, selfless love which can transform the personality and open the doors to the spiritual consciousness. We are seeking the love that leads to a soul-consciousness in which the Golden Triangle becomes a reality in the relationship.

> *It is a Yoga. Therefore, it is necessary to see the divine aspect in each other.*
> *Thus, the woman begins to flower and the man grows by pouring out*
> *Love. When man and woman blend in this intense state, they will invoke*
> *the Holy Presence and the state of the beloved becomes a Divine Yoga.*[149]

What does it mean that the beloved path is a yoga?

In the beloved yoga, through his deep love and devotion to his beloved, the man seeks to see the divine aspect, the true spiritual being of his beloved. Thus he strives to evoke the Divine Presence to be revealed in her. As he begins to truly *see* and *recognize* the Divine Spirit manifesting through his beloved, he realizes that it is really this Divine Spirit that he loves and that he has always loved in his beloved. And through this knowing, this vision, he invokes the woman's acknowledgement and adoration of the Divine Presence within his being and also within her own.

At the same time, the woman comes to *know* that in truth it is the Divine Spirit that causes love to flow through her being. Thus she actualizes her aspiration to become her highest true spiritual self. Her own Spiritual Ideal becomes more present and more the center of her willing and feeling. In aspiring to *see* the Lord of Compassion in her beloved, the woman comes to realize that it is the Divine Being, the Spiritual Ideal, her beloved's True Self, Who is the One she loves and has been loving all along. And as she evokes and worships the Spiritual Being Who is her beloved-one, she knows and feels that, in truth, it is the Divine Lord who is her true beloved.

Thus, when a couple *sees* the Divine in the beloved-other, they are actually pouring their love upon God, the Lord of Compassion or the Holy Mother within their beloved-one. Through their invocation and their deep love and devotion to each other, they begin to see and love the Divine Spirit in and through and *beyond* the person or personality of each other. They see that it is not just another individual person who is their beloved, but the Divine Spirit glowing within and beyond the manifested form.

Thus God becomes a conscious presence in the relationship, known and revered as the One Who is loved.[150] And thus a beloved couple comes to know that it is the Divine who is the true beloved, the One Whom they have always sought, the conscious purpose and goal of their beloved path. When the couple becomes aware that *it is the Divine,* not the person, that they seek and love, it is then that they understand "the beloved path is a yoga." This is indeed a step onto a new level of the path. The Divine Spirit becomes a living Presence in their relationship and is known as the apex and the center of their Triangle of Love. It is *this* love, the light of the Divine Spirit, God's universal compassion, expressed in the mutual love of a man and a woman "that blends into a fire that reaches out to another world" and forms the Golden Triangle.[151]

ഇൻ ര

A further step on the path of the beloved toward a greater love occurs when the lovers realize that the source of their love, indeed of all love, is God, the absolute, Who created the heavens and the earth out of Love. Then they realize that they themselves are not the creators nor the owners of their love, that love does not belong to us as persons and that its power is not ours and has never been ours. They come to see that love does not originate within the personality or ego-consciousness and that it is not a creation of any person. The enlightening awareness dawns within, that Love is a great spiritual energy radiating forth out of the higher worlds creating, forming and sustaining the heavenly and earthly planes of being. And that it can come pouring through our being. And if our aspiration is pure, strong and steadfast, we can become a vehicle for its transcendent light and power.

When we think we are *doing it*—i.e., that we are the ones who are doing the loving— we are participating in the great hypnosis of maya, caught in the very depths of the illusion. Phillip Sherrard says that in this kind of typical illusion spun-out by the ego-consciousness, love seems to be " little more than an expression simply of [our] own ego, to use or abuse as [we] think(s) fit." [We do not have] the recognition that love itself is a Divine Quality and gift and does not belong to [man] in his own right. Thus when [I] say 'I love,' I am really misappropriating something that is not mine, but which is expressing itself through me."[152] We are thinking that we are doing what, in truth, only God can do.

In other words, if we think that we ourselves are doing the loving, then it is our ego claiming something that does not belong to us. This is a universal human "debt" incurred by ego-consciousness and each of us in turn must pay it on our path through life. When we become aware of this eternal truth— that all love comes from God, is God and, therefore, comes from the Divine Spirit, is the Divine Spirit—we know that we can become an "expression" or *vehicle* of *that* love. When this is acknowledged and acted upon in the beloved relationship, it is more than a change in attitude, it is a change in consciousness. Indeed, the personality-consciousness now aspires to realize a pure experience of the soul's union with the soul of our beloved-one. This is a spirit of love that leads us beyond the ego to soul-consciousness, in which the Golden Triangle becomes a *reality*. We know that love is God, and that all love includes God, but we realize that it is up to us, two human lovers, to recognize and live the truth of this holy reality, bringing it into expression through our own life as beloveds. Otherwise we profane the Divine gift and claim it for the ego!

Thus the essence of the Beloved Yoga is to see the divine aspect, the divine Truth of the beloved, to see our beloved-one within the Divine Light, as the Spiritual Being he or she truly is. And to recognize that any other way of love is centered in the personality and, therefore, is solely of *this world*. The way of love that we know and dwell in now is almost completely the personality-way. It is not pure, most often being full of emotional elements and mixed concepts. But when we move into the "love of the soul" we know that, in truth, we can only love at all, if God's Divine love, which descends upon us from the higher planes, is flowing through us. Thus, we realize that only because the sacred power of the Divine is with us and within us, can we BE a beloved couple. Indeed, it is God's Presence, as Love, which makes it so.[153] This realization means that it is only by knowing that we are carriers of God's love, that is, vehicles for divine energies to flow through us, that we, any of us, can truly love at all. And it is the mutual recognition of this fundamental truth that opens the door to the beloved path becoming a divine yoga. Phillip Sherrard summarizes this beautifully:

> "in this ... form of love between man and woman, the real lover—the real subject moving the love within the human lovers—is God Himself, the Lord of Love. ... in each it is God who loves the other. Such a love is physical, insofar as it is focused on and embraces an incarnate image. Yet it is also spiritual ... *What man and woman do in such a relationship is to invest each other with the concrete form of another living being who promotes in each the aspiration to grow towards the perfection for which both have been created.*"[154]

All of the concepts and exercises we have presented on the Way of the Beloved are intended to lead a beloved couple to this understanding: that the Golden Triangle, man/woman/God, is the Reality of their loving.[155]

ႠႠ

As we devote ourselves to the intensification of love on the beloved path, there undoubtedly comes a time when we realize that the physical, emotional, personality-focused loving can no longer offer us the fulfillment, or even the promise, of that which we yearn for and are truly seeking.[156] If we want to proceed further on this path we must seek an explicit transcendent orientation which recognizes God as love and love as God and in which God becomes the "Image," the *body* of our relationship. This can only come about through the *practice*, the *art* of the Way of the Beloved. Again it is Phillip Sherrard who writes:

> Their art—for it is an art to which they are committed—is to transfigure each other by arousing the full potentiality of their creative energies, bringing each other in this way ever more intimately into the presence of God. Seeing each other as the manifestation of the Divine Beloved, the Lord of Love, they spiritualize each other's being by raising it beyond its physical or sensible form to its Divine incorruptible form so that in the end their contemplation of God in each other becomes the highest form of contemplation of which human beings are capable ... [157]

The meditations and practices of Chapters 6 and 7 are a yoga, an *art* of spiritual union. Indeed, here we are designating that which can be considered an *Initiation* process—a stepping through the veils of illusion into the Greater Reality of the Spiritual Worlds. Through this process a couple will move through those extra-ordinary experiences in which our ordinary human conception of love— all of what we have said and all that can be understood through the *language*-of-love—are altogether transcended. And this state of being is open to those loving couples living in today's world, who are willing to do the work to attain it.

By recognizing and actually seeing the Divine in our beloved we experientially overcome the persistent blocks and veils within our consciousness, which prevent the full and unqualified expression of love. The experience of *visioning* the Divine engenders an unshakeable faith in the inherent divinity in our beloved-one. It might be said that we create an *icon*, an *image* or *symbol*, which is a greater *truth* of our Beloved.[158] We have said before that the creative imagination is what makes the ideal image perceivable, manifesting as a *theophanic* experience, and that this *Image* is a spiritual Reality clothed in a recognizable form—our beloved. And, that actually perceiving the inter-relation between the physical person we love and his or her *theophany* is only achievable by transcending the limitations of human, personality-emotional love and our worldly perception. And this transcendence, this theophanic experience, does not negate or cancel-out our experience of the physical manifestation of our beloved. Indeed, both occur simultaneously. As Charles Williams tells us, "The vision of perfection does not at all exclude the sight of imperfection; the two can exist together; they can even ... co-inhere."[159]

One woman confided to us, with a feeling of awe: "I cannot really separate my love for my beloved and my love for the Christ." And another friend wrote:

> This is my approach:
> My beloved actually is Christ. I see this not as a potential state nor do I look at him *as if* he is the Christ. He actually is Christ—because of the fire in the heart. A light that is sometimes dim or sometimes bright is still light. That is its nature. The nature of the beloved is Christ, sometimes revealed perfectly, sometimes imperfectly. Others may not see this when they look at Saul. That is because they do not know him as I do.

We use this Teaching: to see the divine in the beloved. The man, to see that he is living with the Holy Mother. The woman, to see that she is living with the Christ. As I try to do this, I find that it is so. I am living with Christ. Sometimes I forget, but a simple morning when the sun is bright and we offer a stick of incense together, I glimpse that we are living in God and part of this glimpse is the Christ-ness, the Christ-quality of my beloved, the divine, masculine principle in form on earth. All my life I looked for Christ, but Christ is actually already close to me in Saul, in the heart of my beloved.

The *soul-awareness of love*, emerging from and through the theophanic imagination—the eye of the heart—is a form of spiritual consciousness. As it expands within us we develop the vision to perceive that all things and all living beings are divine manifestations—i.e., expressions of God-in-form. This is the fundamental perceptual orientation of soul-consciousness which usually awakens in us by fits and starts. Often it slips away from us for extended periods of time and we again see only separateness everywhere. But our beloved is right there, living beside us, carrying that spark, the spirit of God within the heart. And when we *see* the Divine Spirit in our beloved-one, we become participants in the miraculous process wherein the Spirit is unveiling Him/Her Self, becoming visible and active on this plane, manifesting *here and now, in THIS world*. Through the form and being and life of our beloved and through our mutual intense love and devotion, each of us is revealing to the other, the *divine mystery* hidden in all creation. Again, Phillip Sherrard says it so beautifully:

> Everything is an unveiling of God, a theophany in which God discloses Himself in His own image. Hence in loving each other what they love is God as He has revealed Himself in each of them to the other. Each becomes an ikon to the other; and because God has revealed Himself as an ikon in the form of the living being who is the beloved, so in loving that being the lover will be loving God. In the ikon, it is God who manifests Himself; and what the man loves in the woman is the mystery she discloses as such an ikon, just as what the woman loves in the man is the mystery that he discloses in a similar way. Each thus discloses for the other that unknown being who is the sacred core of their existence and who Himself aspires to find a birthplace in the hearts of both of them.[160]

We become "the image of God," "the Ideal Self," to one another and thusly do we come to know and actually experience that we "live and move and have our being in God."

But we do not know this all the time. Our vision constantly fluctuates, coming and going and it is never completely pure. Most of the time we cannot see that our beloved is a luminous expression of God-in-form, we are too much aware of the personality aspects. But even within our limitations, we aspire to "see the highest that we can conceive of in our beloved, to see the God in him[her] trying to work through a form that is not yet perfected."[161] As Soloviev tells us:

> It is one and the same person in two distinguishable aspects, or in two different spheres of being—the ideal and the real. The first is as yet only an idea. By steadfast believing and insightful love, however, we know that this idea is not an arbitrary fiction of our own, but that it expresses the *truth* of the ... [beloved-one], only a truth as yet not realized in the sphere of external, real phenomena.[162]

Thus, along with all of our spiritual practice, all of our personality purification and our increased capacity for visioning through love, if we are to travel further on the Way of the Beloved, we will need to sustain a love grounded in an intense *faith* in the Divine Spirit which exists as a spiritual potential and an Ultimate Truth within our beloved and within ourself here and now! Only by the power of this Faith can we accept and act as if our theophanic vision is a timeless truth which exists in a Greater Reality than we may be experiencing right now. It is by this Faith that we transcend the here and now and orient ourselves towards the spiritual realms from which our theophanic imagination has brought luminous glimpses.

We have spoken about a kind of faith in our beloved path as an intentional act of Radical Trust (Section 4.3) and as Affirmation (Section 5.3), but the Faith we are referring to now, goes beyond a Radical Trust based on past experience or future hopes and beyond an Affirmation of the beloved-other as a separate, whole and equal person. Max Scheler describes it thusly: [Our] "personal love lives by faith in the ideal self of the other person, that is, by faith in a reality which is somehow already present and is gradually emerging toward full realization."[163] And Nicolai Hartmann said: "Genuine love 'divines' and foresees in the other person the full actualization of his[or her] ideal self. Love senses prophetically, perfection in the imperfect, and infinitude in the finite."[164]

Then, as Soloviev tells us, "The act of faith, under real conditions of time and place, is a prayer." To bring the Presence of the Divine into conscious realization in our relationship, we must make all of our exercises and practices into a great prayer-of-invocation, a meditation which summons the invisible Divine Presence to manifest in our beloved relationship. Moreover, this prayerful invocation changes the fundamental focus of our beloved relationship from a concentration on each other and the purification of our personalities and interactions, into one of mutually invoking the Presence and Power of the Divine to flow into our life together and to transmute our most fundamental ideas and sense of the will-to-love. Our life becomes more and more a constant meditation, a "prayer without ceasing," infused with the conscious orientation of aspiration toward One-ness with the Divine. In this way we move toward Spiritual Union. Indeed, "the aim of love is union; but if lovers desire only union with one another as persons, that love is exhausted in fulfillment ... If on the other hand they desire union with the divine through and by means of one another, instead of being like easily broken and quickly emptied bottles they become conductors from an inexhaustible reservoir of life."[165]

Meditation:[166]

> *When you love deeply and see the divine in your beloved, the veils of illusion and separation begin to dissolve. You shall both blend and become One in Spirit. This unity in love creates a magnetic field that opens the door to the higher Realm, thus lifting you to a higher plane. You move beyond the physical and emotional expression into a sea of Divine Light and Love. This union makes it possible for you to partake of the Divine Nature, to become part of the Spiritual Body of God.*
>
> Mantram: *Through Love and Union with my beloved,*
> *We become one with the Body of God.*

The following ceremony is a guided meditation which we use in our Beloved Retreats. A couple may practice it alone in a meditation area at home. It can also be practiced with others in a small group of beloved couples. The meditation should be read very slowly, with plenty of time for silence in between each paragraph. When a couple is practicing alone, it is best to record (i.e., tape) the reading in advance, so the tape can be played during the actual practice and a couple can remain silent as they listen to their own voices guiding the meditation. If taping is impractical or unavailable, the meditation can be read aloud by the participants during the practice. In a group, a tape can be used, or one couple can read the meditation aloud for everyone.

• GOLDEN TRIANGLE MEDITATION •

Light a candle and incense in your meditation area.
5 minutes: Silent Meditation

Either Person Reads First

When the Will and Love of God came into expression, two great principles carried the Divine Spirit. It was Male and Female, the positive and negative forces throughout creation. When man and woman join, they are partaking of the universal creative process. Through deep love, they move beyond the physical and emotional expression and move into a sea of Divine Light and Love. This union makes it possible for man and woman to partake of the Divine Nature, and to become part of the Spiritual Body of God.

The Other Person reads

As we move into the coming age, the Light of the Divine Feminine is drawing close to humanity. Let us invoke the spiritual presence of God in the feminine aspect, the Holy Mother, who becomes the Feminine Cosmic Principle, in our guided meditation.

First Person Reads

Divine Mother of the world
Your beauty & radiance are the light of God.
Your pure being dwells within the form of every woman;
Thus all that is created by your love, through her, is infused with holy light
Holy Being of Cosmic Fire, we reach out to you,
Pour your divine radiance upon us, so we are risen into spirit consciousness,
to dwell eternally in the fire of your love.

The Other Person Reads

It is written: "Love one another." This is not a platitude. It is a psychic law. Man's love for a woman and a woman's love for a man, blends into a fire that reaches out to another world. Love is the Golden Triangle: Man, Woman, and God.

As we listen to the Golden Triangle Meditation, let us visualize the experience so that we enter into and become the images.

The Man Reads
I sit with my beloved, face to face. We're in a sphere of golden light set at the edge of the world. A pulsing thread of gold links our hearts together, and from each heart, ascending and descending, forms a triangle with the blue of God above. A deep silence pervades this triangle of Love, opening an emptiness in space.

The Woman Reads
The sound of a clear note cuts through this emptiness, and a beam of brilliant blue light flashes out, from which the Holy Mother appears, glowing in pure white raiment. Piercing rays of prismatic fire radiate from her heart to all the directions. She looks upon us with unutterable compassion, & we are showered with holy light and love.

Man
Divine Sophia, Your celestial radiance of light and love charges our being with spiritual fire; May we become One with your Spirit; May you guide us every moment on the path to the spiritual Temple.

Woman
As A Woman I Speak In My Heart: The Light of the Holy Mother pours through my being, and the knowledge dawns within me, that the radiance of this great Divine Being is beyond any manifestation of name and form. And that this Transcendent One is who I can be. I enter the domain of Her Holiness—and I become like the Holy Mother ... My form is fashioned of pure light, and radiant compassion flows through my being. Now my heart overflows with the fire of Her Love, and as I look toward my beloved, I see, he is an emanation of Her cloak of spirit—He is Her messenger to me; and I see that our life in form—all life in form—is Her life, and Her plan. I am beyond time and beyond space, forever—eternal.

Man
As Her Beloved I Answer Her Call: I gaze upon my beloved with the eye of my heart and she becomes the radiant image of my soul. Oh! celestial partner, cobalt angel of my destiny, your unearthly beauty opens my being to the fire

of compassion, and burns away the sense of a separate life-in-form. You are She, Who veils & unveils the mysteries for me, leading me into the still waters of Sophia-wisdom, revealing to me the Divine Purpose of my existence: I unite in love with You, whom I have always sought, for You are the transcendent form of mine own Eternity.

Woman
Divine Sophia, You are the embodiment of the Fire of Compassion;
Your Being covers humanity with a cloak of light and Your song fills all space.
The fires within our heart glow with the pure joy of divine love;
Our being becomes a center for Spiritual Force;
Our eyes carry beams of love;
Our heart radiates Divine Fire;
Our thought blesses everyone we touch.

Man
The Holy Mother flows through our united being, touching all we know and meet, with Sacred Fire.

5 minutes ... Silent Meditation ...
End of meditation.

7.3.5 SERVICE

This is the Yoga for the new age,
The spiritual radiance of the beloved shall light up the world.[167]

Service is a state of spiritual radiation. It is not visible to ordinary physical perception and cannot be measured by tangible results or standards. When man and woman unite through love on all levels, physical, emotional, mental and spiritual, their union becomes an invocation to the spiritual light and their magnetic atmosphere radiates out to touch all they know. Through their intense exaltation of the Divine in each other, they create around them an atmosphere of love. This atmosphere is a radiant sphere of spiritual energy, which carries a tone and a vibration that reaches everyone they see and contact. Everything is touched by the spiritual radiance flowing through them. This happens whether or not they are physically together and without them having to do or say anything in particular. They become a luminous center, touching and helping others even though they do not say a word. A beloved couple thus can serve as they walk the path toward the spiritual heights.

Most of us know all too well that we do not yet dwell in a state of great love and radiant light and our state of mind and heart fluctuates constantly, yet we do not have to wait until we are in that state to be able to serve. Wherever we stand in consciousness, there is always someone whom we can help. It is universally a part of the spiritual teachings that, if we do not give out to others whatever light is bestowed upon us by the Spirit, we will lose it. Light and love are not personal possessions, they are gifts of the Spirit and will be taken away if the selfish ego seeks to covet them for itself.

Among our students we often see that the extremely individualistic philosophy of our society can be transferred, unawares, by a loving couple, to their own relationship or family unit. There is a powerful tendency among loving couples to back away from the terrible stresses and violence of the contemporary world and to retreat into the cocoon of love that they share with each other and their family. This is only natural and Plato recognized it in his own time: "you must not wonder that those who attain to this beatific vision are unwilling to descend to human affairs; for their souls are ever hastening into the upper world where they desire to dwell; which desire of theirs is very natural."[168] However, this separating and protective stance may only be maintained through some kind of artificial isolation. While it is true that to fully participate in our contemporary collective life, one must develop a certain amount of personal impenetrability, yet, as many have pointed out, this leads to an "inauthentic" existence. It is an inescapable fact of our human life on the physical plane that every individual, and couple, is inextricably interconnected with, even interpenetrates, all other beings.[169] Thus to attempt to become impenetrable to others is to limit our ability to love and, therefore, our connection to the Spirit necessarily becomes dimmer. Our Teacher wrote: "A circle of light is drawn around beloveds. It is of different colors and intensity. This circle will lose it's color if one does not step outside of the circle to help a neighbor … The [spiritual] plan is to unite people. If we neglect to pour out the love, the light begins to diminish within, your energy becomes negative, and your Soul cannot come through."[170]

Thus Service is not just an incidental activity for the beloved couple. It is a necessary part of their destiny, because that love for which they strive is a universal spiritual power and its flowering in their relationship makes service an imperative. A beloved couple cannot separate the work of their own spiritual development from the process of worldwide unification through compassion. As Teilhard de Chardin observed:

> There was, perhaps, a time before our own when individuals could still try to better themselves and fulfill themselves, each on his own, in isolation. That time has gone for ever. We now have to make up our minds to recognize that at no moment of history has man been so completely involved … in the value and betterment of all those around him, as he is today. And all the evidence indicates that this regime of interdependence can only become more pronounced in the course of the coming centuries.[171]

Compassion means to feel with others' feeling and this carries with it the impulse to acknowledge, to heal, to ennoble, to be of service to others.[172] With the development of a true compassion in the beloved relationship, the love that the beloveds share overflows and becomes the desire to serve. And this is recognized as a spiritual necessity. It has been a yogic precept for ages that "My love grows when I serve another."[173] In the Bible Christ tells us to not hide our light under a bushel but to "put it on its stand and it gives light to everyone in the house."[174] In today's world, "the house" has become the whole world and when we extend a hand to a neighbor, the love that we share flows forth in the form of service. Our Teacher avowed that the Beloved Path "is the Yoga for the New Age." And when the couple actively turns toward service of others the whole world benefits.

It is in these kinds of considerations that we find the union between the ultimate fullfilment of our own being and the necessity to serve others. Thus, service to others is an integral part of the Way of the Beloved and it is service which will bring about a brighter future for us all.[175]

୫୬ ଓ୫

The world waits
For help. Beloved, let us work so well,
Our work shall still be better for our love
And still our love be sweeter for our work.
Elizabeth Barrett Browning[176]

Through their intense love for each other the Brownings intuitively grasped that "the world waits for help" and that service to others is not only "better for [their] love" but their love is "sweeter" thereby.

For beloveds, service can be a co-intentional decision and activity. Working together as one, the couple becomes a creative vehicle. And when they explicitly intend to serve others, they can develop a form through which they can work and for which they are most suited.

The best place to begin is in the home. To bring new souls into incarnation and prepare them for life in an atmosphere of love is the beginning of Service. In a letter to a couple just starting family life, our Teacher wrote:

> The path of the beloved is the greatest yoga in the western countries because it makes us unearth the best and highest that is within. The home is an entity that sounds forth our note into the world, and when the psychic factors are harmonized, the atmosphere becomes a magnetic field conducive to our higher being. Thus, through the love and devotion of a beloved couple, the home becomes a center glowing with the Radiant Presence, and when we reach out to others, we have a quality of substance that will help them.[177]

Beyond the home, a couple can serve by creating together a service project dedicated to a spiritual ideal or expressing a creative talent, for the purpose of helping others. This project can be a "meditation in action" in which the two "serve the same idea." With this as the motivation, service may take myriad forms and how a couple chooses to serve will vary greatly. For the authors, writing this book together and teaching all our classes together has been motivated by a desire to serve. Among our students who wish to serve, musicians create and perform together, photographers and artists work together and some in 12 step programs become sponsors together.

Some couples are at a loss in seeking for a service project, or some who still have young children have not yet turned toward serving beyond the family. For these, we suggest that they use the mantra from the following meditation:

Meditation:[178]

> *We reach out as high as we can and each of us increases within and we both go forward on the path. Through our union in love, we realize that we are not alone, but a part of a great spiritual Reality.*
>
> *And as the spirit which unites us grows in its intensity in love and light, we shall both, as a unit, move out to touch the people who cross our path. The state of brotherhood for all peoples can become a reality. The path of the beloved has the potential to transform the whole earth.*
>
> Mantram: *As a beloved couple we reach out to serve.*

৩০শ

7.3.6 UNION [179]

> *When man and woman join in deep love their whole being blends into a spiritual magnetic aura that sends out a note heard in the spiritual worlds. When their love and devotion is deep, their union makes it possible for them to partake of their Divine Nature, to become a part of the Spiritual Body of God.*
>
> *As you move toward union through deep love and devotion, your heart will be set afire. On this high level your beloved shall enter your being and live within you; And you shall hear his [her] voice within your heart.* This creates a luminous and fragrant light around you. *And you shall become as one being* because you live within one another. *This holy union will break the hypnotic hold of Maya and free you from the ancient past. For all blocks dissolve before the pure love and devotion for your beloved.*
>
> *Thus the yoga of the beloved has an infinite potential. The union of man and woman fulfills the complete expression of humanity as designed by the Spirit and they move as one toward the Holy City ...* [180]

Yoga means Union. And Love is the bond of spiritual union. Through walking the path of the beloved, a couple attains that spiritual state to which seekers and mystics on the spiritual path of all traditions the world over aspire: Union with the Divine planes of consciousness. The state of spiritual union may be called Nirvana, Liberation, Enlightenment, Spiritual Union or One-ness with God or Christ. Whatever name is used or whichever path is followed, through intensifying love a man and a woman blend with the divine energy currents from the higher worlds. This brings about a spiritual or mystical union with the Divine consciousness. A couple who is aware of living in the Golden Triangle is reaching all the time for union with the Divine. Although they are living on the earth as a woman and a man, they have become One in Spirit and are moving towards the higher planes of consciousness.

A man and a woman who are walking the Path of the Beloved have an intense and one-pointed aspiration to attain "union with the divine through and by means of one another."[181] Thus, for couples on the spiritual path in today's world, the integration with the beloved may be the most creative and important aspect of life.

ॐ

• POLARITY •

When the Will and Love of God came into expression, two great principles carried the Spirit of God. It was Male and Female, the positive and negative forces throughout creation. From a microscopic creature, up to man and out to the stars, there are the male and female forces.[182]

Although the knowledge of the spiritual origin of man and woman has been lost in the Western world (indeed for most of humanity in the last 300 years), mystics in all spiritual traditions from time immemorial offer to us in one form or another a mythico-religious account of our origin, affirming that in some primordial time, i.e., in the spiritual world, the masculine and feminine principles were united in one great being. And when this united, non-physical being descends into physical manifestation, the division of male and female takes place.

The fundamental structure of this story is common, not only to all three of the Abrahamic religions, i.e., Judaism, Christianity and Islam, but also to Hinduism, Buddhism and Taoism. It was also common to the ancient cultures of Egypt, Mesopotamia, Persia and Greece. And in modern times, there have even been a few expressions of this story among contemporary Christian thinkers.[183]

Man and woman, male and female, are thought of and referred to as opposites. And in the world of physical manifestation, as we are often told, the division into opposites takes place throughout the created universe. For example, the Sufi, Hazrat Inayat Khan, says that "There is a pair of opposites in all things; in each thing there exists the spirit of the opposite."[184] However, man and woman are not just opposites, they are *polar* opposites. The two great forces working on this earth and throughout the cosmos manifest in man and woman as a *polarity*.

What does it mean that the relationship of male and female is one of polarity, that man and woman are *polar* opposites? The comprehensive mystical vision of Daniel Andreev (1906-1959)[185] presents in modern, esoteric language, the transcultural and transhistorical narrative of the polar opposites: male and female:

> In manifesting Himself [Herself] externally, the One God reveals His [Her] inherent inner polarity. The essence of that polarity within the Divine is transcendental for us. But we perceive the external

> manifestations of that essence as the polarity of *two principles gravitating to each other and not existing one without the other,* eternally and timelessly united in creative love … Flowing into the universe, the Divine retains that inherent polarity; all spirituality and all materiality in the universe is permeated by it. It is manifested differently at different levels of being. At the level of inorganic matter perceptible by humans it can no doubt be seen as the basis of what we call the universal law of gravity, the polarity of electricity, and much more. In the organic matter of our plane here, the polarity of the Divine is manifested in the distinction between male and female.[186]

Thus the principle of polarity permeates our material universe.[187] It is a law which reigns through all Nature. It is the manifestation of One Divine power by opposite forces—the duality of the opposite forces being the manifestation of a Unity which has its Being in the higher planes of consciousness.

In the Oxford English Dictionary, polarity is defined as "the quality of exhibiting contrasted properties or powers in opposite or contrasted directions; the possession of two points called poles having contrary qualities or tendencies." And the Merriam Webster's Collegiate Dictionary defines polarity as "the quality or condition inherent in a body that exhibits opposite properties or powers in opposite parts or directions." But, even though in a polarity the poles are opposites, they do not contradict each other as in a paradox. Owen Barfield tells us that: "A paradox is the violent union of two opposites that simply contradict each other, so that reason assures us we can have one or the other but not both at the same time. Whereas polar contraries (as is illustrated by the use of the term in electricity) exist by virtue of each other as well as at each other's expense."[188] Thus, polar opposites may be distinguished one from the other, but "there is no possibility of *dividing* them."[189] Polarities are expressive of a dynamic, creative *power*. They are a creative force which when joined together generate a new product: the joining of the opposites poles of electricity produces light, the joining of male and female creates a new *form*.

Owen Barfield sagely advises us that: "the concept of polarity … is not really a logical concept at all, but one which requires an act of imagination to grasp …"[190] And then he adds, "How much use are definitions of the undefinable? The point is, has the imagination grasped it? For nothing else can do so. At this point the reader must be called on, not to think about imagination, but to use it."[191]

One of Teilhard de Chardin's aphorisms captures the contradictory essence of polarity memorably: "Unity in love differentiates."[192] This certainly does not seem logical, but consider the following: "If there are not two (different sexes) not only is the many impossible, but the one is impossible as well."[193] Indeed, as we see in the Way of the Beloved and also in the teachings of the great Wisdom Traditions, it is the development of love which is the primary task of humanity at this point in our evolution and certainly, "A unifying love requires two: 'It takes two to love.'"[194]

• COMMON BLOCKS •

Taking the leap beyond logic and using the imagination to work toward union in the beloved relationship is not easy for a beloved couple in today's world. We live in an era surrounded with powerful thought-forms which contradict and oppose our spiritual aspirations and our attempts to lead a spiritual life. Many students have trouble even conceiving of the concept of a "spiritual union" between the actual manifested polar opposites, a man and a woman. There are several very widespread, popular assumptions, suppositions and inferences which underlie our outlook and make it difficult for many couples, even those who have fully embraced the beloved path, to move more deeply into the work. These assumptions are hidden and act subtly. They rarely come into awareness until a student faces a problem or block. Then, it becomes apparent how strong a hold they have in a person's mind. This awareness is one's opportunity to begin to counteract them.

(1) Materialism
In modern times the universal narrative of the spiritual origin of man and woman has been replaced with a purely materialistic story of evolving physical organisms. Modern Western humanity is habituated to thinking of all life solely as the evolution of material forms, including the development of the mind and consciousness itself. Thus the spiritual descent into form, of the masculine and feminine polarity inherent in the Divine, is turned upside down. The common idea is that man and woman are somehow opposites which have evolved to optimize reproduction. Darwin's purely materialistic theories dominate the current education and outlook of most people. Thus it is usually thought, that if deep-down man and woman are unequivocal, material opposites, then any kind of true *union* is impossible—it would be "against the laws of nature." Indeed, in recent times, the majority of human

beings have believed that a union between men and women is not possible. Without doubt, the logic of Aristotle, which emphasizes the *opposition*, or the unavoidable separation and conflict of opposites, is still very much the dominant way of conceiving of the divergent and contrary things of the world. The idea of the complementarity of opposites, which has acquired a new respectability in quantum physics,[195] has not reached most people and for the most part is puzzling to those that it has.

Modern humanity is so habituated to thinking from the material manifestation up to the immaterial, that a most common error which accompanies speculations regarding the union of man and woman is to concretize the process in much too literal and concrete an image. The tendency is to conceive of the higher worlds as the same as the material, just without the matter[196]

An approach that brings us closer to the truth is to conceive of these processes in terms of *energies*. For instance, we can conceive of a great stream of multifarious energy constantly flowing down from higher realms of Spirit, and, as it descends through various planes of existence, this energy stream spreads out and appears to split, and discrete strands seem to take on separate existences. One may think of the analogy of sunlight passing through raindrops to form a rainbow or through a prism to appear as separate bands of color. When the polar energy of masculine and feminine descends as far as matter it becomes embodied in two different forms, and souls entering the material universe come into one engendered body or the other. Thus, instead of the current material myth of seeing male and female as a blind evolutionary strategy of our genes or of mechanical, material forces, we may describe our gender differences as part of a long-term evolution of human *consciousness* which ineluctably will bring us into a higher, more Divine, state of Being and Love.

Three long-term students immediately come to mind. One man, James, continues giving lip-service to the work year after year, declaring that the beloved path is meaningful and valuable to him, yet protesting vigorously all the while that he does not and cannot believe in "this stuff." Another man, Andrew, could never make the intellectual leap, and, even though he had had a transcendental experience many years before, eventually turned away from the beloved work and all other spiritual pursuits. Alexander, a non-believing intellectual for all of his life, also has a *heart*. He recently wrote the following paper:

This concept of Spiritual union is so esoteric and beyond that which the mind can grasp as to be out of reach, unachievable. It cannot be measured. It does not rest in logic. How can it be believed?

First comes an opening, then a fleeting experience—the paradigm shifts and new possibilities arise. I am not who I once was—no more the skeptic. I have moved beyond tolerance and now accept the reality of this consciousness.

I am grateful for all that has come to me to give me new eyes to see that which has been hidden.

I could not be in this place without love, faith, deep experiences and without my Beloved. She has taken my hand in hers and pointed the way to the Temple door.

(2) "New Age" Assumptions

There are also many today who adhere to what might be characterized as "New Age Thought" and who take the extreme opposite stance from the materialistic view that the universe is composed of separate and distinct material objects. They vaguely assert that, "since *everything* in the universe is "spiritual," then everything is the same thing, because All is One." Antoine Faivre and Jacob Needleman describe this view as an " erroneous supposition" because it assumes "that the inclusion of all levels in the realm of the inner search, and the goal; of a harmonious relationship between all the parts of human and cosmic nature implies the identity of all things, even their sameness."[197]

To take this view, which has a very powerful hold upon its adherents, is to avoid the current reality of our *actual* life. It allows us to avoid the struggle of recognizing and transforming our actual perceptions and consciousness of the *very concrete illusion*—the *Maya*, our differences, our real physical separation and our deep fear and opposition to one another. In other words, this kind of assertion is essentially an egoistic claim to divinity: "We, I, all of us are *there* at the goal already," that is, "I myself am God, you are too, but you don't know it yet!" This is an overt denial of our actual, existential situation, our current state of human consciousness, and such an assertion or belief does not have the power to transform our human nature into Godliness. Indeed, this presumption does not recognize any higher states or planes of consciousness, nor does it acknowledge the path and the effort needed to better oneself. And it is altogether devoid of the necessary element of love.

This approach also lacks the element of discrimination. Marko Pogacnik, a clairvoyant who is popular among new-agers, does not fall into this trap. He cautions his students to stay grounded and to not stop being self-critical: "On the contrary! It is important that the mind should maintain a proper distance even while it accompanies the stream of our perceptions. It should watch us to make sure we are properly grounded and attuned to what we are perceiving. It can warn us if our imaginations go too far and we lose ourselves in fantasies."[198]

We have found in our classes that those who hold on to this "new-age" stance cannot embrace the work needed to walk the spiritual path. They cannot strive for a spiritual goal or ideal. Every student who subscribed to this approach left our classes after a very short time.

(3) Androgyny

There is active today a powerful thought-form which picks up an echo of the traditional myth of our origin in a Being which embodies both masculine and feminine principles and then distorts it by treating it as a description of our physical plane, material existence. This mistaken idea states that our true *human* nature is androgynous, therefore, the actual manifestation of male and female human beings has no intrinsic meaning and our real goal is to reveal and actualize our fundamental, inner androgyny.

Not only does this attitude dismiss the significance of the polarity of male and female, it ignores that the source of these two streams of energy actually emanates from a single locus in *the intangible worlds*. It does not recognize the existence of any other worlds. And more than anything else, it totally obviates the need for ever loving another person. In his book, *The Man-woman Relationship in Christian Thought*, Derrick Bailey writes:

> The androgynous conception of sex [or gender] excludes any idea of genuine meeting and self-communication between man and woman, and tends to find expression only in narcissism or self-regarding love. It also denies the reality of sexual antithesis and complementation, and has no goal but an ultimate fusion of male and female in the undifferentiated unity from which it supposes that they originated. The biblical myth ... on the contrary, recognizes ... [that there are] two primary obligations created by Man's constitution as a "dual being"; these are, the preservation of sexual integrity, and the acceptance of sexual partnership ... The first of these obligations

means the affirmation of sex as a gift from God which Man may neither reject nor seek to transcend in a quest for some "higher" condition of virtual asexuality. From the standpoint of contemporary thought in general, it may seem nonsense to speak of denying or transcending sex—for what can Man do but accept his sex? In terms of biological, physical sexuality there is, admittedly, no alternative; male and female must acquiesce in their respective natures as they received them.[199] But with sex [gender] as a metaphysical phenomenon this is not so, for it is possible to adopt towards one's own masculinity or femininity an attitude which amounts, in effect, to nothing less than a denial of all that sex signifies—a refusal to assent to one of the basic facts of personal existence.[200]

Here is an example of a couple who are sincere seekers, but nevertheless can be described as expressing "self-regarding love":

Hattie and Jacob approached to the Way of the Beloved course as an intellectual venture. At the time that they joined a Beloved class, they were also involved in an academic graduate program of "studying" many spiritual paths. They found the Beloved work to be interesting, but we do not think that they ever tried to do the exercises for reducing selfishness and intensifying love or the Beloved meditations, in fact, it is not at all clear that they actually *practiced* any path. When their class began to work with the Circle of Love, they immediately announced that there was no difference at all between the sexes and that what was being presented was old fashioned and ignored modern feminist ideas—i.e., it was part of a defunct dogma. They believed that men and women are actually the same in all respects, except anatomically, and that each person could achieve a perfect balance of male and female qualities. They kindly offered to be quiet during the class sessions while the other couples delved into the work with the Spiral of Separation and the polarity of gender. They politely tolerated all the classes remaining in the program until they had "completed" the entire course. For some reason, they felt that it was important to attend the course until the very end. During each class, however, they did make it clear (without saying the words outright) that since they had already transcended sexuality and were androgenous, they were further advanced spiritually than the others in the class, including the teachers, and were just being polite to stay. As far as we know, they never explored their own relationship, which was full of turmoil and negativity.

Lastly, Phillip Sherrard gives us a beautiful statement of the *spiritual necessity* for the two different manifestations, masculine and feminine: "It is clear that where human level is concerned the polarization into the two figures of man and woman represent a fuller manifestation of the Divine than a single androgenous figure. It is as if the two complementary principles that we describe as the masculine and the feminine principles, united and reconciled in God Himself, require this polarization on the human plane if the full potentiality of their creative energies is to be actualized."[201]

(4) Love as Duty or Obedience

Another erroneous attitude which limits the possibilities and efforts of love between men and women is the idea that doing one's duty or fulfilling one's responsibilities adequately *is the same as love.*[202] In our empirically and psychologically oriented society, people often confuse love and duty and when they do, the transcendent and mysterious quality of love is utterly lost and it is relegated to the more accepted models of instinct, emotion and ordinary modes of life.

Many people have very fine intentions and, with a generous and positive attitude, are quite willing to do what their beloved-one requests. But, as Thomas Merton tells us, "In practice, this means that love is canceled out and all that remains is obedience. ... The identification of obedience with love proceeds from a superficial understanding of [the saying] 'Love seeks to do the will of the beloved' ... The conformity of duty may perhaps clear the way for love, but it is not yet love."[203]

A beloved couple must be ever watchful of falling into this kind of mechanical relationship. Being kind and considerate and affectionate toward each other is not enough. Moving together harmoniously through life is not yet the beloved path. Without the powerful flow of intense love which seeks to see and love the Divine in the beloved, there is no "Living Spirit" in the relationship and no true path is being followed. An invocation to the Spirit does not reach very high without the power of love in the heart propelling it on its way. It quickly becomes an empty gesture, a mechanical ritual. As Mother Teresa said so often, "It is not how much you do, but how much *love* you put into it."

Some time ago a man came to see us with an unusual question on his mind. He told us the following story.

> He and his wife were childhood sweethearts and had married very young. After some initial years of harmony, there were several years of experiments with drugs, group living and "open marriage," all of which brought upheaval, disharmony, disappointments, betrayals, stormy resentments and emotional exhaustion. They had finally decided that what they really wanted was to do "the right thing" for their children and family, for each other and their marriage. So they had worked out a reasonable way of life for themselves, a sort of "negotiated agreement": to be monogamous, to be fair and kind to each other, to share their social and leisure lives, in short, to lead a good and "righteous" life together. And they were quite successful at it and, in the conventional understanding, they had a relatively satisfactory "love life." His unusual question was, "Isn't this good enough? Or should we be doing more?"

After talking for a while, it became clear that he and his wife really did love each other, but their love was sleeping, covered over by the script they had invented for themselves. We suggested that he talk to his wife about our meeting and, then, for both of them not to do anything very different, except to put as much love as they could into everything that they did with and for each other and see what happened. Well, they both took to the idea with spontaneous enthusiasm. They immediately began to try to infuse love into their interactions and remarkably, it led to an almost instant, re-vivification and transformation of their life. To this day, their love continues to grow. More than five years later, they were still marveling at the alive and beautiful love that they had to share. And, of course, they had begun the beloved classes and had become a devoted and blossoming beloved couple.

(5) Asceticism

Almost universally in the ancient mysteries and, even today in most Eastern religions and many Western ones, a commitment to celibacy, a total denial of the physical side of love, is a necessary precondition for any movement toward the Spirit. However, the world and humanity have undergone enormous changes and the spiritual Teaching is different for this age, but the belief in the necessity for celibacy and detachment from life still haunts many individuals and couples. Throughout Western cultures there are vague and contradictory, but very powerful, ideas which assert that spiritual work can only be done by an individual alone and that he or she must seek to enter the spiritual worlds isolated from the ordinary relationships which are an essential part of our life in this world. (We have elaborated on this issue to some extent in Chapter 7.1: Visioning the Divine, "Obstacles," #2.) Thus the actual manifestation of our beloved-one, that incarnated, bodily, individual person we love passionately, is seen as a hindrance, or even an evil, which dilutes or diverts our love from God.[204]

How can any love be a hindrance to loving God? When marriage is a spiritual path, the love that takes place between a man and a woman includes the erotic or the passionate. Our life in the world involves an acceptance of our physical existence as an essential part of our life and struggle toward the Spirit. Indeed, spiritual development today requires a creative and ensouled meeting of the problems of *all* aspects of our embodied existence. (We discuss this in more detail in the following section called "Sexual Passion.") Without sexual passion marriage can become a lifeless, empty shell, lacking true love. Our Teacher used to tell us that, in today's world, a marriage "without emotional-sexual expression, will cause a couple to dry up *like prunes.*" And Charles Williams, who knew well that the love between a man and a woman can be a path to God, tells us poetically: "Eros need not forever be on his knees to Agape; he has a right to his delights; they are a part of the Way."[205]

We have been surprised at how persistent the ancient ideas of asceticism are and how they lead to a life of intense inner conflict for so many Western seekers. The most extreme example, of course, (which we have encountered only once) is when a married couple resorts to having separate bedrooms and separate meditation practices. Most of the time, seekers with this conflict adapt by leading a sort of "double life." They may have a family and a full married life and be ardent followers of the beloved path, but at the same time they consider their ancient meditation practice to be the primary way by which they must work toward spiritual advancement. Such a couple may do their meditation practice at the same time, "together," even though the practice is world-denying and not focused on the development of love in the heart. Indeed, they may "sit" in the same room, but they are going off in different spiritual directions. They are not developing the love quality. They are not moving together in love towards God!

(6) The Myth of the Individualized Self and the Fear of Union

In our modern era, most of humanity has developed an apprehension of the *self* as a separated ego-consciousness. America is the extreme example of this state of consciousness and our society uses every means it knows to aggrandize the autonomous individual-self. Our educational agendas, our omnipresent media, our churches, our institutionalized, empirical psychology, all perpetuate and sustain the illusion of individualism, self-sufficiency and the total autonomy of the ego-self. We are surrounded with assertions that a single human being needs no one else to become complete and fulfilled. These ideas have fed the inclination to focus with concern almost exclusively on ones own self and have increased our alienation and loss of love for one another. Thus for many, it is extremely difficult to even contemplate that, in truth, it is in the beauty and power of spiritual union that we find our True Self and the completeness and fulfillment of our own individuality. This ideology of excessive focus on the seemingly isolated ego-self knows no love for others and separates us, not only from one another, but from the Spirit. In *The Eclipse of God*, Martin Buber says: "This selfhood that has become omnipotent ... can naturally acknowledge neither God nor any genuine absolute which manifests itself to men [and women] as of non-human origin. It steps in between and shuts off from us the light of heaven."[206]

When we embrace the Way of the Beloved, we know from the beginning, that it is only through the power of a conscious and intentional love for a real person which invokes its flow from an Infinite Source, that an individual or a loving couple can become liberated from self-concern and attain the freedom of a higher state of being. Even though the identification, the seemingly irrefutable experience of being an autonomous man or woman, has become so powerful and so unquestionable, we know that we must develop an unshakable faith that there exists within us and around us, a sea of Divine-love which has a power great enough to unlock that very convincing illusion of separated and alienated existence. In practical terms, this means that, when we give ourselves freely and totally with a love that is unbounded and pure, we will discover the Truth of our own higher Self, of our beloved—and all life, in the higher, Divine planes of consciousness. Thomas Merton describes it this way: "One of the paradoxes of the mystical life is this: that a man [or a woman] cannot enter into *the deepest center of himself and pass through that center into God, unless he is able to pass entirely out* of himself and empty himself and give himself to other people in the purity of a selfless love.[207]

This principle of transformation through love, to "lose oneself in the other" through love, or to "empty" oneself by loving, involves the overcoming of *only the selfish part of us, the egoistic part,* which has, for now, displaced our true spiritual individuality and identification as soul and spirit. We must become pure love itself, to enter into a spiritual union with our beloved-one and to transcend the illusion of the separate self. This pure, selfless love is the only power which can bring about the integration of our individualized self-conscious ego with the true being of our beloved and with the Divine *without losing our sense of self as an individual being.*

No matter how many times we say that in walking the spiritual path one loses only the false *illusion* of self, so many people still are profoundly terrified at the very prospect of this transformation: they cannot bear even the "idea" of losing the smallest part of "who they think they are." In our present stage of the evolutionary process of consciousness this is a most common and understandable reaction. However, if we allow this *illusion*, no matter how convincing it might seem, to dominate our thoughts and actions, our heart will become like a stone and we will never know true love for another being or God.

Some people find that they are too frightened to continue in our classes when they hear about "spiritual union." One woman said, before she left, "I don't want to become One, that's too scary, I just want to be ME." And a man, whose wife had a very strong personality, told us, "Sure we'll beome One, and it'll be HER!" He didn't like that idea very well and soon afterwards they were divorced.

And yet, we all will eventually reach a point in our deep forays into matter when we realize that this fear must be faced and overcome (e.g., see Ch 6.3). Then, we will come to *know* that love in its higher octave has all the power necessary to carry us into a new state of being and that its power can indeed effect the union of two souls who seek its domain. This is what man and woman are in the world *for,* thus, it is the providence of us all to seek and achieve this state.

• THE DRIVE TOWARDS UNITY •

Despite all the problems and fears outlined in the previous section, it is quite apparent, indeed, it is undeniable, that men and women ceaselessly seek each other out with a most powerful and mysterious drive to join. Most people, at least from time to time, are able to disregard or put aside their contrary thoughts and objections and follow those deep inner promptings which tell them that there is something "more," something "else," some great potential "reward" for engaging with the opposite sex. And some will simply go ahead, even with all the conflict and resistance, knowing that in some way they must transform their own selfish ego to find the Truth and Spiritual Fulfillment they seek.

Thus it is demonstrated all around us that men and women are pulled toward each other through a deep and mysterious desire to somehow unite. On this physical plane, the pull toward each other may be the most tangible demonstration of the power of love that we, in our present state of consciousness, can actually see. No doubt, it is a great force, hidden in each one's "secret inwardness." Its concealed power is that which leads us towards greater love for one another and the striving for the Divine planes of consciousness.

> *Male and female are the two great forces working on this earth and throughout the cosmos: the positive and negative polarity. The stars reach toward one another through this great magnetic pull and the psychic center of humanity responds. Thus man and woman have planted in their whole being the pull toward each other. The great drive within a male to seek the female and the great drive within the female to seek the male is the great evolutionary force moving humanity toward God.*[208]

A beloved couple knows that the force that pulls them together is the power of love in a higher octave and that this force can take them toward the realization of their union on the spiritual planes. As they walk the Way of the Beloved, they gradually discover that, through a loving heart and true perception of the divine in the beloved, each of them is becoming one with the consciousness of the other. Indeed, it is a great, but little known, truth that, "When a man and woman love deeply, their forces are truly blended together—hence the saying that 'two shall become one'. This happens on a psychic level and they become so attuned that they are continuously receiving each other's vibration. The beloved yoga is a Royal path to the mountain top. It is the great meditation. This union is the key to the Mysteries!"[209]

This "blending of their forces" through deep love and devotion will lead them to Spiritual Union, and they will move into a higher realm of consciousness. Working toward that higher state of spiritual union becomes the focus of the path for them. They do not have to analyze the meaning of

Spiritual Union or meditate on what it might consist of. But they do need to cultivate and intensify their great aspiration to become psychically blended through intense love in all aspects and levels of their outer and inner life.

To intensify your aspiration, do the following meditation daily for a month or more and use the mantra during the day and evening.

Meditation:

UNION [210]

I become one with my beloved through selfless love,
As a complete being every step through life is a song of joy,
Through deep love and devotion I unite with my beloved on all levels,
physical, emotional, mental and spiritual;
In the intensity of our embrace, our hearts burst into fire.
Hand in hand we walk the path to higher consciousness.

Mantra: I am one with my beloved through deep, spiritual love.

• SEXUAL PASSION •

Sex is an expression of God, and its purpose is to bring human beings together. It is a divine aspect. The physical body is a masterpiece of nature. The body and emotions, as well as the mind, is an instrument for the spirit. [211]

Since a beloved couple aspires to blend through love on all levels of being and the physical, bodily level includes the sexual, sex must be a part of the beloved path. Of course, most couples like this idea very much and are eager to incorporate this aspect of their lives into their spiritual path. Even those who still feel that true spiritual work requires long hours of isolated meditation don't have much problem including sexual union as part of their life together as a couple.

For a beloved couple, sexual communion is the beauty and power of love expressed through their blending on the physical level. It can become a great stimulation towards the union of the opposite polarities, for as the male and female unite at the lowest physical center they are also blending on the emotional and mental levels. Thus, they are harmonizing and integrating their polarized psychic centers through which the masculine and feminine energies circulate.

When love is deep and there is a heightened sense of awareness, blending becomes a process of transferring and interchanging qualities and energies. "There is an exchange of the masculine and feminine streams of force. This exchange is the most important part of the man and woman interchange or contribution to each other. It works for the integration of the two beings and thus for the climbing of the path."[212] It is by this blending, harmonizing and integrating through deep and intense love, that a man and a woman begin to reveal and become aware of those inchoate qualities within the polar opposite, *that cannot be seen or known in any other way.* The power of their Love gives each the capacity to relate with, to embrace, to embody and to comprehend—that is, to *know* —those mysterious and enigmatic, those apparently incomprehensible, aspects of the *other's* being. It is no accident that the Bible refers to sexual union as a man "knowing" a woman.[213] As they move toward an ever deeper blending, this mystery of the polar-opposite, the complementary-other, is revealed through their growing union and they each awaken to a greater Spiritual Reality.

It is because of that which they unknowingly impart to each other through their blending in love that a woman and a man become as one united being. Thus, they move towards the spiritual vision and perception which allows them to rise beyond the ordinary states of consciousness. All true love beween the sexes tends towards the ecstasy of this transcendent state. As each merges with the spiritual being of the other, "there is no loss of individuality or freedom of self. There is a heightening of consciousness and an inflow of wisdom ... Both retain their identities. Each is totally aware and the awareness is so beautiful, filled with pure joy, the greatest joy one can experience on earth."[214]

Many people have told us about having had a glimpse of this blissful state. They always are astounded at how much more beautiful, intense and glorious it was in actuality, than anything they could have imagined previously. They say that they "got so much more" than they had ever even asked for. One woman told us that she had had the experience of "being whole and half" at the same time, a state often described in mystical writings: For example, Erich Jantsch says, "We *are* the stream, source and flow, carrier and carried, the whole stream and yet only part of it—as a water molecule is the river and yet only part of it."[215] And Herbert Guenther writes: "Being is nowhere else than in the what-is, [e.g., the total existential manifestation] and with respect to our existentiality ... this means that we are the whole and yet only part of it."[216]

Here are two descriptions of this process of blending which use words and images that are very different from our own. For instance, Bede Griffiths, the Christian monk, who created an Ashram in India wrote:

> In this union of love man learns to know the woman and the woman learns to know the man, they mutually discover their own masculinity and femininity. This goes far beyond a merely emotional state. It is an awakening to the self. Each discovers a new aspect of his and her self. In every sexual union this self-knowledge is present, but when the emotional union is superficial, self-knowledge remains latent. It is only when the emotional union is deep and lasting that self-knowledge can grow. When this takes place a new level of knowledge is reached. It is no longer a merely physical or emotional intuition, it is a growth in personal knowledge, an awakening to the inner self. Like every intuition it is a reflection of the self on the self, a self-presence, but here the self discovers a new dimension of its being. The passive intellect, the inner vision is awakened to a new level of understanding. In a really profound union of love this may pass into a state of ecstasy. The self goes beyond itself and awakens to the ground of its being in self-transcendence. Then man and woman go beyond the duality of sex and discover their oneness in a love which is total fulfillment.[217]

And in Philip Sherrard's words:

> It is in and through the other that each becomes capable of experiencing and integrating qualities which as separate individuals each of them lacks or has not developed. Indeed, it is only by virtue of such an interchange of qualities that the relationship between them can grow into the fullness of the Divine image and likeness. What makes a man and a woman not simply two isolated individuals each lacking aspects of the integrity of human nature, but two partners who together achieve human perfection, is what is added to each in and through their relationship, in and through what each bestows on

the other. Moreover, this interchange of qualities operates in a way which as it were doubles each of them, since to the being of each as it is in and for itself is added the being of each as it is for the other.[218]

Thus, in a sense, for beloveds, each lives within the other. Each one can say to the other that "all of your being is deeply rooted in mine and through our love, each of us is increased." As Sherrard says above, "this interchange of qualities operates in a way which as it were *doubles* each of them." No matter how many times we may tell this to our students, the telling is never enough to convince those who have not experienced it and it is never enough to lighten the terrible fear that some feel at the very idea of blending or uniting in love with their beloved-one. Only the actual experience, the vision and the realization of Divine Love itself, can prove that we lose nothing of any value or truth through the total selfless giving of pure love, and that we gain the Reality of our True Spiritual Being.

• DYNAMIC TENSION BETWEEN POLARITIES •

The road to God is the unit of male and female. Thus the beloved yoga is for man and woman to unite the masculine and feminine streams of polarized force through the power of deep love and devotion. Neither man nor woman can rise to spiritual heights without the two principles of masculine and feminine fire within.[219]

There is a universal tension inherent in the very nature and destiny of gender, the masculine and feminine streams of force pulling towards each other. As we have suggested before, a useful way to envision this cosmic dynamic is to conceive of humanity as one great center of consciousness, one great Spiritual Being, embodying both principles of the universal life-force. This Being, the *Anthropos*, in order to evolve further has descended into physicality, moving out of its unity in transcendent realms, into a state of apparent polarity, e.g., male and female, thereby generating a dynamic tension within *itself*. Thus, *male* is inconceivable without female and *female* is inconceivable without male; they are indivisible, coinherent and irreducible complementaries. This explanation may bring to mind the well known Chinese image of the *yin/yang*: black and white opposites in all of nature, yet they are polarities circling each other and each with a dot of the opposite in its heart. They are coinciding opposites, polarities, propelled by their inherent dynamic interchange. The tension of this interchange has been expressed since time immemorial as an interminable friction and struggle—i.e., the "war" between the sexes—and simultaneously it is the fundamental, dynamic force working to pull together and reunite this apparent split in the consciousness of all humanity in form. The dynamic interchange of the two principles eventually leads them back to unity in the One Breath that gave them life. This has been called the Hermetic Marriage, which is the fully conscious realization of that which is actually united in spiritual Reality, and this state is the restoration of our true Divine Identity:

> *Holy God-fire split in twain*
> *Like the forked tongue of a cosmic serpent,*
> *Flowing through nature in two streams, descending*
> *Into matter, manifesting man and woman.*
>
> *The positive/negative, yin/yang of the world*
> *Activated by soul magnetism,*
> *Rising Godward, they blend*
> *Through hermetic conflict, combining,*
> *Uniting with the Son-of-two-fires*
> *In the holy explosion of homecoming.*
>
> *Those two forces fuse,*
> *Becoming one light within me.*
> *Through union with my beloved,*
> *I may be like unto Christ.* [220]

Thus our gender differences can be seen as part of a long-term evolution of human consciousness, bringing us into a higher, more Divine, state of Being and Love. Indeed, there is nothing which teaches us how to love more immediately or more potently than the tension between the sexes! It is difficult to overstate the degree to which the power of the tension between the sexes has conditioned and determined the whole course of our global human drama. The pain of separation alternating with the joy of connecting and blending is a constant, dynamic flux. It is the hidden cause of the family, of communities, of societies, and nations—of all that characterizes human social life. It is also the constant and most poignant reminder of the individual's suffering of separation from the Divine as well as the promise, the assurance, of spiritual union through love. As the Way of the Beloved testifies, there is only one solution to the universal existential separation and the suffering that it engenders—and that is selfless love.

> *Whatever are opposites cooperate, and from the*
> *divergent proceeds the most beautiful harmony.*
> —Heraclitus (c. 540 - c. 480 BCE)[221]

• THE PARADOX OF INDIVIDUAL FULFILLMENT •

"Man and woman are one spirit in two bodies—each requires the other for completion."

—Claude Bragdon (1866-1946)[222]

Even though it is acknowleged as mysterious and enigmatic, it is very well known that sexual union can bring about an ineffable sense of completion and fulfillment. For example, even the popular humorist, Joel Stein seemed quite serious when he said, "the real thrill of sex [is]: knowing that another being is freely giving herself to you and that at least for a few minutes, you're not alone."[223]

On a deeper level, we may say that the United Being that is the truth of the beloved couple, becomes a living reality on this plane, when the male and the female are united in Divine love. The blending of their polarized streams of force leads to that integration of the masculine and feminine principles on the higher levels, and this state has been called the Hermetic Marriage.[224] However, in our current state of consciousness, we can only comprehend the polarities once they are manifested in our world of substance, so we think of masculine and feminine in human terms: i.e., in the physical, bodily manifestation. But in less obvious material terms, for example, we may conceive of a celestial body being pulled towards another through the polarity of an attracting/repelling force. Or, as in the electromagnet, a circular flow of energy brings about an attractive force. Or, if you connect the positive and negative poles of a battery, there is a flow of energy—energy to light a bulb or start a car. "So it is for male and female: by their merging through love, they bring illumination, completion and fulfillment. It is so whether it is a star with a star, or a man with a woman. It is taking place throughout the cosmos."[225]

A student asked our Teacher, "Is not a spiritual being both male and female?"

He answered, "Yes, but that is in the spiritual world. On the earth plane, the fulfillment of the plan is through the unity of man and woman in deep love and devotion.

"The most important action of the beloved path is taking place on that higher level, where the soul, or higher self, is both male and female. The spiritual purpose in the union of male and female on this plane, is to achieve the level of soul consciousness and to dwell in the realization that they are complete on the higher planes, as are the spiritual beings. They learn that their union in deep love is a reflection in this plane, of a great spiritual reality.

"Spiritual fulfillment on this plane, comes when a man loves a woman and a woman loves a man. "The woman has a vibration the man needs and the man has a vibration a woman needs. Through love you identify with the divine radiation of your beloved."[226]

Some have said that a man and a woman can become "whole" by trying to balance the masculine and feminine "qualities" within each individual. However, as we have asserted throughout, in modern times, without the exchange of intense love between the actually manifested polar opposites, this integration does not take place.[227] Our Teacher wrote: "To develop the feminine and masculine nature within, the woman does not try to analyze the qualities of the male aspect, nor does the man try for the feminine aspect. This development is more on an unconscious level. The conscious effort you make is to concentrate with love on the Divine within your beloved. *Love is wisdom, and as this principle pours into your system, the qualities you need will be given to you. Love is the conscious force flowing through.*"[228]

Through the state of union, a beloved couple shall rise to a transcendent world of light and wisdom wherein each becomes aware of being at-One with the Divine and of unifying both the male and female principles within. It is thus that marriage fulfills its *spiritual* purpose: it brings about a true Hermetic Marriage within the husband and within the wife. They have become a clear vehicle for spiritual fire. The enigmatic and painful divisions of gender are transcended and overcome.

• SEX AND TRANSCENDENCE •

Sex is the union of man and woman and they unite at the lowest chakra. This stimulation can be used as a power to rise to greater heights in consciousness. Most people are preoccupied with the orgasm and stop there. Sex for the disciple on the Path of Light is to blend with the magnetic and electrical currents that descend from the higher worlds. This can be accomplished by your state of mind and heart. If you approach this exercise as a spiritual experience and see your beloved as a divine form, you raise your vibration to a high level and you make contact with the higher forces. Thus, the orgasm becomes secondary. You will feel a spiritual fulfillment when you make this exercise a sacred meditation.[229]

For a beloved couple, sexual union can have a profound spiritual meaning and potential.[230] Through their joining in love, a man and a woman can aspire to raise their consciousness above the physical plane to an ecstatic awareness not limited to the body and the emotions. Thus they can come to experience that the true purpose of their physical joining is to find fulfillment in union with the Divine.

We have already described that when a man and a woman become a beloved couple they create a magnetic field around them. When such a couple approaches their sexual union as a spiritual experience, they raise their vibration to a higher level and thus can make a contact with higher forces. When they join in love, their magnetic field is intensified and it can open the door to the higher realms where the tone of their union is heard. Through the intense love of their union they invoke energies from the higher levels to stream through their forms, uniting all their psychic centers. Blending with the magnetic and electrical currents that descend from the higher levels, they become a vehicle for that divine radiation to flow through them.

As they join in love, moving as One toward the Spirit of God, a beloved couple partakes of the universal creative process. It is through their many-layered union in love which includes the sexual that a man and a woman become a creative vehicle. Thus, together they invoke new forms to manifest through them, whether this is creating new life in the physical sense, or whether it is creations of art or service or of living compassionately in the world.[231] Yet, most importantly, as they move through their life in the world, *they can create an atmosphere of love* which will touch everyone they know. Indeed, as a couple merges in devotion and love on all levels, the atmosphere in their home, in their work and in their community is transformed into a radiation of compassion. Thus their love touches all that they meet and their radiance is a spiritual service. Indeed, the Anthroposophist and seer, Emil Bock wrote that, "The most important effect of the Sacrament of Marriage is the fact that it releases a whole heaven of higher, superpersonal forces of life which can flow into human communities and civilizations. Where this sphere is active, darkness begins to light up; the burden of life's cares becomes endurable; the torments of bitterness are healed through divine sources of joy."[232]

From time to time, couples have asked us, how can they get more fulfillment, more feelings of merging and blending, instead of just a release of tension or physical pleasure. The answer always is that *love* is the intensifier, it is the love that matters, not physical techniques. None of the physical techniques that humans can devise will lead to the greater union of a man and woman if an abiding and selfless love is not present. The psychic state of a heart and mind overflowing with love is what brings the joy and fulfillment of sexual union. And when a couple intensely aspires to see the divine in the beloved, when their greatest desire is to have a vision of the divine being who is their True Beloved, sex can lead them into a transcendent and mystical state of Unity.

It is not unusual for spiritual seekers to make a comparison between sexual union and the mystical experience. Indeed, historically, the Christian and Sufi mystical literature is replete with sexual metaphors to describe experiences of purely metaphysical union. In modern times, many writers have compared the momentary passing-away of the separate ego-sense which occurs in the heights of sexual passion—orgasm—with the transcendence of the illusory self and its limited state of consciousness. And some modern mystics have acknowledged that the ecstasy of love in sexual union can lead an aspiring couple to spiritual wisdom and to the experience of Divine Reality. For instance, the contemporary Vedantin, Ananda K. Coomaraswamy writes: "In India we could not escape the conviction that sexual love has a deep and spiritual significance. There is nothing with which we can better compare the 'mystic union' of the finite with its infinite ambient ... than the self-oblivion of earthly lovers locked in each other's arms, where 'each is both.' Physical proximity, contact, and interpenetration are the expressions of love ... These two are one flesh, because they have remembered their unity of spirit."[233] And the Christian mystic, Charles Williams, says it this way: "There is no other human experience, except Death, which so enters into the life of the body; there is no other human experience which so binds the body to another being. *The central experience of sanctity is to be so bound to another ...*"[234] The beloved relationship is the arena in which we bind our "body to another being," thus, this union becomes an experience of holiness, a "sanctification" of sex—the man and the woman are thus bound to each other even at the lowest level through mutual love.

This "unity of souls or of spirit" is the consummate experience of the higher planes, which is described by the great mystics. It is the realm where the division and separation of male and female no longer exists. By blending sex with great love, a beloved couple experiences, in full consciousness, the oneness of their higher selves united in the holy fire of spiritual love. The man and the woman find the Truth of their being and they dwell together in the heart of the Divine. Thus a beloved couple feels a spiritual fulfillment when they make their sexual union a sacred meditation. Their love is transmuted from a physical and emotional state to a spiritual union—they are truly reborn in divine beauty and partake of the breath of eternity.

Visualize your beloved as a divine being as you use the following meditation:

Meditation:

> I embrace my beloved with a holy love.
> All my psychic centers are united with my beloved, while I chant, "We are one."
> The breath of God flows from my heart to yours.
> The light of my mind is one with your mind.
> United in pure love our being reaches out toward God.
> There is a response in the higher worlds, for our beings are showered by a golden light.
> I lose myself in my beloved and I find my True Self.
> My Spiritual Being came forth glowing in beauty and pure joy.
> Our love has been transmuted from a physical and emotional state to a Spiritual union.
> We are bathed in fire.
>
> Mantra: In deep love for my beloved
> We shall ascend to the Spiritual heights.[235]

• PSYCHIC CONSIDERATIONS •

Our secular and materialistic society is entirely preoccupied with the sensual aspect of sex. Most people are so involved in seeking physical pleasure that they do not even consider that there might be other dimensions, beyond the physical, involved in sexual union. Indeed, sex can even be a hindrance for seekers on the path, for when it is used indiscriminately or only sensually or to dominate and control others, it becomes negative and harmful. Our Teacher said: "Your sexual emotions are a gift from God. They are also open to the dark forces. It depends on how you direct your emotional drive. When you love your beloved and see the spritual being in her [him], you are using sex for a constructive spiritual gowth. When sex is expressed for its sensation it moves into a negative channel and you are open to dark influences. ... Sex can be divine and can be lower than a worm."[236] He also taught that:

> When you merge with another person completely, you are taking on that person's psyche. Your two auras become one. If you merge just physically, there is not a permanent effect. But if you merge emotionally, mentally and psychically, the blend is much greater than the person realizes. When people have a lot of love affairs their auras are getting muddied up. They bring in all kinds of elements ... they are not oriented. They are also picking up karma and ... psychic disease. In the beloved yoga, where a couple aspires to love very deeply, sex has its proper place.[237]

In the Section on Co-presencing (7.3.2), we have talked about the magnetic chords connecting a man and a woman who are a beloved couple. If there is sexual contact with someone other than the beloved, these magnetic chords are warped and sometimes broken. This dilutes the energy in the beloved relationship and causes a loss of energy to all the people who are involved, which, of course, does not work constructively for the beloved path.[238]

• THE BELOVED PATH •

Wisdom Traditions throughout the world refer to the "mystical path" as having three levels or degrees of attainment. For a beloved couple, these progressive stages lead from the love that they already know to the heights of universal compassion—spiritual realization. The steps to be travelled may be called the Outer, Inner and Invisible or Hidden levels of the path. In *The Way of Beloved* these three divisions correspond to Parts I, II and III of this book.

(1) The Outer level of the path refers to those works that are tangible and visible on the physical plane. For example, a married couple lives in the same house, they may have children and share their possessions and social life. Because they have developed a desire to live harmoniously and intensify their love, they search for books and lessons to read and practice. They may aquaint themselves with various types of exercises designed to bring more communion, harmony and love into their relation. They may attend classes or go to meditation meetings or seek spiritual counseling.

Other Traditions have described this level of the path as the cultivation of an interest and the studying of the teachings. Aspirants will practice exercises, rituals and meditations. The Sufis refer to this level as, "The Lore of Certainty" or "hearing about the *fire* ." Hindus call it the changing of the direction of ones life, a "re-orientation." Christian mystics have called it the stage of "metanoia" and "purification."

(2) "Entering the Way;" is a movement to the Inner Level of the path. A couple entering the *Way of the Beloved* continues with the exercises already learned and also nurtures a desire to deepen their understanding and practices. Indeed, they become aware of the volatile streams of emotion between them and thus they begin the work of becoming more compassionnate by replacing the habitual expressions of negativity with positive and loving responses. They find that they are concerned with a search for meaning and purpose in their life together, and they develop the mental striving to blend in purpose and direction, in other words, to share a common ideal.

Other Traditions may call this level the "Ascent" from the gross to the subtle, i.e., in Vedanta, or the stage of "Illumination" in Christian mysticism. For instance, St. John of the Cross calls it the "night of faith," and the Sufis have called it "The Eye of Certainty," or "seeing the fire."

(3) "The State of the Beloved" or "Spiritual Union" refers to the Hidden, Invisible level of the path, wherein the Reality of our invisible existence is revealed. This level cannot be expressed or taught or described in words. It is the Truth perceived directly, as the seeker's Heart of Perfect Wisdom is awakened through love. A beloved couple becomes acutely, even painfully, aware of the unspoken yearning of their hearts for union with the Divine. They develop a strong desire to purify the love that they know so that they will reach the heights of universal compassion. They learn that their blending through love can move them to higher stages of consciousness.

In the Sufi Tradition this third level is referred to as "The Truth of Certainty" and they compare it to being "burned by the fire"—it is the step leading to being "consumed" by the spiritual fire. For Hindus this level opens to "Identity with Divinity" or realization of *Sat, Chit* and *Ananda*. Christian mystics may call it "Perfection" or "Mystical union with God."

These levels are not rigid, they do not necessarily follow in a strict sequence, they constantly interface and there is a continuous interweaving between them. A couple may move back and forth from one to another or work in more than one at a time. But once a deep commitment has been made to follow the Path, the focus on the Invisible levels becomes foremost and paramount. And, although it may not be apparent to most who know them, both individuals become aware of deep changes in their outlook, in their life and in their inner being. Eventually, as their inner focus develops, their values, their activities and even their friendships undergo a process of change. They have become "disciples" on the path toward the embodiment of a transcendent love.

The invisible Path of the Beloved begins when a couple becomes aware that they are seeking to move to new levels of consciousness on the hidden or imperceptible levels of our existence. They know that more "information" about the physical plane, some call this "horizontal learning," will not help them on the path. Indeed, they are now seeking consciously through their relationship for a "vertical" movement, an ascent toward a higher state of consciousness. Spiritual Traditions teach that at this stage of the path an aspirant, a seeker or a disciple moves through a series of Initiations or expansions of consciousness, culminating in a true *vision*, direct knowledge and experience of the Infinite realms where the eternal Love of God is to be found. Each expansion of consciousness "reveals the hidden mystery that lies at the heart of the solar system. It leads from one state of consciousness to another. As each state is entered the horizon enlarges, the vista extends, and the comprehension includes more and more, until the expansion reaches a point where the self embraces all selves."[239]

In the Beloved Yoga, as a man and a woman blend with each other through deep love and devotion, they realize that they no longer are living only as individuals. Their beings are intermingled and they find that they are psychically living within each other—they have become "as one being." Thus their separate, individual lights are blended to become one light, and the united being that they have become moves as a unit through the stages of Initiation.

It is often said, metaphorically, that we are, each of us, "writing a book" as we live our life. This is the "book of our life" and every experience is recorded in our own psyche, conscious or unconscious, and also in the universal psychic record which is called the *Book of Life* or the *Akashic Record*. At the end of our incarnation, as we cross over to the other side, we review our whole life, i.e., the contents of our book, in the Presence of a Spiritual Being who is our guide on the path.

Before becoming a beloved couple, a man and a woman write the book of their life as individual persons. When they become committed to the path of the beloved and have developed a deep spiritual love they begin together to write one book, the single story of their blended life of love. Turning as one-united-being toward the light of love, they invoke new forces to enter their life and luminous energies pour upon them from the higher planes. As they walk together, they move as one spirit sharing all that they are at this time and all that they ever have been in the past and all that they will become in times to come. And when they meet the storms and trials, joys and problems that life brings to them, they recognize them as spiritual tests of the purity and strength of the love that they have for each other. Thus they move in rhythm and love and create an atmosphere between them that will open the gates to the higher worlds.

Here is a Mantra for couples who are striving to move as One Spirit on the path toward God:

> My spiritual beloved,
> I am one with your radiance;
> Through our destined unity the *divine fire* shall burn within
> the heart
> And we shall live in the Holy City.[240]

Students ask us frequently, "Who knows about this path, has anyone ever followed it?" As far as we know, Charles Williams (1886-1945), author of metaphysical novels and a good friend of C.S.Lewis, may have been the first to write in detail about the relationship between a married man and woman as an approach to the Spirit.[241] Williams was a devout Christian and he wrote in orthodox Christian language, but the concepts and principles that he offers are universal. In his book, *Outlines of Romantic Theology*,[242] he explicitly defines marriage as a "Way of the Soul,"[243] a transformational process which moves a couple towards "Christ-consciousness," i.e., Universal Compassion. He outlines the stages of initiation that a couple goes through as corresponding to stages of the Life of Christ in the New Testament. As a Christian, for him, Divine Love *is* Christ and the path of marriage reflects the course of His life. He says that the life of Christ is also the life of Love in marriage and the "records and commentaries" in the New Testament are applicable to the journey of a couple towards God. For instance, the couple's "business is not to be, but to know that they are, His symbols, and that their marriage is His life."[244] Thus, "each marriage [is] a moment, an "accorded manifestation, of Christ's Life, a 'symbol' of His eternity,"[245] and a couple moves through Initiations which may be called *Birth, Baptism, Transfiguration, Crucifixion* and *Resurrection*.

Recently, in a more popular vein, Barry and Joyce Vissell have written a book called *The Shared Heart* [246] in which they describe their own personal journey on the path of love to the Spirit. They illustrate well the path of the married couple as a *yoga* in which the couple moves on the journey of consciousness through the development of their love for one another.

In general, an awareness of the potential of the marriage relationship as a Spiritual Path is dawning in our world. In addition to the philosophers already mentioned, shelves in stores are filled with books on how to improve and enrich relationships. An awareness of the necessity for love in marriage is at last beginning to be recognized by some.

• REALIZING THE BELOVED •

We wander the earth over long ages of time, restlessly seeking our completion and fulfillment. For a thousand lives we walk alone as we search for a being who embodies the counterpart of our soul.

When two people fall in love the potential is awakened for them to realize the other's higher, eternal self. This cannot be achieved if the relationship is casual or focused only in the material life. It is through the power of love that the transformation takes place. Through the power of love, the fires rise and awaken the higher forcess, to transmute the nature into a temple of light.

The potential is great and the plan is vast. A man and woman can progress in love and harmony for 100,000 years to reach a plateau from which even greater heights can be attained. But when we merge in love with our spiritual counterpart, a tone resounds throughout the universe, and this union cannot be separated. This is the age-long work for which we are called. The possibilities are unlimited.[247]

Students asked our Teacher: "Who is my beloved? Is she [or he] someone I just happened to meet in my travels?"

He answered: "No. It is a design of destiny. It is not in our karmic plan to follow the path with just anyone. We have come together with *this* person because she[he] is the polar opposite who evokes the emotional and mental concept of *the beloved* within us. The beloved is our spiritual counterpart, the one who is, for us, the key to the higher worlds. She evokes in us the qualities necessary for our spiritual growth and helps us to find the path to God. As we move together physically, we are also blending spiritually; thus we evolve on a level where it is creative. Each of us is made a more complete being every moment through the physical and spiritual being of our beloved."[248]

We often use the image of climbing a high mountain when we speak about the spiritual path. A similar image can be used to describe the growth of love and union in a beloved relationship. Torkom Saraydarian gives us a very vivid picture of this process:

> The growth of love between two people can be compared to their ascent of a high mountain. They begin their journey on opposite sides of the mountain, but the higher they climb the closer they come to each other, until one day they meet on the peak of the mountain. To climb the mountain means to raise the level of your being and gradually clear your consciousness, enlarge your horizon of light and service, and enter into deeper levels of responsibility toward each other. Only through such a life is the path of love built.
>
> So we may say that those who love each other most deeply and sincerely are those people who will meet each other more frequently, and more often walk together on the path of love toward the peak. So many people are climbing with us, and in every life we meet some of them. The paths toward the peak are in the form of spirals, and on every turn peoples paths cross. Let us call these crossroads our earthly marriages and lives. For example, on one of the crossroads two people meet each other; they love each other and marry. After they pass the crossing point in the spiral they gradually get further and further apart, until again a crossroad comes and they meet. We cannot say that the same persons will meet each other again and again. It depends on how they walked, what speed they traveled, how they lived …
>
> This meeting at the many crossroads will continue in eternity, and as they get nearer the peak, the two persons will meet more frequently upon every crossroad. They will know each other immediately and

will fall in love, on all levels. They will sacrifice themselves to each other, and do their best to make the life of the other more beautiful, glorious, and supreme.

The day will come when they will meet so often that after a period of time they will never separate, for they will reach the peak of love ... Once you meet on the top of the mountain, he or she is yours eternally. The two of you are one. In this unity of soul and spirit is hidden the glory of love.[249]

As a couple grows in love and devotion they begin to live within each other—physically, emotionally, mentally, psychically and spiritually. When they merge completely they each take on the other's being and each other's Karma and their two auras become one. Thus, the magnetic chords connecting each to the other will remain intact after they leave their physical forms. On this theme, Emil Bock wrote: "The Sacrament of Marriage which blesses the union between two persons does not only concern those directly involved. It involves the higher spheres, where every true union between human souls is continued in an alliance between the Angels of those souls ..."[250] A poetic description of this alliance with the angels, from a different perspective might be the following:

BLENDED RADIANCES

Rejoicing *devas* bend to bless
The blending of man and woman,
Spiritually uniting their Radiance,
In fulfillment of God's design.
This magnetic hermetic blending
Fructifies in *devic* substance
Bringing forth a new angel
Guardian of this holy union,
Whose inhalations raise-up
Their single beating heart
Into a world of sacred light
Fulfilling every vagrant seeking
In the completed unit glowing within.[251]

A very specific and detailed affirmation of the transcendence of the married relationship and the love between a man and a woman is to be found in the work of Emanuel Swedenborg (1688-1772). In his middle-age, the, already famous, Swedish scientist and statesman broke through the psychic veils into the "heavenly" planes of existence. There he came upon a realm wherein dwell those couples who had become blended through deep love for each other in this life, and when they crossed over into the afterlife they remained together as a united angelic being. The couples to whom he spoke appeared as radiant angels, in which the individual man and woman were interweaving in a continuous fluid interchange and interpenetration. A detailed description of his experiences with these couples is in his book *Conjugial Love*.[252] Swedenborg's experiences can provide a vision and an inspiration for couples who follow the beloved path.

From time to time we will hear of someone having a beautiful, if fleeting, experience of other realms. A man told us that at a time of great love, he saw a gold light surrounding his beloved's form and emanating from his hand touching her head. And a woman said that she had felt and seen a silver-blue angelic form above her beloved and herself and it radiated a sublime feeling of pure love.

Couples may use the following visualization and invocation: Visualize the angel of your union as a radiant blue being of glowing light, surrounding and permeating both your forms as you say the invocation:

• Visualization Exercise •

Through deep devotion and love for the divine in my beloved,
We have become blended as One.
We breathe together on a mutual path to the spirit and the veils of illusion begin to dissolve.
Our unity in love invokes a spirit being, the Angel of our spiritual union, who enfolds us with light and guides us every hour.
Our love is lifted up to a higher octave of expression.
It is no longer an emotional or mental expression.
We have become a vehicle for spiritual fire.

How do we know if our husband or wife is our beloved? Some couples have a deep intuitive conviction that they have come together with *this* particular person for a destined spiritual purpose. But many devoted couples have not had such an experience and they wonder whether or not they are with their *true* beloved.

A beloved relationship is not a given. It is not a "package" that is handed to us as established and fixed by destiny. Contrary to what many believe, destiny is not fulfilled by a predetermined event or outcome in our life; destiny is changeable, indeed, our every thought and act changes our destiny. A relationship may be destined, but that is no guarantee of movement on the beloved path. Even if it is destined, the beloved relationship is a creative endeavor. It is continually forged by the way the couple meets the challenges and tests of life's experiences. It is created by the love and invocation of both people as they vivify the truth of their commitment to the path.

Torkom Saraydarian has said that in the beloved couple's circle of love "a magnetic chord is built which extends first from one sex center to the other's sex center; then it connects the couple's solar plexus centers; then it raises to their heart centers and eventually to their spiritual vehicles."[253] This magnetic link must be continually nurtured, enlivened and renewed until a psychic tie is created between the hearts of both people. This is the golden thread through which there is a steady flow and blending of souls. When this spiritual tie is made, no storms in the world or emotional upheavals will disrupt the bond. Indeed, "The magnetic link ... stays unbroken even at the time of death. It is with such a development of union in love that a couple meets each other life after life, helping each other's evolution and together reaching higher levels of achievement. Life by life, they build a few steps higher and higher, until one day the ladder of love is built and the souls can meet each other and be One."[254]

• Visualization Exercise •

Sit with your beloved in a golden circle of light,
See the burning golden thread of love joining both your hearts,
flowing back and forth through one heart and out to the other.

Use the mantram: I am linked to my beloved through the golden thread of love.

• MARRIAGE AS THE WAY •

The song of the beloved has been heard for ages.
It has a potential that does not exist in the mind of man. [255]

Our teacher told us many times that the path of the beloved is a straight path to the spiritual heights and that its potential is unlimited. The revelation of Divine Love is continually evolving in the heart of humanity and the time has come for the transformative power of this love to be most potently realized in the relationship between man and woman. Love as we know it is just the beginning of the Way of the Beloved, and we are only now sowing the seeds of an understanding and expression of its practice.

The very idea that the love relationship between man and woman could be a spiritual path did not exist for humanity before the 16th century. The very possibility had not yet entered into human consciousness. Indeed, it is difficult for most of us even today to comprehend that the word *love*, as we use it, was not part of our language until modern times. C. S. Lewis tells us that in the West, "'love', in our sense of the word, is as absent from the literature of the Dark Ages as from that of classical antiquity."[256] And Denis De Rougemont states that at least until very recently, "what we call 'passionate love' is [has been] unknown in India and China. They have no words to render this concept."[257] In the past, in both the East and the West, marriages were arranged for family or clan interests, political or economic reasons, indeed, love and marriage were not really associated one with the other. In the West, the actual love relationship of a man and a woman in marriage has been considered as a possible path to the spirit only recently, and it has never been considered as such in the East.

The ideal of "romantic love" or "passionate love" emerged in Europe with the courtly poets of the 12th century, but it was not yet connected to the marriage relationship. Its application to marriage did not occur until 400 years later. C. S. Lewis found that

> Two things prevented the men [or women] of that age from connecting their ideal of romantic and passionate love with marriage.
>
> The first is, of course, the actual practice of feudal society. Marriages had nothing to do with love ... So far from being a natural channel for the new kind of love, [i.e., *romantic* love] marriage was rather the drab background against which that love stood out in all the contrast of its new tenderness and delicacy ...
>
> The second factor is the medieval theory of marriage ... according to the medieval view passionate love itself was wicked, and did not cease to be wicked if the object of it were your wife ... [Peter Lombard, d. 1164] quotes with approval from a supposedly Pythagorean source

a sentence which is all-important for the historian ... "passionate love of a man's own wife is adultery."[258]

Thus, believing that passion did not have any role in marriage, it was thought that *true love* is impossible in marriage.

It was also generally believed at the time, that any passion dulled the intellect and subverted reason. But the poets began to recognize that the very opposite was true in the case of "passionate love" between polar opposites. Indeed, "It began to be asserted that 'passion' precisely excited and illuminated the intellect ... [and] that *such a passion could exist as or in marriage.*"[259] By the late 16th century, the idea that there is a spiritual reason or justification for passionnate love in the relationship of man and woman emerged, and it was through the development of this kind of marriage relationship that the very idea of marriage being a spiritual path became *possible.*[260]

Modern communications, technology and air travel have opened a constant interchange between East and West, and we are rapidly becoming as one world of humanity. Also the feminine aspect is gradually coming forward into equality of expression all over the globe. The old patriarchal thought-forms are beginning to fade away. The time is now for the consciousness of humanity to receive a new spiritual impulse. Recognition of the equality of the sexes opens vast new possibilities for millions of couples. Indeed, for the first time in human history, we may be able to dispel centuries of confusion and prejudice and humanity may be ready take the step toward realizing the greater purpose and meaning of the love relationship between a man and a woman.

We can now radically revise the view of human existence as it has been depicted it in our age of individualism and alienation from the Spirit. We have been habituated to conceiving of our "self" as an isolated psyche confronting all the enigmas of life and death and from that solitary place seeking a path toward the spiritual heights. With the path of the beloved, we learn that the "highest manifestation of individual life"[261] is really a transcendence of the *illusory* sense of isolated individuality and that through union in love with our beloved polar opposite each of us finds our true and complete spiritual fulfillment. Our Teacher foresaw that the State of the Beloved is the future for all humanity."[262]

• EXPERIENCING UNION •

Since an experience of *union* occurs on a plane of consciousness that is beyond all language, it is not possible to express it or transmit it through words. It can only be talked "about" or "around." Nevertheless, even a hint of it, when it occurs, is unmistakable. Here is one couple's experience:

There are moments in one's life when everything becomes pure and clear. This is an experience of one of those moments: It happened at the funeral of a long time friend of my husband, Sean. After a short battle with leukemia, Father Patrick Zossima, a 73 year old priest and Carthusian monk, crossed over. Padre Pat, as many referred to him, was a highly spiritual man. He emanated light and love with eyes and a smile that went deep into everyone he met. Now, I'm not sure if it was because of Padre Pat's vibration that I experienced such clarity or that his funeral set the tone, but at any rate it really doesn't matter.

Because of Padre Pat's love for all, his funeral was rather large, approximately 4000 people attended and therefore it had to be held in a basketball stadium. Well, prior to Padre Pat's passing, my beloved was asked to be an honorary pallbearer and to speak at his funeral. Because of Sean's role in the funeral, we were unable to sit together, a fact that initially neither one of us was happy about. Sean was in the procession and sat with the other participants on the stadium floor. I was seated on the second tier of the balcony along the railing. Even though we were as far away physically as one could be in that stadium, we still could spot each other from where we were seated.

Here is that moment of clarity. At some point in the funeral, I felt an overwhelming, all encompassing sensation of love from my beloved course through my body. I looked down at where Sean was seated and he, too, was looking at me, emanating a similar vibration. This love was so great, my being was complete, my smile was complete, my eyes lit up, I felt as if I could leap from the railing and enfold my beloved—I *was* enfolding my beloved and he, me. Time stood still and all was beauty and peace, not a care or worry, just pure vibration of love. That vibration stayed with us for quite awhile and every now and then our eyes would meet and everything was bliss.

The feeling of love for my beloved was so complete and the knowledge of our Divinity made clear. That's what was given to me at that very moment on the day of Padre Pat's funeral.

Here is another example of a couple experiencing that unexpected grace of coming into oneness:

I do not doubt the beloved path, we have had some experiences that have made it very real to us, but I marvel at any demonstration of its truth. Things have always been very intense and dramatic with us and last week was no exception. I don't know why he thought so, but my beloved thought for a moment that I was not there for him and all of a sudden we both felt that the force of connection between us had been withdrawn. The pain of being forsaken and alone was so great, we both were crying, it was so intense, that Michael cried out and sobbed, "I didn't know until now, that *you and your being are necessary for my life*." The power of his revelation was like a tremendous new bond between us that actually lifted us up. We rose, in our hearts and minds and physically, as well, up from our chairs and just stood close together, each of us with one arm around the other, in front of the window. We didn't talk. We had gone into some other realm. We had only one body breathing, yet we each had our own head, but we were flowing within each other in an irridescent field made out of love. We were one being. It was pure love and breathtakingly beautiful. The room was filled with sparkling diamond currents of love, the atmosphere was vibrating with power, the whole place was breathing love and we were made out of love. We wanted to stay there forever, but we couldn't, we had to leave for an appointment. We walked outside and saw that an electric field radiated from our house and yet the house also looked just like it always did. We stayed in that state for a long while. It was still with us days later.

Even though we have outlined the ascent of the beloved path in terms of climbing from one level to another, each couple and each marriage experiences its own timing of movement and development. There is no set sequence of spiritual stages; spiritual experiences will come in an unpredictable order and in mysterious rhythms. Each occurrence is like a "gift" from the Spirit, an immeasurable "grace." A couple may suddenly receive, unannounced and unprepared, as in the two stories above, a glimpse of a luminous, transcendent realm, a glorious moment of pure, Eternal Love. Then, as inexplicably as it came, the experience leaves or lifts and they return to ordinary life and familiar consciousness. This opening and closing of the door is normal and expectable, for the stimulation of the new impulse must be integrated into the whole psyche and fabric of life, and the process unfolds over a period of time. But, as Dante so beautifully wrote, "One glimpse of the 'eternal ray' kindles the desire for that light 'forevermore.'"[263]

Indeed, once a couple has had a transcendent experience, the longing to reach it and know it again becomes their most ardent desire and impassioned quest. Sometimes the psychic effects of the experience will remain as an inner glow or living memory, which comes forward and recedes many times back and forth, sustaining and stimulating both persons as they strive to renew and re-create their ascent in love. This episode in time is poetically recalled by the Kabbalist, Alan Afterman: "As he [she] is turned away, the top of his mind in the afterglow or the impression of the light ... he falls back in the continuous, cyclic process ... But he remains in expectation, the 'silent, thin voice' within inviting in silence, in a state of inner hovering to return."[264] And Charles Williams describes it this way: "Love that was visibly present, a light and a wonder, withdraws ... into the secret and heavenly places; and in His stead there descends upon the lovers the indwelling grace of the Spirit, nourishing and sustaining them."[265]

The practices of the path, the meditations, mantras and exercises for intensifying love, are the means that a couple employs to ascend on the path of consciousness. And although they never know when it shall happen, it is through the intensity of their practice that the couple strives for that actual transcendent experience of union. Yet as we keep on practicing, we may begin to feel that the intervals of our ordinary state of consciousness and familiar quality of love have become interminable. However, we must always know that, in any moment, we may ascend into the joy and beauty of union. Here is a story illustrating that a transcendent experience can come at any time. The couple in this story had been doing the beloved work for only two or three years and their relationship was still full of pain and conflict and turmoil. Their story is an example of how such an experience can occur at a most unexpected time and in a most unexpected way:

> (Helen speaks first) Our marriage has never been an easy road—
> it wasn't based on love at first sight and we have had our share

of challenges. It wasn't until the Beloved work that we began to appreciate our challenges as avenues for our spiritual growth. But after a few years of hard work, one begins to wonder if all this pain has a pay off.

Well on Dec. 24, last year, we got touched by the light of the Divine Union: Ivan and I were at odds for a few days before the holidays. The stress of the holidays just added to our being disconnected. I was getting into my ego satisfying, fearful place of feeling rejected and started demanding that Ivan give me the reassurance of his love—which of course turned him in the opposite direction of "I'm out of here." We were spiraling downward feeling an immense separation.

(Ivan speaks) In the days preceding Christmas this year Helen and I were in a terrible place. She had accused me of not loving her, of loving another more than her, of not being there for her. I, during this, shut down emotionally and shot back several salvos of my own. The result was that we were both in a place of great hurt and anger. Helen told me she wanted me to move out of the house. I told her I was unwilling to leave, but I certainly considered it. I suppose you get an idea how bad it was …

On Christmas Eve, it had even deteriorated. We were driving to my cousin's for dinner, I felt terrible. Then, suddenly, as we were driving past the Arboretum Apartments—I remember the exact spot—my heart suddenly opened! I physically reached over to Helen and said something … maybe, "I love you! or maybe, "I don't want to fight anymore!" I don't remember, but whatever it was, she responded immediately. She looked at me, she touched me, and we felt tremendous love for each other. It was wonderful.

(Helen speaks again) We had our holiday obligations and were heading to a family gathering with our two children in the back seat, neither one of us really wanting to go to a party and feeling void of love toward each other. When out of the blue, Ivan looks over at me and says, "You may think this is crazy, but a feeling just came over me—and I love you with all my heart and soul." He had such a beautiful look on his face and his whole being just glowed with the truth. I could no longer stay closed-hearted. My being opened and I welcomed his love fully. We were One and we were touched by the light of the spirit.

(Ivan) At the party we looked at each other lovingly. We felt close, even from across the room. We felt healed.

(Helen) We remained in this state of loving bliss throughout the party. It was amazing. I've never felt that wholeness before or the radiation of love so profound. If Ivan was in another room, I could feel his love and presence penetrating wherever I was.

All three of the stories presented above demonstrate that, if a couple is "doing the work," an experience of union can come upon them at any time, without expectation and without knowing the hour of the Spirit's descent.

The following meditation tells us of the "pearl of great price," the "jewel within the heart," the great culmination and reward of following the beloved path:

Meditation:

THE ETERNAL TREASURE OF THE BELOVED

The mystics have lived in caves seeking for the jewel in the heart, when near at hand their beloved awaits. The union of beloveds leads them to the Eternal Treasure, for through love and devotion and sacrifice to the other, they find their true, higher Self. In love, as one pours out and leads another on the path, the mystic jewel in the heart begins to glow. A divine love unites two mortals, and they walk together, the path toward God. The two natures are blended on a spiritual tone and the divine plan on earth is fulfilled. With one heart, hand in hand, they walk the path to the mountain top.

Mantram: A divine love unites two mortals and they walk together, the path toward God.[266]

What greater reward is there than for man and woman to blend in their divine nature. This state of the beloved can transform the earth!

☙ ❧

7.3.7 CODA

The foundation of the Way of the Beloved is discovered in the heart of love, itself, where there lives and moves a will to exaltation of the other. To truly love another, is to will the spiritual ideal upon that beloved one. When there is a mutual intention to exalt, infusing the daily life of a man and woman, they enter into the Way of the Beloved.

The free and unlimited intensification of the will to love leads to a literal and transcendent union of the masculine and feminine polarities, embodied in every man and woman. It is through the will to exaltation that we bring the spiritual truth of the loved one into manifestation. The will to exalt coming from the heart of love is an invocation to the spiritual *reality* of the loved one, and is not just a projection of the lover. It is the hidden purpose of the masculine and feminine to manifest through love the highest spiritual being in each other and to copresence that being every hour.

It is well known in the spiritual teachings of the West, that the practice of intensifying selfless love will awaken the seeker's spiritual nature, but in the Way of the Beloved there is a double will to love, crisscrossing into the most intimate recesses of the relationship, purifying, processing and transforming every nuance of egoism. Every couple evokes in their interactions the enigma inherent in the creation and manifestation of the Divine image as masculine *and* feminine—that great cosmic polarity. The deepest regions of the mysteries of love, self and other, the union of opposites, the Hermetic Marriage, all psychology and religion become the arena, the cauldron, of their united striving for spiritual truth. The Way of the Beloved leaves no shred of the ego unscorched, no conceit unlighted, nothing in the psyche escapes the purifying touch of the other's healing love.

Unleashing the transformative power of this double will to reciprocal spiritual exaltation of the other in a marriage, shatters the past and opens new paths for enlightenment, suitable to the coming age of brotherhood and *intentional* relationships. The intensification of love between a man and a woman sharing a life together, will provide them with hourly opportunities for the destined transmutation of the personality. For those couples, who will love, this is the "short path" to spiritual fulfillment in our time.

During this 2500-year historical cycle, the union of opposites as the goal for a man and a woman has been known by only a few, and this true purpose of gender is only beginning to enter the main-stream of humanity. The Way of the Beloved affirms that the purpose of all love between man and woman is fulfilled in the mystical union of "opposites," and that the joining of our sundered beings into a new coherent creation, a spiritual at-one-ment, is the true destiny of gender.

Despite the fears of many, this new union or conspiration does not diminish or obliterate individuality, but fulfills it; each individual is elevated, moving toward her or his full spiritual potential. This new union is not a creation of nature, but the conscious and intentional realization of a *Reality greater than nature* by a man and a woman whose intense love and devotion for each other "enfolds them as one in the seamless cloak of immortality."[267] This may be the first time in history when a man and a woman can unite, through selfless love, the seemingly separate, self-conscious sense of individuality into a greater spiritual whole, thus fulfilling the heretofore mostly hidden, transcendent purpose of gender. Is not this the final consummation of the ancient and enigmatic separation of the sexes, and the next step in the evolution of consciousness for all of humanity?

ೞೞ

· APPENDIX ·

EMOTION WORDS

The following list contains 730 positive and negative emotion words to help you identify and become aware of your emotions and their valence:

POSITIVE N = 223

agreeable
accepting
affectionate
attentive
appreciative
animated
ardent
awed
accommodating
approachable
amorous
amused
aspiring
admiring
altruistic
adaptive
amicable
amenable
amiable
adoring

blissful
buoyant
beatific
bright
blithe
brave
benevolent
beneficent
brisk
bold
blessed
bountiful

cooperative
comfortable
conscientious
compassionate
cheerful
confident
convivial
concerned

courageous
caring
complimentary
calm
contented
cordial
conciliatory
capable
considerate
courteous
clear
competent
communicative
consenting
cherishing
canny
creative
chivalrous
charitable
congenial
controlled

delighted
dauntless
diligent
discreet
devoted

enthusiastic
encouraging
exultant
earnest
encouraged
empathetic
ecstatic
elated
exhilarated
eager
equanimity
ethical
energetic
elevated
excellent

enamored

exalted

forgiving

faithful

focused

festive

frisky

flexible

friendly

firm

fearless

forbearing

gallant

glad

genial

gleeful

generous

grateful

giving

gregarious

gentle

gutsy

good

hopeful

high spirited

happy

hilarious

humorous

harmonious

humble

humane

hospitable

heroic

honest

interested

inspired

impartial

intrepid

intuitive

joyous

jaunty

jolly

jocular

jubilant

jovial

kindly

kindhearted

loving

lively

lenient

lighthearted

lofty

mindful

mirthful

merry

magnificent

magnanimous

malleable

meticullous

merciful

nurturing

neighborly

noble

obliging

outgoing

pleased

patient

peaceful

playful

protected

philanthropic

present

pious

protecting

potent

quick

ready

receptive

resolute

reassured

remorseful

rapturous

radiant

respectful

renewed

reassuring

reverent

romantic

responsive

rhapsodic

restrained

resourceful

spontaneous

supple

supportive

serene

self-controlled

sympathetic

sunny

spirited

sparkling

secure

sociable

satisfied

sensitive

sagacious

sensational

sorry

subtle

self assured

stalwart

sublime

snappy

spry

soft hearted

sensible

strong

tolerant

transported

trusting

tranquil

tactful

truthful

tender

unbiased

unselfish

undaunted

unafraid

unassuming

vigilant

vivacious

valiant

valorous

venerable

wakeful	warm	yummy	zestful
warmhearted	worshipful		zippy
wise			

NEGATIVE N = 507

angry	abnormal	cross	downhearted
anxious	antsy	contrary	dreadful
aghast	autocratic	clouded	discomfited
alarmed		cowardly	disconcerted
appalled	bewildered	cheerless	despairing
apprehensive	bemused	crestfallen	displeased
aggressive	befuddled	contemptuous	disappointed
afflicted	bitchy	crushed	distracted
afraid	boiling	consumed	dull
ashamed	belligerent	careless	deceitful
acrimonious	blaming	cunning	distracted
aching	bitter	caustic	depressed
apathetic	bigoted	craven	dissatisfied
antagonistic	boastful	craving	defiant
annoyed	bored	covetous	disobedient
agonized	baleful	charming	downcast
agitated	beaten	cynical	disconsolate
apathetic	bewitched	crabby	dismal
abased	brazen	curt	dark
abashed	beguiled	cagey	discontented
angst	blue	constrained	disheartened
alienated	brutal	cold	dismayed
argumentative	brash	combative	discouraged
ambivalent	begrudging	covetous	disagreeable
audacious	bellicose	controlling	dejected
authoritarian	base	conniving	despondent
arrogant	bleak	corrupt	dolorous
acerbic	bossy	conceited	disinterested
adverse		cocky	disgusted
alluring	critical	crafty	distrustful
affected	cruel	clandestine	demanding
awful	confused	catty	dreadful

distressed
dour
diffident
dubious
dreary
deceptive
devious
deadly
desperate
disrespectful
domineering
despotic
dogmatic
disloyal
dishonest
doleful
dirty
deviant
depraved
dim
desirous
despicable
degenerate
daring

envious
embarrassed
edgy
equivocal
enraged
enthralled
exasperated
excitable
evasive

fearful
faithless
forlorn

funereal
flat
furious
fuming
fainthearted
fidgety
frantic
flustered
forsaken
frivolous
flighty
frenzied
fruitless
frowning
feeble
forbidding
frightened
fierce
ferocious
fixated
frightful
fidgety
flippant
frigid

giddy
gloomy
glum
grasping
grabby
greedy
grisly
gruesome
grim
grandiose
guileful
guilty
grief-stricken

grouchy
gruff

haughty
helpless
hurt
hostile
heavy-hearted
heartbroken
hot-headed
hopeless
hapless
heedless
horrified
hesitant
humiliated
hate
hysterical
hideous
heated
harsh
hungry
huffy

indignant
inferior
irritated
intolerant
infuriated
inconsiderate
insecure
indecisive
impulsive
incensed
ill at ease
inflamed
impatient
in a huff

indecisive
irate
irresolute
impious
insolent
imperious
irascible
impotent
insipid
incorrigible
intoxicated
irrelevant
irked
impaired
indulgent
intemperate
indiscreet
insensitive
irreverent
insidious
iniquitous
inimical
inhibited
insatiable
infatuated
immoral
impertinent
impudent
inflexible

jealous
judgmental
joyless
jittery
jumpy

kinky
klutzy

kooky	nauseated	patronizing	stubborn
	nonchalant	plaintive	shameless
lazy	nervy	passionless	slothful
lonely	negative	pitiless	superior
loathful	naive	preoccupied	sly
lugubrious	noncommittal	phony	scared
low	narcissistic	pessimistic	submissive
lustful		pushy	suffering
lax	outraged	procrastinating	sad
licentious	oppressed		shaky
lecherous	offended	queasy	shaky
lewd	ornery	querulous	shocked
lurid	obdurate	quirky	suspicious
licked	obstreperous	quarrelsome	scornful
	oblivious		sarcastic
manipulative	obsessed	resentful	somber
malicious	obstinate	rejected	stupid
meek	opinionated	revolted	spiritless
moping	overbearing	reckless	sullen
moody		rebellious	sulky
melancholy	pretentious	rueful	shrewish
mournful	prideful	refractory	self-righteous
menacing	passive	rabid	sassy
misgiving	pathetic	recalcitrant	strict
mean	panicky	reticent	surly
morose	petrified	rancorous	supercilious
malignant	provoked	resigned	snobbish
murky	piteous	rigid	sneaky
militant	prejudiced	repulsed	smug
malevolent	possessive	ravenous	sour
miserly	piqued	rotten	shifty
macabre	permissive	ruthless	shady
maniacal	prickly	repressed	scheming
	perverse	revengeful	skittish
nasty	petulant	rude	stern
nervous	pugnacious		stuck up
negligent	perturbed	sorrowful	seductive
naughty	perfidious	spiteful	spent

sterile

sinful

savage

severe

stringent

short

susceptible

sordid

timid

tortured

tremulous

threatened

timourous

terrified

tyrannical

tenebrous

treacherous

touchy

tough

tricky

tasteless

toxic

unhappy

unreceptive

unaffectionate

unfriendly

up in arms

uncooperative

uncertain

unsympathetic

unruly

unsociable

unmerciful

untrustworthy

unforgiving

unquenchable

unjust

unrighteous

unfruitful

unproductive

unresponsive

unkind

unfair

unscrupulous

untruthful

unethical

unchaste

ugly

uncaring

unworthy

ungracious

unheeding

unreflective

vain

vacillating

virulent

vengeful

vexed

victimized

volatile

violent

venal

vile

vehement

vicious

vindictive

villainous

vulgar

withdrawn

wrathful

worried

woeful

wavering

weary

weepy

woebegone

wanton

wary

washed-out

wasted

weak

wily

wild

whipped

wicked

wishful

wimpy

xenophobic

yeeucky

yappy

zealous

zonked

· REFERENCES ·

Abu Bakr Siraj ad-Din (aka, Martin Lings). *The Book of Certainty.*
The Islamic Texts Society, Cambridge, UK, (revised & expanded ed.), 1992.

Ackerman, Diane. *A Natural History of the Senses.*
Random House, NY, 1990.

Adilaksmi. *The Mother.*
Mother Meera Pub., Dornburg-Thalheim, Germany, (2nd ptg.) 1994.

Affifi, Abul E. *The Mystical Philosophy of Muhyid Dín-Ibnul 'Arabí.*
Cambridge U. Press, 1939. (AMS Press Inc., NY, reprint, 1974)

Afterman, Allen. *Kabbalah and Consciousness.*
The Sheep Meadow Press, Riverdale-on-Hudson, NY, 1992.

Agni Yoga Society. *Agni Yoga 1929.*
Agni Yoga Soc. Inc., NY, (5th. Ed.), 1980.

Agni Yoga Society. *Fiery World 1933.*
Agni Yoga Soc. Inc., NY, 1969.

Agni Yoga Society. *Aum 1936.*
Agni Yoga Soc. Inc., NY, 1980.

Ahmed, Leila. *Women & Gender in Islam.*
Yale U. Press, New Haven, 1992.

Allione, Tsultrim. *Women of Wisdom.*
Arkana, London, 1986.

Altizer, Thomas J.J. *The Self-Embodiment of God.*
Brown Classics in Judaica. University Press of America, Inc., Lanham, MD, 1987.

Amis, Robin. *A Different Christianity: Early Christianity, Esotericism & Modern Thought.*
State U. of NY, Albany, 1995.

Anonymous. *Meditations on the Tarot: A Journey into Christian Hermeticism.*
Amity House, NY, 1985. [Published anonymously, but authored by
Valentin Tomberg]

Anderson, Mary M. *Hidden Power: the Palace Eunuchs of Imperial China.*
Prometheus Books, Buffalo, NY, 1990.

Andreas Capellanus. *The Art of Courtly Love.* (Frederick W. Locke Ed.) (J.J.
Parry trans.)
Ungar Pub., NY, 1976.

Andreev, Daniil. *The Rose of the World.* (Jordan Roberts trans.)
Lindisfarne Books, Hudson, NY, 1997.

Ariel, David S. *The Mystic Quest: An Introduction to Jewish Mysticism*
Schocken Bks. NY 1992.

The Apocrypha: King James Version. (Manuel Komoroff Ed.)
Tudor Pub. Co., NY 1936.

Attar, Farid Ud-Din (Fl. 1150-1200 CE). *The Conference of the Birds.*
Routledge & Kegan Paul Ltd., London, 1967.

Aurobindo, Sri. *Savitri.*
Sri Aurobindo Intl. Univ. Centre, Pondicherry 1954.

Aurobindo, Sri. *The Life Divine.*
India Library Society, NY, 1965. (3rd. Ed.)

Aurobindo, Sri. *Heraclitus.*
Sri Aurobindo Ashram, Pondicherry, India, 1968.

Aurobindo, Sri. *The Problem of Rebirth.*
Sri Aurobindo Ashram, Pondicherry, India, 1969

Avens, Robert. *Imagination is Reality: Western Nirvana in Jung, Hillman,
Barfield, and Cassirer.*
Spring Pub. Inc. Dallas, TX, 1980.

Ayto, John. *Dictionary of Word Origins.*
Arcade Pub., Little, Brown and Co., NY, 1990.

Bachelard, Gaston. *The Poetics of Reverie: Childhood, Language, and the
Cosmos.*
Beacon Press, Boston, 1971.

Bachelard, Gaston. *Air and Dreams: An Essay on the Imagination of Movement.*
The Dallas Institute of Humanities and Culture, Dallas, TX, 1988.

Bahm, Archie J. *Polarity, Dialectic, and Organicity.*
Charles C. thomas Pub., Springfield, IL, 1970.

Bailey, Alice A. *Initiation, Human and Solar.*
Lucis Pub. Co., NY, (7 th ptg.), 1959.

Bailey, Alice A. *Esoteric Psychology V. 1*
  Lucis Pub. Co., NY, 1967.

Bailey, Alice A. *A Treatise on White Magic or The Way of the Disciple.*
  Lucis Pub. Co., NY, (9th ptg.), 1969.

Bailey, Alice A. *Ponder On This.*
  Lucis Pub. Co., NY, (6th ptg.), 1971.

Bailey, Derrick Sherwin. *The Man-Woman Relation in Christian Thought.*
  Longmans, Green & Co. Ltd., London, 1959.

Balzac, Honore' de. *Seraphita.*
  Freedeeds Press, Blauvelt, NY, (revised 3rd. Ed.), 1986.

Baltazar, Eulalio R. *Teilhard and the Supernatural.*
  Helicon, Baltimore, MD, 1966.

Bamford, Christopher (ed.). *The Noble Traveller: O.V. de L. Milosz.*
  Lindisfarne Press, NY, 1985.

Bandler, Richard & John Grinder. *Reframing: Neuro-Linguistic Programming and the Tranformation of Meaning.* Real People Press, Moab, UT, 1982.

Barbach, Lonnie & Geisinger, David L. *Going the Distance: Finding and Keeping Lifelong Love.*
  Penguin Bks., N.Y. 1993.

Barbin, Hèrculine. *Being the Recently Discovered Memoirs of a Nineteenth-Century French Hermaphrodite.* (Richard McDougall trans.) Pantheon Books, NY, 1980.

Barfield, Owen. *Saving the Appearances: A Study in Idolatry.*
  Harcourt Brace Jovanovich, NY, 1957.

Barfield, Owen. *The Rediscovery of Meaning, and Other Essays,*
  Wesleyan U. Press, Middletown, CN, 1977.

Barfield, Owen. *History, Guilt, And Habit.*
  Wesleyan U. Press; Middletown, CT, 1981.

Barney, Stephen A. *Word-Hoard: An Introduction to Old English Vocabulary.*
  Yale University Press, New Haven and London, 1977.

Barnhouse, Ruth Tiffany. "A Christian Speculation on the Divine Intention for the Man-Woman Relationship." in: Gupta, Bina (Ed.) 1987: 116-138.

Barth, Karl. *Church Dogmatics: a Selection.* (B.W. Bromiley trans./ed.)
  Harper & Row Pub., NY, 1962.

Baron, Dennis. *Grammar and Gender.*
  Yale U. Press, New Haven, CN, 1986.

Bell, Joseph Norment. *Love Theory in Later Hanbalite Islam.*
State University of NY Press, Albany, 1979.

Bell, Richard H. (Ed.). *The Grammar of the Heart: New Essays in Moral Philosophy & Theology.*
Harper & Row, Pub., San Francisco, 1988.

Bendroth, Margaret Lamberts. *Fundamentalism & Gender: 1875 to the Present.*
Yale U. Press, New Haven, 1993.

Benz, Ernst. "Theogony and the Transformation of Man in Friedrich Wilhelm Joseph Schelling. In Joseph Campbell, (Ed.) *Man and Transformation*, 1980: 203-249.

Berdyaev, Nicolas A. *The Meaning of the Creative Act.* (Donald A. Lowrie Trans.)
Harper & Bros., NY, 1955.

Berdyaev, Nicolas A. *The Destiny of Man.* (Natalie Duddington Trans.)
Harper & Brothers, NY, 1960.

Bergman, Shmuel H. *Dialogical Philosophy from Kierkegaard to Buber.* (A.A.Gerstein trans.)
State University of NY Press, Albany, 1991.

Berman, Morris. *The Reenchantment of the World.*
Bantam Books, NY, 1981.

Berry, Donald L. *Mutuality: The Vision of Martin Buber.*
State U. of NY Press, Albany, NY, 1985.

Bess, Savitri, L. *The Path of the Mother.*
Ballantine Publishing Group, NY, 2000.

Betanzos, Ramon James. "Franz Von Baader's Philosophy of Love."
Diss. Univ. of Michigan, 1968.

Bhagavad-Gita. (Prabhavanada & Isherwood trans.)
Mentor Books, N.Y. 1951 (13th. Printing)

Biale, David. *Eros and the Jews.*
HarperCollins Pub., NY, 1992.

Binswanger, Ludwig (1882-1966). *The Case of Ellen West.* (Werner M. Mendel & Joseph Lyons trans.) in Rollo May, (et. al. eds.)*Existence: A new dimension in Psychiatry and Psychology*, 1959: pp. 237-363.

Blanton, Smiley. *Love or Perish.*
Simon & Schuster, NY, 1956.

Blavatsky, H.P. *The Secret Doctrine.*
The Theosophical Pub Co. Wheaton, IL, 1888 (1928 reprint).

Blavatsky, H.P. *Isis Unveiled: a Master-Key.*
Theosophical U. Press, Pasadena, CA, 1976.

Bloom, Amy. "The Body Lies."
The New Yorker, July 18, 1994: pp. 38-49.

Blumenthal, H.J. *Plotinus' Psychology. His doctrines of the Embodied Soul.*
Martinus Nijhoff, The Hague; 1971.

Bock, Emil *The Apocalypse of Saint John.*
Floris Books, Edinburgh, 1980.

Bock, Emil. *Moses: From the Mysteries of Egypt to the Judges of Israel.*
Inner traditions Intl., NY, 1986.

Boehme, Jacob. *The Three Principles of the Divine Essence.*
Yogi Pub. Soc., Chicago, IL 1909.

Boehme, Jacob. *The Aurora* (Trans. John Sparrow)
The Attic Press, Greenwood, SC, 1960.

Boehme, Jacob. *The Signature of All Things.*
James Clarke and Co. Ltd. Cambridge & London, 1969.

Boehme, Jacob. *Six Theosophic Points: and other writings.*
U. of Michigan Press, Ann Arbor, MI, 1958.

Boehme, Jacob. *The Way to Christ.*
Paulist Press, NY, 1978.

Boethius (C. 480-524 CE) *The Consolation of Philosophy.* (V.E. Watts Trans.)
Penguin Books, London, (9th ptg.) 1988.

Bohm, David. "On Dialogue."
Noetic Sciences Review, Autumn 1992; pp.16-18.

Bohm, David. *Wholeness and the Implicate Order.*
Ark Paperbacks, London/NY, 1988.

Bohm, David. "Imagination, Fancy, Insight, and Reason in the Process of Thought" In: Shirley Sugerman, *Evolution of Consciousness: Studies in Polarity,* 1976: 51-68.

Bohm, David & B.J. Hiley. *The Undivided Universe: an Ontological Interpretation of Quantum Theory.* Routledge, NY, 1993.

Bohm, David, Donald Factor, & Peter Garrett. *Dialogue—A Proposal.*
The Wisdom Soc. San Marcos, CA, 1991.

Bohm, David & F. David Peat. *Science, Order, and Creativity.*
Bantam Books, NY, 1987.

Bohr, Niels. *Atomic Physics and Human Knowledge,*
Wiley, NY, 1963.

Bokar Rinpoche. *Chenrezig, Lord Of Love: Principles and Methods of Deity Meditation.*
Clear Point Press, S.F., CA, 1991.

Bosker, Rabbi Ben Zion. *From the World of the Cabbalah.*
Philosophical Lib., NY, 1954.

Boswell, John. *Same-sex Unions in Premodern Europe.*
Villard Books, NY, 1994.

Boyarin, Daniel. *Carnal Israel: Reading Sex in Talmudic Culture.*
Univ. of California Press, Berkely, CA, 1993.

Bragdon, Claude (1866-1946). *Delphic Woman: Twelve Essays.*
Alfred A. Knopf, NY, (3 rd. ptg.), 1945.

Briggs, John & F. David Peat. *Turbulent Mirror: an Illustrated guide to Chaos Theory and the Science of Wholeness.* Harper & Row, NY, 1989.

Brinton, Howard H. *The Mystic Will: Based on a Study of the Philosophy of Jacob Boehme.*
The Macmillan Co., NY, 1930.

Bristow, John Temple. *What Paul Really Said About Women.*
Harper San Francisco, CA, 1988.

Brooks, Geraldine. *9 Parts of Desire: the Hidden World of Islamic Women.*
Doubleday, NY, 1995.

Brown, Norman O. *Love's Body.*
Random house, NY, 1966.

Bruce F. F. *New Testament History.*
Doubleday, NY, 1980.

Brumbaugh, Robert S. *Whitehead, Process Philosophy, and Education.*
State U. of NY Press, Albany, NY, 1982.

Brümmer, Vincent. *The Model of Love.*
Cambridge University Press, Cambridge, 1993.

Brunton, Paul. *The Hidden Teaching Beyond Yoga.*
E.P. Dutton & Co., Inc., NY, (4th ptg.), 1946.

Buber, Martin. *I and Thou.* (Ronald G. Smith trans.)
Charles Scribner's Sons, NY, 1958.

Buber, Martin. *The Knowledge of Man: A Philosophy of the Interhuman.*
Harper & Row, Publishers, NY, 1965.

Buber, Martin. *Eclipse of God: Studies in the Relation Between Religion and Philosophy.*
Harper & Row, Pub. NY, (6th ptg.) 1965.

Buber, Martin. *The Origin and Meaning of Hasidism.*
Harper & Row, Pub., NY, 1966.

Buber, Martin. *I and Thou.* (Walter Kaufmann trans.)
Charles Scribner's Sons, NY, 1970.

Buber, Martin. *Between Man and Man.* (Ronald G. Smith trans.)
The Macmillan Co., NY, (8th ptg.) 1972.

Buber, Martin. *Gog and Magog.* (Ludwig Lewisohn trans.)
Syracuse U. Press, 1999.

Bulgakov, Sergei (1871-1944). *Sophia: The Wisdom of God.*
Lindisfarne Press, Hudson, NY, 1993.

Burckhardt, Titus. *An Introductgion To Sufi Doctrine.* (D.M. Matheson
trans.)
Sh. Muhammad Ashraf Pub., Lahore, (reprint) 1963.

Burckhardt, Titus. "Cosmology and Modern Science" in *The Sword of
Gnosis.* (Jacob Needleman ed.) Penguin Books Inc., Baltimore, MD,
1974.

Burr, Chandler. *A Separate Creation: the Search for the Biological Origins of
Sexual Orientation.*
Hyperion, NY, 1996.

Bütz, Michael R. "Negotiation as a Therapeutic Technique in Brief Couples
Therapy."
Mediation Quarterly, v. 8, no.3, 1991:211-223.

Bynum, Caroline W., Stevan Harrel & Paula Richman. *Gender and
Religion: On the Complexity of Symbols.* Beacon Press, Boston, 1986.

Cabezón, José Ignacio (ed.). *Buddhism, Sexuality, & Gender.*
State U. of NY Press, Albany, NY, 1992.

Campbell, Joseph (ed.). *Man and Transformation: papers from the Eranos
Yearbooks.*
Bollingen Ser. XXX • 5. Princeton U. Press, Princeton, NJ, 1980.

Campbell, Joseph. *Myths To Live By.*
Bantam Bks., NY 1988.

Cancian, Francesca M. *Love in America: Gender and self-development.*
Cambridge U. Press, Cambridge, 1987.

Capra, Fritjof. *The Tao of Physics .*
Shambahala, Berkeley, CA, 1975.

Caputo, John D. *The Mystical Element in Heidegger's Thought.*
Villanova University, Oberlin, OH, 1978.

Caputo John D. *Radical Hermeneutics: Repetition, Deconstuction, and the Hermeneutic Project.*
Indiana University Press, Bloomington, 1987.

Carnell, Corbin Scott. "C.S. Lewis on Eros as a Means of Grace" In Charles Huttar, *Imagination and the Spirit.* 1971: pgs. 341-351.

Chadwick, Henry (ed.). *Alexandrian Christianity.*
The Westminster Press, Philadelphia, 1954.

Chauchard, Paul. *Teilhard de Chardin on Love and Suffering.* (Marie Chêne trans.)
Paulist Press Deus Books, NY 1966.

Chia, Mantak (w/ Michael Winn). *Taoist Secrets of Love: Cultivating Male Sexual Energy.*
Aurora Press, NY, (3 rd. Ed.) 1985.

Chidvilasananda, Gurumayi. "Become a Great Doer, A Supreme Enjoyer, and a Great Renunciant" [Talk given 8/23/87] *Darshan.*, March 1994: pg. 40-45.

Childre, Doc Lew. *Freeze-Frame™ Fast Action Stress Relief.*
Planetary Pub., Boulder Creek, CA, 1994.

Chittick, William C. *The Sufi Path of Knowledge: Ibn al-'Arabi's Metaphysics of Imagination.*
State U. of NY Press, Albany, 1989.

Chittick, William C. *The Sufi Path of Love: The spiritual Teachings of Rumi.*
State Univ. of NY Press, Albany, 1983.

Cioran, Samuel D. *Vladimir Solov'ev and the Knighthood of the Divine Sophia.*
Wilfrid Laurier U. Press; Waterloo, Ontario, Canada 1977.

Clairborne, Robert. *The Roots of English: A Reader's Handbook of Word Origins.*
Times Books, NY, 1989.

Clarke, Lindsay. *The Chemical Wedding.*
Ballantine, NY, 1991

Clement of Alexandria (150? CE-220? CE). "On Marriage": *Miscellanies, Book III.* In Henry
Chadwick, (ed.) *Alexandrian Christianity.,* 1954:pgs. 40-92.

Clement of Alexandria. "On Spiritual Perfection": *Miscellanies, Book VII.* In Henry Chadwick, (ed.) *Alexandrian Christianity.* 1954: pp. 93-165.

Codd, Clara M. *The Creative Power.*
The Theosophical Press, Wheaton IL, 1947.

Coff, Pascaline. "Eve, Where Are You?"
   In Bina Gupta, (Ed.) 1987: 17-36.

Cole, William Graham. *Sex & Love in the Bible.*
   Association Press, NY, 1959.

Collins, Steven. *Selfless Persons: Imagery and Thought in Theravada Buddhism.*
   Cambridge Univ. Press, Cambridge/NY, 1995.

Cooey, Paula M., Sharon A. Farmer & Mary Ellen Ross (eds.). *Embodied Love: Sensuality and Relationship as Feminist Values.* Harper & Row, San Francisco, 1983.

Coomaraswamy, Ananda K. "Atmayajña: Self-Sacrifice"
   In *Harvard Journal of Asiatic Studies,* V. 6, 1942: pp. 358-398.

Corbett, Grenville G. *Gender.*
   Cambridge U. Press, Cambridge, 1991.

Corbin, Henry. *The Man of Light in Iranian Sufism.*
   Shambhala, Boulder/London, 1978.

Corbin, Henry. *Creative Imagination in the Sufism of Ibn'Arabi.*
   Princeton U. Press, 1981.

Corbin, Henry. *Cyclical Time and Ismaili Gnosis.*
   Kegan Paul Intl., London 1983.

Corbin, Henry. "The Eternal Sophia" (Moly Tuby Trans.) *Harvest:* Analytical Psychology Club,
   London, V. 31, 1985: 7-23.

Corbin, Henry. *Avicenna and the Visionary Recital.* (William Trask Trans.)
   Princeton U. Press 1988.

Corbin, Henry. *Spiritual Body and Celestial Earth.* (Nancy Pearson Trans.)
   Princeton U. Press, 1989.

Corbin, Henry. *Swedenborg and Esoteric Islam.* (Leonard Fox trans.)
   Swedenborg Fdn., West Chester, PA, 1995.

Corbin, Henry. *The Voyage and the Messenger: Iran and Philosopher.* (Joseph Rowe trans.)
   North Atlantic Books, Berkeley, CA, 1998.

Cousins, Ewert H. (Ed.) *Process Theology: basic writings.*
   Newman Press, NY, 1971.

Cousins, Ewert H. "Male-Female Aspects of the Trinity in Christian Mysticism."
   In: Gupta, Bina (Ed.) 1987: 37-50.

Curtis, Fred A. & Beeke Bailey. "A Mediation-Counseling Approach to Marriage Crisis Resolution." *Mediation Quarterly,* V. 8, No. 2,1990: pp. 137-149.

Cushman, Robert E. *Therapaia: Plato's Conception of Philosophy.* Univ. of North Carolina Press, Chapel Hill, NC, 1958.

Cutsinger, James S. *The Form of Transformed Vision: Coleridge and the Knowledge of God.* Mercer Univ. Press, Macon GA, 1987.

Cutsinger, James S. "Feminity, Hierarchy, and God." in: Nasr, Seyyed Hossein & Stoddart W. (Eds.) *Religion of the Heart.* 1991: 110-131.

D'Arcy, Martin Cyril. *The Mind and Heart of Love.* Henry Holt & Co. Inc., NY, (Rev. Ed.) 1956.

Dalai Lama. *Healing Anger: The Power of Patience from a Buddhist Perspective.* (Thuypten Junpa trans.) Snow Lion, NY, 1997.

Dante Alighieri. *The Portable Dante.* (Paolo Milano ed.) The Viking Press, NY, 1969.

Dante Alighieri (1265-1321). *The Paradiso.* (verse rendering by John Ciardi) New American Library (a Mentor Book), NY, 1970.

Davies, Paul. *God and the New Physics.* Simon & Schuster, NY, 1983.

Davies, Paul. *Other Worlds.* Simon & Schuster, NY, 1980.

Deeken, Alfons. S.J. *Process and Permanence in Ethics: Max Scheler's Moral Philosophy.* Paulist Press, NY, 1974.

de Caussade, Jean-Pierre (1675-1751). *Abandonment to Divine Providence.* Doubleday & Co., NY, 1975.

Delaney, John J. (ed.). *A Woman Clothed With the Sun.* Doubleday & Co. Inc., Garden City, NY, 1961.

de Lubac, Henri. *The Eternal Feminine.* (René Hague trans.) Harper & Row, Pub., NY, 1971.

del Valle, Teresa (ed.). *Gendered Anthropology.* Routledge, London/NY, 1993.

de Nicolás, Antonio T. *Avatara: The Humanization of Philosophy through the Bhagavad Gita.* Nicolas Hays, Ltd., NY, 1976.

de Quincey, Christian. *Intersubjectivity: Exploring Consciousness from the Second-Person Perspective.*
(revised version IIIb), Feb., 1998, Unpublished.

De Rougemont, Denis. *Love in the Western World.*
Shocken Books, NY, 1983. (1940)

Derry, Evelyn Francis. "Marriage in the Gospels." in *Marriage.*
Christian Community Press, London, 1972: pg. 25-29.

Desteian, John A. *Coming Together—Coming Apart: The Union of Opposites in Love Relationships.*
Sigo Press, Boston. 1989.

Dickason, Anne. "The Feminine As a Universal." in Vertterling-Braggin, Mary (ed.) *"Femininity,"*
"Masculinity," and "Androgyny," 1982: pp. 79-100.

Dimont, Max I. *Jews, God and History.*
New American Library Inc., NY, 1962.

Doresse, Jean. *The Secret Books of the Egyptian Gnostics.*
Viking Press, NY, 1960.

Dossey, Larry. *Recovering the Soul: A Scientific and spiritual Search.*
Bantam Books, NY, 1989.

Dostoyevsky, Fyodor. *Notes From Underground/The Double.* (Jessie Coulson trans.)
Penguin Books, Middlesex, England, 1986.

Dowman, Keith. *Sky Dancer: the secret life and songs of Lady Yeshe Tsogyel*
Arkana, the Penguin Group, London 1989.

Dronke, Peter. *Medieval Latin and the Rise of European Love-Lysic, V. 1.*
Oxford Univ. Press, 1965.

Duby, Georges. *The Knight, The Lady & The Priest.*
Pantheon Books, NY, 1983.

Duff, Kat. *The Alchemy of Illness.*
Bell Tower, NY, 1993.

Dworkin, Andrea. *Right-wing Women.*
G.P. Putnam's Sons, NY, 1983.

Eadie, Betty J. *Embraced by the Light.*
Bantam Books, NY, 1994.

Ed-Dîn, Abû Bakr Sirâj. *The Book of Certainty.*
Rider and Co., London, 1952.

Edelman, Joel & Mary Beth Crain. *The Tao of Negotiation.*
HarperCollins, NY, 1993.

Einstein, Albert. *The World as I See It,*
Philosophical Library, NY, 1949.

Einstein, Albert. *Ideas and Opinions,*
Bonanza, NY, 1954.

Eisler, Riane. *The Chalice and The Blade.*
Harper, S.F., CA, 1988.

Eisler, Riane. *Sacred Pleasure: Sex, Myth & Politics of the Body.*
Harper San Francisco, 1995.

Eliade, Mircea. *Mephistopheles and the Androgyne.*
Sheed and Ward, NY, 1965.

Eliade, Mircea. *Patterns in Comparative Religion.*
World Pub. NY, (8th ptg.), 1972.

Elgin, Suzette Haden. *Genderspeak.*
John Wiley & Sons, Inc. NY, 1993.

Erasmi, Gabriele. "Earthly Love and divine Love: A Secular Path to Mysticism in XIII Century Italy." in: Gupta, Bina (Ed.) 1987: 207-220.

Erasmus (1466-1536). *The Essential Erasmus* (John P. Dolan, ed.)
New American Library, NY, 1964.

Erb, Peter C. (ed.). *Pietists: Selected Writings.*
Paulist Press, NY, 1983.

Evola, Julius (1898-1974). *Eros and the Mysteries of Love: Metaphysics of Sex.*
Inner Traditions International, Rochester, VT, 1991.

Evola, Julius. *The Yoga of Power: Tantra, Shakti, and the Secret Way.* (Guido Stucco trans.)
Inner Traditions International, Rochester, VT, 1992.

Faivre, Antoine. *Access To Western Esotericism.*
State U. Press of NY Press, Albany, NY, 1994.

Faivre, Antoine & Jacob Needleman (ed.). *Modern Esoteric Spirituality.*
Crossroad Pub. Co., NY, 1995.

Fang, Thomé H. *Chinese Philosophy: Its Spirit and Its Development.*
Linking Pub. Co. Ltd., Taipei, Taiwan, 1981.

Ferguson, Ann. "Androgyny As an Ideal for Human Development" in Vertterling-Braggin, et. al.
(ed.) *Feminism and Philosophy,* 1977: pp. 45-69.

Ferguson, Marilyn. *The Aquarian Conspiracy.*
Tarcher, Los Angeles, 1980.

Feuerstein, Georg. *Structures of Consciousness: The Genius of Jean Gebser—an Introduction and Critique.* Integral Pub., Lower Lake, CA, 1987.

Feuerstein, Georg. (ed.). *Enlightened Sexuality : Essays on Body-Positive Spirituality.*
The Crossing Press, Freedom, CA, 1989.

Ficino, Marsilio, (1433-1499). *Commentary on Plato's Symposium.*
Univ. of Missouri, Columbia, 1944.

Finley, James. *Merton's Palace of Nowhere: a Search for God Through Awareness of theTrue Self.*
Ave Maria Press, Notre Dame, IN, 1985.

Fisher, R. & Ury, W. *Getting to Yes: Negotiating Agreement Without Giving-in.*
Houghton/Mifflin, NY, 1981.

Fortune, Dion. *The Esoteric Philosophy of Love & Marriage.*
The Aquarian Press, London, (4th. ed.) 1967.

Foucault, Michel. *Mental Illness and Psychology.* (Alan Sheridan trans.)
U. of California Press, Berkeley, CA, 1987.

Foucault, Michel. *Language, Counter-memory, Practice: Selected Essays and Interviews.* (Donald Bouchard & Sherry Simon trans.) Cornell U. Press, Ithaca, NY, 1981.

Foucault, Michel. *Technologies of the Self: A Seminar with Michel Foucault.* (Luther Martin, Huck Gutman & Patrick Hutton Eds.) U. Mass Press, Amherst, 1988.

Foucault, Michel. *The History of Sexuality V.1* (Robert Hurley trans.)
Random House NY, 1990.

Foucault, Michel. *The Use of Pleasure. V. 2.History of Sexuality.*
Random House NY, 1990.

Foucault, Michel. *The Care of the Self. V.3 The History of Sexuality.*
Random House NY, 1988.

Fox-Genovese, Elizabeth. *Feminism Without Illusions: A Critique of Individualism.*
The Univ. of North Carolina Press, Chapel Hill/London, 1991.

Frank, Adolphe. *The Kabbalah.*
Bell Pub. Co., NY, 1940.

Frank, Simeon L. (ed.). *A Solovyov Anthology.*
S.C.M. Press, London 1950.

Freedman, David Noel. *The Unity of the Hebrew Bible.*
University of Michigan Press, Ann Arbor, 1993.

Friedman, Maurice S. *Martin Buber: the Life of Dialogue.*
Harper & Row, NY, 1960.

Friedman, Maurice S. *To Deny Our Nothingness: Contemporary Images of Man.*
Delacorte Press, NY, 1967.

Frings, Manfred S. *Max Scheler.*
Duquesne U. Press, Pittsburgh PA, 1965.

Fromm, Eric. *The Art of Loving.*
Bantam, NY, 1970 (35th. ptg.).

Fuchs, Eric *Sexual Desire and Love: Origins and History of the Christian Ethic of Sexuality and Marriage.* (Marsha Daigle trans.) Seabury Press, NY, 1983.

Furnish, Victor Paul. *The Moral Teachings of Paul: Selected Issues.*
Abingdon Press, Nashville, TN, (Second Ed.), 1985.

Gadamer, Hans-Georg. *The Idea of the Good in Platonic-Aristotelian Philosophy.*
Yale Univ. Press, New Haven & London, 1986.

Gallagher, Kenneth T. *The Philosophy of Gabriel Marcel.*
Fordham Univ. Press, NY, 1975.

Gasché, Rodolphe. *The Tain of the Mirror: Derrida and the Philosophy of Reflection.*
Harvard Univ. Press. Cambridge, MA, 1986.

Gebser, Jean. *The Ever Present Origen.* (Noel Barstad & Algis Mickunas trans.)
Ohio U. Press, Athens OH, 1985.

Geshe Sonam Rinchen. *The Thirty-seven Practices of Bodhisattvas.* (Ruth Sonam, trans. & ed.)
Snow Lion Publications, Ithaca, NY, 1997.

Gibran, Kahalil. *The Prophet.*
Alfred A. Knopf, NY, (59th. ptg.), 1956.

Giffen, Lois Anita. *Theory of Profane Love among the Arabs: The Development of the Genre.*
NY Univ. Press, NY, 1971.

Gilson, Etienne. *Dante and Philosophy.*
Peter Smith, Gloucester, MA, 1968.

Gimbutas, Marija. *The Goddesses and Gods of Old Europe: 6500-3500 B.C.*
University of California Press, Berkeley, 1982.

Ginsburgh, Rabbi Yitzchak. *The Alef-Beit: Jewish Thought Revealed Through the Hebrew Letters.*
Jason Aronson Inc., Northvale, NJ, 1995.

Goethe, Johann W. von. *Elective Affinities.*
F. Ungar Pub. Co., NY, (2nd. ptg.), 1967.

Goicoechea, David (ed.). *The Nature and Pursuit of Love: The Philosophy of Irving Singer.*
Prometheus Books, Amherst, NY, 1995.

Goswami, Amit. *The Self-Aware Universe: How Consciousness Creates the Material World.*
G.P. Putnam's Sons, NY, 1995.

Govinda, Lama Anagarika. *Foundations of Tibetan Mysticism.*
Rider & Co., London 1959.

Govinda, Lama Anagarika. *Creative Meditation and Multi-Dimensional Consciousness.*
Quest Books, Wheaton, IL, 1978.

González-Balado, José Luis &Janet Playfoot (eds.). *My Life for the Poor: Mother Teresa of Calcutta.*
Harper & Row, NY, 1985.

Gray, Donald P. *The One and the Many: Teilhard de Chardin's Vision of Unity.*
Herder & Herder, NY, 1969.

Gray, John. *Men are From Mars: Women are From Venus: A Practical Guide for Improving Communication and Getting What You Want in Your Relationships.* HarperCollins, 1992.

Graybeal, Jean. *Language and "the Feminine" In Nietzsche and Heidegger.*
Indiana U. Press, Bloomington, 1990.

Gregorios, Paulos Mar. *Cosmic Man: The Divine Presence.* [Gregory of Nyssa 330-395 CE]
Paragon House, NY, 1988.

Griffiths, Bede. *The Marriage of East and West.*
Templegate Publishers, Springfield, IL, 1982.

Guénon, René. "The Language of the Birds" in Jacob Needleman (ed.) *The Sword of Gnosis,* 1974: pp. 299-303.

Guénon, René. *The Multiple States of Being.* (Joscelyn Godwin trans.)
Larson Pub. Inc., Burdett, NY, 1984.

Guénon, René. *The Great Triad.* (Peter Kingsley trans.)
Quinta Essentia, Cambridge, UK, 1991.

Guenther, Herbert V. *The Tantric View of Life.*
Shambala, Berkeley, CA, 1972.

Guenther, Herbert V. *Kindly Bent To Ease Us, Part One: Mind.*
Dharma Pub., Berkeley, CA, 1975.

Guenther, Herbert V. *The Creative Vision.*
Lotsawa, Novato, CA, 1988.

Guenther, Herbert V. *From Reductionism to Creativity: rDzogs-chen and the New Sciences of Mind.*
Shambhala, Boston, 1989.

Guggenbühl-Craig, Adolf. *Marriage, Dead or Alive.* (Murray Stein trans.)
Spring Pub., Zürich, Switzerland, 1977.

Gupta, Bina (ed.). *Sexual Archetypes, East and West.*
Paragon House, N.Y. 1987.

Guttmann, Julius. *Philosophies of Judaism.* (David W. Silverman trans.)
Holt, Rinehart and Winston, NY, 1964.

Hacker, Diana. *A Writer's Reference.*
St. Martin's Press, Boston, MA (2nd. Ed.), 1992.

Halevi, Judah. *Book of Kuzari.* (Hartwig Hirschfeld trans.)
Pardes Pub. House, Inc., NY, 1946.

Harper, Ralph. *Human Love: Existential and Mystical.*
The Johns Hopkins Press, Baltimore, 1966.

Hadewijch (13th C.). *The Complete Works.* (Mother Columba Hart trans.)
Paulist Press, NY, 1980.

Handoo, Chandra Kumari. *A Glimpse of the Holy Mother.*
P.C. Chatterjee, Calcutta, 1952.

Hartmann, Franz. *The Life and Doctrines of Jacob Boehme.*
Rudolf Steiner Pub., Blauvelt, NY, 1977.

Hartshorne, Charles. *Omnipotence and Other Theological Mistakes.*
State U. of NY, Albany, 1984.

Hartshorne, Charles. "The Development of Process Philosophy," In Ewert Cousins (Ed.) *Process*
Theology: basic writings, 1971: pp. 47-65.

Harvey, Andrew. *A Journey in Ladakh.*
Houghton Mifflin Co., Boston, MA, 1983.

Harvey, Andrew. *The Hidden Journey: A Spiritual Awakening.*
Henry Holt & Co., NY, 1991.

Harvey, Andrew & Anne Baring (eds.). *The Mystic Vision: Daily Encounters with the Divine.*
Harper, SF, CA, 1995.

Hausman, Bernice L. *Changing Sex: Transsexualism, Technology, and the Idea of Gender.*
Duke Univ. Press, Durham, NC, 1995.

Hassel, David J., S.J. *Searching the Limits of Love: an approach to the Secular Transcendent God.*
Loyola U. Press, Chicago, IL, 1985.

Hayward, Jeremy W. *Shifting Worlds, Changing Minds.*
Shambhala, Boston, MA, 1987.

Heidenreich, Alfred. "The Marriage Sacrament" in, *Marriage.*
Christian community Press, London, 1972: pg. 13-24.

Heisenberg, Werner. *Physics and Philosophy,*
Harper Torchbooks, NY, 1958.

Heisenberg, Werner. *Encounters with Einstein: and Other Essays on People, Places and Particles.*
Princeton University Press, Princeton, NJ, 1989.

Heidegger, Martin. *Being and Time.* (John Macquarrie & Edward Robinson trans.)
Harper & Row, Publishers, NY, 1962.

Heidegger, Martin. *What is Called Thinking?*
Harper & Row, NY, 1968.

Heidegger, Martin. *Early Greek Thinking.*
Harper & Row, Pub., San Francisco, CA, 1984.

Heim, Michael. *The Metaphysics of Virtual Reality.*
Oxford Univ. Press, Oxford & NY, 1993.

Herberg, Will (ed.). *Four Existentialist Theologians.*
Doubleday & Co., Garden City, NY, 1958.

Herbert, Nick. *Quantum Reality.*
Doubleday, NY, 1985.

Herbert, Nick. *Elemental Mind: Human Consciousness and the New Physics.*
Penguin Books USA Inc., NY, 1994.

Herdt, Gilbert (ed.). *Third Sex, Third Gender: Beyond Sexual Dimorphism in Culture & History.*
Zone Bks., NY, 1994.

Hermes, Mercurius Trismegistus. *The Virgin of the World.*
Wizards Book Shelf, Minneapolis, MN, 1977

Hermes, Mercurius Trismegistus *The Divine Pymander.*
Wizards Book Shelf, San Diego, CA, 1978.

Hermetica. (Walter Scott trans. & ed.)
Shambhala Pub. Inc., Boston, 1993.

Heschel, Abraham J. *The Prophets.*
Jewish Pub. Soc. of America; NY, 1962.

Heschel, Abraham J. *God In Search of Man: A Philosophy of Judaism.*
Harper & Row, N.Y. 1966.

Hillman, James. *Re-Visioning Psychology.*
Harper & Row, NY, 1977.

Hillman, James. *The Myth of Analysis.*
HarperCollins, NY 1972. (Harper Perennial edition 1992)

Hocks, Richard A. "'Novelty' In Polarity To 'The Most Admitted Truths':
Tradition and the Individual Talent in S.T. Coleridge and T.S. Eliot."
in Shirley Sugerman, 1976: pp. 83-97.

Hodson, Geoffrey (1887-1983). *The Miracle of Birth: a Clairvoyant Study of a Human Embryo.*
Quest Books, Wheaton, IL, 1981.

Hoodbhoy, Pervez. *Islam and Science: Religious Orthodoxy and the Battle for Rationality.*
Zed Books Ltd., London/NJ, 1991.

Horwitz, Rivka. *Buber's Way to "I and Thou."*
The Jewish Publication Society, Philadelphia/NY/Jerusalem, 1988.

Huttar, Charles A. *Imagination and the Spirit.*
William B. Eerdmans Pub. Co., Grand Rapids, MI, 1971.

Ibn Al-'Arabi. *The Bezels of Wisdom.* (R.W.J. Austin Trans.)
Paulist Press, NY,1980.

Illich, Ivan & Barry Sanders. *A B C: The Alphabetization of the Popular Mind.*
North Point Press, San Francisco, 1988.

Inayat, Taj. *The Crystal Chalice: Spiritual Themes for Women.*
Sufi Order Pub., Lebanon Springs, NY, (2 nd ptg.), 1980.

Irigaray, Luce. *This Sex Which Is Not One.* (Catherine Porter trans.)
Cornell U. Press, Ithaca, NY, 1985.

Irigaray, Luce. *An Ethics of Sexual Difference.* (Carolyn Burke & Gillian Gill trans.)
Cornell U. Press, Ithaca, NY, 1993.

Izutsu, Toshihiko. *Creation and the Timeless Order of Things.*
White Cloud Press, Ashland, OR, 1994.

Jacobson, Nolan Pliny. *The Heart of Buddhist Philosophy.*
Southern Illinois U. Press, Carbondale, IL 1988.

Jacques, Francis. *Difference and Subjectivity: Dialogue and Personal Identity.*
(Andrew Rothwell trans.) Yale U. Press, New Haven/London, 1991.

Jaén, Didier T. *Borges' Esoteric Library: Metaphysics to Metafiction.*
University Press of America, Inc., Lanham, MD, 1992.

James, William. *The Varieties of Religious Experience.*
The New American Lib., NY, (5 th. ptg.), 1958.

Jamgön Kongtrül. *Radiant Wisdom.*
KDK Publications, San Francisco, CA, 1979.

Jardine, Alice & Smith, Paul (eds.). *Men in Feminism.*
Methuen, NY, 1978.

Jaspers, Karl. *Man in the Modern Age.*
Doubleday & Co., NY, 1957.

Jewett, Paul K. *Man as Male and Female: A Study in Sexual Relationships from a Theological Point of View.* Wm. B. Eerdmans Pub. Co., Grand Rapids, 1975.

Johann, Robert. *The Meaning of Love: an essay towards a metaphysics of intersubjectivity.*
Paulist Press, Glen Rock, NJ, 1966.

Joudry, Particia & Maurie D. Pressman. *Twin Souls: a Guide to Finding Your True Spiritual Partner.*
Carol Southern Books, NY, 1995.

Jung, C.G. *Synchronicity: An Acausal Connecting Principle.* (R.F.C. Hull trans.)
Princeton U. Press, Princeton, NJ, 1973.

Jung, C.G. *Aion: Researches into the Phenomenology of the Self.*
Princeton U. Press, Princeton, NJ, 1978.

Jung, C.G. *Mysterium Coniunctionis.* Col. Wks. V. 14. (Hull Trans.)
Princeton U. Press 1989.

Jung, C.G. *The Psychology of the Transference.* (From Col. Wks. V. 16)
Princeton U. Press., (9ᵗʰ. ptg.), 1989.

Kabat-Zinn, Jon. *Wherever You Go There You Are: Mindfulness Meditation in Everyday Life.*
Hyperion, NY, 1994.

Kafatos, Menas & Robert Nadeau. *The Conscious Universe: Part and Whole in Modern Physical Theory.* Springer-Verlag, NY, 1990.

Kaltenmark, Max. *Lao Tzu and Taoism.* (Roger Greaves trans.)
Stanford Univ. Press, Stanford, CA, 1969.

Kalu Rinpoche. *Dharma Teachings.*
Kagyu Droden Kunchab, San Francisco, CA, 1990.

Kalu Rinpoche. *Gently Whispered: Oral Teachings by the Venerable Kalu Rinpoche.* (Elizabeth Selandia, Ed.) Station Hill Press, Barrytown, NY, 1994.

Kalu Rinpoche. *Profound Buddhism: From Hinayana to Vajrayana.* Clear Point Press, San Francisco, CA, 1995.

Kalu Rinpoche. *Luminous Mind: The Way of the Buddha.* (Maria Montenegro trans.) Wisdom Publications, Boston, MA, 1997.

Kamuf, Peggy. "Femmeninism" In Alice Jardine, & Paul Smith, (eds.) *Men in Feminism.* Methuen, NY, 1978: pp. 78-84.

Kasoff, Ira E. *The Thought of Chang Tsai (1020-1077).* Cambridge Univ. Press, NY, 1984.

Kast, Verna. *The Nature of Loving: patterns of human relationship.* Chiron Pub., Wilamette, IL, 1986.

Katz, Jonathan Ned. *The Invention of Heterosexuality.* Dutton, NY, 1995.

Katz, Steven T. (ed.). *Mysticism and Language.* Oxford University Press, NY, 1992.

Katz, Steven T. (ed.). *Mysticism and Philosophical Analysis.* Oxford University Press, NY, 1978.

Keating, Thomas. *Reawakenings.* Crossroad, NY, 1992.

Keating, Thomas. *Open Mind, Open Heart: The Contemplative Dimension of the Gospel.* Amity House, NY, 1986.

Keen, Sam. *Fire in the Belly: on Being a Man.* Bantam Books, NY, 1992.

Keller, Evelyn Fox. *Reflections on Gender and Science.* Yale University Press, New Haven, CT, 1985.

Keller, Evelyn Fox. *Secrets of Life: Secrets of Death.* Routledge, N.Y., 1992.

Kessler, Suzanne, J. & Wendy McKenna. *Gender: An Ethnomethodological Approach.* John Wiley & Sons, NY, 1978.

Keyes, Laurel Elizabeth. *The Mystery of Sex.* Gentle Living Pub., Denver, CO, 1975.

Khan, Hazrat Inayat. *The Complete Sayings of Hazarat Inayat Khan.*
Sufi Order Pub., New Lebanon, NY, 1978.

Khan, Hazrat Inayat. *The Heart of Sufism: Essential Writing of Hazrat Inayat Khan.*
Shambhala, Boston & London, 1999.

Khan, Hazrat Inayat. "Passion"
in: Scott Miners, 1984: pp. 172-175.

Khan, Pir Vilayat (ed.). *A Meditation Theme For Each Day: From the Teachings of Hazrat Inayat Khan*
Omega Pub., New Lebanon, NY, 1992

Kierkegaard, Søren. *The gospel of Suffering And The Lilies of the Field.*
Augsburg Pub. House, Minneapolis, MN, 1948.

Kierkegaard, Søren. *Fear and Trembling & The Sickness Unto Death.* (Walter Lowrie trans.)
Doubleday & Co. Inc., Gaden City, NY, 1954.

Kierkegaard, Søren. *Works of Love.* (Howard & Edna Hong trans.)
Collins, London 1962.

Kierkegaard, Søren. *The Concept of Dread.* (Walter Lowrie trans.)
Princeton University Press, (2nd. ed.), 1969.

Klein, Charles. *How to Forgive When You Can't Forget.*
Liebling Press, Bellmore, NY, 1995.

Klein, Anne Carolyn. *Meeting the Great Bliss Queen: Buddhists, Feminists, and the Art of he Self.*
Beacon Press, Boston, 1995.

Koestler, Arthur. *The Roots of Coincidence: An Excursion into Parapsychology.*
Random House, NY, 1973.

Kohanski, Alexander S. *Martin Buber's Philosophy of Interhuman Relation.*
Associated University Presses, Inc., East Brunswick, NJ, 1982.

Koryé, Alexandre. *From Closed World to Infinite Universe.*
Johns Hopkins U. Press, Baltimore, (8th ptg.), 1991.

Kovacs, George. *The Question of God in Heidegger's Phenomenology.*
Northwestern Univ. Press, Evanston, 1990.

Kriyananda, Swami. (J. Donald Walters) *How to Spiritualize your Marriage.*
Ananda Pub., Nevada City, CA, 1982.

Laing, R.D. *Self and Others.*
Random House, NY, 1969.

Laing, R.D. *Knots.*
Pantheon Books, NY, 1970.

Lakoff, George & Mark Johnson. *Metaphors We Live By.*
   Univ. of Chicago Press, 1980.
Lakoff, George. *Women, Fire and Dangerous Things: What Categories Reveal about the Mind.*
Univ. of Chicago Press, Chigao, IL, 1987.
Lampert, Evgueny. *The Divine realm: towards a theology of the Sacraments.*
   Faber & Faber Ltd., London, 1944.
Landaw, Jonathan & Andy Weber. *Images of Enlightenment: Tibetan Art in Practice.*
Snow Lion Pub., Boston, MA, 1994.
Lemkow, Anna F. *The Wholeness Principle: Dynamics of Unity within Science, Religion & Society.*
   Quest Books, Wheaton, IL, 1990.
Le Pan, Don. *The Cognitive Revolution in Western Culture. V. 1: The Birth of Expectation.*
   Macmillan Press Ltd., London, 1989.
Lerner, Hariet Goldhor. *The Dance of Anger.*
   Harper & Row Pub., NY, 1985.
LeShan, Lawrence. *The Dilemma of Psychology.*
   Dutton, NY, 1990.
Levin, David Michael. *The Body's Recollection of Being: Phenomenological Psychology and the Deconstruction of Nihilism.* Routledge & Kegan Paul, London/Boston, 1985.
Levin, David Michael. *The Opening of Vision: Nihilism and the Post-modern Situation.*
   Routledge, NY, 1988.
Levine, Stephen & Ondrea. *Embracing The Beloved: Relationship as a Path of Awakening.*
   Doubleday, NY, 1995.
Lewis, C.S. *The Allegory of Love: A Study in Medieval Tradition.*
   Oxford Univ. Press, NY, 1958.
Lewis, C.S. *The Four Loves.*
   Harcourt Brace Jovanovich, Publishers, SanDiego/NY/London, 1960.
Lewis, C.S. *The Problem of Pain.*
   Macmillan Pub. Co. Inc., NY, (20th. ptg.), 1978.
Lewis, C.S. *Mere Christianity.*
   Macmillan Pub. Co. Inc., NY, (26th. ptg.), 197.

Lewis, Thomas, Fari Amini & Richard Lannon. *A General Theory of Love.*
Random House, Inc., NY, 2001.

Lings, Martin (aka, Abu Bakr Siraj ad-Din). *Ancient Beliefs and Modern Superstitions.*
Quinta Essentia, Cambridge, UK, 1991.

Louth, Andrew. *The Origins of the Christian Mystical Tradition From Plato to Denys.*
Oxford University Press, Oxford, 1983.

Lowndes Sevely, Josephine. *Eve's Secrets: A New Theory of Female Sexuality.*
Random house, NY, 1987.

Lucas, George R. Jr. *The Rehabilitation of Whitehead: an Analytic and Historical Assessment of Process Philosophy.* State U. Press of NY, Albany, 1989.

Lull, Ramon (1232-1316). *The Book of the Lover and Beloved.* (E.A. Peers Trans.)
Paulist Press, N.Y. 1978.

Luther, A.R. "Marcel's Metaphysics of the We Are."
Philosophy Today, Vol. X, 3/4, 1966: pp. 190-203.

Luther, A.R. *Persons in Love: A Study of Max Scheler's "Wesen und Formen der Sympathie"* Martinus Nijhoff, The Hague, 1972.

MacGregor, Geddes . "A Christian Approach to Sex and Love"
In Scott Miners, 1984: pp. 133-149.

MacKenzie, Gordene Olga. *Transgender Nation.*
Bowling Green State University Press, Bowling Green, OH, 1994.

Macmurray, John. *Persons in Relation.*
Humanities Press Intl., Inc., Atlantic Highlands, NJ, (reprint) 1983.

Marcel, Gabriel. *Metaphysical Journal.* (Bernard Wall trans.)
Henry Regnery Company, Chicago, IL, 1952.

Marcel, Gabriel. *The Philosophy of Existentialism.* (Manya Harari trans.)
The Citadel Press, NY, 1963.

Marcel, Gabriel .*Creative Fidelity.* (Robert Rosthal trans.)
Farrar, Straus & Giroux, NY, 1964.

Marcel, Gabriel. *Being and Having: An Existentialist Diary.* (Katherine Farrer trans.)
Harper & Row, NY, 1965.

Marcel, Gabriel *The Mystery of Being. I Reflection & Mystery.* (G.S. Fraser trans.)
Henry Regnery Co., Chicago, IL, (5th Ptg.), 1969.

Marcel, Gabriel. *The Mystery of Being. II Faith & Reality.* (René Hague trans.) Henry Regnery Co., Chicago, IL, (5th Ptg.), 1968.

Marcel, Gabriel. *Presence and Immortality.* (Michael A. Machado & Henry J. Koren trans.)
Duquesne University Press, Pittsburgh, PA, 1967.

Marcel, Gabriel. *Tragic Wisdom and Beyond.* (Stephen Jolin & Peter McCormick trans.)
Northwestern Univ. Press, Evanston, IL, 1973.

Marías, Julián. *Metaphysical Anthropology: The empirical Structure of Human Life.* (Frances López-Morillas trans.) The Penn. State Univ. Press, U. Park/London, 1971.

Mariás, Julián. *Philosophy As Dramatic Theory.* (James Parsons trans.)
The Penn. State Univ. Press, University Park/London, 1971.

Martin, Luther H., Huck Gutman & Patrick Hutton (eds.). *Technologies of the Self: A Seminar with Michel Foucault.* U. Mass Press, Amherst, 1988.

Massey, Marilyn Chapin. *Feminine Soul: the Fate of an Ideal.*
Beacon Press, Boston 1985.

Matthews, Caitlín. *Sophia Goddess of Wisdom: The Divine Feminine from Black Goddess to World-Soul.* HarperCollins, London 1991.

Maturana, Humberto R. & Francisco Varela. *Autopoiesis and Cognition.*
D. Reidel Pub. Co., Dordrecht, Holland, 1980.

Maturana, Humberto R. & Francisco Varela. *The Tree of Knowledge: The Biological Roots of Human Understanding.* New Science Library, Boston, 1987.

Maximus Confessor (580-662 CE). *Selected Writings.* (George C. Bertthold trans.)
Paulist Press, Mahwah, NJ, 1985.

May, Rollo, Ernest Angel & Henri Ellenberger (eds.). *Existence: A new dimension in Psychiatry and Psychology* Basic Books, Inc., NY, 1959.

May, Rollo. *Love And Will.*
W.W. Norton & Co., NY, 1969.

May, Rollo. *The Discovery of Being: Writings in Existential Psychology.*
W.W. Norton & Co., NY/London, 1983

McClure, Vimala *The Ethics of Love.*
Nucleus Pub. Willow Springs, MO, 1992.

McCraty, Rollin, Mike Atkinson, William Tiller, Glen Rein, & Alan D. Watkins. "The Effects of Emotions on Short-Term Power Spectrum

Analysis of Heart Rate Variability" *The American Journal of Cardiology,* Vol. 76, No. 14, November 15, 1995: pp. 1089-1093.

McCormac, Earl R. *Metaphor and Myth in Science and Religion.*
Duke University Press, Durham, NC, 1976.

McCown, Joe. *Availability: Gabriel Marcel and the Phenomenology of Human Openness.*
Scholars Press, Missoula, MT, 1978.

McGhee, Michael (ed.). *Philosophy, Religion and the Spiritual Life.*
Royal Inst. of Philosophy Supp: 32, Cambridge University Press, Cambridge, UK.

Mead, G.R.S. *The Doctrine of the Subtle Body: in the Western Tradition.*
Solos Press, Dorset, England, 3 rd. Edition, (First Pub., 1919).

Meador, Betty De Shong. *Uncursing the Dark: Treasures from the Underworld.*
Chiron Pub., Wilamette, IL, 1992.

Megill, Allan. *Prophets of Extremity: Nietzsche, Heidegger, Foucault, Derrida.*
Univ. of California Press, Berkeley, 1985.

Meher Baba. *Discourses,* V. III.
Adi K. Irani, Ahmednagar, India, 1967.

Meldman, Louis William. *Mystical Sex.*
Harbinger House, Tucson, AZ, 1990.

Merchant, Carolyn. *The Death of Nature: Women, Ecology and the Scientific Revolution.*
Harper & Row, San Francisco, 1980.

Merejkowski, Dmitri. *The Secret of the West.* (John Cournos, Trans.)
Brewer, Warren & Putnam, NY, 1931.

Mernissi, Fatima. *The Veil and the Male Elite: A Feminist Interpretation of Women's Rights in Islam.*
Addison-Wesley Pub. Co., NY, 1992.

Merton, Thomas. *The Seven Storey Mountain.*
Harcourt, Brace & Co., NY, 1948.

Merton, Thomas. *No Man Is an Island.*
Harcourt brace Jovanovich, NY, 1955.

Merton, Thomas. *Mystics and Zen Masters.*
Dell Pub. Co. Inc., NY, (2nd. ptg.), 1967.

Merton, Thomas. *Life and Holiness.*
Image Books, NY 1964.

Merton, Thomas. *The Wisdom of the Desert: Sayings from the Desert Fathers of the Fourth Century.*
New Directions, NY, 1970.

Merton, Thomas. *New Seeds of Contemplation.*
New Directions, N.Y, 1972.

Merton, Thomas. *Disputed Questions.*
Farrar, Straus and Giroux, NY, (2nd ptg.), 1977.

Merton, Thomas. *The New Man.*
Farrar, Straus and Giroux, NY, 1978.

Merton, Thomas. *The Ascent To Truth.*
Harcourt Brace & Co., San Diego/NY/London, 1981.

Merton, Thomas. *Love and Living.* (Naomi Stone & Patrick Hart, eds.)
Farrar Straus Giroux, NY, 1979.

Merton, Thomas. *The Hidden Ground of Love: The Letters of T.M.,* (William H. Shannon ed.)
Farrar Straus Giroux, NY, 1985.

Metzger, Bruce M. & Michael D. Coogan (ed.). *The Oxford Companion to the Bible.*
Oxford U. Press, Ny/Oxford, 1993.

Mill, John Stuart & Harriet Taylor Mill. *Essays on Sex Equality.*
U. of Chicago Press, Chicago, IL. 1971.

Miners, Scott (ed.). *A Spiritual Approach to Male/Female Relations.*
Theosophical Pub. Hse. Wheaton, IL, 1984.

Miners, Scott. "Divorce and Separation" in Miners, Scott (ed.) *A Spiritual Approach to Male/Female Relations* Theosophical Pub. Hse. Wheaton, IL, 1984: pp. 45-54.

Mingle, Ida. *Science of Love With Key to Immortality.*
School of Liveable Christianity, Chicago, IL, 1926. (1976 reprint, Health Research)

***Mishnah*: Oral Teachings of Judaism.** (Eugene J. Lipman Sel. & Trans.)
W.W. Norton & Co. Inc., NY, 1970.

Moffat, James. *Love in the New Testament.*
Hodder & Stoughton Ltd., London, 1929

Mohler, James A. S.J. *Dimensions of Love: East and West.*
Doubleday & Co., NY, 1975.

Mollenkott, Virginia Ramey. *Women Men & the Bible.*
Abingdon, Nashville, TN, 1977.

Mollenkott, Virginia Ramey. *The Divine Feminine.*

Crossroad, NY, 1991.

Money, John. *Gay, Straight, and In-Between: The Sexology of Erotic Orientation.*
Oxford U. Press, NY, 1988.

Money, John. *The Adam Principle: Genes, Genitals, Hormones, & Gender.*
Prometheus Bks. Buffalo, NY, 1993.

Mooney, Christopher F. *Teilhard de Chardin and the Mystery of Christ.*
Harper & Row, Pub. NY 1966.

Moore, Justin R. (ed.) *Teachings From the Path of Fire: The Life and Works of Herman Rednick.*
Unpublished Manuscript, 1973.

Moore, Thomas. *Soul Mates: Honoring the Mysteries of Love and Relationship.*
HarperCollins, NY, 1994.

Morris, Colin. *The Discovery of the Individual 1050-1200.*
SPCK, London, 1972.

Moseley, Douglas & Naomi. *Dancing in the Dark: the Shadow Side of the Intimate Relationship.*
North Star Pub., Georgetown, MA, 1994.

Moss, Richard M. *The I That Is We.*
Celestial Arts, Berkeley, CA, 1981.

Mother Meera. *Answers.*
Meeramma Pub., Ithaca, NY, 1991.

Mother Teresa. *A Gift for God: Prayers and Meditations.*
Harper & Row, NY, 1975.

Mother Teresa. *Mother Teresa: Contemplative in the Heart of the World.*
Servant Books, Ann Arbor, MI, 1985.

Muktananda, Swami. *Guru.*
Harper Row, NY, 1971.

Muktananda, Swami. "Selections from Baba Muktananda" *Darshan.*
SYDA Foundation, South Fallsburg, NY, March 1994: pg. 23-27.

Murata, Sachiko. *The Tao of Islam: A Sourcebook of Gender Relaltionships in Islamic Thought.*
State University of NY Press, Albany, 1992.

Murphy, Cornelius F. Jr. *Beyond Feminism: Toward a Dialogue on Difference.*
The Catholic University of America Press, Washington, D.C., 1995.

Musil, Robert. *The Man Without Qualities.* (Eithne Wilkins & Ernst Kaiser trans.)
Capricorn Books, NY, (2 Vols.) 1965.

Nanda, Serena. *Neither Man nor Woman: the Hijras of India.*
Wadsworth Inc., Belmont, CA, 1990.

Nasr, Seyyed Hossein. "The Male and Female in the Islamic Perspective"
in: Nasr, S. H (ed.)
Traditional Islam in the Modern World. KPI, London, 1987: 47-58.

Nasr, Seyyed Hossein & William Stoddart (eds.). *Religion of the Heart.*
Foundation For Traditional Studies, Wash. D.C. 1991.

Nasr, Seyyed Hossein (ed.). *The Essential Writings of Frithjof Schuon.*
Amity House, Warwick, NY 1986.

Needleman, Jacob (ed.). *Being-in-the-World: Selected Papers of Ludwig Binswanger (1882-1966).*
Harper & Row, NY, 1968.

Needleman, Jacob (ed.). *The Sword of Gnosis: Metaphysics, Cosmology, Tradition, Symbolism.*
Penguin Books Inc. Baltimore, MD, 1974.

Needleman, Jacob. *A Little Book on Love.*
Bantam Doubleday Dell Pub. Group, Inc., NY, 1998.

Nesfield-Cookson, Bernard *Rudolf Steiner's Vision of Love.*
The Aquarian Press, Great Britain, 1983.

Neumann, Erich. *The Origins and History of Consciousness.* (Trans. R.F.C. Hull)
Bollingen Ser. XLII., NY, 1954.

Neusner, Jacob. *Androgynous Judaism: Masculine and Feminine in the Dual Torah.*
Mercer Univ. Press, Macon, GA, 1993.

Nicholas of Cusa (1401-1464). *The Vision of God.* (Trans. Emma G. Salter)
F. Ungar Pub. Co., NY, (2nd ptg.) 1969.

Nicholoson, Shirley (ed.). *The Goddess Re-awakening: The Feminine Principle Today.*
The Theosophical Pub. House, Wheaton, IL, 1989.

Nicolescu, Basarab. *Science, Meaning, & Evolution: The Cosmology of Jacob Boehme.* (Rob Baker Trans.) Parabola Books, NY, 1991.

Nikhilananda, Swami. *The Gospel of Sri Ramakrishna.*
Ramakrishna-Vivekananda Center, NY, (Abridged Ed.), 1970.

Nirodbaran. *Talks with Sri Aurobindo.*
Sri Aurobindo Ashram Pub., Calcutta; 1966.

Nygren, Anders. *Agape and Eros.* Pt. 1 & 2. (P.S. Watson, trans.)
The Westminster Press, Philadelphia, 1953.

O'Brien, Justin. *Christianity and Yoga: A Meeeting of Mystic Paths.* Arkana, London, 1989.

O'Connell, April & Vincent. *Choice And Change: The Psychology of Holistic Growth, Adjustment, and Creativity.* Prentice Hall, Englewood Cliffs, NJ, (4th Ed.), 1992.

Odin, Steve. *Process Metaphysics and Hua-yen Buddhism: a Critical Study of Cumulative Penetration vs. Interpenetration.* State U. of NY Press, Albany, 1982.

O'Flaherty, Wendy Doniger. *Women, Androgynes, and Other Mythical Beasts.* Univ. of Chicago Press, Chicago/London, 1980.

Oliver, Kelly. *Womanizing Nietzsche: Philosophy's Relation to the Feminine.* Routledge, NY/London, 1995.

Ong, Walter J. *The Presence of the Word: Some Prolegomena for Cultural and Religious History.*
Yale Univ. Press, New Haven & London, 1967.

Oppenheimer, Robert J. *Science and Common Understanding,* Simon & Schuster, NY, 1954.

Ortega Y Gasset, José. *On Love: aspects of a single theme.* (Toby Talbot trans.) The World Pub. Co., Cleveland/NY, 1957.

Otto, Rudolf. *Mysticism East and West.*
The Macmillan Co., NY, 1960.

Owens, Craig. "Outlaws: Gay Men in Feminism" In, *Men in Feminism.* Alice Jardine & Paul Smith
(eds.) Methuen, N.Y., 1987: pg. 219-232.

Pacteau, Francette. "The Impossible Referent: Representations of the Androgyne."
In *Formations of Fantasy,* Victor Burgin, et al., (eds.) Methuen, London, 1986.

Pagels, Elaine. *The Gnostic Gospels.*
Random House, NY, 1979.

Pagels, Elaine. *Adam, Eve, and the Serpent.*
Random House, NY, 1989

Pandit, M.P. *The Yoga of Love.*
Lotus Light Press, Wilmot, WI, 1982.

Parfit, Derek. *Reasons and Persons.*
Oxford Univ. Press, Oxford/NY, 1986.

Parkes, Graham (ed.). *Heidegger and Asian Thought.*
University of Hawaii Press, Honolulu, 1990.

Patai, Raphael. *The Hebrew Goddess.*
Wayne State Univ. Press. Detroit, MI, (3ʳᵈ. Ed.), 1990.

Payne, Richard. "Circles of Love: In Search of a Spirituality of Sexuality and Marriage."
In Gupta, Bina (Ed.) 1987: pp. 51-70.

Pearsall, Paul. *The Ten Laws of Lasting Love.*
Avon Books, NY, 1995.

Peat, David F. *Synchronicity: the Bridge Between Mind and Matter.*
Bantam Books, NY, 1988.

Peck, M. Scott. *The Road Less Traveled.*
Simon & Schuster, NY, 1978.

Pentateuch. Alexander Harkavy (English Trans.)
Hebrew Pub. Co., NY, 1966.

Perry, Whitall N. *The Widening Breach: Evolutionism in the Mirror of Cosmology.*
Quinta Essentia, Cambridge, UK, 1995.

Philo (25 BCE-before 50 CE). In *Three Jewish Philosophers.* (Selections edited by Hans Lewy)
Harper & Row, NY, 1965.

Pike, Nelson. *Mystic Union.*
Cornell U. Press, Ithaca, NY, 1992.

Pintar, Judith. *The Halved Soul: Retelling the Myths of Romantic Love.*
Harper/Collins, NY, 1992.

Pirani, Alix . *The Absent Mother.*
HarperCollins, London 1991.

Plato. *The Works of Plato.* (I. Edman Ed.) (Jowett Trans.)
Random House, NY, 1928.

Plato. "The Seventh Letter." (J. Harward trans.) In *Great Books:* V. 7, *The Dialogues of Plato.*
Encyclopædia Britannica, Inc, Chicago, 1952.

Plato. *Timaeus.* (Francis M.Cornford trans.)
Bobbs-Merril Co. Inc., NY, (6ᵗʰ. ptg.), 1959.

Plato. *The Symposium and The Phaedo.* (Raymond Larson trans.)
AHM Pub. Corp., Arlington Heights IL, 1980.

Plato. *On Homosuxuality: Lysis, Phaedrus, & Symposium.* Jowett trans.
(Eugene O'Connor ed.) Prometheus Bks. Buffalo, NY, 1991.

Plotinus (204-270 CE). *The Enneads.* (S. MacKenna trans.)
Penguin Books, London, 1991.

Pogacnik, Marko. *The Daughter of Gaia: Rebirth of the Divine Feminine.*
Findhorn Press, The Park Findhorn, Scotland, 2001.

Pseudo Dionysius (6th. CE). *Complete Works.* (Colm Luibheid trans.)
Paulist Press, NY, 1987.

Quran. (Abdullah Yusuf Ali, English translation & commentary)
Sh. Muhammad Ashraf Pub., Lahore, No Date.

Rader, Rosemary. *Breaking Boundaries: Male/Female Friendship in Early Christian Communities.*
Paulist Press, NY, 1983.

Ranke-Heinemann, Uta. *Eunuchs For the Kingdom of Heaven.*
Doubleday, NY, 1990.

Rednick, Herman. *The Earth Journey: from Birth to Fulfillment.*
Vantage Press, NY, 1980.

Rednick, Herman. *The Hidden Door to Reality.*
Open Door Pub., Questa, NM, 1982.

Rednick, Herman. *The Beloved Yoga.*
Herman Rednick Archival Project, Memoir #1; H. R. Trust, Questa, NM, 1993.

Rednick, Herman. *The Hermanic Dialogues on Practical Mysticism.*
Herman Rednick Archival Project, Memoir #2; H. R. Trust, Questa, NM, 1993.

Rednick, Herman. *Living in the Presence.*
Herman Rednick Archival Project, Memoir #3; H. R. Trust, Questa, NM, 1994.

Rednick, Herman. *Conversations on the Life and Ministry of Jesus the Christ.*
Herman Rednick Archival Project, Memoir #5; H. R. Trust, Questa, NM, 1994.

Reichmann, James B. (S.J.). *Philosophy of the Human Person.*
Loyola Press, Chicago, 1985.

Remen, Rachel Naomi. "In the Service of Life"
Noetic Sciences Review, Spring, 1996: pp. 24-5.

Rescher, Nicolas. *Process Metaphysics: An Introduction to Process Philosophy.*
State Univ. of NY Press, Albany, 1996.

Richter, Horst-Eberhard. *All Mighty: A Study of the God Complex in Western Man.* (Jan van Heurck trans.) Hunter House Inc. Pub., Claremont, CA, 1984.

Rist, John M. *Eros and Psyche.*
Univ, of Totonto Press, Totonto, Canada, 1964.

Roche de Coppens, Peter. *Divine Light and Fire.*
Element, Inc. Rockport, MA, 1992.

Roche de Coppens, Peter. *Spiritual Perspective II: The Spiritual Dimension and Implications of Love, Sex, and Marriage.* UPA, Washington, DC, 1981.

Roerich, Helena. *Letters of Helena Roerich . V.1.*
Agni Yoga Soc., NY, 1954.

Rosenzweig, Franz. *The Star of Redemption.* (William W. Hallo trans.)
Beacon Press, Boston, MA, 1972.

Ross, Mary Ellen. "The Ethical Limitations of Autonomy: A Critique of the Moral Vision of Psychological Man," in Paula Cooey *Embodied Love,* 1983: pp. 152-168.

Rossi, Alice S. (ed.). *Essays on Sex Equality: John Stuart Mill & Harriet Taylor Mill.*
Univ. of Chicago Press, Chicago/London, 1970.

Rubin, Lillian, B. *Intimate Strangers.*
Harper & Row, NY, 1983.

Sadler, William A. *Existence & Love: a New Approach In Existential Phenomenology.*
Chas. Scribner's & Sons, NY, 1969.

Salzberg, Sharon. *Loving Kindness: The Revolutionary Art of Happiness.*
Shamballa, Boston, 1995.

Sammons, Jeffrey L. *Angelus Silesius.*
Twayne Pub., NY, 1967.

Saraydarian, Torkom. (1917-1997) *Woman: The Torch of the Future.*
A.E.G., Sedona, AZ, 1980.

Saraydarian, Torkom. *The Flame of Beauty, Culture, Love, Joy.*
A.E.G., Sedona, Az., 1980.

Saraydarian, Torkom. *The Psyche and Psychism. V. I & II*
A.E.G., Agoura, CA, 1981.

Saraydarian, Torkom. *Sex, Family, and the Woman in Society.*
A.E.G., Sedona, AZ, 1987.

Sardello, Robert. *Love and the Soul: Creating a Future for Earth.*
HarperCollins, NY, 1995.

Satprem. *Sri Aurobindo or The Adventure of Consciousness.*
Sri Aurobindo Ashram, Pondicherry, 1968.

Schaya, Leo. *The Universal Meaning of the Kabbalah.* (Nancy Pearson trans.)
George Allen & Unwin Ltd., London, 1971.

Scheler, Max. *Ressentiment.* (William W. Holdheim trans.)
The Free Press, NY, 1961.

Scheler, Max. *Selected Philosophical Essays.* (David Lachterman trans.)
Northwestern U. Press, Evanston, IL, 1973.

Scheler, Max. *The Nature of Sympathy.* (Peter Heath trans.)
Archon Books, Camden, CT, 1973.

Scheler, Max. *Formalism in Ethics and Non-Formal Ethics of Values* (Manfred Frings and Roger Funk Trans.) Northwestern U. Press, Evanston, IL, 1973.

Scheler, Max. "On The Idea Of Man" (Clyde Nabe trans.)
Journal of the British Society for Phenomenology V. 9 No. 3, 1978: pp.184-198.

Scheler, Max. *On Feeling, Knowing, and Valuing: Selected Writings.* (Harold J. Bershady, Ed.)
U. of Chicago Press, Chicago, IL, 1992.

Schmidt, Paul F. *Perception and Cosmology in Whitehead's Philosophy.*
Rutgers Univ. Press, New Brunswick, NJ, 1967.

Schmidt, Paul F. *Rebelling, Loving and Liberation: A Metaphysics of the Concrete.*
Hummingbird Press, Albuquerque, NM, 1971.

Scholem, Gershom. *Major trends in Jewish Mysticism.*
Schocken Bks., NY, 1974.

Scholem, Gershom. *Zohar: the Book of Splendor.* (Sel. & Ed.)
Schocken Bks. NY, 1971.

Scholem, Gershom. *On the Mystical Shape of the Godhead.*
Schocken Bks. NY, 1991.

Schor, Naomi. "Dreaming Dissymmetry: Barthes, Foucault, and Sexual Difference."
In *Men in Feminism.* Alice Jardine & Paul Smith (eds.), 1987: pp. 98-110.

Schott, Robin May. *Cognition and Eros: A Critique of the Kantian Paradigm.*
Beacon Press, Boston, 1988.

Schrag, Calvin O. *Experience and Being: Prolegomena to a Future Ontology.*
Northwestern U. Press, Evanston, 1969.

Schrag, Calvin O. *Radical Reflection and the Origin of the Human Sciences.*
Purdue U. Press, West Lafayette, IN, 1980.

Schrödinger, Erwin. *What is Life? and Mind and Matter,*
Cambridge U. Press, London, 1969.

Schuon, Frithjof. *From the Divine to the Human.*
World Wisdom Bks. Bloomington, IN, 1982.

Schuon, Frithjof. *The Transcendent Unity of Religions.*
Quest Books, Wheaton, IL, 1984.

Schutz, Alfred & Thomas Luckmann. *The Structures of the Life-World.*
(Richard Zaner & Tristram   Engelhardt trans.)
Northwestern U. Press, Evanston, IL, 1973.

Sennett, Richard. *Authority.*
Random House, NY, 1981.

Shah, Idries. *The Sufis.*
Doubleday & Co., NY, 1964.

Sharma, Arvind (ed.). *Today's Woman in World Religions.*
State U. of NY Press, Albany, 1994.

Shaw, Miranda. *Passionate Enlightenment: Women in Tantric Buddhism..*
Princeton U. Press, Princeton, NJ, 1994.

Sheldrake, Rupert. *Seven Experiments That Could Change the World.*
Riverhead Books, NY, 1995.

Sheldrake, Rupert. *A New Science of Life: The Hypothesis of Formative Causation.*
J.P. Tarcher, Inc., Los Angeles, 1981.

Shelly, Percy Bysshe *Selected Poetry.*
Bloom, Harold (ed.) Signet, NY, 1966.

Shepperd, A. P. *Marriage Was Made For Man.*
Methuen & Co. Ltd., London, 1958.

Sherrard, Philip *Christianity and Eros: Essays on the theme of sexual love.*
SPCK, London, 1976.

Sherrard, Philip. *The Eclipse of Man and Nature.*
Lindisfarne Press, West Stockbridge, MA, 1987.

Sherrard, Philip *The Sacred in Life and Art.*
Golgonooza Press, Ipswich, U.K., 1990.

Sherrard, Philip. "Man and Woman: An Evaluation of their Relationship in the Christian
Perspective." In Nasr 1991: pp. 256-277.

Sherrard, Philip. *Human Image: World Image: the Death and Resurrection of Sacred Cosmology.*
Golgonooza Press, Ipswich, UK, 1992.

Shestov, Lev. *Athens and Jerusalem.* (Bernard Martin trans.)
Simon and Schuster, NY, 1968.

Shideler, Mary McDermott. *The Theology of Romantic Love: a study in the writings of Charles Williams.* Harper & Bros., NY, 1962.

Schierse-Leonard, Linda. *On the Way to the Wedding: Transformation of the Love Relation.* Shamballa, Boston, 1986.

Showalter, Elaine. *Sexual Anarchy: Gender & Culture at the Fin de Siècle.* Viking Penguin, NY, 1990.

Siegel, Bernie S. *Love, Medicine & Miracles.* Harper & Row, NY, 1986.

Silbury, Lira. *The Sacred Marriage.* Llewelyn Worldwide, St. Paul, MN, 1995.

Simmel, Georg. *On Women, Sexuality, and Love.* Yale U. Press, New Haven/London, 1984.

Singer, Irving. *The Pursuit of Love.* The Johns Hopkins U. Press, Baltimore, 1994.

Singer, Irving. *The Nature of Love I: Plato to Luther.* U. of Chicago Press, Chicago, (2nd. ed.) 1984.

Singer, Irving. *The Nature of Love II: Courtly & Romantic.* U. of Chicago Press, Chicago, 1984.

Singer, Irving. *The Nature of Love III: The Modern World.* U. of Chicago U. Press, Chicago, 1987.

Singer, June. *Androdyny: Toward a New Theory of Sexuality.* Doubleday, NY, 1977.

Sivaraman, Krishna. "The Mysticism of Male-Female Relationships: Some Philosophical and Lyrical Motifs of Hinduism." In Gupta (ed.), 1987: pp. 87-105.

Skolimowski, Henryk. *The Participatory Mind: A New Theory of Knowledge and of the Universe..* Penguin Books Ltd., London, 1994.

Slesinski, Robert. *Pavel Florensky: A Metaphysics of Love.* St. Vladimir's Seminary Press, Crestwood, NY, 1984.

Smith, Huston. *Forgotten Truth: the Common Vision of the World's Religions.* Harper San Francisco, 1992.

Smith, Steven G. *Gender Thinking.* Temple University Press, Philadelphia, PA, 1992.

Smith, Wolfgang. *Cosmos & Transcendence: Breaking Through the Barrier of Scientistic Belief.* Sherwood Sugden & Co. Pub., Peru, IL, (3rd. Ptg.) 1990.

Soble, Alan. *The Structure of Love.*
Yale U. Press, 1993.

Sogyal Rinpoche .*The Tibetan Book of Living and Dying.* (Patrick Gafney & Andrew Harvey eds.)
Harper SanFrancisco, 1992.

Solomon, Robert C. *Reinventing Romance for our Times.*
Simon & schuster, NY, 1988.

Solomon, Robert C. *Love: Emotion, Myth & Metaphor.*
Doubleday, NY, 1981.

Solovyov, Vladimir. *The Justification of the Good: An Essay on Moral Philosophy.* (Nathalie A. Duddington, Trans.) The Macmillan Co., NY, 1918.

Solovyov, Vladimir. *The Meaning Of Love.* (Thomas Beyer, trans. and ed. & Introduction by Owen Barfield) Lindisfarne Press, Stockbridge, MA, 1985.

Sonam Rinchen. *The 37 Practices of Bodhisattvas.* (Ruth Sonam trans. & ed.)
Snow Lion, NY, 1997.

Sorokin, Pitrim A. *The Ways and Power of Love.*
Henry Regnery Co., Gateway edition, Chicago, 1967.

Sorokin, Pitrim A. "The Mysterious Energy of Love"
In Scott Miners, 1984: pp. 55-68.

Soskice, Janet Martin "Love and Attention"
In Michael McGhee, 1992: pp. 59-72.

Spencer, Sidney. *Mysticism in World Religion.*
Penguin Books, Baltimore, MD, 1963.

Spink, Kathryn. *The Miracle of Love: Mother Teresa of Calcutta, Her Missionaries of Charity, and her Co-Workers.* Harper & Row, Pub., NY, 1981.

Spink, Kathryn (ed.). *Life in the Spirit: Reflections, Meditations, Prayers.*
Harper & Row, San Francisco, CA, 1983.

St. John of the Cross (1542-1591). *The Collected Works.* (K. Kavanaugh & O. Rodriguez trans.) Institute of Carmelite Studies, DC, 1979.

St. Teresa of Avila (1515-1582). *The Collected Works,* V.2. (K. Kavanaugh & O. Rodriguez trans.)
Institute of Carmelite Studies, DC, 1980.

Steindl-Rast, Brother David. *A Listening Heart: the Art of Contemplative Living.*
Crossroad, NY, 1983.

Steindl-Rast, Brother David. *Gratefulness, the Heart of Prayer.*
Paulist Press, Ramsey, NJ, 1984.

Steiner, George. *Real Presences: Is there anything in what we say?*
Faber & Faber, London & Boston, 1989.

Steiner, Rudolf .*Metamorphoses of the Soul.* (G. Metaxa trans.)
Anthroposophic Press, NY, ND (1939 ?).

Steiner, Rudolf. *Man's Life on Earth and in the Spiritual Worlds.* (George &
Mary Adams trans.) Anthroposophical Pub. Co., London, 1952.

Steiner, Rudolf. *The Redemption of Thinking: a Study in the Philosophy of
Thomas Aquinas.*
Hodder and Stoughton, London, 1956.

Steiner, Rudolf. *The Case for Anthroposophy.*
Rudolf Steiner Press, London, 1970

Steiner, Rudolf. *Eleven European Mystics.* (Karl E. Zimmer trans.)
Rudolf Steiner Pub. Blauvelt, NY, 1971.

Steiner, Rudolf. *The Wisdom of Man, of the Soul, and of the Spirit.*
Anthroposophic Press, NY, 1971.

Steiner, Rudolf. *An Outline of Occult Science.*
Anthroposiphic Press Inc., Spring Valley, NY, 1972.

Steiner, Rudolf. *Christianity as Mystical Fact: and the Mysteries of Antiquity.*
Anthroposophic Press Inc., NY, (2nd ed.) 1972.

Steiner, Rudolf. *The Riddles of Philosophy.*
The Anthroposophic Press, Spring Valley, NY, 1973.

Steiner, Rudolf *Christianity in Human Evolution.*
The Anthroposophic Press, Spring Valley, NY, (2 ptg.) 1979.

Steiner, Rudolf. *The Origin of Suffering, The Origin of Evil, Illness an Death.*
Steiner Book Center, North Vancouver, Canada, 1980.

Steiner, Rudolf. *Goethe's Secret Revelation and the Riddle in Faust.*
Tresmegistus Press, Ferndale, MI, 1980.

Steiner, Rudolf. "Man and Woman in Light of Spiritual Science" *The
Anthroposophical Review* V.2, No. 1, Winter 1980: pp. 10-13.

Steiner, Rudolf. *Genesis: Secrets of the Bible Story of Creation.*
Rudolf Steiner Press, London 1982.

Steiner, Rudolf .*The Search for the New Isis, Divine Sophia.*
Mercury Press Spring Valley, NY, 1983.

Steiner, Rudolf. *The Reappearance of Christ in the Etheric.*
The Anthroposophic Press, Spring Valley, NY, 1983.

Steiner, Rudolf. *Woman and Society.*
Rudolf Steiner Press, London 1985.

Steiner, Rudolf. *Learning to See into the Spiritual World.*
Anthroposophic Press, Hudson, NY, 1990.

Steiner, Rudolf *Love and Its Meaning in the World.*
Anthroposophic Press, Hudson, NY, 1998.

Steinsaltz, Adin. *The Strife of the Spirit.* (Selected by Arthur Kurzweil)
Jason Aronson Inc. Northvale, NJ, 1988.

Steinsaltz, Adin. *The Long Shorter Way: Discourses on Chasidic Thought.*
(Yehuda Hanegbi trans.)
Jason Aronson Inc. Northvale, NJ, 1988.

Stern, David H. *Complete Jewish Bible*
Jewish New Testament Pub. Clarksville, MD & Jerusalem, 1998.

Stern, David H. *Jewish New Testament.Commentary.*
Jewish New Testament Pub. Inc. Clarksville, MD, (5th Ed.), 1996.

Straw, Carole. *Gregory the Great: Perfection in Imperfection.*
Univ. of California Press, Berkeley/Los Angeles, 1988.

Strémooukoff, Dimitri. *Vladimir Soloviev & His Messianic Work.* (E. Meyendorff trans.)
Nordland Pub. Co., Belmont, MA, 1980.

Stuart, Micheline. *The Tarot: Path to Self Development.*
Shambala, Boston, 1990.

Sugerman, Shirley (ed.). *Evolution of Consciousness: Studies in Polarity.*
Wesleyan U. Press, Middletown, CT, 1976.

Sutton, Jonathan. *The Religious Philosophy of Vladimir Solovyov.*
Macmillan, London, 1988.

Sussman, Irving & Jessey, Cornelia. *Spiritual Partners, Profiles in Creative Marriage.*
Crossroads Pub, NY, 1982.

Suzuki, Daisetsu Teitaro. *Mysticism: Christian and Buddhist.*
Allen & Unwin Ltd, London, (re-issue), 1988.

Swedenborg, Emanuel. *Conjugial Love.*
American Swedenborg Ptg. & Pub. Soc., NY, 1912.

Talbot, Michael. *Mysticism and the New Physics.*
Bantam Books, N.Y. 1981.

Talbot, Michael. *The Holographic Universe.*
HarperCollins, NY, 1991.

Tannen, Deborah. *You Just Don't Understand: Women & Men in Conversation.* Wm. Morrow & Co., NY, 1990.

Tavard, George *Woman in Christian Tradition.* Univ. of Notre Dame Press, Notre Dame, IN, 1973.

Teilhard de Chardin, Pierre. *The Divine Milieu: An Essay on the Interior Life.* Harper & Row, NY, 1965.

Teilhard de Chardin, Pierre. *The Phenomenon of Man.* Harper & Row, NY, (2nd. ed.), 1965.

Teilhard de Chardin, Pierre. *On Love.* Harper & Row, NY, 1967.

Teilhard de Chardin, Pierre *Writings in time of War.* Harper & Row, NY, 1968.

Teilhard de Chardin, Pierre. *Human Energy.* Harcourt Brace Jovanovich, NY, 1969.

Teilhard de Chardin, Pierre. *Christianity and Evolution.* Harcourt Brace Jovanovich, Pub., NY, 1969.

Teilhard de Chardin, Pierre. *Activation of Energy.* Harcourt Brace Jovanovich, NY, 1970.

Teilhard de Chardin, Pierre. *Toward the Future.* Harcourt Brace Jovanovich, NY, 1975.

Teilhard de Chardin, Pierre. *The Heart of Matter.* Harcourt Brace Jovanovich, NY, 1980.

Terrien, Samuel. *Till the Heart Sings: A Biblical Theology of Manhood & Womanhood.* Fortress Press, Philadelphia, PA, 1985.

Theunissen, Michael. *The Other: Studies in the Social Ontology of Husserl, Heidegger, Sartre, and* Buber (Christopher Macann trans.) MIT Press, Cambridge, MA, 1986.

Thompson, Henry O. "Cooperative Contributions to Community." In Bina Gupta (Ed.), 1987: pp. 156-186.

Thunberg, Lars. *Man andthe Cosmos:theVision of St. Maximus the Confessor.* St. Vladimir's Seminary Press, Crestwood, NY, 1985.

Thunberg, Lars. *Microcosm and Mediator: The Theological Anthropology of Maximus the Confessor.* Open Court, Chicago & La Salle, IL, (2nd. Ed.), 1995.

Thich Nhat Hanh. *Living Buddha, Living Christ.* G.P Putman's Sons, NY, 1995.

Tiefer, Leonore. *Sex Is Not a Natural Act.*
Westwiew Press, Boulder, CO, 1995.

Tillich, Paul (1886-1965). *Bibilical Religion and The Search For Ultimate Reality.*
Univ. of Chicago Press, 1955.

Tillich, Paul. *The Dynamics of Faith.*
Harper & Row, NY, 1958.

Tillich, Paul. Theology of Culture. (Robert C. Kimball, Ed.)
Oxford University Press, NY, 1959.

Tillich, Paul. *Love, Power, and Justice: Ontological Analyses and Ethical Applications.*
Oxford Univ. Press, NY, 1960.

Tillich, Paul. *The Eternal Now.*
Charles Scribner's sons, NY, 1963.

Tillich, Paul. *Systematic Theology,* Vol. II.
University of Chicago Press, 1975.

Tillich, Paul. *Systematic Theology,* Vol. III.
University of Chicago Press, 1976.

Tobin, Thomas H. *The Creation of Man: Philo and the History of Interpretation.*
The Catholic Biblical Assn. of America, Washington, DC, 1983.

Tomberg, Valentin. *Inner Development.*
Candeur Manuscripts, Spring Valley, NY, 1983.

Tomberg, Valentin. *Anthroposophical Studies of the New Testament.*
Candeur Manuscripts, Spring Valley, NY, 1981.

Tracy, David & Nicholas Lash (ed.). *Cosmology and Theology.*
The Seabury Press, NY, 1983.

Trebilcot, Joyce. "Two Forms of Androgynism," In Mary Vertterling-Braggin, (ed.)*"Femininity,"*
"Masculinity," and "Androgyny," 1982: pp. 70-78.

Trismegistus, Hermes Mercurius. *The Virgin of the World.*
Wizards Book Shelf, Minneapolis, MN, 1977.

Upanishads. (Swami Prabhavananda & Frederick Manchester trans.)
Mentor books, NY, (6 th. Ptg.), 1957.

Urwick, E.J. *The Platonic Quest.*
Concord Grove Press, Santa Barbara, CA, 1983.

Van Arsdale, Minor Robert. *Poems for the Spiritual Path.*
Vantage Press, NY, 1979.

van Emmichoven, F.W. Zeylmans. *The Anthroposophical Understaning of the Soul.*
Anthroposophic Press, Spring Valley, NY, 1982.

Varela, Francisco J. & Evan Thompson & Eleanor Rosch. *The Embodied Mind: Cognitive Science and Human Experience.* MIT Press, Cambridge, MA, 1993.

Versluis, Arthur. *TheoSophia.*
Lindesfarne Press, NY, 1994.

Vertterling-Braggin, Mary (ed.). *"Femininity," "Masculinity," and "Androgyny"*
Rowman & Allanheld Pub., Totowa, NJ, 1982.

Vertterling-Braggin, Mary, Frederick A. Elliston & Jane English (ed.). *Feminism and Philosophy.*
Rowman and Littlefield, Totowa, NJ, 1977.

Vissell, Barry & Joyce. *The Shared Heart.*
Ramira Pub. Aptos, CA, 1984. (1st. Ed.)

von Balthasar, Hans Urs. *A Theological Anthropology.*
Sheed and Ward, NY, 1967.

von Balthasar, Hans Urs. *Origen, Spirit And Fire.* (Robert J. Daly, Trans.)
Catholic U. of America Press, Washington, DC, 1984.

von le Fort, Gertrud .*The Eternal Woman.* (Marie C. Buehrle trans.)
The Bruce Pub. Co., Milwaukee, 1954.

Waite, A.E. *The Unknown Philosopher: The Life of Louis Claude de Saint-Martin and the Substance of His Transcendental Doctrine.* Rudolf Steiner Pub. Blauvelt, NY, 1970.

Waite, A.E. *The Holy Kabbalah.*
Carol Pub. Grp. NY, 1990.

Wallace, B. Alan. *Choosing Reality: A Buddhist View of Physics and the Mind.*
Snow Lion Pub., Ithaca, NY, 1996.

Wallerstein, Judith S. & Sandra Blakeslee. *The Good Marriage.*
Houghton Mifflin, 1995.

Walter, John L. & Jane E. Peller. *Becoming Solution-focused in Brief Therapy.*
Brunner/Mazel Pub., NY, 1992.

Watkins, Mary. *Waking Dreams.*
Spring Pub. Inc., Dallas, Texas, (3rd. Ed.), 1988

Watzlawick, Paul. *How Real Is Real?*
Random House, NY, 1977.

Watzlawick, Paul. (ed.). *The Invented Reality: How Do We Know What We Believe We Know?*
W.W. Norton & Co., NY/London, 1984.

Watzlawick, Paul. *Ultra-Solutions: or How to Fail Most Successfully.*
WW Norton & Co., NY, 1988.

Watts, Alan W. *Nature, Man and Woman.*
Mentor Bks., NY, (4th. ptg.), 1958.

Weber, Renée. "Plato's Ladder of Love"
In Scott Miners, 1984: pp. 71-82.

Weeks, Andrew. *German Mysticism from Hildegard of Bingen to Ludwig Wittgenstein.*
State Univ. of NY Press, Albany, 1993.

Wehr, Gerhard .*The Mystical Marriage: Symbol and Meaning of the Human Experience.*
Aquarian Press; Northhamptonshire, England 1990.

Weil, Kari. *Androgyny: and the Denial of Difference.*
U. Press of Virginia, Charlottesville, VA, 1992.

Weiner, Philip P. *Leibniz: Selections.*
Charles Scribner's Sons, NY, 1951.

Weiner-Davis, Michele. *Divorce Busting.*
Simon & Schuster, NY, 1993.

Welwood, John. *Journey of the Heart: the Path of Conscious Love.*
HarperCollins Pub., NY, (reissue), 1996.

Whitehead, Alfred North. *Science and the Modern World.*
The Free Press, NY, 1967.

Whyte, Lancelot Law. *The Unconscious before Freud.*
Julian Friedmann Pub., London, 1978.

Wiedemann, Frederic. *Between Two Worlds: the Riddle of Wholeness.*
The Theosphical Pub. House, Wheaton, IL, 1986.

Wilhelm, Richard (trans. & ed.). *The Secret of the Golden Flower: a Chinese Book of Life.*
Harcourt Brace & Co., NY, 1962.

Wilhelm, Richard (trans.). *The I Ching.* (Cary Baynes Eng. trans.)
Princeton Univ. Press, Princeton, NJ, 1967.

Williams, Charles. *The Descent of the Dove: A Short History of the Holy Spirit in the Church.*
William B. Eerdmans Pub. Co., Grand Rapids, MI, 1939, (1972 reprint).

Williams, Charles. *Outlines of Romantic Theology.*
William B. Eerdmans Pub. Co., Grand Rapids, MI, 1990.

Williams, Charles. *The Figure of Beatrice: A Study of Dante.*
D. S. Brewer, Cambridge, (Reprinted) 2000.

Williams, Charles (1886-1945). *Religion and Love in Dante: The Theology of Romantic Love.*
Dacre Press, Westminster, 1994.

Williams, Michael A. "Uses of Gender Imagery in Ancient Gnostic Texts," In Caroline Bynum,
Gender and Religion: On the Complexity of Symbols, 1986: pp. 196-227.

Wilson, Peter L. *Angels.*
Pantheon Bks., NY, 1980.

Wilson, Peter L. *Scandal: Essays in Islamic Heresy.*
Autonomedia. Brooklyn, NY, 1988.

Wilson, Robert Anton. *Quantum Psychology.*
New Falcon Pub., Phoenix, AZ, 1990.

Winterson, Jeanette. *Sexing the Cherry.*
The Atlantic Monthly Press, NY, 1990.

Wojtyla, Karol (Pope John Paul II). *Love and Responsibility.* (H.T. Willetts trans.)
Farrar Straus Giroux, NY, (2 nd, ptg.) 1994.

Yazdi, Mehdi Ha'iri. *The Principles of Epistemology in Islamic Philosophy: Knowledge by Presence.*
State U. of NY Press, Albany, 1992.

Young, Shinzen. "Observing & Opening: A Practical Method for Transforming Physical Pain into Spiritual Growth." *Shambhala Sun*, V. 5, No. 4 (March 1997): pp.50-54 & 57-61.

Zaner, Richard M. *The Problem of Embodiment: some contributions to a phenomenology of the body.*
Martinus Nijof, the Hague, 1964.

Zaner, Richard M. *The Context of Self: A Phenomenological Inquiry Using Medicine as a Clue.*
Ohio Univ. Press, Athens, OH, 1981.

Zerin, Edward. *The Birth of the Torah.*
Appleton-Century-Crofts, NY, 1962.

Zolla, Elémire. *The Androgyne: Reconciliation of Male & Female.*
Crossroad, NY, 1981.

Zweig, Paul. *The Heresy of Self-Love.*
Princeton Univ. Press, Princeton, NJ, 1980.

• NOTES FOR THE INTRODUCTION •

1. Unpublished papers, 1975 approximate date.

2. Herman Rednick (1902-1985) was an artist and spiritual teacher. His paintings depict the spiritual worlds that were the Reality in which he dwelt. Throughout his life people were drawn to seek his counsel and guidance, attracted by his wisdom, compassion, and light. He moved to Taos, N.M. in 1949, where he taught meditation classes which synthesized Eastern yoga techniques with Western Esoteric Christianity. Information about his teachings, his books, and paintings may be obtained from: The Herman Rednick Trust, HC 81 Box 6012, Questa, NM 87556 or www. fireintheheart.net.

3. In 1847 Soren Kierkegaard wrote that, "there is a commonly accepted figure of speech, used by everyone, which compares life to a way. The simile can certainly be used to advantage in many ways, but the necessary unlikeness implied in the figure is not less worth attention. In the material sense the way is an external reality, indifferent as to whether anyone travels on it or not, indifferent as to how the individual travels it the way is the way. In the spiritual sense, on the contrary, the way naturally cannot be physically pointed out. It does in a certain sense indeed exist, whether anyone travels it or not; and yet in another sense it only really becomes a way, or it becomes a way for each individual who travels it; the way is: *how it is traveled* (*The Gospel of Suffering*, 1948: p. 97). It is of the utmost importance, to keep in mind that, "the way is how it is traveled" and thus each person's path is unique. This has been said in many ways and recently the biologist, Francisco Varela, strongly made the point that, "a path exists only in walking" (Francisco Varela *The Embodied Mind*, 1993: p. 241). This certainly seems to echo Martin Heidegger: "We respond to the way only by remaining underway.... In order to get underway, we do have to set out. This is meant in a double sense: for one thing, we have to open ourselves to the emerging prospect and direction of the way itself; and then, we must get on the way, that is, must take the steps by which alone the way becomes a way.... Only when we walk it, and in no other fashion...are we on the move on the way" (*What is Called Thinking?* 1968: pp. 168-9). "Way," "path," "road," "yoga," etc. all have the same meaning in our discussions. We use this designation to refer to the coherent and open-ended "system" of concepts and exercises which we present in this book. We also refer to the the practice of this system as following the "Way of the

Beloved." The Way of the Beloved is not a recipe for enlightenment, but a dynamic life-process—a mode of a loving couple's *being-with* each other and in the world with other persons. In this sense, each religion also offers a "way" which it considers unique, but which is, in many cases, not so open-ended. For instance, Whitall Perry shows us the wide range of the notion of way : "Tao can be rendered simply as 'Way', just as in Buddhism, the Mâhâyâna is the 'Great Way', and in Hinduism, the Deva-yâna is the 'Way of the Gods', while in Christianity Christ says, 'I am the Way.' In Judaism Moses leads the Israelites out of Egypt and shows the Way to the Holy Land, so in Islam the Prophet leads the Way into Mecca. Interiorly this is the 'Straight Way' (*sirat al-mustaquim*; the *Sufiq tariqah* = Way), the 'Straight Way' of the Gospels, and 'Red Road' of the Sioux, or 'Holy Path' (*Shôdô*) of the Japanese....the Way can equally be envisaged as Pilgrimage (to Jerusalem, Mecca, Lhasa, Benares, Ise), or as a Quest (for the Holy Grail, the Terrestrial Paradise, the Fountain of Immortality) or a Voyage" (Perry is quoted in Anna Lemkow, *The Wholeness Principle*, 1990: p. 176). It is an interesting fact that, "if we call the early disciples 'Christians', we may use this as a term of convenience, but such use at this stage [i.e., prior to 41 CE] is an anachronism. The name "Christian" did not come into use until the gentile mission began, several years later; it was Greek-speaking inhabitants of Syrian Antioch who coined it [Acts 11:26]. The disciples themselves called their movement 'The Way'" (F. F.Bruce *New Testament History*, 1980: p. 213). We would also want to include the sense of way mentioned by Martin Heidegger: "By 'way,' or 'how,' we mean something other than manner or mode. 'Way' here means melody, the ring and tone, which is not just a matter of how the saying sounds. The way or how of the saying is the tone from which and to which what is said is attuned" (Graham Parkes *Heidegger and Asian Thought*, 1990: p. 217). Keep in mind that, despite having to refer to *the* path or *the* way as if it were an object (a noun, a container, some*thing* that we are either in or on or not in or on), the Way of the Beloved is a process without "substance" and without a location in space. It has a dialectic, but is a- temporal. One final note from Thomas Merton seems appropriate: "We do not first see, then act: we act, then see. It is only by the free submission of our judgment in dark faith that we can advance to the light of understanding...And that is why the man who waits to see clearly, before he will believe, never starts on the journey" (*The Ascent to Truth*, 1981: p. 48).

4. Claude Bragdon *Delphic Woman: Twelve Essays*, 1945: p. 143.

5. Jon Kabat-Zinn wrote recently about the mountain metaphor: "The mountain climb is a powerful metaphor for the life quest, the spiritual journey, the path of growth, transformation, and understanding. The arduous difficulties we encounter along the way embody the very challenges we need in order to stretch ourselves and there by expand our boundaries. In the end, it is life itself which is the mountain, the teacher, serving us up perfect opportunities to do the inner work of growing in strength and wisdom" (*Wherever You Go There You Are: Mindfulness Meditation in Everyday Life*, 1994: p. 211). In the Way of the Beloved the couple's life together, the structure of their interactions, or their "relationship" becomes the mountain that they are climbing together.

6. Plotinus [204-270 CE] *The Enneads*, 1991: p. 549. Plotinus' image continues to have an impact. Indeed, we even find it used by Claude Bragdon in his book *Delphic Woman* which is an eloquent endorsement of conjugal love: "The right conditions for liberation through love have always been so rare in the East, by reason of the age-old subjugation of woman, that there the path to spiritual emancipation is the lonely one of the yogi and the ascetic, just as in the West, up to now, sainthood has been associated with celibacy, and deeply concerned with 'the sins of the flesh,' with woman as their symbol. Now although *the Great Work* is and must ever be self-initiated, singly pursued and solely consummated, for the reason that it is 'the flight of the alone to the alone'; and although it is and must be a *via dolorosa* in that it involves the immolation of the personal self and a disciplining of the carnal nature, there is absolutely no reason why the love between man and woman should act as a deterrent to spiritual illumination; there is every reason, on the other hand, why it should act rather as an energizing and accelerating force" (Claude Bragdon *Delphic Woman: Twelve Essays*, 1945: pp. 72-3). We would agree, with qualifications, that, entering any spiritual path must be "self-initiated," but the intent of our book is to demonstrate a way which is not "singly pursued," "solely consummated," or which constitutes solely a "via dolorosa." These are lingering shadows of the very attitude that Bragdon is trying to dispel in his very good and useful book.

7. A useful autobiographical account of the struggle with the contradiction between ascetical, world-denying practices and the need for an active life of service is to be found in the first 2 Chapters of Paul Brunton's, *The Hidden Teaching Beyond Yoga*. 1946: i.e., "Beyond Yoga" & "The Ultimate Path." More recently John Welwood addressed this situation, albeit in a psychological

way: "Never before have intimate relationships called on us to face ourselves and each other with so much honesty and awareness. Maintaining an alive connection with an intimate partner today challenges us to free ourselves from old habits and blind spots and to develop the full range of our powers, sensitivities, and depths as human beings. In former times, if people wanted to explore the deeper mysteries of life, they would often enter the seclusion of a monastery or hermitage. For many of us today, however, intimate relationships have become the new wilderness that brings us face to face with all our gods and demons" (*Journey of the Heart: the Path of Conscious Love*, 1996: p. 1).

8. There are three good studies of the Tantric way of working with the male/female polarity: Herbert Guenther, *The Tantric View of Life*, 1972; Keith Dowman, *Sky Dancer: the secret life and songs of Lady Yeshe Tsogyel*, 1989; & Miranda Shaw, *Passionate Enlightenment: Women in Tantric Buddhism*, 1994. Books are being published all the time which purport to tell Western couples the "secrets of Tantra." However, these are almost always sensualist distortions of the Eastern teachings and are ineffective for the intensification of love.

9. *Passionate Enlightenment: Women in Tantric Buddhism*. 1994: p. 5. A spiritual path for the couple was also formulated within Taoism. It is called the way of "Dual Cultivation" (Mantak Chia, *Taoist Secrets of Love*, 1985: pp. 41-49).

10. Richard Payne has commented on this situation as follows: "Of the seven sacraments, the most frequently used by the largest section of the population is the sacrament of sex, yet a theology of sex remains to be written: nowhere in existence in our day is there an exhaustive delineation of the male-female relationship on the spiritual, psychological, and physical levels insofar as this relationship is willed by God and leads to him" ("Circles of Love" in Bina Gupta, *Sexual Archetypes, East and West*, 1987: p. 65). Even historically in the West there are only two interesting exceptions to this absence of a spiritual purpose for marriage. First, in Jewish mysticism, where, since Old Testament times, the sexual relations of husbands and wives have had a connection to the spiritual world and a purpose in events of a higher order than just reproduction. For instance, as David Ariel has written: "Jewish mystics exhibit a candid and comfortable attitude toward sexuality within the strict parameters of what is permissible under Jewish law. Within these limits the mysteries of human sexuality are seen as reflections of processes and sexuality within God" (*The Mystic Quest*, 1992: p. 130). Second, according to

Charles Williams, there was an attempt (now almost forgotten) in the first two centuries after the resurrection of Christ to put into practice what Williams describes as the revolutionary New Testament teachings on the equality of the sexes and spiritual potential of love between men and women (*The Descent of the Dove*, 1939: pp. 12-14, 56-57 & 129-131). Williams tells us that "The great experiment had to be abandoned because of 'scandal'." This issue is also discussed by Richard Payne in his, "Circles of Love," 1987, see particularly the section titled "Sex as Sacred in the Judeo-Christian Tradition," pp. 63-67). The story of why this teaching was not carried forward is yet to be told, even though, the history of *ascetic* heterosexual relationships in this period is detailed by Rosemary Rader in her excellent study, *Breaking Boundaries: Male/Female Friendship in Early Christian Communities*, 1983. Rader's study makes the important point that "heterosexual friendship" was a "distinctive phenomenon within early Christian societies" which crossed accepted social boundaries and suspended the norms of male/female relationships. Also it was suppressed and eventually eliminated by the church. For the interested reader, we are familiar with several detailed and useful studies of the history of the man/woman relations in the West: In the Christian tradition, see Derrick Sherwin Bailey, *The Man-woman Relationship in Christian Thought*, 1959; Ruth Tiffany Barnhouse, "A Christian Speculation on the Divine Intention for the Man-Woman Relationship" in Bina Gupta, *Sexual Archetypes, East and West*. 1987: 116-138; John Bristow, *What Paul Really Said About Women*, 1988; Eric Fuchs, *Sexual Desire and Love: Origins and History of the Christian Ethic of Sexuality and Marriage*, 1983; Victor Furnish, *The Moral Teachings of Paul : Selected Issues*, 1985; Paul Jewett, *Man as Male and Female: A Study in Sexual Relationships from a Theological Point of View*, 1975; Virginia Mollenkott, *Women Men & the Bible*, 1977; Samuel Terrien, *Till the Heart Sings: A Biblical Theology of Manhood &Womanhood*, 1985; & the excellent work by Philip Sherrard, *Christianity and Eros: Essays on the Theme of Sexual Love*, 1976. In the Islamic tradition, see: Leila Ahmed,*Women & Gender in Islam*, 1992: Joseph Bell, *Love Theory in Later Hanbalite Islam*, 1979; Geraldine Brooks, *9 Parts of Desire: the Hidden World of Islamic Women*, 1995; Lois Giffen, *Theory of Profane Love among the Arabs*, 1971; Fatima Mernissi, *The Veil and the Male Elite: A Feminist Interpretation of Women's Rights in Islam*, 1992; Seyyed Nasr, "The Male and Female in the Islamic Perspective" in Nasr (ed.), *Traditional Islam in the Modern World*, 1987: 47-58; Peter Wilson, *Scandal: Essays in Islamic Heresy*, 1988. And in the Jewish tradition: David Ariel, *The Mystic Quest: An Introduction to Jewish Mysticism*, 1992; David Biale, *Eros and the Jews,* NY, 1992; Daniel Boyarin, *Carnal Israel: Reading Sex in Talmudic Culture,* 1993; Rabbi Yitzchak Ginsburgh, *The Alef-Beit,* 1995; Raphael Patai, *The Hebrew Goddess,* 1990; & A.E. Waite, *The Holy Kabbalah,* 1990.

11. In the nineteenth and twentieth centuries there have been some less well-known proponents of the spiritual potential inherent in the man-woman relationship: e.g. Franz von Baader, Vladimir Solovyiev, Nicholas Berdaiev, Max Scheler, O. V. de L. Milosz, Karl Barth, Gabriel Marcel, Claude Bragdon, Clara Codd, Henry Corbin, Thomas Merton, Torkom Saraydarian, Derrick Sherwin Bailey, Joyce & Barry Vissell, Paul Pearsall, Paul K. Jewett, Jacob Needleman and Philip Sherrard. Relevant books by all of these authors are listed in the bibliography.

12. This prediction was made by our Teacher, Herman Rednick (1902-1985), more than 20 years ago. In a meditation given on 5/4/75 he said, "A divine yoga has been given to humanity. [This yoga] is through the positive and negative streams of spiritual force. When united by man and woman through deep love and devotion, it gives them the potential to fly to the spiritual heights....This is the yoga for the new-age. Thus, the spiritual radiance of the beloved shall light up the world" (*The Earth Journey: From Birth to Fulfillment,* 1980: p. 138 & The Beloved Yoga, 1993: p. 17).

13. We will use the pronominal constructions "he or she" or "she or he" (also "him or her" or "her or him") as this still seems the most accepted way in English of referring to a person of either sex. See Diana Hacker, *A Writer's Reference,* 1992: pp. 73-75, ("Avoid sexist language" and p. 103 note). For a fascinating discussion of how English has attempted to deal with the gender pronoun problem see Dennis Baron, *Grammar and Gender,* 1986: Chapter 10, "The word that failed" (pp. 190-216).

14. Teilhard de Chardin brilliantly developed this idea, expressing it simply, and unforgettably, in the phrase, "unity differentiates" (*Human Energy,* 1969: pp. 63-4). Teilhard is not speaking abstractly, but quite concretely, as he makes clear: "the essential aspiration of all mysticism," is "*to be united* (that is, "*to become* the other") *while remaining oneself*" (*The Divine Milieu,* 1965: p. 116. For discussions of this important concept, see Christopher Mooney, *Teilhard de Chardin and the Mystery of Christ,* 1966: pp. 179-181 & Donald Gray, *The One and the Many: Teilhard de Chardin's Vision of Unity,* 1969: pp. 133-135).

15. M. Robert Van Arsdale *Poems for the Spiritual Path*, 1978: p. 46.

16. Toward the Future, 1975: p. 71.

17. A corollary to these observations, is the fact that *all* paths of development are not open to *all* people. For instance, the path of celibacy (e.g., the Catholic priesthood, the Hindu *sanyassin*, or Buddhist monk) is not really open to the loving couple—rejecting love to gain it, is contradictory. Also there are several, but increasingly fewer, paths which are only open to those who are born into a particular culture, sex or race (e.g., Shintoism, the Masonic orders or the black Muslims). Also there are those traditions which are moribund and have no living teachers (e.g., the Egyptian mysteries, Valentinianism or Catharism). That spiritual realization through the path of the beloved is limited and significantly diminished for single persons, same-sex couples, the vast majority of Moslems, most tribal peoples, or atheists should not be seen as the result of some arbitrary exclusionism or prejudice, but as inherent in the nature of the path itself.

18. Vincent Brümmer has commented that, "mystics frequently divide their journey to God into three stages. This threefold division which medieval mystics might have derived from neo-Platonism occurs so often in the mystical tradition that it is probably the most adequate way of describing the mystical experience of the journey to God" (*The Model of Love*, 1993: p. 59). A discussion of the possible origins of these stages is to be found in Andrew Louth *The Origins of the Christian Mystical Tradition From Plato to Denys*, 1983: pp. 54-56. An even more complete treatment of this issue is found in Lars Thunberg *Microcosm and Mediator: The Theological Anthropology of Maximus the Confessor*, 1995: pp. 332-368. St. Gregory of Nyssa (ca 330-395) provides an early delineation in which the three degrees of the ascent to God are symbolized "in the degrees of illumination and darkness through which Moses journeyed to God. Moses first saw God in the burning bush. Then he was led by God across the desert in a pillar of cloud. Finally he ascended Sinai, where God spoke to him 'face to face' but in divine darkness" (Thomas Merton, *The ascent to Truth*, 1981: pp. 50-1). Pseudo-Dionysius (6th. CE) discusses these three stages of the path, calling them "purification," "illumination," and "perfection"—see CH 165C-168A (see also EH 504A-509A), in *Complete Works*, 1987. Thomas Merton sees "a clear correspondence between Saint Gregory of Nyssa's digress of obscurity and the Night of Saint John of the Cross" (*The ascent to Truth*, 1981: p. 52). St.

John of the Cross (1542-1591), "makes this threefold division of his night into a night of sense, night of faith, and night of pure contemplation or mystical union with God" (Ibid. p. 336, Ch. III, n. 4). And coming from an entirely different direction, Antoine Faivre suggests a "rapprochement between these three stages" and the alchemical stages of *"nigredo* (death, decapitation, of the first matter or of the old man), *albedo* (work with white), and *rubedo* (work with red, philosopher's stone)" (*Modern Esoteric Spirituality,* 1995: p. xviii). In the Christian mystical tradition the three states of the via *mystica* are called Purification, Illumination, and Ecstasy. Some Sufis (Islamic mystics) refer to these stages as: "the Lore of Certainty"—Faith, "the Eye of Certainty"— Vision, and "the Truth of Certainty"— Gnosis (Abu Bakr Siraj ad-Din *The Book of Certainty,* 1992: pp. 1-2). Huston Smith says that the first of these is "likened to hearing about fire, the second to seeing fire, and the third to being burned by fire" (*Forgotten Truth,* 1992: p. 88). Tibetan Buddhists refer to the path as an ascension from: Hinayana as the "Outer," Mahayana as the "Inner," and Vajrayana as the "Secret" or "Hidden" (Kalu Rinpoche *Dharma Teachings,* 1990: p. 74). For discussions of Buddhist conceptions of the threefold path, see Kalu Rinpoche *Luminous Mind,* 1997: pp. 97-99 & 173-75 & Tsultrim Allione,*Women of Wisdom,* 1986: p. 25.

19. Pseudo Dionysius, quoted in Vincent Brümmer *The Model of Love,* 1993: p. 61.

20. On Love, 1957: p. 37.

21. Alice Rossi (ed.), *Essays on Sex Equality: John Stuart Mill & Harriet Mill,* 1970: p. 40.

NOTES FOR PART 1

1. . Adapted from *The Beloved Yoga,* 1993: p. 82.

• NOTES CHAPTER 1 •

1. *Human Energy,* 1969: p. 32.

2. We do not intend this expression to be either trite or hackneyed, but as a familiar way of indicating the true ontological primacy of love. Paul Tillich (1886-1965) said it very unambiguously: "If we speak of the ontology of Love we indicate that Love belongs to the structure of Being itself, that every special being with its special nature participates in the nature of Love since

it participates in Being itself" ("Being and Love" in Will Herberg Ed. *Four Existentialist Theologians*, 1858: p. 300). (This essay first appeared in Ruth Nanda Anshen ed. *Moral Principles of Action*, Harper, 1952: pp. 661-672.) In a Chapter with the same title published 2 years later, (i.e., *Love, Power, and Justice*, 1960: Chapter II "Being and Love," p. 25), Tillich says that "life is being in actuality and love is the moving power of life. In these two sentences the ontological nature of love is expressed. They say that being is not actual without the love which drives everything that is towards everything else that is. In man's experience of love the nature of life becomes manifest." Without love there can be no actual beings, i.e., world, nature, persons, etc.

Throughout his writings, Teilhard de Chardin also asserts that love is the ontological basis of the whole of creation, its continued existence, and the ongoing evolution of this cosmos: e.g., "The most telling and profound way of describing the evolution of the universe would undoubtedly be to trace the evolution of love" and, "Love is a sacred reserve of energy; it is like the blood of spiritual evolution" (Teilhard de Chardin *Human Energy*. 1969: pp. 32-34). He also asserts that, "Considered in its full biological reality, love—that is to say, the affinity of being with being—is not peculiar to man. It is a general property of all life and as such it embraces, in its varieties and degrees, all the forms successively adopted by organized matter...." (*The Phenomenon of Man*. 1965. pp. 264-5).

Thomas Merton takes a very similar position on the cosmic significance of love: "Love then is not only our own salvation and the key to the meaning of our own existence, but it is also the key to the meaning of the entire creation of God. It is true, after all, that our whole life is a participation in that cosmic liturgy of 'the love which moves the sun and the other stars'" (Thomas Merton, *Disputed Questions*, 1977: p. 99). This is a very famous aphorism and it appears in Dante (*The Divine Comedy: Paradise*, XXXIII, 145), but Dante got it from the Roman philosopher, Boethius, who said it more than 750 years earlier; i.e., Boethius. (C. 480-524 CE) *The Consolation of Philosophy*, 1988: Bk. II poem 8, l. 29, p. 77. (See the discussion of this aphorism by Watts in his Introduction to Boethius, p. 8).

Also the ontological primacy of love is the foundation stone of the philosophy of Max Scheler: "'*Man is, before he can think or will, ens amans.*' This proposition of Scheler's is the core of his philosophy of man....Love is *the* fundamental spiritual act. It is an irreducible and spontaneous movement" (Manfred S. Frings, *Max Scheler*, 1965: pp. 67-8).

In this beginning discussion we will do well to heed what Claude Bragdon had to say about love, "It is useless to try to *mentalize* love as it is foolish to sentimentalize it, for it cannot be understood by the mind nor is it subservient to the will or the emotions….love is preëminently a spiritual experience, *a great flame* which purifies all the gold and burns up all the garbage in man's nature" (Claude Bragdon *Delphic Woman: Twelve Essays*, 1945: p. 106)

3. Quoted in Pitirim A. Sorokin *The Ways and Power of Love*. 1967: p. 3. Paul Tillich was a consistent voice for the primacy of love: e.g., "love is unconditional. There is nothing which could condition it by a higher principle. There is nothing above love. And love conditions itself. It enters every concrete situation and works for the reunion of the separated in a unique way" (*Theology of Culture*, 1959: p. 145). This observation has been enunciated since early times, e.g. Boethius (C. 480-524 CE): "But who to love can give a law? Love unto itself is law" (*The Consolation of Philosophy*, 1988: Bk. III poem 12, l.47-8, p. 114).

4. The relationship between love and feeling has been discussed in several popular books: Eric Fromm *The Art of Loving.*, 1970: p. 3; C.S. Lewis *Mere Christianity*, 1978.p. 99; Rollo May *Love And Will*, 1969: p. 286; & M. Scott Peck The Road Less Traveled, 1978: pp. 116 & 119. Martin Buber gives us a succinct and cogent statement of the relationship of feelings to love in his famous book, *I and Thou:*, "Feelings accompany the metaphysical and metapsychical fact of love, but they do not constitute it. The accompanying feelings can be of greatly differing kinds…but the love is the one love. Feelings are 'entertained': love comes to pass. Feelings dwell in man; but man dwells in his love" (*I and Thou*, 1958: p. 14). The Spanish philosopher Julián Marías has also analyzed this issue: "I believe that the fact that love has been understood primarily as a 'feeling,' secondarily as an 'affection' or 'tendency,' has clouded our understanding of it to an indescribable degree. Naturally there are amorous 'feelings.' they are those which *go along* with love, the concomitant phenomena with which love is brought into being and out of which it is in part nourished, but love is not a feeling. The psychological interpretation of love reduces it to the sphere of psychic life. There is not doubt that that life [i.e., psychic] is affected by love and that there could be a psychology of love, but love is a reality of biographical life. Nor can love be reduced to an act or a series of acts, which is what the use of the verb 'to love' suggests. Love is primarily an *installation,* in which a person is located and from which he caries out acts—among them, specific acts of love. In other words, when a person is

installed in love, many things are done out of it, and one of them its to love" (*Metaphysical Anthropology: The empirical Structure of Human Life*, 1971: p. 182). We can give a concommitant meaning to Tillich's use of "dwells" and Marías' use of "installation." Those interested in a further ontological analysis of love and emotion are referred to Paul Tillich *Love, Power, and Justice*, 1960: pp. 3-5 & 26-27.

5. In Judaism, Islam and Christianity God commands that we love others, e.g., "thou shalt love thy neighbor as thyself. I am the Lord; you shall keep My law": Lev. 19:18-19 and "This is my commandment, That ye love one another as I have loved you": Jn. 15:12. (This commandment to love others is repeated just 5 verses later: Jn. 15:17). However, if love is that one thing which one must freely give to another person, how can God command us to do it? This paradox has confused many people over the centuries and we will give just a few notes for the reader's consideration: Martin Buber said that "the Bible overcomes the paradox in a precisely contrary fashion. The Bible knows that it is impossible to command the love of man. I am incapable of feeling love toward every man, though God himself command me. The Bible does not directly enjoin the love of man, but by using the dative puts it rather in the form of an act of love (Lev. 19:18, 34). I must act lovingly toward my rea, my 'companion' (usually translated 'my neighbor'), that is toward every man with whom I deal in the course of my life, including the ger, the 'stranger' or 'sojourner'; I must bestow the favours of love on him, I must treat him with love as one who is 'like unto me.' (I must love 'to him'; a construction only found in these two verses in the Bible.) Of course I must love him not merely with superficial gestures but with an essential relationship. It lies within my power to will it, and so I can accept the comandment. It is not my will which gives me the emotion of love toward my 'neighbour' aroused within me by my behaviour" (Eclipse of God, 1965: p. 57). In the New Testament "there is the new interpretation of neighbour, and the extension of this love to one's enemies, [e.g., "I tell you, Love (agapate) your enemies" (Mt. 5:44). See also Lk. 6:27 & 35] which superseded the lex talionis. Finally, there is the organic connexion between all this love and love to God or God's love, which maintains the religious basis of the ethical teaching. Christian love, as we might say, loves each man in god and God in every man" (James Moffat, Love in the New Testament, 1929: p. 97. See Part A, Section III, pp. 97-130, for a very useful discussion of these issues). The importance of this fundamental Western perspective is that we (whether Jew, Christian or

Moslem) are commanded by God to act in a loving manner toward all other persons. We can accept this command because we can will to act in a loving manner whether we *feel* love or not. The will to love is truly creative, therefore, its expression (action) is spontaneous and may take almost any form. Also we cannot know before the will to love what would constitute an expression of love in any given situation. This is a major precept of The Way of the Beloved and we will return again and again to learning how to love our beloved-one no matter what the circumstances might be. The Way of the Beloved is a path which moves in the middle of the stream of Western teachings on love, it is just the application of these teachings to the relationship between man and woman has been temporarily lost.

6. Many people today become confused when the word "love" is used in this kind of context. They feel that they don't know what *love* means nor do they know what to do about it. Indeed, students often ask us to define the word "love," as if a definition could clear up the current situation which was so well expressed by the French poet, O.V. de L. Milosz: "To this word, love, the ignorance and coarseness of the epochs which separates us from the Middle Ages have given many puerile or irreverent meanings, and even those minds that are the least false in these horrible times...do not seem to wish to express with it anything other than passion, pleasure or curiosity" (Christopher Bamford, *The Noble Traveller: O.V. de L. Milosz*, 1985: p. 240, "Epistle to Storge," written in 1916). It is obvious that this degeneration has become more widespread than when Milosz was writing, probably most persuasively exemplified by the omnipresence of puerile TV sit coms and soap operas. However, as Paul Tillich said, "in spite of all the misuses to which the word *love* is subjected, in literature and daily life, it has not lost its emotional power. It elicits a feeling of warmth, of passion, of happiness, of fulfilment, whenever it is used. It brings to mind past or present or anticipated occasions of loving or being loved" (*Love, Power, and Justice*, 1960: p. 3). In the Way of the Beloved it is critical to *express* your love for the other person, whatever that means or does not mean to you. It is only through the *will-to-love* or the *doing* that we will *know* anything about love. As Herman Rednick said, "Of course, the term 'love' does not capture or explain its nature, but he who expresses love, develops a quality or vibration which greatly facilitates his evolution and illumination. On the higher octave, love is the power that holds the solar system in its place. That power is stepped down...until it reaches a level that the human being can tolerate. At the human level, this power expresses itself

in the attraction for the opposite sex. When... [a person] learns to transform his instinctive nature, he develops a quality of love that includes everyone. But even this level of love is far removed from the pure essence that is referred to as the Divine Essence or Compassion. This is the force that sustains the solar system; it emanates from the true sun, which is behind the physical sun" (Justin Moore *Teachings From the Path of Fire: The Life and Works of Herman Rednick.*, 1973: Q 61).

7. Ramon Betanzos, *Franz Von Baader's Philosophy of Love*, 1968: p. 267.

8. We have been unable to find the location of this quote.

9. In speaking about the use of the imagination, Herman Rednick said that one "can derive considerable benefits from cultivating the ability to create and sustain images. For example, when a person concentrates on the image of a spiritual ideal within the heart, he attracts the higher forces associated with that image. He also becomes sensitive to images that will be impressed upon his consciousness from the other plane. So the proper use of the imagination makes the person more receptive to forces and concepts from the higher dimensions. It is the entrance to the higher plane." (Justin R. Moore, ed. *Teachings From the Path of Fire: The Life and Works of Herman Rednick.*, 1973: Q161) We develop these concepts further in Section 7.2.

10. A deeper consideration of cause and effect in relation to motives, goals and vision may be useful for some. For instance, Saraydarian has said, "To cause means to have a vision, to have a motive, to have willpower. Motive is the picture, vision is the projection, and willpower is the energy which is projecting the motive. Together they are the cause. So cause is will, motive and vision. The motive is the picture within you which is going to actualize and be projected into your future. You are projecting yourself into the future. You are becoming the future. The image you are building about yourself for the future is projected by willpower into space toward the future. When it is projected by will power, as an arrow shot toward the space, it creates a tremendous magnetism. You become your own cause." Torkom Saraydarian, *The Psyche and Psychism.* 1981: V. I, Chapter 29 "The Will-To-Be-A-Cause." pp. 267-8. Examining our motives, being clear about our goals, honoring our commitments, and creating a vision will free us from the past and open up new possibilities. Rudolf Steiner takes this issue of our relationship to vision and the future to another level when he says that "the riddles of consciousness will be solved and the whole peculiar nature of the soul life clarified if you

start with the premise that the current of desire, love and hate comes to meet you out of the future, and meets the current of visualizations flowing out of the past into the future. At every moment you are actually in the midst of this encounter of the two streams, and considering that the present moment of your soul life consists of such a meeting, you will readily understand that these two currents overlap in your soul. *This overlapping is consciousness* " (Rudolf Steiner *The Wisdom of Man, of the Soul, and of the Spirit.*, 1971: p. 122) (Italics in original). Clearly, visualizing the highest potential for our beloved relationship is no idle fantasy. Indeed we are already *that* in the present! This orientation is difficult for people educated in our materialistic culture to grasp. The Spanish philosopher, Julián Marías has provided us with a comprehensive and brilliant analysis of the vectorial structure of life, but scant attention has been given to it. Briefly, he points out that, "we are dealing with the future, and more generally with possibility. The reality of the future, *a priori*, cannot be material. And the *fact*—we are dealing with a fact, though not only with it—the inescapable fact, is that we live primarily in the future. I am not future—let me make myself clear—but perfectly real and present; however, in Spanish there is a marvelous suffix *-izo,* which indicates inclination, orientation, or propensity…very well then, I am *futurizo*—present, but oriented toward the future, turned toward it, projected toward it. I am in *this* world and in the *other:* the world I anticipate, project, imagine, the world that is not there, the world of tomorrow. And this world, the world of my plans, that unreal world in which I am 'I,' is the world which confers its worldhood—its character as a world—on this material and present world, which without the future-oriented 'I' would not be a world at all" (*Metaphysical Anthropology: The empirical Structure of Human Life,* 1971: pp. 14-15). For more see Chapter 12, "The Vectorial Structure of Life" pp. 89-96).

11. This story recently appeared in Richard Bandler & John Grinder *Reframing: Neuro-Linguistic Programming and the Transformation of Meaning,* 1982: p. 1. These authors begin their book with this story as an illustration of the reframing of socially accepted meanings of events. We have rewritten the old farmer's responses to better illustrate, not just a *change* of meaning, but a change into a *higher* meaning—in this case, gratitude. Our emphasis throughout is to reframe experience according to *higher* principles or meanings.

12. Indeed, there is a similar tradition in Western thought which goes back, at least, to the New Testament: e.g., "Give thanks in all circumstances" (I Thessalonians 5:18, RSV). And "I have learned, in whatever state I am, to

be content. I know how to be abased, and I know how to abound; in any and all circumstances I have learned the secret of facing plenty and hunger, abundance and want" (Philippians 4:11-12 RSV). This teaching is echoed by Boethius (C. 480-524 CE). He said that, "nothing is miserable except when you think it so, and vice versa, all luck is good luck to the man who bears it with equanimity" (Boethius *The Consolation of Philosophy*, 1988: p. 63). Despite the fact that Boethius was a Roman convert to Christianity, his approach to fate is Neoplatonic. For instance, see Plotinus [204-270 CE] *The Enneads*, 1991: First Ennead; Fourth Tractate: Happiness, pp. 30-44.

13. April O'Connell & Vincent O'Connell, Choice And Change, 1992: p. xvi. This is a current textbook used in university psychology courses.

14. Arthur Versluis, *TheoSophia.*, 1994: p. 88. In talking about gratitude with students for the first time, we have found an almost universal misunderstanding about the relation of gratitude to passive acceptance, approval of whatever the other does, "going along to get along," enduring abuse, and even denial of wrongdoing by one's partner. These attitudes represent the antithesis of gratitude. Some of the problem may lie in the different English translations of the New Testament. In the New International Version (NIV), Paul concludes the First Epistle to the Thessalonians by telling the members of this harassed new church to "be joyful always; pray continually; *give thanks in all circumstances*, for this is God's will for you in Christ Jesus" (1 Th. 5:16-18, our emphasis). Both The King James and The Jerusalem Bible render the passage (i.e., 5:18) as "in everything give thanks." The New English Bible says, "give thanks whatever happens." This may explain why so many people misunderstand what it is that we should be grateful for. Paul Tillich pointed out that even though the King James text says, "'In everything give thanks!' This does not mean—give thanks for everything, but give thanks in every situation!" (*The Eternal Now*, 1963: p. 179). This distinction in the meaning is critical. To say, "be grateful *in* every circumstance" is very different from saying that we should be grateful "*for* every-*thing*." Becoming grateful for our *experience* of evil is very different from becoming grateful for evil things in themselves. Indeed, mistakenly trying to become grateful for evil things in themselves contradicts both the teaching that one should either oppose evil or "turn from it." Belief in the notion that gratitude ("it is God's will for us"), means to become passively accepting of the unjust and harmful things done to us has led many into helpless victimhood, passivity in the face of injustice, and even suicidal despair. A proper understanding and practice of gratitude

for our *experiences in all circumstances* will lead us into greater freedom and power in life.

15. In talking about gratitude with students for the first time, we have found an almost universal misunderstanding about the relation of gratitude to passive acceptance, approval of whatever the other does, "going along to get along," enduring abuse, and even denial of wrongdoing by one's partner. These attitudes represent the antithesis of gratitude. Some of the problem may lie in the different English translations of the New Testament. In the New International Version (NIV), Paul concludes the First Epistle to the Thessalonians by telling the members of this harassed new church to "be joyful always; pray continually; *give thanks in all circumstances*, for this is God's will for you in Christ Jesus" (1 Th. 5:16-18, our emphasis). Both *The King James* and *The Jerusalem Bible* render the passage (i.e., 5:18) as "in everything give thanks." *The New English Bible* says, "give thanks whatever happens." This may explain why so many people misunderstand what it is that we should be grateful for. Paul Tillich pointed out that even though the King James text says, "'In *everything* give thanks!' This does not mean— give thanks for everything, but give thanks in every situation!" (*The Eternal Now*, 1963: p. 179). This distinction in the meaning is critical. To say, "be grateful *in* every circumstance" is very different from saying that we should be grateful "*for* every-*thing*." Becoming grateful for our *experience* of evil is very different from becoming grateful for evil things in themselves. Indeed, mistakenly trying to become grateful for evil things in themselves contradicts both the teaching that one should either oppose evil or "turn from it." Belief in the notion that gratitude ("it is God's will for us"), means to beome passively accepting of the unjust and harmful things done to us has led many into helpless victimhood, passivity in the face of injustice, and even suicidal despair. A proper understanding and practice of gratitude for our *experiences in all circumstances* will lead us into greater freedom and power in life.

16. This statement probably came from the talk that the Dalai Lama gave in Sept. 1993, in Tucson AZ, which was reported in The Snow Lion Newsletter. The precept that our oppressors give us precious opportunities to be grateful has been expressed by many diverse teachers: Christ taught, "Love your enemies, bless them that curse you, do good to them that hate you, and pray for them which despitefully use you, and persecute you" (Mt. 5:44). The Zen Buddhists say that when one meets problems or encounters difficulties it is as if "a great teacher has arrived." Gandhi said, "problems are opportunities in

disguise" and Don Juan tells Carlos Casteñeda that he is very lucky to have a boss who is a tyrant (*pinche tirano*), it is truly a *gift* for it is the fastest way to learn many difficult lessons. And Meher Baba said unforgettably, "When you are kicked, be like a football and go higher!'

17. Torkom Saraydarian, *The Psyche and Psychism*, V.II., 1981: p. 1075.

18. Men leaving the toilet seat up, has almost become an apocalyptic event in American marriages. The "problem" is always defined as finding a way to get the man to put the seat back down into its "proper" position. This has even been called the "chivalrous" thing for a man to do. Indeed, in the typical American way, a Florida man, ("Inventor Flushed With Pride" *Albuquerque Journal* 5/13/95) "who set out to conquer all the gripes," has invented a toilet that automatically lowers the seat when the toilet is flushed. He calls it the "Marriage Saver." Eventually all toilets may come equipped with Marriage Savers which will mechanically do for you what you are *supposed* to do to spare your spouse "a chilling encounter with cold china." This new invention is a significant improvement over "The Peacekeeper," which has been manufactured by Kohler for years, and requires the man to put the seat down before the toilet can be flushed. However, the potential success of these two inventions has been overshadowed in 1997 by introduction, in a mail-order catalog, of a $12.99 electronic device, the Beep Seat*, that attaches to the underside of the toilet seat with a self-adhesive strip and sounds an alarm if it is left in the up position for more than 60 seconds! No one ever suggests the reciprocal possibility of the woman raising the seat so the man would not have to do it every time.

19. Herman Rednick, *The Earth Journey: from Birth to Fulfillment*, 1980: p. 185. The "temple" is the one built without hands—the temple of love.

20. *The Eternal Now*, 1963: pp. 179-80.

• Chapter 2 NOTES •

1. Ramon Lull *The Book of the Lover and Beloved*. 1978: p. 44, § 123.

2. This is not surprising because, as the Sociologist, Francesca Cancian, points out, "recent surveys showing that good communication is valued above all other qualities…suggest that there has been a major rise in valuing good communication since the sixties" (*Love in America: Gender and self-development*, 1987: pp.47-8).

3. The ubiquitous word "communication" has been called an "amoeba-word" and it is part of a modern vocabulary that has been called "Uniquack." Ivan Illich & Barry Sanders caution that "we must be forever conscious of the fact that we do not know what those terms [amoeba-words] mean. We use the words like words from Scripture, like a gift from above. Furthermore, we gratefully transfer the power to define their meaning to an expertocratic hierarchy to which we do not belong. The word... ["communication"] is used neither with common sense, nor with the senseless precision of science, but almost like a sublinguistic grunt—a nonsense word...like sexuality, transportation, education, communication, information, crisis, problem, solution, role, and dozens of other words..." (*A B C: The Alphabetization of the Popular Mind*, 1988: p. 106).

4. See for instance: Deborah Tannen *You Just Don't Understand: Women & Men in Conversation* 1990; John Gray *Men are From Mars: Women are From Venus.* 1992; Suzette Elgin *Genderspeak.* 1993.

5. R. Fisher & W. Ury Getting *to Yes: Negotiating Agreement Without Giving-in.* 1981.

6. Steindl-Rast, Brother David, *Gratefulness, the Heart of Prayer,* 1984: pp. 194-5. There are much deeper levels of the relation between "speech," "communion" and "listening" than we will be able to discuss in this beginning section, but just to open a window on these vistas we will quote a brief and intriguing passage from Altizer's meditative study of speech: "Distance and intimacy are mutually established by speech, but they are established not as distinct and isolated fields, but rather as mutual and ever-present poles of one continuum. While neither can be fully or wholly distinguished from the other in the presence of speech, it is also true that each remains itself in the act or embodiment of speech, for so long as speech speaks both distance and intimacy are maintained by the presence and actuality of voice. Communion or coinherence may be realized by the act of speech, but never union or identity. Union and identity are realized only by silence, never by speech, and speech can only prepare the way for union by ever more fully ceasing to speak. So long as speech speaks distance is at hand, and at hand not simply in its distinction from silence, but also in the very intimacy which its voice establishes. To listen to speech, as opposed to listening to silence, is to be open to otherness, an otherness impossible apart from distance, and an otherness which is real only in the context of distance. Yet the otherness established by speech is not

an empty or vacuous otherness. It is far rather a present and actual otherness, even an intimate otherness, an otherness which is not only distant and apart but which is likewise and simultaneously near at hand" (Thomas J.J. Altizer, *The Self-Embodiment of God*, 1987: p. 12). We will take up some of these issues which involve "otherness," "presencing" and "union" in Sections 7.2 and 7.3.

7. All religions, Eastern and Western, have affirmed for thousands of years that there is in truth an underlying *Unity of Being*. The current materialistic and secular notions of separate existence are a temporary illusion of the experience of matter. According to modern Quantum Physics even matter has an underlying unity.

8. "Maya" and "Cloud of Illusion" are conventional terms for the "illusion" referred to in footnote #7.

9. We will discuss the important issue of the relationship between love and knowledge in Section 7.1. "Vision Through Love."

10. Quoted in: Vissell, Barry & Joyce *The Shared Heart*. 1984: p. 17. Also found in Hazrat Inayat Khan, *The Complete Sayings of Hazarat Inayat Khan.*, 1978: p. 90 § 760.

11. Thomas Merton underscored this when he said that, "Communion is the awareness of participation in an ontological or religious reality: in the mystery of being, of human love, of redemptive mystery, of contemplative truth" (*Love and Living*, 1979: p. 68). He further elaborated that, "Communication takes place between subject and object, but communion is beyond the division: it is a sharing in basic unity. This does not necessarily imply a 'pantheist metaphysic.' Whether or not they may be strictly monistic, the higher religions all point to this deeper unity, because they all strive after the experience of this unity. They differ, sometimes widely, in ways of explaining what this unity is and how one may attain to it" (Ibid. p. 73).

12. *The Hidden Ground of Love*, 1985: p. x. These two passages are quoted in the Introduction by the editor, William Shannon. He comments that Merton wrote the first in notes he prepared for a talk to be given in Calcutta at the end of Oct. 1968. The second is what he actually said in the talk. This was only 2 weeks before his accidental death in Bankok on Dec. 10.

13. From a letter by Herman Rednick sent to a student, who is a psychotherapist (9/29/61)

14. "When we speak of the heart, we mean the center of intuition, and not the physical heart. When the conflict in the mind and emotions has been stilled, the voice of the heart comes into play. The intuition that flows through the heart is straight knowledge, for it comes from the higher levels of consciousness where one does not have to seek an answer—for the answer is there as you turn toward it. The intuition of the heart increases with the quality of compassion. The more the heart is trusted, the more it becomes the guiding force in a person's life. It is the guidance of knowing where to go and what to do at the appointed hour. And it is the voice that knows the people that cross your path." (Herman Rednick The *Hermanic Dialogues,* 1993: No. 17, p. 5) The important, but nearly neglected philosopher, Max Scheler (1874-1928) said that, "the 'heart' of man, is no chaos of blind feeling-states which are attached to, and detached from, other so-called psychic givens by causal rules of some sort. The heart is itself a *structured counter-image* of the cosmos of all possible things worthy of love; to this extent is a *micro cosmos of the world of values."* And that, "the unity of this realm of love lies, therefore, on another plane." ("Ordo Amoris" in Max Scheler, *Selected Philosophical Essays.,* 1973: p. 116). For further discussion of *heart* see: Henry Corbin *Creative Imagination in the Sufism of Ibn 'Arabi.* 1981: Chapter IV "Theophanic Imagination and Creativity of the Heart", pp. 216-245; and Robert Sardello *Love and the Soul.,* 1995: Chapter 8 "Heart and Soul", pp. 147-160. For an essay on "A Listening Heart" see Brother David Steindl-Rast *A Listening Heart: the Art of Contemplative Living,* 1983: pp. 9-14.

15. Mother Meera, *Answers,* 1991: p. 50.

16. This "dialogue" approach was developed by David Bohm and his colleagues. Bohm had great hope for this technique: "Possibly it could make a new change in the individual and a change in the relation to the cosmos. Such an energy has been called 'communion'. It is a kind of participation. The early Christians had a Greek word *koinonia,* the root of which means 'to participate'—the idea of partaking of the whole and taking part in it; not merely the whole group, but the *whole.* This, then, is what I mean by 'dialogue.' I suggest that through dialogue there is the possibility for a *transformation of the nature of consciousness,* both individually and collectively." David Bohm On Dialogue. *Noetic Sciences Review,* Autumn 1992: p. 18 & David Bohm, Donald Factor & Paul Garrett *Dialogue—A Proposal* The Wisdom Soc., San Marcos, Ca. 1991. For the recent historical development of the concepts

which underlie Bohm's work with dialogue see: Shmuel Bergman, *Dialogical Philosophy from Kierkegaard to Buber*, 1991.

17. In part, adapted from the Dialogue Questions of Episcopal Marriage Encounter®.

18. David Bohm "On Dialogue" *Noetic Sciences Review*, Autumn 1992: pp. 16-7. (Italics in original)

19. Herbert V. Guenther, The Tantric View of Life, 1972: p. 44.

20. The first four lines of a poem by Herman Rednick, titled "The Spoken Word" (*The Hidden Door to Reality*, 1982: p. 74), reads:

> A spoken word carries the tone of your being
> in whatever state you may be in.
> You can ride in upon the vibration of a word
> and enter the inner recesses of a man's being.

21. Suzette Haden Elgin, *Genderspeak*,1993: p. 27.

22. Suzette Elgin has called this approach "Miller's Law," and states it in the following way: "1. Assume (not accept, just assume) that what you heard is true. 2. Ask yourself: What could it be true of? In a world where it is true, what else would have to be true?" (*Ibid.* p. 28) A similar approach is used by the psychologists, Richard Bandler & John Grinder, "assume that people want to communicate in such a way that they get what they want, *and* that they want to respect the integrity and the interests of the other people involved. That assumption may not be true, but it's a very useful operating assumption, because it gives you something to do that can be very effective. If you make that assumption, it's always possible to find another solution—not a compromise—that satisfies both parties." (*Reframing*, 1982: p. 147) This understanding is also used in divorce & family mediation, i.e. John Allen Lemmon *Family Mediation Practice*. 1985: pp. 43-48.

23. "…it's the old formula 'Message intended is not necessarily message received.'" Richard Bandler & John Grinder (*Reframing*, 1982: p. 144-162.) present a step by step technique of what they call "couple reframing," which is one useful way to reach an "agreement frame" or an intention/meaning understanding between the parties.

24. As the relationship grows and develops a greater depth it may be possible to reestablish our communication around a new focal point. For instance, Robert Sardello has thought deeply about these possibilities and writes that, "Rather than a focus, as in the traditional form of relating, on expression of personal feelings to keep in connection with how we are getting along, an open conversation is needed. Not what do I feel and what do you feel, and what do we feel about each other, but how does what we are making together feel—is it whole, comprehensive; does it belong to the world, or is it being imposed on the world; are we still working out of imagination, or have we begun to lose this focus? These and a thousand questions like these can form a new mode of intimate conversation." (*Love and the Soul*, 1995: p. 186).

Chapter 3 NOTES •

1. Paul Zweig *The Heresy of Self-Love.* 1980: p. vi.

2. Concern with this issue is not new. Indeed Maximos the Confessor (580-662 CE) called egoism (*Philautia* in Greek), "the mother of all the vices" (Lars Thunberg *Man and the Cosmos: The Vision of St. Maximus the Confessor.*, 1985: p. 95).

3. *The Art of Loving.* 1970: p. 99.

4. Before the term "self-esteem" became so popular and widely used, Paul Tillich wrote: "One may call the right self-love self-acceptance, the wrong self-love selfishness, and the natural self-love self-affirmation. In all cases the word 'self,' as such, has no negative connotations. It is the structure of the most developed form of reality, the most individualized and the most universal being. Self is good, self-affirmation is good, self-acceptance is good, but selfishness is bad because it prevents both self-affirmation and self-acceptance" (*Theology of Culture*, 1959: pp. 145-6).

5. Denis De Rougemont *Love in the Western World.* 1983: p. 52. (Our emphasis)

6. This is an important issue for those who wish to gain a deeper understanding of the effects that love has on egoism. A consideration of the following may be useful: "We are surrounded by innumerable living and conscious beings... But rather than knowing that they really exist and that they are as much alive as we ourselves, it nevertheless appears to us that they have a *less real existence* and that they are *less living* than ourselves. For us it is WE who experience the

full measure of the intensity of reality, whilst other beings seem, in comparison with ourselves, to be less real; their existence seems to be more of the nature of a shadow than full reality. Our thoughts tell us that this is an illusion, that beings around us are as real as we ourselves are, and that they live just as intensely as we do. Yet fine as it is to say these things, all the same we feel ourselves at the center of reality, and we feel other beings to be removed from this center. That one qualifies this illusion as 'egocentricity', or 'egoism', or *'ahamkara'* (the illusion of self), or the 'effect of the primordial Fall,' does not matter; it does not alter the fact that we feel ourselves to be more real than others." (Valentin Tomberg *Meditations on the Tarot.* 1985: p. 125) Why do we experience others as less real? For an analysis of the ontological status of others from the point of view of egocentrism, refer to: Max Scheler *The Nature of Sympathy*, 1973: pp. 58-61.

7. There have been quite a number of studies from very diverse viewpoints about how this situation may have come about in Western societies: e.g. C.S. Lewis, *The Allegory of Love: A Study in Medieval Tradition.* 1958; Denis De Rougemont, *Love in the Western World.* 1983; Anders Nygren, *Agape and Eros.* 1953; M.C. D'Arcy, *The Mind and Heart of Love.* 1956; Paul Zweig, *The Heresy of Self-Love.* 1980; Owen Barfield, *Saving the Appearances: A Study in Idolatry.* 1957; Riane Eisler, *The Chalice and The Blade.* 1988; Erich Neumann, *The Origins and History of Consciousness.* 1954; Derrick S. Bailey, *The Man-woman Relationship in Christian Thought.*, 1959; Philip Sherrard, *Christianity and Eros: Essays on the Theme of Sexual Love.*, 1976; & most recently, Riane Eisler, *Sacred Pleasure: Sex, Myth & Politics of the Body.*, 1995, Part 1 "How did we get here?" pp. 15-157.

8. Some call this kind of unselfish love "compassion" or "altruism" or use the Greek term, *Agape.* For discussions see Pitrim A. Sorokin, *The Ways and Power of Love.* 1967: pp. 3-35; M. Scott Peck, *The Road Less Traveled.* 1978: pp. 81-180; John Boswell, *Same-sex Unions in Premodern Europe.*, 1994: Chapter 1 ("What's in a Name?" The Vocabulary of Love and Marriage) pp. 3-27; Vladimir Solovyov, *The Meaning Of Love.* 1985; Denis De Rougemont, *Love in the Western World.* 1983: pp. 299-323; M.C. D'Arcy, *The Mind and Heart of Love.* 1947; Anders Nygren, *Agape and Eros.* Pt. 1 & 2, 1953; Irving Singer, *The Nature of Love I: Plato to Luther,* 1984; Irving Singer,*The Nature of Love II: Courtly & Romantic,* 1984; & Irving Singer,*The Nature of Love III: The Modern World.*, 1987. It is interesting to note that the discussion of the relationship between "eros" and "agape" has had a somewhat involved history. Anders Nygren, a Protestant Bishop in Sweden, published his, still

controversial *Agape and Eros,* first in 1932. Then, in 1945 M.C. D'Arcy, a Jesuit, published, *The Mind and Heart of Love* which was taken as an "answer" to Nygren's perspective (Denis De Rougemont's, *Love in the Western World*, published in 1940, is also considered and answer to Nygren). And now Irving Singer, a Jew, has given his version of the eros/agape debate with 3 volumes that comprehensively traces the history of the concepts from Plato to modern times. These are all very serious and deep studies of the nature of love and they demonstrate that the recognition of the importance of love for an understanding of the phenomena of man has increased enormously in the last 50 years. Indeed, Irving Singer has spent the last 40 years studying the history and nature of love in the Western World. A useful appraisal of his work has recently been published, David Goicoechea (ed.) *The Nature and Pursuit of Love: The Philosophy of Irving Singer,* 1995.

9. "To realize what I call the wisdom of compassion is to see with complete clarity its benefits, as well as the damage that its opposite has done to us. We need to make a very clear distinction between what is in our *ego's self-interest* and what is in *our ultimate interest;* it is from mistaking one for the other that all our suffering comes. We go on stubbornly believing that self-cherishing is the best protection in life, but in fact the opposite is true" (Sogyal Rinpoche, *The Tibetan Book of Living and Dying,* 1992: pp. 189-90; Italics in original).

10. Meher Baba *Discourses* V. III., 1967: p. 19 (Italics in original)

11. Pierre Teilhard de Chardin *Human Energy,* 1969: p. 63. Addressing the issue of the fear that many have of "losing themselves" if they love another, Teilhard points out that "A person cannot disappear by passing into another person; for he can only give himself *as a person* so long as he remains a self-conscious unity, that is to say *distinct.*" (*Ibid* p. 67) (Italics in original). Teilhard said this more succinctly, if not more paradoxically, when in one of his wedding addresses he asked the question, "How, being two, will you be more truly one?" And then answering it himself he said, "By never relaxing your effort to become more yourselves by the giving of yourselves." (Pierre Teilhard de Chardin *The Heart of Matter,* 1980: p. 141) For other statements by Teilhard de Chardin on how love fulfills our individuality see: *The Phenomenon of Man,* 1965: p. 265 & *Toward the Future,* 1975: p. 71. We will adress this issue again and again in the course of our presentation.

12. The way to change these qualities is discussed at length in the next Section. 3.2 "Transforming Negativity"

13. Ramon James Betanzos, "Franz Von Baader's Philosophy of Love," 1968: p. 106.

14. How one person can effect changes in the relationship is discussed in: Section 3.2, the part titled, "Why Should I Change?"

15. Hazrat Inayat Khan *The Complete Sayings of Hazrat Inayat Khan*, 1978: p. 245.

16. Robert Sardello *Love and the Soul: Creating a future for Earth*, 1995: p. 126.

17. Mother Teresa *My Life for the Poor: Mother Teresa of Calcutta*, 1985: p. 41.

18. Luminious Mind: The Way of the Buddha, 1997: p. 248.

19. The discussion of emotions is often difficult, and dividing it into the "experiencing" of emotional states and the "expressing" of these states is very useful. For the purposes of this exercise we are primarily concerned with the "expressing" or the "acting out" of negative emotions and how they affect our patterns of interaction within the relationship. However, it is necessary to delve into our "experience" of emotions in order to identify our own negativity. For an interesting perspective see Jeremy W. Hayward *Shifting Worlds, Changing Minds*, 1987: Chapter 7 "Feeling and Emotion": pp. 81-94.

20. "Falling in love" is such a common expression that very few people ever question it, however there are negative consequences which arise from such a view of "'love." Thomas Merton elaborated some of the corollaries of conceiving of love as a "falling into": "We speak of 'falling in love,' as though love were something like water that collects in pools, lakes, rivers, and oceans. You can 'fall into' it or walk around it. You can sail on it or swim in it, or you can just look at it from a safe distance. This expression seems to be peculiar to the English language. French, for instance, does not speak of '*tomber en amour*' but does mention 'falling amourous.' The Italian and Spanish say one 'enomors oneself.' Latins do not regard love as a passive accident. Our English expression 'to fall in love' suggests an unforeseen mishap that may or may not be fatal...To speak of 'falling into' something is to shift responsibility from your own will to a cosmic force like gravitation. You 'fall' when you are carried off by a power beyond your control. Once you start you can't stop. You're gone...A certain rudimentary theology regards the whole human race as 'fallen' because Eve tempted Adam to love her. That is bad theology. Sex

is not original sin…The expression to 'fall in love' reflects a peculiar attitude toward love and toward life itself—a mixture of fear, awe, fascination, and confusion. It implies suspicion, doubt, hesitation, in the presence of something unavoidable—yet not fully reliable. For love takes you out of yourself. You lose control. You 'fall.' You get hurt. It upsets the ordinary routine of life. You become emotional, imaginative, vulnerable, foolish. You now have to let yourself be carried away with this force that is stronger than reason and more imperious even than business!" (*Love and Living,* 1979: pp. 25-6). As Merton says, this is indeed a "peculiar" attitude toward love and life.

21. We said at the beginning of Section 1.1 "The Invocation of Love" that, "What most of us experience as love is, no doubt, a mixture of illusion and longing, romanticized desires and fantasy; yet at the same time, it is a reflection of a great truth…" We are not referring here to the loss of the illusion, but the loss of that "reflection of a great truth." We lose the True Love!

22. Aurobindo refers to the identification with the emotions as the "vital ego", see discussion in: Sri Aurobindo *The Life Divine,* 1965: pp. 476-7.

23. See Jeremy W. Hayward *Shifting Worlds, Changing Minds.* 1987: p. 82: "emotions are usually felt to be very real and definite, almost solid things. We think we have a repertoire of emotions: the emotion of anger, the emotion of love, the emotion of jealousy and so on. 'Anger,' 'love,' and 'jealousy' are all nouns; we think of emotions as things we can experience, like a rock or the sky. And when we experience these things we are in the corresponding state: when we experience anger, we are angry. We would not say to a friend, 'I am experiencing anger toward you.' We would simply say, 'I am angry with you.' Thus, when the emotion is a part of our present experience, we name it and identify ourselves with it. 'I' becomes that emotion."

24. This "collection" may be referred to as "the emotional nature" or "the affective nature", and most people have little knowledge or understanding of this side of their being beyond an awareness of what they like and dislike. One of the few modern thinkers who has delved deeply into the emotional nature is Max Scheler: "For Scheler the emotional sphere in man possesses its own lawfulness of acts not deducible from reason and will, and that the emotional has its own *a priori* content, which can only be exhibited in ethics, and not in logic. The seat of the value-*a priori* in acts of feeling, preferring (or rejecting), and ultimately in love and hatred, where cognition of values

and value intuition take place." (Manfred Frings, *Max Scheler*, 1965: p. 67) (Emphasis in original). Scheler uses the Latin term *Ordo Amoris* to describe "the order or ordering of love", and for a valuable analysis of the structure and purposes of the emotional nature see: "Ordo Amoris" in Max Scheler, *Selected Philosophical Essays.*, 1973: pp. 98-135. See also Max Scheler, *Formalism in Ethics and Non-Formal Ethics of Values*, 1973: Pt II, 5.2 "Feeling and Feeling-States" pp. 253-264.

25. Thomas Keating, *Reawakenings*, 1992: p. 28.

26. Dramatic new research has been able to scientifically demonstrate the harmful effects of short-term negative emotional states. An eclectic group of researchers at the Institute of HeartMath in California have done extensive and sophisticated measurements of the heart's power spectrum when subjects recall negative and positive emotions. Not only have they demonstrated that negative emotions (i.e., anger) produce chaotic and harmful responses in the heart's electrical profile, but positive emotions (i.e., appreciation) produce a harmonious heart rate variability spectrum. See Rollin McCraty, et. al., "The Effects of Emotions on Short-Term Power Spectrum Analysis of Heart Rate Variability", 1995. These results are also presented in Doc Lew Childre, *Freeze-Frame™ Fast Action Stress Relief*, 1994: Chapter 4 "The Scientific Basis of the Freeze-Frame Technology", pp. 38-55. An interesting appraisal of the work of the HeartMath Institute has been recently presented in *Vibrational Medicine* by Richard Gerber (Bear & Co, S.F., NM, 1996: pp. 588-90). Gerber also cites the discussion in D. Winter *et. al.*, *Alphabet of the Heart, Sacred Geometry: The Principle of Language & Feeling* (Crystal Hill Farm, Eden NY, 1993).

27. It is beyond the scope of our presentation to discuss, in more depth, the complexities and purposes of these "dark" emotions. Suffice it to say, that the usually offered options of 'express' or 'repress' do not represent a valid solution or a path to growth for a person. Indeed, this common approach to the dark side of human nature is simplistic and ignores the holistic view of humans as more than a "collection" of various parts that can be analyzed as if they were separate from any dynamic whole. Useful studies of the real scope and purpose of the negative emotions are rare, but the interested reader would do well to see "The Mission of Anger" in Rudolf Steiner, *Metamorphoses of the Soul*: pp. 17-44. & Max Scheler, *Ressentiment*, 1961. Aso of interest, is the new book by the Dalai Lama, *Healing Anger: The Power of Patience from a*

Buddhist Perspective. Within a more Western psychological perspective, but with positive usefulness is Hariet Lerner's *The Dance of Anger*, 1985.

28. Tantric Buddhism has enunciated this perspective for, at least 1600 years: "Thus, in general, the method of the Inner Tantras is not to suppress emotion (as in the *hinayana*) or to transform it into its opposite (as in *mahayana*), but to transmute it into its real nature and use its inherent energy. When incisive insight into the nature of mind, from which emotion is inseparable, removes the sting of passion, passion becomes an inexhaustible source of energy, power and awareness. Following the middle path, emotional feeling is the *sadhaka's* best ally" (Kieth Dowman, *Sky Dancer*, 1989: p. 237).

29. This exercise was given by Pythagoras (6th. Century B.C.) to the students in his Crotona Mystery school, and it has been recommended and used by various spiritual teachers in different traditions all over the world. For instance, a daily review was also recommended by Pythogaras' contemporary, Confucius: "Every day I examine myself on these three points: in acting on behalf of others, have I always been loyal to their interests? In intercourse with my friends, have I always been true to my word? Have I failed to repeat (and so keep in memory) the precepts that have been handed down to me? (Analects: I, 4). For contemporary discussions see, Torkom Saraydarian The *Psyche and Psychism.* V.II., 1981: Chapter 80 (Evening Review) pp. 791-800; Rudolf Steiner *Learning to see into the Spiritual World.*, 1990: Lecture 1 (The Development of Independent Thinking & The Ability to Think Backward) Pp. 1-21; & Herman Rednick in Justin R.Moore, (Ed.)*Teachings From the Path of Fire: The Life and Works of Herman Rednick*, 1973: "On the Spiritual Path in the Aquarian Age,": Q100-105. Michel Foucault discusses the uses of this technique in Hellenistic and Roman times in *Technologies of the Self,* pp. 26-28. Emil Bock said that "Memory is a remnant of the ancient powers of supersensible vision. Calm, patient exercises in remembering, such as looking back in the evening and reviewing the events of the day, raise the soul slowly back to those heights from which it has fallen." (*The Apocalypse of Saint John*, 1980: p. 39).

Since most ancient times, Eastern and Western spiritual practices have included instructions for the control or transformation of the emotional nature and the actions that result from these emotions. For example, Kalu Rinpoche gives a basic outline of how the different divisions of Buddhist practice "process" emotions: e.g., Hinayana Buddhism and Zen Buddhism reject emotions through non-action. (Similarly, Christianity has traditionally recommended rejection of the emotions as the only sure way to "life in the Spirit.") Mahayana Buddhism seeks to transform the emotional nature through compassion and concern for the well-being of others. And Vajrayana Buddhist practice instructs the practitioner to simply recognize emotions in *Mahamudra* medititation, wherein the mind dwells in itself without distraction, e.g., *Mahamamudra* practice is so powerful that it "tears samsara to pieces" (*Profound Buddhism: From Hinayana to Vajrayana*, 1995: p. 176). Kalu Rinpoche offers a useful caution in respect to these practices: "Even today, many people develop such erroneous views when they hear Mahayana teachings, and the very profound transformative techniques of the Vajrayana tantras are equally open to misinterpretation. If these people hear, for example, that in the Vajrayana there is theoretically no need to suppress or alter emotional confusion, because simply seeing the nature of emotional conflict is sufficient for Liberation, they can easily misunderstand, and take this to mean that nothing has to be done about the emotions. Some people even think the Vajrayana teaches that lust and anger should be indulged when they arise in the mind" (*Dharma Teachings*, 1990: p. 14). In these times of total access to spiritual teachings, this is not an uncommon problem for Western practitioners, who are not properly prepared for these advanced teachings or who do not have the guidance of a qualified teacher.

Varela, Thompson and Rosch describe the approach presented in the Mahayana Buddhist teachings called the *Abhidarma* which is congruent with our practice as it is discussed in this Section: "the Abhidharma contains various sets of categories for examining the arising of the sense of self....The most popular set of these categories, one that is common to all Buddhist schools, is known as the five aggregates..."(Francisco Varela, Evan Thompson & Eleanor Rosch. *The Embodied Mind:* 1993: p. 63). What concerns us here is the third aggregate called, discernment and "this aggregate refers to the first moment of recognition, identification, or discernment in the arising of something distinct, coupled with the activation of a basic impulse for action toward the discerned object." (Ibid. p. 66) Discernment "normally arises inseparably with feeling. Through mindfulness...the meditator may recognize impulses of passion, aggression, and ignoring for what they are—impulses that need not automatically lead to action....one may thus be able to choose wholesome rather than unwholesome actions. Eventually, when sufficient freedom from habitual patterns has been obtained, perception/discernments can... automatically give rise not to self-based impulses of passion, aggression, and ignoring [i.e. avoidance] but to impulses of wisdom and compassionate action." (Ibid. p. 120) The process for transforming negativity presented in this Section is basically similar to this Buddhist approach, except that we unfold and elaborate the recognition of impulses and we provide a step by step process to stop the automatic response to unwholesome impulses by substituting a specific course of action based on wisdom and compassion.

30. Refer to discussion on reframing in Section 1.3 "Gratitude."

31. See Section 4.1 "Responsibility", for a detailed analysis of 'changing ourselves.'

32. Weiner-Davis 1992: "It Only Takes One To Tango," p. 99.

33. *Ibid.* 1992: pp. 132-3.

34. The Institute of HeartMath in California uses a similar technique, developed by Doc Lew Childre and presented in his book *Freeze-Frame: Fas Action Stress Relief, 1994*. There are five steps in the Freeze-Frame process (p. 27). It may also be useful to compare the six-step reframing process developed by Bandler and Grinder (*Reframing,* 1982: pp. 114-5). They also have a modified six-step exercise for couples, see pp. 147-8 of their book.

• NOTES FOR PART 2 •

1. Moore, Justin R. (ed.) *Teachings From the Path of Fire: The Life and Works of Herman Rednick,* 1973: Q231.

2. As indicated by the title, The Way of the Beloved, we shall be using the word "beloved" throughout this book. It will take on many shades of meaning, and it may be useful at this point to consider the statement by Max Scheler that, "in all human love relations, such as marriage or friendship, a distinction must be made between a 'lover' and a 'beloved,' and the latter is always nobler and more perfect. He is the *model* for the lover's being, willing, and acting" (Max Scheler, *Ressentiment,* 1961: p. 85).

• Chapter 4 NOTES •

1. Saraydarian, Torkom *Sex, Family, and the Woman in Society.* 1987: p. 44.

2. The English root of responsibility is "**spend-**, to make an offering, perform a ritual when L[atin] *spondere, spons-,* make a solemn promise, whence the

SPOUSE who's made such a promise, and the SPONSOR who, at a baptism, promises to be RESPONSIBLE for the infant's moral upbringing. If you make someone such a promise, they're supposed to RESPOND ("promise back"); if they don't, you may become idiomatically DESPONDENT. And if you promise of your own accord it's SPONTANEOUS." Clairborne, Robert. *The Roots of English: A Reader's Handbook of Word Origins.*, 1989: p. 228.

3. Michele Weiner-Davis, *Divorce Busting.* 1993: p. 69.

4. Refer back to Transforming Negativity Section 3.2

5. Gurumayi Chidvilasananda, "Become a Great Doer, A Supreme Enjoyer, and a Great Renunciant" [Talk given 8/23/87] *Darshan*, March 1994: pp. 40-45.

6. Quoted in Peggy Kamuf "Femmeninism", 1978: p. 83. (The full quote found in Kamuf reads: "it therefore seems to me that admiration is the first of the passions, and that it can have no contrary; this because, if the object that presents itself has nothing in itself which surprises us, we are not moved in the least and can consider it without any passion.") It is certainly interesting that Luce Irigaray uses a different translation of Descartes which says that "wonder is the first of all the passions; and it has no opposite, because if the object which presents itself has nothing in it that surprises us, we are in nowise moved regarding it, and we consider it without passion" (Luce Irigaray *An Ethics of Sexual Difference*, 1993: p. 13). (She quotes from *The Philosophical Works of Descartes*, trans. E.S. Haldane & G.R.T. Ross, Cambridge U. Press, 1931: reprinted Dover, 1955: I: 358) There is certainly an interesting link between "admiration" and "wonder," however they are not equivalent and for our purposes admiration is more appropriate.

7. *The Poetics of Reverie: Childhood, Language, and the Cosmos*, 1971: p. 190

8. Herman Rednick *The Beloved Yoga*, HRAP Memoir #1, 1993: p. 75.

9. Torkom Saraydarian, *The Flame of Beauty, Culture, Love, Joy.* 1980: p. 156.

10. "We have what Jung called an *enantiodromia*— the thing has turned into its opposite. What was positive is now negative, and vice-versa" (Desteian, John A. *Coming Together—Coming Apart.* 1989: p.136). Besides the things that we admire, this reversal of affect occurs in other areas of a dynamic relationship between people.

11. "If a woman cannot admire a man, she wants to be rid of him...When she does not find anything to admire in him, he becomes dead for her... Admiration offers the only solution to many problems" (Torkom Saraydarian, *Sex, Family, and the Woman in Society*. 1987: pp. 216-17).

12. Gabriel Marcel *Creative Fidelity*, 1964: p. 48.

13. Ibid.

14. *Ibid.* p. 47.

15. *Ibid.* p. 48

16. Torkom Saraydarian, *The Flame of Beauty, Culture, Love, Joy*, 1980: p. 125.

17. For many people it may sound like we are talking about faith, specifically when we refer to trusting in "something higher." Indeed, in the epigram, Steiner uses faithfulness in this sense. However, in Robert Clairborne's, *The Roots of English*, we find that historically the words "faith" and "trust" came into English from different root sources, and their meanings may not have been interchangeable in the past. Yet, today the term "faith," according to Paul Tillich, "is more productive of disease than health. It confuses, misleads, creates alternately skepticism and fanaticism, intellectual resistance and emotional surrender, rejection of genuine religion and subjection to substitutes. Indeed one is tempted to suggest that the word 'faith' should be dropped completely..." (The Dynamics of Faith, 1958: p. ix). Almost twenty years later Tillich still found it necessary to point that, "There are few words in the language of religion which cry for as much semantic purging as the word 'faith.' It is continually being confused with belief in something for which there is no evidence, or in something intrinsically unbelievable, or in absurdities and nonsense. It is extremely difficult to remove these distorting connotations from the genuine meaning of faith" (*Systematic Theology Vol. III.*, 1976: p. 130). Another twenty years have elapsed and the misuse of the term "faith" may not have improved very much. Tillich said that, "The most ordinary misinterpretation of faith is to consider it an act of knowledge that has a low degree of evidence. Something more or less probable or improbable is affirmed in spite of the insufficiency of its theoretical substantiation. This situation is very usual in daily life. If this is meant, one is speaking of *belief* rather than faith" (The Dynamics of Faith, 1958: p. 31). Even though "trust is an element of faith," we should make it clear that in this Section we are not speaking about "faith," but in increasing our trust in what we believe to be true about our

beloved relationship through expanding our knowledge and perception of the basis and dynamics of our interaction. The distinction is important because, "faith is more than trust in even the most sacred authority. It is participation in the subject of one's ultimate concern with one's whole being. Therefore, the term 'faith' should not be used in connection with theoretical knowledge, whether it is a knowledge on the basis of immediate, prescientific or scientific evidence, or whether it is on the basis of trust in authorities who themselves are dependent on direct or indirect evidence" (Ibid. p. 32). Tillich has made it quite clear that all "knowledge of our world (including ourselves as a part of the world) is a matter of inquiry…It is not a matter of faith" (Ibid. p. 33).

18. It should be pointed out, again, that the practices and exercises presented in this book are, with few exceptions, adaptations for the use of couples of widespread methods of transformation found throughout the world's spiritual teachings. For instance, in the fourteenth century the Tibetan Lama, Gyelsay Togmay Sangpo (1295-1369), wrote *The Thirty-seven Practices of Bodhisattvas* and Chapter 4 is titled "Trusting." Apparently, the basic human dilemma has not changed much in 600 years: "We need a refuge we can trust and which will not let us down. The Three Jewels are such a refuge, for they will never fail us. Taking refuge in them, we look upon the enlightened beings [Buddhas] as those who show us our true protection. We regard their teaching [Dharma] as our actual refuge and the spiritual community [Sangha] as our companions and role-models. When we are overwhelmed by obstructions, feel afraid or are in pain, we have a support and a source of strength and hope. Feeling this trust is taking mental refuge, expressing it in words is taking verbal refuge and making any gesture of homage is taking physical refuge. We then try to live by the refuge precepts. When we see no way out, when we look to our right and left but no one, not even enlightened beings and our spiritual teachers, can do anything directly to help us, there's no need for despair because the virtue we ourselves have created will act as our refuge and protection. If we imagine our spiritual teachers and the Three Jewels before us, thinking again and again of their excellent qualities, we'll remember them not only during our waking hours but during the night as well. Through such prolonged familiarity we will, hopefully, also recall them when we're dying" (Ibid. pp. 34-35). It is obvious that, in the West, Christianity recommends a similar practice using the image and vision of the Christ as *refuge*. In Part 3 we will discuss concepts and exercises specifically related to couples who are truly following the spiritual path of the Beloved.

19. This Section is intended only to help us disbelieve the illusions created by the powerful negative emotional states which inevitably arise in love relationships. This is also why we use the word "radical" to describe the kind of trust that is powerful enough to overcome our naive belief in the truth of our perceptions for the sake of love. Techniques for developing a clearer vision and increasing our ability to assess the dynamics of our relationship with more wisdom are presented in Chaps. 5 & 6.

20. It is in the very nature of love and devotion to seek a greater union with the loved one. In other words, a loving relationship could be called a "positive co-dependency"—one in which the parties rely on being treated with care and respect. This is probably not a useful term because it is the opposite of the normal use of "Codependency." As Robert Sardello explains, "Codependency means that one person relies on being treated badly by the other person and vice versa, but the whole thing is disguised as obsessive love. When a person becomes obsessed with another person, this obsessiveness is not about love, but about fear…All obsession cannot be traced back to what one did not receive as a child…the work is not perhaps to strengthen our ego in order to be in control of our self, but to decide to work on becoming a creative being who creates through love" (Robert Sardello, *Love and the Soul*, 1995: pp. 159-60). Some have used the following terms for this union or blending: "interdependency," "symbiosis," "conspiration", "convergence", or "syzygy" (for a discussion of syzygy see Vladimir Solovyev *The Meaning Of Love*, 1985: pp.113-117 & note 5). The mystery of personality transformation through a loving interdependency with another person is central to the Way of the Beloved and will be addressed more fully in Section 5.4.

21. Written as part of an exercise at the Winter 1995 Beloved's Retreat.

Chapter 5 NOTES •

1. Mother Teresa, *A Gift for God: Prayers and Meditations*, 1975: p. 12.

2. The general *romantic fog* surrounding our conceptions of love relationships has prevented the spread of the understanding that "there is a general law of life which states that every organic reunion constitutes a more profound and solid reality than the union which had been broken or damaged. The reason for this is…because the uniting principle [love], when actual separation or even just the solicitation to it occurs, has to regather its energies within itself in a more profound way for a new emanation; by means of this deeper emanation

drawn from itself it unites what has to be united in the same relationship more deeply and inwardly" (Ramon Betanzos "Franz Von Baader's Philosophy of Love", 1968: p. 242). Von Baader put it poetically when he said, "The heart's blood spilled in misunderstanding is sometimes the very 'cement' of a deeper and more lasting union" (*Ibid.* p. 238).

3. C.S. Lewis, *Mere Christianity*, 1978: Forgiveness, p. 104.

4. Consider why so many TV and movie dramas are based on the hero, leading character, or protagonist seeking a *righteous revenge*. And how the killings in Northern Ireland, Bosnia, Palestine, etc. go on and on because no one can break the cycle of revenge.

5. Torkom Saraydarian, *The Psyche and Psychism*, V.II., 1981: p. 1111. Saraydarian mentions even worse consequences of not forgiving others, "Unforgivingness is the best way to cultivate those characteristics which you hate in another person. Unforgivingness continuously channels into your system those forces which emanate from the thought form built around the event you hate. Unforgivingness leads to moral and physical degeneration" (Ibid).

6. Robert Clairborne, *The Roots of English: A Reader's Handbook of Word Origins*, 1989: p. 107.

7. For useful definitions & history of anger, revenge and forgiveness, and some practical and creative techniques for facilitating forgiveness, see Kenneth Cloke "Revenge, Forgiveness, and the Magic of Mediation" *Mediation Quarterly*. v. 10 (3), 1993: pp. 67-78.

8. This power of higher love is called "God" in many traditions.

9. Franz Hartmann, *The Life and Doctrines of Jacob Boehme.*, 1977: Fn. p. 302 (our emphasis).

10. Sogyal Rinpoche, *The Tibetan Book of Living and Dying*, 1992: pp. 212-3 (our emphasis).

11. If no person can forgive another person's sin, why do we so often hear that we should forgive ourselves and others? It may be that the two aspects of the meaning of "forgiveness" are not made clear and distinct in ordinary speech. Our vernacular would seem to use "forgiveness" imprecisely, combining or mixing its two aspects. As we pointed out, in one sense, the injunction to

"forgive oneself and others" is asking us to dissolve and move on from our own negativites. But if I say, [1] forgive you because "your heart cannot see" or "you know not what you do," I have either abrogated to myself the power of selfless love (God) or I am giving an excuse for not transforming my own negativity. Even Christ on the cross said, [Father], forgive them for they know not what they do!" (Lk. 23:34). It is a profoundly different act to pray for the liberation of the person who has harmed you and to say, I love you, and I have compassion for you; therefore, I ask that you [be] forgiven. Desiring the liberation of the other person from his or her negativity may be a positive part of one's inner work to love and forgive, but if there is any sense of superiority in your attitude, it is the ego speaking. If you believe that you are practicing forgiveness by pointing out the moral or spiritual inferiority of the person who has harmed you, you are in truth just veiling your arrogance. How can forgiveness flow from condescension? This kind of self-deception leads to a life of hidden resentments. Max Scheler has given us a detailed phenomenology of the roots and dynamics of resentment (See Ressentiment, 1961: pp. 43-77 for some of the workings of condescension; note particularly pp. 96-7).

12. *Divorce Busting*, 1993: p. 231.

13. Quoted in Bernie S. Siegel, *Love, Medicine & Miracles*, 1986: p. 196.

14. Frederic Wiedemann, *Between Two Worlds: the Riddle of Wholeness*, 1986: p. 143.

15. In his recent book, Rabbi Charles Klein, observes that, "One of the questions most frequently asked is, 'How can I forget what was done to me?' For them, forgetting is the biggest obstacle to forgiveness. However, forgiving does not demand that we simultaneously perform the more difficult task of forgetting" (*How to Forgive When You Can't Forget*, 1995: p. 43). And to take this a step further, Jon Elster shows that "The will to forget is an example of what has been called 'to want what couldn't be wanted,' an impossibility, since it relies on the confusion of active and passive negation. Forgetfulness, or indifference, is a passive negation—simply the absence of consciousness of x—while the will to forget requires the consciousness of the absence of x. Wanting to forget is like deciding to create obscurity from light. Just like forgetfulness, or indifference, states of mind like sincerity, spontaneity, innocence, or faith could never be created by an act of intentional will" ("Active and Passive Negation: An Essay in Ibanskian Sociology" in Paul Watzlawick *The Invented Reality*, 1984: p. 185). In speaking specifically of

forgiveness, Herman Rednick said that, "The object is not to be free from memory, but free from the pull of negative emotions and thought-streams that come into consciousness from memory." He goes on to say that even when a person's vibration has become "so strong that all negative elements will be repelled and nullified....he [or she] will not be freed from his [or her] memory..." (Justin Moore, *Teachings From the Path of Fire*, 1973: Q179).

16. It could be said that the Apostle Paul prefigured pre-forgiveness when he said, "Bear with each other and forgive whatever grievances you may have against one another" (NIV Col. 3:1). Despite the common objection that to forgive a person who has done wrong is to readmit him or her back into the community of the *righteous* (i.e., to make just the unjust), forgiveness is nonetheless imminently practical (and Christian) because how else may we reunite with those who have done wrong or acted unjustly? Is not the highest justice that which rejustifies the sinner and turns him or her back toward righteousness? Paul Tillich has brilliantly untangled the issues of forgiveness and justice in the following way: "The third and most paradoxical form in which justice is united with love is forgiving. Their unity is indicated in the Pauline term: justification by grace. Justification literally means: making just, and it means in the context of Paul's and Luther's doctrine to accept as just him who is unjust. Nothing seems to contradict more the idea of justice than this doctrine, and everybody who has pronounced it has been accused of promoting injustice and amorality. It seems to be utterly unjust to declare him who is unjust, just. But nothing less than this is what has been called the good news in Christian preaching. And nothing less than this is the fulfillment of justice. For it is the only way of reuniting those who are estranged by guilt. Without reconciliation there is no reunion. Forgiving love is the only way of fulfilling the intrinsic claim in every being, namely its claim to be reaccepted into the unity to which it belongs...In accepting him [her] into the unity of forgiveness, love exposes both the acknowledged break with justice on his [her] side with all its implicit consequences and the claim inherent in him [her] to be *declared* just and to be *made* just by reunion" (Paul Tillich, *Love, Power, and Justice*, 1960: p. 86). In the beloved relationship we are trying to establish a dynamic mutual forgiveness which Tillich calls "the fulfillment of creative justice." But, as he points out, "mutual forgiveness is justice only if it is based on reuniting love... Only god can forgive, because in Him alone love and justice are completely united. The ethics of forgiveness are rooted in the message of divine forgiveness. Otherwise they are delivered to the

ambiguities of justice, oscillating between legalism and and sentimentality. In the holy community [beloved relationship] this ambiguity is conquered" (Ibid. p. 121). A mutual pre-forgiveness based on reuniting (i.e., spiritual or unselfish) love resolves the difficult issue of how to reunite with a loved one without sacrificing the recognition and consequences of the hurtful, selfish, or unjust acts that he or she has committed. If we believe, as many do, that the necessary consequence of wrong-doing is to never be reunited in love again (i.e., forever unforgiven), then we are unjustly denying of the other's inherent, and thus, legitimate claim to rejustification. Forgiveness declares the other rejustified and reunion makes the other rejustified. Seeking revenge or permanently *casting out* wrong-doers is the antithesis of justice and of anything even resembling spiritual love. It would seem that the forgiveness of a reuniting love is part of the true meaning of Christ's sacrifice on Golgotha, and a part that humanity has experienced as nearly impossible to practice.

17. We cannot find a precise location for this quotation. However, Mother Teresa has voiced the same idea in many other places e.g., Kathryn Spink, *The Miracle of Love*, 1981: p. 184 & Mother Teresa *A Gift for God: Prayers and Meditations*, 1975: p. 13.

18. In our secular and individualistic society this meaning has almost been lost. For most people sacrifice means loss, and the fear of loss is at an all time high in our consumer oriented (or every-desire-must-be-fulfilled) culture. Robert Clairborne shows sacrifice coming from the roots DHE- to set or do, and SAK- to make SACRED, CONSECRATE, or SANCTIFY, whence SAINT (*The Roots of English*, 1989: pp. 84 & 207). The saint is a sacred (holy) person who has achieved this status through sacrifice. Clairborne says that, "to SACRIFICE something originally meant 'make it sacred'" When we freely choose to sacrifice our self (part or whole) for the sake of love for another, we make that self sacred. It may be useful to think of sacrifice as more of a process of transubstantiation as in the Eucharist or the Mass. As Torkom Saraydarian has said, "Sacrifice comes from a Latin word meaning 'to make whole or sacred.' In sacrificing something one sets it apart to be used for a higher and more noble purpose. In sacrifice, the physical, emotional and mental bodies are prepared to be a unified vessel for a highly-burning essence" (*Sex, Family, and the Woman in Society*, 1987:p. 90).

19. There are several other terms that are commonly used for this higher love. In the Christian tradition the Greek word *Agape* is often used (Denis De

Rougemont, *Love in the Western World*, 1983). Scholars seem to prefer the word "Altruism," when referring to unselfish love (Sorokin, Pitirim, *The Ways and Power of Love*, 1967). For many of us "Compassion" is equivalent to "Spiritual love," and the terms used for spiritual love in the Eastern Spiritual Texts (i.e. *karuna*) are usually translated as "compassion" (Bokar Rinpoche *Chenrezig, Lord Of Love: Principles and Methods of Deity Meditation*, 1991). Francisco Varela says, 'The Sanscrit term translated here as 'compassion' is *karuna* …there is no other satisfactory English term" (*The Embodied Mind*, 1993: p. 277 n. 11).

20. For our purposes here, we take "self," "personality," and "ego" to be equivalent. We mean these to be simply, "the image we construct of the apparent experiencer of our everyday actions, thoughts, and feeling" (Amit Goswami, *The Self-Aware Universe*, 1995: p. 202). Or, "This 'self' which we take to be 'me' and which feels so present and real to us is actually an internalized image, a composite representation, constructed by a selective and imaginative 'remembering' of past encounters with significant objects in our world. In fact, the self is viewed…as a representation which is *actually being constructed anew from moment to moment*." (Jack Engler in *Transformations of Consciousness*, 1986: p. 21. Quoted in Jeremy Hayward, 1987: p. 125.)(Italics in original). A good discussion of the recent origin of the modern usage of the word *self* (dating only from 1674) and the western cultural specificity of all our ideas about "self," "personality," etc., is to be found in *Meeting the Great Bliss Queen* by Anne Klein (Chapter 2).

21. Those interested in a deeper understanding of the complexities and paradoxes of "self-interest," are referred to the detailed study by Derek Parfit, *Reasons and Persons*, 1985.

22. *Sex, Family, and the Woman in Society*, 1987: p. 90.

23. Von Baader expressed it poetically, if not enigmatically, "The giver is not the gift, nor is the gift the giver, and yet the giver gives himself in his gift *to the extent that he loves*, and the recipient receives the giver in the gift *to the extent that [she] he loves him[her]*. If I do not give you myself, my heart, in my gift, then I do not love you, and if you do not receive *me* in my gift, then you do not love me" (Ramon James Betanzos, "Franz Von Baader's Philosophy of Love", 1968: p. 278; Underlining and brackets added).

24. There is much confusion surrounding the Sanscrit word *karma*, but there is no word in English that will do the job. The closest concept to *karma* in the

West would be "original sin." As Martin Lings has pointed out, "The truth of the *samsara*, with its pre-terrestrial states, is partially expressed in the doctrine of original sin, which serves to single out and stress the essential fact that man is not born into this world in a state of innocence. The same truth is also implicit in the Islamic doctrine that each man's sense of responsibility began when he was created as a seed in the loins of Adam and not merely after his birth into this world. For a Hindu the doctrine of original sin is self-evident: birth into this world necessarily means imperfection...because a being that had reached perfection in a pre-terrestrial state would thereby have already excaped from the *samsara* altogether. Without sharing this perspective, our Western ancestors nonetheless saw that the doctrine of original sin, that is, the doctrine that babies are no longer born into the world as Saints, corresponds to an obvious fact; and indeed this fact could only arouse question in a community which has lost all sense of the human ideal..." (*Ancient Beliefs and Modern Superstitions,* 1991: p. 63). However, for most Westerners, the notion of original sin is probably more confusing than that of *karma*. Some thinkers have equated *karma* with the "will of God, but this would take us too far afield.

The following, simple definition of *karma* by Kalu Rinpoche is all that we are implying here: "to realize the full potential of being human, we must examine the concept of *karma*, the process of cause and effect, especially the relationship between our actions and their results. We need to recognize fully the unfailing connection between what we do now and what we experience later" (*Dharma Teachings,* 1990: p. 44). *Karma* is like our *natural laws*, impersonal and unfailing in their functioning. And like our natural laws, "the law of *karma* is not considered absolute, and therefore negative karmic fruitions can be eliminated through applying correct purification methods..." (Kalu Rinpoche, *Gently Whispered,* 1994: p. 244). It is important not to get trapped in the popular negative notions about *karma* (or original sin) which limit our freedom of action and induce passivity. Herman Rednick has explained that "we are living in a psychic sea. It is filled with all kinds of psychic forms, some strange and grotesque and some very beautiful and radiant. There are millions of currents in this sea; and you are attracting one of the psychic currents. It brings to you the ideas and experience that is your karma to go through. Therefore, every experience comes to you with a purpose to teach you and help you to reach the mountain top. No experience is accidental. It is a design of nature. When you realize that all your experience is according to a plan, you will face it with courage, knowing that it is your problem to solve. You will not resent it. But if you resist the experience, it will repeat itself until you have learned the lesson" (Herman Rednick, *The Earth Journey: from Birth to Fulfillment*, 1980: p. 220). Sacrifice is a correct purification method, as is the Way of the Beloved, in general.

25. In India this sense of sacrifice has not been lost since Vedic times. Indeed, as Mircea Eliade has written, "it is certain that from the time of the Brahmanas sacrifice became chiefly a means of restoring the primordial unity....by sacrifice the scattered limbs of Prajapati are reunited, that is to say the divine Being, immolated at the beginning of Time in order that the World may be born from his body, is reconstituted. The essential function of sacrifice is to put together again (*samdha*) that which was broken up *in illo tempore*. At the same time as the symbolic reconstitution of Prajapati, a process of reintegration takes place in the officiant himself. By ritually reuniting the fragments of Prajapati, the officiant 'recollects' (*samharati*) himself, that is to say endeavours to regain the unity of his true Self. As Ananda Coomaraswamy writes, 'the unification of the act of becoming oneself represent at the same time a death, a rebirth and a marriage.' That is why the symbolism of the Indian sacrifice is extremely complex; one is concerned with cosmological, sexual and initiatory symbols, all together. Sacrifice conceived as the preeminent method of unification is one of the numerous examples illustrating the irrepressible aspiration of the Indian spirit to transcend the contraries and rise to a complete reality" (Mephistopheles and the Androgyne, 1965: pp. 97-8). Eliade's quoting of Coomarsaswamy is particularly pertinent. This passage is from Coomaraswamy's article, "Atmayajña: Self-Sacrifice" (*Harvard Journal of Asiatic Studies*, V. 6, 1942: pp. 358-398; p. 388). This article is the best discussinon of *self-sacrifice* that we have seen. Coomaraswamy makes it quite clear how one's whole future evolution hinges on self-sacrifice, e.g., "The [Upanishad] passage sums up in a few words the whole thesis of 'self-sacrifice,' i.e. the sacrifice of oneself to one's Self, 'this self's immortal Self'...Whoever will not make this sacrifice is 'damned': 'Whosoever hath not [possessed his Self], from him shall be taken away even that [self] he hath,' Mark XIII.12" (Ibid. p. 378, Fn. 57). The sacrifice of the individual ego for the sake of becoming a greater being or "self" is ultimately unavoidable—one can choose to delay it, but not circumvent it. This is fundamental to all spiritual traditions. Indeed, if a teaching does not contain a dimension of sacrifice, we can confidently label it as a false teaching.

26. Clara M. Codd, *The Creative Power*, 1947: p. 21 (our emphasis). See also, Scott Miners, (Ed.) *A Spiritual Approach to Male/Female Relations*, 1984: p. 109.

27. Vladimir Solovyov, The *Meaning Of Love,* 1985: p. 41.

28. See Section 3.1 "Transcending Selfishness."

29. Ramon Betanzos, "Franz Von Baader's Philosophy of Love", 1968: p. 247.

30. Indeed, it is at this basic level of extreme self-absorbtion that we seem to have lost our way as a healthy civilization because we have obscured what is most fundamental to human relations. As Martin Buber (1878-1965) has said, "The inmost growth of the self is not accomplished, as people like to suppose today, in man's relation to himself, but in the relation between the one and the other, between men [and women], that is, pre-eminently in the mutuality of the making present—in the making present of another self and in the knowledge that one is made present in his own self by the other—together with the mutuality of acceptance, of affirmation and confirmation" (*The Knowledge of Man: A Philosophy of the Interhuman*, 1965: p. 71). Buber's concept of "confirmation" is congruent with our concept of "affirmation" presented in this Section. Also refer to the discussion in Section 5.2 "sacrifice."

31. A useful explication of negative bonds is to be found in Richard Sennett's, *Authority*. Commenting on negative bonds in marriage he says, "Most of us have observed marriages in which one partner complains endlessly about the other but never manages to leave. And often what we are hearing is not hatred or disgust which the person is too weak to act upon. Instead…[the negative bond is] masked, rendered safe by declarations of rejection. Rejection of and a bond to the other person are inseparable" (*Authority.*, 1981: pp. 27-28). This has also been called "co-dependency."

32. See Section 4.1 "100% Responsibility." & Section 3.2 "Transforming Negativity."

33. It has even been said recently that "neither men nor women can fully exist unless they are being affirmed by the love of another. The richest possibilities of such affirmation are to be found in some form of heterosexual encounter" (Cornelius Murphy, *Beyond Feminism: Toward a Dialogue on Difference*, 1995 p. xvii).

34. Michele Weiner-Davis, *Divorce Busting*, 1993: p. 58.

35. For those who are interested in the philosophical issues involved with affirmation it is worth noting that Michel Foucault called this kind of unconditional affirmation "nonpositive affirmation." This term may seem, at first, to be a contradiction. Foucault defines it by saying that "this affirmation contains nothing positive: no content can bind it, since, by definition, no limit can possibly restrict it." And he points out that "when contemporary philosophy discovered the possibility of nonpositive affirmation, it began a process of reorientation..." (All the Foucault quotes are from his, *Language, Counter-memory, Practice*, 1981: pp. 36-7). It is not clear when philosophy discovered nonpositive affirmation since a clear statement is found in René Guénon, *The Multiple States of Being*, 1984, a book originally published in 1932: "Any direct affirmation expressed in language must, in fact, be a particular and determined affirmation—the affirmation of something—whereas total and absolute affirmation is not any particular affirmation to the exclusion of others, for it implies them all equally. It should now be simple to grasp the very close connection which this has with universal Possibility, which in the same way embraces all particular possibilities" (p. 30). Can nonpositive affirmation open up a realm of unlimited possibilities? Hopefully, we can reorient our habitual approach towards rejection and affirmation. Could nonpositive affirmation also be called "compassion"? Our purposes here are much more specific than were Foucault's (or Guénon's, for that matter), yet Foucault opens some inspiring vistas which anticipate our Chapters 6 & 7. It was unusual for Michel Foucault to speak about spiritual matters, yet nonpositive affirmation "opens onto a scintillating and constantly affirmed world, a world without shadow or twilight, without that serpentine 'no' that bites into fruits and lodges their contradictions at their core. It is the solar inversion of satanic denial. It was originally linked to the divine..." Philosophy may be just discovering these regions, but the poets have perhaps always ascended to them. Speaking about one of his favorite poets, O. V. de L Milosz, Gaston Bachelard describes him "rising into the clouds, toward the world of luminous repose, Milosz had the impression of a brow that conquered its light and attained the 'absolute place of Affirmation'" (Gaston Bachelard, *Air and Dreams*, 1988: p.122). Milosz himself said that "the home of all things, its Logos—'the absolute place of Affirmation'—is love" (*The Noble Traveller: O.V. de L. Milosz*, 1985: p. 56).

36. The most common term for "Spiritual Self" is "soul." But there are other terms which we also use interchangeably, e.g., "Higher Self," "True Self,"

Eternal Self," "Solar Angel" or perhaps, "Atman." Consider the following definition by Herman Rednick, "The Higher or True Self is a pure entity which is working through one's personality and physical equipment in the attempt to bring more light and spiritual expression through the person. It is also known as the Solar angel. This is the eternal Self.... [A person] is constantly evolving towards that Self as his [or her] mind and heart increasingly take on its vibration" (Justin R. Moore, *Teachings From the Path of Fire: The Life and Works of Herman Rednick*, 1973: Q. 115). We have delayed introducing these terms because they have become so debased in current usage that most people, who have even been exposed to the notion of "higher self," think that they know "all about that." In order to counter the naive, the psychological, and the secular uses of these terms, we will use the following quote from Thomas Merton: "that the inmost center, that scientilla animae, that 'apex' or 'spark' which is a freedom beyond freedom, an identity beyond essence, a self beyond all ego, a being beyond the created realm, and a consciousness that transcends all division, all separation. To activate this spark is not to be, like Plotinus, 'alone with the Alone,' but to recognize the Alone which is by itself in everything because there is nothing that can be apart from It and yet nothing that can be with It, and nothing that can realize It. It can only realize itself. The 'spark' which is my true self is the flash of the Absolute recognizing itself in me. This realization at the apex is a coincidence of all opposites...a fusion of freedom and unfreedom, being and unbeing, life and death, self and nonself, man and God. The 'spark' is not so much a stable entity which one finds but an event, an explosion which happens as all opposites clash within oneself. Then it is seen that the ego is not. It vanishes in its non-seeing when the flash of the spark alone is. When all things are reduced to the spark, who sees it? Who knows it? If you say 'God,' you are destroyed; and if you say no one, you will plunge into hell; and if you say I, you prove you are not even in the ballgame" (*Love and Living*, 1979: pp. 9-10). We should make it clear that this higher self or soul is not an absolute being, but can be considered as a higher state of consciousness and as a temporary spiritual station on an ascending arc of unlimited potential.

37. Norman O. Brown *Love's Body*, 1966: p. 252. Also quoted in Thomas Moore *Soul Mates*, 1994: p. 162.

38. We are sometimes asked by people who have a background in psychology or who have been in therapy, "Don't we just reinforce or enable people's negativity if we affirm their happiness in their own terms? Unless we apply our

own standards and ideas of what is right, won't our blanket affirmation lead to a co-dependent relationship?" The key to this confusion is to remember that by affirming another we are not seeking to satisfy all of the wants and desires of his or her personality—this would be impossible anyway! Nor is the goal to "let the other do what he or she wants" which is what many think will happen if they do not keep "the other person's 'bad' tendencies under control." In so far as our love is truly unselfish, it will not enable the loved one to indulge in selfish and negative behavior. On the other hand, it is an observable fact that constantly saying "no" to another "brings out the worst." To affirm or say "yes" to our beloved may mean that we have the greater wisdom to also say a firmer, more loving "no" to the destructive impulses of his or her personality. When we radically affirm our beloved from a heart full of love, we will not be nurturing negativity or inviting co-dependency because unselfish love only supports what is higher and more noble in the beloved one.

39. It will take more than an intellectual understanding to overcome our fear of losing who we believe we are. Only an unshakeable faith in the power of spiritual love can give us that courage. Franz von Baader (1765-1841), approached this issue from the broadest of contexts, as Jean Gebser makes clear: "It must be pointed out that Baader is in no way advocating an abolition of the self through love. On the contrary, he argues that the only way to achieve genuine self-discovery and self-determination is through love which, paradoxically, exacts a self denial: 'one who freely loves allows himself [herself] to be filled by his [her] lover, without thereby losing his [her] self-determination....' It is the gospel message all over again; 'He who loses his life for My sake will find it' (Mt. 10:39), and 'Unless the grain of wheat falls into the ground and dies, it remains alone... He who loves his life, loses it' (Jn. 12:24-25)" (Jean Gebser, *The Ever Present Origen*, 1985: p. 248). Thomas Merton wrote a very clear and pertinent description (despite the androcentric language) of our next evolutionary step, "Adam, perfectly whole and isolated in himself, as a person, needs nevertheless to find himself perfected, without division or diminution, by the gift of himself to another. He needs to give himself in order to gain himself. The law of self renunciation is not merely a consequence of sin, for charity is the fundamental rule of the whole moral universe. Without it, man will always be imprisoned within himself. He will be less than a man. In order to be fully himself, man needs to love another as himself. In order to realize himself, man has to risk the diminution and even the total loss of all his reality, in favor of another, for if any man would

save his life he must lose it. We are never fully ourselves until we realize that those we truly love become our 'other selves'" (*The New Man*. 1978: p. 90). Through the Way of the Beloved we can overcome the illusion of the false ego and discover, not only a truer Self, but also our *other selves*.

40. *Between Man and Man*, 1972: pp. 61-2 (our emphasis). There is a surprising and very interesting reason that Martin Buber could write so convincingly and poetically about the potential of marriage. The philosopher Maurice Friedman, who knew Buber well, tells us in his recent biography that "Buber's relationship to his wife Paula was probably more decisive for the development of his *I-Thou* philosophy as a whole than any of the events and meetings with which we have dealt. Buber's dialogical thinking could have grown only out of his marriage to this strong and really 'other' woman, this modern Ruth who left her family, home, and religion, and finally even her country and people for him. The fundamental reality of the life of dialogue—that it is a confirmation and inclusion of otherness—was understood and authenticated in the love and the marriage, the tension and the companionship, of his relationship to Paula…One can go further and say that the existential trust that underlies *I and Thou* and all of Buber's mature works would have been unthinkable without his relationship to Paula. This is perhaps the unique case of a philosopher whose thinking did not emerge from his individual being but from the 'between', which he knew first and foremost in his marriage" (*Encounter on the Narrow Ridge: a Life of Martin Buber*, 1993: pp. 132-3). We will use more of Martin Buber's philosophial insights in Chapter 7. We believe that there are other modern thinkers whose work was strongly influenced by their marriage relationship—e.g., Jacob Böehme (1575-1624), Franz von Baader (1765-1841), John Stuart Mill (1806-1873), John Pordage (1607-1681), & Max Scheler (1874-1928).

41. Paul Pearsall *The Ten Laws of Lasting Love*, 1995: p.43.

42. The coordinating of the physical breathing has been known since ancient times. The modern Taoist master, Mantak Chia, says that "'Chi' means 'breath' in Chinese. Life is breath. All living activity has the quality of inhalation, exhalation, or some combination of the two. This is why Chinese philosophy classifies everything as Yin (exhalation or Yang (inhalation) to a greater or lesser degree. The act of love is essentially an act of respiration… Physically breathing together unifies the two partners and focuses the rhythm of all of their energies" (*Taoist Secrets of Love: Cultivating Male Sexual Energy*,

1985: p. 146). See also Stephen Levine & Ondrea Levine *Embracing The Beloved: Relationship as a Path of Awakening*, 1995: pp. 86-7.

43. Paul Pearsal The Ten Laws of Everlasting Love, 1995: p. 42.

44. Usually we take common English words that we use everyday for granted. Certainly the pronoun "we" is of irreplaceable importance, especially to a beloved couple. Yet *we* has a history. According to the *Dictionary of Word Origins.*, (John Ayto, 1990): *"We* goes back ultimately to Indo-European **wei,* which also produced sanskrit *vayám* 'we.' The precise process by which this evolved into German *wir*, Dutch *wij*, Swedish and Danish *vi*, and English *we* has never been unravelled." Ivan Illich & Barry Sanders in their brilliant book, *A B C: The Alphabetization of the Popular Mind*, discuss some of the history and use of this simple pronoun: "The *we* that we have used emphatically in this book is morphologically an English plural. Semantically, however, it is close to a dual, for which English, some time during the Anglo-Saxon period, has lost a special form. Other Indo-Germanic languages—for instance, the Slavonic ones—have preserved this form. And, like thought and the word, like narration and the lie, *we* has a history. The *we* on which we want to reflect is...the personal pronoun, with which he who speaks refers to the first person in the plural. Now, what is that first person? The answer is rather easy when we deal with person in the singular: 'I,' the first person, speaks to 'you,' the second person. In doing so, I tell you something about a third, who neither is speaking nor is being addressed. By addressing a person whom I designate 'you,' I make that person at that moment unique to me—and distinguish that 'you' from any third: person or thing. Thus, *you* is almost as unique as *I* . Even abuse will not detract from the poser intrinsic to the spoken *you* to estsablish this exquisite bond....This univocal precision of the *I* is a condition for the formation of plurals. In fact, with almost the same directness with which all languages oppose the addressing *I* with a *you* who is addressed, they also provide some kind of *we* . Quite arguably, the opposition of *I* and *we* is a more fundamental category than the opposition of singular and plural. For the English speaker, it seems natural that the existence of a third person singular—the *he-she-it*—requires that there be a third person plural—a *they*. But this is just not so in all languages...however, the difference between the *I* and the *we* is clear. No language seems to lack a pronoun that says, 'I and . . ..'" (Ibid., "Postscript: Silence and the We," pp. 123-4).

The obsolete plural form of "we" mentioned by Illich & Sanders is "wit." The OED tells us that it was also "wyt," "wet," & "witt" and means "we two."

Perhaps we should revive this form to describe the first person plurality of the true beloved relationship. It is certainly interesting that "the noun *wit* [OE] and the verb [OE]…originally meant 'see,' in which sense it has given English *visible, vision,* etc., but it developed metaphorically to 'know,' and it is this sense that lies behind English *wit.* The noun to begin with denoted 'mind, understanding, judgement, sense' …" (John Ayto, *Dictionary of Word Origins,* 1990). Much of this meaning has been lost since the 16th century, but it can be seen in the word "interview" in which two people "see each other." In addition to the extensive material in the OED, see the entries for "wit" in Robert Clairborne, *The Roots of English: A Reader's Handbook of Word Origins,* 1989, and "witan" in Stephen Barney, *Word-Hoard: An Introduction to Old English Vocabulary,* 1977: p. 15, §96.

45. Paul Pearsal, The Ten Laws of Everlasting Love, 1995: p. 44.

46. For instance, Paul Pearsall reports that "my own experience and clinic observations indicate that spouses in miracle marriages begin to breathe together. They breathe much more slowly and deeply when in each other's presence than when they are alone or with others." Pearsall suggests that, "the synchronized, slower breathing pattern that evolves between lovers… [is] a form of…metronome ticking by the cadence of the couple's own 'conspiracy.'… the miracle marriage seems able to live at its own unique life rate, and the couple conspire together to make their own time" (*The Ten Laws of Lasting Love,* 1995: p. 126).

47. On this issue Pearsall, a psychologist himself, goes on to point out that "traditional psychology, marriage counseling, psychiatry, and most psychotherapies…offer little to help in making a miracle marriage. The mental health movement has evolved largely alongside the Me Myth, so it does not acknowledge or understand marriage other than as a vehicle for self-actualization or source of guaranteed availability of romantic love, unequivocal support, or convenient sex. To be 'happily married' has become similar to becoming 'fulfilled in our career' and 'self-actualized.' It has become a secondary objective to larger life goals and a place we live while we are busy 'doing our own thing.' Marriage often becomes something we use to help us get what we want for ourselves instead of something we are making with someone else" (Ibid. p. 54). Pearsall even quotes psychologist, Lawrence LeShan, who says that "Psychology has so lost contact with real human experience that there would be no point in asking it to solve major human

problems" (*The Dilemma of Psychology,* 1990: p. xiii). Also, in this regard, it is worth noting the work of James Hillman: e.g., *Re-Visioning Psychology,* 1977 & *The Myth of Analysis,* 1972.

48. Ibid. p. 47. (Italics in original)

49. These ideas were expressed by Herman Rednick as follows: "Wherever you go and whatever you do will be an expression of your love for your beloved. As both of you move…and blend spiritually your heart will be fused with your beloved and any other activity will carry the same atmosphere. Your time shall be enriched when you carry your beloved with you. What greater treasure is there, than your beloved?" (The Beloved Yoga:, 1993 Unpublished: p. 71).

50. It was taken for granted until quite recently in Christian countries that a married couple shared in all the catastrophies and blessings that might befall each of them. St. Teresa of Avila (1515-1582) wrote, "what honorable woman is there who does not share in the dishonors done to her spouse even though she does not will them? In fact, both spouses share the honor and the dishonor. Now, then, to enjoy a part of His kingdom and want no part in His dishonors and trials is nonsense" (*The Collected Works,* V.2, 1980: p. 86).

51. From a letter by Herman Rednick written on 2/4/62 (Beloved Yoga, 1993: p. 140).

52. From a story sketch by a friend, 1981.

53. As our companion in this Section, Paul Pearsall, points out: "The use of the word 'conspiracy' to refer to a positive collusion and 'breathing together' is found in M. Ferguson, The Aquarian Conspiracy, 1980: p. 19" (Ten Laws of Lasting Love, note 6 p. 310).

54. That is, *"we have reached a decisive point in human evolution,* at which the only way forward is in the direction of a common passion, a 'conspiration'" (Pierre Teilhard de Chardin, *Human Energy,* 1969: p. 153). And in speaking about the this *greater life* of humanity he says that "We cannot therefore fail to come to the following idea—which coincides moreover with one of the oldest and commonest intuitions of our consciousness: 'the *conspiration* ' of activities from which the collective human soul proceeds presumes at its beginning the common *'aspiration'* exerted by a hope" (Ibid. p. 139).

55. Henry Corbin says that "Ibn 'Arabi…invests the concrete form of the beloved being with an 'angelic function' and, in the midst of his meditations,

discerns this form on the plane of theophanic vision. How is such a perception...possible? To answer this question we must follow the progress of the dialectic of love set forth by Ibn 'Arabi...it tends essentially to secure and test the sympathy between the invisible and the visible, the spiritual and the sensible, that sympathy which Jalaluddin Rumi was to designate by the Persian term *ham-dami* (litt. *conflatio*, blowing-together), for only this 'conspiration' makes possible the spiritual vision of the sensible or sensible vision of the spiritual, a vision of the invisible in a concrete form apprehended not by one of the sensory faculties, but by the Active Imagination which is the organ of theophanic vision" (Henry Corbin, *Creative Imagination in the Sufism of Ibn'Arabi,* 1981: pp.144-5).

NOTES FOR PART 3 •

1. A paper written by a student at the July, 1994 Beloved Retreat in Northern New Mexico.

2. The mantras we will be using are generally brief statements of the concept presented in the meditation. Sogyal Rinpoche gives a simple and useful definition: "The definition of mantra is "that which protects the mind." That which protects the mind from negativity, or that which protects you from your own mind, is called mantra. When you are nervous, disoriented, or emotionally fragile, chanting or reciting a mantra inspiringly can change the state of your mind completely, by transforming its energy and atmosphere … when you chant a mantra, you are charging your breath and energy with the energy of the mantra, and so working directly on your mind and subtle body" (*The Tibetan Book of Living and Dying,* 1992: p. 71).

3. Based on several beloved meditations given by Herman Rednick, Beloved Yoga, 1993.

• NOTES FOR CHAPTER 6 •

1. HRAP Memoir #1: p. 103.

2. Dante Alighieri, *The Paradiso,* 1970: Canto V. line 7, p. 62. Indeed, when Dante was only 9 years old he saw Beatrice for the first time and the "Eternal Ray" inflamed his heart forever. See the opening paragraph of *La Vita Nuova, The Portable Dante,* 1969: pp. 547-549.

3. Allen Afterman, *Kabbalah and Consciousness,* 1992: p.19.

4. *Ibid.*

5. "Beginning" means different things to different people, but whether one thinks of the beginning of humanity's embodiment in a biological evolutionary sense, as a mammal, or whether one sees our beginning as in Genesis 1:27, we are a species composed equally of males and females. This is obviously true for so many life-forms on our planet and certainly at a biological level our binary nature is undeniable. As James Reichmann cogently says, "The sexual division between the male and the female means that *biologically* neither the woman nor the man is completely human. Rather, each depends upon the other for the achievement of biological fullness. Just as no individual human can claim, 'I am humanity,' so no individual man or woman can say, 'I am biologically fully human,' for each of us lacks the perfection and capabilities of those individual humans of the other sex" (*Philosophy of the Human Person.*, 1985: p. 221).

6. Irigaray points out that "man and woman, woman and man are always meeting as though for the first time because they cannot be substituted one for the other. I will never be in a man's place, never will a man be in mine. Whatever identifications are possible, one will never exactly occupy the place of the other—they are irreducible one to the other" (*An Ethics of Sexual Difference*, 1993 p. 13).

7. *Men are From Mars: Women are From Venus: A Practical Guide for Improving Communication and Getting What You Want in Your Relationships*, 1992: p. 5.

8. As Luce Irigaray has said, "Sexual difference is probably the issue in our time which could be our 'salvation' if we thought it through" (*An Ethics of Sexual Difference*, 1993: p. 5). We propose that we must "live it through" with another person working to resolve and transcend our differences by intensifying love and creating a new synthesis.

9. *Men are From Mars and Women are From Venus*, 1992: pp. 6-7.

10. There are many other ways that the male/female polarity has been described, indeed since ancient times every culture has maintained a binary system of male/female differences. Long before we described the male and female aspects as "centrifugal" and "centripetal," Claude Bragdon used the terms: "it is clear that behind all the complexities of form and phenomena there are two powers—twin aspects of one power—the first of which manifests the characteristics of the thunderbolt, and the second shares with

sentient nature that soft resistant force which defies destruction; the one masculine, *centrifugal*, revealed and symbolized in igneous action; the other feminine, *centripetal*—aqueous action" (*Delphic Woman: Twelve Essays*, 1945: p.12). It may be that Bragdon's source of this metaphor was actually José Ortega y Gasset. In his book *On Love*, Ortega find the following: "Under equal conditions, the feminine psyche is closer to potential contraction than the masculine; for the simple reason that the woman has a more centripetal, integrated, and elastic mind. As we noted, the function charged with giving the mind its structure and cohesion is the attention... In contrast to the concentric structure of the feminine mind there are always epicenters in that of the man. The more masculine one is, in a spiritual sense, the more his mind is disjointed in separate compartments. One part of us is deeply dedicated to politics or business, while another devotes itself to intellectual curiosity and another to sexual pleasure. The is lacking, then, a tendency toward one unified gravitation of the attention. In fact the contrary predominates, which leads to dissociation. The axis of attention is multiple" (pp. 74-5). Now *even* the secular humanist psychologist, John Welwood, uses the terms "centrifugal" and "centripetal" to describe male and female differences (*Journey of the Heart: the Path of Conscious Love*. HarperCollins Pub., NY, 1996: p. 146).

The binarisms that are most familiar to us have been largely used to sustain and justify antifeminist agendas, for example, active/ passive, dominant/ submissive, rational/irrational, reasoning/emotional, strong/weak, etc. However, there have been other attempts to describe differences without characterizing women in essentially negative ways. For instance, Beatrice Bruteau commented that "We are used to contrasting masculine and feminine as active and passive, bright and dark, positive and negative. I propose a different set of pairs: specialization and generalization, partiality and wholeness, analysis and synthesis. The two aspects of our consciousness do have a complementary relation to one another and do alternate in their emphasis in our lives. However, by putting the contrast in this way, I believe we can see more readily why we all feel that the feminine is our source and why reunion with it is what makes us feel complete, whole, and 'at home at last'" ("The Unknown Goddess" in Shirley Nicholoson, (ed.) *The Goddess Re-awakening: The Feminine Principle Today*, 1989: pp. 72-73). Clearly, the binarisms that we choose to delineate the major gender differences will support or deny whatever we wish, whether it is male superiority, female superiority, androgyny, or something else. There is a price to pay no matter what kind of descriptive system one chooses. The important thing is to know that you are making a *choice*, and to have some idea about what that choice leaves out.

11. A more sociological approach to the way in which men and women experience love is presented by Francesca Cancian. She begins her chapter on "Feminine and Masculine Love" with a statement which thematizes much of her orientation: "Most Americans have an incomplete, feminine conception of love. We identify love with emotional expression and talking about feelings, aspects of love that women prefer and in which women tend to be more skilled than men. We often ignore the instrumental and physical aspects of love that men prefer, such as providing help, sharing activities, and sex... Our feminine conception of love exaggerates the difference between men's and women's ability to love, and their need for love. It reinforces men's power advantage, and encourages women to overspecialize in relationships, while men overspecialize in work" ((Love in America, 1987: p. 69).

12. We are indebted to the architect, Christopher Alexander for creating and introducing us to the use of this format in his exquisite book, *The Timeless Way of Building*, Oxford U. Press, 1979.

13. We use the phrase "vicious circle" to describe a relationship where one person's negative reaction feeds, encourages and initiates the other's negative reaction; which in turn escalates the first person's negativity, etc. The people are caught in a downward spiraling loop which is quite common in relationships today where two egos are battling for supremacy and control. For instance, a "co-dependent" relationship is a vicious circle. In Hindu and Buddhist thought the very structure of the world of appearance (the Maya) is that it "goes in circles" (i.e., *samsara*).

14. It is a fact of our experience that it is women, and not men, who ask, "Do you love me?" In fact, in more than 20 years we have only twice had a man confess that it was important to him to have his beloved answer this question in order for him to feel loved. Almost universally men feel that it is wholly unnecessary for them to ever ask, "Do you love me?" This illustrates a fundamental gender difference. Since men do not need to ask, they do not comprehend why a woman should have to do so. Women, on the other hand, cannot comprehend how it would be to not need to ask.

15. Francesca Cancian comments that, "The masculine conception of self-development that is still influential today is rooted in this nineteenth-century

male ideal. Independence, self-control, and achievement are the major values of this ideal self while intimacy, emotional expression, and other feminine qualities are devalued" (Love in America: Gender and self-development, 1987: p. 21).

16. An excellent exposition of this vicious circle, which results from the different responses of male and the female to interpersonal stress, is found in John Gray's popular book, Men are From Mars: Women are From Venus, 1992. See Chapter 3 "Men go to their caves and women talk" pp. 29-41.

17. This pattern has been also called "demanding-woman/witholding-man" and it is well known in the social science literature. Francesca Cancian did an extensive study of couples in the middle 1970's which found that "about half fit the pattern" (*Love in America: Gender and self-development*, 1987: p. 92).

18. The different ways in which men and women experience fear, in relation to their interactions with each other, is well known. For instance, Sam Keen has said, "Men and women seem to have different styles of fearing. Men's fears focus around loss of what we experience as our independence, and women's around the loss of significant relationships. We most fear engulfment, anything that threatens to rob us of our power and control. Women most fear abandonment, isolation, loss of love (*Fire in the Belly: on Being a Man*, 1992: p. 140).

19. Torkom Saraydarian has made the point that this is true of woman even on the emotional level. This is important because "most women are anchored in their emotional vehicles. This gives the woman an advantage over man and makes her sensitive to the environment, to the people and their conditions. Her physical changes translate themselves into various emotions. She speaks a language of emotions no matter what words she uses...Man mostly speaks a physical language, or if he is educated, he speaks a mental language and translates the speech of the woman either into physical or mental language. Thus, there is a gap between man and woman, but this gap is less for the woman because emotions are INCLUSIVE, whereas body or thoughts are EXCLUSIVE. Body or thoughts act and think mostly for their own. Emotions are communions, sharing;..." (*Sex, Family, and the Woman in Society*, 1987: pp. 183-4).

20. Torkom Saraydarian, *Sex, Family, and the Woman in Society.*, 1987: p. 121.

21. Ibid. p. 211.

22. Men and women are constantly becoming entangled in these kinds interactions where meaning and intent are misunderstood in an escalating spiral. R.D. Laing called these interpersonal entanglements "knots" (Knots, 1970), and he says that "Interpersonal life is conducted in a nexus of persons, in which each person is guessing, assuming, inferring, believing, trusting, or suspecting, generally being happy or tormented by his fantasy of the other's experience, motives, and intentions. And one has fantasies not only about what the other…experiences and intends, but also about his fantasies about one's own experience and intentions, and about his fantasies about his fantasies about one's experience, etc.…There are some people who conduct their lives at several fantasy steps away from their own immediate experience or their own intentions. Family interactions are often dominated by these issues" (R.D. Laing, *Self and Others*, 1969: p. 154). Richard Zaner refers to Laing's knots as "webs of *Maya* " and he relates a common knot that is relevant to the discussion of hurt: "I can see, and I know this clearly, that you have hurt me with your words; I know that I didn't do anything to warrant your hurting me, and it is especially painful that you don't see even that you've hurt me and are wondering why I am so grieved; why can't you see that you've hurt me twice—by doing what you did, and not seeing that you did it to me? Etc." (Richard Zaner, *The Context of Self*, 1981: p. 241).

23. This is the 'vicious circle' described by many authors as the "demanding-woman / witholding-man" and its dynamic is described by the sociologist, Francesca Cancian, as follows: "Insofar as marriage is defined as the wife's 'turf,' an area where she sets the rules and expectations, the husband is likely to feel threatened and controlled when she seeks more intimacy. If the couple believes that love is shown through the activities that the woman prefers and in which she is more skilled, i.e., intimate talk as opposed to sex, his negative feelings will be aggravated. Talking about the relationship as she wants to do will feel to him like taking a test that she has made up and he will fail. Blocked from straightforward counterattack insofar as he believes that intimacy is good and should not be opposed, he is likely to react with withdrawal and passive aggression" (*Love in America: Gender and self-development*, 1987: p. 93).

24. This situation is illustrated by the story of Sara and Eric in Section 2.3 "Patterns of Sharing."

25. Men are From Mars: Women are From Venus, 1992: p. 15.

26. Ibid. p. 76.

27. Francesca Cancian believes that "sexual intimacy is the only 'masculine' way of expressing love that is culturally recognized in our society…" (Love in America, 1987: p. 77).

28. In regard to this gender difference, Torkom Saraydarian said, "For many men, love equals sex and not much else. But for women, love is a combination of sex, sensuality, games, intellect, spirit, dreams, visions, and goals. Man's downfall is his failure to understand women. Women stand for lovingness, tenderness and touch, but men think women want sex in the same way they do. Women are more sane about sex than men because women are naturally subject to sexual cycles" (*Sex, Family, and the Woman in Society*, 1987: p. 216).

29. In his book, Woman: The Torch of the Future, Torkom Saraydarian speaks at length of woman as the "torchbearer," the flame and light of man and humanity. Indeed she "is a link between the fiery world and the physical plane. In her these two worlds meet, and that is why she is aware of the fiery world, psychic realms, and the orientation of the physical world to them" (p. 211). Indeed, it is actually women who hold the vision, the light, and "have been inspirers in all ages, and they will increasingly inspire more and more until all departments of human endeavor are oriented towards a life based on the Teaching… In esoteric philosophy, women are identified with the principle of the Holy Spirit, which inspires, gives vision, and works for all" (Ibid. pp. 202-3). Even the New Testament identifies the Holy Spirit as feminine and as fire. For example, at Pentecost the Holy Spirit appeared as "cloven tongues of flame" which "sat upon each of them" (Acts 2:3).

30. An interesting presentation of the recent history of women's, so called, "specialization in relationship skills" is found in Francesca Cancian, *Love in America: Gender and self-development*, 1987: Chapter 2 "The feminization of love in the nineteenth century", pp. 15-29.

31. Tsultrim Allione, *Women of Wisdom*, 1986: p. 14. The late Torkom Saraydarian (1917-1997) often spoke and wrote about woman's superior spiritual affinities. In terms of the aura he said, "A person is his aura. the aura is the combined radiation of a person's etheric, astral (emotional), mental, intuitional and higher bodies. It is the radiation of the entire person on all levels and an energy field around him…A twelve-foot aura is a magnetic station for the twelve signs of the Zodiac, which acts as a transmission station

for their energies within you....Women in general are sensitive to the energies of the Soul of zodiacal signs....The higher levels of zodiacal signs transmit impressions related to the future, which advanced women receive in their auras....The machine of a woman is much more complex than the machine of a man, as is her subtle mechanism to run that machine....A woman is an ethereal being; she belongs to etheric realms more than to the physical realm...." (*Sex, Family, and the Woman in Society,* 1987: pp. 109-10). "Woman is the bridge who links the subjective and objective world, the world of soul and the world of body, within herself. Psychologically woman has a closer contact with the spiritual world than man due to her intuitive perception and sensitivity" (*Woman: The Torch of the Future,* 1980: p. 209).

32. Herman Rednick *The Earth Journey: from Birth to Fulfillment,* 1980: p. 111. Indeed, "that is why in Elusinian, Zoroastrian and Egyptian mysteries, the connecting link between the subjective and the objective worlds were virgins who acted as mediators between the world of wisdom and vision and the world of everyday life and its problems. Virgins, in the mystery temples, esoterically were those women whose focus of consciousness was totally anchored in the intuitional plane...Because of this, they were able to contact higher forces and become transmitters of great visions, ideas, and revelations. Many women in history, after having a contact with the supernatural, lifted their focus of consciousness to the intuitional plane and gave humanity a supreme Teaching and a great beauty..." (Torkom Saraydarian, *Woman: Torch of the Future,* 1980: p. 210).

33. As Saraydarian said, "Men's auras usually are blocked by many worldly preoccupations, and higher impressions often are distorted by their auras" (*Sex, Family, and the Woman in Society,* 1987: p. 109).

34. For instance, Tsultrim Allione wrote that "women tend to have a natural affiliation for the receptive states of meditation, intuitive knowing and compassion, but have a harder time seeing clear ways of working with concrete problems and acting assertively and effectively in worldly situations" (*Women of Wisdom,* 1986: pp. 17-8). All this is not to imply that women cannot function in the philosophical/intellectual or the pragmatic/material modes, but rather that in the realms of spirituality and human relationships, women's way is more sure and direct because she functions more through the heart.

35. Indeed, there are also many forms of latent misogyny for example, hatred and fear of women is deeply encoded in the metaphorical structure

of our language and culture, see the important work of George Lakoff, e.g. *Metaphors We Live By*, 1980 & *Women, Fire and Dangerous Things*, 1987.

36. It has been suggested that men and women live in separate social and ideational spheres, created in the last 200 years. Francesca Cancian says that in the nineteenth century, "As the daily activities of men and women grew further apart, a new world view emerged. It exaggerated the differences between 'the home' and 'the world' and polarized the ideal personalities of women and men" (*Love in America: Gender and self-development*, 1987: p. 19). Cancian details the split between the private sphere and the public sphere brought on by capitalism and her description of the separate ideals that developed for men and women fits well with the polarized conflict we see in contemporary relationships: "In sum, the ideology of separate spheres reinforced the new division of labor, and portrayed a world of independent, self-made men and dependent, loving women. The ideal family was portrayed as a harmonious, stable, nuclear household with an economically successful father and an angelic mother" (ibid.).

37. Indeed, we often hear women say that many of our contemporary social problems would be solved if men were more like women. For example, in commenting on the sexual harassment trials at Aberdeen and elsewhere, Kate Clinton "conclude[d] that it's time to get men out of the military. In war, let women be men; in peace, let men be women." *The Progressive,* June 1997; quoted in *Utne Reader,* Sept-Oct 97: p.37.

38. Dante Alighieri, *The Paradiso*, 1970: Canto V. line 7, p. 62.

39. From the title of Søren Kierkegaard's book, i.e., *Fear and Trembling & Sickness unto Death.* We have called this section somewhat extravagantly the "fear that has no name," and that is true in our secular society, but within philosophy, theology and existential psychology it is well known. For instance, Rollo May gives a succinct and enlightening account of this state in Chapter 7 of his excellent book, *The Discovery of Being.* He speaks of it as "anxiety" and we have avoided that term because of the common, and misleading, associations which seem to be irrevocably attached to it at present. Also we have characterized it as "fear," even though May makes it clear that it is not: "anxiety strikes at the central core of his[a person's] self-esteem and his sense of value as a self, which is the most important aspect of his experience of himself as a being. Fear, in contrast, is a threat to the periphery of his existence; it can be objectivated, and the person can stand outside and look at it. In greater or

lesser degree, anxiety overwhelms the person's discovery of being, blots out the sense of time, dulls the memory of the past, and erases the future" (Ibid. p. 110). The important thing of note here is May's description of "anxiety" as an ontological condition of being and not just one affect among others. He describes anxiety as "an experience of threat which carries both anguish and dread, indeed the most painful and basic threat which any being can suffer, for it is the threat of loss of being itself…anxiety always involves inner conflict…Anxiety occurs at the point where some emerging potentiality or possibility faces the individual, some possibility of fulfilling his existence; but this very possibility involves the destroying of present security, which thereupon gives rise to the tendency to deny the new potentiality" (Ibid. p. 111). In the context of our discussion of the spiral of separation it would seem that it is a question of: "to love, therefore, to be; or not to love and therefore, not to be." May adds: "If there were not some possibility of opening up, some potentiality crying to be 'born,' we would not experience anxiety. This is why anxiety is so profoundly connected with the problem of freedom. If the individual did not have some freedom, no matter how minute, to fulfill some new potentiality, he would not experience anxiety. Kierkegaard described anxiety as 'the dizziness of freedom,' and added more explicitly, if not more clearly, 'Anxiety is the reality of freedom as a potentiality before this freedom has materialized'" (Ibid. p. 112). This is precisely what this section (6.2.7) is about.

40. We have also spoken with many women, who, whenever they have had any hints of this fear, have gone immediately to a therapist. Psychotherapy almost always identifies this fear in women as fear of abandonment caused by a reserved, uncaring father or a father who walked out on the family, etc. A "psychological reason" or "cause" can, and will, be found in any individual's past experiences because it is one of the a priori, grounding assumptions of modern psychology.

41. Herman Rednick Archival Project, Memoir #1: p.14 (Meditation given 2/27/1974).

42. The view that humans are random collections of genes and culturally conditioned characteristics is dominant today in our secular psychology and the social sciences. These traits, characteristics and roles that we label variously as male and female are so culturally conditioned that they change constantly and in the twentieth century with increasing rapidity. For instance, just 40

years ago in many of the social strata within our own culture, "sensitivity" in a man was viewed as highly undesirable. Indeed, even today there is considerable ambivalence on this issue. This is demonstrated by the very popular TV show, "Home Improvement." In this show, which airs daily, a major dynamic in virtually every episode is created by the "quaint macho" husband whose never-ending ambivalence and apparent inability to maintain a caring and sensitive interaction with his wife is the central issue in the story line. In addition to the rapid change of gender roles and traits there is a growing lack of consensus on which traits are "really" male and which are female.

43. This may happen eventually. However, "Women seeking acceptance within professional and intellectual communities are often expected to exhibit qualities of thought and action that characterize the lives of men. And if their performance does not meet standards established by men, it is likely that nothing significant will be expected from them" (Cornelius Murphy, *Beyond Feminism: Toward a Dialogue on Difference*, 1995: p. 44). This situation is not confined to business and the professions but is found equally in the practice of science, e.g., Evelyn Keller, *Reflections on Gender and Science*, 1985.

44. Not only has the "true" nature of gender been reduced to mere opinion outside of medical circles, but an intellectual or rationalistic "understanding" is seldom a motive for releasing our attachments to past patterns of action. This can perhaps be seen most clearly in the continuing and intensifying practices of misogyny which permeate all cultures on the planet. Despite "modern" psychological and sociological knowledge and widespread rationalistic education, misogyny not only persists, but is on the increase. A dramatic documentation of this was presented by Barbara Ehrenreich ("For Women, China Is All Too Typical" *Time Magazine* 9/18/95: p. 130): "instead of advancing, women, on average, seem to be losing ground....the percentage of women elected to national legislatures has dropped worldwide almost 25% in the past seven years. Human Rights Watch reported in August [1995] that such traditional abuses as wife beating remain rampant everywhere and usually unpunished, while new problems—like the transnational traffic in female sex slaves—have grown unchecked. There is...a worldwide 'war on women.' ...When it comes to women's rights, there is no single 'evil empire' that can be isolated and embargoed. Thanks to religious conservatism and official indifference, misogyny is making a comeback everywhere." More recent evidence of the fact that women are losing ground, was presented in

Parade Magazine (3/24/1996: p. 24): "Even though more women are being elected to national office worldwide, the vast majority of legislators still are men. Worldwide, only 11.3% of the parliamentary seats are now held by women. They reached a record number in 1988, when women held 14.3% of all parliamentary seats. In the United States, women now hold just 10.9% of the seats in the House of Representatives and 8% of the seats in the Senate." Clearly the United States is below the world average. Sweden is the highest with 40.4% women in their legislature and even South Africa has 25%! The current (1996) political rhetoric that the long history of injustices towards women and minorities has been corrected is a transparent attempt to return to the discriminatory practices of the past which keep white males in power.

45. *You Just Don't Understand: Women & Men in Conversation,* 1990: p. ix.

46. *Ibid.* p. 298. Also see her Chapter 10 "Living with Asymmetry" pp. 280.

47. One of the deepest and most immediate ways of illustrating that men and women really do not understand each other's ways of expressing love is the realization that speech itself is gendered. This is not a new discovery, indeed as Ivan Illich & Barry Sanders recently pointed out, "the way men and women speak contrasts in many ways: linguists, anthropologist, and sociologists recognize about two dozen criteria describing these contrasts. In no two places is their configuration the same. The gender contrast in speech is just as fundamental as the contrast in phonemes, but it has barely been remarked" (*A B C: The Alphabetization of the Popular Mind.,* 1988: p. 8). Five years later Suzette Elgin observed that, "the idea that men and women use language very differently continued to thrive as conventional wisdom over the decades. It was generally taken for *granted* that the difference existed, that it was as natural and inevitable as the difference between ovaries and testicles, and that it was one of the mysteries of the universe. Few believed that it should be investigated, or that anything could or should be done about it" (*Genderspeak,* 1993: p. 5). Nonetheless, "with every utterance, the speaker refers back to himself and his gender. It is always the total quality of speech that refers the listener to the speaker's gender, not the grammatical gender of the pronoun 'I'...In a culture, what sounds feminine and what sounds masculine is determined by convention, and not by the biological nature of the vocal cords" (*A B C:The Alphabetization of the Popular Mind.,* 1988: p. 8). In some languages (e.g. Japanese) the differences between men's speaking and women's speaking are so profound that some linguists refer to them as

"genderlects" (Ibid, p. 22-23). A comparative study of gender as a grammatical category in more than 200 languages has been published by the British linguist, Greville Corbett, *Gender*, 1991. However, in the case of English speakers the idea that the differences between male and female speech would constitute a genderlect is highly debatable. Suzette Elgin has made it clear that "even if genderlects of American Mainstream English [AME] exist, both genders have the resource of that process for *negotiating* meaning available to them. That's a vast improvement over 'speaking different languages.' However, there are two major problems with the process of communication by negotiation when it takes place between AME-speaking women and men. First: The two varieties are so much alike on the surface, so much alike in the words used and the rules applied to the words with regard to things like word endings and word order, that the speakers tend to *assume* no nontrivial differences exist. Men and women can go to a meeting, carry on a discussion, and go away with quite different perceptions of what went on there and what decisions were made—*without being aware that the different perceptions exist.* Second: speakers of both dialects tend to feel that they shouldn't have to *worry* about communication in this way, that the other speaker *ought* to understand without a struggle. Particularly when the man and woman involved are a couple, they feel that communication between them *ought* to be easy. When it's not, there's a strong and dangerous tendency for each half of the couple to suspect that the other one isn't trying—doesn't really want to communicate; is deliberately obstructing communication; has some kind of secret agenda; and so on. The better the two know each other, and the longer they have spent much of their time together, the worse this problem tends to be" (Ibid, p. 26; emphasis in original). Every person probably has some vivid memories of the times of separation when it was like our partner was speaking in a foreign tongue, and we attributed all kinds of false motives to him or her.

48. "Several studies show that enduring commitment has persisted as an ideal and has not declined as a reality. In the massive study, *American Couples*, Philip Blumstein and Pepper Schwartz found that 'an intimate enduring relationship' remains a central aspiration for Americans." And "…another study points out that 96% of all Americans held to the ideal of two people sharing a life and a home together (in other words permanent marriage), according to surveys done in 1970 and 1980; and they acknowledge that 'the satisfactions of marriage and family life have been increasing.'" (Francesca Cancian, 1987: p. 106) The ideal of an enduring relationship is also the stated desire of most same-sex couples.

49. Herman Rednick, The Beloved Yoga, 1993: p. 108.

50. *Op.cit.,* pp. 30 - 40

51. The Wisdom of the Desert, 1970: p. 17.

52. We discussed the "will to love" in The Introduction and it should be noted that all the components of the work to break the spiral of separation have been presented in previous Sections.

53. See Section 6.2.7.

54. The Wisdom of the Desert, 1970: p. 18.

55. In the last few years there has been a dramatic increase in the concern with the question of manhood in post-modern American society. There has been considerable speculation on the changing nature of maleness in our culture. For instance, many people are familiar with the work of Robert Bly, e.g., *Iron John*; and others like *Fire in the Belly* by Sam Keen and the writings of Herb Goldberg, *The New Male* and *The Inner Male*. Therefore, due to the volatile and problematic nature of the current debate on maleness, we will focus on, what is perhaps, the most basic and pervasive model of American maleness.

56. This term came into common usage in late nineteenth century America and expressed the endpoint of a process of individualization begun in the Enlightment. The profound influence that the myth of individualism continues to have on us is not very well understood because it is still a dominant force in the ideational structure of American life. As Elizabeth Fox-Genovese said, "American democracy has grounded its hegemony in the theory and practice of individualism. All men, according to our founding text, are born free and equal" (*Feminism Without Illusions: A Critique of Individualism*, 1991: p. 58). America is truly the bastion of the individual, and the rugged individualist is the extreme expression of this dead end philosophy. The books of Ayn Rand are probably the most complete presentation of individualism carried to its logical conclusions. In addition to the above mentioned book by Fox-Genovese, see Cornelius Murphy, *Beyond Feminism: Toward a Dialogue on Difference*, 1995: "Individualism and Equality in an Age of Abstraction," pp. 52-59.

57. That the door to true freedom lies in loving relationships is one of those "hidden" teachings of the New Testament (perhaps hidden by the American obssession with the personal ego). We are just beginning to emerge from 2

451

1/2 millennia of this hypnosis. Thomas Merton was an eloquent voice for the path of love, and this path is also being opened in "dialogic philosophy." As Michael Theunissen says: "That expression of Jesus handed down by Luke (17:21), which Luther renders as; The kingdom of God is inside of you,' reads in another, and today almost universally recognized, translation, 'The kingdom of God is *in the midst of you.*' It exists *between* those human beings who are called to it, as a present future....The will to dialogical self-becoming belongs to the striving after the kingdom of God in such a way that its future is promised in the present love of human beings for one another " (*The Other*, 1986: p. 383). This is a the kind of spiritual perspective which underlies The Way of the Beloved. At the very end of his book, Theunissen raises the whole discussion to a higher level with a quote from the quite obscure philosopher, Ferdinand Ebner, who was a seminal influence on Martin Buber and Franz Rosensweig: "The kingdom of love is also the kingdom of God. And Jesus has said that this dwells inwardly in man. A few now want the *entos hymon* of the original German text translated into the German as 'in the midst of you' and understood as such. They are right. For the kingdom of God is not in human being in the inner solitude of its existence, in the solitude of its I, but lies in this, that the I has been disclosed to the Thou in the word and in love, and in the word and in the act of loving—and then it is also 'in the midst of us' as the community of our spiritual life" (*Ibid.*, pp.383-4). The purpose of this discussion is to point to the possibility that there are alternatives to the common notions that God, Truth, and true individuality lie solely in the isolated ego, the one, who has turned away from the love of any other but God. Historically, this has been strongly supported by the persistent falsehood that asceticism is the only worthy path to Spiritual Being.

58. "Antifeminism, in any of its political colorations, holds that the social and sexual condition of women essentially (one way or another) embodies the nature of women, that the way women are treated in sex and in society is congruent with what women are, that the fundamental relationship between men and women—in sex, in reproduction, in social hierarchy—is both necessary and inevitable. Antifeminism defends the conviction that the male abuse of women, especially in sex, has an implicit logic, one that no program of social justice can or should eliminate; that because the male use of women originates in the distinct and opposite natures of each which converge in what is called 'sex,' women are not abused when used as women—but merely used for what they are by men as men...in general the massive degradation of

women is not seen to violate the nature of women as such" (Andrea Dworkin, *Right-wing Women*, 1983: pp. 195-6). This pervasive cultural orientation, despite its basis in known falsehoods, can become an effective way for a man to categorically deny the necessity of truly loving any woman as an equal.

59. *Sex, Family and the Woman in Society*, p. 211

60. *Ibid.* p. 218

61. *Ibid.* p. 211.

62. See Section 6.2.5

63. See Section 4.3

64. Torkom Saraydarian, *Woman Torch of the Future*, 1980: p. 191.

65. See Section 6.2.5.

66. We must remember that the techniques of the yoga of the beloved should only be practiced with love and for the sake of love. If any person tries to use the techniques to manipulate and take advantage of another person or to get their own way in a relationship, their motive is selfish and is not consistent with the path of the beloved. Misuse of the beloved practices can correctly be called "co-dependency."

67. *Sex, Family, and the Woman in Society*, 1987: p. 207.

68. *Woman Torch of the Future*, 1980: pp. 191- 2.

• NOTES FOR CHAPTER 7 •

1. Quoted in Bernie Siegel *Love, Medicine & Miracles*, 1986: p. 196.

2. From Herman Rednick in Justin Moore, *Teachings From the Path of Fire: The Life and Works of Herman Rednick*, 1973: Q. 184-5.

3. *Conversations on the Life and Ministry of Jesus the Christ*, 1994: p. 19.

4. *Ibid.*

5. Herman Rednick *The Beloved Yoga*, 1993: p. 35.

6. The understanding that love and wisdom are intimately linked is found at the very roots of Western thought, for as Plato said: "wisdom has to do with the fairest things and Love is a love directed to what is fair; so that

Love must needs be a friend of wisdom, and, as such, must be *between* wise and ignorant" (*Symposium* 204b). (The capitalizing the "L" in Love indicates that Plato is referring, not to eros, but to "love of ideal Being.") Rudolf Steiner expressed Socrates' point of view as follows: "Plato's 'dialogue on love,' the *Symposium*, describes an 'initiation.' In this initiation, love appears as the herald of wisdom. If wisdom, the eternal Word or *Logos*, is the son of the eternal world creator, then love has a motherly relationship with this Logos" (*Love and Its Meaning in the World*, 1998: p. 13. This passage is from *Christianity as Mystical Fact*, 1972: p. 71, which is a different English trans.). In other words, without Love, one cannot enter into Wisdom. In one of the very best books ever written on Plato, Robert Cushman comments that, "Love of reality, the *theia mania*, is an inherent uplifting force in the soul and pertains specifically to the whole mind. Once again, Plato is telling us in a figure that the mind of man is axiologically engaged, that is, it is solicited by the Good as the ultimate and privileged object of human volition" (*Therapaia: Plato's Conception of Philosophy*, 1958: p. 204). We would call Plato's "love of reality" selfless love or compassion. Surely, compassion "solicits" us from higher regions. Since the higher regions are unknown to us, the impulse of love which draws us upward toward Logos is usually seen as a dark and dangerous *daemon*. With the advent of the Christ, a fundamental change in the relationship between Love and Wisdom takes place: "Christ who came forth from the realms of spirit, has united wisdom with love, and this love will overcome egoism. Such is its aim. But it must be offered independently and freely from one being to the other" (Rudolf Steiner *Love and Its Meaning in the World*, 1998: p. 188). The uniting of Love and Wisdom is of utmost importance for each of us, whether we know it or not, for as Steiner said: "Love united with wisdom—that is what we need when we pass through the gate of death, because without wisdom that is united with love we die in very truth" (Ibid. p. 187). That love had become wisdom was well understood by the early Christian Fathers: e.g. Gregory of Nyssa (330-395), see Paulos Gregorios, *Cosmic Man*, 1988: pp. 208-210; Maximus the Confessor (ca. 580-662), see Lars Thunberg *Microcosm and Mediator*, 1995: "Charity and knowledge," pp. 320-22; Gregory I (590-604), see Carole Straw *Gregory the Great*, 1988: p. 226.

7. Max Scheler, *The Nature of Sympathy*, 1973: p. 157. Buddhism also recognizes that love brings a clearer vision. Herbert Guenther says that, "Usually we say 'love is blind' precisely because by tradition we have associated everything

positive with the Devil; but Buddhism, not suffering from a power-inflated straitjacket of dehumanizing dogmatism, recognizes the observable fact that love can be more perceptive than non-love" (Herbert Guenther, *The Tantric View of Life*, 1972: p, 42).

8. Justin Moore *Teachings From the Path of Fire: The Life and Works of Herman Rednick*, 1973: Q. 13.

9. Scheler says that love functions in just the opposite way than the old proverb would have us believe: "It can certainly be said that true love opens our spiritual eyes to ever-higher values in the object loved. It enables them to see and does not blind them." And he adds: "Love is the awakener to knowing and willing—she is, in fact, the mother of spirit and reason itself" (*The Nature of Sympathy*, 1973: p. 157).

10. *Disputed Questions*, 1977: p. 103.

11. Alfons Deeken, *Process and Permanence in Ethics: Max Scheler's Moral Philosophy*. 1974: p. 184. The passages quoted by Deeken are to be found in Max Scheler *The Nature of Sympathy*, 1973: p. 160.

12. *The Meaning Of Love*, 1985: pp. 59-61.

13. *Kabbalah and Consciousness*, 1992: p. 18.

14. This famous phrase is actually found much earlier than the New Testament in Plato's Phaedrus (c. 350 BCE), and it would seem that the intended meaning is the same. Plato gives a more detailed account of the process: "every soul of man has in the way of nature beheld true being this was the condition of her passing into the form of man. But all men do not easily recall the things of the other world; they may have seen them for a short time only, or they may have been unfortunate when they fell to earth, and may have lost the memory of the holy things which they saw there through some evil and corrupting association. Few there are who retain the remembrance of them sufficiently; and they, when they behold any image of that other world, are rapt in amazement; but they are ignorant of what this means, because they have no clear perceptions. For there is no light in the earthly copies of justice or temperance or any of the higher qualities which are precious to souls: they are seen but through a glass dimly; and there are few who, going to the images, behold in them the realities and they only with difficulty" (250 b). Plato pursues these thoughts further and reveals his understanding of the

process of visioning the divine in the beloved: "he whose initiation is recent, and who has been the spectator of many glories in the other world, is amazed when he sees anyone having a god-like face or form, which is the expression or imitation of divine beauty; and at first a shudder runs through him, and again the old awe steals over him; then looking upon the face of his beloved as of a god he reverences him, and if he were not afraid of being thought a downright madman, he would sacrifice to his beloved as to the image of a god" (Phaedrus 251 b). It may be noted that for Plato and other Greeks of his time the beloved is referred to as male!

15. Henry Corbin uses the term "Theophanic Imagination. For a most enlightening discussion, see Corbin's *Creative Imagination in the Sufism of Ibn 'Arabi*, 1981: pp. 184-95. He also uses the terms "Soul," "Active Imagination" and "Creative Imagination" somewhat as synonyms.

16. Commenting on this tendency Charles Williams says: "The second point is the use of the word 'Imagination.' It is generally employed to mean a vague and uncontrolled fancy. In fact, it needs only right direction, and it may then become power. Wordsworth said it was 'absolute power.' It may become the union of the mind and the heart with a particular vision" (*Outlines of Romantic Theology*, 1990: p. 92).

17. Cf. Herman Rednick in Justin Moore *Teachings From the Path of Fire: The Life and Works of Herman Rednick*, 1973.

18. Quoted in Patricia Joudry & Maurie D. Pressman *Twin Souls: a Guide to Finding Your True Spiritual Partner*. 1995: p. xi (uncorrected proof).

19. James Cutsinger, *The Form of Transformed Vision: Coleridge and the Knowledge of God*, 1987: pp. 27-8.

20. Henry Corbin, Creative Imagination in the Sufism of Ibn 'Arabi, 1981: p. 154.

21. This is a central practice in Tibetan Buddhism (Vajrayana Tantra), and Herbert Guenther has written a comprehensive account of these practices, i.e., *The Creative Vision*, 1988. Revisioning the whole world of the Maya is a widespread activity of Tibetan practitioners. For instance, as a culmination of the *Chenrezi* (Avalokiteshvara, Lord of Love) meditation (*Puja*), which is a basic Kagyu practice, we are to visualize that, "light emanates from Chenrezi's noble form and purifies all manifestations of impure karma and confusion.

The place becomes Dewachen (e.g., heaven). The body, speech, and mind of all beings becomes Chenrezi's: appearance, sound, and thought inseparable from emptiness" (Sarah Harding Trans.). Also see the "Ten visualizations" in Bokar Rinpoche *Chenrezig, Lord Of Love: Principles and Methods of Deity Meditation.*, 1991: pp. 78-87.

22. Creative Imagination in the Sufism of Ibn 'Arabi, p. 154.

23. For example, see Vladimir Solovyev, "The object of true love is not simple, but twofold. We love, in the first place, the ideal being (ideal not in the abstract sense, but in the sense of belonging to another higher sphere of being), the being whom we ought to install in our ideal world. And, in the second place, we love the natural human being, who furnishes the living personal material for the realization of the former, and who is idealized by means of it, not in the sense of our subjective imagination, but in the sense of its actual objective transformation or regeneration. In this way true love is both *ascending* and *descending*... The whole process of the cosmos and of history is the process of its realization and incarnation in a great manifold of forms and degrees" (*The Meaning Of Love*, 1985: p. 92).

24. Pictures or representations of spiritual beings are reflections and symbolic portrayals of a Spiritual Reality. If *authentic* they are not forms or projections of human desires or human personalities. Our Teacher wrote that if we meditate on a representation we will find that, "Images are not blocks, but open doors... At first it is an emotional response. When one continues it becomes a psychic living symbol within, and when one continues further, it becomes a spiritual living being..." (*Beloved Yoga*, 1993: p. 140).

25. Herman Rednick, edited and compiled from unpublished ms. material.

26. Until we truly see with the eye-of-the-heart, this may be a reasonable view. However, as Thomas Merton said: "This world is illusory only insofar as it is misinterpreted to fit our prejudices about our limited ego-selves" (*Mystics and Zen Masters*, 1967: p.284. Quoted in James Cutsinger, *The Form of Transformed Vision: Coleridge and the Knowledge of God*, 1987: p. 108, Fn. 39).

27. These ideas have been deeply embedded in Christian religious thinking for 2 millennia. Of particular importance for the corruption of nascent Christianity, were the teachings of many Gnostic sects which blended decaying pagan ideas with the new impulse from the Christ. The heritage of these theologies is still with us. As Henry Corbin has pointed out: "It has generally

been assumed that the only way to arrive at a true idea of spirit, was to regard it as the opposite of matter in every respect. They reason in this way. Matter has form, therefore spirit has none. Matter has substance, therefore, spirit has none. In this way they deny to spirit all possible modes of existence. The Christian stops here, and ends by simply affirming its existence, but denies that we can know anything more about it. But many push this destructive logic a step further, and deny the existence of spirit altogether. And this is the logical result, for denial can never end in anything but negation and nothing. This is inevitable; and the Christian escapes this conclusion only by stopping before he reaches it. We must admit that there is a spiritual substance, and that this substance has form, or we must deny the existence of spirit altogether. No other conclusion is possible" (Creative Imagination in the Sufism of Ibn 'Arabi, 1981: pp. 139-40, Note 109).

28. This is evident, for example, in the writings of such diverse teachers as Thich Nat Han, Mother Teresa, Ammachi, The Dalai Lama, Mother Meera, Herman Rednick, Torkom Saraydarian, Thomas Merton, Teilhard de Chardin, Vladimir Solovyev, Philip Sherrard, and Henry Corbin.

29. Henry Corbin, Creative Imagination in the Sufism of Ibn'Arabi, 1981: pp. 87-88.

30. Henry Corbin, *Creative Imagination in the Sufism of Ibn'Arabi*, 1981: pp. 87-88.

31. Hazrat Inayat Khan, *The Heart of Sufism: Essential Writing of Hazrat Inayat Khan*, 1999: p. 52. This story applies, not only, to one's beloved but also to any object of devotion. As Inayat Khan continues: "Therefore if we wish to regard the object of devotion of whatever faith, of whatever community, of whatever people, we have to borrow their eyes, we have to borrow their heart. It is no use disputing over each historical tradition: they have often sprung from prejudice. Devotion is a matter of the heart, and is offered by the devotee" (*Ibid.*). By the way, *majnun* means crazy in Arabic! And indeed, spiritual seekers are often considered by the worldly to be "out of their minds" or "fools."

32. Herman Rednick, edited and compiled from unpublished ms. material.

33. The problem of reducing symbols to empty concepts through "abstract thinking" is not just a 20th century phenomenon. Rudolph Steiner even provides us with a history of the development of abstract thinking and the

loss of "living thinking," see *The Redemption of Thinking: a Study in the Philosophy of Thomas Aquinas,* 1956. In the "Synopses of Lectures" we find a brief tracing of the process: "A hundred years after Augustine's death, Justinian banished from the Roman Empire the Plotinistic philosophers at Athens. As a result the awareness of spirit-reality as a background to life and thought gradually faded in Europe, and philosophy dried up into logic. The only conception of the spirit-world was that expressed in the dogmas of religion. In these, freedom of thought and direct perception had no longer a place. With the loss of this consciousness of spirit-reality and with the growing sense of his own individuality, man was faced with the necessity of producing the spiritual as an abstraction from his own experience... The question the medieval scholastics put to themselves was this: What is our relationship to a world of which all we know is derived from concepts which can arise only out of our own experience as individuals? It was a different world from that of Plotinus and Augustine...Aquinas fashioned his theory of the "universals" not as intellectual abstractions, but as objectively real links between the physical and the yet-more-real spiritual worlds. Two centuries later the new, man-born, earth-tied thinking of science arose, with its boundary of sense-observation. Once more a different world came into being. Almost immediately after Aquinas' death, the intuitive perception of spirit-reality and its formative relation to the physical died away again. Thinking was given no higher origin than man's brain, the sense-world no significance beyond itself, and philosophy no basis in spirit-reality. Two centuries later science awoke to vigorous sense-directed life, and philosophy sank into the anarchy of a self-mistrustful existence. Six centuries after Aquinas, materialistic science bestrode the realm of human certainty, indifferent to the bewilderment of philosophy, and the suspicion and alarm of religion. Except for a flash of intuition in Spinoza and the inspired scientific observation of Goethe, there has been no intellectual certainty of the ever-present reality of spirit." Rudolf Steiner was not the only one to recognize this process. However, he put the situation into the context of the evolution of consciousness—our *spiritual* evolution. Another source of insight into the development of abstract thinking as the *only* acceptable mode of mental functioning can be seen in the rise of empirical psychology, where the concept of *the unconscious* has grown apace with the disappearance of the presence of the divine in our perceptions and cognitions.

34. Strangely this has been a contentious subject for millennia. Yet it seems perfectly logical, if not commonplace, to recognize the fact that people are

constantly loving (and engaging in many other activities besides) in different modes of *levels* simultaneously. Indeed this is an illustration of a cognitive faculty necessary to the normal functioning of the human mind: "In this regard, Islamic philosophy maintains that the mind is constituted by its nature to function in different ways at the same time; being perceptive of intelligible substances on the one hand, and speculative about sensible objects on the other" (Mehdi Yazdi, *The Principles of Epistemology in Islamic Philosophy: Knowledge by Presenc.*, 1992: p. 9).

35. In *The Man of Light in Iranian Sufism*, Henry Corbin describes the theophanic vision of the divine in the face of the beloved: "When the circle of the face has become pure, writes the Shaykh, it effuses lights as a spring pours forth its water, so that the mystic has a sensory perception (i.e., through the suprasensory senses) that these lights are gushing forth to irradiate his[or her] face. This outpouring takes place between the two eyes and between the eyebrows. Finally it spreads to cover the whole face. At that moment, before you, before your face, there is another Face also of light, irradiating lights; while behind its diaphanous veil a *sun* becomes visible, seemingly animated by a movement to and fro. In reality this Face is your own face and this sun is the sun of the Spirit (*shams al-ruh*) that goes to and fro in your body. Next, the whole of your person is immersed in purity, and suddenly you are gazing at a person of light...who is also irradiating lights. The mystic has the sensory perception of this irradiation of lights proceeding from the whole of his person. Often the veil falls and the total reality of the person is revealed, and then [in] the whole of your body, you perceive the whole. The opening of the inner sight...begins in the eyes, then in the face, then in the chest, then in the entire body. This person of light...before you is called in Sufi terminology the suprasensory *Guide*. It is also called the suprasensory *personal Master*... Najm Kobra refers to the Guide of light as the Sun of the heart...the spiritual Sun of the Spirit" (pp. 84-5).

36. See 7.3.4 "Presencing the Third."

37. *Creative Imagination in the Sufism of Ibn'Arabi*, 1981: p. 154.

38. Herman Rednick, edited and compiled from unpublished ms. material.

39. *The Complete Sayings of Hazarat Inayat Khan*, 1978: p. 245.

40. As Joyce and Barry Vissell have said, "Your mind will naturally seek the easiest person to be with, one with whom there is no struggle, no rough edges

to work out, one with whom it is easy and comfortable. But your heart, your true inner self, will seek the person who can best help you in your search for truth. The mind seeks an easy relationship. The heart seeks a spiritual partner" (*The Shared Heart*, 1984: loc. cit.).

41. We usually think of "purification" in relation to the *refiners fire* which smelts or burns away the impurities of our untransformed nature. Max Scheler describes it in this way: "Purification...means a continuous falling away (in our value-estimations and spiritual observation) from all that does not belong to our personal essence. It is an ever increasing clarification of the center of our existence for our consciousness" (Max Scheler, *Formalism in Ethics*, 1973: pp. 347-8). Clarification of our "essence" through a change in our "value-estimations and spiritual observation" certainly constitutes a movement on the spiritual path.

42. Adapted from *The Earth Journey: from Birth to Fulfillment*, 1980: p. 146, & *The Beloved Yoga*, 1993: p. 1.

43. Rudolf Steiner, *The Origin of Suffering*, 1980: p. 3.

44. Even outside the "spiritual" teachings we can find objections to the current views of Western civilization has towards suffering. For instance, in 1864 Dostoevsky asked, "And why are you so firmly and triumphantly certain that only what is normal and positive—in short, only well-being—is good for man? Is reason mistaken about what is good? After all, perhaps prosperity isn't the only thing that pleases mankind, perhaps he is just as attracted to suffering. Perhaps suffering is just as good for him as prosperity. Sometimes a man is intensely, even passionately, attached to suffering—that is a fact" (Notes From Underground, 1986: p. 41). This was written before Freud and before the modern psychologization of these issues.

45. For the logic and dynamics of polarities see: Archie J. Bahm, *Polarity, Dialectic, and Organicity*, 1970: Chapters 1 & 2, pp. 5-59. For an enlightening discussion of the most advanced applications of the concept of complementarity see: Menas Kafatos & Robert Nadeau. *The Conscious Universe: Part and Whole in Modern Physical Theory*, 1990: Chapter 7, "The Road Untraveled: Enlarging the New Logical Framework of Complementarity" pp. 127-146.

46. This myth reflects our erroneous belief in our superiority to the rest of humanity, i.e., those peoples who are less industrialized, and it totally ignores the fact that there has actually been an enormous increase in pain

and suffering in the modern world. Moreover, we refuse to believe that most of the increase in global suffering has occurred as a direct result of the industrialization, technological development and subsequent exploitation of less developed cultures by the military power and economic hegemony of the West. See Thomas Merton, *Disputed Questions*, 1977: pp. 97-8, & *Mystics and Zen Masters*, 1967: p. 263. Also see Max Scheler's essay, "The Meaning of Suffering," in *On Feeling, Knowing, and Valuing*, 1992: pp. 94-5.

47. The moral/spiritual vacuum in today's world has led to what some have called, *psychological man*, e.g., "becoming the dominant national character type." And for "psychological man the self is the only sound organizing principle...Psychological man eschews grand schemes of meaning that call for virtue, even heroism, and concentrates on living as comfortable and stable a life as possible. He allows himself periods of instinctual release and no longer feels guilt over this...the reigning American cultural theme is the prudent pursuit of pleasure, entailing both the command to be disciplined and controlled— eat right, exercise, work hard, don't waste any time—and the exhortation to consume a universe of products..." (Mary Ellen Ross, "The Ethical Limitations of Autonomy," 1983: p.154- 155). The term "psychological man" was coined by P. Rieff, and is discussed at length in his *The Triumph of the Therapeutic*, 1966.

48. Blaming the victim is very often the response of the medical establishment toward illnesses which are difficult to diagnose, especially chronic illnesses. Blaming the victims of rape also comes to mind. Indeed, our culture goes to great lengths to save the appearances specified in the myth of superiority. Kat Duff recently wrote that "sickness...is not only a breakdown of normal health but a personal failure, which explains why so many sick people feel so guilty and ashamed—or angry at anyone who intimates that they have done something wrong...When symptoms persist and illness becomes chronic, we often find fault with the victim; we call it a lack of will power, a desire for attention, an unwillingness to work or change, rather than question the hidden assumption that it is within our power as human beings to overcome sickness and, in fact, it is our job to do so" (*The Alchemy of Illness*, 1993: p. 41). Kat Duff provides an excellent discussion of how and why the sick are blamed for their own illness in Chapter 3, "Toxic Health: Cultural Assumptions and Illusions" (*Ibid.* pp. 34-58).

49. "Observing & Opening: A Practical Method for Transforming Physical Pain into Spiritual Growth." *Shambhala Sun*, V. 5, No. 4 (March 1997): pp. 51-2.

50. Thomas Merton, *The Seven Storey Mountain*, 1948: pp. 82-3.

51. Indeed, Rudolf Steiner has argued that pain lies at the very root of consciousness itself. For instance, "All that gives rise to consciousness is originally pain. When life manifests externally, when life, air, warmth, cold encounter a living being then these outer elements work upon it... Consciousness first arises when these outer elements come into opposition with the inner life and a destruction takes place. Consciousness must result from destruction of life. Without partial death a ray of light is not able to penetrate a living being...Consciousness within matter is thus born out of suffering, out of pain" (*The Origin of Suffering*, 1980: pp. 10-1).

52. *The Prophet*, 1956: p. 11.

53. As Rudolph Steiner said, "the origin of purification, the lifting up of human nature, lies in pain." (*The Origin of Suffering*, 1980: p. 15). And Nickolas Berdyaev remarks, precisely for our purposes, that, "in a true marriage that has meaning husband and wife have to suffer and bear each other's burdens, since life upon earth is always full of pain. And true love means tragedy and suffering" (The Destiny of Man, 1960: p. 234). And more recently Mother Teresa of Calcutta declared that, "suffering will come, trouble will come—that's part of life; a sign that you are alive. If you have not suffering and no trouble, the devil is taking it easy. You are in his hand" (*Mother Teresa: Contemplative in the Heart of the World*, 1985: p. 129).

54. Paraphrase by Norman O. Brown Love's Body, 1966: p. 178.

55. Boethius *The Consolation of Philosophy*, 1988: p. 97.

56. Farid Ud-Din Attar, *The Conference of the Birds*, 1967: p. 102. It is not inconceivable that Attar actually got this from the Roman philosopher, Boethius, who was very well known throughout the "world" in Medieval times.

57. *The Collected Works*, 1979: p. 663.

58. The term "Dark Night of the Soul" comes, of course, from St. John of the Cross (1542-1591). He tells us that, "Trials will never be lacking in religious life, nor does God want them to be... Since He brings souls there to be proved and purified, like gold, with the hammer and the fire, it is fitting that they encounter trials and temptations from men and from devils, and the fire of anguish and affliction" (*The Collected Works*, 1979: p. 663).

59. *The Hidden Journey: A Spiritual Awakening*, 1991: p. 38.

60. For a most enlightening discussion of "orientation" see Henry Corbin, *The Man of Light in Iranian Sufism*, 1978: Chapter 1 "Orientation," pp. 1-12.

61. Adapted from Herman Rednick, *The Earth Journey: from Birth to Fulfillment*, 1980: p. 220 and other unpublished writings.

62. *The Long Shorter Way: Discourses on Chasidic Thought*, 1988: p. 173.

63. *The Eternal Now*, 1963: pp. 179-80.

64. See Section 1.3 for the idea of gratitude *for every experience.*

65. Adapted from Herman Rednick's unpublished writings.

66. This process is mentioned by Vincent Brümmer: "According to Simone Weil, 'the extreme greatness of Christianity lies in the fact that it does not seek a supernatural remedy for suffering but a supernatural use for it'. This supernatural use lies in the fact that affliction can make us aware of our vulnerability and so help to free us from the illusions of personal worthiness which prevent us from receiving divine love as a gift. Through affliction we can achieve what she calls 'spiritual nakedness' before God" (*The Model of Love*, 1993: p. 231). Without love the fear of "nakedness," expressed as an indefatigable and unrelinquishable defense of our egoism, is the driving motive in life.

67. Thomas Merton *The Wisdom of the Desert*, 1970: p. 18.

68. Andrew Harvey *The Hidden Journey: A Spiritual Awakening*, 1991: p. 86. This took place in Ladakh in 1981, when Thuksey Rinpoche was dying.

69. Andrew Harvey, *A Journey in Ladakh*, 1983: pp. 182-3. These words of the Buddha were given to Andrew Harvey by the young Rinpoche Drukchen on that same 1981 journey to Ladakh.

70. Adapted from *The Beloved Yoga*, 1993: p. 14.

71. *The Long Shorter Way: Discourses on Chasidic Thought*, 1988: p. 168.

72. From Herman Rednick, *Living in the Presence*, 1994: p. 1 and p. 14

73. W. James, The Varieties of Religious Experience (New York: Longmans Green, 1980) as quoted in Paul Pearsall, The Ten Laws of Lasting Love. 1995: p. 254.

74. *The Beloved Yoga*, 1993: p. 14.

75. *The Meaning Of Love*, 1985: p. 45.

76. Robert Sardello, *Love and the Soul: Creating a future for Earth*, 1995: p. 151. Emphasis added.

77. *The Phenomenon of Man*, 1965: p. 265.

78. From Solovyev: "There is only one power which can from within undermine egoism at the root, and really does undermine it, namely love, and chiefly sexual love" (*The Meaning Of Love*, 1985: p. 45).

79. Ibid. He says further, "simply by the facts love ... [compels] us not by abstract consciousness, but by an internal emotion and the will of life to *recognize for ourselves the absolute significance of another*. Recognizing in love the truth of another, not abstractly, but essentially, transferring in deed the center of our life beyond the limits of our empirical personality, we by so doing reveal and realize our own real truth, our own absolute significance, which consists just in our capacity to transcend the borders of our factual phenomenal being, in our capacity to live not only in ourselves, but also in another" (*Ibid.*, italics added).

80. Solovyev's eloquent presentation of the spiritual purpose of *marriage* is the following:

"Egoism is a power not only real but basic, rooted in the deepest center of our being, and from thence permeating and embracing the whole of our reality—a power, acting uninterruptedly in all aspects and particulars of our existence. In order genuinely to undermine egoism, it is necessary to oppose to it a love equally concretely specific, permeating the whole of our being and taking possession of everything in it. So then this other force, which is to emancipate our individuality from the fetters of egoism, must possess a correlation with the whole of that individuality, must be equally real and concrete, a completely objectified subject like ourselves. Moreover, in order to really be another it must in everything be distinguished from us; i.e., possessing all that essential content which we also possess, it must possess it in another mans or mode, in another form. In this way every manifestation of our being, every vital act would encounter in this other a corresponding, but not identical, manifestation, in such a way that the relation of the one to the other would be a complete and continual exchange, a complete and

465

continual affirmation of oneself in the other, with perfect reciprocity and communion. Only then will egoism be undermined and abrogated; abolished, not in principle alone, but in all its concrete reality. Only under the action of this, so to speak, chemical union of two beings, of the same nature of equal significance, but *on all sides* distinct as to form, is the creation possible (both in the natural order and in the spiritual order) of a new human being, the real realization of true human individuality. Such a union, or at least the closest approximation to it, we find in sexual love, for which reason we attach to it exceptional significance, as the necessary basis of all further perfection, as the inescapable and permanent condition under which alone a human can really be in the truth" (*The Meaning Of Love*, 1985: pp. 45-6).

81. This paradoxical exhortation appears in all four gospels, e.g., Mt. 10:39 & 16:25; Mk. 8:35; Lk. 9:24 & 17:33; & Jn. 12:25. Interestingly it does not appear in the New Testament outside of the gospels. Herman is here quoting Matthew 10:39 (NIV), i.e.: "Whoever finds his life will lose it, and whoever loses his life for my sake will find it." Matthew's use of the Greek *heureo*, "find" or *sozo*, "save" and *apollumi*, "lose" which is typical of the other gospels except Jn. 12:25 who uses *phileos*, "love" and *miseo*, "hate." This renders John's statement even more paradoxical: i.e., "The man who *loves* his life will lose it, while the man who *hates* his life in this world will keep it for eternal life."

82. *The Phenomenon of Man*, 1965: p. 265.

83. Adapted from meditations in *The Beloved Yoga*, 1993.

84. *The Beloved Yoga,* Herman Rednick Archival Project, Memoir #1, 1993: p.9 (from 11/26/72).

85. According to the OED, "presencing" has been in use since 1638, and "copresent" was used first by Coleridge in 1817, so *copresencing* is not exactly a neologism. Arthur Versluis uses the term "compresence" in his recent book *TheoSophia* (1994: p. 142), but the OED gives this form as "obs.-rare." Apparently these terms were used at one time in the seventeenth century to refer to the 'copresence' of the bread and wine in the Eucharist, where they were 'consubstantiated' together. Henry Corbin also uses the form "compresence." In his translation of a passage by 'Abd Al-Karim Jili (d. 1403), he presents the following sentence: "Now the one and the other involve unawareness of reciprocal *compresence* with God. That is why these people are asleep, whereas one who is *compresent* with the Divine Presence is a Watcher, an Awakened

One (an *Egregoros*); his degree of awakening is proportionate to his reciprocal *compresence* with God" (Henry Corbin, *Spiritual Body and Celestial Earth*, 1989: p. 152). The term "co-presence" has also been used recently by two philosophers. Gabriel Marcel said in a late work, *Creative Fidelity*, that "To encounter someone is not merely to cross his path but to be, for the moment at least, near to or with him. To use a term I have often used before, it means being a *co-presence*." (p. 12). Building on Marcel, Richard Zaner says in the final chapter ("The Vivid Presence") of his book, *The Context of Self*, that "*vivid co-presence is a veritable achievement, and it is one which,...deeply marks* the selves co-presenced 'with' one another." (p. 236)(emphasis in original). In relation to the experience of co-presencing, Zaner further submits that there is a "'going-beyond" in spatial terms...[and] in temporal terms...the "here" and the "elsewhere," so "past" and "future"...are here transcended... one experiences a kind of timelessness" (p. 237). We will be expanding on these aspects of copresencing in this Section.

86. Paul Pearsall's Sixth Law of Love is basically the same as "copresencing." He calls this "The Transcendent-Love Law." He also calls this "nonlocal Love" p. 214. Pearsall has had considerable personal experience of copresencing with his wife and he develops the concept in his own unique way in Chapter 10 of his book, i.e., "The Quantum Leap of Love: Coming Together Anywhere" (*The Ten Laws of Lasting Love*, 1995: pp. 211-225). The interested reader will discover that our exercises and directions for couples are quite different from Pearsall's, however we admire the work that he is pioneering in this field.

87. *The Beloved Yoga*, 1993: p. 28.

88. For instance, the traditional and ubiquitous notion that we are homeostatic organisms which are self-regulating, operating as separate systems, is no longer valid. This nineteenth century idea has been shown to be false and humans are neurologically and physiologically dependent on information from and a connection to other persons to regulate our "hormone levels, cardiovascular function, sleep rhythms, immune function, and more," just to function properly. See Thomas Lewis, Fari Amini & Richard Lannon *A General Theory of Love*, 2001.

89. It is possible to speak of copresencing at a mental or ideational level. For example, Rudolf Steiner once wrote that, "Paradoxical as it may sound, it is true: the idea which Plato represented to himself and the same idea which I represent to myself are not two ideas. They are one and the same idea. And

there are not two ideas, one in Plato's head, the other in mine; rather in the higher sense Plato's head and mine interpenetrate; all heads which grasp the same, *single* idea, interpenetrate; and this unique idea exists only once. It is there, and the heads all transport themselves to one and the same place in order to contain this idea." The Greeks knew this, but it has temporally become unknown to us. As Sophocles expressed it, so long ago, "The long unmeasured pulse of time moves everything. There is nothing hidden that it cannot bring to life, nothing once known that may not become unknown" (*Ajax*).

90. Clara Codd, The Creative Power, 1947: p. 28.

91. The legacy of Plotinus' "alone to the alone" is very pervasive in esoteric and religious teachings, however the Way of the Beloved directly challenges these notions. Recent philosophical thought (e.g. Martin Heidegger, Gabriel Marcel, Alfred Schutz, George Kovacs, Richard Zaner Max Scheler & Tielhard de Chardin) demonstrates that, "The conception of the 'I' as a monad, independent and without real connection with other beings, is false in two senses...we are never alone, nor are we one" (Joe McCown, *Availability: Gabriel Marcel and the Phenomenology of Human Openness*, 1978: p. 43). This orientation is grounded in Heidegger, i.e., "Heidegger concludes, there is no isolated 'I' without the 'other.' This is an important principle according to Heidegger's phenomenology. The 'other' is ontologically given with the 'World'; the 'other' is an existential" (George Kovacs, *The Question of God in Heidegger's Phenomenology*, 1990: p. 72). For Martin Heidegger's analysis, see *Being and Time*, 1962: § 116-124. The largely neglected philosopher, Max Scheler developed his ideas about *person* along similar lines: "two factors stand out in Scheler's metaphysical view of reality: the uniqueness of persons in their being, and the unity of the primordial concrete existential situation...A person for him is in no sense a thing, is in no sense given as finished or complete. A person is a center of originality, a creative source, a richness of possibility fundamentally unique. In Scheler's phenomenological view persons are the same in their uniqueness, and this uniqueness is the intrinsic coherence of a dynamic orientation. Persons are irreducible. The being and value of a person is absolute...Scheler sees the existential situation as unitary and this primordial unity as relational. There is, for Scheler, a direct and immediate involvement among beings. More precisely all beings *are* their involvement with other beings; beings *are* participations in Being. There are not first of all beings isolated and apart from Being and then a coming together which is a participation. Participation, involvement, living exchange, dialogue are given primordially.

"The relational unity here described as participation can be understood as a dialectical relation. This dialectical relation is a relatedness in which each term of the relation is meaningful only as a reference to the other, and in which one term without the other at least implied is an abstraction" (A.R Luther *Persons in Love*, 1972: pp. 41-2).

92. The Ten Laws of Lasting Love, 1995: p. 211.

93. Chardin's term.

94. The soul for the Jews is the Hebrew *nefesh*, and for Moslems it is the Arabic *nafas*, both of which mean breath.

95. Thich Nhat Hanh uses the term "interbeing, " see *Living Buddha, Living Christ*, 1995: *loc. cit.* Martin Buber uses the term *interhuman* which intentionally does not include the whole cosmos, see *The Knowledge of Man: A Philosophy of the Interhuman*, 1965.

96. HR quoted in Justin Moore *Teachings From the Path of Fire*, 1973: Q 719.

97. *Toward the Future*, 1975: p. 71.

98. *The Ten Laws of Lasting Love*, 1995: pp. 28-9 and pp. 219-220.

99. *The Beloved Yoga*, 1993: p. 136 and *The Earth Journey:*, 1980: p. 291.

100. Adapted from: *The Beloved Yoga*, 1993: p. 4 & 66.

101. Enneads, V, 8, 4. Jorge Luis Borges cites this passage often, (e.g., Other Inquisitions: p. 69; Ficciones: p. 43; & The Aleph & Other Stories: p. 33). These references are from Jaén Didier *Borges' Esoteric Library: Metaphysics to Metafiction*, 1992: p. 71 & 77.

102. Hermetica, 1993: p. 211,*Libellus* XI (i), § 6a.

103. "Hundred Gates to the Sea of Ideas of the Flowery splendor Scripture." Wing-tsit Chan (trans.) in *A source Book in Chinese Philosophy*, 1963: pp. 420-424. Quoted in Steve Odin, *Process Metaphysics and Hua-yen Buddhism*, 1982: pp. 21-22.

104. Thich Nhat Hanh, *Living Buddha, Living Christ*, 1995: p. 185.

105. *From Reductionism to Creativity: rDzogs-chen and the New Sciences of Mind*. 1989: p. 190.

106. Quoted in Ibid.

107. *Of Learned Ignorance*, 1954: pp. 83-4. Quoted in Steve Odin, *Process Metaphysics and Hua-yen Buddhism*, 1982: p. 218 Note 14.

108. Philip P. Weiner, (Ed.), *Leibniz: Selections,* 1951: pp. 300-1.

109. Science and the Modern World, 1967: p. 91.

110. Phenomenology of Perception, 1978: p. 421. Quoted in Steve Odin, *Process Metaphysics and Hua-yen Buddhism*, 1982: p. 104.

111. *Wholeness and the Implicate Order*, 1988: p. 177.

112. Murray Sargent, Marlan Scully & Willis Lamb, Laser Physics, 1974: p. 228. Quoted in Arthur Zajonc, *Catching the Light: The Entwined History of Light and Mind*, 1993: p. 322.

113. "Quantum Cat Tricks" in *Discover*, Vol. 17, No. 10, October 1996: p. 26.

114. Overcoming the, still ubiquitous, but erroneous concept of *simple location*, which is the basis of our belief in the absolute separation of material objects in space, was accomplished independently by Einstein and Whitehead in 1905. See Paul F. Schmidt, *Perception and Cosmology in Whitehead's Philosophy*, 1967: p. 4 & Chapter VI.

115. Allan Megill comments that, "We must distinguish here between the two senses of the word *presence*. There is the temporal sense, in which the present is distinguished from the past and the future, and the spatial sense, in which something is 'present at' or 'in proximity to' something else. In German, these two senses are marked off, as they are not in English, but the distinction between *Anwesenheit*, which means the presence of someone at some place or occasion, and *Gegenwart*, which may mean 'presence at,' but which more often means presence in the temporal sense" (*Prophets of Extremity: Nietzsche, Heidegger, Foucault, Derrida*, 1985: p. 124).

116. These are the final words of Goethe's, Great Work, *Faust,* and are uttered by the "Chorus Mysticus." There are many different translations of *Faust* into English and we have used the one given in Rudolf Steiner's *Goethe's Secret Revelation and the Riddle in Faust*, (1980: p. 134). Steiner comments that, "What is 'unattainable' for the material world is within the reach of spiritual vision….in this Chorus Mysticus he[Goethe] points out to us how that which is indescribable in material words is done, when the language of imagery is used: how the soul, by means of the eternal womanhood in it is

drawn into the spiritual world." This really sums-up this Section of the *Way of the Beloved*.

117. Actual visions of the Eternal Feminine are not that uncommon, even in modern times. Indeed, visionary encounters with the Virgin Mary have become important signs within the Roman Catholic Church world-wide. We will list briefly the better known visions of Sophia, as Mary, which have taken place within the last 170 years (with one exception from the 16th century): One of the most famous visions, and one with astonishingly widespread consequences, was that of the Virgin of Guadalupe in Mexico (1531). More recently there has been a remarkable series of appearances of "Our Lady" beginning in 1830 in Paris, 1846 in La Selette, Lourdes (1858), Knock (1879), Fatima (1917), Beauraing (1932), Banneux (1933), Cairo (1954), and, more recently, at Mudjeggore (1960's). Needless to say, these appearances have a tremendous importance for millions of Catholics and also for many non-Catholics. The appearance of the Holy Mother is never taken lightly, particularly in times of peril, when she is regarded as a spiritual comforter (Paraclete) and healing force from God.

In the last 400 years there have been many well-known, but less publicly acclaimed, experiences of the Eternal Feminine among mystics and esotericists. Indeed, the great majority of modern mystics and theosophers have reported profound and transformative encounters with Sophia and many have subsequently based their theosophical writings on an outspoken sophiology. Those who have reported actual visions of Sophia would include, Gillaume Postel, Paracelsus, Jacob Böehme, the Baal-Shem-Tov, Immanuel Swedenborg, Karl Ekhartshausen, Georg Gichtel, Gottfried Arnold, John Pordage, Jane Leade, Louis Claude de Saint-Martin, William Blake, Franz von Baader, Vladimir Solovyov & Sergei Bulgakov.

118. There is probably not a single culture which does not have some concept or myth of the Holy Mother, the Eternal Feminine. We would like to list some of the names for the Eternal Feminine; we will use these interchangeably in the text as the mood suits us, however in most places we will use the more neutral, "Sophia." This list will include names of both the aspects of creation and destruction or, as some designate this difference, the White Goddess and the Black Goddess. Some commonly used Christian and Western names are: Mary, Mother of God, Holy Mother, Divine Mother, Virgin Mother, Blessed Virgin, Divine Feminine, Creative Feminine, Cosmic Feminine, Eternal

Feminine, Feminine Archetype, Feminine Principle, The Goddess, Universal Mother, Mother of the Universe, Cosmic Mother, Mother of the World, the Veiled One, World Soul, Eve, Universal feminine, The World Mother, Universal feminine consciousness, Fire of original awareness, Creative feminine principle, Cosmic feminine principle, etc. Jewish names include: Shekinah, Hokhmah, Malkhut, God's Glory, Wisdom of God, the fourth member of the Kabbalist tetrad, Matronit (Matron), or just, Wisdom and, of course, Lilith. In the ancient Near East, She was called Inanna in Sumer, Ishtar in Akkad, & Anath in Canaan, also Asherah, Astarte, Lilith & Naamah. In Islam She is called, Fâtima or sometimes Maryam. The Greeks had many different manifestations of Her: e.g., Sophia, Gaia, Sapientia, Hera, Demeter, Athena & the incomparable Aphrodite in both Her celestial designation, Aphrodite Urania, and as the World Soul, Aphrodite Anadyomene/Pandemos. Likewise, the Hindus recognize many aspects of Her: Pârvatî, Shakti, Sarasvatî, Prakriti, Kâli & Durgâ. The Egyptians look to Isis, the Chinese to Kuan Yin and the Buddhists to Tara. Among the ancient Celts there were Macha, Brigitt, & Mórrígan. And the ancient, pre-Islamic, Persians called Her, Spenta Armaiti, Archangel of the Earth and mother of Daêna, the Celestial I.

119. Primary, useful sources for an orientation to modern spiritual modes of thinking about the Eternal Feminine have included: Henry Corbin *Creative Imagination in the Sufism of Ibn 'Arabi*, 1981; Henri de Lubac *The Eternal Feminine*, 1971; Sergei Bulgakov *Sophia: The Wisdom of God*, 1993; Keith Dowman *Sky Dancer: the secret life and songs of Lady Yeshe Tsogyel*, 1989; Herbert Guenther *The Tantric View of Life.*, 1972; Caitlín Matthews, *Sophia Goddess of Wisdom: The Divine Feminine from Black Goddess to World-Soul*, 1991; Torkom Saraydarian *Woman: The Torch of the Future*, 1980; Miranda Shaw *Passionate Enlightenment: Women in Tantric Buddhism*, 1994; Philip Sherrard *Human Image: World Image: the Death and Resurrection of Sacred Cosmology*, 1992; Vladimir Solovyov *The Meaning Of Love*, 1985; Arthur Versluis *TheoSophia*, 1994; Gertrud von le Fort *The Eternal Woman*, 1954; Mother Meera. *Answers.*, 1991 & Adilaksmi *The Mother*. 1994.

120. This paragraph contains phrases from HR and Adilakshmi's Introduction to *The Mother*, 1994.

121. Devi Surta, *Rig Veda* quoted in Andrew Harvey & Anne Baring *The Mystic Vision*, 1995: p. 77.

122. Daniel Andreev, *The Rose of the World*, 1997: pp. 356-8.

123. Torkom Saraydarian, *Woman, Torch of the Future*, 1980: p 201.

124. The title of Torkom Saraydarian's book is *Woman, Torch of the Future*.

125. *Ibid.*, p.191.

126. Taj Inayat *The Crystal Chalice: Spiritual Themes for Women*, 1980: p. 64.

127. *Savitri*, 1954: pp. 355-6. Aurobindo began *Savitri* in the late 1920's and he continued to revise and "raise it up into the *supramental*," until his death in 1950. The above text continues:

> *The Sun from which we kindle all our suns,*
> *The Light that leans from the unrealised Vasts,*
> *The joy that beckons from the impossible,*
> *The might of all that never yet came down.*
> *All Nature dumbly calls to her alone*
> *To heal with her feet the aching throb of life*
> *And break the seals on the dim soul of man*
> *And kindle her fire in the closed heart of things.*
> *All here shall be one day her sweetness's home,*
> *All contraries prepare her harmony;*
> *Towards her our knowledge climbs, our passion gropes,*
> *In her miraculous rapture we shall dwell,*
> *Her clasp will turn to ecstasy our pain.*
> *Our self shall be one self with all through her.*
> *In her confirmed because transformed in her,*
> *Our life shall find in its fulfilled response*
> *Above, the boundless hushed beatitudes,*
> *Below, the wonder of the embrace divine.*

128. We have not mentioned the subject of "beauty" which is of profound importance, but let us just indicate its connection: "Beauty is the supreme theophany, but it reveals itself as such only to a love which it transfigures. Mystic love is the religion of Beauty because Beauty is the secret of theophanies and because as such it is the power which transfigures" (Henry Corbin *Creative Imagination in the Sufism of Ibn 'Arabi*, 1981: p. 98). And "Beauty is God: You know the saying that God is love, but it is not often realized that beauty is God. ...When there is Love in your heart you can see beauty everywhere because God is everywhere. For a greater manifestation of the

beautiful, turn and look at your beloved. The structure and color of the eye is the manifestation of the Holy Spirit; and when she smiles, the spiritual Sun is radiating at you. ...Through Love I live in beauty, through beauty I live and breathe in the presence of God" (Herman Rednick *Beloved Yoga*, 1993: p. 135). And in view of this it should be mentioned that, "Something that is the reverse of what we observe in the physical world takes place in higher creative work: there the woman fertilizes the man, who conceives the idea and brings it to life...If we plumbed the depths of the creative process of the majority of geniuses of the arts, we would find that it was women who sowed the spiritual seed of the geniuses' immortal works into the depths of their subconscious, into their innermost creative recesses" (Daniil Andreev *The Rose of the World*, 1997: pp. 354-5).

129. See Chapter 6 for an explanation of the ideas in this and the next 3 paragraphs.

130. Epigram for Hazrat Inayat Khan *Passion* in Scott Miners, 1984: p. 172.

131. Robert Van Arsdale, *Song of the Beloved*, 1980 (unpublished).

132. The concepts presented in this paragraph are detailed in Chapter 6.

133. This was the weekly meditation given by Herman Rednick on Sunday, July 29, 1973:

THE HOLY MOTHER

With the New Age, the forces of Light are changing their vibration. It was in the past one of power, forcing humanity in the path of evolution through warfare and destruction. They fought their way through the ages. This is fading into abstraction as we enter the New Age.

The Holy Mother, radiant in Love and Peace is approaching.

Sometimes She is very distant, part of the heavens, impersonal and abstract. Another time She is a young woman with a sweet fragrance, radiating eternal Love. And again, She is a woman of mystic power, with a vibrant blue being containing all the mysteries of the heaven and the earth.

Through Her Presence, true brotherhood shall descend upon humanity.

Mantram: *The Holy Mother fills me with love for my brother.*

134. These ideas are discussed in Chapter 6.

135. Refer to "Three Obstacles to Revisioning" detailed above.

136. *Passionate Enlightenment: Women in Tantric Buddhism*, 1994: p. 41.

137. Herbert Guenther, *The Tantric View of Life*, 1972: p. 73.

138. Many women who come to us with this "problem" believe that it is a psychological problem stemming from some lack in their childhood. They are surprised to hear that it is a well known and universal situation for beloved couples.

139. See 7.1 "The Test of Fire."

140. This corresponds to the relationship in Tantric Buddhism, described by Miranda Shaw: "While a woman's relationship with Vajrayogini is one of identity, for a man it is primarily one of devotion that he must extend to women as her living representatives... For men, meditating on women as embodiments of Vajrayogini and transferring their reverence for Vajrayogini to all women was a way to remedy their ordinary views of women and purify their vision. This process was not an arbitrary exercise in deconstruction of social conditioning, but a means of perceiving women accurately—as embodiments of female divinity, inherently divine and sacred in essence..." (*Passionate Enlightenment: Women in Tantric Buddhism*. 1994:p. 42). Also Keith Dowman comments: "Despite the ubiquitous practice of celibacy within Buddhism, the tantrics developed a metaphysic of woman which elucidates the same comprehension of the relationship of woman to the Divine Feminine as the Sufis. Tantric metaphysics are derived principally from the Prajnaparamita-sutras, and...the tantric view [is] that there is no distinction between the ultimate metaphysical nature of woman and the relative human reality. Woman is the Dakini [feminine Goddess] and is to be worshipped as such" (*Sky Dancer*, 1989: p. 253). Within modern Sufism it has been described as follows: "When a woman discovers the Veiled One within herself, the Veiled One appears as the Mother of the World. When a man becomes conscious of the Veiled One, she appears as the Beloved. A woman becomes her embodiment and a man becomes her protector" (Taj Inayat *The Crystal Chalice*, 1980: p. 58). In the Hindu religion, "Partnership is a path to enlightenment. When Indian couples get married in the thousands-of-years-old Vedic wedding ceremony, the woman is accepting her husband as her guru and god, and the man is accepting his wife as creatrix and goddess" Savitri, L. Bess *The Path of the Mother*, 2000: p. 123). And there is yet another approach

to spiritual union with the Eternal Feminine Principle of the universe, which has been mostly hidden in the West. Henry Corbin explains that in the Sufi approach, "Woman is the mirror...in which man contemplates his own Image, the Image that was his hidden being, the Self which he had to gain knowledge of in order to know his own Lord" (*Creative Imagination in the Sufism of Ibn 'Arabi*, 1981: p. 161). Thus, it is the Eternal Feminine that is the Image of the Ideal which actually *manifests* in the beloved. And Vladimir Soloviev says: "Hence also is derived the legitimate place of that element of adoration and boundless devotion which is so peculiar to love, yet possesses so little meaning if it relates only to the earthly object, in separation from the heavenly one... The heavenly object of our love is only one, always and for all humans one and the same—the eternal Divine Femininity. But seeing that the task of true love consists not in merely doing homage to this supreme object, but in realizing and incarnating it in another lower being of the same feminine form, though of an earthly nature..." (*The Meaning Of Love*, 1985: pp 92-94). Thus, when one *looks again* into the face of our beloved with the eye of the heart, the transformed vision of the beloved reveals the Image of the Eternal Feminine—*Sophia aeterna*. Indeed, on this path, the Eternal Feminine *is* the Image of Divinity. Both man and woman see the *same* Symbol, i.e., Sophia *is* the Image of God. However, The Symbol, Sophia, may *appear* or *image* in infinite forms. Indeed, Tantric Buddhists speak of seeing the Buddha in the man and to Western mystics it is the Christ who appears. Thus, both a man and a woman will see the Image of his or her own soul—the True Self as disclosed to the eye of the heart!

141. This declaration, which sounds so alien to our egalitarian ears, is from the Prajnaparamita-sutra. Quoted in Keith Dowman, *Sky Dancer*, 1989: p. 253.

142. This precept is stated by Keith Dowman in the following way: "it cannot be sufficiently stressed that in the realm of tantric practice there is no distinction between woman in her every day reality and the all-inclusive divine female archetype that permeates her being and dominates her mind (the Yidam Vajra Yogini, for instance). Every woman *is* the Dakini...Whether or not woman knows herself as the Dakini, the Guru and *yogin* see her only in her divine form. A *yogin* can evaluate the maturity of his practice by judging the constancy and depth of his vision of woman as the Dakini" (*Sky Dancer*, 1989: pp. 254-5).

143. Henry Corbin, *Creative Imagination in the Sufism of Ibn'Arabi*, 1981: p. 339, N. 48.

144. This ceremony was inspired by Ramakrishna, Ammachi, the Golden Triangle Meditation, (See 7.3.4 "Presencing the Third"), and Buddhist ceremonies described in Miranda Shaw and Keith Dowman. For instance, a ceremony that Ramakrishna performed with his wife was described as follows: "As if to show that the ideal of marriage is a union of the spirit or atman, Sri Ramakrishna went a step further. In June 1872 on the day of the Phalaharini Kale Puja, he made arrangements for the worship of the Divine Mother in his own room. It was 9 p.m. He asked the Holy Mother [i.e., Sarada Devi, his wife] to sit on the seat meant for the Deity. With invocations and ceremonial offerings, he worshipped her as the Mother of the Universe. The Holy Mother went into samadhi immediately, and Sri Ramakrishna in deep ecstasy offered his rosary and the fruit of his sadhana at her feet, and at the end himself fell into deep samadhi. Both were united in God-consciousness, where time and human personality cease to have any meaning. It was a deeply significant action in many ways. It established perfect communion between the two. It showed the world a new idea of conjugal harmony and happiness. Worship of the husband had been a path of God-realization for women in India since time immemorial, but the worship of the wife was rare and was perhaps meant by Sri Ramakrishna as a path for men of future generations. In any case, to look upon all women as manifestations of the Divine Mother was definitely a way of noble living established by Sri Ramakrishna" (Chandra Kumari Handoo *A Glimpse of the Holy Mother*, 1952: pp. 11-12).

145. Philip Sherrard "Man and Woman, An Evaluation of their Relationship in the Christian Perspective," in Nasr, Sayyed Hossein & William Stoddart, *Religion of the Heart*, 1991: p. 269.

146. These are all quotes from *The Beloved Yoga*, 1993: pp. 18, 24, 46, 100 & 136.

147. For instance, Plato said: "But two things alone cannot be satisfactorily united without a third; for there must be some bond between them drawing them together. And of all bonds the best is that which makes itself and the terms it connects a unity in the fullest sense…" (*Timaeus*. 1959: 31b-c). As we have asserted so many times, the only bond which "makes itself and the terms it connects a unity in the fullest sense" is the bond-of-love.

148. For instance, Christ said, "When two or more are gathered in my name, there I am." Clearly, to "gather in His Name" is to come together with *some* love.

149. *The Beloved Yoga*, 1993: p. 25.

150. Kierkegaard elucidates this idea with a brilliant argument which even includes reference to the inherent triangular nature of the man-woman love-relationship: "The world can never get through its head that God in this way not only becomes the third party in every relationship of love but essentially becomes the only loved object, so that it is not the husband who is the wife's beloved, but it is God, and it is the wife who is helped by the husband to love God, and conversely, and so on. The purely human conception of love can never go further than mutuality: that the lover is the beloved and the beloved is the lover. Christianity teaches that such a love has not yet found its proper object: God. The love-relationship is a triangular relationship of the lover, the beloved, love—but love is God. Therefore to love another person means to help him to love God and to be loved means to be helped" (*Works of Love*. 1962: p. 124). More recently, Teilhard de Chardin had much the same things to say about the love-relation of man and woman and its interconnection with God: "the centre towards which the two lovers converge by uniting must manifest its personality at the very heart of the circle in which their union wishes to isolate itself. Without coming out of itself, the pair will find its equilibrium only in a third being ahead of it. What name must we give to this mysterious 'intruder'...Love is a three term function: man, woman and God. Its whole perfection and success are bound up with the harmonious balance of these three elements" (*Human Energy*, 1969: pp. 75-6).

151. Indeed, Kierkegaard maintains that some form of *God-relationship* is necessary for "genuine love." For instance: "The God-relationship is the mark whereby love towards men is recognized as genuine love." Furthermore, "As soon as a love-relationship does not lead me to God, as as soon as I in a love-relationship do not lead another person to God, this love, even if it were the most blissful and joyous attachment, even if it were the highest good in the lover's earthly life, nevertheless is not true love" (*Works of Love*. 1962: p. 124).

152. Phillip Sherrard, "Man and Woman: An Evaluation of their Relationship in the Christian Perspective." In: Seyyed Hossein Nasr, & William Stoddart, *Religion of the Heart*, 1991: p. 265.

153. Sherrard says it this way: "Yet there is more than this. For if the lover recognizes that the love with which and in which he beholds the beloved is a Divine Quality, he will be seeing the beloved in God. He will be seeing her in the light of the love that in its essence is divine. He will not be loving her therefore outside or apart from God. In the fallen—or profane type of consciousness—it is quite possible for a man and woman to love each other outside and apart from God, at least where their own awareness and intentions are concerned, and to see each other as beings that have no relationship with God and are quite independent of Him. But in the paradisal state, man and woman love each other in God, aware that it is only by being in God that they can love at all" ("Man and Woman: An Evaluation of their Relationship in the Christian Perspective," 1991: p. 265).

154. Ibid., 1991: p. 266, Italics added.

155. This is especially true of the exercises presented in 7.2 (e.g., Exaltation & Visioning the Divine) and in 7.3 (e.g., Copresencing & Service), which lead us directly to the realization of God's presence as a Coinherent aspect of the Beloved Relationship.

156. I.e., "the centre of physical union from which [our love] was radiating is found to be incapable of accepting any further intensification. The focus of attraction suddenly shifts further and further—endlessly, indeed—ahead. If the lovers are to be able to continue to increase their mutual possession in spirit, they have to turn away from the body and look for one another in God" (Pierre Teilhard de Chardin *On Love*, 1967: p. 29-30). See also *Toward the Future*, 1975: p.85.

157. "Man and Woman: An Evaluation of their Relationship in the Christian Perspective," 1991: pp. 266-7. This is word for word what Sherrard had already said in The *Sacred in Life and Art*, 1990: p. 118.

158. As Solovyev confirms, "This true idea of the beloved object, though it shines through the real phenomenon in the instant of love's intense emotion, is at first manifested in a clearer aspect only as the object of imagination. The concrete form of this imagination, the ideal image in which I clothe the beloved person at the given moment, is of course created by me, but it is not created out of nothing" (*The Meaning of Love*, 1985: p. 89).

159. *The Figure of Beatrice*, 2000: p. 35.

160. Phillip Sherrard, "Man and Woman," 1991: p. 266.

161. Herman Rednick *The Beloved Yoga*, 1993: p35

162. Vladimir Solovyev *The Meaning of Love*, 1985: p. 89.

163. Alfons Deeken, *Process and Permanence in Ethics: Max Scheler's Moral Philosophy*, 1974: p. 192.

164. Quoted in Ibid. For the discussion in Nicolai Hartmann, see *Ethik*, 1962: p. 533. And as Vladimir Soloviev says: "We must, by faith in the object of our love, understand the affirmation of this object as it exists in God, and as in this sense possessing everlasting significance. It must be understood that this transcendental relation to one's other, this mental transference of it into the sphere of the Divine, presupposes the same relation to oneself, the same transference and affirmation of oneself in the sphere of the absolute. I can only acknowledge the absolute significance of a given person, or believe in him (without which true love is impossible), by affirming him in God, and consequently by belief in God Himself, and in myself, as possessing in God the center and root of my own existence. This triune faith is already a certain internal act, and by this act is laid the first basis of a true union of the man with his other and the restoration in it (or in them) of the image of the triune God" (*The Meaning Of Love*, 1985: p. 88). We do not intend to discuss the possible relationship of the concept of the Golden Triangle to the "Triune God," the *Trinity*; it is outside the scope of the Way of the Beloved.

165. Claude Bragdon *Delphic Woman: Twelve Essays*, 1945: p. 84.

166. Adapted from *The Beloved Yoga*, 1993: pp. 18, 60 & 100.

167. *The Beloved Yoga*, 1993: p. 17.

168. The Republic, 517c.

169. See Co-Presencing (7.3.2) for further discussion of coinherence and interpenetration.

170. *The Beloved Yoga*, 1993: p. 102.

171. "The Evolution of Responsibility in the World" In *Activation of Energy*, 1970: pp. 207-214.

172. Perhaps one way to grasp the connection between love and service is with the thought of Max Scheler: "Love discloses its creative character as a dynamic

movement towards deeper value participation and value fulfillment. It lets the other person be as he is and encourages him to become more fully himself. A wider fullness and a greater richness become actualized in the process of interpersonal love in both the lover and the loved person. The dynamism of love is directed more to the fuller realization of being than to this or that particular value. Scheler quotes with approval a statement of Karl Jaspers to the effect that it is not particular values which are discovered in love, but that 'in the movement of love everything becomes more valuable'" (Alfons Deekins *Process and Permanence in Ethics: Max Scheler's Moral Philosophy.* 1974: p. 191). When other persons become more valuable to us, i.e., when we lovingly *share* their passion, it becomes more than a desire to *help*. Certainly, there are many who help others without compassion—for example, compassion is not a requisite for social work. Indeed, as Rachel Remen has pointed out, "Serving is different from helping. Helping is based on inequality; it is not a relationship between equals. When you help you use your own strength to help those of lesser strength...Serving is also different from fixing. When I fix a person I perceive them as broken, and their brokenness requires me to act" ("In the Service of Life" Noetic Sciences Review, Spring 1996: pp. 24-5). If one has a sense of "inequality" and of "fixing" others with one's own strength or expertise, then it is not service!

173. Our Teacher wrote: "My love grows when I serve another. With intense love I enfold my beloved and family. When I include other families, I carry out the spiritual plan for humanity. I begin at home, and with my beloved I become a radiant center. Thus, I can reach out to others, and have a quality of substance that will help them" (*The Beloved Yoga*, 1993: p. 93).

174. Mt. 5:15-16.

175. Vladimir Solovyev has discussed some of the philosophical grounds and implications of the necessity for serving others and reaching out beyond the circle of the couple's intimate sphere: "So long as the individual's achievement is confined to its proximate object—the amendment of the distorted personal relation between two beings—it remains of necessity without final success and is limited to this its own immediate concern. For the evil with which true love comes into collision, the evil of material separateness and impenetrability, and of the external resistance of two beings who internally fulfill one another— this evil is a particular yet typical instance of the general distortion to which our life is subject, and not ours alone, but the life of the whole world.

"An individual can really be saved, i.e., can regenerate and immortalize his individual life in true love, only conjointly or together with all others. He possesses the right and the obligation to defend his individuality from the basic law of general existence, but not to separate his own welfare from the true welfare of all living beings. From the fact that the deepest and most intense manifestation of love is expressed in the mutual relation of two beings who fulfill each other, it by no means follows that this mutual relation can separate and isolate itself from all the rest, as something self-sufficient. On the contrary, such isolation is the death of love, for in itself the sexual relation, in spite of all its subjective significance, proves (objectively) to be only a transient empirical phenomenon. In just the same way, from the fact that the perfected union of two such single beings will always remain the true and fundamental form of individual life, it does not at all follow that, when this life-form sets its keystone in its individual perfection, it is bound to remain empty, since, on the contrary, by the very nature of the human being, it is capable and predestined to be filled with universal content. Finally, if the moral meaning of love demands the reunion of that which is wrongfully separated, demands the identification of oneself with another, then to separate the problem of our individual perfection from the process of worldwide unification would be contrary to this same moral meaning of love, even if such a separation where physically possible" (The Meaning of Love, 1985: pp. 101-2).

176. Elizabeth Barrett Browning, Aurora Leigh., Quoted in Alice Rossi, (ed.) *Essays on Sex Equality: John Stuart Mill & Harriet Taylor Mill*, 1970: p. 44.

177. From an unpublished letter dated [V&A date?]

178. Adapted from Herman Rednick's unpublished writings.

179. We use the term *Union* in the mystical and, not the religious sense. The Islamic philosopher, Mehdi Ha'iri Yazdi, explains that "At this point it may be objected that such a sharp exclusion of religion from the essential features of mysticism is not consistent with the idea of 'union with God,' expressed so frequently by Western religions as the religious principle. Furthermore, it has been remarked that the drive toward mystical union is the vital principle of all religious life. 'Without it religion withers away in sterile ritualism or arid moralism.' Yet despite all this, when one turns one's attention to the matter of an examination of the meaning of this religious union, especially in comparison with the mystical sense of unitary consciousness, one finds that that which religious authorities try to indicate by the expression 'union' is far

from being mystical. It is a religious union that is no more than an 'association with,' or a 'devotion to,' the divine Will, such that in this union the distinction between subject and object is highly emphasized and is never disregarded. Even if the meaning of religious union were more than this, it could never, on the basis of any understandable hypothesis, proclaim a complete elimination of the subject-object relation, expressed in the 'lover-beloved' opposition, or the beatific vision....the sense of mystical unity is no less than an existential union to which religion cannot, at least theoretically, commit itself, although religion and mysticism are not contradictory. However, the major claim of mysticism is a complete dissolution of the finite self into the infinite Unity, such that phrases like 'be Thou our guide...' are no longer meaningful." (*The Principles of Epistemology in Islamic Philosophy: Knowledge by Presence.*, 1992: pp. 111-2).

180. Adapted from *The Beloved Yoga.* 1993. "Holy City" refers to Shamballah or the New Jerusalem.

181. Claude Bragdon *Delphic Woman: Twelve Essays*, 1945: p. 84.

182. *The Beloved Yoga*, 1993: p. 18.

183. For instance, in 1959 Derrick Bailey wrote: "When God created Man as male and female, he did not make two independent, self-subsistent beings—two 'individuals', ontologically separate and bound together by no closer tie than that of a common humanity and the need to co-operate in social life and in the propagation of the species. On the contrary, he created one dual 'being', and *'adham,* consisting of two empirically distinct yet correlative personal components, one male (*zakhar*) and the other female (*neqebhah*) . Each, though completely and autonomously human, postulates and is naturally orientated towards the other, so that together they are impelled to realize their mutual belongingness as the constituent elements of Man in the many forms of relationship through which sexual fulfillment can be achieved—and chiefly that of union as one-flesh in marriage" (*The Man-woman Relationship in Christian Thought.*, 1959: p. 271).

184. Pir Vilayat Khan (Ed.), *A Meditation Theme For Each Day: From the Teachings of Hazrat Inayat Khan*, 1992: May 17, p. 43.

185. Released in 1957 after 10 years in Lubyanka prison, Andreev's transcendental vision arose out of that deep well of Russian mysticism. Andreev's intricate account is based on his actual transcendental experiences

while imprisoned, and the full text of his work, *The Rose of the World*, did not appear until 1991—it was not available in English until 1997.

186. *The Rose of the World*, 1997: p. 348.

187. For a complete explication of the "logic" of Polarity see, Archie Bahm, *Polarity, Dialectic, and Organicity*, 1970 and Owen Barfield, What Coleridge Thought, 1971.

188. Owen Barfield, What Coleridge Thought. p. 84. Barfield considers himself an Anthroposophist, but he is recognized as a very independent thinker and just about the only contemporary one who has studied the principle of polarity.

189. *What Coleridge Thought*, 1971: pp. 35-36.

190. Owen Barfield, *Speakers Meaning*, 1967: pp. 37-8. On the truth of contradictory propositions Barfield quotes Coleridge as follows: "[Plato] leads you to see that propositions involving in themselves a contradiction in terms are nevertheless true; and which, therefore, must belong to a higher logic— that of ideas. They are self-contradictory only in the Aristotelian logic, which is the instrument of the understanding" (*What Coleridge Thought*, 1971: p. 188).

191. *What Coleridge Thought.*, 1971: pp. 35-36. In clarifying the structure of polarity, Archie Bahm said that, "polarity involves at least three general categories—oppositeness, complementarity, and tension—and various subcategories" (*Polarity, Dialectic, and Organicity*, 1970: p. 5). The subcategories of complementarity are: supplementarity, interdependence, dimension, & reciprocity. The subcategories of tension are: tendency, extra-tension, duo-tension, con-tension, dimensional tension, inter-level tension, polari-tension, rever-tension, rhythmi-tension & organi-tension" (*Ibid.* pp. 5-21). Therefore, "systems of polarity relations" can vary in structure and exhibit much greater complexity than is usually assumed of simple bi-polar interactions.

192. *Human Energy*, 1969: pp. 63-4.

193. Kelly Oliver *Womanizing Nietzsche: Philosophy's Relation to the Feminine.*, 1995: p. 55.

194. *Ibid.*, p. 56.

195. See particularly the thought of Niels Bohr: *Atomic Physics and Human Knowledge*, 1963: *loc. cit.*

196. We should point out that the erroneous concept of "soul-mates" arises from this kind of thinking; and even though humans are split into two forms which embody separately the energies of masculine and feminine, this does *not* mean that the physical "skins" or the bodies we inhabit are actual *parts* or halves of some *particular* higher being. Indeed, it has been written that souls will usually alternate between male and female forms when they reincarnate. So the idea of the two sexes being actual substantial halves of some particular transcendent being, and that our task-of-love is to find our particular or specific "other half," is a materialistic interpretation of much more enigmatic process which only finds its faint reflection in the substantially engendered men and women of our life-in-form.

197. *Modern Esoteric Spirituality*, 1995: p. xxviii.

198. Earth Changes, Human Destiny, 2000: p. 55.

199. Bailey notes here: "So-called 'changes of sex' in human beings, though much publicized when they occur, are very rare phenomena (comparatively speaking), and cannot be accepted as in any sense a refutation of the proposition here stated. In any case, we know very little about the nature, causes, and consequences of of such 'changes' especially from the personal and metaphysical standpoint" (*The Man-woman Relationship in Christian Thought*, 1959: pp. 275-6). Of course, when he wrote this in 1957, transexualism appeared to be "very rare," however, now with improved hormones and sophisticated surgery it is much more common. These issues are discussed at length in Robert Van Arsdale *Gendering*, (not yet published).

200. Derrick Bailey *The Man-woman Relationship in Christian Thought*, 1959: pp. 275-6.

201. Quoted in Sayyed Nasr & William Stoddart *Religion of the Heart*, 1991: p. 261. And Thomas Merton adds: "Each of them incarnates in a positive manner an aspect of the Divine; and any attempt on the part of either to deviate from, suppress or eliminate this God-given qualification, with the consequent loss or attenuation of masculinity in man and femininity in woman, represents a step away from perfection and an obstacle to it" (p. 262).

202. Thomas Merton pertinently discusses the common Christian tendency to identify love with obedience and thus to confuse love with will: "For a great many present day Christians, 'love' and 'obedience' are so perfectly equated with one another that they become identical. Love is obedience and obedience is love. In practice, this means that love is canceled out and all that remains is obedience—plus a 'pure intention' which by juridical magic transforms it into 'love.' The identification of obedience with love proceeds from a superficial understanding of such dicta as: 'Love is a union of wills,' 'Love seeks to do the will of the beloved.' These sayings are all very true. But they become untrue when in practice our love becomes the love of an abstract 'will,' of a juridical decree, rather than the love of a real person—and of the persons in whom He dwells by His Spirit! A distinction will be useful here. To say that love (whether it be the love of men or the love of God) is a union of wills, does not mean that a mere external *conformity* of wills is love. The conformity of two wills brought into line with each other through the medium of an external regulation may perhaps clear the way for love, but it is not yet love. Love is not a mere mathematical equation or abstract syllogism. Even with the best and most sincere of intentions, exterior conformity with a regulation cannot be made, by itself, to constitute a union of wills-in-love. Why? Because unless 'union of wills' means something concrete, a union of hearts, a union of spirits, *a communion between persons*, it is not a real enough union to constitute love. A communion between persons implies interiority and depth. It involves the whole being of each person—the mind, the heart, the feeling, the deepest aspiration of the spirit itself. Such a union manifestly excludes revolt, and deliberate mutual rejection. But it also presupposes individual differences—it safeguards the autonomy and character of each as an inviolate and unique person. It even respects the inevitable ambivalences found in the purest of friendships. And when we observe the real nature of such communion, we see that it can really never be brought about merely by discipline and submission to authority...Hence as the Gospel teaches us (Mt. 25:31-46), a Christian loves not simply by carrying out commands issued by Christ, in heaven, in regard to this 'object' which happens to be a fellow Christian. The Christian loves his brother because the brother 'is Christ'" (*Disputed Questions.* 1977: pp. 117-119). The common confusion of love and will has been investigated at length in Rollo May's classic study, *Love And Will*, 1969.

203. *Disputed Questions.* 1977: pp. 117-119.

204. Indeed, the Catholic Church's traditional policy remains, albeit recently somewhat ameliorated by Vatican II, that sex in marriage is only to serve the purposes of procreation, all other expressions of sexuality, even in marriage, are evil. Interweaving pagan asceticism with Greek misogyny, for nearly 1400 years the Church denied that passion had any role in *love*, and thus emerged the belief that "true love" is impossible in marriage. Romantic, passionate love in marriage became equated with adultery. Of course, this is not the case with all Catholic writers in modern times. Thomas Merton was one who understood clearly, and in depth, the nature and potential of the love between man and woman. And he cut through the pesky problem we keep bumping into in the widespread erroneous assumption that somehow "love is blind," and it was usually asserted that this was because Eros-love involved *passion*. And it was erroneously assumed that passion, even the passion of love, blocked our access to the spiritual. We have spoken about this before, but in the current context it is worth quoting from Merton: "On the contrary, the subjectivity essential to love does not detract from objective reality but adds to it. Love brings us into a relationship with an objectively existing reality, but because it is love it is able to bridge the gap between subject and object and *commune in the subjectivity of the one loved*. Only love can effect this kind of union and give this kind of knowledge-by-identity with the beloved" (*Disputed Questions*, 1977: p. 103).

205. Outlines of Romantic Theology, p. 111.

206. *Eclipse of God*, 1965: p. 129.

207. *New Seeds of Contemplation*, 1972: p. 64. We must forgive Merton's gender-specific language here; it was written in the 60s!

208. Adapted from *The Beloved Yoga*, 1993: p. 46 & 47. And similarly, in the *Symposium* (189c), Plato describes the primordial androgynous human-being as likened to a sphere which, at the time of its external manifestation in the physical realms, became split into two equal halves which have sought to reunite ever since.

209. Cf. Justin Moore (Ed.) *Teachings From the Path of Fire*, 1973.

210. The *Beloved Yoga*, 1993: p. 9.

211. Justin Moore (Ed.) *Teachings From the Path of Fire*, 1973: pp. 9-10.

212. Justin Moore, (Ed.) *Teachings From the Path of Fire*, 1973: pp. 1-2. Herman also said that it is possible for this interchange to take place without

the physical relation, but that this is the ancient path and not the Beloved path.

213. In his discussion of Camus' writing on Don Juan, Maurice Freidman notes: "Camus speaks of Don Juan's way of knowing as 'loving and possessing, conquering and consuming' and refers in this connection to the Biblical use of 'knowing' in connection with the carnal act. But for the Bible this word means mutuality, real mutual contact, and mutuality is the one thing that Don Juan entirely lacks as he goes from one woman to another" (*To Deny Our Nothingness: Contemporary Images of Man.*, 1967: p. 332). English translations of the Bible seem to have completely lost the idea of mutuality or of the interrelationship implicit in the sexual act. This is not surprising since Christianity is still perpetuating an ancient and disgraceful misogyny and, particularly the Roman Church; it continues to regard the sex act, even in marriage, as a sin and not at all as a loving, mutual exchange.

214. Justin Moore, *Teachings From the Path of Fire:* 1973: Q 235.

215. Quoted in Herbert Guenther *Reductionism to Creativity: rDzogs-chen and the New Sciences of Mind.* 1989: p. 190.

216. *Ibid.*

217. *The Marriage of East and West*, 1982: pp.160-2.

218. *Man and Woman: An Evaluation of their Relationship in the Christian Perspective*, 1991: p. 269.

219. Adapted from *The Beloved Yoga*, 1993: p. 19

220. Robert Van Arsdale, *Poems for the Spiritual Path*, 1979: p. 18.

221. Quoted in Denis De Rougemont, *Love in the Western World*, 1983: p.3.

222. *Delphic Woman: Twelve Essays*, 1945: p. 39.

223. Joel Stein, "Will Cybersex be better than real sex?" Time Magazine, June 19, 2000: p.64.

224. The "Hermetic marriage" is not the same as, and should not to be confused with, the notion, now associated with Jung and many others, of the balancing and blending of the *animus* andthe *anima archetypes* in the individual person. This has led to some serious misinterpretations of our "dual nature," i.e., being actual *men* and *women*, manifestations of two cosmic

forces, and not some kind of androgyne in an obscure "inner," or psychic sense.

225. Adapted from an unpublished H.R. fragment.

226. Adapted from *The Beloved Yoga*, 1993: pp. 54 & 112.

227. In ancient times and for very high initiates today, it is possible to unite with a Divine focal point (like the Holy Mother or the Christ) who has both principles within. Thus they attain the Hermetic Marriage in the transubstantial realms. Our Teacher taught that this kind of union of opposites is the "old path" and that the Beloved Yoga is the path for today.

228. *The Beloved Yoga*, 1993: p. 108.

229. *The Beloved Yoga*, 1993: p. 7.

230. It has been known for millennia that the exchange of energy between a man and a woman during sexual intercourse can be used as a power to rise to greater heights in consciousness. In the ancient spiritual traditions, yogas, of India, Tibet and China sexual union was recognized by some as having a spiritual potential. The practices which grew out of this knowledge were designed to raise the consciousness of the practitioners above the physical plane. It was discovered that these, otherwise celibate, monks and nuns could soar to the heights of the spirit through very specific and rigourous *tantric* practices. They also came to believe that the production of offspring was of secondary importance and children were not born to these tantric practitioners.

However, we should be very clear that these tantric practices had nothing to do with a loving relationship between a man and a woman. These were not married couples, indeed, they were not couples, except sexually. They were *initiates*, and they had no relationship outside of those regulated and ritualized sexual practices. It is worth noting here that the explicit knowledge of these sexual yogas and of the transcendent possibilities of sex were unknown in the West until very recently. And, expectably, these practices are not used today for a spiritual purpose, as they were intended. For one thing, these practices were only for those who had already achieved a high stage of initiation before they were allowed to engage in any of the Sexual Tantras. Nonetheless, in our modern culture, tantric practices are usually heralded as "spiritual sex," etc. In the secular West, we have actually debased the spiritual intent of the

Tantras, and now seek to intensify physical pleasures through them, not to seek God. The ancient monks were certainly not seeking to intensify physical sensations and this is not the goal of sex in the beloved relationship. Moreover, outside of the monastic and cultural context in which they were developed, the practices of Tantra become an inversion of their original intent. Indeed, our historical, religious and cultural context is the opposite of regarding sex as a potential way to the spirit. We all know that, except for Judaism, Western religions have made all sex into a sin and have limited its approved expression solely to reproduction.

231. The Slovenian artist and seer, Marko Pogacnik tells us that, "First of all the Goddess made it clear that the essence of sexual intercourse is not bound to the act of procreation, but rather represents an autonomous tranformational process in which both partners participate during their union...Finally, bouyed by the love bonds created between the two partners, the archetypal power of regeneration surfaces to enrich their daily life" (*The Daughter of Gaia: Rebirth of the Divine Feminine.*, 2001: pp. 142-3).

232. *The Apocalypse of Saint John,* Floris Books, Edinburgh, 1980, pp. 140-141

233. *The Dance of Shiva: Fourteen Indian Essays.*, 1957: pp. 124-134.

234. *Outlines of Romantic Theology,* 1990: p. 24.

235. The Beloved Yoga, 1993: p.12.

236. The Beloved Yoga, 1993: p. 56.

237. *Ibid.*

238. Torkom Saraydarian describes this in Woman, Torch of the Future: "A married couple eventually builds a magnetic cord...Sexual contact with men or women other than the wife or husband... [causes] a breakage of the magnetic link between the two partners....[The] magnetic chords break if loyalty is violated. During marriage one must try to exercise a very high loyalty through the physical body, the emotions and the mind, and never allow an intruder to sever the link" (p. 47).

239. Alice Bailey *Ponder On This*, 1971: p. 198.

240. This mantra was created for the authors by Herman in 1976. We have adapted it slightly for the purposes this book.

241. For instance, *Outlines of Romantic Theology* written in 1924-5 and *Religion and Love in Dante: The Theology of Romantic Love* published in 1941.

242. *Outlines of Romantic Theology*, 1990: p. 92.

243. We have not seen the specific term "way of the soul" used by anyone else, but there are other words which mean the same thing. For instance, Herman Rednick often used the term "Yoga" to refer to fact that the marriage relationship was a way of spiritual development—a Way to God. Below we list those others (that we are familiar with) who have understood and, explicitly stated, that the loving relationship of a man and a woman has, in modern times, become a most powerful and appropriate path to the Spirit: Rabbi Judah Loew of Prague (1512-1609), Jacob Böehme (1575-1624), John Pordage (1607-1681), (who had a spiritual awakening simultaneously with his wife, Mary, in 1654), Gottfried Arnold (1666-1714), Emanuel Swedenborg (1688-1772), Friedrich Christoph Oetinger (1702-1785), Franz von Baader (1765-1841), Vladimir Solovyiev (1853-1899), Claude Bragdon (1866-1946), Nicholas Berdaiev (1874-1948), Max Scheler (1874-1928), O. V. de L. Milosz (1877-1939), Martin Buber (1878-1965), Pierre Teilhard de Chardin (1881-1956), Karl Barth (1886-1968), Paul Tillich (1886-1965), Gabriel Marcel (1889-1973), Sergei Bulgakov (1871-1944), Ludwig Binswanger (1882-1966), Henry Corbin (1903-1978), Daniel Andreev (1906-1959), Thomas Merton (1915-1968), Derrick S. Bailey (1910-?), Torkom Saraydarian (1917-1997), Philip Sherrard (1922-1995) and Barry & Joyce Vissell.

244. *Outlines of Romantic Theology*, 1990: pp.14-5.

245. *Outlines of Romantic Theology*, 1990: p. 27.

246. I.e. Barry & Joyce Vissell, *The Shared Heart*, 1984.

247. Adapted from *The Beloved Yoga*, and unpublished ms.

248. *The Beloved Yoga*, 1993: p. 124 & Moore p. 14.

249. *The Flame of Beauty, Culture, Love, Joy*, 1980: pp. 158-9.

250. Emil Bock, *The Apocalypse of Saint John*, 1980: pp. 140-1.

251. Minor Robert Van Arsdale unpublished.

252. I.e., *Conjugal Love*, 1912. For those who are interested, there are more recent editions, and it is still being published.

253. *Woman, Torch of the Future,* 1980: p. 47.

254. *Ibid.*

255. *The Beloved Yoga,* 1993: p. 64.

256. *The Allegory of Love: A Study in Medieval Tradition,* 1958: p. 9.

257. *Love in the Western World,* 1983: p. 9. De Rougemont continues: "When I am asked: 'Does the word *love* express the same realities now as it did before?' I answer: 'What love, what realities, what before?' The European languages alone have included all these realities in one single word. The West is distinct from other cultures not only by its invention of passionate love in the twelfth century and the secular elaboration of conjugal love, but by its confusion of the notions of eros, agape, sexuality, passion. Classical Greek used at least sixteen different terms to designate love in all its forms: *eros* for physical love, *agape* for altruistic love, *philia* for tender or erotic feelings, etc." (*Ibid.*). De Rougemont's book was published only 1 year after Lewis' and there were others at this time who were investigating the origins of passionate love or romantic love, notably: Anders Nygren, *Agape and Eros,* 1953 (pub. in 1932), Charles Williams *The Descent of the Dove: A Short History of the Holy Spirit in the Church,*1939 and M. C. D'Arcy, *The Mind and Heart of Love,* 1956 (pub. in 1947). It might be noted that in Arabic there are 22 different words for expressing different states and levels of love.

258. *The Allegory of Love,* 1958: pp. 13-14. In the same year that Lewis' comprehensive study on the origins of romanticism appeared, Charles Williams published *Descent of the Dove,* in which he quotes from Lewis; they were close friends and each knew what the other was working on. In the same vein as the quote from Lewis, Williams wrote about the problem of passion (sexual love) in marriage with regard specifically to the teachings of the Church: "The effort in Christendom of the polarizing of sex-relationships towards God had been officially disapproved since the Councils of Elvira and Nicaea [i.e., 325 CE] except in marriage…In the general effort of establishing and maintaining a settled civilization marriage had become rather a fixity of social life than a dynamic of divine things.…[the Church] affected by her early passion of devotion and her later passion for Reason, she deprecated sexual passion altogether. 'The medieval theory finds room for innocent sexuality; what it does not find room for is passion, whether romantic or otherwise.…In its Thomist form the theory acquits the carnal desire and the

carnal pleasure, and find the evil in the *ligamentum rationis,* the suspension of intellectual activity.' [quoted from Lewis] From this point of view passion towards a man's wife was as bad as passion towards somebody else's wife. The unlimited remark of Messias that a man who desired a woman—nor did he exclude wives—committed adultery with her was taken literally..."(*Descent of the Dove,* 1939: pp. 129-30).

259. *Descent of the Dove,* 1939: p. 131.

260. See *Descent of the Dove*: "Passion was no longer to be only a morally dubious, because unintellectual, quality of marriage which was itself but a degree of justice working itself out in the world. The discovery of a supernatural justice between two lovers was passion's justification, and yet not only justification, but its very cause. There was vision (or conversion) and there was co-inherence and there was faith and hope and the Christian diagram of universal goodwill...But there has been more to it than this. In certain states of romantic love the Holy Spirit has deigned to reveal, as it were, the Christ-hood of two individuals each to other" (p. 131).

261. Vladimir Solovyev says in *The Meaning Of Love,* "Involuntary and immediate feeling reveals to us the meaning of love as the highest manifestation of individual life, which finds in union with another being its own proper infinity" (p. 97).

262. *The Beloved Yoga,* 1993: p. 31. Although the Beloved path is a direct path to realization, we do not mean to imply that it is the only path or that every couple will follow this path. There are always many paths to the spiritual mountain top. At this time, most of the fundamental spiritual representations upon which the Way of the Beloved depends are strenuously opposed in our secular culture. In our 30 years of working directly in the Way of the Beloved we have seen over and over that there are only a few who are ready and willing to walk this path. But, as Charles Williams made clear "the possibility is always there" (*Outlines of Romantic Theology,* 1990: p. 26). It is most important for all couples to know this, for as long as men and women lose their hearts in love for one another they will marry and perhaps follow a path to union with each other and, at the same time, union with the Divine.

263. *The Paradiso,* 1970: Canto V. line 7, p. 62.

264. *Kabbalah and Consciousness,* 1992: p.76.

265. *Outlines of Romantic Theology,* 1990: p. 25.

266. Adapted from H.R.

267. Minor Robert Van Arsdale *Poems for the Spiritual Path,* 1978: p. 46.

TRUE DIRECTIONS
An affiliate of Tarcher Perigee

OUR MISSION

Tarcher Perigee's mission has always been to publish books that contain great ideas. Why? Because:

GREAT LIVES BEGIN WITH GREAT IDEAS

At Tarcher Perigee, we recognize that many talented authors, speakers, educators, and thought-leaders share this mission and deserve to be published – many more than Tarcher Perigee can reasonably publish ourselves. True Directions is ideal for authors and books that increase awareness, raise consciousness, and inspire others to live their ideals and passions.

Like Tarcher Perigee, True Directions books are designed to do three things: inspire, inform, and motivate.

Thus, True Directions is an ideal way for these important voices to bring their messages of hope, healing, and help to the world.

Every book published by True Directions– whether it is non-fiction, memoir, novel, poetry or children's book – continues Tarcher Perigee's mission to publish works that bring positive change in the world. We invite you to join our mission.

For more information, see the True Directions website:

www.iUniverse.com/TrueDirections/SignUp

Be a part of Tarcher Perigee's community to bring positive change in this world! See exclusive author videos, discover new and exciting books, learn about upcoming events, connect with author blogs and websites, and more! www.tarcherbooks.com

TRUE DIRECTIONS
AN AFFILIATE OF TARCHER PERIGEE